THE WORLD OF Europe

THE WORLD OF

Europe

NEIL J. HACKETT
JAMES W. ALEXANDER
GEORGE S. ROBBERT
DE LAMAR JENSEN
A. LLOYD MOOTE
RALPH W. GREENLAW
BRISON D. GOOCH
AMOS E. SIMPSON
VAUGHAN B. BAKER

FORUM PRESS
Saint Louis

Printed in the United States of America.

Library of Congress Catalog Card Number: 72-97972

ISBN: 0-88273-300-1

First Printing March 1973

Cover Design by Richard C. Bartlett

Contents

Preface

THIS BOOK is designed for use as a core book for European and Western Civilization courses where there is some emphasis upon supplementary readings on special topics. It is available in one volume for one-semester courses and in two and three volumes for two-semester or quarter courses. For additional flexibility, it is also available in nine 64-page minibooks, each covering a major period. A Self-Learning Program, prepared by Robert V. Schnucker, Northeast Missouri State University, and an Instructor's Supplement by James Waltz, Eastern Michigan University, are also available.

The World of Europe presents the essence of man's experience in Europe from primitive times to the present day. Each of the nine authors, a specialist in the period he covers, has concentrated on major trends and developments without losing sight of particular people and their problems. Fact and interpretation are carefully balanced and there is as much attention to social and economic developments as to political and cultural. The authors' aim has been to provide the student with a brief and readable survey which will point the way to further reading on his own.

The authors are: Neil J. Hackett (*The Ancient World*); James W. Alexander (*The Medieval World*); George S. Robbert (*The Renaissance World*); De Lamar Jensen (*The Sixteenth Century*); A. Lloyd Moote (*The Seventeenth Century*); Ralph W. Greenlaw (*The Eighteenth Century*); Brison D. Gooch (*The Nineteenth Century*); and Amos E. Simpson and Vaughan Baker (*Death of an Old World, 1914-1945* and *Genesis of a New World, 1945 to the Present*).

The authors wish to thank the following people for their critical reading of various sections of the book: William J. Miller, Saint Louis University; W. A. Fletcher, University of Delaware; Robert Zaller, University of Miami (Florida); George D. Balsama, Kent State University; Robert E. Herzstein, University of South Carolina; Otis C. Mitchell,

University of Cincinnati; Jeffrey B. Russell, University of California, Riverside; Carleton Curran, Eastern Illinois University; Howard Evans, Central Michigan University; Hugh Bonar, California State University, Los Angeles; Walter Simon, University of Colorado; Robert Bush, Nebraska Wesleyan University; Jack Ridley, University of Missouri (Rolla); James Chastain, Ohio University; Alexander Niven, Meramec Community College; Maxine Taylor, Northwest Louisiana University; David Trafford, University of Maine; Sidney Lipshires, Manchester Community College; Andrew Heisserer, University of Oklahoma; John Scarborough, University of Kentucky; Richard Glenn Eaves, Auburn University; Dale Gaeddert, University of Nebraska (Omaha); Delno West, Northern Arizona University; Donald Wilcox, University of New Hampshire; Jay Hammond, El Centro College; James Seaver, University of Kansas; David Hicks, New York University; Frank Bartholomew, California State University, San Diego; Richard E. Sullivan, Michigan State University; Jane Schulenberg, University of Wisconsin; and John Yost, University of Nebraska. The authors would especially like to thank Robert G. Clouse, Indiana State University, for his many helpful and constructive suggestions for improving one portion of the manuscript.

THE
ANCIENT
WORLD
TO 800 A.D.

1

The Ancient Near East

HISTORY is the reconstruction and interpretation of mankind's existence. An historian has two basic objectives: to recreate the past as accurately as possible, and then to reflect on this recreation in order to evaluate and interpret it as best he can. The modern historian is no longer an antiquarian, or one who undertakes a study simply because it gives him pleasure. Rather, the historian must be concerned to rediscover man's past by establishing what actually happened in history, and then to evaluate his findings in order to make history meaningful to the present.

Through the examination of his past, modern man is able to learn much about himself and his world. Certainly all that he learns is not hopeful, or encouraging, or even memorable. Yet all of human history points toward one inescapable conclusion: that man was and is a remarkable creature, capable of goodness and evil, brillance and ignorance, idealism and desperation. The motivations and actions of our ancestors are worthy of examination, for in many ways we are their reflections.

The term prehistory is used generally to refer to the past before man left written evidence of his existence. The prehistoric period, then, was extremely lengthy, since the first writing systems were devised by the Sumerians and Egyptians less than 6,000 years ago. Since writing is one of man's more recent innovations, the prehistoric era covers at least 95 percent of human existence. Our knowledge of this crucial period in the history of man depends on the work of archaeologists and anthropologists, who have discovered, and are continuing to discover, much information about the origins of man, his society, and his way of life.

The chronology of human history is usually divided into three broad categories: the Old Stone Age, or Paleolithic Age (1,750,000-12,000 B.C.), the New Stone Age, or Neolithic Age (12,000-5,000 B.C.), and the Age of Metals (5,000 B.C. to the present). Each category takes its name from the type of tools or weapons produced during the period: the Paleolithic Age is typified by the use of roughly worked and crudely shaped stone tools, the Neolithic by flint tools and weapons capable of being given a sharp cutting edge, and the Age of Metals by the use of bronze, copper, and finally iron.

• Homo Sapiens and the Neolithic Age

Homo sapiens is a relatively new creature on earth, when we consider that our species first made its appearance only about 50,000 to 100,000 years ago. Anthropologists now believe that men like ourselves are descended from earlier "hominids," the exact line of descent being uncertain because of the discovery of many varieties of other anthropoid, or man-like, forms. All of these early anthropoids possessed some of the distinguishing characteristics of *Homo sapiens,* such as sharp focusing eyes, a generalized hand and grasping thumb, the ability to stand and walk erect, the power of speech, and a reasoning brain, but never until *Homo sapiens* were all these characteristics to be found in one creature.

The noted African anthropologist L.S.B. Leakey has suggested that at the start of the Paleolithic Age there existed a man-like being which he named *Homo habilis,* "man having ability," who inhabited eastern Africa. He probably walked erect, and he produced crude stone tools and weapons. Although arguments still rage in scholarly circles over the evolution and chronology of our remote ancestors, we are safe in assuming that *Homo habilis* was one of the oldest "men" to inhabit the earth.

Africa seems to qualify as the birthplace of early man, but for reasons presently unknown the earliest African hominids made little evolutionary progress, and some 500,000 years ago they gave way to several types of more advanced creatures, commonly called Java Man and Peking Man. Java Man walked erect and probably could talk, although his cranial capacity was only two-thirds that of modern man. Peking Man was a cave dweller, was able to use fire, and made crude stone tools.

Several hundred thousand years elapsed before a creature more similar to *Homo sapiens* came into existence. This was Neanderthal Man

(*Homo neanderthalensis*), who inhabited most of Europe and the Near East from roughly 100,000 to 50,000 B.C. Neanderthal Man bore more obvious physical similarities to modern man than did older ape-men, he was able to produce tools and weapons more skillfully worked than his ancestors, and he took great care in burying his dead, a fact which seems to indicate that he had some awareness of some form of life after death.

Homo sapiens originated when Neanderthal Man was still inhabiting the earth, sometime around 50,000 B.C. He was a superior type of animal who demonstrated the power to adapt to his environment, or even to change it, much more readily than any of his predecessors. The best known variety of these first true men is Cro-Magnon Man, named from the cave in France where his remains were discovered. Apparently Neanderthal Man yielded to modern man by being absorbed through interbreeding, or by Cro-Magnon Man's extermination of his rival creature. In any event, by 40,000 years ago *Homo sapiens* came to dominate all other hominids, and finally eliminated them.

From the beginning, *Homo sapiens* seems to have been a social animal. Paleolithic Man lived with his fellow creatures first in caves, and later, when he had greater confidence in his weapons and in the strength of his group, he took to open country. The pattern of life must have been a very simple one. The earliest men were hunters, fishers, and root grubbers, and the greater portion of each day centered on the unending search for food. Most Paleolithic communities were not well enough organized or wealthy enough to make war continually on their neighbors. Even prehistoric art bears witness to early man's first priority – a full stomach. As early as 10,000 B.C. man engraved, and later painted, on the walls of caves strikingly realistic pictures of bison, reindeer, mammoths, and other creatures.

Paleolithic art also gives us a glimpse of what must have been the religion of early man. Perhaps Cro-Magnon Man thought that the act of drawing a picture of a game animal on a cave wall would somehow aid him in capturing and killing the real article. We can infer from prehistoric man's formulated and consistently practiced burial rites that he had a creative imagination capable of forming religious conceptions. This prehistoric religion is generally given the name animism, or the belief that all the world is alive and filled with forces which might have a good or evil effect on man. Most prehistoric religious practices with which we are familiar – the performances of magical rites and rituals, the care in burial, the superstitious avoidance of "unholy" places – all indicate that fear played a major part in the day-to-day lives of our remote ancestors.

Man's entrance into the Neolithic Age has been called the Neolithic Revolution, since the changes devised by the human community around

12,000 B.C. were of such magnitude that the pace of progress increased tremendously. Man now began to produce more effective and better worked tools and weapons by grinding and polishing the implements instead of simply chipping or fracturing the stone. Perhaps more importantly, he ceased being a food *gatherer* and became a food *producer* by planting his own crops and domesticating animals. Tilling the soil and keeping herds and flocks provided him with a dependable supply of food for the first time, and early in the Neolithic period he began to make pottery, and spin and weave his own clothing. Such advances made it possible for man to become less of a nomad in search of migrating game and seasonal wild crops and to establish more permanent residence in a hospitable area; villages grew and prospered so that the food supply was more than adequate for an ever growing population.

• The Bronze Age

The Neolithic Age came to an end in the Near East around 5,000 B.C. when man first began to use metals in the production of his tools and weapons. Along with the technological advances made possible by the use of first copper, then bronze, an alloy of 90 percent copper and 10 percent tin, came the more extensive use of boats as means of trade and communication between villages. The primitive self-sufficiency of the Neolithic village was altered immeasurably by an increase in the amount of trade and commerce and contact with outsiders. In an ancient version of the "arms race," villages without an adequate supply of copper or tin were forced to trade some desirable commodity for the necessary metals or be faced with conquest or extermination. Trade necessarily brought about contact with outsiders, and as a result the knowledge possessed by one village was imparted to others. The increasing complexity of life is indicated by the fact that men became more and more specialized in their occupations, and with this specialization of labor came an increasing dependence of the individual on the community, the collection of specialists. Certain individuals were more gifted at metal working, or farming, or shipbuilding, or hunting, or praying than were others, and these occupations gradually became full-time concerns, with each "specialist" relying on the other to supply his physical or social needs.

This complexity of life, in addition to a steady growth in population, led to two further developments in the Bronze Age: the urban revolution and the invention of writing. Since men were forced to depend on each other more and more, and since the population was ever increasing, the great river valleys of the Near East became dotted with sizable villages and later, towns. The economics of urban life also grew more complex, and soon the necessity of keeping systematic records of wealth, possessions, and offerings given to kings or priests produced the invention of writing. By 4,000 B.C. the simplicity and primitive atmosphere of the Neolithic village had been replaced by thriving towns and trading centers, the shops of merchants, craftsmen, and artisans, and the temples and palaces of priests and kings; in short, Neolithic culture had given way to Near Eastern civilization.

• The Egyptians

The Nile valley in Egypt and the Tigris-Euphrates valley in Mesopotamia gave birth to the two oldest civilizations on earth, but we are unable to discover why these two great Near Eastern river valleys, rather than any others, produced such results. The land near the great rivers was rich and fertile and men congregated there in the early Neolithic Age. The river valleys also provided men with a common challenge – the land had to be cleared and irrigated, marshes and swamps cleared, canals dug, levees built, water rights settled. Some sort of political and economic organization had to have been present for such a well-disciplined effort to meet with success, for projects so vast and cooperative efforts so large had to have been directed by a centralized organization. Whatever the process of settlement, it appears that the great river valleys of the Near East brought men together in true political organizations under the absolute authority represented in the person of a king or chief priest.

By 4,000 B.C. the Egyptians had created a complex culture and society which was destined to last for over 3,000 years in the great river valley of the Nile. The keystone of Egyptian civilization was always its great river which served as a great highway through the land, providing a means of trade, communication, and unification. The land of Egypt itself was composed of Upper Egypt, the valley of the Nile winding its way 800 miles from the second cataract to the Delta, and Lower Egypt, the Delta itself, a wedge-shaped area 100 miles in length. Most of the people of Egypt lived in the flood plain of the Nile which flooded regularly and calmly once every year, providing enough new silt and soil for fertilizing. The Nile valley was protected on all sides from foreign invasions and unwelcome interuptions by natural barriers: to the east and west were inhospitable deserts, to the south the rugged, rocky terrain of the Upper Nile, and to the north the Mediterranean Sea. A sense of security and freedom from concern with hostile neighbors afforded the Egyptians the advantage of focusing their interests on other matters, such as religion, art, and architecture. The regularity and predictability of the Nile, the stability of the climate, and the geographic isolation of the nation created an atmosphere of changelessness and regularity in the minds of the Egyptian people.

Early in the Neolithic Age in Egypt (5,000-3,200 B.C.) small independent city-states dotted the Nile valley. Slowly, by conquest and consolidation, two kingdoms emerged – Upper Egypt in the south and Lower Egypt in the north. The two kingdoms were allegedly united by a certain Menes, the founder of the first dynasty of Egyptian pharaohs, or rulers of a united kingdom of Upper and Lower Egypt. The dates given to Menes (c. 3,200) and the first dynasties of Egyptian pharaohs are more or less mythical, but much more is known of the deeds of the third dynasty pharaohs, who ruled all Egypt with autocratic authority from their capital at Memphis, and founded the Old Kingdom (3,200-2,250 B.C.). The period was one of great centralization and regimentation under the rule of the pharaohs who were believed to be divine beings, actually sons of the sun god, Re. The pyramids of Gizeh, the burial monuments of the Old Kingdom's fourth dynasty, still stand as lasting reminders of the absolute power of the god-kings of Egypt, and likewise bear testimony to the dedication of the Egyptian people themselves to the pharaoh and the state.

• The Middle Kingdom and the New Kingdom

Gradually the power and wealth of the Old Kingdom pharaohs diminished and much of their authority was usurped by ambitious nobles, so that the Old Kingdom disintegrated into a period of decentralization in which no one pharaoh was able to assert his authority effectively over the whole state. Reunification was brought about by the pharaoh Amenemhet I, who founded the Middle Kingdom (2,000-1,750 B.C.), which had its capital at Thebes in Upper Egypt. During the Middle Kingdom Egypt expanded her boundaries southward into Nubia, east into Sinai, and west into the Lybian desert; traders and merchants carried on an active commerce with Syria, Crete, and other Mediterranean seaports, art and architecture developed into their classic Egyptian forms. But the Middle Kingdom was brought to an end by an invasion of foreign conquerors, the Hyksos, or Rulers of Nations, who came apparently from Palestine or Asia Minor, and not until the sixteenth century could the Egyptians rid themselves of their foreign masters and reestablish native rule. The New King-

An Unfinished Stela from the Era of the New Kingdom.
Courtesy, Museum of Fine Arts, Boston.

dom (1,570-1,085 B.C.) brought with it the militarization of Egypt, since for the first time in her history Egypt made use of a standing professional army to conquer new territories and bring in tribute money from her subject states throughout the Near East. The city of Thebes, with its magnificent temples built across the Nile at Luxor and Karnak, became the most majestic capital in the world.

Curiously, at the height of its imperial power and opulence, Egypt produced a pharaoh who seemed to care nothing for his vast empire, but turned his attention instead to religious reform and ideological battle with the powerful and wealthy priests of the god Amon. Amenhotep IV (1,369-1,353 B.C.) attempted to revolutionize Egyptian religion by insisting on the worship of the sun disk Aton in place of Amon and all the other

Egyptian deities. Amenhotep changed his name to Ikhnaton ("Pleasant for the sun disk"), left Thebes to found a new capital dedicated to Aton, and spent the rest of his life worshipping his one god and composing hymns. Ikhnaton and his reforms were opposed by Egypt's priests and army leaders, who in turn persuaded the people of Egypt to reject Ikhnaton's self-imposed monotheism, and the pharaoh's reforms were overturned after his death. Egypt never quite recovered its full vigor after Ikhnaton's death, and aside from the conquests of several warrior pharaohs named Rameses in the thirteenth and twelfth centuries, her greatest days of expansion were at an end. From the end of the New Kingdom in 1,085 until Alexander the Great incorporated Egypt into his empire in 332 B.C., weak native rulers and foreign usurpers from Libya and Ethiopia rivaled each other for control of the Nile.

• Egyptian Religion, Science, and Art

Egyptian religion pervaded every aspect of life and influenced the whole of Egyptian civilization. The religion of the Egyptians was polytheistic, or one which recognized the existence of many gods and goddesses, whose activities and motivations were explained through myths and legends. Eventually Egyptian religion evolved an intricate theology in which certain divine beings were considered more significant or influential than other lesser gods. Among the most prominent gods of Egypt were Amon Re, the sun god and the supreme cosmic power; Osiris, the god associated with the fertilizing power of the Nile and the god who provided immortality to his worshippers; and Isis, the wife of Osiris and the goddess of the fertility of the earth. Pharaoh himself, the son of the sun god, was looked upon as the divine being who controlled the destiny of all Egypt. Originally the Egyptians apparently believed that pharaoh alone could achieve a life after death, but gradually even the common Egyptian searched for immortality which could be guaranteed by the worship of such life-giving gods as Osiris and Isis. A quick glance at the remains of Egyptian civilization might give one the impression that Egypt developed a style of life morbidly preoccupied with death. Most likely just the opposite was true – the Egyptian paid so much attention to death because he loved life and wished to see that life perpetuated in the tomb.

Science and technology were well developed by the Egyptians, as is attested by their magnificent architecture and their invention of a solar calendar of 365 days, the average period between inundations of the Nile. Arithmetic was limited to addition and subtraction, multiplication and division, a simple knowledge of algebra, but a considerable skill at practical geometry, which was a necessity for the construction of ramps, dams, and irrigation systems, and the walls and ceilings of temples. Egyptian architecture was and remains so impressive that the Egyptians have been called the greatest builders in history. From the magnificent temples at Thebes to the more than eighty pyramids constructed in the Old Kingdom, Egyptian architecture reflects a concern with size, simplicity of construction, massiveness, and repose. Art was almost always of a religious nature, and remained conservative and traditional throughout most of Egyptian history; tomb paintings and statues reflected a solid, stately quality to the scenes and individuals they depict.

The economy of Egypt was always controlled by the state; all trade and agricultural enterprise was under the watchful eye of pharaoh and his bureaucracy. Although Egypt was primarily an agricultural state, industries such as bronze production, tanning, weaving, pottery making, and enameling were mastered by the Egyptians, and the goods of Egypt were carried by land and sea up and down the Nile, to Phoenicia, Crete, Greece, Syria, and even Mesopotamia.

The Egyptian social structure was a simple one, consisting of the upper class of priests and the court nobility, the middle class of merchants and craftsmen, and the lower class, made up of laborers. Both men and women dressed with great care, using cosmetics extensively; the status of women in society seems to have been high in comparison with other Near Eastern societies.

• Mesopotamia

The plain between the Tigris and Euphrates rivers, in what is now Iraq, was in the ancient world called Mesopotamia, the land between the rivers. The geographic features of this region created different hardships and concerns than did the peaceful Nile. Although the two rivers usually flooded annually, the flood waters could come in torrents, or could never reach a level sufficient to supply water for irrigation. Storms and violent winds very often destructive in their intensity added to the uncertainty of both the urban and rural resident of Mesopotamia. In addition, the Mesopotamian valley was virtually open on all sides to invasion, since the alluvial plain of the valley gives way to rolling hill country and flatlands to the north, east, and west. Such geographical conditions partially account for the unstable political situation characteristic of Mesopotamian life, and perhaps are responsible in part for the Mesopotamian view of the world, which was essentially insecure and pessimistic.

The first people to inhabit Mesopotamia were the Sumerians, who settled in the southern portion of the valley around 5,000 B.C. To the north of Sumer was Akkad, and to Akkad's north Assyria, both of which regions were settled by peoples of a Semitic origin. For well over a thousand years (4,000-2,400 B.C.) the Sumerians possessed the most advanced civilization in Mesopotamia; they were an urban people, fiercely guarding the independence of their city-states and resisting any attempts to create a unified state in Sumer. For a brief time the Akkadian Kingdom (2,400-2,100 B.C.) to the north was able rid itself of Sumerian domination, and under the leadership of its great warrior king Sargon the Great, Akkad posed a threat to future Sumerian independence. However, the rise of Akkad was interrupted by the invasion of hostile and primitive nomads, the Amorites from the west and the Elamites from the east, and Akkadian preeminence gave way to a century of renewed strength by the Sumerians. Sumer was eclipsed once and for all by the rise of the Babylonian Empire (2,000-1,650 B.C.), which succeeded in dominating all central and southern Mesopotamia from the great capital city of Babylon, but the sway of the Babylonians was brought to an end by still more invaders, the Kassites, who reduced all the central valley to a state of political chaos for the next 400 years. Next the Assyrians were able to create a sound and thoroughly centralized empire in the Mesopotamian valley (1,200-612 B.C.), with Assyrian military might and high-handed dominance extending as far as Syria, Palestine, and even Egypt. A brief revival of Babylonian strength was able to overthrow the Assyrian hold on the valley, and from 612 to 539 B.C. the so-called New Babylonian, or Chaldean, Empire attempted to exert its influence, but Babylon and the rest of the Mesopotamian valley fell captive to the advancing Persian Empire in 539.

• Mesopotamian Civilization

The development of Mesopotamian civilization was affected by the geographic and political uncertainties of life in the Tigris-Euphrates valley. Mesopotamian religion in its broad characteristics was similar to that of Egypt, in that it was polytheistic, ritualistic, and mythmaking, but the people of Mesopotamia came to look upon the universe as a kind of a state in which the gods were the only citizens. Man was considered to be no more than a slave to his gods, who owned their own cities and the people within them. The god himself was thought to live in his temple, or ziggurat, in his chosen city-state, and govern through his human representative on earth, the *patesi,* or priest-king, who oversaw the activities of the city on the god's behalf. The only purpose of man was to serve his gods; there was no promise or hope of a pleasant existence after death.

The social hierarchy of Mesopotamia was composed of the upper-class priests and nobles, an active and vibrant middle class of merchants and craftsmen, the farmers and laborers, and finally the slaves, upon whom the Mesopotamians relied more heavily than the Egyptians. Although slaves seem to have been treated with some degree of fairness and respect, perhaps this attitude came about because of the ever present possibility that one who owned slaves could well be enslaved himself, due to the various misfortunes made possible by life in Mesopotamia.

In general, the Mesopotamian view of life seems to have been largely negative, full of desperation, pessimism, and superstition. Yet art and architecture in Mesopotamia reflected the people's creativity and resourcefulness. The huge ziggurats constructed entirely out of mud-brick, the mighty walls of Babylon and Nineveh, and the complex irrigation canals bear witness to the Mesopotamian's inventiveness and originality. The sciences were investigated further in Mesopotamia than in Egypt; astronomy and mathematics developed a sound and definite body of knowledge which was passed on to the Greeks. Law in Mesopotamia was codified and published, the most outstanding example of which is the Code of Hammurabi, the great king of Babylon in 1800 B.C. Hammurabi's code is primitive by modern standards, but it is a code which guarantees at least some rights for all segments of Babylonian society, even for slaves. The influence of Mesopotamian civilization was long-lasting, as one observes from the impact Mesopotamia had on the next great power which came to prominence in the Near East, Persia.

• Persia

The ancient Persian Empire was centered in present-day Iran, and extended east to the Indus River, north to the Caspian Sea, west to Mesopotamia and the Mediterranean, and south to Egypt. The Persians, who originally called themselves Iranians, entered their new homeland from the northeast around 900 B.C. and soon established themselves as rulers and aristocrats over the earlier residents. Immediately to Persia's north, another group of invaders, the Medes, entered the region and created the Median Empire, which was soon strong enough to incorporate the Persians to the south. But in 550 B.C., a successful revolt, led by the young Persian king Cyrus (559-529 B.C.), overthrew the Median Empire and catapulted the Persians to prominence in the Near East. Cyrus the Great became one of the world's most effective warrior kings, conquering the Lydian Kingdom in 546, establishing Persian control as far as the Indus River in the east, and accepting the capitulation of the New Babylonian Empire, and all Mesopotamia, in 539 B.C. Following his death, his son Cambyses conquered Egypt, and the successors of Cambyses, Darius I and Xerxes, began a series of campaigns against the Greek mainland in the first decades of the fifth century. After Xerxes' defeat by the Greeks in 479 the Persian Empire was able to hold most of its subordinate states until Alexander the Great conquered all Persia for himself in 331.

• Persian Civilization

The great success Persia had in ruling a far-flung empire was achieved through an efficient and well-organized governmental structure. Almost all of the Persian kings proved themselves to be talented conquerors and administrators. The Great King, as he was called, was an absolute monarch, aided by the advice of the nobility and the loyalty of a hand-picked bureaucracy. The empire itself was divided into twenty-one satrapies, each of which was governed by a satrap, or governor. To serve as a check on the power of the satrap, a secretary and a military official were stationed in each satrapy and took their orders directly from the Great King. In addition, officials known as "the eyes and ears of the King" were sent out to each satrapy to discover any evidence of discontent or possible rebellion against the empire. The Persian empire was the first Near Eastern state to attempt to govern many different racial and cultural groups on the principle of equal rights and responsibilities for all people; as long as the subject states of the Persians were peaceful and paid their taxes, the Persian central government was content to let them order their own affairs in the manner which they preferred.

Persian religion was an ethical religion founded by the prophet Zoroaster around 660 B.C. Zoroastrianism consisted of the teachings of the god Ahura-Mazda as revealed in the sacred book, the *Avesta.* The religion itself was what is called theological dualism, or the belief in two gods: the supremely good god Ahura-Mazda, and Ahriman, the god of evil. In every man there was a struggle between the good and evil forces controlled by these two gods, but each man had the obligation to assist the good in order to one day achieve eternal life with Ahura-Mazda in paradise (a Persian word). The Persian belief that there would be a last judgment at the end of the world, at which Ahura-Mazda would punish all evil men, was influential on Judaism.

Persian civilization was in its content and style very similar to Mesopotamian civilization, since the Persians, proving themselves eager learners, adopted much of the more advanced culture of their Mesopotamian subjects as their own. In art the Persians borrowed heavily from the Assyrians and Babylonians. Their most outstanding contribution was in palace architecture, the remains of which can still be seen today at the ancient Persian capital at Persepolis. The Persian system of roads was the most efficient in the Near East; every part of the empire could be reached within three days time by swift riding messengers, whereas it might take as long as three months to make such a journey on foot. Although the Persians were never innovators in science and technology, they served an important function in preserving the knowledge amassed by Mesopotamia and passing that knowledge on the Greeks, and later the Romans.

• The Hebrews

The political impact of Hebrew civilization was never of great significance in the ancient Near East, and Hebrew culture was much the same as that of their Semitic neighbors, but the Hebrews fundamentally affected the development of western civilization through the evolution of an intricate and influential religion.

Ancient Palestine was a very small country, approximately 150 miles north to south, and ranging from 30 to 60 miles in width. The geography of this tiny area varied from the smooth coastline of the Mediterranean on the west, followed by the rich coastal plain, then rough hill country. The hills yield to the richer land of the Jordan River valley to the east, which is in turn followed by more rugged and rocky hill country.

The people, who were mostly Semitic, seem to have originated in the Arabian desert, and as early as 2,000 B.C. these *habiru,* or wanderers, had started a long migration which eventually carried them to the shores of the Mediterranean and Palestine. By 1,350 B.C. the Hebrews were of such number and strength in Palestine that they successfully overthrew the cities of the more advanced and older residents of the area, the Canaanites, who inhabited northern Palestine. Here the Hebrews formed a political organization known as the Confederation of Israel, a loose union of ten tribes who acted as a unit only in times of national emergency.

At the same time when many Hebrews were migrating into Palestine, many other nomadic Hebrews were moving from Arabia southward into Egypt, where they eventually increased to such numbers as to pose a threat to the Egyptians, and they were enslaved. After a period of about 400 years in bondage in Egypt, the Hebrews, under the leadership of Moses, freed themselves of Egyptian control and left the land in around 1,200 B.C.; their migration from Egypt ended just to the south of Israel, where the Confederation of Judah was established.

The two confederations of Hebrew states in Palestine were headed by officials called judges, who held no official political power, but were respected and followed by the people because of their exemplary deeds and wisdom. But the informal power of the judges was not sufficiently centralized to cope with the invasion of a seafaring people, the Philistines, who threatened to destroy the southern confederation around 1,100 B.C., and Judah established a monarchy to better equip itself to meet the Philistine threat. Under the leadership of the first king of Judah, Saul, the Philistines were defeated and Judah's next king, David (c. 1,000), was able to bring the Confederation of Israel into a united monarchy of Israel and Judah and to establish a strong central government with its capital at Jerusalem. David's son Solomon seems to have had dreams of empire and taxed the people heavily in his search for revenue, which made him an unpopular monarch; at his death the northern confederation dissolved the united monarchy and proclaimed its own king.

For the next few centuries Israel was the stronger of the two Hebrew states and eventually attracted the interest of the Assyrian Empire; in 722 the Assyrians conquered Israel and scattered the ten tribes, but Judah was spared such a fate until 586 when the New Babylonian Empire took the city of Jerusalem and carried off the majority of the Hebrews to Babylon. In 539, when Cyrus the Great overthrew the Babylonians, the Hebrews were granted permission to return to Palestine where they remained at peace with the Persian Empire until the conquest of the Near East by Alexander.

The religion of the Hebrews underwent a long evolution before the establishment of true monotheism, the belief in one god. Early in Hebrew history Yahweh seems to have been a god closely associated with nature and one god among many. Moses, however, seems to have enforced monolatry, the belief that one god should be worshipped to the exclusion of all other gods, on the Hebrews in Egypt. In the time of David and Solomon, Yahweh was looked upon as a national god – one who guarded the fortunes of his favored people, but it was not until around 700 B.C., with the teachings of the prophets Isaiah and Jeremiah, that the Hebrews seem to have achieved true monotheism. Through centuries of speculation, reflection, and theological refinement, by 500 B.C. the Hebrews had developed one of the world's most sophisticated and ethical religious systems.

• The Hittites, the Lydians, and the Phoenicians

Several states in the ancient Near East often receive slight attention, since they failed to achieve the political prominence displayed by the great Near Eastern powers; nonetheless many of these minor civilizations had an impact on the future of western civilization. The empire of the Hittites, for instance, at one time rivaled Egypt in strength, but failed to create a civilization of stability and high cultural attainment. The Hittite Kingdom in Asia Minor reached its apex between 2,000 and 1,100 B.C. The people were Indo-Europeans from the Danube River region, and they spoke a language quite similar to those of the Greeks and Romans. Throughout its existence the Hittite state was a warrior nation constantly in conflict with its neighbors; perhaps their militarism was encouraged by the fact that they were the first Iron Age culture in the Near East. For a nation dedicated to war, the Hittites displayed an interesting tolerance of the customs of foreigners, as is reflected in their ready acceptance of foreign gods and goddesses, and in the Hittite legal system, which generally sought reparation for wrong-doing rather than retaliation.

The Lydian Kingdom, also in Asia Minor, reached its highest development under its famous and tolerant King Croesus (569-546 B.C.). The Lydians seem to have originated the idea of minting precious metals into coins, and this innovation stimulated trade throughout the Mediterranean.

The Phoenicians, a Semitic people inhabiting the coastline of what is now Syria and Lebanon, by around 900 B.C. had become the greatest sea merchants and traders of the ancient world. From their great cities of Tyre, Sidon, and Byblos, Phoenician shipping carried their famous purple dye, woolen goods and carpets, tin, spices, and perfumes to Mediterranean ports as far away as eastern Africa and Italy. Early in their history the Phoenicians had developed an accurate system of record keeping and writing which was adopted by those with whom they traded, in particular the Greeks; in this way the alphabet we use today originated.

In retrospect, the debt western civilization owes to the ancient Near East is not an easy one to define or evaluate, perhaps due to the tremendous gulf of time which separates the ancient and modern worlds. Certainly it is easier to see the more obvious contributions of the Near East to later ages: Mesopotamian astronomy and mathematics, the Egyptian basilica, the Hebrew Bible, the Phoenician alphabet, Lydian coinage, and so on. But perhaps the ancient Near East becomes more meaningful, and therefore more relevant, to us when we consider that many of our present political institutions, our social patterns and habits, our economic systems, even our thoughts about religion have their precedents in ancient civilizations. Policies of expansion, conquest, and agression were practised with great regularity and vigor; greed, racial hatred, religious intolerance, and man's inhumanity to man – all were displayed in the Near East. Yet ancient man searched for political order, individual dignity, religious freedom, and cultural excellence no less than his modern counterpart; the old saying that there is nothing new under the sun may be more accurate than we realize.

2

Greek Civilization

NO OTHER PEOPLE of the ancient world seem more like ourselves than the Greeks; perhaps this is true because modern institutions, even modern patterns of thought, have their origins and early formative development in the classical world of Greek civilization. It was the secularism and rationalism of the Greeks which first glorified the individual and liberated men of the conception that he was a pawn of the gods or the state. Hellenic political theory, philosophy, science, and literature have remained of timeless value to later civilizations of the West. Perhaps it is because of their great influence on the culture of the present western world that we too often think of the Greeks as austere and removed from the day-to-day cares of life – a race of geniuses set apart from human frailty. Nothing could be farther from the truth; they were at times passionate, they were one of the most bellicose peoples in the history of all the West, and they were above all curious and greatly uninhibited in their search for knowledge. Greek civilization, long after Greek political dominance had faded, was adopted and incorporated by the Romans from whom that inheritance was transferred to the modern world. It is to the lasting credit of the Hellenic world that even in the twentieth century western civilization remains, at its very foundations, Greek.

Greece is a poor country – poor in farmland and in mineral resources – and a very small land, only 150 miles in width from its eastern to western coasts, and about 220 miles from north to south. Four-fifths of the Greek peninsula is mountainous, and because of this extremely rugged terrain inland communication is difficult and flows slowly through the mountain passes and valleys. From the first the Greeks were interested in the sea and came to depend on it, not only as a means of communication but also as a source of food and way by which to trade with other cultures of the Eastern Mediterranean.

The Greeks themselves were an Indo-European people who first began their migrations from the region of Europe near the Danube River around 2000 B.C. By 1700 the whole peninsula had been settled by these nomadic tribes; they were illiterate, unsophisticated in their religious practices, unknowledgeable of husbandry, and hostile to the indigenous population with whom they mingled. The migrations came to an end with the Greeks settled in small, isolated villages in the mountain valleys.

• Mycenaean Greece

Gradually the Greeks learned to navigate the sea, and the growth of trade with other Aegean peoples began to break down the economic backwardness and cultural isolation of mainland Greece. As early as 1600, in the southernmost region of Greece, the Peloponnesus, the development of a strong economy and the growth of several politically well-organized urban centers had produced a level of civilization which has been named Mycenaean, in honor of its most outstanding city, Mycenae. Splendid palaces, richly furnished and decorated with frescoed murals, rock-cut chambered tombs elaborately adorned with the riches of kings and queens, and gold and silver artifacts all attest that Mycenaean civilization was a brilliant one. Even a writing system, called Linear B, was adapted from the Cretan written language and used by the Greeks to keep record of their riches.

By 1400 B.C. the Mycenaean Greeks had become such adept sailors and warriors that they were able to launch a successful raid on the island of Crete, the site of the older and more advanced Minoan civilization. The Minoans, who were probably of an eastern origin, had arrived in Crete as early as 3000 B.C. and had developed a rich and powerful civilization by 1600. Before 1400 the Minoans had been masters of the eastern Mediterranean, dominating trade and commerce, and probably controlling the economy of mainland Greece. The Cretan royal palace at Knossos has shown us the tremendous wealth of the Minoan kings, who were absolute rulers over their subjects, and its art and architecture clearly indicate that before 1400 Minoan civilization was much more advanced than Mycenaean. Yet the

Greek raid toppled the power of the Minoan kings at its very height, and for the next 300 years Mycenaean Greeks ruled in Knossos, usurping Minoan trade and commerce and absorbing the culture of the older, more developed civilization.

• The Dorians

Mycenaean civilization was ended in both Greece and Crete around 1200 B.C., when another wave of invaders entered northern Greece and slowly worked their way south, destroying the sites of Mycenaean power. The new Greeks were called Dorians, a group of tribes much less civilized than their non-Dorian cousins. Because of their almost complete destruction of the Mycenaean political order, the Dorians once again plunged Greece into darkness; the Dorians, who first brought iron weapons to the peninsula, found the older residents no match in combat, and burned the Mycenaean cities to the ground. Since their needs were simple the invaders found no need of retaining an active trade with other Aegean peoples, did not possess the skills of Mycenaean artists and craftsmen, and found no use in keeping written records.

The period known as the Dark Ages, or the Middle Age, lasted in Greece from 1200-800 B.C., and was a definite step backward in the development of Hellenic civilization. The Dark Ages were marked by the Greek migrations, large movements of peoples who were forced to leave their homes and villages due to a steady increase in population in a land which could not support such an increase, and by the efforts of many non-Dorians to flee from the advance of the hostile Dorian invaders. These migrations carried groups of Greeks in an easterly direction, out into the Aegean Islands or to the coasts of Asia Minor in search of a place of refuge. Politically, the Middle Age was an unsophisticated time; the king of a village or town was called upon to be the commander in war, the chief priest, and the supreme judge of his people. The king was assisted by a Council of Elders, composed of only the noblest and wisest of the citizens, who gave advice to the king when he requested it. In addition, each village had an assembly of all adult males, the only full citizens of the village, which had very little influence in the decision-making process. Most villages isolated themselves in the Dark Age, since there was very little need or advantage in wandering far from home; travel was dangerous and difficult, and trade declined appreciably, as well as interest in cultural pursuits. This isolation and loss of contact with foreign influences during the Dark Ages was responsible for the development of a distinctive variety of culture by each village or town, and an individuality and exclusiveness which later became a typical feature of Greek life in the city-state.

• The Emergence of Greece

The period from 800-600 B.C. sometimes is called the era of the Emergence of Greece, because the momentous changes and developments which transpired during that short period were eventually to influence the growth of classical Hellenic civilization. Early in the period kings lost their political hold on their states and were usually forced to relinquish power by the noble aristocrats, whose great wealth had given rise to political ambition. The aristocracy governed their respective city-states through the Council of Elders, or in several states a narrower oligarchy of the wealthiest nobles was able to exert political influence through its control of the Council and the assembly. Aristocratic government was responsible for a revived interest in trade and commerce throughout Greece, since many wealthy nobles wished to exalt themselves by acquiring the luxuries brought by overseas trade. They encouraged the codification of the law in their cities and they sponsored poets, artists, and craftsmen in order to enhance the prestige of their respective states. But soon, the non-noble citizens grew restless under the economic and political hold of the aristocrats.

Tyranny made its first appearance as a Greek political institution around 650 B.C. In the Greek sense of the word, tyranny was merely the establishment of a man in power in the state through unconstitutional means; a tyrant was usually a noble who seized control illegally in his city because of the overwhelming support he received from the middle classes and common citizens. Most tyrants, in order to gain control, promised the commoners of their city-states more of a part in governing its affairs through the assembly, and more freedom to engage in trade and industry. Tyrants were responsible for further broadening the political base of the Greek state, for the encouragement of a strong and active middle class through sponsorship of trade and commerce, for beautifying their city-states through investment in public works, and for an increased activity in cultural affairs by their sponsorship and patronage of artists, writers, games, and festivals. Tyranny itself was a step toward the establishment of a democratic form of government due to the increased responsibility the tyrant gave to the average citizen. As many tyrants became more autocratic, and thus more unpopular, in their respective states, a democracy was established in the tyrant's place; when their tyrants were expelled,

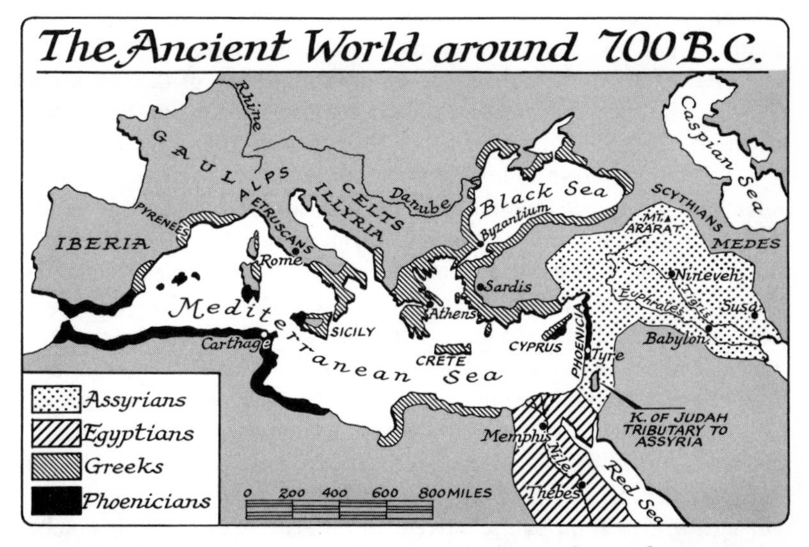

most Greek city-states returned to an aristocratic form of government, although some, notably Athens, continued on the path toward democracy.

• The Polis

The Emergence of Greece also witnessed the origin and development of the *polis,* or city-state, which included the city proper and its surrounding territory. The highest and most easily defended area of each city was known as the *acropolis,* which was usually fortified from enemy attack, and contained the main temples and civic buildings of the *polis.* To an ancient Greek the *polis* meant the city *and* its people, both linked to one another inseparably. Every one of the more than 100 *poleis* on the Greek mainland alone were fiercely individualistic, proud of their gods and traditions, and protective of their independence from their neighbors.

Economic activity began to increase steadily in this period, spurred on first by the interest of the aristocrats, and later by the tyrants, many of whom encouraged the Greek's use of coinage instead of the older barter system. The expansion of economic activity furthered the Greek colonisation movement, which began around 750 B.C. Because of a need for new markets for trade, for additional sources of raw materials, and for new settlements to help relieve the pressure of a constantly growing population, more than 150 colonies were sent out from their mother cities in Greece to occupy promising sites throughout the Mediterranean area and beyond. Greek colonists found their way to the Black Sea, to Egypt, to southern Italy, and even to the southern coasts of France.

Before 700 B.C. warfare was the private preserve of the Greek aristocracy, who fought on horseback. But after that date the brunt of responsibility for defending the *polis* fell to the common citizen because of the military reform known as hoplite tactics. A hoplite was a heavily armored infantryman, equipped with a spear and a shield, who fought side by side with his fellow citizens in a phalanx, or close order formation. Because of his new military importance, the common citizens of many states increased their demands to have a more active part in politics, since it did not seem fair to them to be asked to fight and die for an aristocracy which excluded them from political activity. The army itself, then, became a factor in broadening the political base of the Greek *polis.*

Around 800 B.C., after the Greeks had adapted the Phoenician alphabet to their own language, they began to write once more. The two most famous epic poems of the Greeks, Homer's *Iliad* and *Odyssey,* were put into written form by the very end of the Dark Ages, and thus stood at the beginning of written Greek literature to serve as models not only for future Greek literature but Greek life in general.

The two centuries which followed the Dark Ages were of tremendous importance in the shaping of Hellenic civilization. By 600 B.C. most of the city-states of Greece had acquired the cultural characteristics which typified Greek public and private life in the next few centuries. It would be an immense task to examine the particular brand of civilization developed by each of the major Greek *poleis,* but certainly the political and cultural development of Greece's two most influential states, Sparta and Athens, is worthy of our attention.

• Sparta

Sparta was a *polis* in the eastern Peloponnesus, centered in the region called Laconia. The Spartans themselves, the only full citizens of the state, were of Dorian descent, tracing their ancestry back to the invaders who conquered Laconia in around 1100 B.C. A second and lesser class in Sparta were the *perioikoi,* or "dwellers around," who were ruled by the Spartans but had the freedom to engage in trade and commerce. Last and least were the helots, non-Dorian serfs who were bound to the land in service to their Spartan overlords and who were totally deprived of any political voice in the state.

Although Sparta was eventually the most militaristic of all Greek city-states, such had not always been the case. From 800 to 600 Sparta had been a cultural leader among the Greeks, and a state well noted and admired for its outstanding poets and lyricists. But around 650 B.C. the helots, both in Laconia and in Messenia, an eastern region of the Peloponnesus previously conquered by the Spartans, revolted from their Spartan overlords and began a war which took the Spartans over ten bloody years to win. In order to insure their security from any future rebellions by the helots, the Spartans coldly decided to reverse the natural growth and development of their *polis* by turning the state into an armed camp. Through a series of political and social reforms, Sparta attempted to safeguard her existence by placing the whole emphasis of the state on military readiness in general and the preservation of the Spartan caste in particular. These reforms eliminated all but military pursuits as undesireable; Sparta was never beautified by stone temples and civic buildings, its streets were never paved, and literature with other than a patriotic theme was banned. Bravery, cunning, and fearlessness became the greatest of Spartan virtues; Spartan children purposely were not fed enough or clothed warmly enough so that they were forced to learn the necessity of stealth and endurance. Through a program of regimentation and physical fitness, Sparta produced the best soldiers and most feared army in Greece. The training of Spartan youth began at age seven, when they were taken from their parents to live in military barracks, and ended at sixty. During all those years it was the primary duty of each Spartan male to condition himself into a military machine. The army which resulted from such a program was indeed formidable and soon earned the reputation of invincibility and inhuman strength; it was said that the Spartan phalanx preferred to fight rather than train, since the Spartan training program was more demanding than actual combat. The women of Sparta also were expected to keep fit, mainly so that they could bear more Spartan boys to fill the ranks of the army.

The Spartan constitution reflected the conservatism and inflexibility of the Spartan social order. There were two kings who were commanders in war and the chief priests of the state, but the greatest authority in Sparta rested with a board of five officials called ephors, who assisted the kings, checked on their activities, presided over the Council and the assembly, and ran the system of military training. The Council of Elders was composed of 28 Spartans, all over age sixty, and the two kings; it served as a court for all criminal cases, and it prepared measures to be submitted to the assembly. The assembly, consisting of all adult male Spartans, was little more than a rubber stamp to the legislation put before it by the Council and the ephors.

The pros and cons of the Spartan system have been weighed and discussed ever since the fifth century B.C. Although most Greeks would have never traded places with a Spartan, the dedication and resolve of the Spartan state was admired and respected. The system was successful over the short term, for Sparta was able to dominate her helots and to protect her interests away from home through the use of its army. Yet in the long run Spartan militarism accounted for the downfall of the state; her army fought so much that its ranks eventually became depleted, and due to the Spartan's establishment of a closed caste system the birth rate declined steadily. Through endless war and a racist social program, the Spartans had virtually eliminated themselves as a major Greek state by the mid-fourth century.

• Athens

In stark contrast to the Spartan *polis* stood the democratic state of Athens. The Athenian state had developed normally according to the usual Greek political pattern, and in 600 B.C. Athens seemed no more than an average Greek *polis.* By this date the king had been replaced by a board of nine executives called archons, who governed the state with the aid of the Council of Elders and the assembly. Largely because of the economic domination of the lower classes by the aristocratic land owners, an archon named Solon was appointed in 592 for a term of two years, during which time he would reform the state and solve the growing economic crisis. Solon abolished slavery for debt, encouraged trade and industry, gave more power to the assembly, and opened the major offices of the state to those who had the most wealth, rather than restricting them to the aristocracy of birth.

Solon's reforms provided only temporary relief for Athens, and discontent with the constitution continued to grow as the economic and political gulf between nobles and commoners grew larger. In 560 the tyrant Peisistratus seized power in Athens with the promise of aiding the middle class and common citizen in their struggle with the aristocracy. Peisistratus, and later his son Hippias, ruled Athens until 510, during which time much of the land was redistributed to the poor, trade was encouraged and fostered by the state, a large program of public works was begun, and the arts were patronized. But in his later years Hippias grew autocratic, and he was driven from power in 510 to be replaced by the archon Cleisthenes, the true founder of Athenian democracy. Cleisthenes increased the powers of the Athenian assembly at the expense of the aristocratic Council of Elders, with the result that the assembly of the citizens became the most important Athenian legislative body. He reorganized the tribal structure of the state, creating ten new tribes which determined their membership on the basis of residence in Attica rather than hereditary membership; the aristocrats could no longer control politics in Athens through their domination of the old system of four hereditary tribal units. Many new citizens were given the franchise and encouraged to engage in trade and industry, and the major administrative officers of Athens were now chosen by lot from among the body of Athenian citizens wishing to hold office. Archons held office for a one year term, and then were never again permitted to hold that office; generals were chosen by the assembly, and were soon given the privilege of holding successive terms. In the mid-fifth century magistrates and jurors were paid for their services, thus enabling every citizen to afford to be politically active if he wished. The end result was a direct democracy in which almost every citizen had an opportunity to participate.

• The Persian Wars

The beginning of the fifth century B.C. witnessed not only the birth of Athenian democracy but the beginning of a monumental struggle between the Greeks and the Persian Empire. The Persian Wars, from 500-449 B.C., began when several Greek states, including Athens, sent help to the Greeks in Asia Minor who were attempting to free themselves of Persian control. The revolt failed, the Persian king Darius vowed revenge on Greece, and in 490 his army arrived by sea in Greece at the plain of Marathon, just to the north of Athens. The Athenians marched out to meet the invaders, and although they were outnumbered by more than three to one, they defeated the Persian host decisively. Ten years later Darius' son Xerxes invaded Greece from the north with 700 ships of war and an army in excess of 150,000 men. In 480 an attempt was made by the Greeks to stop the Persian advance at Thermopylae, a narrow pass in central Greece. After a valiant stand, 300 Spartans under the command of King Leonidas perished to the last man, and the Persians marched south to Athens. But in the Bay of Salamis off the coast of Attica, the Persian and Athenian fleets engaged. The result was a stunning Athenian victory which destroyed the entire Persian navy. The disheartened Persian army started home in 479, only to encounter the full Spartan army in central Greece. At the battle of Plataea the Spartans won a decisive victory, and all hopes of a Persian conquest of Greece vanished forever; the loosely united Greeks had defeated the greatest empire of the day.

In 479 Athens and her allies formed the Delian League, the purpose of which was to free all Greek states still in Persian hands. Technically the league was a union of equals, but it soon became clear to all that Athens intended to dominate the organization; she fixed the tribute to be donated by each member state, and oversaw its collection, she furnished most of the ships and all of the admirals of the league fleet, and she appointed the league's treasurers. Soon Athens was forcing states to join her league, as well as using force to keep her resentful allies under domination. In 449, the formal peace treaty ending the Persian Wars was made, but Athens chose not to disband the league and continued to enforce membership, collect tribute, and use the league treasury in any way she wished: the Delian League had clearly become the Athenian Empire.

• Athenian Democracy

The creation of an Athenian Empire was well received by the ordinary Athenian citizen, who realized that Athenian imperialism would bring increased revenues to the state and the citizen body at large. The shipyards of the harbors of Athens thrived, merchants grew rich on trade with the allied states, and the coffers of the treasuries of the state grew full. Most of Athens' citizens linked the empire with their democracy and thought that imperialism was a natural product of a thriving democratic state; to the Athenian, the empire was completely justifiable. But Athens' domination of her allies was not popular with most of the subject states, who longed for the day when their freedoms could be restored.

Athens, under the brilliant leadership of her famous general and politician Pericles, had fared well in the creation of an empire on both land and sea in the middle years of the fifth century. But Athenian power reached such great proportions by 431 that Sparta was forced to take action to stop further Athenian aggrandizement. The Peloponnesian Wars (431-404 B.C.) pitted Athens and her empire against the Spartans and their allies and from the first the Athenians fared badly. In 429 a plague decimated the city and claimed many victims, among whom was Pericles. Since no other politician was able to fill the void left by Pericles' death, the citizens turned to political demagogues, such as Kleon, the most influential politician after Pericles. In 413 the Athenians rashly become involved in a large war with the city-state of Syracuse in Sicily, and because of hasty preparation and poor leadership almost the whole Athenian fleet was destroyed. Athens continued to fight until 404 when she was forced to surrender unconditionally to the Spartans.

The Temple of Cerere at Paestum. Courtesy, Italian Government Travel Office.

• The Golden Age of Athens

The years immediately before and during the Peloponnesian Wars are referred to as the Golden Age of Athens, for in those few decades the school of Hellas produced the best poets, dramatists, sculptors, architects, philosophers, and historians in the history of Hellenic civilization. These were also the years during which Athens reached her fullest development as a democracy; but there were flaws in that democratic fabric which eventually brought ruin to the state. Since the archonship was decided by lot and one could hold that office for only one year, Athenian politicians who wished to continue in power were forced to seek election as generals, for the generals could hold successive terms. Many politicians proved themselves bad generals and many generals made poor politicians. Further, although the Athenians had the opportunity to participate directly in politics, most became apathetic and were willing to let professional politicians lead them and determine state policy on their own terms. Pericles, for instance, was elected general forty-two times in his career and his policies most times were unquestioned by the populace. The basic cause of the failure of Athenian democracy was not Sparta, nor the mistakes of Athens' leaders, but the apathy of the people as a whole.

With the defeat of Athens, Sparta made a brief attempt at establishing an empire, but she, and later the *polis* of Thebes, failed to dominate the peninsula. In the middle years of the fourth century a new threat to Greek independence rose in the north from the kingdom of Macedon, under the leadership of an ambitious and resourceful young king, Philip II. In 338, at the battle of Chaeroneia in central Greece, the Macedonians defeated a combined force of Greek states and Philip was master of all Hellas. With the Macedonian victory at Chaeroneia, the era of the independent city-state was ended and the Hellenic world could never be the same. The beginning of the Hellenistic world was at hand.

• Greek Civilization

The contributions of Greek civilization to modern civilization are countless. Greek religion is an exception – its influence was felt by the Romans but not by later civilization. The polytheistic religion of the Greeks existed on several levels; there were the austere and official cults of the Olympian gods and the protecting deities of each *polis,* and there were the emotional and frenzied mystery cults of the common people. Religion was undogmatic and unorthodox in most cases, since the Greeks never developed a hierarchy of priests or any centralized authority to oversee religious practices. The state gods and goddesses, Zeus, Athena, Apollo, and the rest, demanded recognition and worship from the *polis* in general, but on the private level individuals were permitted great latitude in their religious conduct.

Greek philosophy, however, still stands at the base of most western speculation. The Greeks practically invented the discipline in the sixth century, when thinkers from the Asia Minor city-state of Miletus first turned their attention to inquiries on the nature and substance of the physical world. They believed that all things could be reduced to a primary, original substance: Thales, the founder of this Milesian school, thought that substance was water, Anaximander called this substance which contained and directed all things the Boundless, and Anaximenes determined it to be air. Although somewhat primitive, the Milesian school broke with the Greek mythological explanations of the origin of the world and at least attempted a rational view.

Before the end of the sixth century, Greek philosophy became involved not only with the study of the nature of the universe, but with an examination of the meaning of being, the meaning of truth and goodness, and the nature of man. The Pythagoreans taught that the essence of things was not a material substance and drew sharp distinctions between spirit and matter; Heracleitus held that the universe was in a constant state of flux, and that the real essence of things was change; and the atomists believed that the universe was composed of infinite and indestructible atoms. The Sophists concerned themselves with a search for a better understanding of man, and determined that "man is the measure of all things," and that goodness, truth, beauty, and such ideas were relative to each individual.

The last and greatest of the Sophists was Socrates, who was born in Athens in 469 B.C. He taught that man could learn the true meaning of things and understand himself and the universe through the use of dialectic, the exchange and examination of opinions through which the truth could be obtained. Socrates' greatest pupil was Plato, who was born in 427 B.C. Plato developed the doctrine of Ideas, or that there existed eternal forms, the Ideas, of goodness, truth, beauty, and the like, which cannot be perceived by man's senses. Man must rid himself of the influence of knowledge gained through sensual experiences and seek the Ideas, in particular the Idea of the Good, through use of his reason. Aristotle, the last of the great philosophers of the Hellenic world, agreed with Plato that the Ideas were real and that knowledge derived from the senses was inaccurate, but he maintained also that both form (the Ideas) and matter were each worthy of examination in the search for true knowledge, and that by an understanding of individual things, the particulars, man could come to a more full realization of the general, or the forms.

Greek literature, in its many and varied forms, still retains its value and quality. Homer's *Iliad* and *Odyssey,* long epic poems full of emotional intensity, served as models and inspirations to future writers who chose to deal with the relationship of gods to men and the frailties of human nature. Elegy, a more informal and personal variety of poetry, dealt with love, patriotic themes, and the difficulties and disillusionments of life. Lyric poetry, which was intended to be sung to the music of the lyre, dealt with a great variety of themes and moods – Sappho used it to describe the beauty of love and nature, while Pindar wrote to glorify the deeds of athletes and the benefits of Greek civilization.

Drama was invented by the Athenians. The tragic dramas of Aeschylus, Sophocles, and Euripides were intended to purge their audiences of pity and fear; all of these dramas dealt with tragic topics derived from Greek mythology and legend, and all intended to shed light on man's struggle with his surroundings and the eventual triumph of justice. Comedy, best represented in the works of Aristophanes, was a biting satire of contemporary political events or social problems.

Critical history was likewise begun by the Greeks. Herodotus, the "father of history," was born in 484; he determined to write an account of the Persian Wars, which he appraised to have been a great turning point in human history. His account was intended to be a critical look at the forces which brought the Greeks and Persians into conflict, and a history of the various peoples who constituted the Persian Empire. Thucydides, the historian of the Peloponnesian Wars, was more critical than was Herodotus in his examination of his sources; he carefully sifted the evidence, eliminated hearsay and legend, and rejected biased opinion. In his account of the clash between Athens and Sparta, he determined that greed and ambition were the two most important motivations of man in his quest for political superiority.

The Greeks were much more interested in speculative and artistic endeavors than in pure science, and scientific progress in the Hellenic world was slight. Mathematics and geometry were furthered by the contributions of Thales, and especially by the philosopher Pythagoras, who discovered several important geometric theorems. Anaximander was one of the first Greeks to advance a crude theory of evolution, and was one of the first biologists. Biology was greatly advanced by Aristotle, who conducted many experiments to shed light on the structure and growth of plants and animals. Medicine, also examined first by the philosophers, was furthered by Hippocrates of Cos, who believed that every disease had a natural cause; he dissected animal bodies and greatly improved surgical techniques.

Greek art and architecture typifies Hellenic civilization, in that the art of Greece glorified man as the most important being in the universe, and employed the elements of balance, harmony, simplicity, and moderation. Greek vasework remains a supreme example of ceramic art; sculpture, best represented by the work of the fifth century master Phidias, emphasized dignity, patriotism, and grandeur in almost perfect combination with simplicity and restraint. The architecture of Greece also reflected concern with simplicity of design; the magnificent temple architecture, best represented by the Parthenon in Athens, seems to have been intentionally designed to appear simple and balanced to the eye, yet magnificent in its visual effect.

• Alexander the Great

Although the Hellenistic era was influenced by the older Hellenic civilization, the world of Alexander the Great and his successors was vastly different than that of the Golden Age of Athens. After 338 and Philip of

Macedon's successful subjugation of all Greece, the *polis,* that vibrant force of Hellenic individuality and creativity, ceased to exist, for Philip organized the various Greek city-states into a league which functioned under his watchful eye. Soon after his mastery of Greece was complete, the Macedonian king planned to invade the Persian Empire and he was anxious for the cooperation of the Greek states. But Philip was assassinated in 336, and the throne of Macedon and the league of Greek states were claimed by Philip's young son, Alexander (356-323 B.C.).

Alexander was only twenty years old when he became king in Macedon. From his early youth he had proven that he was an exceptional human being. He was a high-strung, nervous man, average in appearance except for his eyes, which had the appearance of looking through anyone with whom he talked. His mother Olympias had a great influence and hold on him all through his life; from childhood she had filled his mind with suggestions that he was something more than human and that the gods had chosen him to accomplish great tasks. Alexander's curiousity and range of interests seemed boundless: he was interested in philosophy, perhaps because he had been tutored by Aristotle when a youth, he loved sports and games. Everything he did, he seemed to do exceptionally well.

Alexander's first task as king was to solidify his claim to the throne in Macedon; he enforced his will on the restless Macedonian nobles and retained his father's generals and confidants to serve as his own advisers and friends. When the young king was busy settling affairs in the north, the Thebans, resentful of Macedonian domination, decided to revolt and leave the Greek league. Alexander quickly turned south and razed the city of Thebes to the ground – the fate of the Thebans was to serve as an object lesson to the rest of the Greeks. After restoring control in Greece, Alexander departed for Persia in hopes of accomplishing the goal his father never realized. The Macedonian army marched through Asia Minor, down the coast of the Mediterranean, and reached Egypt, which was added to the king's conquered states in 332. After being hailed as a god by the Egyptians, he struck deeply into the heart of the Persian Empire and defeated the armies of Darius III once and for all in 331. For the next seven years Alexander was constantly on the move, campaigning as far north as southern Russia, east to the borders of classical China, and south past the Indus River. He probably was planning even further conquests in 323, but in that year, at the age of thirty-three, he was taken ill and died; in only thirteen years as king Alexander had created one of the largest empires ever known to man.

• The Hellenistic World

Since Alexander was deprived of the opportunity to rule his empire and order its affairs before his death, it will never be certain in what manner the young conqueror would have organized his vast holdings. But his conduct seems to have indicated that he intended to rule each portion of the empire in as much accord with local, traditional political customs as was possible. Alexander was an idealist, and he seems to have been deeply convinced that one way of uniting his empire would be through "hellenizing" his subjects: Greek culture would be established as the common bond uniting all the peoples of the eastern Mediterranean. In line with this policy, Alexander encouraged marriages between his soldiers and non-Greek women; the king himself took the daughter of Darius III as his wife. He also founded many Greek cities throughout his domain, in hopes that the native population would be educated and inspired by these outposts of Hellenic culture. In general, Alexander promoted Panhellenism, or the belief that all men should be united as brothers under the aegis of Greek culture.

The world will never know whether Alexander could have achieved his lofty goals. After his death, the king's generals and friends divided his empire between themselves, and they and their successors ruled what became the Hellenistic world, until Roman power reached the shores of the eastern Mediterranean in the first century B.C. Three great states emerged out of Alexander's empire, the strongest and most successful of which was Hellenistic Egypt, where the general Ptolemy and his heirs ruled as pharaohs in the land. The Seleucid Empire, named after its first ruler, the Macedonian general Seleucis, was comprised of western Mesopotamia, Syria, and Asia Minor. The weakest of the three empires was Greece and Macedonia, which was ruled by the general Antigonas and his successors. Until the Roman conquest, the three Hellenistic empires constantly engaged in wars and boundary disputes with one another; each time one of the states threatened to disrupt the balance of power, the other two empires took to arms. Alexander's successors ruled as absolute despots over their subjects, and many of them styled themselves as divine beings.

The economic pattern of life in the Hellenistic world was markedly different from that of Hellenic Greece, in that all trade and industry was regulated and controlled by the state for its own financial benefit. Factories were established by the government, harbors were improved, better roads and canals were constructed, and merchant fleets were sent out to canvass Mediterranean markets. Large cities, such as Antioch in Syria and Alexandria in Egypt, became centers for commerce and refuges for men dissatisfied with the increasing rigors of rural life. Economic prosperity was limited to the upper classes – the nobles and the merchants – as farmers and laborers suffered from inflation and unemployment.

• Hellenistic Civilization

The culture of the Hellenistic period was a culture limited to the upper classes, namely the Greeks, for although Panhellenism was the ideal, the Greek minority in the Hellenistic empires was never successful in replacing the native patterns of civilization. Greek was the official language of all three empires, and Greek art, architecture, and literature were sponsored by the state, but the Hellenic influence never penetrated successfully to the lower levels of society. Further, much of Hellenistic civilization was nothing more than an empty imitation of the earlier Hellenic culture. Hellenistic literature, for instance, lacked originality and thoughtfulness; art and architecture reflected a concern with size and the display of power and wealth, an exaggerated realism in which features were distorted in pain or violent emotion, and a loss of that sense of balance and simplicity which had typified Hellenic art.

On the other hand, the Hellenistic Age was one of the great eras in the history of science. Old Babylonian and Egyptian knowledge of astronomy was improved upon by the astronomers of the Hellenistic world. Aristarchus of Samos, for instance, advanced the heliocentric theory – that the earth and the other planets revolve around the sun – although the geocentric theory – that the sun and other planets revolve around the earth – proved to be more popular and was unquestioned until the sixteenth century. Mathematics was advanced by Euclid through his studies in geometry, and by Hipparchus, the father of plane and spherical trigonometry. Geography was studied by Eratosthenes, who computed the earth's circumference with an error of less that 200 miles, composed the most accurate map of the world to that date, and proposed the possibility of reaching India by sailing west. Perhaps the greatest medical mind of the Hellenistic world was Herophilus, who was one of the first to practice human dissection, and who conducted researches in the circulation of the blood. Archimedes of Syracuse advanced the knowledge of physics with his discovery of the law of specific gravity and the invention compound pulley. In general, man's knowledge of pure science was increased greatly by Hellenistic scientists, but progress in the applied sciences was relatively small, perhaps because human labor was abundant and there seemed little need to develop labor saving devices.

Along with its scientific contributions, the Hellenistic world produced two very influential schools of philosophy, Epicureanism and Stoicism. Epicureanism advanced the notion that it was the task of man to achieve peace of mind in the world through the pursuit of intellectual and spiritual pleasure and the avoidance of pain, while Stoicism expounded the doctrine that the world was ordered according to rational principles and that all earthly activity was in agreement with an orderly pattern. Man, to be happy in this world, had to accept his fate and perform his duty, even if it led to physical and mental suffering. The Stoics believed that man should concentrate on overcoming the influence of his emotions; they also furthered belief in a universal brotherhood of all mankind. Much of the teachings of both the Stoics and Epicureans was to have an effect on the attitudes of the Romans toward life in a complex and impersonal world, and several elements of both schools later came to have an influence on the development of early Christian philosophy.

Perhaps the greatest failure of Hellenistic civilization was lack of confidence in its own future and a preoccupation with the past. Although the political order of things had changed, and science and philosophy progressed, the effort to recapture Hellenic civilization seems to have possessed Hellenistic artists and writers. By the time of the Roman conquest of the eastern Mediterranean, the Hellenistic world was in the process of undergoing not only political decline but a period of cultural stagnation.

3

Roman Civilization

IF IT IS TRUE that modern western civilization looks to the Greeks as the founders of the basic cultural fabric of the West, then it is equally true that the Romans laid the foundations of the more practical aspects of western civilization. Perhaps our most influential inheritance from Rome has been the idea of the sovereignty and absolute power of the state and the notion that a world-wide empire, directed and held together by a people of superior civilization, could be desirable. Many of the characteristics of the Romans as a people attract us as virtues to be admired in today's world: sobriety, sense of purpose, devotion to duty and country, and high moral character. Certainly there is much to admire in the Roman sense of practicality and dogged determination reflected in their creation of one of the most successful and generally constructive empires known to man. Our debt to Rome increases when we realize that Greek civilization, long after Hellenic political dominance had past, was adopted and incorporated by the Romans, from whom that inheritance was transferred to the modern world.

The Italian peninsula is seven hundred miles long, about four times the area of Greece. In the north, the huge and fertile valley of the Po River gives Italy its richest soil, while in the south the Apennine mountains divide the peninsula into valleys, yielding on the western coasts to the coastal plains of Tuscany, Campania, and Latium. The city of Rome itself came to be located on the plain of Latium in west central Italy on the banks of the Tiber River.

• The Etruscans and the Greeks

Italy was inhabited at least as far back as the Upper Paleolithic Age by Mediterranean peoples who probably came to the peninsula from Spain, Gaul, and northern Africa. Around 1000 B.C. or slightly before, Indo-European peoples, the ancestors of the so-called Italians, began to work their way over the Alps and down to Italy. One of these groups of invaders were the Latins, who settled in west central Italy; the Romans themselves were of Latin origin. In the eighth century two other civilizations became established on the Italian peninsula: the Etruscans in the north, and the Greeks in the south and on Sicily. The Etruscans arrived in northern Italy with a fully developed civilization. Although the question of where the Etruscans came from has never been satisfactorily solved, their art, the organization of their villages, and their religion seem to point toward an origin in Asia Minor. The Etruscan written language used an alphabet based on the Greek, but has never been translated. Etruscan civilization was largely militaristic in character, and in a short time after their arrival in Italy they had carved out a sizable kingdom in northern and central Italy. They were skilled metal craftsmen and architects in addition to being effective soldiers.

The Greek colonisation movement began to affect Sicily and southern Italy by 750 B.C., when colonies of Greeks took hold and grew into centers of trade and commerce. Caught between these two military and economic powers was the small agricultural community of the Romans.

• The Roman Monarchy

According to their own legends, the Romans were descended from the Trojan prince Aeneas, who escaped the destruction of Troy and traveled by sea to finally reign as king in Latium. Several hundred years later were born twin boys, Romulus and Remus, who were in the royal line of inheritance established by Aeneas, but the boys' wicked uncle usurped their rights and exposed the twins on a hillside to die. Such was not the will of the gods, for a she-wolf found the twins and raised them to manhood, whereupon they claimed their rightful place as kings among the Latins. Soon thereafter Romulus killed Remus in a dispute and founded the city of Rome; the date the Romans assigned to this foundation was 753 B.C.

Somewhat suprisingly, archaeologists have found that although there is evidence of habitation on the site of Rome before 800, the middle of the eighth century witnessed an increase in the number of inhabitants around Rome and an organized effort to clear marshes and drain the swamps along the Tiber. Still the settlement remained small, and the Romans numbered just one among the several Latin tribes in the vicinity.

The earliest period in Roman history is that of the Roman monarchy, for from the first Rome seems to have been ruled by kings. The kings of Rome held a powerful position in the state, exercising command of the army in war, serving as the chief priests of the city, and acting as the supreme judges in major legal cases. The kings were assisted by a powerful Senate, or Council of Elders, which was composed of the elder members of the Roman nobility. The Senate was to advise the king on all matters of state and to veto any measures which went against ancient custom. In addition to the Senate, an assembly, composed of all male citizens of military age, was called on occasion, but that body had little power other than to ratify the proposals of the king and the Senate.

Roman society in the time of the monarchy was dominated totally by the patrician class, or the nobles, most of whom were the descendants of old clan and tribal leaders, and all of whom were wealthy landowners. Only patricians could serve in the Senate, hold positions of command in the army, and become priests of the various state cults. The plebeians, or commoners – farmers, craftsmen, and laborers – had little or no voice in any aspect of Roman society, and many of them served as clients and dependents of the great patrician families, who gave the plebeians protection in return for political and economic support.

In the sixth century the Etruscans to the north of Rome began to take much more notice of the Greeks, and in an effort to control the lines of communication connecting northern and southern Italy, Rome was taken over by her northern neighbors and an Etruscan kingship was established in the city. The Etruscan kings of Rome did much to improve the physical appearance of the city by draining swamps and marshes, constructing stone civic buildings and temples, and instructing Roman artists and craftsmen in the ways of a more advanced civilization. Yet the Romans resented this domination by a foreign power and a revolt by the Roman aristocrats succeeded in driving the Etrucsans from the city somewhere near the traditional Roman date of 509 B.C. Although later Romans were fond of retelling of the military exploits of their ancestors in expelling the Etruscan kingship, the truth of the matter seems to be that the Etruscan empire had overextended itself by 500 B.C. and was under pressure from enemies both north and south, which aided the Romans immeasurably in their revolt.

• The Roman Republic

The Etruscan kingship at Rome was replaced by the Roman Republic, which was actually the oligarchic rule of the patrician class, whose members held virtually all of the executive offices of the state. The powers of the king were given to two officials, the consuls, who were elected for one-year terms and served as commanders of the army and the chief administrators of Rome. Each consul had veto power over the other's initiative, and thus unity was required to enact any kind of major legislation. In times of emergency, the two consuls might be asked to relinquish their authority to a dictator, who was chosen by the Senate to exercise complete control in the state until the particular crisis was solved. Praetors were officers who functioned as assistants to the consuls, financial officials, and city administrators; later in Republican history they often served as governors of the Roman provinces. Finally the censors were commissioned to take the census of the state in order to determine who was eligible for military service; they also came to examine the personal lives of men who wished to hold major office to determine if such men were morally qualified for such duty.

In addition to the authoritative Senate, the Romans had three other major assemblies: the tribal assembly, which had existed under the Roman monarchy, the army assembly, made up of all Roman soldiers, which elected most of the major magistrates and passed most legislative enactments; and the plebeian assembly, initially created to govern the plebeian community alone, for which purpose the commoners elected ten officers, the tribunes.

The first 200 years of the Republic was a time of almost continual warfare, but the Romans found themselves in possession of the whole Italian peninsula by 264 B.C. After the establishment of the Republic, Rome continued to fight with the Etruscans for over 100 years, steadily widening her possessions in the north. Immediately after the Etruscan expulsion the Romans had joined with their Latin neighbors in a league, but soon Rome attempted to dominate the Latin League; when the Latins resisted Roman leadership they were forced into submission. In 390 the city of Rome itself was sacked by the Gauls, a primitive people from the north, but the invaders were eventually driven back to their homelands. Throughout the fourth century Rome occupied herself with campaigns against the Samnites, the rugged mountain peoples to the east and south of Latium. Finally the Greeks were subjugated; in 281 the Greek city of Tarentum called upon King Pyrrhus of Epirus to help his Greek kinsmen against Roman advances into Greek territory, and after losing two battles to the Greek king, the Romans defeated him decisively in 264. With the fall of the Greek cities in the south all of Italy fell to the control of Rome.

It is difficult to give a satisfactory explanation for the militarism of the early Republic. Were the Romans naturally so proud and aggressive that they set out to conquer the peninsula? Were they, by their very natures, imperialists? Perhaps it would be best to say that the Romans practiced defensive imperialism: they feared the aggression of the Etruscans and Latins, later the Samnites, and finally the Greeks, and to protect their own interests, the Romans conquered all their neighbors. Roman foreign involvements were also complicated by the Roman custom of engaging every state with which she came into contact in some kind of a treaty, usually a defensive alliance. Thus if one of her allies were drawn into war, the Romans were obligated to give aid, and if a Roman ally broke its treaty, such action was always viewed as hostile by the Romans. Through such a system of "entangling alliances," the Romans were constantly drawn into confrontations with her neighbors.

The manner in which Rome chose to govern Italy was unusual in that the Romans did not create a centralized empire, but preferred to rule through a confederation, in which the Roman allies were given rights and privileges depending on their loyalty and ability to practice Roman citizenship. If an allied state proved worthy, Rome might even grant it full Roman citizenship: permission to vote on Roman magistrates and in the assemblies, the right to trade in the Roman marketplace, and the right to marry Roman citizens. Most of the members of this Roman confederation actively sought good relations with Rome in hopes of eventual citizenship, with all its rights, privileges, and prestige.

• The Plebeians

The early Republic was also an age of great domestic conflict in the Roman community itself, for throughout the period the plebeian class continually exerted pressure on the patricians to gain political and social equality. In addition to being excluded from holding major office and from participation in the priesthoods, the commoners were compelled to pay heavy taxes and forced to serve in the army. The interpretation of Roman law was also in the hands of the patrician class. The plebeian community chose to protest their lot through a series of strikes, which brought the economic and military activities of Rome to a virtual standstill. Such a strike, in 450 B.C., gave birth to the plebeian assembly and the election of the ten tribunes. Soon the patricians were forced to take the demands of the commoners seriously: the plebeian assembly was granted legal status as an official Roman legislative institution, the tribunes were recognized as legal Roman magistrates, and by the fourth century even the consulship was opened to the plebeian order. Around 300 B.C., after more than 150 years of conflict between the two orders, the plebeians had gained access to all political and social privilege on an equal footing with the patricians; in their long quest for equality the commoners had been amazingly peaceful and patient, having rejected the use of violence as a means to their end. After 300 Rome ceased to be an aristocracy of birth, but gradually became instead an aristocracy of wealth; the wealthy (*optimates*) practiced the same degree of political, economic, and social discrimination on the poor (*populares*) as had the patricians on the plebeians.

• The Punic Wars

The middle years of the Republic (264-133 B.C.) was the period in which Rome became undisputed master of the Mediterranean world. Her first great enemy was the city of Carthage, on the coast of northern Africa, a state which had established a great economic empire in the western Mediterranean. Through a series of three wars, the so-called Punic Wars, the Romans eliminated Carthage as a major power. The First Punic War (264-241) saw Rome extend her sovereignty over Sicily, Sardinia, and Corsica. The Second Punic War (218-201) was one of Rome's most taxing conflicts, for the Carthaginians were led by the youthful and brilliant general Hannibal, who decided to strike at the Roman homeland by marching his army of over 40,000 over the Alps and down into the middle of Italy. Hannibal defeated two consular armies in the first year of the war; the Romans probably lost more than 50,000 men in that year alone. In 216 a Roman army of 80,000 met Hannibal at Cannae, near the Adriatic coast where Hannibal overwhelmingly defeated an army twice the size of his own; nearly all the Roman troops lost their lives. But Hannibal did not feel strong enough after Cannae to march on Rome, and instead marched to southern Italy where the Romans sealed him up until 202. In 204 Rome launched an invasion of Africa under the direction of the general Scipio, who was able to defeat the Carthaginians and bring the war to an end.

The Third Punic War (149-146 B.C.) was an unnecessary one, for Carthage was finished as a major power, but Roman imperialism and outright vindictiveness demanded the elimination of their old rivals. The city of Carthage was razed to the ground and the citizens who remained were sold into slavery.

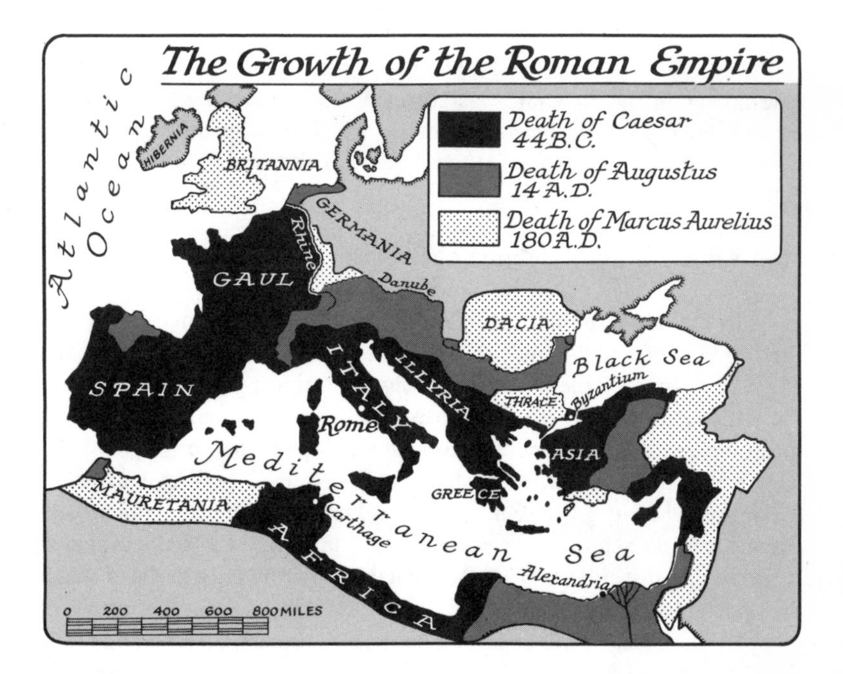

• Roman Imperialism

There seems little doubt that by the end of the Second Punic War Rome had embarked on a policy of conquest for conquest's sake, and that the state was blatantly imperialistic in its motivation. Roman generals and aristocrats reaped the benefits of successful wars and the wealth of empire whetted the appetites of the aristocratic Senate. By 146, Rome controlled all of Italy, Sicily, Sardinia, Corsica, Spain, part of southern France, northern Africa, Greece, and Macedonia; Egypt had been made a protectorate, and Roman armies were active in Asia Minor. There seemed no limit to the expansion of the empire, no end to Roman imperialism. The armies of the state were by no means invincible and on many occasions the Romans suffered disastrous defeats; yet Roman manpower, drawn from her own citizens and her allies, seemed endless. In less than 100 years Rome came to dominate most of the civilized Mediterranean world.

Unlike the manner in which she ruled Italy, the Romans chose to create an empire in the Mediterranean, controlled by governors in charge of the various Roman provinces. The Romans seemed to have been reluctant to construct a vast bureaucracy to deal with the problems of empire, and as a result the provincial governors were given almost complete power to rule as they wished in their own provinces. The governor was in charge of the army, he collected taxes, and he oversaw the law courts. Provincial government in the Republic was generally poor, for many governors enhanced their prestige through lucrative wars, or augmented their own wealth by extortion and graft at the expense of the local residents.

• Mob Violence and Attempts at Reform

In the late Republic (133-27 B.C.) the Romans continued to widen the frontiers of the empire, yet one domestic crisis after another had the effect of destroying the traditional forms of Republic government. Italy in the late second century was a country stricken with serious economic and social ills: small farms were decreasing in number because of the growth of large estates run by Roman aristocrats, and Roman rural residents were flocking to the city in alarming numbers due to their disillusionment and despair. The number of poor and unemployed in the city itself continued to grow, and the number of citizens eligible for army duty declined steadily, since only Romans who owned land were subject to conscription.

In the midst of this crisis two political reformers, Tiberius and Gaius Gracchus, proposed reform legislation which would redistribute much of the land of Italy to the poor, but their measures met with opposition from the conservative aristocracy. The Gracchi brothers began the practice of inciting mobs of poor and unemployed city residents to place political pressure on the Senate, and soon the aristocrats employed the same tactic against the reformers: both Tiberius and Gaius were killed in mob violence, and a precedent was set for the use of unconstitutional force by any politician who wished to enforce his will on the state.

After the affair of the Gracchi, the aristocratic Senate tried to reestablish its dominance of Roman politics, only to be challenged again by the rise of the general Marius in the early first century. Marius, the hero of the *populares*, determined to force his way to supreme power in Rome through the recruitment of his own army, which was more loyal to him than to the Roman state. With his army behind him Marius defied the Senate and was elected to the consulship in seven successive years. Eventually the aristocrats attempted government by force and found their military champion in the person of Sulla, who defeated Marius in the First Civil War (88-82 B.C.). Sulla ruled as dictator in Rome for three years after his defeat of Marius and attempted in that time to revive the failing powers of the Senatorial nobility, but several new leaders soon emerged to champion the cause of the people. The most successful of these new heroes

The Head of Augustus on a Gold Coin, 29 B.C. Courtesy, Museum of Fine Arts, Boston.

were Pompey the Great (106-48 B.C.) and Julius Caesar (100-44 B.C.), who for a time attempted to combine their resources in order to control the state. Soon the two politicians became rivals for absolute control of Rome and their armies engaged in the Second Civil War (49-45 B.C.), in which Caesar eliminated his rival.

With his victory over Pompey in 45, there remained in Rome no one who dared to challenge Caesar's power, which was so well established that in 44 B.C. he declared himself dictator for life. Caesar attempted some reforms during his dictatorship, such as a revision of the Roman calendar, a reduction in the distribution of public grain, the codification of law, and the conferring of citizenship to many Gauls and Spaniards, but he failed to take the proper measures to strengthen the position of the Senate as the foundation of Republican government. He ignored that body, and took for himself nearly all the executive power of Rome. In 44 B.C., amid rumors that Caesar planned to name himself king, a group of aristocratic Romans assassinated him in the hope that the Republic would be restored by the dictator's death.

After the murder of Julius Caesar the fortunes of the Republic continued to grow worse, for there now developed a struggle for control of the state between Octavian (63 B.C.-14 A.D.), Caesar's grandnephew and heir, and Mark Antony, the dictator's close friend and powerful ally. The two politicians disliked each other intensely, but found it best to join forces to gain revenge on the Republican aristocrats who had caused Caesar's death; in 42 B.C. the armies of the Republican forces were shattered and Octavian and Mark Antony personally directed the affairs of the empire. However, by 32 B.C. the two men found it impossible to cooperate any longer and war was the result. Octavian had little difficulty in defeating the forces of Mark Antony and his ally Cleopatra, queen of Egypt; by 27 B.C. he was sole master of the whole Roman Empire.

• Augustus and the Roman Empire

Octavian, later to be called Augustus, was the true founder of the Roman Empire. Never before had any politician been able to so completely dominate the state and manipulate the Republican constitution. Augustus was commander-in-chief of all the armies of Rome, consul, dictator, censor, tribune, and chief priest at various times in his career, and the Senate was packed with his supporters. Fortunately, Augustus was a brilliant administrator and it is a lasting tribute to him that the empire stood on such a solid foundation by the time of his death in 14 A.D. that it was able to withstand a great number of inefficient emperors for the next two centuries. The Princeps (first citizen), as he chose to be called, created an efficient and loyal bureaucracy to help in the task of administrating a vast empire. Augustus himself assumed direct control over the provincial governors and did much to eliminate graft and corruption in provincial administration.

Upon his death in 14 A.D., Augustus was succeeded by a series of four emperors, all of whom were related to him – the so-called Julio-Claudian dynasty. Of those rulers, Tiberius (14-37 A.D.) and Claudius (41-54 A.D.) were capable men who strengthened the state, but Caligula (37-41 A.D.) and Nero (54-68 A.D.) were autocratic and unpopular despots who proved to be inept administrators. The three emperors of the Flavian dynasty – Vespasian (69-79 A.D.), Titus (79-81 A.D.), and Domitian (81-96 A.D.) – were generally popular and intelligent rulers who

The Roman Arena and Ampitheater of Arles. Courtesy, the French Government Tourist Office.

placed increasing confidence in the army to insure their power. The Flavians were succeeded by the so-called "five good emperors" – Nerva (96-98 A.D.), Trajan (98-117 A.D.), Hadrian (117-138 A.D.), Antoninus Pius (138-161 A.D.), and Marcus Aurelius (161-180 A.D.) – all of whom proved to be humane and gifted statesmen. Through their talents and abilities the empire enjoyed peace and prosperity, and a general sense of security and permanence never before evidenced in Roman history.

• Roman Civilization

When Rome first became involved with the political fortunes of Greece in the third century B.C., Roman civilization was still in the formative stage and was shaped by the customs and traditions of a rural, conservative society. It was only natural that the Romans adopted and transformed much of Hellenic culture and made it their own; Roman art, architecture, literature, philosophy, and religion came to be patterned closely after the Hellenic models. Roman religion was more highly ritualized and ceremonial than was Greek, but the major deities of the state were similar in both religious systems. Roman religion was political to a great degree, in that the gods were worshipped so that they might bring benefit to the state; in the later days of the Republic the state gods were neglected by individuals who sought immortality and a sense of personal importance through the mystery cults imported from the east, or through philosophy.

Stoicism and Epicureanism were the most popular schools of philosophy in Rome, especially among the upper classes. Rome's greatest Epicurean was Lucretius (98-55 B.C.), whose didactic poem *On the Nature of Things* attempted to explain the orderly pattern of the universe in order to free man from all fear of the supernatural and thus gain peace of mind. Stoicism claimed many influential Roman public figures, one of whom was Cicero (106-43 B.C.), the famous orator and politician. Roman Stoicism found its greatest spokeman in the emperor Marcus Aurelius, whose *Meditations* are the thoughts and questions of a philosopher who found himself burdened with the responsibility of governing the empire.

The Hellenic influence was also felt by Roman literature, and several Roman writers have shown themselves to have been equal to the Greeks in creativity and artistry. Some of the finest examples of Roman poetry were produced by Catullus (84-54 B.C.), who wrote passionate love poetry, and Horace (65-8 B.C.), whose *Odes* proclaimed the glories of Rome and the Stoic doctrine of devotion to duty. Vergil (70-19 B.C.), the author of the epic poem the *Aeneid,* traced the travels and adventures of Aeneas in much the same way Homer described the voyages of Odysseus, and at the same time extolled the benefits of the empire and the virtues of Augustus. Although Roman tragedy was generally lifeless and dogmatic, satirical and witty comedies were produced by such authors as Plautus (254-184 B.C.), Terence (185-159 B.C.), and Juvenal (60-140 A.D.). Almost all of Roman history was concerned with an explanation of why Rome had been chosen for greatness and how that greatness might best be preserved. Rome's greatest historian was Livy (59 B.C.-17 A.D.), whose *History of Rome* attempted to trace Rome's rise to prominence and to appeal to Roman patriotic emotions.

Much of Roman art was unoriginal, in that Hellenic and Hellenistic models and modes of representation were copied by later Roman artists and sculptors; yet Roman art differed in its penchant for realistic detail and ornamentation. Architecture in Rome was primarily civic in nature, and designed to give evidence of the glory of empire and the power of the state. Nearly all Roman architecture was massive in proportion and solid in construction; private homes, civic buildings, temples, amphitheaters, and public baths all bore witness to the grandeur and magnificence of the state.

The Romans seem to have had little interest in the pure sciences, and Rome produced no major advances in scientific knowledge significant enough to increase the status of the discipline beyond Hellenistic achievements. Roman science remained much more practical in its applications than did Greek and the Romans became the greatest engineers of the ancient world. The roads in Italy and throughout the empire were solidly constructed and well designed, Roman aqueducts are still utilized in many parts of Europe, and Roman bridges stand as testimony to the brilliance of the empire's engineers.

The creativity of Roman civilization left its mark on later western civilization primarily through the influence of Roman law, one of the most fair and humane legal systems devised by man. Roman law was comprised of three great branches, the first of which was the *ius civile,* or civil law, the law of Rome and her citizens. But the Romans also believed in a *ius gentium,* or a law of peoples, the law which was considered to be common to all men regardless of their citizenship. Finally Roman legal thought advanced the notion of a *ius naturale,* a natural law which is common to all peoples and is of an order higher than any law imposed by any state.

It is inaccurate to declare that Rome's only gift to the future was the preservation and transmission of Hellenic civilization to the West. Roman developments in art, architecture, and engineering continued to be of influence in Europe long after the empire's fall, and Roman legal thought has become firmly entrenched as the basis of most western legal systems. In addition, one of Rome's most influential gifts to the West has been the idea that a single government, motivated and directed by high ideals and a superior brand of civilization, might successfully impose a political unity over a large area, or even over all the world, and thereby provide mankind with lasting peace and prosperity. After Rome's demise several states have attempted such lofty goals, and all of them, like Rome, have failed; nevertheless the idea of a new *Pax Romana,* a lasting peace through world order and concord, continues to remain influential in the West.

4

Barbarian Europe

THE FALL OF ROME has stirred more interest, caused more debate, and inspired more writing than has the death of any other civilization. A numerous variety of explanations for Rome's decline and fall have been advanced ever since Latin writers themselves as early as the second century A.D. began to examine the empire and find it wanting. Some historians busied themselves with a search for the single most important factor behind Rome's decline from Mediterranean preeminence; the great eighteenth-century historian Edward Gibbon, in his monumental history of *The Decline and Fall of the Roman Empire,* determined that the coming of Christianity and its destruction of ancient Roman values and morals was more at fault for Rome's fall than any other reason. Modern historians, hoping that they know better, usually agree that a variety of factors brought on the collapse of Rome.

In addition, the problem of the fall of Rome is complicated by the fact that no one date can be given for the end of the Roman Empire, since Rome's collapse was gradual and lasted for over 300 years. Similarly, no one date can be given for the beginning of Rome's decline, since a good argument can be made for tracing some of the political, economic, and social problems which contributed to Rome's fall back as far as the Republic. Nevertheless, if one begins to examine the empire in 180 A.D., the year of the emperor Marcus Aurelius' death, several indications of serious trouble for the state appear obvious.

• Causes for the Fall of Rome

The second century A.D. was perhaps the most happy and prosperous period in all Roman history: most of the Roman emperors in that period were outstanding, trade and commerce flourished, and the whole Mediterranean world benefitted from the *Pax Romana,* the "Roman peace" which created an atmosphere of safety and contentment. Yet after 180, for the next hundred years, the empire was plagued by civil wars, and of twenty-seven emperors or would-be emperors all but two met violent deaths. Persia rebelled under Roman rule, in Europe the Germans broke through the Roman frontiers into the empire, the Roman middle class became virtually non-existent, and farmers and laborers were reduced to serfdom. It seems clear that the causes of Rome's decline had been developing long before 180 A.D. and had finally worked their way to the surface to hasten the decline and fall.

Several political problems of the late Roman Empire seem to stand out as partial causes of the Roman decline. The empire had never established a constitutional method of selecting a new emperor, and although Augustus' immediate successors usually adopted the man they chose to succeed them, later emperors more and more often named their natural sons as their heirs. Often this practice weakened the empire, since very often the sons proved to be not as capable as their fathers.

Early in the history of the empire the Roman army began to realize that it had the power to create or destroy emperors almost at its pleasure, since every emperor after Augustus began more and more to rely on the support of the army. The emperor Septimius Severus (193-211 A.D.) went so far as to advise his sons to "pamper the army and despise the rest." The army could also be turned against an emperor by ambitious and usually wealthy generals who wished to seize power in Rome; if a general could depend on the loyalty of his troops, or if he could buy their support, he could easily use the army to force his way to power in the state.

Apathy toward political matters by the Roman people must have accounted for a weakening of Roman political institutions, since a general lack of interest in politics by the Roman populace had the effect of increasing the political importance of the emperor and the army. Had the citizens of Rome wished to protest or take political action no effective means were at hand by the third century, since the assemblies were never called, and the Senate consisted of men hand-picked by the emperor.

An important factor in the political decline of Rome was that the empire had become too large and unwieldy for any but the most efficient of administrations to administer. A topheavy bureaucracy, weak emperors, overextended commitments to defend far-flung borders, and a weary army created an almost impossible political situation. The soldier-emperor Diocletian (284-305 A.D.) seemed to realize the problems of ruling the empire singlehandedly and attempted to strengthen the state by splitting the empire into two halves, naming a co-emperor to rule the western section while he himself retained the east. The emperor Constantine (306-337 A.D.) completed the administrative reforms of Diocletian, and although the Eastern Roman Empire benefitted from the personal attention of both these competent rulers, the Western Empire was never able to halt its steady political decline.

The economy of the Western Roman Empire, in dire circumstances long before 180 A.D., was another factor which weakened the state. Since the early days of the empire more and more of the Roman aristocracy fled the turbulent conditions of city life and sought refuge in huge rural estates (*latifundia*), which were intended to be self-sufficient. The great landholders continually enlarged their estates at the expense of the small farmers, who found it increasingly difficult to compete with their more wealthy rivals and became tenant farmers or serfs in service to the rural aristocracy. The "back to the farm" movement on the part of the aristocracy not only deprived Rome of the political participation of the nobility, but of their economic resources as well; the lack of capital investment by the Roman aristocracy in trade and commerce all but destroyed the Roman middle class. Rome steadily became a city parasitic on the eastern portion of her empire; food and luxury items were imported from the east, Rome paid for such goods in gold and silver, and the result was a monumental gold drain from west to east. Inflation in the empire reached ridiculous proportions as emperors continually debased the coinage in an effort to meet the costs of administration and military expenses.

In an effort to remedy the economic ailments of the empire, Diocletian attempted to stem the runaway inflation by issuing new standard silver and gold coins, and by imposing maximum prices and wages for goods and services, but such regulations proved impossible to enforce.

Roman society in the late empire seemed to reflect some of the ills of the empire itself. Throughout the empire a noticeable increase in the amount of slaves was apparent, and an increasing reliance on slave labor, both in the city and on the *latifundia,* indicated a change in Roman values. The common people, apathetic to politics and work, became more and more interested in eastern and oriental religions and cult practices, thereby reflecting a disillusion with the traditional Roman gods and western ethics.

There are, of course, many more causes of the decline and fall of Rome than have been enumerated here, and more theories on Rome's fall certainly will be forthcoming. Recently studies have been undertaken to explore the effects of pollution and ecological imbalance on the city of Rome; the possibility that the Roman aristocracy lost its vigor partially due to the effects of lead poisoning from the use of lead cooking vessels and utensils is being examined; and the implications of the loss of a native citizen base to the Roman army by the third century, at which time 98 percent of the army was German, continue to be explored. The two major factors hastening the decline of Rome – the coming of Christianity and the Germanic Invasions – have yet to be fully examined.

• The Origins of Christianity

Christianity had its origins in the teachings of Jesus of Nazareth, who was crucified in the Roman province of Judea in around 29 A.D. Immediately after Jesus' death, the community of his followers was small and restricted to Jews in and around the province of Judea, but the infant religion began to grow rapidly due to the missionary work of the Apostles, and especially because of the efforts of Saul of Tarsus who later became known to the Christians as Paul. After his conversion to Christianity, Paul became an ardent teacher and missionary of the Christian message, who took as his personal mission the bringing of Christianity to the non-Jews, the Gentiles, of all the Roman Empire.

Our only dependable record of the teachings of Jesus is the Gospel, the oldest book of which was not written until a generation after Jesus' death. According to these records, Jesus revealed himself to be the Christ, the Son of God, who was sent to die for the sins of mankind. His followers were convinced that he had risen from the dead and ascended into heaven, and that he would come again to judge the world. From the Gospels, it is clear that the basic teachings of Jesus were: a belief in the brotherhood of man, forgiveness of one's enemies, self-denial, the avoidance of rituals and ceremonies in religion, the impending end of the world, and the resurrection of the dead and the establishment of the kingdom of Heaven.

Paul took the basic message of Jesus and succeeded in making it attractive to the non-Jews throughout the empire by ridding Christianity of any of the restrictions and constraints of Hebrew law, and by emphasizing the importance of faith in Jesus as God and Savior. Jesus had given no indication that he intended to found a church, but Paul became the principal creator of a unified Christian church and personally saw to its instruction through missionary journeys and by writing letters, or epistles, to many of the major Christian communities. By the time of his death in around 65 A.D. Christian communities had been established throughout the Mediterranean world with predominantly a Gentile membership.

• The Triumph of Christianity

Christianity's success by 100 A.D. must have seemed astounding to the non-believers in the Roman Empire; yet there were many reasons why a religion such as Christianity would have met with success in the world of the first century A.D. The average Roman citizen had grown apathetic to the ancient cults of Rome, which seemed unfulfilling and detached from the cares of the common man; Christianity was a religion which stressed a personal bond between the individual and his god, who would provide immortality for his faithful followers. The Christian message was a message of love, and one which emphasized the value of each individual soul – no Roman citizen felt the love of the state gods, whose business it was to care for and protect the empire, not the individual. Christianity was one of the rare religions of Rome which preached the spiritual equality of the sexes, and it was a relatively easy religion to practice, since it involved no elaborate rites and rituals. But perhaps the most decisive strength of the new religion was that it was highly adaptable and flexible, in that no rigid doctrines or dogmas had been established for the young church. The Christians, working from the basic framework of belief created by Jesus and Paul, were free to formulate the tenets of their religion so that they could meet and refute successfully any theological challenges placed in their path, no matter whether those challenges came from learned pagan philosophers or the members of the various mystery cults of the empire.

The persecution of the Christians began immediately after Jesus' death in the province of Judea and were carried out because of the insistence of the orthodox Hebrews that the new sect posed a threat to Judaism. As long as the Christian communities were small and scattered throughout the empire, Roman authorities paid little attention. Yet soon after Paul's death large groups of Christians had established themselves in Rome and the other cities of the empire where they were quickly regarded as dangerous. The persecutions were regarded as prosecutions by the Roman authorities who judged the followers of Jesus to be traitors to the state, since the Christians refused to worship the state gods of Rome and denied the divinity of the emperor himself. Christians referred to this world as transitory and evil, they looked forward to the coming of a new kingdom called Heaven, and the fact that they met in secret gave rise to all sorts of rumors that they practiced cannibalism and performed sacrilegious ceremonies.

The Roman prosecutions of the Christians as traitors were sporadically carried out for more than 200 years, and of course all such attempts to suppress the new religion failed miserably. In fact, the persecutions increased the popularity of the faith, since martyrdom was quite convincing to many non-believers that the Christian faith was a compelling one – few followers of either the state cults or mystery religions were willing to lay down their lives for their convictions. The persecutions also forced the Christians to unite and form a stronger, tightly disciplined, and well organized church.

Early in the development of the faith certain members of the congregation were selected to serve as priests, the leaders and teachers of the faithful; in the larger cities of the empire an official called the bishop was given the responsibility of leading and instructing all the Christian communities in his city. Naturally the bishops of the oldest and largest cities of the empire – Rome, Constantinople, Antioch, and Alexandria – were the most influential church officials, and by the fourth century the bishop of Rome, or the pope, had achieved primacy over all other churchmen in the Western Roman Empire.

The fourth century marked an important turning point for the Christian religion, for in 313 A.D. the emperor Constantine, convinced that the Christian symbol of the cross had aided him in battle, issued the Edict of Milan, which provided that Christianity be henceforth tolerated throughout the empire. Now the Christian message could be spread overtly and in 395 Christianity was proclaimed to be the official and sole religion of the Roman Empire.

By 600 A.D. the Christian church had proven its stamina, resilience, and determination and had become an institution strong enough to outlast the Western Roman Empire. This Roman Catholic Church had become a wealthy institution and even a powerful political force, for on many occasions the popes were called upon to give political guidance in times when weak and ineffective emperors and kings attempted to rule in the West. The bishops of Rome had wisely exercised their authority to direct the policies of the Roman Catholic Church and the papacy had achieved moral and spiritual power over the lives of all the faithful; by the reign of Pope Gregory I the Great (540-604), the papacy had proven itself to be the single most important, as well as the wealthiest, office in the steadily centralizing hierarchy of the Church.

The popes, in addition to the Fathers of the Church, who were influential theologians and writers on behalf of the Christian cause, had established much of the doctrine which constituted the Catholic faith; writers and philosophers such as Augustine and Jerome had founded Christian belief on a solid philosophical base capable of withstanding and refuting the attacks of the best of the pagan philosophers. In its effort to enforce orthodoxy on the Catholic community, the Church turned her attention to the elimination of heresy, or beliefs which were found to be contrary to the standard doctrines of the faith. The Arian heretics, for example, posed a danger to Christian unity of belief by insisting that Christ could not be the equal of God the Father, since the Son was created by the Father and could not have been co-eternal with him. The orthodox Roman Catholic view, that the members of the Trinity were all equal and composed of the same substance, was reaffirmed by a Church council, and Arianism was suppressed. The Gnostic heresy, which held that all matter was evil and that Christ was all God and could have no human nature, was likewise condemned by the Church.

• The Barbarian Invasions

By 600 A.D. the Western Roman Empire had ceased to exist; perhaps the most important reason for its eventual political collapse was its inability to cope with the migrations of Germanic peoples into the empire. The Barbarian Invasions, or Germanic Invasions, were actually long-lasting migrations of Germanic tribes and their movements into the empire were usually not hostile onslaughts, but rather peaceful attempts to gain admission to the protecting boundaries of the Roman world. Rome had been aware of the primitive and nomadic German tribes to the north of the empire ever since the early years of the Republic, when they had presented no consistent threat to Rome's northern defenses. But in what has come to be called the crisis of the fourth century, when the Germans pushed across the Roman frontiers in increasing strength and numbers, Rome found itself unable to halt or even absorb the steady stream of new and backward peoples who steadily forced their way south.

The migrations of the Germans in the 300's A.D. may have had several causes. Perhaps the demands of a steadily increasing population forced the Germans to look for new and more hospitable lands to the south, or perhaps many of the German tribes were under pressure to flee their traditional homes due to the violent entrance into northern Europe of Asiatic migrating tribes such as the Slavs and Huns. Many Germans wished to have a part in the security, wealth, and opulence of the Roman Empire and attempted to gain admission not to overthrow Rome, but rather to benefit from its civilization. Unfortunately, the Germans found that the cultural gulf between their own more primitive existences and the fully developed and complex culture of Rome was too vast to close, and their resultant anger and frustration was catastrophic for the political and cultural order of the empire.

Through their invasions, the barbarians brought about the total collapse of Roman civilization in the West. The Visigoths, for example, a tribe of Scandinavian origin, was granted permission to enter the Eastern Roman Empire in 360 as a Roman ally, but all attempts to Romanize the tribe failed, and the Visigoths rose in rebellion, defeated a Roman army at Adrianople in 378, and killed the emperor Valens. The Visigoths were persuaded to go west by Valens' successor, and under the leadership of their ruthless leader Alaric they moved northward through Italy, sacking the city of Rome itself in 410. From Italy the tribe made its way to Spain where they settled permanently. Another Germanic tribe, the Vandals, abandoned their traditional grounds in the north and moved through eastern France and Spain to the northern coasts of Africa. From their African kingdom, the Vandals, led by their brutal but brilliant king Gaiseric, disrupted commerce in the western Mediterranean, and even sacked Rome in 455. The Ostrogoths, another tribe of Scandinavian origin, migrated first to the Eastern Roman Empire, then to the West, where they established the Ostrogothic Kingdom of Italy. Their king, Odoacer, refused to uphold the incompetent western emperor Romulus Augustulus, who was murdered by the Ostrogoths in 476. Romulus Augustulus was the last of the western Roman emperors, for never again was that position necessary in a region so decentralized and disorganized.

Perhaps the most unsettling of the barbarian invaders of Rome were the Asiatic Huns who were led by the warrior king Attila, known by the Romans as the Scourge of God. The Huns moved south into Italy and threatened to take the city of Rome itself, but Attila's hordes were stopped in northern Italy by Pope Leo the Great, who perhaps persuaded Attila to spare southern Italy and turn northward. For whatever reason, the Huns withdrew, Attila died shortly thereafter, and the most dreaded of the barbarian invaders dispersed in Eastern Europe and Russia.

Many other migrating Germanic tribes shifted position in the third century and weakened the frontiers of the empire as a result. The end of the sixth century found the Burgundians firmly entrenched in southern France, the Angles, Saxons, and Jutes in Britain, and the Franks in western Germany and France; few could have predicted that the latter tribe would play what perhaps was the most important role in the shaping of medieval Europe.

• The Eastern Roman Empire

While the West was shattered by the assault of the Germans, the Eastern Roman Empire was enjoying a better fate. The ancient city of Byzantium served as the capital of the empire, although it was renamed Constantinople in 330 when the emperor Constantine chose to make his base of operations there. The two halves of the old Roman Empire gradually drifted apart over the years, so that by the reign of the Eastern Emperor Justinian (547-565 A.D.) we may speak of the old Eastern Empire as having developed a civilization substantially different than that of the West – a civilization produced by a blending of Roman and native eastern, "oriental" influences. Justinian was the last emperor to hold on to the dream of a united Roman Empire and he unsuccessfully attempted a series of invasions of Germanic kingdoms in the West in hopes of reestablishing Roman order. However, under Justinian and his successors, the East was governed by emperors who ruled as absolute monarchs, who personally controlled both church and state. The Eastern Roman Empire gradually evolved into the Byzantine Empire, which was strong enough to survive until the fifteenth century.

• The Early Middle Ages

In Western Europe the course of civilization was radically different than in the East, for by 500 A.D. the political unity and order once provided by Rome had given way to the decentralization and regionalism of the Germanic states. Barbarian Europe had no need for the complicated and intricate organization of Roman politics and law; the various German states were governed by kings or chieftains whose main duty was to lead the state in time of war. The king was aided by a council of advisers composed of the great nobles and warriors of the tribe. Germanic law seems crude and unsophisticated in comparison with the Roman legal system: it was based on the common body of law customary to a particular tribe, an accused man was presumed guilty until proven innocent, and many times innocence could be established only by the successful completion of an "ordeal," such as trial by combat. Since the barbarians devoted themselves mainly to farming and fighting, trade all but ceased between east and west. The Germans preferred their own simple and more primitive art and architecture to that of the classical world, and everywhere Roman temples, civic buildings, and villas fell into a state of disrepair.

Education in the early Middle Ages was mainly utilitarian, and almost entirely in the hands of the Church. The Catholic Church in the West must be given credit for the transmission of classical culture to the new medieval civilization in the process of formation in Europe. The works of the great Greek and Roman authors were preserved and recopied in monasteries throughout the continent, to be reabsorbed into the mainstream of Western thought in the ninth century. Almost all of early medieval literature itself was produced by those within the Church, and that literature, of course, dealt primarily with religious subjects, and both knowledge of and interest in the Greek and Roman classics was not wide. One notable exception to this rule was the philosophical work *The Consolation of Philosophy* by Boethius (480-524 A.D.), who attempted to determine the relationship of man to the universe through what was essentially a non-Christian viewpoint.

• The Franks

The first of the Germanic successor states to the Western Roman Empire to found a viable and long-lasting kingdom in Europe were the Franks. Largely through the abilities of one man, King Clovis (481-511 A.D.), the founder of the Merovingian dynasty of Frankish kings, the Franks were able to conquer nearly all of what is now France and a portion of Germany besides. Clovis was able to establish his authority over all of the other great nobles of the Frankish realm who might attempt to usurp power and to increase the prestige of the royal house. Early in his reign Clovis was converted to Roman Christianity and became a valuable ally of the Catholic Church in its fight against non-Roman Catholic and pagan peoples. Clovis' dynasty remained in power until 751; his heirs followed Clovis' policies of expansion and annexation, domination of the Church, and personal aggrandizement until 639, when the royal line began to degenerate. The so-called "do-nothing kings" of the later years of the dynasty lost themselves in the pursuit of pleasure, cared little for political concerns, and delegated most of their authority to their principal subordinates, the mayors of the palace.

Through personal ambition and sagacious politics, the mayors of the palace increased their authority in the kingdom to the point where they became more powerful than the Merovingian kings themselves. Mayors of the palace such as Pepin of Heristal (687-714) exercised more and more control of the Frankish nobility and passed their positions of dominance on to their sons and heirs. Pepin's son Charles Martel (714-741), called "the Hammer," was not only a good administrator but an excellent warrior who led the Franks to victory in 732 over an invading Moslem force at Tours, only 100 miles from Paris. After 632, the year of Mohammed's death, the Islamic world had successfully spread its influence over much of Asia, all of northern Africa, and most of Spain. The Moslems, dedicated to the conquest of all the world for Allah and the conversion of that world to Islam, posed an immediate threat to Christian Europe from their Spanish base of operations. At Tours the Moslem advance was halted successfully by the Franks: all Europe, with the exception of Spain, now seemed safe from the threat of Moslem conquest.

• Charlemagne

Charles' son Pepin the Short (741-768) was able, with the blessings of the pope, to remove the Merovingian dynasty from power and to replace it with his own family, the Carolingians, as kings of the Franks. Pepin's son Charles the Great, or Charlemagne (768-814), proved to be the greatest ruler in the history of early medieval Europe, transforming the kingdom of the Franks into the centralized and far-flung Carolingian Empire.

Charlemagne was essentially a warrior king who was also a gifted politician; he was not a formally educated man, but he possessed a keen mind and took an active interest in cultural developments in his empire. The first Frankish emperor was involved constantly in campaigns against the Franks' hostile neighbors, such as the Saxons and Avars to the east, the Moslems in the south, and the Lombards in Italy; in the forty-six years of his reign he engaged in no less than fifty-four wars. Yet conquest was not his only interest, for he successfully strengthened the empire from within by dominating the Frankish nobility and constructing a loyal and efficient bureaucracy. Although he sometimes sought the council and advice of the great nobles and churchmen of his empire, Charlemagne always took the most active part in the governing of the state. He increased the efficiency of royal government by dividing all Frankish territory into 300 administrational units called counties, each of which was headed by a count, a noble appointed by the emperor to oversee local government, collect taxes, and administer justice. To keep a watchful eye on the activities of his counts, Charlemagne sent out *missi dominici,* literally "those sent by the king," to all the counties of the realm.

The emperor was involved deeply in the welfare of the Church throughout his lands and personally encouraged reform and the elimination of abuses in the practices of the Catholic hierarchy; the appointments of all major churchmen in the empire were controlled by him. This domination of the Church has led later authors to describe him as having practiced Caesaropapism, or the control of the Church by the secular head of society. Learning and the arts received much of his attention; he sought to provide schools throughout his kingdom which would provide for the needs of churchmen and laymen alike, and he surrounded himself with the greatest scholars and writers of the day at his court in Aachen.

On Christmas Day, 800 A.D., Charlemagne was crowned by the pope as King of the Romans, and the Carolingian Empire officially was created. The significance of this event seems to be that the idea of empire had never died in the West, and although the Carolingian Empire was never as large or pervasive as was the Roman, Charlemagne had come closer to restoring a semblance of unity to the West than had any other political force since the demise of the Roman Empire.

Charlemagne died in 814 A.D. and the Carolingian Empire declined soon after the death of its founder. The dream of a politically united Europe seemed far from reality in 814, yet the beginnings of political, economic, and social change were not far removed, and the early medieval period gradually was giving way to the full flowering of medieval civilization.

Suggestions for Further Reading

Albright, W.F., *The Archaeology of Palestine* (1960)

Alfred, Cyril, *The Egyptians* (1963)

Artz, F.B., *The Mind of the Middle Ages* (1954)

Bailey, Cyril, ed., *The Legacy of Rome* (1924)

Bark, W.C., *Origins of the Medieval World* (1958)

Bloch, Raymond, *The Origins of Rome* (1960)

Breasted, James H., *History of Egypt* (1912)

Burn, A.R., *Minoans, Philistines and Greeks* (1930)

Ceram, C.W., *Gods, Graves and Scholars* (1951)

Chiera, Edward, *They Wrote on Clay* (1951)

Dawson, C. H., *The Making of Europe* (1932)

Duckett, E.S., *The Gateway to the Middle Ages* (1938)

Freeman, Kathleen, *The Greek City-States* (1963)

Kitto, H.D.F., *The Greeks* (1957)

Kramer, S.N., *History Begins at Sumer* (1961)

Lot, Ferdinand, *The End of the Ancient World* (1931)

Mattingly, Harold, *Christianity in the Roman Empire* (1967)

Moscati, Sabatino, *The Face of the Ancient Orient* (1962)

Muller, H.J., *The Uses of the Past* (1952)

Olmstead, A.T.E., *History of the Persian Empire* (1948)

Somervell, D.C., ed., A.J. Toynbee, *A Study of History*, 2 Vols, (1947-1957)

Spengler, Oswald, *The Decline of the West,* 1-vol. ed. (1934)

Tarn, W.W., *Alexander the Great* (1956)

Tarn, W.W., *Hellenistic Civilization* (1952)

Wilson, J.W., *The Culture of Ancient Egypt* (1951)

Zimmern, A.E., *The Greek Commonwealth* (1911)

THE MEDIEVAL WORLD

5

Medieval Society, 800-1300

CHARLEMAGNE had made himself the dominant political figure in the West, and through his "renaissance" western culture had been rejuvenated by the recovery of patristic and Latin classical learning. Yet, within half a century of the great emperor's death, his empire had collapsed. The Carolingian state folded before internal and external challenges which arose in the ninth century: Viking and Magyar invasions, feudalism with its devolution of governmental and military authority to the local level, and failure to develop institutions sophisticated enough to cope with the problems of ruling such a vast area with so many different peoples.

The Northmen covered a generous area in their raiding, from the eastern coast of North America to the heart of European Russia. The Vikings had not participated in the development of Christian European civilization; still primitive, these seafarers, attracted by the comparative wealth both of Greek and Latin Europe, swept up the rivers in their long boats, trading where resistance was strong, raiding where it was not. These pirate/merchants were devastating visitors, but by the middle of the tenth century they were proving valuable settlers in Normandy, as they did later in England, Sicily, and the Latin states of the Holy Land. Beyond undoing the destruction which they had caused, the Vikings – particularly those known as Normans – made important contributions to medieval civilization in architecture, government, and social institutions after adopting Latin civilization.

• Early Feudalism

One response of the weakening empire to these last barbarian invasions was to invite the brigands to settle; another was feudalism in its rudimentary form. Feudal institutions, as so many elements of ninth and tenth century society, were a bridge connecting the late classical world with that of the high middle ages. Ninth century feudalism was largely a response to Viking invasions against which the central (imperial) government could afford no protection. Feudal institutions had precursors in the late Roman Empire: Diocletian had bound men to occupations into which they were born, the agricultural classes were depressed into a state of dependence upon great rural landowners themselves gathering more land and authority into their hands, the church became a great landholder, and the pope exercised governmental functions which the emperors could (or did) not themselves utilize.

Feudalism entered public law in the Carolingian Empire in 847 and 877, when it was decreed that every man and each parcel of land must have a lord. Feudalism was not yet the complicated structure which it was to become, however; at this time (ninth through mid-eleventh centuries) it meant personal dependence of warriors (the vassals) upon their lords in a freely-chosen *personal* (and nonheritable) relationship expressed in terms of the lord's obligation to provide land as a form of income for his vassal, who in return followed him to war.

Before the end of the period, feudalism had begun to involve more complex relations: in 1020, Fulbert of Chartres explained the obligations of vassalage to William, Duke of Aquitaine, thus: the vassal should treat his lord so as to be "harmless, safe, honourable, useful, and cooperative" and should also give counsel and aid. Of course, the central obligation was still military. The feudal landscape on the eve of the high middle ages, then, was still rudimentary: political power had devolved to the area commanded by a castle and upon its owner, still an armed thug rather than the chivalrous knight of literature. Public powers – for example, police and legal jurisdiction, taxing authority, defense, lawgiving – were at this time enforced by private individuals, a situation analagous to that found in the Old American West. By the mid-eleventh century powers of government were in the hands of local strong men, against whose jurisdiction there was no appeal. The justification for this monopoly of power lay in the essential attribute of the knight: only he was a warrior, and with his status (as in the ancient and in the Germanic civilizations) went both the highest degree of personal freedom and the right to lord it over others less able to be fighters.

• The Peasant

The knight's authority lay most heavily upon the peasants who lived under his jurisdiction. The rural workers, like the knights, lived a life dominated by nature to a degree unimaginable to us: lacking watches, their lives were regulated by the hours of daylight; lacking the chimney, the night and the winter were bleak, occupied by quasi-hibernation; lacking the most rudimentary sanitation, life was short and racked by illness; lacking sufficient food, the quality of their wretched lives was miserable. More domestic animals than humans in their existence, the peasants suffered through a dreary life on earth sustained by the hope of a glorious life to come, much as American slaves did. Though peasant life improved throughout the high middle ages, merry and jolly it never was.

Peasant communities, scattered and isolated by forest, bog, watercourse, slow and poor means of transportation, and by the dangers of travel, lived almost entirely to themselves. In the early twelfth century, a journey from London to Rome took six weeks. Their low-yield farming was supplemented by food gathered in the woods and fished from the streams; livestock were half-starved and bony – when there is not enough for people to eat, animals fare even worse. Nor did the rustic have an honorable relation with the lord whose land he worked; to the contrary, he was totally dependant and had no appeal rights against his authority, no defense against his greed but flight.

Where the noble did not work, the peasant did little else; where the noble had sufficient to eat, the peasant did not: where the knight had all powers, the peasant had none; still, men of all classes shared terror in the face of darkness, misery in the face of cold, vulnerability to infection and illness, and defenselessness in the face of natural forces. Life was grim, coarse, and extraordinarily barren.

• Culture

Although the church had entered into the structures of feudalism and had become a great landowner and governor, her bishops fighting men and her peasants little better off than those of secular lords, the Benedictine monks had so come to dominate the gentler side of life that the years from the sixth through the eleventh centuries are known as the "Benedictine Centuries." Society at all times has certain needs which must be filled; the knights filled the need for defense and government, the church satisfied the spiritual requirements, and the good monks fulfilled many functions which are now associated with government or with private philanthropy: education, scholarship, maintenance of libraries, missionary work, hospital and inn management, innovation of scientific farming methods, and direction of charitable institutions and functions. Monasticism did not mean withdrawal from the world and its needs.

Largely as a result of the Carolingian Renaissance, the classical and patristic heritage had been recovered for Europe, and had been conveyed to areas which had not shared in the culture of the Roman Empire. This period is more notable for the transmission of preexisting learning than for new creativity, but this was a necessary step in the intellectual flowering of the West which was shortly to come. Europe acquired cultural uniformity in educational tools and equipment, in Latin as the language of the European learned, and in curriculum elements. Beyond this limited area, the continent in the middle ages was a kaleidoscope of diversity and of social and geographical mobility; there may be models, but there was no "typical" fief, manor, kingdom, individual, social group – it is this variety which gives the period its color and interest.

In the ninth and tenth centuries there was a slow substitution of mechanical power for human and animal strength. New agricultural methods included the heavy wheeled plow, capable of turning deep furrows; the three-field system, which allowed only one third of the arable land to lie unplanted every year; the nailed horseshoe and the horsecollar with lateral traces; mills powered by water and (later) by wind; and wheels mounted on axles rather than on vehicle bodies, later to be employed in fulling machines and iron forges. For the knight, the introduction of the stirrup was fundamental; now he could rise and hurl his lance as a missile weapon.

• Lord and Vassal

It is customary to speak of a "feudal system," but feudalism was anything but systematic. The core of feudalism was confusion, among personal, property, political, legal, and social rights, and among noble, ecclesiastical, and royal jurisdictions. Yet, the confusion which was feudalism did have certain basic parameters, expressed in the mutual loyalty of lord and vassal. The specific obligations of man to lord, and of lord to man, were subsumed within that basic principle. The lord who had replaced public authority with his own also assumed its duties, not as a function of theories of feudal lawyers, but as a matter of practicality. The voluntary association of free men with one another had begun to be transformed into a property relationship, hereditary and formal rather than personal, dependent upon the physical proximity of the contracting parties.

The Monastery of Mont Saint Michel, built between 1203 and 1208. Courtesy, French Government Tourist Office.

While there was no "typical" feudal relationship between lord and vassal, and while many parts of Europe were never feudalized at all, there were some elements which appeared often enough in the lord-man relationship where it did exist to justify describing them here. By the ceremonies of homage and fealty – swearing by a vassal to be his lord's man and to be faithful to him – a knight incurred the responsibility of military service for a stated number of days annually (usually 40, except in England) and the obligation to share in garrisoning the lord's castles. He also had the duty to provide hospitality to the lord, and to give him advice and counsel on matters affecting the lordship as a collective entity. As well, the vassal was obliged to proffer money on certain stated occasions: relief (a token of renewal of the feudal bond when either lord or vassal died), a gift when the lord's eldest son were knighted and his eldest daughter married, and ransom when the lord was captured. When the obligations of personal service began to be commuted to money payment, as happened in England before the end of the eleventh century when military service was commuted for some to payment of *scutage* (shield money), an economic relationship came to replace the personal one. Feudalism thereby began to be both transformed and undermined.

The lord's duties to his vassal were related to those of his vassal to himself – rights imply obligations. The vassal had to supply knight service; the lord had to provide protection for his man. The vassal was obliged to attend his lord's court for counsel; the lord was expected to provide justice for his vassal at his court – judgment by peers (vassals holding of the same lord). The vassal was to treat his lord with honor, respect, and courtesy; so the lord was to hold his vassal in similar state. The vassal owed his lord wardship, the custody of his widow and orphans should he die before they were of age. This custom protected the lord's permanent interest in the fief; it also provided a form of life insurance for the vassal, whose survivors would be protected and provided for. As with any agreement, the complex of mutual obligations between lord and vassal depended on good faith, and failing that on force. Should the lord fail to fulfill his obligations, the vassal had the right to defy him and renounce his homage and fealty; should the vassal fail in his duties, the lord had the right to reclaim the lands which he had let out as fief. In either case, the right depended upon might.

• The Noble Lord and Lady

The life of the noble lady and man, of the high middle ages was more comfortable and "civilized" than that of their predecessors of the ninth and tenth centuries. Their home – the castle – was designed as a fortress and it did not lose this character until the end of this period. Cold, drafty, dark, humid, these grim towers came more and more to be constructed of stone after the turn of the twelfth century. They were aswarm with armed retainers, prostitutes, servants, and hounds. Simple stone towers (keeps, baileys) at the beginning of the period, castles by the end of it often adopted the sophisticated concentric architecture of (for example)

Edward I's great structures at Conway, Carnarvon and Harlech, aesthetically attractive as well as militarily functional. During the same years, life within them became more comfortable: chimney flues appeared in the twelfth century, enabling warmth to be generated within the castle; window glass appeared by the fourteenth century, cutting down the chill drafts which howled across the gigantic rooms; tapestries, one of the glorious artistic media of the middle ages, hung out from the walls to provide insulation; plumbing, while primitive, did exist. Rooms came to be smaller and more numerous, showing a growing desire for privacy and intimate conversation, itself a sign of cultural refinement.

When not fighting, the noble preferred to occupy his time in hunting, not only for the game but also for the practice in armsbearing; it was a way for him to keep in shape. It was customary to eat only twice daily, but the amounts of food and drink were such that we need not pity the nobility, greedy gluttons with gross manners and grosser behavior. Evening relaxation varied from gentle pastimes such as chess and backgammon through singing and enjoying stories and poems (whether read or recited) to a good hanging or animal-baiting. When seasons permitted, the outdoors played a large part in the life of medieval man – few were the castles which had no parks and formal gardens, and the forest was ever nearby. With the slow spread of the commercial revolution, more and more nobles acquired money and developed a great talent for spending it in the way most approved by the feudal code: largesse, wasting freely, giving it away perhaps, or at least giving a riotous party. Bourgeois ideas of thrift were totally alien to the noble and his lady. A good deal of the knight's money was spent for jewelry, fine brocaded cloth, illuminated manuscripts, reliquaries and other enameled pieces, eating and drinking vessels, and so forth. The knightly class evolved. Accurately described as thugs in Carolingian times, by the end of the thirteenth century knights had come much closer to the idealized picture found in Sir Walter Scott's *Ivanhoe* and other romantic writings.

The noble lady, too, evolved in her relation with her society. Ladies of the earlier middle ages were physically tough, uncouth in language, loose in personal conduct, and foul of smell. Yet, by the end of the thirteenth century she was firmly atop the pedestal which has lasted until our own day. But, as the fourteenth-century *Book of the King of La Tour Landry* copiously illustrates, life could be hard indeed for the noblewoman who held what her husband viewed as a too exalted view of her position in life; the book resounds with thwacks and thumps. The noblewoman had different occupations and entertainment than did her husband – childbearing was of course her prime justification for existence and her most important role, but beyond that her pastimes were amusements of the mind (reading, music, and so forth), hawking, and religion. Her practical functions as a unit of society included supervision of the domestic side of the fief, overseeing medical services for its inhabitants, and governing it when her husband was absent (which was often). Unable in the eleventh century even to hold land in her own right, by the end of the thirteenth she could do homage for a fief and testify in court. Queens were in a different category, and some of the greatest people of the middle ages were queens, such as Eleanor of Aquitaine, Blanche of Castile, and Margaret of Anjou.

• Chivalry and Courtly Love

The improvement in women's lot coincided with the development of chivalry and courtly love, and with the great rise in the popularity of veneration of female saints (especially the Blessed Virgin). Chivalry may best be described as the system of rules and regulations which should govern the professional and personal conduct of the ideal knight. Heavily influenced by the Church, which – as in the Peace and Truce of God – had attempted to exert some degree of influence over the warrior's behavior, particularly as it affected the weak, the defenseless, and the noncombatant, chivalry attempted to civilize the knight in his relations with other knights and with noble ladies. It involved training for knighthood, a distinct change from the earlier dubbing. The candidate for knighthood was expected to undergo some training both in arms and in "courtesy" at his lord's castle, at the conclusion of which regimen he underwent a complex investiture with the order of knighthood, closely supervised by the church.

We can sum up the practical impact of chivalric ideals by saying that chivalry bears the major responsibility for changing the nobility from the class of armed roughnecks into a cultured aristocracy; the change is demonstrated in numerous ways. Respect for noblewomen was translated into formal behavior toward them; men even began to speak with them for enjoyment, quite a change from the previous attitude that talk was wasted, assault was not. Slowly the program of chivalrous conduct between one knight and another became actuality – sneak attacks became infrequent, thus the knight no longer had to ride about encased in metal under a blazing sun (he would have time to arm after the challenge). Knights were no longer imprisoned after capture in pestilent, mouldy dungeons, but were paroled on their word in anticipation of the payment of ransom. Tournaments, originally great brawls, became pageants which, while still dangerous and still a source of profit for knights-errant, at least followed

From Valturius, "De Re Militari." An illustration in one of the earliest books printed in Italy. Courtesy, Museum of Fine Arts, Boston.

certain rules intended to make them less bloody. Standards of gentlemanly courtesy slowly spread (for example, since the sword was drawn across the body with the right hand, a handshake of greeting occupied the arm which might otherwise perhaps be engaged in baring steel).

Other signs of the evolving civilization of the feudal caste may be found in the literature intended for their enjoyment. One is the new cult of courtly love, which arose in southern France in the early eleventh century. A literary rather than a social movement, courtly love nevertheless ameliorated the knight's behavior toward ladies, and gave him new ideas of what a proper heterosexual relationship should be as well as a manual with rules of the game, such as, Andreas Capellanus' *Art of Courtly Love.*

The beginnings of courtly love literature are found in the poetry appearing in southern France in the eleventh century. This vernacular poetry was written mostly by laymen and for laymen, unlike the Latin poetry which was written largely by clerics for their own class. By the end of the twelfth century, in the more culturally aware courts of France, England, and Germany, the masculine epics characteristic of the earlier feudal age – for example, *Beowulf,* the *Song of Roland,* the *History of the Kings of Britain* by Geoffrey of Monmouth – were being superseded by romances, devoted less to war than to ladies and their courting. The more popular romances were organized into cycles over the years, associated with Charlemagne, with the heroes of classical antiquity, and with King Arthur and his knights. Unlike the epics, most romances were written in prose, they did not pretend to be history, and they were intended to be read rather than recited. They were also much more inventive, thickly populated with magic spells, enchanted forests and people, wizards, and the like. By the turn of the thirteenth century, Lancelot, Tristan and Isolde, Galahad, Percival, Merlin, and Guinevere were well-known in courtly circles.

Before the end of the thirteenth century, chivalric literature in its maturity was joined by new literary forms, in part dependent upon the epic, romance, and courtly love, in part original. *Aucassin and Nicolette* is a delicious piece of irony, treating elements of the epic and romance with irreverent humor. William of Lorris' part of the *Romance of the Rose* culminates the courtly tradition; its latter two thirds, written by Jean of Meung about 1275, is of totally different character, learnedly allegorical, humanistic, rational, almost a textbook of humanistic education presented for the court nobility of the fourteenth century. The book and gracious behavior slowly became as important to the knight as was the ability to hack with a sword and splinter an ash spear on another's breastbone. Civilization has never been an instant process.

• Serfdom

The peasant slowly worked his way from serfdom to freedom, from personal dependence to that sturdy peasant independence so characteristic of the farmer. In western Europe, much of this evolution had been accomplished by about the turn of the fourteenth century; in eastern Europe, the process was slower, and in Russia, full legal serfdom was not even imposed on the peasantry until 1785.

One naturally thinks of the medieval peasant as a serf; yet there were areas of Europe which never knew a personally dependent peasantry, and degrees of dependence varied considerably. Further, to be free did not necessarily mean to be a peasant without obligations to a lord. Seignorialism is the word medieval historians prefer to describe both the complex of relations between a lord and his serfs, and the economic organization of the farming unit, the manor. Seignorialism should not be confused with feudalism; while both involved social relationships, the former was the *economic* system which supported the latter, primarily a *political* arrangement. Further, the tie of lord and vassal was contractual, mutually and voluntarily accepted, an honorable agreement among free men; the tie of lord and serf was also mutual, but involuntarily accepted by the serf who, unlike the knight, inherited his status. Seignorialism did *not* involve honorable, voluntary association among free and equal partners; it was a relationship between a superior and his inferiors.

A "typical" manor or a "typical" lord-peasant relationship did not exist; economic and social relationships described here never existed on any single manor, but most of the elements in our model were common on most of them. A manor was the economic unit which supported the knight. Ordinarily a village would comprise land of several manors, and thus be subject to several lords. While the peasant's social and labor associations were defined in terms of the village, his legal and political relations both with his fellows and with his lord were determined by his affiliation with a specific manorial government.

A minimal description of the manor lord's rights over his peasants would include the following elements, all of which supported the lord in order that he need not work, but could spend his time in war, training for war, governance, and leisure. The various dues and services described below took the place of taxes, insurance payments, military service, and other obligations of modern man. Like most men of the underdeveloped world of our own time, what the medieval peasant most wanted was security, and this he had, if in less measure than his lord. The lord's land in the manor was planted, cultivated and harvested for him by his peasants, who delivered its fruits to his barns; in addition, he had the right to a stated share of produce from land other than his own, such as hay from the meadows, pasturage for his animals, and firewood. As well, he had the right to a specified number of days of work performed by his peasants weekly, to their labor in maintaining roads and bridges, and to tax them generously. He could also charge them fees in kind for the performance of economic functions over which he held the monopoly: if the peasant could gather deadfall in his lord's woods, he had to provide firewood for his lord; if he could let his livestock graze in the common pasture, he had to provide cheese for the lord; when he was permitted to fish in his lord's waters, the lord received a portion of the catch; when his swine fed in the lord's wood, the lord received some of their pork; similar dues arose from the peasant's use of his lord's brewery, winepress, flour mill, baking ovens, and so forth. The peasant's resentment against his obligations arose less from the specific matters set forth above than from the fact that in theory, and often in practice, the lord could order him about at will, so that on any given day the countryman would not know what he would be doing on the following day.

But, in this hierarchically-ordered world with its complex relations of man to man, the peasant did have rights, important, if few. Like the manorial obligations, they varied greatly, but the following were common. First, the serf was dependent only in his relations with his master; among others below the knightly caste, he was a legal person, with the right to sue and be sued in court, to witness and to assist in judgment, and he could not be subjected to any lord other than his own. Unlike the slave, the serf was bound to the land which he worked; this gave him the security of steady labor and income arising from it – of course, from the point of view of the ruling class, this custom ensured a steady labor supply. This practice meant, too, that the land which he worked could not be taken from the peasant. Although in theory the lord owned all the serf's property, the accumulation of savings by peasants indicates that the theoretical right was not enforced in practice. In addition to dues in kind, the serf owed the tithe to his parish church, the headtax (hated as a sign of serfdom), and certain other money payments which tended to multiply both in number and in kind as money came more and more to rival the fruits of the land as the symbol of wealth and status.

Even in this rough society, the superior had obligations to his lesser fellow as well. Custom (law) and tradition gave the peasant some relief from his life of constant drudgery: he had a great number of religious holidays on which he could not work; he had a garden plot of his own which lay beyond the lord's confiscatory rights; he did not have the obligation of military service unless his own settlement were attacked, nor indeed any of the rights and obligations of citizenship; he was fed by his lord on the days when he worked the lord's land; and he could participate vicariously – often the best way – in the festivities and pageantry of the knightly class, watching tournaments, attending fairs, enjoying executions. Further, his lord owed him definite obligations. Foremost among these were protection and land, the two things which the peasant most needed. In addition, the lord provided a church, a priest, seed at planting time, and the services for which the peasant had to pay in kind (mills, etc.). There were as well external restrictions on the lord's conduct toward his peasants – law in many regions, the teachings of the church as expressed in sermons and in theological treatises, the contractual nature of the relations of the two groups, and pragmatism – one did not abuse willfully a valuable economic resource.

It would be ungenerous also to disregard the element of humaneness in most men as a restriction on their behavior; it is significant that Thomas of Marle, accused by early twelfth-century writers of atrocities against his dependent men, received universal condemnation for his savagery in northern France. It was seldom the lord who oppressed his peasants, rather it was his officials (usually drawn from the peasants) who milked the lord's rights to the fullest, to their own advantage. We should not overestimate the kind feelings of most knights for their serfs, however. Language often signifies reality, and it is no coincidence that the medieval Latin word meaning the peasant's family is translated as "litter." And the manorial courts, sometimes hailed as great safeguards of the peasant's interests, rendered impartial judgment only between peasants. When the customals came to be written down in the thirteenth century they were prejudicial to the peasants' rights as against their lords, whose courts they were. The lords' judicial authority included what we would now call police or magistrate's court jurisdiction, and often extended upward to include high justice, the right to punish by maiming of limb or deprivation of life. This is a further example of the devolution of public authority into private hands. Possession of a gallows by a lord was the ultimate status symbol.

The peasants in these two and a half centuries infrequently expressed themselves in writing, their tools seldom survived the ravages of time, their hovels are known only through imprecise pictures in art works of the time, their furniture and utensils are rare. What is certain are constant change and steady improvement in the peasant's economic lot, owing to economic and technological factors, their impact assisted by a growing public order and security. After the mid-eleventh century there was a slow spread in the use of the tools and machines already extant. The importance of mills, horsecollars, and similar inventions was the replacement of human by mechanical and animal power, thus freeing time and manpower for other uses, and leading to an improvement in nutrition. By the mid-twelfth century, metal, especially iron, tools were more common, and perhaps the most important of these (other than the wheeled plow with the moldboard) was the great clearing axe, the peasants' chief means to force back the forest and add more arable land to that under cultivation. It is during the twelfth century as well that the three-field system of crop rotation became common in northern Europe, leading to greater production of cereal crops, which in turn still further improved peasant nutrition.

• The Serf Becomes Free

Because of the increase in available food the subsistence level of existence became a thing of the past; the countrymen could now depend upon a more predictable and sufficient supply of food. Adequate nutrition also contributed to an increase in family size, since people lived longer and infant mortality dropped astonishingly. Population density increased across the twelfth century in those regions where the agricultural innovations were employed, but somehow it managed to stay just behind the increase in the means to support it. As so often in history, he who had, profited first; the lords had less need of their peasants' labor owing to changes in technology and the increase in yields. In many areas of France and other advanced agricultural regions, many peasants found that most of their onerous obligations to the lords had been commuted into money payments, thus transforming their relations with their lords in a way analogous to those of lord and vassal, also increasingly commuted to money payments across the twelfth and thirteenth centuries. Not that all obligations were wiped away – there remained, and would remain for centuries to come, the *corvée* and other customary obligations – but they lay on all the rustics alike, serf or free, and most of the farmers of economically progressive regions managed their own affairs in considerable independence.

What were the changes in the status of the peasants from the turn of the ninth century to the close of the thirteenth? Chattel slavery was an institution of the past by the mid-eleventh century in most of Europe. Serfs were not slaves; the serf was dependent upon his lord, but his lord was neither his master nor his owner, although perhaps to the serfs on some of the more primitive manors run by the rougher type of lord the distinction might have seemed a poor joke. The serfs did have security, which some free peasants did not – those who hired themselves out as farm laborers and held no land upon the fruits of which they could depend. By no means were all peasants serfs, and the proportion of unfree to free peasantry steadily declined during this period; again, it is important to bear in mind that the free peasants had virtually all the liabilities of economic dependence which the serf had.

There are many reasons why the servile status of the peasantry was alleviated so rapidly during the twelfth and thirteenth centuries, in those areas where this was indeed the trend. In Germany's eastward-moving frontier and in those vast tracts of newly reclaimed agricultural land in northern France, the principal factor in the improvement of peasant status was the need for rural labor; a lord could hardly lure settlers to come to these lands newly open for settlement by promising them serfdom – he had to do better than that, and consequently those peasants who went to these pioneer areas went as free men, often further enticed by the lords' providing them with tools, homes, and a church. The new status for frontier peasants filtered back to affect the lot of those who stayed behind, less because of the goodheartedness of the lords than because they did not wish their serfs to run off to areas where conditions were better. Other serfs bought their freedom. The commutation of services into payments in kind and in money freed the peasants' time and labor for their own betterment.

The serf could also escape his status through manumission, which was not uncommon by the end of the thirteenth century, and by becoming a clergyman, since the unfree were not permitted to take Holy Orders. If a serf could escape and settle in a town for a stated period, usually a year and a day, he was free. There were, more rarely, migrations of entire villages; there were also instances of villages joining together to negotiate with their lords for charters of liberty which defined their obligations, privileges, rights of self-government, and so on. It seems that revolt would be an obvious means by which serfs could gain their freedom; but just as was the case with slave rebellions in the old South, peasant revolts in the middle ages were never successful in gaining freedom.

• The Commercial Revolution

It is largely from the peasant class that the bourgeoisie, the middle class – founded on commerce, industry, and the town – descended. The commercial revolution was fully as revolutionary as was to be the industrial revolution of the eighteenth and nineteenth centuries. Beginning late in the eleventh century, roughly contemporaneous with, but not caused by, the beginning of the crusading movement, the commercial revolution had its origins in a revival of trade. The causes of the commercial revolution are difficult to sort out, since the nature of the evidence is often obscure and it is difficult to determine which element in the cause-and-effect equation was which. What is here presented as a sequence of events in time was actually a number of processes and events taking place at once, interracting upon and catalyzing one another. It is impossible to have commerce without transportation and without both industry and raw materials to supply it; this is hardly startling information, but the point is that there was not before the later eleventh century the presence of all these elements at once. A number of factors operated at one time to produce the revolution's beginnings: the reappearance of long-distance transportation from the Italian maritime states, particularly Venice, Pisa, and Genoa, ambitious to engage in long-distance trade; the availability of goods from the east which were both light and expensive (for example, spices, fine eastern cloth, jewels), an ideal combination for merchant sailors; the availability either of money or of some other commodity desired by the merchant at the location to which he took his wares; the emergence of England as a source of wool, and of the Flemish towns as manufacturing centers of fine woolens; and a rising demand for the natural products of the Baltic littoral. These are the principal factors in the revival of trade.

When international commerce began to revive, so too did local trade and cities located in an advantageous location for trade. Older cities which happened to be well-situated for commerce burgeoned – London and Paris, Rouen, Hamburg. All of the international, and most of the interprovincial, trade was by water, the cheapest and fastest means of transport; the combination of evil roads, beset by robber barons and common thieves, and poor and small vehicles, further argued for sea and river transport. Prosperity followed the navigable watercourses. Ideas, too, followed the paths of trade, a trend paralleled in the spread of Christianity in the ancient world and in that of the Protestant movement in the sixteenth century.

Before the end of the twelfth century, many new techniques of enterprise had been developed, particularly by the Italian merchants; among the new instruments of business were the joint-stock company, maritime insurance (from which all other forms of insurance descend), merchant law which in special courts protected the trader's and investor's legitimate interest, banking as a means both of currency exchange and of investment, commercial moneylending, cheques, individual credit (and usury), and annuities.

Local industry came into being to claim a share in the reviving trade. We must not think of manufacturing plants but of small shops in which a small number of craftsmen both made and sold their products, whether for local consumption or for trade. Of course there were some large manufacturing centers, particularly the clothmaking towns of Flanders and northern Italy, but these were exceptional. Many towns tended to specialize rather than to be locales of general manufacture, for example Limoges, renowned for its exquisite enamelware. And there was the lush Gascon wine trade, a source of profit both to Englishmen and to Gascons.

The craftsmen were ordinarily organized into guilds, less analagous to our labor unions than to a combination of union, civic or service club, and fraternity. The guilds, unduly romanticized by some modern social critics, were insufficiently flexible to be a permanent element in society. Originally they comprised both the manufacturer (craftsman) and seller, but the obvious divergence of interests of these two groups quickly led to the formation of two kinds of guilds, craft and merchant. The craft guilds performed many functions: they closely regulated (and thereby limited) conditions of manufacture, pricing, competition, and sale, criteria of quality, standards of admission to the guild; so detailed and cumbersome were most of the guild regulations that they tended to stifle initiative and creativity.

Although artisans initially sold their wares in their own shops, it did not take long for the merchant to appear, the man who purchased his products from the craftsman and sold them elsewhere. The final step in this process was the system whereby a merchant would furnish the raw materials to the manufacturer and then buy the finished product for resale. Just as the seignorial and feudal relationships contained elements of social insurance, so too did the guild perform similar functions. The guild ordinarily made available a form of life insurance to its members, by the apprentice system which ensured that a dead member's surviving sons would learn their father's trade, bore some fiduciary responsibility to a man's widow, and engaged in many acts of corporate worship and other forms of solidarity. But the guilds, as functioning economic units, withered away well before the end of the middle ages. The reasons are clear; they were too particularistic in their concerns, they fell more and more under the control of their most powerful and wealthy brethren, they did not adapt to meet the competition and other and larger forms of capital enterprise, and they became so exclusive that well before the end of the middle ages it was virtually impossible for an apprentice or journeyman to become a master (thus a full member of the guild). This last factor was one of the important elements in the appearance of a new class: the urban worker who would never be a manager or entrepreneur – the proletarian.

• The Origins of Towns

While there is considerable debate about town origins, the towns here to be considered are those which arose from commercial settlements. A town may be defined as any settlement in which merchants and artisans supported themselves by their occupations and bought their food elsewhere; such a place would not have been possible without the agricultural revolution which made a surplus possible in the countryside. The town-dweller of bourgeois status differed from his bucolic cousin in significant ways: he had freedom of movement, necessary for the merchant; he had fixed, rather than arbitrary, obligations, else there would have been no incentive to accumulate capital; he had, with his fellows, a large measure of self-government, but this was emphatically *not* democracy, since ordinarily participation in government was confined to guild members. Further, the overlord of a town customarily retained important powers over it.

The towndwellers usually taxed themselves, and agreed to military obligations to the town's lord. They ran under their own laws, although it was uncommon for a lord to surrender the privileges of high justice to his towns. Like the serf's freedom, town charters could be gotten in many ways, and as with the serfs, rebellion was not a viable means to establish mercantile rights. The usual methods of obtaining charters were negotiation, purchase, or gift. Gifts were not as common as the other means, since it was a rare lord or king who was astute enough to recognize the advantages to himself of a town; in fact, many established them on the lands of their enemies, since the town could be a contentious political and social unit.

Among the principal type of towns would be those which had charters of limited privileges, described above; those in which the population remained servile; privileged towns, virtually autonomous; and the communes. Communes differed from other types of towns in that they governed themselves, those who held town office being responsible to those whom they ruled. They could be difficult neighbors indeed, particularly the communes of Flanders, some areas of northeastern France, and northern Italy, and they could fight well enough to win major battles at Legnano and Courtrai against the finest orthodox military men and tactics of the day. They were sufficiently troublesome to their royal, feudal, and episcopal neighbors to have received an almost universally bad press from those chroniclers not of their own municipalities. Their relations with neighboring nobles differed; in Italy and in southern France, nobles were compelled to become citizens and then generously treated, whereas in Flanders and northern France the noble remained the traditional enemy.

Towns often joined in leagues for mutual protection against common enemies; these leagues were particularly common in Flanders, northern Italy, and around the littoral of the Baltic (the Hanse, the great northern trading association). The Lombard League was to be the doom of the Italian ambitions of Emperor Frederick Barbarossa, and the Flemish towns alternated between defiant obedience and successful opposition to the king of France.

As the status of the newly-freed serf, now a free peasant, ameliorated that of his fellow still bound in a dependent relationship to his lord, so too the developments in the towns affected developments in the countryside. The more towns and the larger, the more demand for the fruits of the earth and the better the prices paid. Coinciding with the enormous expansion of the arable and the more intensive cultivation of all farmland, the growth of consumer demand enabled the peasant materially to improve his lot, and encouraged him to produce surplus which could be sold. Foodstuffs even entered into international trade – wine is the obvious example. There was a growing class distinction among the peasantry themselves, however, since in a period of expansion and dazzling opportunity there are always some more clever, more industrious, more opportunistic, more ambitious than their fellows. Some peasants became men of such substance that they entered a more privileged status and at the same time became objects of scorn, like their bourgeois cousins, because money enabled them to euchre their way into positions theirs neither by nature nor by grace. Resentment was quick to rise against those who lived in as much comfort as their betters. It is the way of the world that those who have, resent those who want a share.

For the peasant, the commercial revolution meant opportunity; for the noble, its impact was more mixed, although there is little reason to assume that the noble was such a simpleton that he neither realized nor took advantage of the new situation. While money enabled the base-born to achieve a material equality with his lord, particularly if the lord were impoverished, new barriers to status appeared: aristocracy rose to defend its privileges by new standards – birth, delicacy, formality, culture, unearned but inherent privilege. Nevertheless, many nobles – especially those of limited resources – suffered from the commercial revolution. While their income tended to remain relatively stable, noblemen's expenses rose precipitously; not only was waste and display a constant drain, but practical expenses also rose rapidly – armor became more elaborate and expensive, housing more comfortable and costly, and oblations formerly made to religious establishments in land now were offered in money. As their status was undermined by the wealth of others, the nobles' reaction was largely ineffective; they were fighting a holding action at best. The impoverished knight would see his child married to a spouse of lower class but of higher material endowments, just as impoverished European nobility in the years surrounding the turn of the present century married their sons to the daughters of newly rich Americans. Social mobility became the reluctant order of the day for these lesser knights, but it was met by a stronger stress on birth and breeding as a criterion of social superiority.

Throughout western history, cities have been the catalyst of change and the centers of intellectual innovation, and so they were in the high middle ages. The medieval environment was primarily rural, but the city was the source of many distinctively medieval cultural developments, among them the university with its philosophical and theological, scientific, medical, and legal teaching and writing; bourgeois literature and drama; and that most characteristically medieval of urban architectural remains, the Gothic cathedral. The period from the mid-eleventh to the late twelfth centuries was distinguished by that remarkable creative movement known as the Renaissance of the Twelfth Century, which marked less the coming of medieval civilization to maturity than its exciting adolescence. The cultural renaissance centered in the cities owing to their wealth and to the patronage of those who held that wealth; once more, ideas followed trade.

• Education and Thought

The medieval university established the now-traditional approach to higher education, including the division into undergraduate and graduate or professional curricula and degrees. The bachelor's degree was, then as now, directed less at specialized training than at broad learning, defined in terms of the seven liberal arts (the term itself is medieval): grammar, rhetoric, and logic, the arts of expression, literature, and clear thinking; mathematics, geometry, astronomy, and music, the scientific disciplines. Graduate work led to either the master's degree (in the arts) or the doctorate (in the professional disciplines). The organization of the university could be dominated either by the students or by the faculty; in either case, the corporation was hierarchically stratified. Not only do our degree designations and academic costume come from the medieval universities, so too do our customary teaching methods of reading and lecture, our basic liberal arts undergraduate curriculum, the university's traditional autonomy from the civil jurisdiction within which it is located, and the association of libraries with formal instruction.

Ideas follow trade routes; they also are transmitted in those areas where two cultures intermingle. While it seems reasonable to attribute the introduction of Greek and Arabic learning into the West to the Crusades, in fact the centers of this transmission were in Spain, southern Italy, and Sicily. Since few could read Greek, and even less Arabic, in the Latin west in the twelfth century, translations were prepared. The new logic was as old as Aristotle, but the lack of its availability in a familiar language had denied its use to Latin-reading thinkers.

In the eleventh century the burning intellectual issue was the question of the propriety of applying dialectical methods (logical reasoning as then developed) to theology, the science of God and of His revelation. Lanfranc of Bec, later archbishop of Canterbury (died 1089), made the use of dialectic respectable in theological disputation by using it successfully against the unorthodox Berengar of Tours (died 1088), thus establishing the usefulness of logic in defending revelation and doctrine. Anselm, Lanfranc's successor at Canterbury (died 1109), put the use of dialectic in proper medieval perspective: it follows, but does not supersede, faith – faith seeks understanding. Anselm also produced a rational proof for the existence of God, the ontological argument: all men can imagine some Being than Whom he can conceptualize nothing greater or more powerful – this Being we call God. Another important controversy centered around the problem of universals: do general concepts (for example, man) have a reality of their own, or are they merely convenient words which express common features shared by individuals (men)? While this may seem an arid schoolboy's argument, it touched deep questions of theology.

Peter Abélard (died 1142) was a man whose brilliance of mind is overshadowed in history by his disagreeable personality and by his famous romance with Heloise. Abélard was an important figure in the history of western thought less because of his teachings (wrongly condemned as heretical) than because of his challenges to traditional patterns of thought and method; he raised questions rather than answered them. What was the proper role of reason in relation to revelation? If one arrives by reason at conclusions which differ from the teachings of received authority, is he humbly to submit to authority or to follow his own path? Abélard urged that reason be the guide, although he protested "I would not be an Aristotle if this were to part me from Christ." His analytical method was later followed by the commentators on the law, and by the great Aquinas: collect the opinions of the authorities, show them in conflict, reconcile the conflict by logic.

In Thomas Aquinas (died 1274) we confront one of the giants in the history of western thought. This southern Italian noble was a man whose philosophical system, serene, logical, learned, complex, still commands the respect of thinking persons. Nothing escaped his careful attention and everything had a proper role in his hierarchically-ordered universal philosophy; like the music of Bach, every note is in the right place. His application of reason to theology was so complete that, while he strongly affirmed the existence of mystery (those truths of theology not explicable by human reason), he stated that mystery could not be *contrary* to reason. Nor, taught Aquinas, is the very existence of God beyond the power of the mind to prove. Since all movement is caused by something which sets it in motion, we are driven logically to a Mover Who is Himself unmoved; like the first Cause of a series of causation, this is God. He also argued the existence of a perfect Source of virtues against which imperfect virtues are measured as a standard; this, too, is God. Aquinas also demonstrated by logic that Intelligence must have planned an orderly and integrated universe. Finally, there is the argument from contingency: the existence of beings and things which are, but need not be, extant leads us by logic to the existence of a necessary Being without Whom those which need not exist are brought into existence.

• Science and Medicine

Not confined to the universities, scientific work made valuable progress in the high middle ages; it was one of the disciplines (another was architecture) in which the practitioners of the period excelled their fellows of the Italian Renaissance. The scientific renaissance of the twelfth century owed a great debt both to translations from Greek and Arabic and to the technological developments discussed earlier. Technology "developed power machinery based on water-, wind-, and ox- or horse-driven mills and such automatically self-adjusting machinery as the mechanical clock. It was inventive and active in applying inventions as shown by the clock, the compass, cartography, spectacles. It made a strong move toward precision, as in metallurgical assaying and in astronomical and mathematical instruments and computers, which provided the prototypes for scientific instrumentation."[1]

The principal scientific achievements of the eleventh through thirteenth centuries can be summarized as follows: mathematics benefited from Arabic influence – the introduction of Arabic numerals, algebra, and trigonometry were fundamental not only to pure mathematics but to the development of quantification and of precision measuring, and the introduction of the zero made higher mathematics possible. Astronomy was another area in which there were notable advances, many based on the newly-translated Greek and Arabic texts, aided by the development of new astronomical instruments, particularly the astrolabe and the quadrant. Its more popular (because more practically useful) brother, astrology, enjoyed a great vogue; it remained respectable until early modern times, when its beautiful symmetry was destroyed by the disproof of the geocentric theory. Great strides were made in optics – for example, by the end of the thirteenth century, spectacles were common.

Medicine, also the beneficiary of newly translated authorities, advanced remarkably in the eleventh through thirteenth centuries. Its discoveries were largely restricted to the universities, of which the most important centers for medical studies were Salerno, Padua, Bologna, and Montpellier. At the time of the Crusades medical practice in the East was more sophisticated than that of the West. The principal improvements in the West came in the areas of surgery (dissection was often part of the medical curriculum), gross anatomy, pharmaceutics, and wound treatment. While the germ theory of disease causation is modern, medical practitioners were aware that disease spread from one who is ill to those who are not.

The isolation of individuals striken by disease was a major stride forward in medical history. Crude anaesthesias were employed, and sterile fields were achieved either by the application of distilled or fermented beverages or by cauterization with hot metal, the latter particularly com-

[1] A. C. Crombie, "The Relevance of the Middle Ages to the Scientific Movement," in Katherine Fischer Drew and Floyd Seyward Lear (eds.), *Perspectives in Medieval History* (Chicago, 1963), p. 39.

The walls of the fortress of Carcassonne. Courtesy, French Government Tourist Office.

mon in the treatment of amputations and of flowing wounds. While the physician was a recognized professional by the early thirteenth century, the preferred medical practitioner was the lord's wife, the barber, or the leech, the paramedics of the day.

• Literature of the City

The literature of the city was different from that of the monastery and of the castle; in the late middle ages and in the Renaissance, Chaucer Dante, Petrarch, Boccaccio, Villon were all city-dwellers. From the town and from the universities came the bourgeois and student literature: the *fabliaux,* the songs of the "wandering scholars," and the drama. The first of these genres was satirical, coarse, didactic. Short stories pointing morals and mocking the pretensions of the nobility not only provided the material for much of the later work of such masters of the short piece as Chaucer and Boccaccio, but many are familiar in the form of nursery rhymes and tales, such as the cycle of stories associated with Reynard the Fox (a clever bourgeois).

From the city environment came, too, the Little Flowers of Francis of Assisi (written about a century after Francis' death by a Franciscan friar), a charming collection of didactic vignettes of the life of St. Francis and of other notable Franciscans. Like the Little Flowers, the medieval drama emerged from a religious ambience; coming from the liturgy of the Mass, the miracle and mystery plays are the direct ancestors of modern drama. In about the middle of this period, the language of the people came to replace Latin as the medium of performance. There were three chief types of medieval religious drama. First was the mystery play: the subject and usually the text came from Biblical stories of an inherently dramatic type. In the twelfth century appeared the miracle play, which presented the lives and deeds of the saints; and in the following century, the morality play, which allegorized the story and its leading characters.

• Architecture

The typical architecture of the countryside in the high middle ages was the castle, thousands of which still dominate their landscapes, grim, powerful, strongholds which convey both the power and isolation of the feudal class. Peasant dwellings have not survived the decay of the years, although many houses of towndwellers have; those extant in Nürnberg were effectively utilized in the Nazi propaganda film "The Triumph of the Will," to symbolize the continuity of Hitler's regime with the German Empire of the middle ages, and to walk in Chester is to walk in the middle ages. The architectural picture which springs to the mind when the middle ages is mentioned however is the towering, light-filled, graceful Gothic cathedral; the product of communal efforts of the citydweller, the cathedral is the expression both of their faith and of their civic pride.

As with feudalism and siegnorialism, not every region of Europe knew the Gothic, and in Italy, in Spain, and in southern France, the Gothic style appears very different than it does in England, in northern France, and in Germany. The Gothic order owed much to its predecessor, the Romanesque. They shared essential features, including a long nave, towers at the front (usually the west) face, an apse circled by chapels behind the altar (usually at the east end of the church), and the setting of rose windows above the front doors and at the ends of the transepts (the cross-bars of a cruciform ground plan). At the beginning of this period the Romanesque was the customary ecclesiastical architectural order in most of western Europe. It was characterized by the round barrel vaulting which supported the stone roof, massive side walls and piers to shore up the great weight of the stone vaulting, small windows except in the clerestory (that part of the wall which supported the ceiling over the main nave, and extended above the roofs over the side aisles), and the rounded arch.

The Gothic order was probably developed at the French royal abbey of St. Denis in the early twelfth century. Its immediate impact is quite different from that of the Romanesque: it is airier, much lighter visually, more fancifully decorated with statuary, rood screens, brilliant stained glass windows, and more complex, more delicate. By comparison, the Romanesque seems squat, solid, dark, plainer, although in most instances the murals which originally covered the interior walls have not survived. Many cathedrals combine both orders, since they were built when one order was dominant and completed under another.

Unique to the Gothic are the flying buttress, the pointed arch, columns carved into statues (giving the typical Gothic sculpture its lean and hungry look), the light-flooded interior, the impression of soaring height, the marvelous balance of the whole structure. The flying buttress was a support outside the main side- and endwalls carrying the thrust of the weight both of the roof and of the walls, which tend to buckle outward with the weight of the structure, to the ground. These enabled the walls to be filled with glass since they no longer had to bear the weight of the building. Pointed arches allow a higher and more open structure than the round arch, architectonically limited in the height to which it can spring by geometrical ratios; the pointed arch allowed more freedom in design. The problems of weight, force, thrust and counter-thrust were carefully and scientifically worked out, as surviving architects' notebooks and manuals demonstrate. Gothic architecture, like the philosophy of Thomas Aquinas, was perfectly balanced, complex and admirable in the care and integrated logic with which it was constructed.

The culture of medieval society was not a panorama of national cultures – it was European, and Italians studied and taught in France,

England and Germany (Aquinas, Lanfranc, Anselm were all from Italy), English scholars such as John of Salisbury, Stephen Langton, and Robert Pullen made their reputations in France, and most wandering scholars were exactly that. It is important to stress the common bonds of medieval society as we turn to the more particularistic units of Church and the states of Europe in the period from the ninth through the thirteenth centuries.

6

The Church and the State in the High Middle Ages, 800-1300

IN THE ELEVENTH CENTURY Latin Europe began an imperialistic expansion which has lasted to our own times. Well before the eleventh century, the Moslems had established themselves firmly in the littoral of the Mediterranean, sweeping from Syria through the Holy Land, across North Africa and thence to the point where they held two thirds of Spain. Yet before the end of the eleventh century, the Moslems at both ends of the Mediterranean were under severe assault by European Christians, beginning a hostility not concluded until the end of the First World War and still a factor in international politics.

The thrust against the Crescent began in Spain where the enemy was convenient for attack, then spread to southern Italy and Sicily. Before 1100 Europeans were settling in the newly-recaptured Holy Land. Many elements coincided to bring about this first age of European imperialism in the post-classical world. The dominant religious ingredient was a desire to expel the Moslems from lands which they had not held in the days of the early Church. Christianity was becoming more militant, as shown by the new concept of the Christian soldier, "Christ's knight." Increased public order added restraint on the behavior of the knightly class – perhaps a more useful release for these men's proclivities could be found fighting the enemies of Christ rather than His servants?

• The Spanish Reconquest

The Spanish Moslem (Moorish) states were ripe for attack. While they luxuriated in an advanced material civilization and enjoyed a good standard of living, their weakness lay in their disunion and quarreling. The first crusade in Spain began in 1018; there were five more before the end of the century, maintaining a relentless pressure and slowly pushing back the area of Moorish control. The Moslems, divided by the ambitions of their leaders, were unwilling to cooperate against their common enemy. Christian forces frequently had Moorish allies, a situation to be repeated in the Holy Land. Aragon, Castile and Portugal emerged as the strongest Christian states and bore the heaviest responsibility in future conflicts. After the mid-thirteenth century the outcome of the struggle was not in serious doubt. The future history of Spain was conditioned by her nearly five-century war against the Moors. Spain in the middle ages and in early modern times differed from the rest of Europe – her religious orthodoxy was intensely militant and the development of her political and social institutions was retarded by the perpetual crusade.

• The Kingdom of Sicily

Compared with the relatively simple situation in Spain, that in southern Italy and Sicily was complex. By the end of the tenth century Saracens possessed Sicily, representatives of the Byzantine Emperor held eastern and southern Italy, and the rest of the south was subject to other rulers. A local rebellion was in progress against the Byzantine authorities when some Normans headed home from the Holy Land joined the rebels in 1016, and soon great numbers of Normans were employed as mercenaries by whoever would hire them; their relations with the Lombard authorities became more regularized when the Duke of Naples gave these brigands a county (Aversa) of their own.

Shortly before the mid-eleventh century, three sons of the knight Tancred de Hauteville arrived and established themselves as chiefs of the Normans in south Italy. Shortly after receiving the pope's formal acknowledgment, the Norman rulers successfully campaigned against Byzantine and Moslem power in south Italy and Sicily, a prelude to their aggressive leadership during the First Crusade. The south Italian and Sicilian Norman states were not united until 1127, when the new Kingdom of Sicily emerged under Roger the Great as the first cosmopolitan kingdom of the high middle ages, the seat of a civilization which combined Byzantine, Moslem, and Norman cultures and institutions into a dynamic whole under

a highly centralized monarchy and a professionalized administration. The cultural and religious toleration practiced in this polyglot state came about not because it was theoretically desirable but because it was realistically necessary. The same rough accommodation arose in the relations among Christian settlers and the indigenous Moslems in the states founded by the crusaders.

• The Crusades

The expeditions to the Holy Land were anticipated by the Spanish Reconquest, by the Norman incursions into southern Italian lands, and by the Norman Conquest of England in 1066, undertaken beneath banners blessed by the pope. Unlike their predecessors, these Crusades went beyond the home continent, although Palestine was familiar to west Europeans and their goal was a particularly sacred place, the lands where Christ had walked, taught and prayed, and where He died. Finally, papal impetus for these great movements was overt; the first Crusade was called by Pope Urban II at Clermont in 1095. The Byzantine Emperor, Alexius, had asked the pope for assistance against the Turks, although it is unlikely that he envisioned this help as independent of his own control. The pope was quick to respond, since he both had a dream of reuniting Christianity again into one organic institution (the Eastern and Western churches had separated in 1054).

From the first eastern crusade (1096) to the fall of the Latin Kingdom of Jerusalem (1291) there were problems and conflicts which, despite the stunning success of the First Crusade and the establishment of the Crusader States in the Levant, despite the devout integrity of many crusading leaders, despite the very real Christian motivation of thousands of faithful men who made the arduous journey to the east, were to spell the ultimate military failure of the crusading movement. In the Holy Land the Saracen leaders finally were able to unite and the crusader states' doom was certain. Each arriving army conflicted with the Latins who had settled and who did not welcome the prospect of seeing their peaceful relations with the local Arabs stirred up by men who had come to kill infidels. While the crusading armies fought well, and while their leaders knew strategy and tactics, command was terribly flawed since the feudal nobility were a proud lot who did not take naturally to discipline. Consequently, impatience repeatedly endangered promising battle situations, as did the refusal of many leaders to take orders from others; nor were these armies usually under unified command, fighting instead as separate feudal hosts.

The failure of the Byzantine Empire enthusiastically to support the crusaders embittered the westerners and contributed to the diversion of the Fourth Crusade, which never reached the Holy Land, instead plundering Constantinople and establishing Latin rule in the European precincts of the Empire. The longer the crusading movement lasted the more the leaders went for other than religious reasons, and the more was the temptation to the papacy to use crusades to further political ambitions, exemplified by Boniface VIII's declaration of a crusade against a rival family.

Men learned a great deal more about their world from undertaking the Crusades, and there were notable advances in geographical knowledge, in navigational technology, and in comfortable living – the last since the crusaders who returned home brought with them new tastes, new styles, and new demands which only could be satisfied by trade, to the great profit of the Italian trading towns. Franciscan missionaries penetrated legendary central Asia and China, and before the end of the thirteenth century were followed by that remarkable merchant traveler Marco Polo. The crusaders developed specific improvements in military technology both from the Moslems and from the environment of the Near East; these included changes in design and function of castles and the wearing of a cloth outergarment over armor to keep off the heat of the sun – this garment (the coat-of-arms) came to bear a heraldic symbol identifying the wearer. These results were a poor return for the enormous expenditure of lives, energy, and wealth, all of which better might have been used to hasten the development of Europe.

• Medieval Law and the Benedicts

Earlier medieval law was customary and traditional rather than the product of jurisprudence. Lacking a systematic integration of principle and practice, lacking even a rationalization of legal doctrines, medieval legal thinking could make little progress until a framework of rationally-organized law was developed. As so often in the intellectual history of the high middle ages, those who pursued legal studies found their inspiration and model in the ancient world. The Justinian Code, compiled in sixth-century Byzantium, was a rational integration of the Roman legal experience, offering not only a systematic organization of the law but also jurisprudential principle. Around the turn of the twelfth century the Code appeared in legal instruction at Bologna, and rapidly dominated the legal thinking of the period. A sophisticated collection of material, it attracted the attention of glossators, men who wrote commentaries and interpretations of the Code. These served to make the Code a suitable medium for use as a textbook for legal scholars.

Political theory and legal study developed largely within the medieval Church, beginning with Pope Gregory I (died 604), in whose reign occurred important changes which justify regarding this pontificate as a major turning-point in the history of the Church. He began the significant alliance between the papacy and the Benedictine monastics, he established the primacy of the Roman See throughout the western Church, and he put the power of his office on a secure economic and administrative base.

The monks who followed the monastic rule of Benedict of Nursia (died about 544-547) played the major cultural and social part in the history of the western Church during the period from Gregory the Great to the late eleventh century. What made the Benedictine Rule successful in the West was its commonsense approach to the religious life. It required vows of stability (monks were to remain at the monastery where they made their initial profession unless released by authority), poverty (they were to own nothing as individuals), chastity, and obedience to their abbot, customarily elected by the monks. The daily routine of the monks kept them busy but not oppressed. Time was set aside for sufficient rest, for leisure, and for solitude, as well as for corporate worship (the *Opus Dei*) and for work. When the rough Lombards invaded southern Italy in the sixth century, the brethren fled to Rome, where their mission underwent a significant transformation. They became linked with the papacy and were active missionaries in the West for the popes.

• The Feudalization of the Church

One must not overstate the vigor and spirituality of the earlier middle ages; the secular (non-monastic) aspect of the Church presents a different picture. Since bishops and other great churchmen controlled large amounts of land, they fell naturally into the feudal order, and the conflict between a churchman's role as servant of God and his position as secular magnate and ecclesiastical baron was never satisfactorily resolved. With lay nobles, clerical aristocracy had the responsibilities and opportunities of lordship; they owed homage and fealty to their overlords, they participated in feudal government, they managed vast estates with dependent serfs, they exercised authority over lower clergy and over their knights, and they amassed considerable wealth, not always employed in the service of the Church. And the way of life of many of these men was as rough, violent, and sensual as that of the lay nobility. The conditions of the time demanded that the bishops be governors as well as pastors, and it was difficult to behave more like the latter than the former.

Unfortunately for spiritual values, a bishop and tenant-in-chief of the crown had public functions; thus it was necessary, from the viewpoint of kings and great secular lords, that the ecclesiastics who held lands of them, and acted as surrogate wielders of their authority, be loyal to them (their "man"). Thus these laymen demanded a voice in the election of a bishop, then later acquired in many areas of Europe the right to select this man who was to be Caesar's servant as well as God's. It was surprising neither that these churchmen had trouble sorting out their loyalties and responsibilities, nor that reforming spirits among the clergy should call for a reordering of priorities. Periodically various provinces of the Church underwent reforms (as under Charlemagne), but these rejuvenations did not have lasting effects because they were not sufficiently institutionalized and because they were local rather than general in the western Church.

The feudalization of the Church was the background from which the Gregorian Reform emerged; it was also the Reform's immediate cause. In the mid-eleventh century there was no clear distinction between church and state, nor was there agreement on precisely what the powers of the laity ought to be over churchmen. From the period when Christianity was recognized as the state religion in the Roman Empire emperors had exercised great power over the Church, even claiming that their offices came from God as much as did those of the clergy, and that they had a responsibility before God to answer for the good order of the Church (theocratic kingship). Those who opposed this tradition argued, not that it was not traditional, but that it was wrong.

The Mountain of Prayer. Title page to *Monte delle Oratione.* Courtesy, Museum of Fine Arts, Boston.

• The Gregorian Reform

It is ironic that the great Church reform of the eleventh century was initiated by a layman, Emperor Henry III (died 1056), who was canonized by the Church in recognition of his holy life and works. When Henry became emperor in 1039, the papacy was the captive of Roman courtiers and unworthy popes who had brought the prestige of the Fisherman's

Throne to its low point in the history of the Church. Popes were made and unmade to suit the family interests of the Roman nobility. Henry III hastened to Italy where he held a council which directed the deposition or resignation of the three putative reigning popes. After the probable murder of two succeeding popes, Henry appointed Bruno of Toul as Pope Leo IX (1049-54), the first saintly reformer of the high middle ages. Henry's appointment, while uncanonical, did remove the papacy from the control of the great Roman noble houses, and Leo was careful to insist that he be properly elected after his arrival in Rome. Leo held reform councils all over northwestern Europe, but perhaps his chief contribution to ensuring that reform would be an ongoing process was to associate the papacy with an influential and uncompromising group of monastic reformers who can properly be called revolutionaries.

One pole of Church reform was to be found in the monastic orders. The older Benedictine monastics, so often a source of reform within the Church, had themselves fallen in need of reform in the eleventh century. They were not corrupt or immoral, rather they had become too comfortable and too wordly. New orders arose during the eleventh century, advocating a return to old, pure ways. These new orders – Carthusians, Cistercians, Grandmont – shared a severely ascetic life, a refusal to become involved with the world (as had both the Benedictines and their tenth-century reformed Order, the Cluniacs). They advocated a simple liturgy and church architecture and as little involvement with the feudal order as was compatible with existence.

Monastic reform was aimed at the monastic orders; the Gregorian Reform, coinciding with it, was aimed at the whole Church and at revolutionizing the Church's relations with the world. The attack of the Gregorian reformers on abuses and corruption in the Church from about 1060 to about 1120 was carried out with an intemperate determination. Clerical celibacy was a principal target of the reformers' ire. If the Church were to succeed in her mission of leading men to salvation, she had to control the appointment and tenure of her clergy, an argument also intruded into the quarrels over canonical elections and lay investiture. Married clergy tended to establish clerical dynasties and provide for their own children in the Church. It took many decades and repeated denunciations and excommunications for the clergy of the West to accept the monastic requirement of unmarried clergy as part of their discipline, and perhaps this would not have happened at all had not economic forces come into play which made a married priesthood less a moral than a financial liability.

Another viciously attacked moral flaw was simony. This is not simply the purchase of church offices; to the Gregorians, it was a heresy because simony is *any* interference with the free operation of the Holy

Spirit in designating candidates for clerical office through free election. This was a serious matter, for to have an unworthy bishop was to endanger the eternal lives of the faithful; hence the violence with which simony, celibacy, and lay investiture were attacked.

Lay investiture was a particularly difficult practical problem, since it was commonplace throughout western Europe. As a result of the feudalization of the Church, appointment to higher church offices which owed secular obligations tended to fall into the hands of kings and magnates. Canonical election was reduced to a formality. The initiation of the College of Cardinals in 1059 removed the papacy from lay control; Gregory VII and his successors ferociously fought to remove bishops and abbots from a similar state.

Lay investiture consisted of a king or baron granting to an ecclesiastic the *symbols* of his spiritual office – in the case of a bishop, his ring and staff. While this symbolized an ecclesiastical function performed by a theocratic king, it implied *no* sacramental power; a bishop is consecrated by other bishops laying their hands upon his head to bestow the apostolic succession, not by the investing of symbols of office. Nevertheless, if the lay investor refused the symbols, the bishop could not function as diocesan ordinary. The attack against lay investiture began in 1059, and was pursued with increasing determination in the Eastern Synod of 1075, which laid stringent penalties both on any who accepted or gave royal investiture.

This revolutionary program was inconsistently applied, because no pope, even the redoubtable Gregory VIII, could afford to antagonize all rulers at once and fling Christendom into probable schism. The king of England was sympathetic to Church reform in those areas where it did not adulterate his own rights as he saw them, and had already reformed the English Church. The king of France allowed synods and councils to meet, even if he ignored their decisions. But since the Holy Roman Emperor was in deep trouble with his nobility over his firm attempts to wrest back crown lands and powers usurped during his minority, Gregory VII decided to strike at the distracted Empire. As well, it was in Germany that the great churchmen had been associated most closely with the lay power; they were indispensable to the emperor as counsellors and ministers and as the source of much of his military strength.

But where control of church personnel was central to the success of the Gregorian Reform, Henry IV thought his own control essential to the success of his policy in the Empire; since each contending party regarded the stakes as uncompromisable, conflict was unavoidable. Gregory VII was not a lovable person, nor was he inclined to be reasonable or conciliatory. His pontificate (1073-1085) saw the Gregorian Reform program, personified in the pope, become the offical policy of the Church, and marked the radical extreme to which papal power had laid claim. With Gregory the Holy See became a monarchical papacy, the pope claiming absolute obedience within the Church and without, and the right to judge (and therefore to command) secular rulers. Gregory's determination was matched by his arrogance and self-righteousness. His famous papal letter, the *Dictatus Papae,* was registered in 1075; a collection of quotations carefully selected from extant canon law collections, it supported the High Gregorian view of papal power.

This view of supremacy of papal power over all other powers and jurisdictions was a revolutionary doctrine which challenged the existing social, political, and religious environment as it affected church-state relations, as well as relations among the bishops, abbots and pope. Naturally the old order found defenders, who included many archbishops and bishops, as well as the ablest canon lawyers of the day. Secular rulers were even less pleased at the prospect of Gregory's success. The conflict between the papacy and the empire long outlived the original protagonists, although the immediate issues surrounding lay investiture were settled in 1122. The Concordat of Worms provided for canonical election of bishops, but in the presence of the emperor or of his representative who was thus able to influence the election process.

To misunderstand the dual role of the pope as head of the Church and of an ecclesiastical state is to misconstrue the papacy of the middle ages and of the Renaissance. The papal state had its own monarch, the pope; once elected, his authority was more absolute over his citizens – Christians – than that of any medieval ruler over his subjects. The Church state had its princes, the Cardinals, and its hierarchy of archbishops, bishops, and lesser dignitaries, just as the medieval state had a hierarchy of nobility. As each state had a law code, so the Church had canon law. The Church had its diplomats, the legates, central both to the process of the Gregorian reform and for later papal diplomacy, keeping the center of power in close touch with the outlying areas. Like any state, the Church had a cabinet and an administration, indeed the most advanced and innovative administration of the medieval period, and a professional civil service. She had armed forces, both permanent and called up for such special expeditions as the Crusades. And the Church had the most elaborate taxing structure of the middle ages. Only the greatest popes – Alexander III, Innocent III – were able to serve both ecclesiastical and monarchical functions equally well.

As a result of the Gregorian Reform, papal authority was a reality over the Latin Church, and reform of the clergy of the West thus was facilitated. Hence, simony, clerical marriages, and incontinence were less and less common, a genuine rarity after 1200. The success of Gregory VII in deposing Henry IV and releasing his subjects from their obedience not only made good a radical new claim, but gave future popes a tempting weapon to use against recalcitrant monarchs.

• Innocent III

The medieval papacy reached its greatest power in the high middle ages under its ablest pontiff, Innocent III (ruled 1198-1216), whose great achievement was to preserve papal leadership in the face of the forces emerging from the Renaissance of the Twelfth Century. His success, like that of Aquinas in philosophy, was so complete that little more could be done to enhance the prestige and power of the papacy until new standards for judging it appeared; this did not occur until the reforming popes of the sixteenth century reemphasized the spiritual role of the papacy at the expense of its administrative and political aspects. Trained as a canon lawyer, Innocent became pope at 37 – it is characteristic of the high middle ages that most rulers were young. His achievements are astounding; he never lost a conflict with a secular ruler, although he contested with the rulers of most European states. This pope made papal administration the most complex, sophisticated, and efficient of any administration for decades to come. But he is chiefly interesting as a reformer; as the Gregorians responded to the problems arising from the feudalization of the Church, Innocent responded to those arising from the impact of towns, university scholarship, and laxity of discipline. Innocent stands with the great reformers in Church history, by his own example of saintly life, but above all by his great work in supervising the deliberations of the Fourth Council of the Lateran (1215) and in his confirmation of the first mendicant orders, the Franciscan and the Dominican.

The Fourth Lateran Council ranks with Nicaea and Trent as the most important councils in the history of the Church; it was largely a response to the problems raised by the urban environment and from the commercial revolution. One problem was the spread of heresy. To combat heresy, the Council decreed annual sacramental confession (to nip heretical ideas in the bud and reconcile the man in error by instruction) and reception of the Holy Eucharist, reaffirmed the ancient doctrine that there was no salvation outside the Church. The Council required the cooperation of secular powers in the detection and punishment of heresy, founded the Roman inquisition, and enacted reforms which would not only tighten up casual discipline but would make the conduct of the clergy less likely to offend devout people and thus cause them to abandon the Church.

Equally important, in themselves and as weapons against heresy, was Pope Innocent's authorization of the mendicant friars. Members of the Order of Friars Minor (Franciscans) and the Order of Preachers (Dominicans) were not monks; they were a new phenomenon in the history of the Church, secular clergy who lived under rule. Francis of Assisi (died 1226) was an apostle to the city, and his Order was intended to be a dedicated band of urban missionaries. Francis spoke to the thirteenth century; he would have been out-of-place in an earlier time. His gentleness, love of all creation, humility, courage, fine intelligence, ebullient joy, do not differentiate his from many wholly lived lives. He is, rather, historically important for his embrace of Lady Poverty, a continuity with the pristine monastic virtue, important to monk and friar for the Christian discipline of nonattachment to possessions in order to free the ascent of the soul to God. As well, Francis had a deep distrust of formal learning, fearing it could lead to pride and vainglory among his "little brothers." Francis viewed his friars as missionaries to the urban poor, among whom they begged and lived as an essential part of their apostolate. This missionary emphasis colored the later history of the Order, and Francis himself set the example for later missionary work among the heathen by attempts to convert a bemused sultan during the Fifth Crusade. Franciscans were the first missionaries to central Asia, China, and India.

Different in emphasis were the Dominicans, founded by Dominic (died 1221), a highly-educated Spaniard. While they were situated in the cities, like the Franciscans, they stressed education as a weapon against heresy, and became eminent university professors. Both orders moved among the people, and were authorized to take confessions, to preach, and to perform all the other duties of a parish priest, which led to unseemly squabbling between parish priests and wandering friars in the later middle ages. The most beloved of the religious orders, the mendicant friars, by reason of their holy lives and ardent mission in their daily work, marked the accommodation of the Church to conditions of the thirteenth century. Among their members were most of the great intellectuals of the thirteenth century: Thomas Aquinas and Albertus Magnus from the Dominicans and Roger Bacon, Robert Grosseteste, and Bonaventure from the Franciscans.

• The High Medieval Church

After Innocent III the Church became more bureaucratized and dominated by canon lawyers, and she became less flexible, less responsibe to the demands of the time, less imaginative, more embedded in routine and legalism against problems and movements with which her leadership seemed unable to cope effectively – heresy, social protest movements, and the rise of the national state. The high medieval papacy fittingly ends with Pope Boniface VIII (1294-1303) who, while not without great legal ability and intelligence, bureaucratic skill and administrative genius, brought the papacy to its lowest point of effective power since the beginning of the Gregorian Reform. He stands in marked contrast with Innocent III, whose intellectual and administrative abilities he shared – sadly, he did not share Innocent's holiness of life, serene temperament, sound common sense, and grasp of the realities of power.

Failing in his attempts to forbid royal taxation of clergy in France and in England, Boniface renewed the conflict with Philip IV of France only to lose disastrously once again. He was temporarily captured by servants of the French king in 1303. Boniface was succeeded by a Gascon, Clement V (after a short intervening pontificate), and before Clement's death (1314) the papacy had been captured by the King of France. The Roman See could no longer command from a position of strength. This owed less to papal decline and to Boniface's policies than to the fact that other powers had gained strength in the century so that they could afford cheerfully to ignore Peter's successor.

One reason for the triumph of the Church was her efficient and highly centralized organization; but bureaucracy seldom inspires deep devotion in men, so we must look beyond this explanation. Essential to the Church's dominating position in the middle ages was her role in the intellectual and artistic life of the age, so open to different schools of thought and art. The Church was the civilizer of Europe, and as in the Roman world men were defined as civilized when they entered the Roman cultural and institutional sphere, so in the middle ages Christianization meant civilization. Civilizer of barbarians, transmitter of classical culture, inspirer of art, architecture, and literature, the Church also sponsored a specific ecclesiastical culture.

The fundamental reason why the Church was the dominant force in European society was her success in satisfying the religious needs of Europeans. One source of strength was her flexibility, her willingness to embrace a variety of religious beliefs and practices so long as essentials were maintained. Her discipline was also important: the regular administratiion of the sacraments, the orderly provision of spiritual guidance, the presence of the Church and her ministers at life's great crises and joys, from birth through marriage and death, gave men the comfort which comes from routine.

Another element of mediation between God and man was the sacramental system; a sacrament is the outward and visible sign of an inward and invisible grace, a gift of God mediated through material or human agencies. As Peter Lombard defined them in the twelfth century, they were seven. Baptism, conveyed by anointing with water, made the recipient a member of the Church, the Mystical Body of Christ, and marked his adoption as a child of God. Confirmation, bestowed by the laying on of hands by the bishop or by anointment of the confirmand with holy oil blessed by him, made the subject a full participant in the sacramental and institutional life of the Church. The Holy Eucharist (Mass) is bread and wine, transformed by God through the priest's prayer of consecration into the objective Body and Blood of Christ (doctrine of the Real Presence). The Mass makes the communicant a participant in the benefits of the Sacrifice of Calvary in a mystical fashion. Holy Unction, or unction of the sick (incorrectly known as Extreme Unction or the Last Rites), the vehicle for which is holy oil administered by a priest, is intended to assist in the cure of the ill, or to fortify and strengthen the souls of the dying. Penance, the sacrament of confession and priestly absolution of sins sincerely repented, is liturgical in form and is not conveyed by material media, as is also the case with Holy Matrimony, the marriage of two baptized people, which blesses the union and makes it a type of the mystical union between Christ and His Church. Holy Orders, given by bishops in the laying-on of hands, makes a man a bishop, priest, or deacon, depending upon the order being bestowed.

Here, then, the believer could find solace, hope, and comfort – the Word, the sacraments, the support and encouragement of discipline, the regularity of worship, faith and order, and the varieties and flexibilities of a Church confident in her mission. Yet this magnificent institution which had successfully guided the spiritual and creative life of the continent for centuries was showing signs of decline before the end of the thirteenth century.

• Waldensianism and Albigensianism

After the turn of the thirteenth century, there was a growing rigidity in faith and order, an erosion of the flexibility which had been one of the sources of the Church's strength. As the structure and doctrine of the Church became better-defined and more precisely articulated, deviation from established norms became more common. Heresy became a great medieval problem for the first time in the late-twelfth century. Many heresies, such as Waldensianism, were urban in origin. Heresy – religious nonconformity – could be dealt with in several ways. The friars, with their preaching and apostolic lives, were one response. Another was conversion, the attempt to return the erring to the fold of the Church by teaching. Yet another was that followed by Innocent III, the reform of the Church where she had fallen from standards of purity and order. The least-preferred measure in the early thirteenth century became increasingly popular during the middle ages: slay the unrepentant and obstinate who persisted in their heresies.

To comprehend the violence of the medieval reaction against heresy one must understand that many heretical movements were unlovable – pillaging, slaughtering the faithful, burning, blaspheming. This is particularly the case of those heresies which converged with social protest movements, and of the violently intolerant Albigensians. Further, to medieval men, nothing was more important than the salvation of their eternal souls, and those who endangered this salvation should be dealt with as one deals with an inflamed pancreas: excise it before it causes more trouble.

In the earlier middle ages, most heresies had been intellectual, so abstruse in their arguments as to leave the common man indifferent or bewildered, much like the recent "death of God" theology. This ceased to be the case in the late twelfth century. The Gregorian Reform sowed the seeds of the dangerous idea of apostolic poverty; they bore fruit now, and the undercurrent of criticism of shortcomings and abuses in the Church became a torrent. But these new movements of dissent were practical, not intellectual; even the appeal of the Albigensians seems to have lain principally with their practical criticism of the Church and with their anticlericalism than with their repellent doctrines.

In some ways a forerunner of many Protestant groups, Waldensianism began when its founder, Peter Waldo, felt called to a life of apostolic poverty in 1173. Among Waldensian doctrines were an emphasis on vernacular services, omission of hymns, and a symbolic interpretation of the Eucharist. Other Waldensian beliefs which reappeared in sixteenth-century reformation churches were complete pacifism, a denial of the validity of infant baptism, and a rejection of purgatory. Heretical these ideas may have been in the context of the time, but they were at least Christian.

Albigensianism was not, strictly speaking, a heresy (erroneous interpretation of Christian doctrine), but another religion. Emerging in southern France and northwestern Italy in the late twelfth century, Albigensians (or the Cathari, the Pure Ones) shared beliefs composed of early Christian heretical ideas, elements of eastern mystery religions, and Manichaeism. Their most important doctrines were that there were an evil god and a good one, contending both in history and in individuals for victory; that the clergy of the Catholic Church and most of their doctrines were in grave error and perverted; and that all matter (including their own bodies) was evil and created by the evil god. Pacifistic in theory, in practice they were anything but.

The Albigensian Crusade was declared in 1209 by a reluctant Innocent III, after the failure of attempts to convert them by preaching and by other means (excommunication, interdict, and the like). This crusade, the first major one in a district of Europe which had not seen a like expedition in the eleventh century, was a stunning success from the point of view both of the ecclesiastical and feudal authorities, as well as of the French king who exploited the resulting confusion of conflicting feudal claims, but it was conducted with that monstrous barbarism on both sides which so often characterizes wars over conflicting ideologies.

Another instrument to combat heresy was the Roman Inquisition, founded in 1233 after the failure of similar diocesan tribunals to establish themselves successfully as ferrets of truth. The inquisition was a court which ran under Roman principles of investigation and interrogation, but which did not provide the safeguards for the accused found in the English common law, nor did this institution always abide by its own procedural rules. Inquisitors were sent out from the papacy to hold tribunals. The sequence of events when the inquisitors came to town was as follows. First, heretics were given a period of time within which to appear voluntarily and renounce their errors; those who did so were discharged with a light penalty. Then all were summoned to tell the inquisitors of heretics of whom they knew; while there were some safeguards for the accused, the advantage in the trial lay with the prosecution, particularly after the introduction of torture in 1252. At this stage a confirmed confession would deliver the heretic to a heavy penance and punishment. If the accused maintained his innocence or refused to renounce an admitted heresy, he was delivered to the secular authorities, condemned as a heresiarch, and, since heresy was a capital crime in secular law, he was executed. Punishment at the stake was comparatively rare.

• The Decline of the Church

The decline in the respect and authority of the Church was due in part to her internal loss of flexibility, failure of leadership, and growth of an overcentralized bureaucracy, and in part to her failure to meet effectively new external challenges arising in the thirteenth century: urban heresy, social protest linked with urban violence, the rise of competing intellectual interests coming with a more sophisticated society, a growing lack of response to the needs and aspirations of the lower classes, and the growing attitude that attacks upon defects in the institutional Church were attacks upon Christ and His Vicar as well.

Also, the papacy made fatal errors of policy. The Crusades gradually were diverted to the political and even personal interests of the popes:

those declared against Frederick II, against the great crusading House of Aragon, against Florence, and against the personal enemies of Boniface VIII, all contributed to the debasement of the crusading ideal and to questioning of the moral foundations of the See of Peter. By the end of the century, Rome was making exalted claims far out of line with reality. The popes had done well in exerting the political interests of the papal state, but at the expense of the moral and religious majesty which alone gave their political authority its credibility. The groundwork of the calamitous events in church history of the fourteenth and fifteenth centuries had been laid all too well in the preceding years; Clement V had moved the Holy See into the orbit of France, leading to the Avignonese papacy and the Great Schism; the growth of ideas of representation in the Church led to the Conciliar Movement; the failure of the Church to find a viable place in a changing society exemplifies the fate of institutions which fail to adapt as times and contexts change about them. It would take a crisis shaking the Church to the point where the very foundations and mandate of her being were challenged in the sixteenth century to bring her again to her primary mission – saving souls.

One important element in the decline of the Church in its relation to society was the growing dominance of secular values over religious ones, and with it the growth of the feudal monarchies, which came to compete successfully for the loyalty of Europeans as against the Church. People give their allegiance to those institutions which best seem to satisfy their most important needs. Certainly in the rise of feudal monarchy we see a response, if grudging, to the needs of its citizens, as great as we have seen in the history of that Body which claimed all Christians as its citizens. Perhaps this slow transfer of loyalties from Church to state also reflects a growing materialism, and a satisfaction with this life which made the rewards of the life to come less important, because less immediate and tangible.

• Feudal Monarchies

In 1050 England, France, and the Holy Roman Empire were governed by similar political and social institutions, and the Holy Roman Empire which had descended from Charlemagne was the strongest of the three; yet by the end of the thirteenth century, the Holy Roman Empire had become a legal fiction, its ruler endowed more with title than with effective power, the French state had emerged as the first power of Europe under a monarchy close to despotic, and England was on the way to that constitutional monarchy which has made her the Mother of Democracy.

There were various opportunities open for kings to increase and consolidate their powers. One important element in a king's potential was his conversion of feudal rights (suzerainty) into royal rights (sovereignty) by effective use of his position as feudal overlord, a policy followed both by the medieval kings of England and of France, but never consistently in the Empire. Another potential source of great strength was the royal prerogative, that area within which the king could act politically without restriction by a parliamentary body or by other means of opposition. Royal power expanded by extension of the prerogative, and when the prerogative seemed to influential political groupings with the state to be overexpanded, rebellion could result, as happened in England in 1215 and almost again between 1297 and 1300, and in France between 1314 and 1316. No king could simply use his title to acquire power.

The royal domain, the area under the king's direct control, could be used to enhance royal power. In England after the Conquest, the domain was scattered, thus the king's direct authority was present in virtually every English county. In France the Capetian royal domain was not scattered across the country; it was astride the middle Seine basin, well-located to become the cultural and economic center of northern France; it became the nucleus for the expansion of the power of the French kings. In Germany the domain was neither large nor wealthy enough to provide a base for the expansion of imperial power, and lands were constantly being eroded from it to purchase support for the emperor. Related to the domain in each country is the question of how intelligently the monarch utilized his resources; the English kings consistently and efficiently exploited their resources to such a degree that their methods were copied by the kings of France. The Holy Roman Emperor dissipated his in pursuit of impossible dreams of Italian empire.

The Church could be a great support of the monarchy, as under the Capetians and often in Norman and early Angevin England, or it could bring a powerful monarchy to ruin, as in the Empire. The nobility were another politically articulate group whose interests had to be considered by the king; English kings were most successful in cooperation (not always voluntarily), Holy Roman Emperors least. The strong monarchs were those who most successfully identified their interests with those of their politically important subjects; this category did not include the peasants (the majority). Of course no one in the period 800-1300 thought that the people had sovereignty; the ruler and the law were sovereign. The history of English kingship from 1066 to 1307 includes some of the greatest kings of England – William the Conqueror (1066-1087), Henry I (1100-1135), Henry II (1154-1189), and Edward I (1272-1307); each was great because he exploited the elements of royal power to the maximum.

The Capetian kings of France (987-1328) were biologically lucky, ruling in regular succession with few regencies; unlike the English kings, their accessions were generally peaceful and accepted by the influential classes. Their power lay in first consolidating their authority within the royal domain, the great work of Louis VI "The Fat" (1109-1137), then in the slow extension of their power both by the geographic expansion of the royal domain and the extension of their feudal rights (such as justice) beyond the domain, a process begun by Louis VII (1137-1180). Philip II "Augustus" (1180-1224) engineered a quadruple increase in the French royal domain, not least by the conquest of all lands in northern France which had been held by the kings of England as vassals of the French king; by the time of his death, the French monarchy was the most powerful in Europe. The founder of the bureaucratic state, he began a trend of strong central government intensified by his grandson Louis IX (1226-1270) and brought to completion by Louis' grandson, the enigmatic Philip IV "The Fair" (1285-1314).

The Holy Roman Empire had a quite different history; where Henry III (1039-56) was unquestionably the strongest European ruler, the emperor by 1300 was a phantom in terms of actual power. There were fewer great German emperors after the mid-eleventh century than either French or English kings: Frederick I "Barbarossa" (1152-1190), Henry VI (1190-1197), and Frederick II (1212-1250), and even their greatness was as much personal as in their record as emperors. The causes for the ruin of the medieval Empire are apparent; in general, they do not include changes in dynasty, which did not permanently weaken (for example) English kingship, except as such changes were articulated in factional feuding and in rebellion. First, there was the opposition of the Church to Henry IV (1056-1106) which permanently weakened the Empire and undermined the emperor's authority. Chosen by the Holy Roman Emperor in the mid-eleventh century, the popes had become the masters of imperial destinies by the turn of the thirteenth. It was customary for the pope to anoint the emperor which implied papal veto power, just as investiture with temporalities by the emperor implied imperial veto over episcopal candidates. The popes also were not slow to intervene in factional feuds, supporting candidates who seemed more favorable to the pontiffs' policies.

Then there was the Italian problem. After Barbarossa's revival of the German dream of rule over north Italy (part of the Empire) and the invasion which followed, "The first step led to others: in three generations the emperors were to change from Germans to Italians and transfer their capital from Goslar to Palermo, while Germany became a confederation of almost independent fiefs and towns."[1] Frederick I had married his son

[1] Robert S. Lopez, *The Birth of Europe* (New York, 1966), p. 220.

(the future Henry VI) into the Sicilian ruling house, establishing a dynastic claim to that Normanized land which was to cause endless trouble and result eventually in the obliteration of the Hohenstaufen line of emperors. At the turn of the thirteenth century, Innocent III chose Frederick II, son of Henry VI and Constanza of Sicily, to rule; the result was the practical, if not the theoretical, division of the Empire into its German and Italian components. The last major reason for the shattering of the medieval Empire was the triumph of the elective principle; a candidate for the imperial throne was to be elected, thus he had to bargain for the election, which came before long to mean that he promised not to increase the power of his office while he held it. Thus the emperors were not able to accrue power in successive reigns, and were not able to build slowly the imperial authority as the kings of England and France built theirs.

• Government in England, France, and the Holy Roman Empire

The history of central administration, and of the centralization of power in the king's government shows clearly why the English kings so rapidly developed great power in their tight little island, why the French kings did so both more slowly and differently, and why the Holy Roman Emperors never did develop an effective central government after the eleventh century. Anglo-Saxon England, its rulers replaced by Normans in 1066, had developed some institutions of government and society so effective that the Norman kings continued them. The divisions of local government (the shire and the smaller hundred) held great promise for self-government and were the seat of the popular courts. The sheriff was the king's agent in the shire.

The Normanization of government began under the Conqueror, as the Normanization of its personnel had begun under Edward the Confessor (1042-1066). By the turn of the twelfth century, the English kings had developed an administration so effective that the country could be governed during the king's frequent absences in Normandy. The Norman kings continued and elaborated the Anglo-Saxon chancery (originally the department of state which drafted aud authenticated royal letters of command called writs) although the chancellor (its chief) did not become a great officer of state until early in the reign of Henry II. The nerve-center of government, the chancery came around the turn of the thirteenth century to keep sophisticated records of its work. Another important institution was the curia regis, the king's court, where the nobles assembled to counsel the king and otherwise to participate in governance and in legal judgment; from the curia, the council (a formal consultative body, appointed by the king) emerged. Before the end of the reign of Henry I, specialization of government departments, a sign of growing modernity in institutional history, had begun. Financial administration and its legal enforcement were confided to the exchequer. Royal justice began to be professionalized, its operation increasingly delegated to justices and sheriffs as the king began to withdraw from judgment in all but the most important cases. Henry I also inaugurated a new official, the justiciar, effective head of the administration and viceroy in the king's absence. The growth of professionalism and of more complex record-keeping continued throughout the history of England in the high middle ages. Bureaucrats developed formulas, precedents, and routines of government.

England was fortunate in having no long-lasting noble dynasties to usurp control from the king; hence she was more easily unified under law and under central administration than were France and the Empire. Administrators, then as now, needed careful checking, and the history of England from 1170 on is studded with great inquests to ensure that the officials were faithful to their royal masters' interests. England was unique in having an unpaid body of substantial citizens who did much of the government's work performed elsewhere by hired bureaucrats; this helped to keep the size of the bureaucracy down and to involve more people in the work of government, an important factor in the growth of English self-government. These local worthies included coroners, justices of the peace, jurymen, keepers of castles and of the forest, and a host of other officials. As other politically significant groups came to exercise more influence over the royal government in the reign of Henry III, the king developed new institutions dependent on himself and amenable neither to baronial nor other control; they included the wardrobe, a personal financial department accountable only to the king, and the privy seal, which was used to authenticate the king's own letters and orders, the great seal having become institutionalized in chancery.

France, a kingdom created from the union of many almost sovereign lordships and principalities, had an administrative history quite different from that of the more homogeneous England. In law and financial administration, French institutional growth was less rapid, less directed from the center, and less carefully thought out in the twelfth century than was England's. Unlike the English kings, French monarchs had to face the problem of inherited offices; inheritance of function put officials beyond the king's power to control by deprivation of office. In the tenth and eleventh centuries, French central administration was inferior to that of many of the great feudal states of France, its chancery neither as sophisticated nor as efficient as England's. Even by the end of the twelfth century, the king's institutions really functioned well only in the land directly ruled by the monarch. By 1300, this was no longer true.

During the thirteenth century, the rapid expansion of the royal domain meant not only the expansion of the geographical area covered by the definition "domain," but also the invigoration of royal institutions by new challenges requiring responses. English local government was staffed both by professionals sent from the central government and by local people; in France, provincial government was directed by royal agents sent out from Paris, who administered local customs and local administrative machinery.

The uniformity of law and institutions which governed England was absent in France, hence her administrative structure was much more complicated than was that of England, with a far larger bureaucracy and complex chain of command. The father of the bureaucratic France was Philip "Augustus," a king impressed by Norman administrative machinery and institutions and intelligent enough to recognize their superiority over his own institutions. While adopting such Norman practices as administrative inquests of knight service and of lands, he continued such older practices as the use of agents sent from the court with miscellaneous administrative and judicial duties, quite like those of the English sheriff. In St. Louis' reign occurred the beginning of specialization of function in government and a galloping growth of the bureaucracy, over whose workings he established itinerant officials as watchdogs. The royal bureaucrats kept constant pressure upon the rights and claims of other sources of public authority, such as the feudality, in the course of defining royal rights, necessary for the rationalization and clarification of royal power.

The reign of Philip "the Fair" marked both a culmination of previous trends toward centralization and bloated bureaucracy and a turning point in French history. The reign saw the gestation of the French absolute monarchy of the early modern period, more sordid in its birth than in its maturity. What the kingship of France lost in terms of prestige and respect it gained temporarily in terms of Philip's and of his house's power. Forerunners of modern totalitarian techniques of rule were present in his menacing reign: the use of legal forms to work injustice, attacks on the Church in defense of God, slander and blackmail, blatant hypocrisy, division of possible opposing forces in the state, and propagandizing rather than explaining. These succeeded in the short run, but the price of immediate success was a loss of faith in the French monarchy which would cost it dearly in years to come. Fortunately for Philip and his successors, Frenchmen were so divided by geographical and class considerations that concerted opposition to the king was impossible.

From the eleventh century on, the government of the Holy Roman Empire could not govern. The Empire was too large for effective government and included too many peoples. Even the greatest medieval emperors were unable to resolve the problems of state-building, because of trying to rule both Germany and Italy, each unwilling to be governed by a highly-centralized government, each fractious and fragmented. Frederick II attempted to centralize Italy, placing the fiercely independent city-states of northern Italy under officials responsible to himself. The plan never worked owing to the determined opposition of the city governments and people. While England and France solved the problems of government and of central administration in the twelfth and thirteenth centuries, forming feudal monarchies on a territorial basis, the Holy Roman Empire fell victim to localism and to the enmity of a resurgent papacy, the sole rival claimant to universal authority.

• The Development of Law in England and France

While administration demonstrates the success of a ruler in governing, the law defines the rights both of state and society. Anglo-Saxon law was popular law, enforced both by popular and royal courts. After the Conquest, civil and criminal jurisdiction became a monopoly of the king and those to whom he chose to give it; the king was nothing if not lawgiver and fount of justice. Shire courts were royal courts under the presidency of the sheriff, while the hundred courts continued to administer the customary Anglo-Saxon law among the peasants. These courts were often granted to barons, less for the judicial powers than for the profits which lay in fines.

In England, all disputes involving land possession and rights went to the king's court. Most cases fell into classifications for which the government developed standardized forms of judgment and process. As the volume of cases to be taken by the king's court increased in the twelfth century, the legal system became more complex. By the end of that century there were not only the king's court with himself as judge, but also the circuit courts held by traveling justices, the court of exchequer, that of common pleas, and others. The proliferation of courts, controlled by and responsible to the king, was more fortuitous than planned, and occurred because justice had to be both quick and effective.

The reign of Henry II (1154-1189) was pivotal to the history of the English law; first, it saw the jury introduced into royal justice. The jury, which first appeared in Anglo-Saxon England, functioned in trials involving judgments in customary law; Henry II was the first king to impanel the jury in *royal* courts. Less like modern trial juries than like present witnesses, the jury was required by royal agents to swear to what it knew concerning crimes committed in the area from which they were drawn. Introduced first into land cases to determine which party had the better claim to possession of land, in the thirteenth century juries were introduced into criminal trials. Not only were juries important in replacing older methods of trial (ordeal and combat), but since they were composed of non-noble people, the juries were regarded by Englishmen as a defense against royal and noble tyranny.

The use of common legal procedures and itinerant justices who judged in the same way all over England contributed to the growth of that unique English constitutional development so vital to our own legal system, the common law, the law enforced as common to all Englishmen. Judge-made law, stressing the importance of precedent, built common law jurisprudence. So successful were the judicial reforms of Henry II, and so well did they fill an obvious need, that when the rebellious barons forced the Magna Carta from King John in 1215, they were careful to make reforms in the law and its administration to make it work better.

Before the reign of Philip "Augustus," French kings struggled to make their legal authority effective in the royal domain; only sporadically was appeal made to royal justice from outside this limited area. As medieval society became less violent, the king's judicial authority became more effective in the duchies and counties; a society evolving toward peaceful settlement of conflicts had no other ultimate judicial recourse. As in England, justice slowly evolved into a state, rather than a private, function. In part a matter of natural evolution, in part an aspect of the king's slow conversion of suzerain into sovereign rights, the process hastened in the reign of Philip "Augustus," in which there was an infusion of the principles and practices of Roman law into French jurisprudence.

St. Louis, the personification of goodness and justice, established the king as the source of justice available to all. Not only did he sit under the oak at Vincennes receiving appeals from his people, he also professionalized the judiciary under men who were judges trained in the Roman law rather than administrators who handled judicial duties among other assignments. The *Parlement* of Paris, a judicial rather than a legislative or representative body, was established at the summit of the judicial system. It extended royal legal jurisdiction and enhanced the authority of the king's courts at the expense of feudal and church tribunals. Philip "the Fair" used the law as an agency of despotism, thus undermining the faith of Frenchmen in royal courts which harassed them in the interests of the state rather than in the service of justice. Most of this king's leading counsellors and administrators were lawyers trained in the Roman law, and they turned it, as they turned administrative policy, to the service of the royal bureaucracy and its master.

The Holy Roman Empire did not develop an effective centralized legal system because the emperor's justice was too personal and thus insufficiently institutionalized, because the lands over which a judicial system would have had to rule were too diverse and too large, and because of the triumph of localism in justice as in virtually all else in the medieval imperial government. The great law schools of Italy did not provide the Emperor with the system which he needed. This was also the case with taxing authority, another important foundation of royal and imperial power: a state, to function effectively, must be able to command the resources of its citizens, and the Empire was never able consistently to utilize the rich resources of either the wealthy Rhenish and Lotharingian cities or of the turbulent communes of north Italy. In fact, the Empire had no general taxing authority until the fifteenth century, although both the Italian and the German principalities and communes which formed it did exercise this power. The emperor maintained himself and his administration from the resources of a steadily-diminishing personal domain.

• The Development of Taxation in England and France

The English financial administration was the most advanced secular fiscal structure of its time. The Norman kings of England started off with the first regular land tax in Europe, the Danegeld, inherited from the Anglo-Saxon kings. During the reign of the Conqueror, general taxes became a royal monopoly, and the king was careful to see that he got his due; the unique medieval survey, *Domesday Book,* was primarily a fiscal document. As a feudal suzerain, the king also enriched himself from feudal taxes and from exploitation of the royal domain, as well as from scutage. The royal courts also delivered their fines to the king's treasure chest.

It is very well to have rights; to make them effective by institutionalization of procedure and by professionalization of personnel required persistence. During the reign of Henry I, so fertile in institutional developments, the exchequer was established to ensure the king a dependable, regular income exploiting all sources of royal wealth. The first European department of government to leave a guidebook of procedure to posterity (the *Dialoque on the Exchequer*), its professional staff not only collected and accounted for the king's income from many sources, but also kept an impressive series of records of receipt known as pipe rolls.

As heavyhandedly efficient in taxation as in administration, King John found his financial enterprise trimmed in Magna Carta, which required him to limit both the occasion and the amount of aids which he could take by prerogative, and further stated that in future no extraordinary taxes could be levied without the "common consent of the realm." This last, the seed from which parliamentary control of taxation was later to spring, was most important in differentiating English from French practice. Where the French king and his agents had to negotiate taxation with regional assemblies, the English king dealt with one body rather than with shire and hundred.

In France, before the reign of Philip "Augustus," the king was fortunate if he could enforce his claims to taxation within his domain. By the end of the reign of Philip "the Fair," royal taxing powers were generally acknowledged in France. Financial procedures improved in technique owing to the example of accounting procedures in the Duchy of Normandy, its exchequer practice (similar to England's) grafted onto French administrative tradition following the duchy's conquest by France in 1204. Owing to the extensive territorial acquisitions of Philip "Augustus," new sources of revenue accrued to the crown, quadrupling the royal income in this reign. Louis IX established the Chamber of Accounts, and combined taxation by royal fiat with that obtained by negotiations with local assemblies and notables to augment greatly the crown income. Philip IV refined existing institutions, staffing them with professional bureaucrats. Sacrificing long-range good for short-range gain, he expropriated and expelled three important financial resources of the kingdom (the Jews, the "Lombard" bankers, and the Templars) and made fluctuation of coinage an economic policy in order that he might borrow in dear money and repay in cheap, which may have been good for the king but was bad for the kingdom.

• The Growth of National Monarchy

Feudalism was imposed on England by William the Conqueror. Before this king, England did not know knight service, homage and fealty, devolution of extensive powers of justice and local government upon the nobility by the king's grant, nor the nobility's involvement in central government by virtue of being tenants-in-chief of the king. The strength of feudal institutions in England was proved in the reign of Henry II, who quickly reestablished order and a rough cooperation with the magnates after Stephen's weak reign (1135-1154). Yet Henry intended to exploit his feudal rights for all they were worth, as did his son and successor Richard "Lionheart," as sorry a king as he was splendid a warrior. King John caught the backlash, and Magna Carta reminded the king of his limitations and of the barons' power. If redress of grievances through the legal system or by baronial cooperation in the royal government did not answer the magnates' grievances, rebellion seemed the only alternative; it was to seem so again in 1258, 1264, 1327, 1399, and frequently throughout the fifteenth century. Among the more important feudal clauses limiting despotism were the scutage clause, limitations on overseas service required of the feudal host, and reforms relating to wardship, marriage of heiresses, and the limitation of aids to three specific occasions: knighting of the king's eldest son, marriage of his eldest daughter, ransom of himself.

During the long reign of Henry III (1216-1272), the barons tried to achieve an institutionalized voice in the government rather than to subvert or to overthrow it. In this king's minority (1217-1227) the magnates directed the country, joining with royal administrators in the appointment of the king's ministers and in governance. The barons did not forget the good old days when they had a vital role in the government of England, and they regularly worked to convert the feudal right of counsel into the constitutional right of participation in making the decisions which affected their interests. Failing thus to limit the monarch's powers, they attempted between 1258 and 1265 to take over the governance of the state and failed, owing both to a division among the baronial leaders and to their failure to find an escape from the dilemma of restricting the king in a manner too revolutionary for thirteenth-century Englishmen to accept. Feudal developments of the reign of Edward I are twofold: baronial reaction against the over-rapid centralization of royal power, expressed between 1297 and 1300 in the Confirmation of the Charters and in the Articles on the Charters, both of which obliged the king to recognize traditional restrictions on his prerogative and powers, and in the Statutes of Westminister II and III, which provided for the reversion of lands to the crown if the line which held these lands died out. By the end of Edward I's reign, feudalism was a dying institution as a means of government, and feudal monarchy had turned the corner toward becoming national monarchy.

In England, rule was participatory (often against the wish of the king), the barons sharing in government; in Capetian France, the king slowly extended his authority and superimposed it upon a reluctant nobility who did not share in governance. A dominating theme of French medieval history is the slow overcoming of feudal principalities by the crown and their addition to the royal domain. At the turn of the twelfth century, the French king was delighted if he was able to get his own vassals of the royal domain to perform homage and fealty; during that century, he achieved that and as well random success in enforcing obligations upon his vassals elsewhere in France, although at the vassals' initiative rather than his own (as in appeals to the royal court). Yet, in the thirteenth century the forces of the feudality were overcome by the power of the monarchy, which found the tools to assert its power: encroachments of royal upon private justice, administrative expansion, the slow conversion of suzerainty into sovereignty, the superimposition of the structure of royal governance upon the French lands. Unlike in England, the barons of France felt no unity against the crown; hence the king was able to erode their traditional position until the nobles found themselves powerless. The rebellions which occurred in 1314-1316 were unsuccessful; sharing with the revolt which led to Magna Carta a resistance to royal centralization, they are unlike that English rising of 1215 in being disunited, provincial rather than national, and lacking both strong leadership and a definite program of reform.

In the Holy Roman Empire before the early twelfth century, feudalism existed only in the western part of the Empire, formerly included in the Carolingian Empire. The opposition to centralization of the Empire came less from feudal nobles than from the great dukes, the rulers of such duchies as Swabia, Franconia, Lorraine, and Saxony, who combined strong personal leadership with their landed wealth, ecclesiastical influence over the Church in their duchies, and ancient tribal loyalties. In Germany the trends of centralization, dynastic stability, legal institutionalization, and so on, must be sought in the duchy rather than at the imperial court. When feudalism was imposed on Germany in the early twelfth century, the feudal ties and obligations ended with the dukes and did not converge on the emperor; hence he could not utilize his position as suzerain to become sovereign. The internal history both of the German and Italian possessions of the Empire is a dismal one of constant civil war against the emperor and among themselves, cheerfully stoked by papal intervention. The decentralizing tendencies in both regions overcame centralization, but little of this was feudal.

• The Growth of Representative Institutions

A ruler could deal with opposition to royal authority in three ways: he could engage in headlong conflict with it, as in the Holy Roman Empire; he could subvert it, as in Capetian France; or he could institutionalize it, as in Norman and early Angevin England. The origins of representative institutions are complex; one source lies in the feudal right of counsel. Another is the growing self-awareness of the politically conscious and articulate classes. Both from a feudal and a Roman civil law background came the principles that decisions in matters affecting the community should be made publicly, that customary ways should not be altered without the consent of the community of the realm, and that decisions affecting particular groups should not be made without their consultation and consent. Like the law courts, parliamentary bodies were official instruments used by the ruled to inhibit and eventually to limit the powers of the ruler, a phenomenon found in representative assemblies of towns and Church as well. Few representatives were elected in this period, although their decisions bound those whom they represented.

England worked out the most historically important representative institution, Parliament, which was in its infancy around 1300. As an instrument of political opposition, it had precedents in the rebellion of 1191, when leaders of the English baronage rose against those ruling in the name of the absent Richard I and forced their replacement. This may be the first constitutional opposition in English history; it was a rebellion against misgovernment in the king's name, but not against the king whose loyal opposition the rebellious leaders remained. Then, Magna Carta of 1215 embodied the fundamental principle that the king is bound by the law; should he not exercise his rule with self-restraint, others will provide restraint.

Henry III's reign was fruitful in parliamentary precedents; one was the repeated refusal of the barons to grant taxes to the king unless he granted redress of their grievances. His increasing stubbornness led to the Provisions of Oxford (1258), a plan of reform which placed royal power in control both of a group of baronial representatives and officials and of royal administrators, ruling in the interests of the community of the realm; too revolutionary for the times, it is important for the assertion of principles. This is true as well of the rule of Simon de Montfort (1264-1265), which saw the convocation of a Parliament attended by selected barons, churchmen, country gentry, and townsmen. Such assemblies were increasingly consulted from 1260 on; they derived what power they had as a function of royal authority, since they were convoked and prorogued by the king, served at his pleasure, and their decisions were of no effect without his approval; thus, parliament was dependent upon the king for its authority and for its very existence. By the end of the reign of Edward I, this was no longer so certain.

The medieval English parliament in Edward I's reign received its basic form. Its responsibilities were legal, administrative, and financial, although it handled miscellaneous matters which the king chose to bring before it. Inclusion of ever-increasing numbers of members not of the noble class gave further impetus to "self-government at the king's command." Edward's parliaments represented the whole country, not constituent geographical parts of it; hence they were more and more spokesmen for the community of the realm. Rather than command, the king was compelled by political realities to compromise and discuss, to yield something to the representatives in return for what they yielded to him. Parliamentary power thus forced Edward to respect tradition, law, custom, counsel; his control over council and parliament was not unchecked (unlike that of his contemporary Philip "the Fair"). He was compelled to be a limited monarch by political realities.

Philip IV of France did not have to worry about institutionalized opposition; as Parliament gained an essential place in the political life of England at the turn of the fourteenth century, so the French Estates-General found a place in his reign, but it was neither a necessary one nor did it serve to institutionalize opposition.

Philip "the Fair" summoned the Estates-General three times. In 1302, when he was about to press his campaign against Boniface VIII, this body heard the king's case against the badgered pope. The Templars, already harried by Philip's hounds, were the subject of the 1308 Estates, which received the royal bill of accusations against this unfortunate Order; support of the Estates was not sought by the king – rather he wished to influence public opinion. In 1314, the representative assembly was convoked to approve the levy of a tax, although not its amount. With the same feudal and Roman law antecedents as the English Parliament, why did the Estates-General never come to hold a similar position in the French polity?

An obvious reason is the differing political traditions and development of the two countries, but there are specifically French explanations as well. In England, representatives had to attend the meetings to which they were summoned; in France, delegates could send substitutes. In England, Edward insisted from the first that sheriffs summon representatives with full powers to discuss and vote on any issues which might be raised; the customary French practice was to send delegates empowered to treat with the king only on specifically announced matters. England's parliament had the capacity to receive individual and group petitions, and to use these in the grievance procedure, but in France petitions to the king were received by the *Parlement* – a judicial body – rather than by the Estates-General. Where by 1300 the Parliament had the right to consent to taxation, and to use consent as a lever to compel the king to grant redress, the Estates-General did not develop this power; many noblemen and ecclesiastics were immune from taxation (and approved only of taxes on their subjects, not on themselves), and the amounts were haggled for in local assemblies and with local notables rather than with the general representative body. Then, France was a large country; attendance was a burden to the delegates, and often the Estates did not represent the vast region lying below the Loire. Philip did not need to fear baronial control or revolt, whereas in England Edward had the precedents of baronial opposition from 1191 on to remind him that he had to take the interests of the barons into consideration lest they force him to do so. This made him a

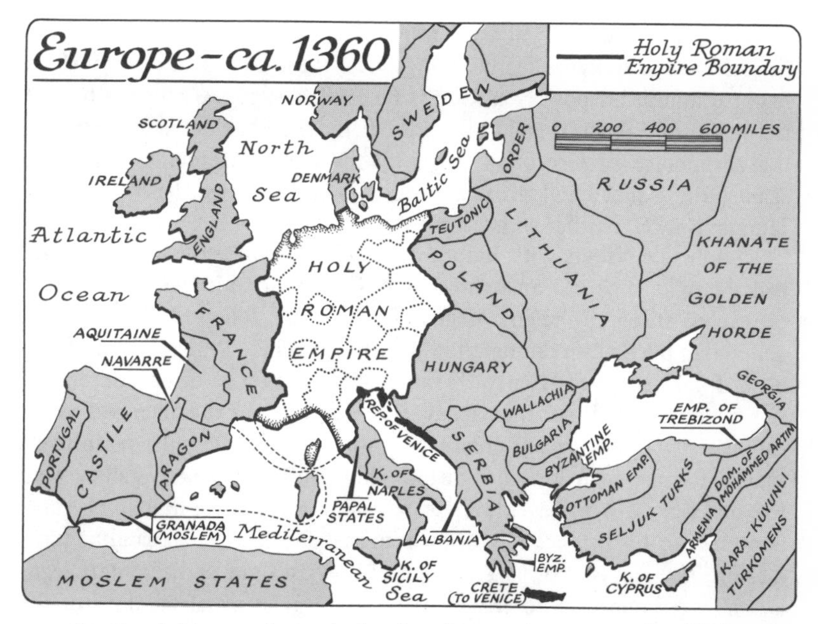

constitutional king, and the lack of such restraint meant that Philip was not a constitutional king.

The Holy Roman Emperors at the turn of the thirteenth century shifted their residences and principal interests from Germany to Italy. Frederick II virtually abandoned Germany to the control of the great lords, who quickly cast off effective imperial authority to the point where the emperor was merely first among equals. Yet in Italy the imperial power also deteriorated rapidly, due both to papal interference in imperial affairs and to Italian resistance to imperial authority. The empire disintegrated in the late thirteenth century: after 1273, a divisive feudalism triumphed in Germany. In 1279, Emperor Rudolf von Hapsburg renounced all claims to Sicily and the Papal States, and a successor's attempt in the early fourteenth century to reassert imperial authority failed. Both Germany and Italy came to find a cultural unity not joined by political unification until the late nineteenth century.

• The Nation and the Church

By the end of the thirteenth century the secular state successfully claimed the first allegiance of its members, and the Church had been reduced to a private society. Following the Conquest, the English Church was reformed on the Norman model: the king influenced episcopal appointments, considered himself responsible for the good order of the Church, and exercised effective control over those aspects of reform which might diminish his powers as king of England. The ecclesiastical history of the reigns of William II and Henry I is chiefly remarkable in demonstrating the acceptance of Gregorian ideals by the English clergy. A last battle against the claimed rights of the Church was fought by Henry II against Thomas Becket; neither won entirely.

John's conflicts with Innocent III were based on the question, who had the right to choose an archbishop of Canterbury, his reigning temporal or ecclesiastical sovereign? Magna Carta, which followed this conflict, stated that the English Church should be free to adhere to the Roman obedience. John's successor Henry III more than lived up to this promise; himself under the thumb of the papacy, Henry's reign was characterized by his submission to the papacy combined with a growing popular resentment against Roman incursions into English church life. Particularly galling were the invasion of papal agents in search of money, appointment of papal nominees to English ecclesiastical vacancies, and the ever-expanding jurisdiction of the papal court. The reign of Edward I saw parliamentary legislation, indifferently enforced by the king, against papal taxation of the clergy and interdiction of clerical taxation by secular authority, against provision of papal appointees to English livings, against legacies to the Church without royal permission, and against undefined canon law jurisdiction in England. Similar protests had occurred in France since 1247, and in both countries the enforcement or statutes and decrees depended upon the royal pleasure; usually, king and pope found mutual accommodation in matters of appointment and taxation.

In France, from the reign of Philip I until that of Philip "Augustus," there was a virtual alliance between the French and papal monarchies. Like the English kings, the Capetian monarchs supported reform where it did not infringe their own political and sovereign rights. St. Louis' reign was similar to that of England's Henry III in encompassing growing unrest against papal abrasions with nationalistic emotions; while the power of the French monarchy vis-a-vis the Fisherman's Throne increased, there was no reason to fear the King of France – as long as that king was Louis IX. His successors, unfortunately for the Church, lacked his piety, moderation, and rationality. The longstanding alliance between the Capetians and the Roman pontiff ended with the reign of Philip "the Fair," suppressor of the Templars, captor of Boniface VIII, and persecutor of the French church, who reigned when the Babylonian Captivity of the Church, the settlement of the Roman Pontiff in the French border city Avignon, began. With the Bishop of Rome no longer in his see city, his prestige and position suffered irreparable hurt.

In the tenth and eleventh centuries the Holy Roman Emperor exercised direction over the Church and her head; in the twelfth and thirteenth centuries, the situation altered to the point that the Church exercised increasing control over the empire, even to designating her head at the turn of the thirteenth century. While the emperors could invade papal lands and set up antipopes, the pontiffs had greater powers: spiritual sanctions, manipulation of factions and of ambitious would-be emperors, sanctification of rebellion as an act pleasing to God, interference in imperial elections, encouragement of pretenders, and a continuity which the empire did not have – broad was the strategy, many the tactics which armed the universal pope against the universal emperor. Their conflict doomed both to a loss of their earlier medieval positions.

• The Byzantine Empire

To turn to eastern Europe is to turn to another world – the Byzantine Empire, the direct heir of old Rome and of the Hellenistic heritage. The vast Empire, encompassing more linguistic groups and races than all the states of western Europe, gave a distinctive civilization to eastern Europe. This empire always had to struggle for survival against a succession of enemies; Arabs, Turks, Bulgars, Franks, and wild central Asian barbarian tribes. The history of the Empire is complicated; from 585 to 716, she maintained her existence while developing a distinctive civilization and institutions, both strongly stamped with Hellenistic as well as Roman antecedents. From 717 to 1056, she was the mightiest, most culturally advanced, and wealthiest state in Europe. But from the late eleventh century she began a slow but steady decline, invaded by Turks and Latins, her cultural life stagnating, her internal problems more and more difficult to solve, until she fell in 1453 to the last wave of Asian invaders to strike Europe, the Ottoman Turks.

Why did the Byzantine Empire endure for so long? One explanation was the strength of her governmental institutions. Theocratic absolutism reposed in the emperor who chose the Patriarch of Constantinople (no nonsense about lay investiture here) and endured no check upon his conduct but death or deposition, and who was served by a smoothly-functioning professional bureaucracy. Of equal importance were her well-paid and well-trained army and navy, their members chosen from among the Byzantine population; there were no barbarians in the Eastern Roman army. A complex bureaucracy, a large military establishment, and a rich and varied culture all require economic support, and the Byzantine economy flourished throughout most the high middle ages. Urbanized and industrialized, minutely regulated by the state, rich in commerce, East Rome enjoyed a prosperity which most of the West did not achieve in the middle ages. Fortune seemed to favor the Empire in dangerous times, for she usually found herself with capable rulers when she most needed them.

Her problems, as impressive as her strengths, were eventually to overwhelm the Empire. The absence of established rules for succession to the imperial throne led frequently to palace revolution, to deposition (or worse), to plots, and to vicious feuding among political groups. The political struggles too often were brought to the streets of Constantinople, where the unstable crowds were whipped to a frenzy of violence. Revolts by the army were as common as they had been in the late Roman Empire, and they had similar results. And then there was that touch of softness which comes from too good living, sensed even by the rough men of the First Crusade – the Greeks were somehow too sly, too given to luxury, too effete. The Byzantine Church, mother of the great Eastern Orthodox communion of our day, did not differ in theological essentials from the Western Catholic Church; the principal bases of unique Orthodox practice were more cultural than theological. The Eastern Church was less legalistic, more mystical and speculative in her theology, than the Latin Church, more majestic in liturgics, and differentiated as well by ceremonial observances. Her religious conflicts were more violent than those of the Western Church; where Catholics tended to ignore or deplore heterodox opinions until the late twelfth century, the Orthodox debated heretical teachings with a passion beyond the comprehension of our secularly-oriented time, which reserves passion and bloodshed for political occasions and sports events. The schism formalized between the Eastern and Latin communions in 1054 is still not completely healed.

As the Roman Church was the civilizer of western Europe, so the Eastern Church was the civilizer of the East. Russia, her civilization centered at Kiev, was a mighty state in the high middle ages; through commerce, dynastic marriage (with France), and Christianity, she was a European state. She entered the Byzantine orbit with Vladimir the Great's Christianization of his country in 990, which initiated an age glorified in Russian epic literature and folklore, that of Holy Russia, a time when Russian culture, like that of the West, was directed and dominated by religious influence. Serfdom was then unimportant in Russia and the city was a vital force earlier than it was in the West. Russian political institutions were freer than those of the West, and her non-noble classes important in the governance of the realm. But Kievan Russia was more a conglomeration of autonomous princedoms than a unified state, despite her unity in dynasty and Church. Struggle for supremacy among members of the princely house, rivalries among the cities and principalities which composed the state, and the growth of a caste nobility helped to disrupt the realm; then came the Mongol hordes in the early thirteenth century, who isolated her from the rest of Europe, dropping an iron curtain. Already lacking the heritage of classical Latin civilization, she was sundered from such essential formative experiences of the West as feudalism, the medieval political, philosophical, and religious heritage, the Renaissance and Reformation, the influence of exploration and discovery of a wider world, and the Enlightenment.

The historical importance of the high middle ages for subsequent developments in the West is fundamental. The cultural contributions of the period are obvious: preservation and transmission of classical culture, creation of a colorful and varied literature, introduction of Greek and Arabic learning to the West, building of an elaborate philosophical system, evolution of the university, developments in medicine and in natural science, and the invention both of the Romanesque and Gothic architectural orders. The agricultural revolution which for the first time since the classical epoch enabled men to live at better than a subsistence level and to accumulate surplus food coincided with the commercial revolution to provide a basis of economic wealth which supported the advancing civilization.

It is customary to view the late middle ages, the years from roughly 1300 to roughly 1500, as an era of decline, decadence even – medieval civilization had become a slightly overripe fruit by the early fourteenth century. It is impossible to agree with this pessimistic view when one considers the continued development of the modern state system, of universities, of architecture, and so forth. An old hymn includes the phrase "change and decay in all about I see" – the two words are not synonymous.

Suggestions for Further Reading

Lyon, Bryce D., *The Origins of the Middle Ages* (1972)

Wood, Charles T., *The Quest for Eternity: Medieval Manners and Morals* (1971)

Brooke, Christopher, *The Structure of Medieval Society* (1971)

Brondsted, Johannes, *The Vikings* (1965)

Bloch, Marc, *Feudal Society* (1964)

Ganshof, F. L., *Feudalism* (1964)

Painter, Sidney, *French Chivalry* (1957)

Jackson, W. T. H., *Medieval Literature* (1966)

White, Lynn, Jr., *Medieval Technology and Social Change* (1964)

Homans, George C., *English Villagers of the Thirteenth Century* (1970)

Rörig, Fritz, *The Medieval Town* (1967)
Lopez, Robert S., *The Commercial Revolution of the Middle Ages, 950-1350* (1971)
Holmes, Urban T., *Daily Living in the Twelfth Century* (1953)
Haskins, Charles Homer, *The Renaissance of the Twelfth Century* (1957)
Heer, Friedrich, *The Medieval World* (1962)
Baldwin, John W., *The Scholastic Culture of the Middle Ages, 1000-1300* (1971)
Southern, R. W., *Medieval Humanism* (1970)
Francastel, P., *Medieval Painting* (1967)
Male, Emile, *The Gothic Image* (1958)
von Simson, Otto, *The Gothic Cathedral* (1964)
Harvey, John, *The Gothic World, 1100-1600* (1969)
Haskins, Charles Homer, *The Rise of Universities* (1957)
Knowles, David, *The Evolution of Medieval Thought* (1962)
Copleston, Frederick C., *Medieval Philosophy* (1961)
Leff, Gordon, *Medieval Thought* (1958)
Douglas, David C., *The Norman Achievement* (1969)
Southern, R. W., *Western Society and the Church in the Middle Ages* (1970)
Russell, Jeffrey Burton, *A History of Medieval Christianity: Prophecy and Order* (1968)
Barraclough, Geoffrey, *The Medieval Papacy* (1968)
Cohn, Norman, *The Pursuit of the Millenium: Revolutionary Millenarians and Mystical Anarchists of the Middle Ages* (1970)
Strayer, Joseph R., *On the Medieval Origins of the Modern State* (1970)
Ullmann, Walter, *A History of Political Thought: the Middle Ages* (1965)
Brooke, Christopher, *From Alfred to Henry III, 871-1272* (1966)
Holmes, George, *The Later Middle Ages, 1272-1485* (1966)
Haskins, George L., *The Growth of English Representative Government* (1960)
Luchaire, Achille, *Social France at the Time of Philip Augustus* (1967)
Barraclough, Geoffrey, *The Origins of Modern Germany* (1963)
Waley, Daniel, *The Italian City-Republics* (1969)
Hussey, J. M., *The Byzantine World* (1961)
Jenkins, Romilly, *Byzantium: The Imperial Centuries, 610-1071* (1969)

THE RENAISSANCE WORLD

7

The Material Basis for the Renaissance

THE FOURTEENTH and fifteenth centuries, often referred to as the Age of the Renaissance, experienced marked and profound changes which characterized Europe's transition from the medieval to the early modern period. Individuals and nations alike saw a concatenation of opposites, of exaltation and despair, boundless enthusiasm and a depressing awareness of death, great wealth alongside grinding poverty. With the growing importance of city life these extremes often appeared side by side.

What the man of the Renaissance experienced is also reflected in the institutions within which he functioned. Politically, the same opposing counter-forces were at play. The national monarchies were rising with greater strength and forcefulness, together with their smaller counterparts, the city-states of Italy. At the same time, their aggressiveness was balanced by the fear of invasion and destruction by the Turkish empire. In the economic sphere, expansion of organized commerce and industry occurred in certain areas and yet there was a general feeling of economic depression and retrenchment. In the church this same dichotomy was felt as the rigidity of formalized and institutionalized worship and increased financial exactions were challenged by the idea of freeing the soul for its search for unity with God in mysticism. The church was also beset with problems such as the forces of secularism which, reacting with groups within the church, brought about the Great Schism and lead to the Conciliar Movement.

The men of the Renaissance evinced a growing awareness of the world around them and especially of its material aspect. They seem to be more irreligious than their medieval ancestors, more secular and more "worldly," but this is merely a shift in emphasis and priorities. While the medieval serf or peasant, working on his lord's manor, looked from the furrow he was plowing up to the sky and heavens to God who ruled His world, the Renaissance man looked around him and was aware of what his neighbor was doing, the clothes he was wearing and the status in which he was held by his fellowmen. This new attitude represents the transition from a predominately barter agricultural society to the beginnings of a capitalist economy. This transition marks the beginning of the modern feeling that although money isn't everything it is ahead of whatever is in second place.

• Trade and Commerce

During the Middle Ages the Mediterranean Sea and the North Sea had been the centers for most European trade and commerce. In the later Middle Ages and the Renaissance these two areas were connected as commerce developed. This was aided by technological advances – ship building, better maps, and especially the increased demand for varied products and the ability to pay for them. In the twelfth and thirteenth centuries western Europeans desired more of eastern and Far Eastern products, such as spices and silks. The luxuries of one generation had become the necessities of the next.

Northern Italy occupied the center of the economic stage in the Mediterranean Sea area with Lombardy and the Mediterranean Sea the chief corridor for goods to and from the east. Lumber, metals, and slaves for Moslem workshops and harems were carried to the eastern Mediterranean in exchange for cargoes of Byzantine fabrics, spices from the Far East, and raw materials for western craftsmen. Venice tapped the stream of oriental goods that moved westward above the Caspian Sea and into the Black Sea provinces as well as those passing through Alexandria in Egypt. Genoa early vied with Venice for her share in this trade. In 1261 the Genoese helped seize Constantinople and gained a foothold in the Byzantine world. There were numerous commercial wars among the various rival Italian cities. For example, Marco Polo (1254-1324) son of a Venetian merchant, dictated the account of his famous travels to Asia in a Genoese prison after being captured in one of the frequent commercial wars between Venice and Genoa.

Lombardy assumed the leadership in trade and industry, because of the access to the Alpine passes which lead northward to the lands drained by the Rhine River. The passes of St. Bernard and Mont Cenis led into the heart of France, and ultimately to Flanders which was a center of the northern commercial and industrial development. The textile industry had developed there, importing wool and dyes and exporting finished cloth. Merchants from central and southern Europe came to this area via the valleys of the Rhine, Meuse, and Scheldt Rivers. Englishmen from the west and Scandinavians from the north brought wool and fish while German merchants used Flanders as an entrepot between the east and the west. However, there was a difference between northern European and Mediterranean trade. In the north commerce consisted largely of necessities such as grain, fish, wool, cloth, iron, timber, pitch, and tar; while exotic items such as spices, silks and brocades, sweet wines, fruits, carved ivory, gold and silver plate dominated the Mediterranean trade.

Between these two great commercial movements, one centering on the southern shores of Europe and the other along the northern shores lay the great mass of continental Europe, feudally oriented in politics and economically retarded in comparison with Flanders and northern Italy.

• The International Fairs

Among the early developments in the expansion of trade in Renaissance Europe were the international fairs, "oases of commercialism" which arose in the county of Champagne, east of Paris, and in Flanders. Lasting from one to six weeks, each of these fairs was the center of long-distance, wholesale trade, as distinct from the local markets which dealt in retail goods. At the fair, Venetian, Genoese, and Pisan merchants exchanged luxury goods for German linens, English wool, Flemish cloth, Russian furs, and Scandinavian naval stores. During the fourteenth century the Champagne fairs declined, as rival fairs developed in Geneva, Lyons, Frankfurt on the Main, Strasbourg, Paris, Winchester, and Westminster.

To meet the needs of these fairs new trading agencies developed. Venice inaugurated the Flanders Fleet in 1317 when galleys sailed through the Straits of Gibraltar to England and Flanders. Sailing annually this fleet provided the first regular all-water service between Italy and northern Europe. With no tolls to pay and no danger from robbers and with the advantage of only one loading for each trip, this fleet provided greater security and economy for the merchants.

• The Hanseatic League

Another trading agency, the Hanseatic League, reached the height of its power during the fourteenth and fifteenth centuries. This league was a confederation of northern mercantile cities, ranging from Bergen and Novgorod, to London, and Bruges, with its center usually in Lübeck, Germany. The League was formed to insure protection from piracy and to achieve security which was not given by the feudal governments in northern Europe. The League operated its own merchant fleet and navy, sailed under its own flag, and behaved like an independent power. Herring was the commodity of greatest value in the Hanseatic trade but furs from Russia, grain from the Baltic, and forest products were exchanged for wool, tin, hides, and cloth from the more southern members.

These commercial activities encouraged the development of new courts and legal systems – traditional legal practices of medieval Europe had made no provision for a merchant operating in an international economy. There was also a growing need for a code of laws which would deal with problems arising on the high seas such as piracy or shipwreck. Legal solutions were found in the Rhodian Sea Law of the second and third centuries, B.C., which was preserved in the *Digest* of Justinian. This was adopted in the Rolls of Oleron and as maritime law by the Atlantic and Baltic nations. The Laws of Wisby, based partially on the Rolls of Oleron, were the basic legal code used by the Hanseatic League. *The Consulate of the Sea* of Barcelona or, more properly, the *Book of the Consulate* ordered by James I of Aragon confirmed the maritime regulations prepared by the merchants and guild officials of the city of Barcelona in the Iberian peninsula. This was the most widely used code of mercantile law in the Mediterranean.

Medieval merchants developed a separate commercial law and separate law courts for use at the fairs. These were the "pie-powder" or dusty-foot courts, so named because the merchants would come into these courts with the dust of the road still on their feet. There was no formality – often lawyers were not allowed to attend – but there was speedy justice in contrast to the slow moving justice of the royal or ecclesiastical courts. The decisions of the court were rendered by a jury of merchants, and generally half the jury were foreigners, especially if one of the litigants was a foreigner. Land disputes and murder were not considered but virtually all other types of cases arising because of the fair were considered. Transgressions were usually of a commercial nature, such as nonpayment of debts or cheating on weights or measures.

• The Rise of Towns and Guilds

The expansion of trade was stimulated by the industries that furnished the textiles, metals, ships, and commodities needed by the merchants. Basic to this industrial development was the rise and growth of urban centers of population. Medieval towns had grown up next to feudal castles, or on the remains of old Roman cities – these areas offered safety from attack and attracted merchants who built shops and huts near the fortified walls. Such a fortified center was called a *burg* in the German language. The inhabited areas outside the burg, called *faubourg* (suburbs in modern English), in the course of time were also enclosed by a wall, and additional suburbs spread out.

Medieval society lacked strong central governments with the power to protect life and property. For their own defense traveling merchants joined together in voluntary associations of merchant guilds. As they settled in towns the wealthy merchants were the most influential citizens in obtaining charters of freedom for their town from their feudal overlords. The merchant guildsmen naturally became the leading officials of the city and the guilds became a political, as well as a commercial, force in society.

In the craft guilds which had grown up in medieval Europe there were three levels of membership: apprentice, journeyman, and master. The apprentice gave his services to the master while he learned the craft. The journeyman, or day laborer, travelled from place to place and gained further experience by working for wages under a master. The master craftsman owned his own shop and sold all the goods produced in it directly to the consumer.

With the growth of commerce during the Renaissance, merchants began to control the production of certain craft guilds. Under the "putting-out" system the merchant supplied the craftsman with raw materials and then purchased the finished product for resale in distant markets. Under this system the producer sold his labor to the merchant who controlled both the price of the finished product and the wages of the craftsman. The manufacture of woolen cloth was the most tightly organized industry in the late Middle Ages and the Renaissance.

• The Wool Industry

During the thirteenth century the Flemish cloth industry was dominated by a group of merchant-manufactures who purchased raw wool from England and "put it out" to artisans in Flanders. The finished cloth was then collected and sold in distant markets, usually through the Champagne fairs. Some craftsmen, such as highly skilled master dyers, were relatively well off, but the mass of workers were badly exploited. About 1280 a number of poor journeymen known as the Blue Nails, because of the condition of their hands, revolted in a violent class war. For more than a century civil war raged between the poor craftsmen and the rich merchant manufacturers. In addition to social unrest, the uncertain conditions resulting from the Hundred Years War, financial pressures of the Dukes of Burgundy, and the emigration of Flemish workmen to England caused the Flemish textile industry to decline after 1350 and northern Italy, especially Florence, became the center of the industry. The rise of the Florentine wool industry rested in part upon its long tradition (probably extending back to Roman times), its ready access to alum mines, the unparalleled development of its dyeing processes, and its abundant capital. Florentine cloth industry had two large guilds, the *arte de Calimala,* which was surpassed in the fourteenth century by the *arte della lana.* The organization of the *lana* guild was capitalistic – merchant bankers furnished raw materials to the workers and took the finished products to market in Europe and the orient. All the operations involved in cloth-processing (there were more than 20) were sub-contracted to craft specialists by the merchant guild which paid extremely low wages. Workers were forbidden to organize for their own protection and in many cases were bound to individual masters, who kept them in servitude by paying in advance and then making them work off their wages. By the guild rules, no employer could hire a laborer who had not fulfilled all his obligations to his current master. Workers who gained reputations as trouble-makers were blacklisted and could never find a job. This condition was particularly discouraging since the city government was often controlled by a clan of wealthy employers who used their political power to keep the workers in subjection. Even when a revolt destroyed for a time the control exercised by the great merchant guilds, only the lesser guilds profited and they had no interest in the poor workers of the larger industries. Generally, the lesser guilds feared violence and so sided with the wealthy in their attempt to keep law and order.

Under these circumstances it is not surprising that there were many riots. During the fourteenth century the aim of the wool-workers was to form a guild of their own so that they might bargain collectively and gain a share in the city government, such as that exercised by the members of the lesser guilds. Between 1379 and 1382, a rebellion of the Ciompi, or lowest class of workers, succeeded in accomplishing a democratic, political revolution, and for a time the common working men and the lesser guilds held control. However, in 1382 the wealthier merchants, manufacturers, and bankers maneuvered themselves back into power and executed more than one hundred and fifty leaders of the rebellion. In the end the wealthy Medici family, posing as champions of the common people, seized power in Florence (1435) and controlled the city until two years after the death of Lorenzo the Magnificent in 1492.

The Ciompi revolt illustrates the makeup of Renaissance industrial society. The revolt failed, not only because of a lack of effective leadership, but also because the violence frightened the artisans of the lesser guilds and even many workers. After the counter-revolution the guild of the Populo Minuto or Ciompi was suppressed and the merchant oligarchy was re-established. In the fifteenth century the decline of the Florentine wool trade reduced the number of workers and made revolt more difficult.

In both Italy and Flanders other industries grew to take the place of the wool trade. These were controlled by wealthy merchants rather than craft guilds and the workers lacked the organization and tradition of revolt of the wool workers. It is possible also that after a century of attempted revolt the proletariat gave up in its attempt to change the situation. Although the new capitalist leaders liberally patronized art and culture it is well to remember that the economic roots of Renaissance life were sunk in the seething misery of the workers suburbs.

• Money and Credit

Early medieval Europe had been largely an agrarian society with few coins in circulation and trade conducted mostly by barter because there were few precious metals. In the ninth century silver mines were opened in Alsace, and in the tenth century in the Black Forest and the Harz Mountains, and in the mid-twelfth century in Freiburg. Between 1100 and 1300 new gold and silver mines were found in Bohemia, Transylvania, and the Carpathian Mountains. With the increase of available metal, many new coins were minted. Florence began to issue the silver florin in 1252; Venice the ducat in 1284; France, England, and Spain rapidly followed with both gold and silver coins.

By the middle of the twelfth century, both the Church and the Empire accepted notarial cartularies as legal documents. The notaries recorded contracts of trade and exchange which evolved into bonafide credit instruments in the late twelfth century. This shift toward credit is seen at the merchant fairs where banking first began to develop. (The term bank comes from the Italian *banca,* the bench or table used by money changers.) Merchants came to the money changer to exchange one coin for another, and because the money changer had to have many types of coins on hand and the facilities to protect this considerable amount of cash, merchants began to deposit their money with him for safe keeping and pay him for this privilege. The money changer then began to lend money to a merchant to be repaid at the next fair. There was risk involved and, at times, security was required. More often, however, the money changer would accept the good name of the merchant and a promissory note and these notes developed into letters of the fair. But the Church prohibited usury, that is, interest on loans, and to disguise the interest and to avoid the accusation of usury, the loan was often repaid in a different coinage. In other cases, a contingency, or risk clause, or a penalty clause was added to avoid the taint of usury. These letters of the fair created credit, enabling the merchants to engage in business without carrying large sums of cash.

During the Crusades certain semi-military orders, such as the Knights Templar, provided banking services. With centers in various European cities, they made loans to crusaders and merchants alike. By the beginning of the fourteenth century dozens of important banking firms were located in Florence – two of the greatest were run by the Bardi and the Peruzzi families. Both families made substantial loans to the English crown during the Hundred Years War and were driven into bankruptcy in 1345-1346 when Edward III repudiated his debts.

The Medici house of Florence became the chief bankers of Europe in the fifteenth century. Beginning as merchants and bankers with minor interests in industry and mining, the Medici expanded until they had branches in Paris, London, Bruges, Lyons, Venice, Rome, Genoa, Naples, and eight other cities. Their business organization resembled a modern holding company and consisted of a number of legally independent firms in which members of the Medici family held a majority interest and exercised effective control. With such an organization most of their business consisted of foreign trade and exchange. The Medici also had controlling interest in their industrial enterprises, one of which made silk cloth and the other wool cloth. They handled papal income and transferred it to Rome from branches throughout Europe. It was due to this Church connection that they gained a controlling share in the alum mines in the papal states, and two members of the family became popes, Leo X and Clement VII. Cosimo dé Medici used his wealth to control the government of Florence from 1434 to 1464. He did this from behind the scenes in a manner that has been compared to the tactics of a modern city boss. He avoided as far as possible a show of power, using his economic resources in an indirect manner to get his way and often got crushing income taxes imposed on his opponents. This made it unnecessary for him to engage in the brutal terrorism that characterized many Italian city-states. Called Pater Patriae by the people of Florence he and his son Lorenzo were great patrons of the arts. Although their political power waned, socially the family remained important and two of its members, Catherine and Marie, later became queens of France.

With the decline of the Italian banking community in the second half of the fifteenth century a group of south German firms, most notably the Fuggers, rose to prominence. Jacob Fugger, the most prominent member of this banking family, built the wealth and reputation of the firm by lending money to the Hapsburgs and receiving mining and other monopolies from them. The great banking families were destined to lose their power to state banks, the first of which was started in Barcelona in 1401.

• Land and Agriculture

Up to 1350, along with the expansion of trade, commerce, and industry, went a comparable increase in arable and pasture lands. Forests were cleared, marshes were drained, and the German peoples moved eastward into areas thinly settled by Slavic peoples. Much of this expansion was organized, financed, and carried out by religious orders, especially the Benedictines and the Cistercians who, by the rules of their order, were farmers.

With more coins in circulation and with profit to be made from the sale of agricultural surplus, landlords and peasants had an incentive to produce more than they needed themselves. Commutation, the substitution of money payments for manual service, began very early in the history of the manor system and by the thirteenth century, the lords of the manor, hard up for money, were eager to receive commutations from their peasants who then became tenant farmers. With the value of land and the price of agricultural products gradually rising small freeholders profited, but the landlord who lived on fixed rents saw his real income decline.

After the mid-fourteenth century, European agriculture suffered from dislocation and disaster, which affected both landlords and peasants. The expanding economy of the Middle Ages had come to an end, due to a slow decline in population, a decline that reduced both the supply of labor and the market for goods produced. When agricultural prices declined during the fourteenth century peasants who had to pay a fixed rent to the lords could not meet their obligations. Since the old bonds that had held the peasant to the land had broken down, lords found their peasants moving away and land dropping out of cultivation. Some peasants settled in more properous areas and others went to the town, thus pressuring the lords to lower rents. Since the prices of non-agricultural goods tended to hold firm or increase, the landholding class was caught between lower prices for what they sold and generally higher prices for what they bought. Some lords tried to solve this problem by hiring laborers to work the land but with the labor shortage caused by the Black Death rural wages tended to rise. Attempts to roll wages back through government intervention – such as the English Statute of Laborers (1351) and later laws which required workers to accept wage rates that had been in effect before the plague – failed. (This maximum wage law makes an interesting comparison with today's minimum wage.) The difficult condition prevailing in the late fourteenth century closed the medieval agricultural frontier and caused the interests of the peasants and their lords to clash.

• The Black Death and Peasants Revolts

In 1348 and 1349, a bubonic plague, the Black Death, was brought to Europe from the Orient, carried by lice on the rats which traveled westward with the caravans and in ships. The plague appeared in Venice, then swept through north and central Italy, south and central France, and on to Flanders, Germany, and England. The spread of the plague followed the main trade routes, since it was carried by merchants. Its symptoms were boils in the groin and arm pit; the victim's skin turned black, he suffered excruciating pain, and died within a day or two. The Black Death destroyed as much as thirty to forty percent of the population in some areas, while others were almost untouched. After a brief period, the plague returned again in the 1360's and 1370's, and at regular intervals thereafter.

Because of the Black Death there were not enough peasants to work the land and the surviving peasants demanded higher wages. The ravages of the plague, the misery caused by the Hundred Years War in France from 1337 to 1453, and the reactions to the legal attempts to curtail wages provoked a series of peasant revolts throughout Europe during the fourteenth and fifteenth centuries. In France the most serious of these revolts was the Jacquerie which broke out in 1358. It took its name from Jacques, a common French nickname for the peasant. Led by Guillaume

Cale (William Carle), and with the help of lower class Parisians, groups of desperate peasants made plundering expeditions, attacked the manor houses, and committed atrocities. One lord was stuck on a spit and burned in the presence of his family. The dauphin Charles (who later ruled France as Charles V) succeeded in turning the Paris mob against its leader, Etienne Marcel, who was killed. Then the French lords united to suppress this revolt and killed thousands of peasants.

England's most famous peasant revolt occurred in 1381. The insurrection began in the county of Kent, a center of discontent at the enforcement of the Statute of Laborers. Wat Tyler assumed leadership of the uprising among the peasants aided by John Ball, an excommunicated priest with a long career as an agitator for the rights of common people. Ball influenced the already angry mob with talk of equality and an age to come when there would be no rich or poor. The peasants marched on London in June, 1381 and were welcomed into the city by many sympathetic citizens. At the moment the royal government was in a weak position because of war on the Scottish border and so King Richard II negotiated with the insurgents. They wished recognition as free men, with rights to justice, cheap land, and free trade. Faced by the rebels ready for battle Richard annulled the Statute of Laborers by issuing charters which provided for civil emancipation and amnesty for the revolutionaries. The government still had resources and soldiers, however, and the king's minister had no intention of honoring the agreements that Richard had made. The mayor of London and his men tricked and killed Wat Tyler. Without their leader the rebel bands were persuaded to leave London and the revolt was put down with great brutality. John Ball, the people's prophet, was hanged, disemboweled, and quartered.

Peasant revolts did not break out in Germany until the end of the fifteenth century culminating in one of the bloodiest of all peasant uprisings in southern and western Germany in 1524-1525.

• Voyages of Discovery

The age of the Renaissance was a period of discovery as European nations in a series of daring voyages reached the New World and also found new and better routes to the Far East. Until the recent space probe, this was the era of mankind's greatest adventure. The knowledge of the non-European world available to these early discoverers consisted of some sketchy charts and maps, academic treatises, and traveller's tales. The traveller's accounts, both real and imaginary, often described the unknown in frightening terms. The Atlantic Ocean was believed to be an unnavigable "green sea of darkness" and the frigid and torrid zones of the earth horrible uninhabitable places. For Asia, however, many of these accounts such as the one by Marco Polo were dependable.

Several travelers journeyed to the East in the thirteenth century including John of Plano Carpini, William Rubruck, and John of Monte Corvino, but the most famous of all was Marco Polo. Between 1262 and 1269 the two Polo brothers, Niccolo and Maffeo, traveled to China and back, and between 1271 and 1296 they made a second journey and took with them Niccolo's son, Marco. Marco won the confidence of Kublai Khan, the Mongol ruler of China, served under him, and was privileged to travel throughout China. On his way back to Europe he travelled through southern Asia and the Middle and Near East. His account, the *Travels of Marco Polo,* greatly influenced western Europe by correcting mistaken geographical notions and by demonstrating that the wealthy East could be reached by water.

The discoverers were also encouraged by academic treatises, such as the *Imago mundi* (c. 1410) by the famous conciliarist Pierre d'Ailly. This vast storehouse of knowledge brought together classical, biblical, and Arabic cosmological learning. Columbus used this book and his copy still survives in the Colombina at Seville. Like all the accounts that Columbus used, d'Ailly exaggerated the east-west extent of Asia and the proportion of land to sea on the globe. Most theorists like d'Ailly accepted Ptolemi's *Geography.* His work attached southern Africa to Asia, thus making the Indian ocean an inland sea, estimated the distance around the world at three-fourths of the actual figure, and extended the land mass of Asia too far east. However, it was these very errors that encouraged the fifteenth century explorers in their attempts to sail around Africa and to sail westward to Asia.

In addition to geographical theories that encouraged the voyages of discovery, there were various technological changes that made these journeys possible. Advances in the arts of navigation and cartography, such as the compass, astrolabe, and better charts, enabled sailors for the first time to observe and record the position of a point on an unknown coast. New methods in the design of ships which combined the Roman, Viking, and Arab ships into the caravel and the nau made it possible not only to make long voyages of discovery but to repeat them and establish regular communication with new found lands. The development of ship-born artillery gave European explorers a great advantage over even the most civilized continent that they might discover and enabled them to establish colonies and trading ports in lands where their enemies had great numerical superiority.

The people of northern Europe desired to establish direct contact with the Indies and China because they were dependent for the purchase of the spices, silks, and other luxuries of the East upon a host of middle men such as Italians, Greeks, Turks, Chinese, and Indians, and because these goods were increasing in price and had to be bought with gold and silver. Many Europeans also were motivated by a missionary or crusading desire to outflank the Muslims and convert them to Christianity. The legend of Prester John encouraged their dreams. He was supposed to be a Christian emperor who ruled a vast state in Africa and would make a ready ally in a Christian war against Islam. Prince Henry believed that Prester John had an army of over one million and that he had already conquered much of Africa.

The lead in these voyages of discovery was taken by Prince Henry the Navigator (1404-1460) a younger son of the king of Portugal. As a young man he participated in a crusade against the Moors which culminated in the Portuguese conquest of Ceuta in Morocco. Then he devoted himself to the encouragement of exploration along the African coast in order to find the kingdom of Prester John and open a sea route for the Portuguese to the Far East. Henry established a school on the Portuguese coast at Cape St. Vincent where he studied mathematics, navigation, astronomy, cartography and gathered together experts in all these areas. He sent out annual voyages to explore the coast of Africa, heard the reports of returned ship captains, and studied their logs. After his death in 1460 the exploratory activity slackened until the reign of King John II (1481-1495). The Cape of Good Hope was rounded by Bartolomeo Diaz (1487), who found the waters of the equator to be navigable and the possible existence of an all-water route to the Far East.

In 1497 Vasco da Gama's expedition of four ships rounded the Cape of Good Hope and went up the eastern coast of Africa as far as Malindi. There he picked up an Arab pilot who guided the ships to Calicut on the Malabar Coast of India. He returned in September, 1499 with a cargo of pepper and cinnamon that was worth sixty times the cost of the expedition. This was probably the greatest voyage in the history of navigation up to that time – da Gama was out of sight of land for ninety days (three times as long as Columbus on his voyage to the New World), and covered about twenty-eight thousand miles. This voyage established the pattern for later Portuguese expeditions, gave them a monopoly of the Far Eastern spice trade, and established Lisbon as the pepper capital of Europe. Another Portuguese sailor, Cabral, intending to make the usual trip around Africa to the Spice Islands, was blown off course by a storm and driven westward until he touched the eastern coast of Brazil which he claimed for Portugal (1500). From the Malabar Coast and Goa in India,

Portuguese merchants and missionaries moved eastward until they reached Sumatra, Java, the Spice Islands, and north along the eastern coast of Asia reaching Canton (1517) and arriving in Japan (1542).

Before the Portuguese had found the all-water route to India and the Spice Islands, a Genoese sailor and map-maker, Christopher Columbus, had offered to find a western route for the Portuguese. When they turned him down he persuaded King Ferdinand and Queen Isabella of Spain to finance an expedition. On August 3, 1492, his first expedition of three ships and eighty-six men set out from Palos, Spain and on October 12 they sighted land, probably one of the Bahama islands, which Columbus named San Salvador. He explored the West Indies for about three months and left some of his men to establish a settlement on the island of Haiti. The rest of the group returned to Spain in July, 1493.

Columbus had no difficulty collecting men and money for his second voyage whose purpose was settlement and colonization. On September 25, 1493, seventeen ships, twelve hundred men and three stowaways weighed anchor at Cadiz. They found that the old colony at Haiti was gone but discovered a new island, Santo Domingo. The second trip proved to be a failure, and Columbus returned to Spain with his reputation shattered.

Spain planned another expedition to stake out her claims, even though investors in the second voyage were still clamoring for returns on their money. The third attempt left Spain in spring, 1498 and took Columbus to the South American coast near the mouth of the Orinoco River. Columbus never realized he had discovered a new continent; he had failed to obtain wealth from the islands, and in October, 1500 he and his two brothers were sent back to Spain in chains. He returned to the new world on a fourth voyage (1502-1504) filled with hazard and mutiny and returned to Spain for the last time, broken in body and spirit.

Portugal and Spain were the most active and successful among the nations making voyages of discovery in the fifteenth and early sixteenth century. To keep peace between these two powers the papacy established a Line of Demarcation (1493), which separated the Spanish and Portuguese areas of discovery and confirmed Columbus' discoveries to Spain. Portugal and Spain signed the treaty of Tordesillas in 1494 which established a line 370 leagues west of the Azores and Cape Verde Islands as the frontier between the two empires. This confirmed to Portugal a monopoly of all lands east of the line (Brazil, Africa, and Asia) and to Spain a monopoly of all lands to the west (North and South America). These nations developed two different types of empires. The Portuguese empire was primarily commercial, setting up factories or collection depots in India and the Spice Islands to which ships would go once or twice a year. The contents of the warehouses would be transferred into the holds of the Portuguese ships which would then return to Lisbon.

The Spanish empire was colonial rather than commercial. Following the expeditions of Cortes to Mexico and of Pizarro to Peru, the Spaniards confiscated unbelievable amounts of Inca and Aztec gold and silver which they shipped to Spain. After this profitable beginning, the Spaniards developed a system of Spanish colonies in the New World. By 1575 their rule extended from South America to North America and dominated 175,000 Spaniards, 40,000 Negroes, and about 5 million Indians engaged in mining, cattle ranching, and agriculture.

The new discoveries affected Europe economically during the Renaissance. During this period spices from the east and gold and silver from America accounted for an overwhelming proportion of the products received from the newly discovered lands. The influx of precious metals trebled Europe's supply of money during the sixteenth century. As the quantity of money increased, the price of goods rose thus making a time of inflation. Grain prices increased three- to four-fold during this period. Another important item of trade was slaves. The Arabs had been trading in black slaves since medieval times and in the early fifteenth century the Portuguese joined them. Between 1450 and 1505, 140,000 slaves were shipped out of Guinea alone. Later in the sixteenth and seventeenth centuries the trade with the new world and Asia would broaden to include such products as coffee, tea, sugar, and tobacco.

Commercially, the age of discovery meant that the Mediterranean Sea was no longer the focal point of European trade. Venice lost her monopoly of the Far Eastern spice trade and in 1532 the Flanders Fleet made its last voyage. Venetian losses were duplicated in Genoa, Marseilles, Barcelona, and other Mediterranean ports. These towns were replaced by the nation states with harbors on the Atlantic, such as Seville, Cadiz, Lisbon, Bordeaux, Amsterdam, Southampton, Bristol, and London.

It seems strange that the new discoveries did not attract more attention. It was not until the seventeenth century that western man would expand his mental horizon to match these great geographical expansions. Fascinated by their attempt to recover ancient knowledge, the most powerful intellects of the Renaissance scarcely noticed the new world.

8

The Church and the State in the Renaissance

EUROPE between 1300 and 1500 was in a period of transition from medieval to modern institutions. In these centuries the medieval idea of the universality and unity of all society as expressed in the Holy Catholic Church and the Holy Roman Empire was challenged by the rise of the territorial state. The national states in France and England, and the principalities in Italy and Germany, developed with the cooperation of monarchs and a comparatively new group of men – the townsmen. Actively engaged in such non-feudal pursuits as commerce, industry, and banking, the townsmen saw advantages to be gained from an increase in centralized political control. Their interests thus coincided with those of the monarchs who wanted to curtail the political power of feudal lords and the church. Townsmen wanted equality under the law, representation in government, and social prestige; the kings, in turn, needed their money.

• Royal Justice

Administrators and lawyers, drawn from the new towns and trained in Roman law at the universities, were able to justify a centralized monarchy by the use of two political theories. They advanced the idea that for the good of the entire territory or state the ruler must be absolute, above the law and the legal and military powers of the nobility. The second theory asserted that the king received his power directly from God and therefore ruled by divine right. This theory destroyed the secular power of the church and the papacy.

The immediate problem facing the monarchs was to recover the governmental functions they had lost to the feudal nobles during the medieval period. The monarchs of France and England moved toward centralizing the administration of justice, the military organization, and the collection of taxes. As supreme feudal lord the king claimed the right to hear appeals from the courts of his vassals and sub-vassals. As consecrated king he had the duty to see that justice was done to all within his kingdom. In England, the king was able to spread a uniform royal justice (i.e. common law) throughout the land as early as the twelfth century. By the end of the thirteenth century, Edward I, called the English Justinian because he was a great legislator, like the Roman Emperor, brought under royal jurisdiction most of the administration of justice. An example of the way he was able to do this was a long series of judicial proceedings based upon inquests of 1274-1275. In these trials a lord who held judicial power was asked "by what warrant" or authority he held his power. If he could produce a royal charter giving him or one of his ancestors a legal position then he received a confirmation of his grant. Most lords, however, based their power on precedent and could not defend themselves with documentary evidence. Many local authorities lost their power this way, but an even more important outcome was that the royal government could supervise and intervene in the administration of the local courts. In the following century the justices of the peace, who were loyal local gentry appointed by the crown, brought what remained of feudal jurisdiction under royal supervision.

In France where feudalism was more fully developed the triumph of royal justice was delayed. Unlike England, the French feudal courts existed side by side with the royal courts until the French Revolution. In practice, however, appeals to the king's justice were heard by royal officials who were paid from the fees and fines levied by the royal courts. These men increasingly insinuated themselves into the administration of local, feudal, and church courts with the result that both laws and legal procedures became more effective and uniform and the authority of the monarchy was entrenched and extended. By the sixteenth century the monarchs of both England and France had recovered much of the administration of justice from the feudal nobility.

• A Royal Army

In the early Middle Ages the king neither paid for nor equipped an army but called upon his chief vassals to provide the military service due to him under their feudal contract, usually about forty days service for a mounted knight per year. This was sufficient for repulsing an invasion or pursuing a short offensive expedition, but it was totally inadequate for waging a long foreign war. England in the late thirteenth century took the first step toward the formation of a national army. The kings of England had imposed upon their knights the scutage, the payment of money equal to the cost of hiring a substitute. With these and other revenues Edward I was able to supplement his feudal cavalry with an infantry of freemen armed with the newly introduced long bow. In the fourteenth century both feudal levies and the national army were inadequate and the monarchs relied more heavily upon paid armies of mercenary soldiers. The emergence of a middle-class urban infantry required a large, well-trained, permanent, and salaried force, and only a strong government supported by revenues derived from taxation could afford such an army. In the fifteenth century the introduction of gunpowder and firearms increased the expenses of warfare. War had become big business, much too expensive to be indulged in as a private sport by feudal nobility.

• Taxation

The cost of larger royal administration and of armies forced the kings to supplement their traditional sources of revenue from crown lands, feudal dues, customs duties, mint rights, and commodity monopolies with new taxes. Various expedients such as forced loans or borrowing against future revenues did not solve the problem. The conclusion that was reached by both the French and English monarchs was that taxes had to be collected more frequently and regularly. In order to expand royal revenues greater reliance was placed upon representation of the people. These assemblies included elected citizens from the town and the landed gentry as well as the great council of the king. These bodies, such as the Parliament in England and the Estates General in France, were expected to establish closer contact between the royal government and the people, though the king was primarily concerned with raising taxes.

In France, the crown established its right to collect in time of peace special taxes that had been exacted to finance the war. In addition to the king's ordinary income from royal landholdings and customary taxes, were added the salt tax or gabelle, a sales tax, and the real estate tax or taille. King Charles VII used these taxes to create a standing army and he created a professional officer corps recruited from the nobles to command permanent garrisons scattered throughout France. In addition to suppressing the lawless mercenaries who devastated France in the early fifteenth century, the king's force caused the submission of unruly nobles such as the dukes of Bourbon and Orléans.

The English crown's efforts at raising taxes which were developing in the fourteenth century were hampered in the fifteenth century by the development of what has been called "bastard feudalism." The monarchy was forced to pay large amounts of money to the important nobles ostensibly for the service of soldiers, but actually as bribes. This enabled these magnates to expand their private armies and challenge the royal power itself. After the Wars of the Roses (1453-1485) and the victory of Henry VII royal finances were reorganized. The king was a very frugal man and he extracted as much as he could from the traditional sources of royal income such as revenues for the crown lands, feudal dues, customs duties and ecclesiastical revenue. He also cut down on military expenditures and imposed fines and granted pardons for "dead letter" crimes or the slightest misdemeanors. Generally, however, Henry was able to increase royal income without serious new taxes because of the cooperation of parliament in granting him special subsidies.

While in central Europe and northern Italy common interests developed within city states and smaller principalities, in western Europe the new monarchies extended their jurisdiction to the larger area of the nation state. Nationalism has become dominant in the nineteenth and twentieth centuries. In a certain sense its roots go back to the Renaissance monarchies when men first became aware of speaking a common language, obeying a single ruler, and sharing economic and political interests.

• The Hundred Years War

The French and English people were brought to national consciousness during the weary struggle known to history as the Hundred Years War (1337-1453). The actions of Edward III, king of England from 1327 to 1377, precipitated the war. An earlier dispute between England and France had been settled by the Treaty of Paris of 1259 which left England in possession of the duchy of Aquitaine (Guienne and Gascony), one of the most important wine-producing areas in France. Edward III was fearful of losing his Aquitanian holdings to the French kings who were completing the territorial unification of France and hoped to bring Aquitaine under their direct control. Flanders, another fief of the French crown, was important to England because the Flemings purchased approximately 80 per cent of their raw wool from England. The French king, Philip IV, had joined the Count of Flanders in defeating the rebellious Flemish merchants and artisans at Cassel (1328). French control over the woolen industry in Flanders would have been a serious economic blow to England. In addition to these provocations, the French kings had been encouraging the Scots to resist English attempts to rule them.

In 1337 Edward III announced his claim to the French throne. It has been disputed whether he was serious, since his claim was poor. Edward's mother was Isabella, daughter of Philip IV, but the Salic law of the French prohibited the transmission of the crown through the female line and the throne had gone to Philip VI, nephew of Philip IV.

The course of the war can be divided into three periods. In the first period, 1337-1360, England was victorious. The English destroyed the French fleet at Sluys (1340); this cleared the Channel and made possible an English invasion of France. At the Battle of Crécy (1346) the English longbowmen wiped out the much larger French army. In 1356 the English won the battle of Poitiers, confirming once more the decision of Crécy that mounted feudal knights were no match for the middle-class infantry with their long bow. The French king, John, was captured and by the Treaty of Brétigny (1360) Edward received full sovereignty over Aquitaine and Calais and renounced his claim to the French throne, thus ending this period of the war.

When Charles V (1346-1380), ascended the French throne he turned over the prosecution of the war to his ablest mercenary captain, Bertrand du Guesclin, who was responsible for the French victories during the second phase of the war, 1369-1400. He laid greater emphasis upon infantry than cavalry and created a more efficient fighting machine for France. He also used new tactics which involved avoiding direct contact with the English except for small skirmishes, devastating the surrounding country, and then retreating into previously provisioned fortresses. When the English besieged these forts, bands of French free companies harassed them and cut their supply lines. By using this method of guerrilla warfare, du Guesclin was able to reconquer most of the English possessions in France. With the death of Edward III in 1377 and Charles V in 1380, the second phase of the war ended.

In the interim a bitter struggle developed between two factions of the French nobility: the Burgundians and the Orleanists (also called the Armagnacs) and the third phase of the Hundred Years War (1415-1453) was accompanied by a civil war between these two factions. The English king, Henry V, reactivated the conflict when he declared himself King of France and invaded France (1415). Met by a number of Armagnac knights at Agincourt the English won a decisive victory and by 1419 the English, who had made an alliance with the Burgundians, had conquered most of northern France. The following year the French were forced to sign the ignominious Treaty of Troyes in which they recognized Henry V as heir to the French throne and regent of France during the lifetime of the French king Charles VI. To cement the agreement the English king married Catherine, the daughter of the French sovereign. In 1422 both monarchs died and Henry V was succeeded by his nine-month-old son Henry VI (1422-1461). Charles VI was succeeded by his son Charles who was forced to remain in southern France as the uncrowned dauphin because of the English. Even though Charles did little to regain his crown, opposition to the English intensified in France, largely due to a seventeen-year-old girl, Joan of Arc. Convinced by visions that it was her duty to defeat the English and crown the dauphin, she was placed at the head of the army. She went from victory to victory until it was possible for the dauphin to be crowned at Reims, and much of northern France returned to support the king. However, Joan was captured by the English and the ungrateful Charles made no effort to ransom her. She was turned over to the court of the Inquisition at Rouen where she was tried for heresy and sorcery by the Bishop of Beauvais and was condemned and burned at the stake in May, 1431. The death of Joan excited the enthusiasm of Frenchmen and even of the apathetic Charles; the French armies seized northern France and took Paris in 1436. With the capture of Bordeaux in 1453 all of France except Calais was in French hands and the Hundred Years War was over.

The war resulted in the weakening of both the French and English feudal nobility, many of whom died in battle and left no heirs. According to feudal law, their lands returned by escheat to the king who was able to award these lands to loyal followers and create a new barony. New methods of warfare also lessened the value of the feudal cavalry. The artillery and cannon of the Hundred Years War rendered useless the castle as the supreme defensive weapon of the knight. Castles turned into country estates with picture windows instead of slits from which to fire arrows, and formal gardens instead of moats of stagnant water.

In France, following the war, royal power was consolidated. The French king extended the royal domain over all France. Public opinion associated peace, order, and the explusion of the English with the monarchy. Taxes which had been established to finance the war were continued on a permanent basis and a permanent army was established, for in addition to the English, the government was forced to wage campaigns against unemployed mercenaries who roamed the country. The people gladly paid taxes for a force to protect them from these bands of outlaws.

In England, Parliament gained authority, for whenever the king needed money to carry on the war he had to have the consent of the people's representatives and they demanded concessions before they would vote the funds. The years of war and those immediately following permitted the development of a constitutional monarchy. The monarchs lost their continental lands and thus were forced to concentrate on domestic problems. The English baronial class divided into two factions, the Houses of Lancaster and York; the Lancastrians had as their emblem the red rose and the Yorkists, the white rose. Both sides struggled for control of Parliament and the monarchy in a lengthy civil war, the Wars of the Roses (1453-1485), and the feudal nobility virtually exterminated one another, enabling Henry VII of the house of Tudor to come to power. The Tudor dynasty was destined, through Henry VIII and Elizabeth I, to fashion England into a strong state.

• Italy in the Renaissance

In the fourteenth and fifteenth century Italy was a geographical area which lacked political unity among its many independent states. While France and England developed into nation states because their monarchs succeeded in centralizing their authority at the expense of the feudal nobility, the territorial states of Italy, particularly the city-states of northern Italy, grew because of the expansion of commerce between western Europe and the eastern Mediterranean. These wealthy Italian city-states were able to profit from the hostility between the German emperor to the north who considered Italy as part of his Holy Roman Empire, and the pope who occupied the Patrimony of Peter to the south. When the imperial power was broken after 1254 and the papacy was transferred from Rome to Avignon in 1309, the political vacuum in Italy was filled by these city-states, each ruling the area around it and quarreling with its neighbors over land and the control of trade routes. This was a period of power politics and of shifting political alliances. Most of these city-states had had a republican form of government in the Middle Ages. At the beginning of the Renaissance, however, a significant change was taking place as the republics were being replaced by despots, or, as the Italians called them, *signori.* The development of despotism was similar in many Italian city-states. An able or particularly aggressive leader, perhaps a condottieri or podestá, took power for a limited time; the term was then extended because of internal or external crisis and then he sought to make his succession hereditary. These rulers would often try to expand their territory so they could appeal to the pride and patriotism of the citizens and also insure hostile neighbors so that the state of crisis which kept them in office would continue. A city where this pattern is most evident was Milan.

• Milan

Milan, in the fertile Po River valley, had led the Lombard League of Italian cities against the emperor Frederick Barbarossa in the twelfth century. Razed by the emperor and rebuilt by the league, Milan rapidly expanded with an economy based on armor-making, the wool trade, and silk manufacture. A new aristocracy of wealth began to challenge the old aristocracy of land and demand their share in political power. With its growing commercial strength and territory, Milan rivaled both Venice and Florence in wealth and prestige in the Renaissance. In the twelfth and thirteenth century its republican government was based on a *parlamento* or grand council in which all the free citizens were represented and a group of twelve men who served as executive officers for one year. In 1277 this republican government was overthrown by Otto Visconti and by 1395 this family was made the hereditary ruler of Milan by the Emperor. The Visconti continued to rule until the death of the Filippo Maria in 1447. During the next seven years his son-in-law, Francesco Sforza, a condottieri or mercenary captain, defeated Venice and conquered the Lombard plain and assumed the title of Duke of Milan. The Sforza dynasty ruled Milan until 1535 when Milan came under direct Spanish rule with the death of Francesco II Sforza.

• Florence

Florence, like Milan, was a republic with a prosperous economy and an unstable political tradition. The control of the city did not pass into the hands of military leaders, however, but was held by merchant bankers. The townsmen revolted against the imperial party of the Tuscan nobility and in 1293 established a republican constitution which stated that only members of the seven greater guilds could hold office. The constitution provided for an executive council of priors composed of seven elected

The Cathedral in Milan. Courtesy, Italian Government Travel Office.

officials. Florence had a popular assembly, the *arengo,* but the chief direction of its government remained with the priors who instituted a bureaucracy with important secretarial positions which attracted both lawyers and humanists.

The production and export of woolen cloth was the most important economic activity in Florence, employing about one-third of the population. The great cloth merchants became international bankers and were influential in creating the constitution which disenfranchised the nobility. The men of more modest means in the craft guilds supported the great merchant guildsmen who controlled Florence, even in the fourteenth century when the city was weakened by depression and bank failures. In 1434 the Medici family, posing as champions of the common people, controlled the city until 1494 when Charles VIII of France invaded Italy.

Under the Medici, particularly Cosimo (1434-1464), and Lorenzo the Magnificent (1478-1492), Florence pursued a policy of diplomacy and political maneuvering which made this city the center of an Italian balance of power system. Financially prosperous during this period she was also the center of the humanistic and artistic culture of the Renaissance. The Medici were magnificent patrons of learning and the arts.

• Venice

Venice was the most stable, and, at the same time, the perhaps least democratic of the Italian city-states. The city was built on mud flats in the Adriatic Ocean which gave it open communication on the sea and kept it safe from siege and conquest. Venice was also fortunate is not having any feudal countryside with which to deal. The whole life of *La Serenissima,* the most serene lady (as Venetians called their state) was centered in commerce controlled by a few patrician families who established control over the city government and refused to share governmental functions with the people. In 1297 these ruling families closed the Great Council to all except their descendants. The functions of the Council were to elect the head of state, the doge, to choose the Council of Ten, charged with the maintenance of public order and welfare, and appoint the other councillors and magistrates. Throughout her long history, Venice remained a republic, but it was a republic ruled by as arbitrary an oligarchy as any single despot could be.

• The Papal States

South of these city-states and stretching like a band across the peninsula lay the Papal States. From 1309 to 1378 the popes lived in Avignon on the border of France. The states of the church had never been thoroughly centralized and, under this absentee lordship, they became even more fragmented as destructive feuds raged between rival cities and between warring families such as the Orsinis and the Colonnas. In 1347

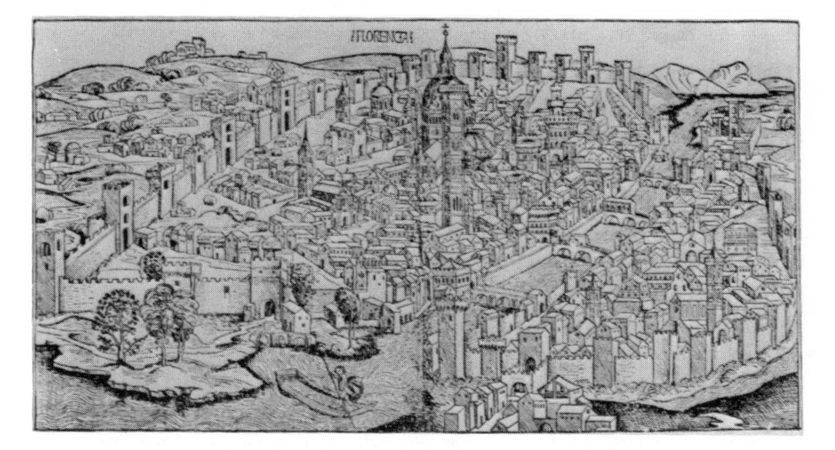

Florence in the fifeenth century, from a contemporary drawing.

Cola di Rienzi gathered the support of the populace at Rome, and overthrowing the rule of the upper classes set himself up as a tribune of the people, attempting to free them from the corrupt nobility and reestablish the glory of classical republican Rome. His rule proved to be a failure, and when he was slain by a mob the nobility resumed control (1354). Pope Innocent VI (1352-1362), sent a legate, the Spanish Cardinal Albornoz, to Italy to reestablish papal authority in these church lands. Within a decade he restored order and paved the way for the return of the popes to Rome. Not until the end of the conciliar movement, however, were the popes able to give the Papal States their attention and ultimately set up a strong monarchical state.

• French Invasion of Italy

The year 1492 marked the death of Lorenzo the Magnificent in Florence and the expulsion of the Moors from Spain. The first of these events upset the diplomatic balance of power among the north Italian states and the second marked the unification of Spain under Ferdinand and Isabella. At this same time the king of France, Charles VIII, felt secure enough to test his strength in Italy where he claimed the crown of Naples because a branch of the French royal family had ruled south Italy in the early fifteenth century. In 1494 he was invited to take Naples by the regent of Milan, Ludovico Sforza, *il Moro,* who was seeking revenge against the King of the Two Sicilies. The French king marched triumphantly through Italy and entered Naples on February 22, 1494. This sudden victory was lost almost as quickly as it was won. King Ferdinand of Aragon resented the French incursion into Naples which his family ruled and he formed a league of Italian states which drove the French out of Italy by 1496. This marked the beginning of a long struggle between France and Spain which continued into the sixteenth century.

• Germany

During the fourteenth and fifteenth centuries Germany was developing differently from France and England. While they were becoming more centralized and a spirit of nationalism was growing within them, in Germany the forces of particularism won out over the central government.

The conflict between the empire and the papacy in medieval times resulted in a lack of political unity in which the individual territorial units of Germany and its rising cities were able to maintain their relative independence. Because of this struggle several of the German emperors were more concerned about extending their control over Italy than with conditions in Germany. Again, the popes were often interested in establishing rival emperors in Germany so that they could find a leader with whom they could work out a political settlement. The critical period of the Interregnum (1254-1273) during which there was no emperor or king, further intensified this political fragmentation.

In 1273 the electors – the three archbishops of Mainz, Trier and Cologne and the Count Palatine of the Rhine – chose Rudolph of Hapsburg as emperor king because they thought he was financially and politically weak and no threat to their independence. Rudolph, wisely discarding the old imperial ambitions of ruling Italy, restricted himself to laying the foundations of a strong royal domain in southwest Germany by appropriating the lands of those feudal lords who died without heirs. The king of Bohemia, Ottokar II had illegally appropriated the Babenberg inheritance of Austria, Styria, Carinthia, and Carniola in 1270. Rudolph defeated and killed him in 1278, seized these lands and gave them to members of his own family, creating the royal domain of the Hapsburg dynasty which remained in their possession until 1918. Following Rudolph's death in 1291 the electors chose emperors from various German houses which tended to paralyze the imperial government and shift the balance of power from the emperor to the German princes.

The new electoral mechanism was legalized in 1356 with the publication of the Golden Bull, the nearest approach to a constitution the empire ever acquired. The Bull designated seven princes as electors of the German Emperor: the archbishops of Mainz, Trier, and Cologne; the king of Bohemia; the duke of Saxony, the Margrave of Brandenburg; and the Count Palatine of the Rhine. Upon the death of an emperor, these seven electors were to meet at Frankfort on the Main and select a successor, and they were declared to have full sovereign rights within their own territories. Each electoral territory was to be inherited as a unit and was never to be divided between joint heirs. The Golden Bull completely omitted any reference to the papal claims to confirm or veto an election and to administer the empire during a vacancy which effectively removed papal intervention in imperial elections.

The sovereignty of the territorial state was thus firmly established. These separate German principalities were no substitute for the strong national state in maintaining internal security and peace and for the next century and a half Germany experienced a period of lawlessness unequalled in the early Middle Ages.

• The Catholic Church

During these same centuries the church developed into a monarchy which rivaled the nation states. Pope Boniface VIII (1294-1303) began the conflict with the national monarchs because he felt that temporal authority owed obedience to the church and he was challenged by the kings of France and of England, each of whom taxed the clergy without permission of the pope, which violated the medieval concept of clerical immunity. Boniface answered by issuing the bull, *Clericis Laicos* (February, 1296), in which he forbad secular governments to tax clerics without papal authorization. In answer, Edward I of England withdrew royal protection from clergy and church lands and the church in England promptly voted the king a gift to support the war with France. Philip IV sealed the borders of France and forbad export of all money, jewelry, or precious metals. When the Italian bankers and papal tax collectors protested, the pope issued *Etsi de statu* (August, 1297) which rescinded the prohibitions of *Clericis Laicos.* The first phase of the conflict was a victory for the state.

In 1301 Philip IV tried and condemned the Bishop of Pamiers on a charge of treason and demanded that Boniface degrade him before his execution. The pope issued the bull, *Ausculta fili* (December, 1301), ordering the bishop freed, suspending all privileges of clerical taxation, and summoning the French bishops to a council to take action against the king. Philip countered by calling the first meeting of the Estates General, an assembly of clergy, nobles, and townsmen which supported his position. In November, 1302, Boniface issued the bull, *Unam sanctam,* an extreme argument for papal authority which ended with the statement that subjection to the Roman pontiff was absolutely necessary for salvation. The next year the Estates General charged the pope with various crimes and heresies and the king's representative, William Nogaret, was sent to bring the pope to France for trial. Nogaret seized Boniface at his summer home in Anagni but a mob freed him. Exhausted by the experience the pope died about a month later – no ruler in all Europe had come to his aid and no succeeding pope punished Philip. More than any other event this showed the power of the national monarchy and the weakness of the head of the church.

Boniface's successor died after a rule of a few months and a Frenchman, Clement V, was chosen pope. He created ten new cardinals, nine of whom were Frenchmen, and moved the papal court from Rome to Avignon (1309), thus beginning the Babylonian Captivity of the church. The popes at Avignon were French and papal policy was pro-French. The most important pope during this period was John XXII, a financial genius, who reorganized the entire fiscal system of the church and developed many new forms of revenue for the papacy.

• The Great Schism

In 1377 Pope Gregory XI left Avignon and returned to Rome to save the papal states from the power struggles of Italy. Rome welcomed his return for the papacy was the main industry of Rome and, in its absence, the city had degenerated into a sleepy village. When Gregory died the following year the Romans were determined at all costs to keep the papacy in their city and clamored wildly for a Roman, or at least an Italian, pope. The presence of mob violence terrified the cardinals and they chose an Italian, Urban VI (1378-1389), who treated the French cardinals with such brutal contempt that some observers suspected his sanity.

The French cardinals left Rome and declared the election of Urban invalid, because it had taken place under threat of violence, and elected a French pope, Clement VIII (1378-1394). Thus began the Great Schism which was to divide catholic Christendom for nearly forty years and deal a severe blow to papal prestige. There were now two popes and each pope claimed the power of the keys which governed admission to heaven. Thus no one could be certain that the sacraments upon which salvation depended were administered by a validly ordained priest. The money to maintain two separate papal courts came from a divided constituency which meant increased financial exactions from the faithful. Anti-clerical and anti-papal sentiments reached threatening proportions as the schism continued and there was agreement that something must be done to heal the schism but neither pope was prepared to abdicate. Only a pope could call a general council which might heal the schism but neither pope represented the entire church.

Several theories were advanced to solve the dilemma. A group of writers at the University of Paris, known as conciliarists, suggested that a general council possessed an authority superior to the pope and therefore could act independently of papal control. Marsiglio of Padua, writing in his *Defender of the Peace* (1324), asserted that in both state and church the sovereign power rested with the people and was only delegated to the rulers as long as they fulfilled their function by ruling wisely. He asserted that the papacy was a human institution without any authority except that given it by the Christian people and all important questions of faith should be referred to a general council representing the entire Christian community. All clergymen, from deacon to pope, should be subject to the state and its laws.

The first effort to break the impasse came when a majority of the cardinals of both papal obediences joined to summon a general council to meet in Pisa in 1409. The result was unfortunate because each pope refused to accept the sentence of deposition and to acknowledge a third pope elected by this council. However, the failure of the Council of Pisa did not discredit the conciliar movement. Pressure was brought to bear upon the Emperor Sigismund to summon a general council to meet in Constance and the Council of Constance (1414-1418) had a three-fold agenda: heal the schism, suppress heresy, and reform the church. It secured the deposition or abdication of the three contemporary popes and elected a new pope, Martin V (1417-1431), to be the sole head of the church. It was less successful in dealing with the problem of heresy, however. Although John Hus was summoned to the Council and executed for his heretical beliefs, his followers in Bohemia regarded him as a martyr and continued to struggle for his ideals. Also, the council made little progress with the problem of reform. The council of Constance did issue the decree, *Sacrosancto,* which declared that a general council, representing the entire church, received its authority directly from Christ and that even the pope must obey its decisions. The Council provided for the future by issuing the decree *Frequens* which called for a meeting in five years, another seven years following that, and successive councils every ten years thereafter. Later fifteenth century councils were called to meet the problems of the Hussites, reform of the church, and unification of the Byzantine and western churches. However, the popes of the fifteenth century had no intention of diminishing their power, and they consistently worked against the conciliar movement until it was officially ended by Pope Pius II with the bull *Exercrabilis* (1460).

At the end of the Renaissance period, the Catholic Church was neither as monolithic nor were its followers as satisfied as during the high Middle Ages. Although there were intellectual and theological difficulties within the church, perhaps the most serious problem was that by the end of the fifteenth century the popes had failed to provide the spiritual leadership of the church and had become for all interests and purposes, Renaissance princes. Their desire to build a strong state in central Italy so that the problems of the Avignon papacy would not be repeated seemed sensible at the time. In retrospect, however, it was a tragic decision which set the stage for the Protestant Revolt of the sixteenth century.

9

The Mind of the Renaissance

THE UNCERTAINTY and ferment of the fourteenth century caused the medieval synthesis of theology, philosophy, and the arts to crumble. Subject to the pressures of socioeconomic upheavals caused by the Black Death and the Hundred Years War, as well as the psychological shock of the Avignon Papacy and the Great Schism, the European outlook of the fifteenth century was not as well organized as during the high Middle Ages. Traditional views continued among the upper classes in northern Europe and even enjoyed an Indian summer in Burgundy, but new ideas emerged among the Hussites in Bohemia, the Brethren of the Common Life in the Netherlands, and especially in northern Italy where the Renaissance brought a conscious change from medieval traditions.

• Late Scholasticism

Although humanism had created a new form of learning in Italy during the period from 1300-1500, this did not affect northern Europe to any great extent until later. The fourteenth century witnessed a continual debate between realist and nominalist thinkers at universities such as Oxford and Paris. The achievement of the great thirteenth-century thinkers, such as Thomas Aquinas, of reconciling Aristotle and the Christian faith was subjected to criticism by fourteenth-century scholars. Perhaps the most important of these anti-Thomist thinkers was an Oxford trained Franciscan, William of Ockham (d. 1349). His major contribution was to demolish the system of philosophy which had furnished a rational basis for theology. The medieval platonists, called realists, taught that there are certain immutable forms or ideas (universals) which exist in the mind of God and can be perceived by divine illumination, without reference to particular things. Aquinas had asserted that in order to reach these forms one must gain knowledge through the apprehension of objects. Ockham stated that only individual things actually exist and that universals have no real existence, for if they did they would be individual and so could not exist in a number of things. Thus universals are merely names or terms, and his philosophy is called nominalism from the Latin word *nomen*; Ockham's logic led to the rejection of proof for God based upon observed data. As a devout Franciscan he did not wish to destroy faith in God, rather he felt that he was freeing Christianity from the shackles of reason. One could continue to believe in God, but not because of logical necessity. His reasoning also did away with the need for the data of divine revelation as far as human knowledge of the world is concerned. In this sense, Ockham is one of the founders of modern science. His followers, such as Jean Buridan (d. 1358) and Nicholas Oresme (d. 1382), anticipated the cosmological ideas of Copernicus and Galileo.

Nominalism was also applied to the problems of the state when men asked, "Where does political authority actually reside?" Their answer was: in the individual citizen, not in the idea of the state (a universal). When applied to the question "What is the church?", the answer was: the church is composed of individual Christians, and is not a divine institution with a life of its own. Thus nominalism provided a seed-bed for ideas that were used fruitfully by political theorists and by those advocating the superiority of councils over the papacy.

• John Wyclif

Another late scholastic who attacked the medieval synthesis was John Wyclif (1330-1384). Called "the morning star of the Reformation," he was born in the village of Wyclif, Yorkshire, but spent most of his life at Oxford University. In two pamphlets, *On Divine Dominion* and *On Civil Dominion* (issued 1375 and 1376), he declared that dominion, which is lordship over all things, belonged solely to God. Although God has granted a measure of lordship to human beings in return for service, if a man sins his condition of being in a state of grace is in jeopardy; therefore he is delinquent in his service to God and forfeits his right to lordship. Wyclif's basic premise is that all possessions and all power, civil and ecclesiastical, are contingent upon their possessor being in a state of grace. Thus, even the authority of the pope is not absolute but is contingent upon his personal character. A cleric whose life manifested a lack of grace should be deprived of his lordships (his benefices), and if the church failed in this disciplinary action the state should perform the function.

In *On the Church*, completed toward the end of 1378, Wyclif claimed that formal membership in an ecclesiastical organization is no guarantee of salvation. The church is defined as the spiritual company of believers with Christ at their head. Salvation is an individual matter between a man and Christ, and the pope is the head only of the portion of the visible church at Rome. After 1380, Wyclif came to the radical conclusion that the pope was the Antichrist. He also began to teach that the doctrine of transubstantiation was wrong and that believers should look on the holy communion as a celebration of the spiritual presence of the body and blood of Christ.

Wyclif was an eloquent and persuasive teacher. During his last years he built up a body of "poor preachers" or itinerant evangelists who travelled through England preaching his doctrines. Since a knowledge of the Bible was basic to his entire approach he encouraged the translation of the Scriptures into English. These editions, together with Wyclif's sermons and tracts, were widely spread by the Lollards, as the followers of Wyclif came to be called. Following the passage of the statute *De haeretico comburendo* in 1401, Lollardy was forced underground. Little record of their activity in England remains and their influence on the coming Reformation is doubtful.

Wyclif's teachings were transplanted to Bohemia where they flourished. Charles IV (1346-73) had made Prague a center of international culture, founded the University of Prague, and encouraged the growth of Czech nationalism. In 1382, Anne of Bohemia, sister of King Wenceslas, married Richard II of England, taking a large number of Czechs to England with her. Among them were students who studied at English universities and returned with copies of Wyclif's philosophical and theological writings. These found a favorable reception among the Czechs in the university, one of whom was John Hus (1369-1416).

• John Hus

Hus, a professor at the University of Prague and popular preacher at Bethlehem Chapel, began to demand reforms similar to those desired by

Wyclif, and won a large following when he attacked the papacy and the hated German upper class. In disputations, he defended Wyclif's opinion that the church consisted of all persons predestined to salvation but he did not deny the doctrine of transubstantiation. He was instrumental in inducing King Wenceslas IV (1378-1419) to change the constitution of the University of Prague to give the Czech masters a decisive voice in university affairs. As a result, the German masters and their students migrated to ducal Saxony where they organized the University of Leipzig. Hus preached against the sale of indulgences, challenged the primacy of the pope, and emphasized the supreme authority of Scriptures. In 1409 he was excommunicated by the Archbishop of Prague which served to heighten his opposition to the hierarchy of the church, and in 1412 he publicly condemned the papal preaching of a crusade against the king of Naples and the accompanying sale of indulgences to finance it. Wenceslas withdrew his support and Hus left Prague wandering through Bohemia for the next two years, preaching, writing, and gaining wider audiences.

The Emperor Sigismund, wishing to deal with the trouble in Bohemia, persuaded Hus to go to the Council of Constance and defend his position. Although the emperor had given Hus a letter of safe-conduct the cardinals accused him of heresy and imprisoned him. Rather than jeopardize the council, the emperor decided to sacrifice Hus. The council had earlier condemned all of Wyclif's writings and was in no mood to deal lightly with one who adhered to many of Wyclif's teachings. Hus was tried, condemned as a heretic, turned over to the secular authorities and burned at the stake in July, 1415.

The followers of Hus, infuriated at his treatment, rebelled against the Holy Roman Emperor plunging Bohemia into a religious war. Under the leadership of their brilliant general, Jan Zizka, the Hussites, though outnumbered, were always victorious. Zizka utilized new mobile guns, called wagon forts, and with this maneuverability and psychological advantage it was not unusual for the opposition to retreat in disorder when they heard that the Hussite armies were coming. However, a division in the Hussite movement, between a radical group, the Taborites, and the more moderate majority, blunted their campaign against the imperial establishment. The moderates then defeated the Taborites and made peace with Rome in 1436. They accepted papal supremacy in return for the right of the laity to receive both the bread and the cup in communion and for the abolition of abuses among the clergy. Many Hussites would later become involved in the Protestant Reformation of the sixteenth century. By that time, however, the wars, shifting trade routes, and transfer of the imperial interests to Vienna had reduced Bohemia to a backwater. Still, the Hussite movement had insisted on national self-expression, a fateful principle in western history.

• The Brethren of the Common Life and Mysticism

In addition to the teachings of Wyclif and Hus, movements of popular piety, such as mysticism, were important in fourteenth- and fifteenth-century Europe, especially in Germany and the Netherlands. These popular currents, outside the formal structure of the church, were revolts against the rigid institutionalism of Rome – the teaching that salvation comes through the sacraments only when they are performed by a validly ordained priest. The mystics emphasized personal morality and the inner life of the spirit and believed a pure life was a necessary accompaniment of the higher religious experience. In place of the sacraments and priesthood as a saving institution, they put Christ Himself as mediator between the soul and God. Therefore there was little need for the intercession of the priesthood. This movement was concentrated in the cities where secular education had provided a reading public for the sermons, tracts, and devotional books of the mystics, most of which were in the vernacular.

The most prominent of the German mystics was the Dominican friar, Johannes Eckhart (1260-1327), usually known as Meister Eckhart. He sought the soul's union with God and taught in his sermons and writings that such a union was possible. When God was born in a man's soul, he was filled with a love for the pious life. What made Eckhart such a force in the spiritual life of the German people was his ability to express his ideas with a clarity born of personal experience and conviction. Speaking in a clear, simple vernacular, Eckhart created the vocabulary he needed to present these ideas to unlearned men and in so doing was a formative influence in the development of the German language. After his sermons had been copied down by the nuns to whom he preached, they were printed and often excerpted in devotional books and so reached an even wider audience.

Mysticism became a vital force in the Netherlands due to the efforts of Gerard Groote (1340-1384). He urged men to strive for communion with God and transform their lives by imitating the life of Christ. The essence of religion, he felt, could be perceived only after a person had freed himself from sin and lived his religion in day-to-day activity. Instead of abstruse theological speculation, he emphasized morality, piety, and work. In 1383 he settled in Deventer and gathered a band of Disciples around him; after his death in 1384 this little group formed an association known as the Brethren of the Common Life.

The Brethren were an order of laymen who lived under self-imposed regulations but were not bound by monastic vows. They led a life of service to the poor and teaching for the young and became so successful that they controlled over 200 schools in various parts of the Netherlands and Germany. With their emphasis on mysticism they were hostile to scholasticism and adopted some of the new humanist education from Italy – Deventer, their famous school, had the most advanced teaching north of the Alps. Some measure of their success can be appreciated by the fact that John Gerson, Nicholas of Cusa, Desiderius Erasmus, and Thomas a Kempis, all leading writers of the age, were students at Brethren schools.

Probably the best and clearest expression of the mysticism of the Brethren is the devotional book, *The Imitation of Christ,* written by Thomas à Kempis (1380-1471) of the congregation at Windesheim. Thomas stressed thorough study of the Bible, prayer, introspection, and a sincere attempt on the part of the Christian to lead a pure life. Only the pure in heart can achieve that close communion with God which transcends the bounds of human intellect and is the goal of every mystic.

Although centering in the low countries and northwest Germany, mysticism had representatives in other parts of western Europe. In England, Richard Rolle, and the author of *The Cloud of the Unknowing,* in Sweden, Saint Brigitta (1303-73), and in Siena, Saint Catherine (1347-80) – all advocated a mystical approach to the problems of life.

These mystics, led by the *devotio moderna* of the Low Countries, presented a threat to the established church. Although they did not criticize orthodox doctrine, their emphasis on ethics and disdain for speculative theology reduced the importance of official catholic teaching, and their concern with the inner spirit and the direct relationship between the individual and God reduced the significance of the sacraments and clergy, leading to a laicization of religion. The dark side of much of this mysticism during the fifteenth century was a belief in witches – the easiest explanation for many of the troubles of the times was to blame a witch. These beings were supposed to have special dealings with the devil who gave them power to torment Godly people; witches were believed to use special images and charms to destroy crops and kill livestock. In an age of high infant mortality, midwives were often accused of being sorceresses and some witches were believed to be able to transform themselves into animals, or ride broomsticks, or possess the bodies of men with which to seduce women. Pope Innocent VIII issued a bull in 1484 defining witchcraft as heresy and instructing the inquisition to destroy it; later two inquisitors published a manual called *Malleus Maleficarum* (*Hammer of Witches*) which explained how to deal with the phenomenon. The coming of more modern times did not eradicate a belief in witches, as the occult revival of the twentieth century has proven.

• Burgundy and Traditionalism

For many years the wealthiest and most brilliant court in northern Europe was that of the dukes of Burgundy. Although vassals of the kings of France, these dukes tried to build a new state. Through the marriage of Duke Philip the Bold and Margaret of Flanders (1369) the Burgundian domains were extended to include much of the low countries, and to gain independence from France later Burgundian rulers, such as John the Fearless (1404-1419) and Philip the Good (1419-1467), allied themselves with the English. In 1435 Charles VII of France succeeded in breaking these alliances but the French monarch and his Burgundian vassal were never on good terms. Philip spent his energies trying to transform the duchies and counties he had inherited into a territorial state, a difficult task because the states were separated from one another by intervening territories and the inhabitants spoke many different languages and dialects and had diverse economic interests. The strongest support for unity came from the nobles who Philip organized into the order of the Golden Fleece, the most colorful of all the orders of knighthood. These men furnished leaders for the army as well as administrators for the provinces. Through a central judicial system, control of coinage, and an Estates General the dukes worked to strengthen their hold but with the death of Philip's son, Charles the Bold (1467-1477), the dream of transforming Burgundy into a kingdom came to an end.

The Burgundian court became a center for the preservation of medieval intellectual, social, and art forms, and its courtly outlook was shared by the feudal nobility everywhere in Europe outside of Italy. Literature during the fifteenth century in northern Europe clearly illustrates the fact that the chivalric tradition still gripped the minds of the upper classes. In addition to translations of classical authors, such as Livy and Cicero, which praised the courage and patriotism of Roman "knights," the cycle of stories about King Arthur remained popular. These tales were designed to furnish models for manners, education, martial bravery, and political action to contemporary nobles. Poets relied on medieval symbolism, archaic forms, courtly conventions, and florid rhetoric in their verse. Courtly tradition also dominated society as evidenced by the elaborate ceremonies developed by the dukes of Burgundy which remained the model for European monarchs for the next 300 years. In art, the growing influence of Burgundian craftsmen caused a change in the International style growing from the High Gothic of north France. The two leading painters of fifteenth century Netherlands, Jan van Eyck (c. 1380-1441) and Roger van der Weyden (1400-1464), illustrate this change. Van Eyck was court painter to the duke of Burgundy and Van der Weyden was the official painter of the city of Brussels, although both artists held commissions from wealthy merchants and nobles as well. Their paintings were more natural than medieval works through an application of correct perspective, an effective use of light and shadow, and refinement of linear rhythm. Van Eyck used luminous colors, made possible by new discoveries in oil paints which made greater clarity possible. While he concentrated on everyday objects and natural phenomena his painting was religious. Light, for example, which symbolized the divine presence, is presented in his work as the sun's rays pouring through a window or a burning candle. Such painting techniques had a Europe-wide influence.

In architecture, the great age of cathedral building had passed, and both architects and sculptors were beginning to work for wealthy, as well as royal patrons, in the construction of town halls, and private residences, and private chapels. Although Gothic styles were still used there was an increasing tendency toward elaboration and refinement. This flamboyant style is illustrated in the home of the wealthy French capitalist, Jacques Coeur at Bourges.

• The Renaissance in Italy

The artistic and intellectual innovations which occasionaly appear in northern Europe during the fourteenth and fifteenth centuries were outdone by the great cultural achievements of Renaissance Italy. For many years historians have taken their understanding of this period from a book written by the great Swiss historian Jacob Burckhardt, *The Civilization of the Renaissance in Italy* (1860). He believed that the Renaissance was the spontaneous creation of the Italian people during the fifteenth century, something new with no roots in the past – a new expression of individuality, an outburst of genius that found expression in magnificent art and immortal literature. Several preconceptions distorted Burckhardt's interpretation, such as his concern with culture and ideas, which caused him to neglect the religious, political, social, and economic factors of history. He also believed in the "great man" theory of history which led him to ignore mass movements. In spite of these weaknesses, his work remains a classic of historical interpretation.

Certainly, the men of the times thought that the Renaissance was a rebirth of ancient Greek and Roman civilization. Modern scholars, however, are more likely to emphasize the interpretation that it was a transitional period between medieval and modern times. Thus while some of the ideas of the Renaissance were taken from the past, and some stretch into the future anticipating modern life, others are unique to the period itself. Most would agree that the Renaissance was characterized by restless curiosity, especially about man himself, and it was out of this emphasis on man that the most distinctive features of the Renaissance emerged. In this sense, Burckhardt is correct, the Renaissance did burst with creativity and the artists of the period were among the finest that western civilization has produced.

• Dante

One of the earliest individuals who displays some of the characteristics of Renaissance individuality is Dante Alighieri (1265-1321). There are elements in his complex personality of medievalism as well as of the modern world. The details of Dante's life are rather sketchy, although it is known that his Florentine family background was respectable and that he was active in the politics of the city, rendering military service, serving as a guild officer, and as a prior (1300). There were two factions in Florence at this time, the Cerchi (Whites) and the Donati (Blacks). Dante's Whites lost power and several hundred of them including the poet himself were banished from the city; until his death in 1321 he was an exile and never returned to Florence again. Dante's principal works include *On the Possibilities of the Vernacular, Monarchy, La Vita Nuova* (The New Life), and the *Divine Comedy.* The latter two works written not in Latin, but in Italian, have brought Dante his greatest fame.

La Vita Nuova established the sonnet in Italian. In this work, composed of prose sections followed by sonnets, he expresses his love for a young woman of Florence, Beatrice Portinari (his platonic love for her did not prevent his marriage to Gemma Donati, by whom he had four children.) Dante began his masterpiece, the *Divine Comedy* in 1302 and completed it during his long years of exile and travel. The poem covers the three days from Maundy Thursday to Easter of the year 1300. His subject is the state of the soul after death, or, more simply, his subject is man. The poem is an allegory of man's attempt to gain salvation, but unlike most medieval works on this subject, it does not focus on personified abstractions. Rather, the poet uses actual historical persons to describe, in a figurative manner, the realities of Christian thought: sin and punishment, remorse and repentance, and God's love and mercy which sent his Son. Dante passes successively through Hell, Purgatory, and Paradise with three guides to lead him. For the first two regions the poet Virgil directs his steps; for most of Paradise, it is Beatrice; and, for the final empyrean of God, Saint Bernard of Clairvaux. In this work Dante shows an astonishing knowledge of science, theology, history, and the classics. Through the *Divine Comedy* Dante created the modern Italian language and the work is considered as the summation of medieval life and thought. However, there are aspects of the poem which do not fall into the medieval outlook. It rejects the claim of the church to control every aspect of an individual's life, and Dante was not afraid to consign several popes to hell for heresy, simony, cowardice, and avarice. The treating of pagan and Christian elements side by side showed a respect for classical culture that was not characteristic of most medieval writers. The *Divine Comedy* exercised a profound effect on people of fourteenth-century Italy and within one hundred years of his death professorships to study the poem were established at Florence, Venice, Bologna, and Pisa.

• Humanism

The major development in learning during the Renaissance was the growth of humanism. The term *humanism* is derived from *humanitas,* a Latin term used to describe the civilizing force of art and literature in the widest sense. Medieval scholars had of course known the classics but the Renaissance men approached these texts in a different manner. No longer were classical works merely sources for homiletics or tools for logic, but now they were appreciated for their own sake. In fact, the humanists coined the term "middle ages" to heap abuse upon the long period which separated their era from a previous golden age, ancient Greece and Rome.

Before the study of the classics could begin, however, they had to be collected. The despots of the Italian cities and the popes were great collectors and spent vast sums of money buying manuscripts of the Latin and Greek classics. The Vatican Library had its beginning when Pope Nicholas V assembled around five thousand manuscripts – many of these manuscripts had been copied three to four hundred years earlier and were damaged by fire or water, others were worm eaten. In other cases, medieval copyists had made additions and comments to the text which had to be removed, to restore the pure text, by comparing a number of manuscripts of the same text copied by different scribes, working independently of each other. Finally, dictionaries, books of reference, and encyclopaedias of the classics had to be composed so that men beginning to study the classics would have at their disposal a body of reference material to aid in the understanding of various references and allusions.

• Petrarch

One of the most important leaders in the recovery of the classical heritage was Petrarch (1304-1374), often called the father of humanism. Born in Arezzo, a small town close to Florence, after his father had been exiled from the city together with Dante, the family moved to Avignon in 1312. Petrarch studied law at the universities of Montpellier and Bologna, but when his father died he gave up his legal studies and returned to Avignon where he took minor orders so as to be eligible for benefices from wealthy patrons. He was able to live comfortably and travel extensively throughout western and central Europe before finally settling in Italy during his last years.

Petrarch, interested in the classics from childhood, imparted his passion to many of his acquaintances and through them to an ever-widening group of scholars. He discovered manuscripts of the works of Vergil, Horace, Livy, Ovid, Cicero, Seneca, and Juvenal, among others, and inspired many humanists to search for copies of the classics. His epic poem *Africa* which glorified the conqueror of Hannibal, Scipio Africanus, won him the poet's crown in Rome and set the vogue of glorifying classical times. He also wrote a collection of biographical sketches of famous Romans of ancient days, *Concerning Illustrious Men,* to show their great accomplishments and superior wisdom and virtue. Petrarch's most important works by modern standards were his Italian sonnets which describe his love for Laura. Most of them breathe the spirit of the medieval troubador, pleading for a lady's love that could not be gained. Each little contact with Laura was treated in careful detail, for example, the theft of her glove took three sonnets to describe.

• Boccaccio

The third of the great Florentines to influence Renaissance literature, Boccaccio (1313-1375), was born in Florence and apprenticed at the age of ten to the Florentine banking house of the Bardi. He was sent to their branch in Naples where he pursued a thoroughly secular life. At the age of seventeen he met Fiammetta (little flame) who at first rejected his advances but later accepted him. Inspired by her love, Boccaccio produced a number of verses, romances, and prose works. When she turned against him and the house of Bardi failed (1346), he returned to Florence to become a successful merchant and public official. It was here in 1350 that he met Petrarch who imbued him with love of the classics.

Boccaccio is best known for his *Decameron,* a collection of one hundred stories, written in Italian, supposedly told by ten young Florentine men and women to entertain each other in a rural retreat while the Black Death was sweeping Florence. These tales, ranging from witty anecdotes to licentious stories, were produced to amuse a bourgeois audience. The didactic moralism of the Middle Ages has vanished completely and a secular spirit pervades the *Decameron.*

After he became absorbed in Latin scholarship Boccaccio pointed others to ancient Rome in the hope of teaching moral lessons, as well as a better style. His passion for classical manuscripts became a mania and he spent almost all his money buying and having copies made of manuscripts by authors such as Livy, Cicero, Tacitus, and Varro. He wrote about classical times in works such as *On the Vicissitudes of Famous Men* and *On Famous Women.* Boccaccio also learned Greek and spent the last few years of his life lecturing in Florence on Dante's *Divine Comedy.* In studying the ancient classics to find moral guidance and cultural inspiration individuals like Petrarch and Boccaccio laid the foundations for humanism in the Italian Renaissance.

• Civic Humanism

A number of scholars, such as Coluccio Salutati (1331-1406), who became chancellor of Florence in 1375, and his successor, Leonardo Bruni (1370-1444), followed in their steps. Both of these men were directly involved in government and exerted an impressive influence on the advancement of classical and humanistic learning through the development of what has been called "civic humanism." The humanists, faced with a challenge in the rise to power of the Visconti of Milan who tried to unite Italy as the Capetians were doing in France, attempted to strengthen internal politics to make the state immune to outside pressures, by developing diplomatic policy and by the formation of civic humanism. They believed that the city states should be modelled on the cities of classical times and that each citizen should be allowed to rise to a position of responsibility and power if he showed the aptitude. Competition was to be based upon a knowledge of the classics because they developed the type of person best fitted to rule. There should be freedom between city-states because rivalry, on the economic and cultural level, would produce the finest civilization.

The revival of classical studies at first was concerned only with Latin for the early humanists could not read Greek. The first professor of Greek, Manuel Chrysoloras, who came to Italy in 1396, had been sent by the government in Constantinople as an ambassador to appeal for military aid against the Turks. The following year he began to lecture on Greek in Florence, remaining there for three years and spending an additional three years in Milan and Pavia before returning to Constantinople in 1403. Contact with Greek scholars encouraged Cosimo de Medici to found the Platonic Academy in Florence. This was a small group of individuals who met to discuss Plato's philosophy and problems of the day in the light of his teachings. In order to facilitate such discussions, Cosimo de Medici provided Marsiglio Ficino (1433-99) with a villa and an endowment which enabled him to spend the rest of his life translating and interpreting Plato. The Platonic Academy flourished throughout the fifteenth century and numbered among its members outstanding scholars, such as Giovanni Pico Della Mirandola (1463-1494) who introduced the study of Hebrew to Christians in western Europe, and attracted students to Florence from as far away as Germany and England. The Medici foundation served as a prototype for similar academies, not only in other Italian cities but eventually throughout Europe.

Most of the scholarship produced by the humanists was not original but consisted of guides to understand the material they were recovering – grammars and lexicons, philological rules and techniques, and commentaries on ancient works. One of the outstanding humanist contributions is the science of textual criticism. Despite the naiveté of some fourteenth- and fifteenth-century scholars who accepted as authentic such fraudulent works as the Chaldaic Oracles, many humanists began to question the assumptions and conclusions of medieval scholarship. The most famous example of Renaissance textual criticism was the work of Lorenzo Valla in demonstrating that the *Donation of Constantine* was a forgery. The document claimed to be the record by which the emperor Constantine (fourth century) had given the western part of the Empire to the papacy. Valla demonstrated by philological and historical arguments that the document could not have been written in the fourth century, but was of much later origin. He showed that the word *satrap* used in the document was not in existence this early and that the Roman Senators did not wear stockings as the *Donation* states. By collecting many of these anachronistic words and customs he convinced his contemporaries that the document was an eighth-century compilation. His critical method was to find an echo in sixteenth-century Germany when Luther would openly acknowledge Valla as one of his authorities.

• The Printing Press

There had been previous classical revivals in European history, such as that under Charlemagne in the eighth century and a second during the twelfth century led by scholars such as John of Salisbury. One of the reasons why these movements did not have the lasting effect of the Italian Renaissance was the fact that the classical movement of the fifteenth century was captured in print. Printing led to cheaper books, a wider reading public, and a new outlook. Paper, ink, and the techniques of block printing from carved wooden blocks or metal dies had long been known, but this process was slow and expensive, because each letter had to be carved separately. About 1450 Johann Gutenberg of Mainz, Germany, began to make interchangeable metal letters instead of wooden blocks; since this metal type could be used over and over again, the printing of books became relatively inexpensive. With incredible speed this new technique spread throughout Germany and to other European countries, and by 1501 there were printing presses in over one hundred European communities which had published no fewer than thirty thousand editions totalling between six and nine million volumes.

One of the most important fifteenth-century printers was Aldus Manutius (1449-1515) of Venice. Imbued in his youth with a fondness for Greek literature he was painfully aware of the lack of accurate Greek manuscripts and a dearth of good grammars and lexicons to aid in the study of the language. His goal in life was to remedy these deficiencies. Designing his own type and making his own ink, which became known as Venetian red, he began to publish Greek works. His first book was an improved grammar published in 1494, followed by a lexicon and an edition of Aristotle in five volumes appearing between 1495 and 1498. He produced other Greek classics, vernacular literature, including Dante's *Divine Comedy,* and works by scholars such as Erasmus. He also designed his own Latin type, supposedly derived from the handwriting of Petrarch, which became known as Aldine in Italy and as italic in other parts of Europe. Another innovation was his decision to issue the Latin classics in a new format called octave which was smaller and less expensive than the customary folio volumes. Beginning in 1501, the Aldine Press issued a new

A printing shop in the fifteenth century.

volume almost every two months for over fifteen years, providing the humanist and scholarly world with one hundred and twenty-six separate editions.

• The Universal Man

The ideal of the Renaissance humanist was not a scholar working in an ivory tower but rather a man of the world, an individual who mastered all kinds of activities: intellectual, social, and physical. Such universal men as Leonardo da Vinci (1452-1519) and Leon Battista Alberti (1404-1472) were their models. Alberti was a great architect who worked in Rome, Rimini, and Florence, but even more important were his theoretical works on architecture, painting, and social thought. In his search for fame and glory, Alberti was the antithesis of a twentieth-century specialist, for he was proficient in many arts and a superb athlete. He played ball, hurled the javelin, ran, leaped, wrestled, delighted in mountain climbing, and excelled at archery and horsemanship. With his feet together, he could leap over the shoulders of a man and for show he would hurl an apple beyond the highest city roofs or a coin to the top of the great cathedral.

Although Alberti learned music without the aid of teachers, he composed music and was an expert organist who provided musicians with valuable advice. In literature he was accomplished in both verse and prose and his mastery of Tuscan was so superb that fellow citizens took his quotations to make their orations in council more eloquent. He mastered canon law, mathematics, physics, and he tried to learn something from everyone, even cobblers. He was utterly disinterested in material gain and gave of his means freely to help his friends. His will power was so great that he could overcome weaknesses of the body. With his catholicity of interest it is little wonder that Alberti's contemporaries even believed that he could foretell the future.

An even more famous example of *l'uomo universale* was Leonardo da Vinci (1452-1519) who ranks among the most versatile geniuses of all time. Engineer, sculptor, inventor, musician, empirical scientist, and above all painter, his mind was so filled with ideas that few of them were ever realized. His notebooks contain hundreds of drawings and comments based upon his dissections of animal and human cadavers, his observation of the flight of birds, and other natural phenomenon. He also included designs for submarines, machine guns, airplanes, and other modern inventions. Despite all these other activities he regarded himself primarily as a painter. An illegitimate child, he had been apprenticed to Verrochio as a boy and had gone on to enter the painters guild of Florence. Lorenzo de Medici was his patron during the years 1477-1483 before he left Florence to work for the Duke of Milan. He then spent some time in Rome and Florence before going to France to end his days at the court of Francis I. In his paintings Leonardo experimented with a form of perspective that brought the whole picture forward to a plane directly in front of the viewer, thus increasing attention on the activity within the picture. He also developed further the use of chiaroscuro, the blending of light tones into dark. In the *Last Supper* painted on the walls of a monastery refectory in Milan he attempted to portray the moment when Jesus said: "one of you shall betray me." The facial expressions and the gestures of the apostles are brilliant psychological studies of man. The *Mona Lisa* also penetrates human personality; observed from one angle she is sad, but from another the young lady seems to be smiling. In the *Virgin of the Rocks,* the play of light and shadow lends an air of mystery to the atmosphere and brings a new element in the portrayal of distance. One writer sums up Leonardo: "He was the most relentlessly curious man in history. Everything he saw made him ask why and how. Why does one find sea-shells in the

The first printed illustration of an amputation.

mountains? How do they build locks in Flanders? How does a bird fly? What accounts for cracks in walls? What is the origin of wind and clouds? How does one stream of water deflect another? Find out; write it down; if you can see it, draw it. Copy it out. Ask the same question again and again and again. Leonardo's curiosity was matched by an incredible mental energy. Reading the thousands of words in Leonardo's note-books, one is absolutely worn out by this energy. He won't take yes for an answer. He can't leave anything alone – he worries it, re-states it, answers imaginary antagonists. Of all these questions, the one he asks most insistently is about man. . . ."[1]

• Machiavelli

Another side to the Renaissance man that provided the driving force for the artist or the despot was virtú. This term expresses a commitment to achievement through force of personality, strength, and resolute will. A man was to be judged by the skill and bravery with which he achieved his personal goals and by the subtlety of the means employed. In pursuit of virtú, not to be confused with virtue, conscience was irrelevant. This is the message that Niccoló Machiavelli (1469-1527) communicates in his political theory. A Florentine from a family with a commitment to Republican government, he rose to a position of leadership (1498-1512) after the Medicis were forced to leave the city. When they returned to power he was exiled and had the leisure to write.

He produced a number of works, including a play, *Mandragola, The Art of War,* and *History of Florence,* but it is on *The Discourses* and especially *The Prince* that his literary fame rests. *The Discourses on the First Ten Books of Livy* present his comments on ancient and contemporary problems of politics, based on a discussion of themes from Livy's history of the Roman Republic. The work tends to glorify republican government, something that Machiavelli had supported during his active career as a politician. *The Prince,* written in 1513 but not published until 1532, advocates the necessity of a strong prince who is above the law in order to bring about peace and a strong state. Morality must not be permitted to stand in the way of expediency, and the welfare of the state is above all law, either civil or ecclesiastical. The ruler must realize that people are primarily selfish and egoistic. It follows that the successful leader must appeal to man's baser instincts of fear and credulity and not to love, honor, or the search for truth. In serving the state, a prince should

[1] Kenneth Clark, *Civilisation,* New York: Harper & Row, 1969, p. 135.

appear honest, but if it suits his purpose he should not hesitate to lie. Again it is well if the prince can be loved, but if necessary he should not hesitate to take actions that will cause his subjects to fear him. In fact, if the choice is necessary it is better to be feared than loved since men love as they wish, but fear is controlled by others. The ruler is also given other advice by Machiavelli; such as to appear religious, but not to be a genuine man of faith; to be stingy with money but to seem liberal, and to use scapegoats whenever possible.

Some have tried to explain Machiavelli's work by stating that the *Prince* represents his short-term goals, while the *Discourses* is what he desires in the long run. Others believe that *The Prince* was a satire. It was dedicated to the Medici, who were hated by Machiavelli, and it contains statements which would embarrass them.

• The Renaissance Popes

Men of virtú also came to hold the office of pope during the fifteenth century. From the accession of Nicholas V to the papal throne (1447) until the sack of Rome in 1527 humanism triumphed at the center of the Roman Catholic Church. Most of the popes who ruled during these years were convinced that what the church needed was a strong state in central Italy and their lives and interests were generally secular. Men were chosen as popes who were good statesmen, and as leaders in Renaissance society they had excellent tastes in the arts. Nicholas V was a great patron of arts and letters who carried out an elaborate building program in Rome. When he came to power the city was in ruins after almost a century of neglect. He had bridges, roads, palaces, churches, and fortifications built, and to decorate these new buildings he invited artists, such as Fra Angelico, from many parts of Europe, especially Florence, to come to Rome. He also commissioned tapestries, the ornamentation of rich vestments, and work in precious metals.

His greatest interest, however, was in books. He employed agents to search for rare copies of classical manuscripts and humanists to translate and correct them. Many ancient Greek writers, including the Greek fathers, were translated into Latin and thus made available to those who could not read the language. Nicholas left a collection of several thousand manuscripts to the Vatican Library. On his deathbed (1455) he made a speech claiming that he had patronized the arts not because of any personal interests but in order to make Rome outstanding and thus strengthen allegiance to her.

Perhaps the most fascinating of the Renaissance popes was Pius II (ruled 1458-1464), a skilled humanist whose *Commentaries* give us penetrating insights into his life and times. Coming from a poor noble family, he left his home in Siena to take a position with a church leader who went to the Council of Basel. He changed masters and rose rapidly in the council's service but sensing the futility of the conciliar movement he took a position with the German Emperor Frederick III (1442). Much of his work was diplomatic and he travelled to Scotland, France, Norway, the Low Countries, and England. Later he went to work for the papacy becoming Bishop of Siena, Cardinal, and then Pope. Pius was a brilliant Ciceronian orator, claiming that he could hold an audience spellbound for a two- to three-hour speech. Although not a man of piety, he was an excellent diplomat and during his pontificate organized a crusade to halt the advance of the Turks in Central Europe. He died at Ancona before the ships could sail against the Turks.

Corruption became apparent in the papacy during the reign of Innocent VIII (1484-1492). After a profligate youth at the court of Naples, Cibo (Innocent's surname) had become a priest. Rising in the Church's service, he became pope but his habits did not change to any great extent. He fathered sixteen children, openly acknowledging them and celebrating their weddings in the Vatican. He was constantly engaged in wars and disputes with other Italian states and forced the church into debt to finance these campaigns. The cynicism and corruption that permeated the curia during his reign is illustrated by the papal official who stated: "The Lord desireth not the death of a sinner, but that he should live and pay."

At the time of his death Innocent is supposed to have implored the cardinals to choose a pope better than himself. They did not listen to him and with the rule of Alexander VI (1492-1503) the papacy reached a spiritual low. Rodrigo Borgia (Alexander's given name) came from a Spanish family one of whose members had been pope (Calixtus III). Rodrigo had risen rapidly in the church, becoming a cardinal when he was twenty-five. A shrewd businessman he accumulated a fortune which he used to help him gain the papacy. Pius II had warned him of his immorality:

Dear Son: We have learned that your Worthiness, forgetful of the high office with which you are invested, was present from the seventeenth to the twenty-second hour, four days ago, in the gardens of John de Bichis, where there were several women of Siena, women wholly given over to worldly vanities. . . . We have heard that the dance was indulged in in all wantoness; none of the allurements of love were lacking, and you conducted yourself in a wholly worldly manner. Shame forbids mention of all that took place, for not only the things themselves but their very names are unworthy of your rank. In order that your lust might be all the more unrestrained, the husbands, fathers, brothers, and kinsmen of the young women and girls were not invited to be present. You and a few servants were the leaders and inspirers of this orgy. It is said that nothing is now talked of in Siena but your vanity, which is the subject of universal ridicule. Certain it is that here at the baths, where Churchmen and the laity are very numerous, your name is on every one's tongue.

The warning went unheeded and Alexander fathered several children. Although he managed papal finance very carefully his goal was to build a principality in central Italy for his family. He turned this project over to his son, Cesare Borgia, who became legendary as an unscrupulous murderer and assassin. Alexander's daughter, Lucretia, who was given control of the papal palace, was an immoral young woman, married three times by age twenty-two, although she became pious in later life. When Alexander died of fever, his son Cesare was forced to leave Italy. Although the Pope had supported Portuguese missionary work in the New World and negotiated the Line of Demarcation, keeping Spain and Portugal from war, he left the church in disrepair. Julius II (1503-1513), his successor, tried to repair the damage and attempted to recover territories that the papal states had lost, eliminate simony, and reduce nepotism. He led his armies in person and was a man of such restless, fierce temper that men spoke of him as terribilitá. By the time of his pontificate, Rome had replaced Florence as the center of Renaissance culture, and to emphasize the grandeur of Rome Julius tore down the basilica of St. Peter, and with plans drawn by Bramante began the construction of the greatest church in Christendom, St. Peter's Cathedral. He commissioned among other works by Michelangelo, the frescoes on the ceiling of the Sistine Chapel, portraying the creation and fall of men and assigned to Raphael the decorating of the Julian apartments.

Leo X (1513-1521), who succeeded Julius, was the second son of Lorenzo the Magnificent and had been made an archbishop at the age of eight, a cardinal at thirteen, and pope at thirty-seven. A man of expensive tastes, he was convinced that the head of the church should not live the austere, simple life of Christ and the Apostles. At his coronation he entered Rome in gorgeous robes, passing through arches erected in his honor, as though celebrating an ancient triumphal procession. During his administration, Leo packed the curia with members of the Medici family, either as churchmen or in various high places in the papal states, and justified it by saying, "God has given us the Papacy, let us enjoy it." His love of art, music, and the theatre made Rome the cultural center of Europe, but it was also very expensive. Julius II had been a frugal pope, but the vast sums he had accumulated were soon exhausted and Leo even mortgaged the Papacy for 400,000 ducats.

The Renaissance papacy was shot full of nepotism. Relatives who were often incompetent or underage were given positions in the church. At times these were "nephews," or bastard sons such as Casare Borgia, and many of the popes themselves, such as Julius II, Alexander V, and Leo X, got their start in church politics because of nepotism. The exquisite tastes, expensive lifestyles, and political involvements of the Renaissance popes led to many fiscal abuses. Church offices were bought and sold through the Medici bankers and Julius II and Alexander V were elected because they bribed a majority of the College of Cardinals. Indulgences were sold with great regularity and there were even attempts to forge and sell papal bulls. The Renaissance popes shared the outlook of a majority of their fellow nobles who felt that an extravagant life would gain respect for their office. While this made possible some of the finest art of the Renaissance it also led to widespread criticism of the papacy.

• Savonarola

Many, especially among the lower classes, disapproved strongly of the Renaissance style of life of the clergy. In Siena, for example, a hermit sent a child carrying a skull through the streets with a call to repentance in the face of imminent destruction. In Milan, a prophet of doom seized the pulpit of the cathedral and promised God's judgment would soon strike. In other parts of Italy preachers of repentance drew great crowds to hear them denounce the abuses of the people and clergy, including the pope. Among these fiery evangelists of repentance none is better known than Girolamo Savonarola (1452-1498). His life and ministry illustrate the fact that the Italian Renaissance was not as secular and worldly as many have claimed. Born into a family in Ferrara of modest means, trained in the humanist tradition, destined for a career in medicine, at the age of twenty-two he entered the Dominican order and was sent to Florence (1482). His sermons were filled with apocalyptic prophecies which reinforced his call for repentance and conversion, and the times were ripe for such a message since the Medici regime in Florence was at war with France, there was a major depression, and food was scarce. The Medici had become too powerful, too obvious in their political control of the city, and not only the lower classes but also merchant families now reacted to the Medici display of wealth and luxury. The Church of San Marco, where Savonarola delivered his powerful sermons, filled with people anxious to hear his latest pronouncements against the Medici and other high-living princes and ecclesiastics. Many repentants contributed lewd books, nude pictures, costume jewelry, false hair, and frivolous attire to be burned in huge bonfires of vanities.

Savonarola's popularity reached its height when he persuaded the French King, Charles VIII, who had invaded Italy, not to sack Florence. The Medici's rule collapsed and when a new republican government was formed it was heavily influenced by Savonarola's preaching. He began to predict that a great disaster would come to Italy, but then the golden age would dawn in Florence and spread to other communities. Florentines, including such well known humanist scholars as Marsilio Ficino and Giovanni Pico Della Mirandola, enthusiastically supported these predictions. Pope Alexander VI was worried about the situation in Florence because of the city's friendship with France; he did not wish to have a state on the flank of the patrimony of Peter that was allied with the French king. Thus, the austere Dominican was pitted against the most infamous of the Renaissance popes. Alexander tried to persuade Savonarola to leave the city, and when this failed Alexander tried to bribe him by offering him the position of cardinal. Still not successful, the pope finally excommunicated Savonarola (1497). The friar claimed, however, that the excommunication was not valid and that only God could cut him off from fellowship. He continued to preach and hold mass, but the city government threatened with an interdict asked him not to perform his duties.

The Franciscan community in Florence took the lead in opposing Savonarola. They proposed an ordeal in which a representative of their order and a follower of Savonarola would march through a fire. If the Dominican survived, Savonarola's claim to occupy a prophetic role would be vindicated. On the day the fire was kindled, the champions argued over what they would carry and wear and while this was going on a violent rainstorm came up and put out the fire. Savonarola was discredited by the event and was tried for heresy, tortured, and executed. For all his passion for reform he had not argued with the dogmatic content of the church. A true verdict to his trial would have been not guilty.

• Renaissance Art

Since the Renaissance, no other age has produced such splendid works of genius in painting, sculpture, and architecture – these works have set standards for the art of the western world ever since. Within this period of almost three centuries there were three crucial eras. The first came at the beginning of the fourteenth century and was dominated by Giotto (1266-1336). The second period of advance was in the early fifteenth century and featured the painting of Masaccio (1401-1428) and the sculpture of Donatello Bardi (1386-1466). The final achievement spanned the late fifteenth and early sixteenth centuries and produced the works of Leonardo da Vinci, Raphael Sanzio (1483-1520), and culminated in the art of Michelangelo.

It is difficult to explain how Giotto got the inspiration and ideas to paint in the manner that he did. Italian painting, influenced by Byzantine conventions, was a flat, flowing linear style based on a traditional approach that had not changed in half a millennium. During these years painting had been a church art that was designed to teach those who could not read. To accomplish this, however, it was necessary to remove all unnecessary details, so that the viewers attention would not be distracted from the main theme, and to draw Biblical characters in a conventional manner. Often three or four events were put into the same picture and gestures were exaggerated to make a point. Painting is an attempt to convey on a two-dimensional medium a three dimensional world. To a person of medieval times a painting of a man was "real" if it reminded him of a real man, just as a child's stick figure drawing would be "real" in the sense that it reminded him of a man. To present a more accurate illusion of reality it was necessary for artists to learn how to give a sense of perspective through the use of proportion and of light and shadow. Giotto broke with the medieval symbolic world and painted in a way that made direct references about people and things. He made men stand in lifelike positions and groups, interrelated as men usually are. Although he did not know the laws of perspective his people look round, solid, and statuelike. He may have painted in this fashion because he started life as a herdsman, far from the influence of medieval painters and so was able to record what he saw according to his own instincts. Giotto painted many pictures of St. Francis such as those found in the church at Assisi and the Bardi chapel in Florence. He also dealt with a variety of other religious themes, all of which he treated with his new naturalist approach.

Renaissance art did not move toward its culmination in Michelangelo in an unfaltering fashion. When the Black Death swept over Italy in the mid-fourteenth century Giotto's approach, with its emphasis on man, was cast aside and men for a time turned back to more traditional modes of expression. By the end of the century, however, the crisis was over and artists again picked up the thread of realism. The movement that Giotto had begun revived by a competition to select an artist to design the bronze

Giotto's Bell Tower in Florence. Courtesy, Italian Government Travel Office.

doors for the Baptistery of San Giovanni in Florence (1401). Two of the city's most respected sculptors, Filippo Brunelleschi (1377-1446) and Lorenzo Ghiberti (1378-1455), entered the contest. The panel that the artists were to produce depicted the sacrifice of Isaac by Abraham. Although Brunelleschi's panel showed a greater intensity of religious feeling, the judges chose his rival's because of its superior unity of mood and greater attention to the classical nude. When the doors were finished Michelangelo would claim that they were fit to serve as "the gates of paradise." His defeat caused Brunelleschi to devote his attention to architecture and he adapted the classical style of ancient Rome to the architecture of his day. He applied these principles to the construction of such buildings as the great cathedral of Santa Maria del Fiore, the Pitti Palace, and the Pazzi Chapel in Florence.

The frescoes of Masaccio (1401-1428) also revived the realistic approach of Giotto. Brunelleschi had discovered the laws of perspective by which the size of objects are reduced in the background and Masaccio used these in his "Holy Trinity" on the walls of the church of Santa Maria Novella in Florence. He produced in his short career works that were exceptional in their physical realism and portrayal of emotion and character, such as *Christ and the Tribute Money* and the *Expulsion From Paradise.* At the same time that Masaccio was introducing a new style of painting in Florence, Donatello was breaking with traditional patterns of sculpture. A student of Ghiberti, he worked in Florence, Rome, Padua, and Mantua. He freed sculpture from its medieval function of embellishing architecture, reduced the details in his statues and gave them a solid, heavy, determined air. Much of the inspiration for his work came from the study of anatomy. In the equestrine statue of Gattamellata at Padua, the subject was an Italian condottieri who is presented in the pose of an ancient Roman horseman. The condottieri displays the hard, suspicious, astute outlook which made for success among the Italian Tyrants. Although many artists such as Fra Angelico (1387-1455) did not follow Masaccio's lead, others like the Umbrian Piero della Francesca (1416-1492) were impressed by the principles of perspective. Piero wrote a mathematical treatise, *On Perspective Painting,* and gave form to his ideas in a series of masterful frescoes in the church of San Francesco in Arezzo.

The Italian artists of the later fifteenth century felt that they had mastered the art of depicting nature through painting and began to search for deeper meanings. At first, the Renaissance artists had been members of the craft guilds and without much education, but as they secured patrons among the upper classes, they began to rub shoulders with philosophers and humanists and picked up new ideas from the intellectual elite. The

Florentine Platonic academy and Marsilio Ficino taught that love of the physical world is but one of the steps leading to love of God. Artists tried to introduce this idea into their work by making the human body look more attractive than it is. The more beautiful nature became, they believed, the closer it would be to God. This led them to study the human body more carefully than ever and to place a much greater emphasis on nudes. Sandro Botticelli (1444-1510) was a leader in this new style. A Florentine who enjoyed the patronage of the Medici, his *Primavera* (Spring) and *Birth of Venus* are fragile, delicate attempts to demonstrate Renaissance neoplatonism through the medium of art. The three best known artists of the high Renaissance, Leonardo da Vinci, Michelangelo, and Raphael, all owe something to Botticelli. Although da Vinci was more interested in science, with Michelangelo Platonism triumphs. A versatile genius, he idealized the human form in statues such as the David in Florence or the Pietá in Rome. Born a Florentine, taken into the Medici family circle while still a young man, he left his hometown in 1494 for Rome where he spent much of the remainder of his life. In addition to sculpture, he painted, designed buildings, and wrote poetry. His composition on the ceiling of the Sistine Chapel is probably the most imposing single painting of the Renaissance. The design consists of nine scenes from the early part of the Book of Genesis, surrounded by figures of slaves, putti, prophets, and Sybils. It is a magnificent synthesis of pagan form, Christian thought, and Old Testament subject matter. The third of the great trio, Raphael, was born in Urbino, went to Rome in 1508 and remained there until his death. In his Madonnas he tried to achieve a beauty greater than that found in nature. His art combines the naturalistic goals of earlier fifteenth-century artists with the idealization of the human form found in Michelangelo.

The Renaissance broke with the medieval subjective approach, which used art in order to teach a lesson or present a doctrine, and experimented with light and shade, tactile values, and line and atmospheric perspective to present three-dimensional reality. Toward the end of the Renaissance the exploration of the inner life of man, encouraged by Platonic ideals, was to end in a new subjective emphasis.

• The Age of the Renaissance

The fourteenth and fifteenth centuries constituted a time of testing of ideas and institutions that had held sway for centuries. The economic base of the period consisting of urban populations, a money economy, and the beginnings of capitalism was a late medieval heritage. However, with the voyages of discovery and the wealth of the new world a dynamic age of capital expansion began. While long sea voyages opened the rest of the world to European exploitation, at home, in despair over the failure of feudalism, many Europeans turned to strong monarchs and the national states they were building. The idea of Europe, as the *Respublica Christiana* ruled over spiritually by the pope and materially by the Holy Roman Empire, broke down. In the process of redefining its role, the Roman Church was to lose its spiritual leadership, thus setting the stage for Reformers of the sixteenth century. The growing dynastic states were supported by the bourgeoisie or middle class, and aided by advances in technology and improved credit techniques this small group was to become the dominant class in Europe, leading western civilization and the world toward industrialization.

In the non-material realm, the Renaissance, which owed a tremendous debt to the past, in a paradoxical way prepared society for the future. While the humanists worked to recover what they believed to be the lost intellectual and moral grandeur of the classical world they handed on to posterity new ideas and attitudes. Methods of government articulated by Renaissance scholars became the basis for modern theories of constitutionalism. Attempts by painters, sculptors, and architects to reproduce classical masterpieces led to new discoveries in technique and design. Historians, in their efforts to understand the work of antiquity, not only developed a modern historical outlook, but also sparked a parallel Christian attempt to return to the sources, thus leading to the coming Reformation. In testing and rejecting many of the insights of medieval Europe the humanists, critics, adventurers, artists, and discoverers were laying the foundations for the modern world.

Suggestions for Further Reading

Baron, Hans, *The Crisis of the Early Italian Renaissance,* 2 vols. (1966)

Berenson, Bernard, *The Italian Painters of the Renaissance* (1952)

Brucker, Gene A., *Renaissance Florence* (1969)

Cassirer, Ernst, *The Individual and the Cosmos in Renaissance Philosophy* (1963)

Cheyney, E. P., *The Dawn of a New Era, 1250-1453* (1936)

Chubb, Thomas C., *Dante and His World* (1967)

Cohn, Norman, *The Pursuit of the Millennium* (1957)

Dannenfeldt, Karl H., ed., *The Renaissance: Medieval or Modern?* (1959)

Ehrenberg, Richard, *Capital and Finance in the Age of the Renaissance* (1963)

Ergang, Robert, *The Renaissance* (1967)

Ferguson, Wallace K., *The Renaissance in Historical Thought: Five Centuries of Interpretation* (1948)

Hay, Denys, *Europe in the Fourteenth and Fifteenth Centuries* (1966)

Heaton, Herbert, *Economic History of Europe,* 2nd ed. (1948)

Jacob, Ernest F., *Essays in the Conciliar Epoch,* rev. ed. (1963)

Jensen, De Lamar, ed., *The Expansion of Europe: Motives, Methods, and Theory* (1967)

Kristeller, Paul Oskar, *The Classics and Renaissance Thought* (1958)

Kristeller, Paul Oskar, *Eight Philosophers of the Italian Renaissance* (1964)

Lerner, Robert E., *The Age of Adversity: The Fourteenth Century* (1968)

Lodge, R., *The Close of the Middle Ages,* 5th ed. (1922)

Lucki, Emil, *History of the Renaissance, 1350-1550,* 5 vols. (1963-65)

McKisack, May, *The Fourteenth Century 1307-1399* (1959)

Mallot, G., *The Popes at Avignon, 1305-1378* (1963)

Panofsky, Erwin, *Renaissance and Renaissances in Western Art,* 2 vols. (1960)

Penrose, Boies, *Travel and Discovery in the Renaissance, 1420-1620*

de Roover, Raymond, *The Rise and Decline of the Medici Bank, 1397-1494* (1963)

Schwoebel, Robert, *Renaissance Men and Ideas* (1971)

Thrupp, Sylvia, *The Merchant Class of Medieval London, 1300-1500* (1948)

Tierney, Brian, *Foundations of the Conciliar Theory* (1955)

Wicksteed, Philip, *Dante and Aquinas* (1913)

Wilkins, Ernest H., *The Life of Petrarch* (1961)

Wöfflin, Heinrich, *Classic Art: An Introduction to the Italian Renaissance,* rev. ed. (1952)

Woodward, W. H., *Studies in Education During the Age of the Renaissance* (1965)

THE SIXTEENTH CENTURY

10

The Reformation

THERE WERE MANY chinks and fissures in the structure of Renaissance society. Some improvements had been made in the daily lives of many people since the Middle Ages, but for the masses life was still hard, uncertain, and short. The degree of private security and political stability that gradually had been achieved in some areas of Europe was unknown in others. While France, Spain, and England, for example, profited from the advantages (and paid for the disadvantages) of a strengthening monarchy, much of Italy and Germany fluctuated between the extremes of intense despotism and rampant anarchy. These pulsations of political dysphoria were both the cause and the result of many other disorders and tensions in the society of sixteenth-century Europe.

Within the area of the Holy Roman Empire the problem was particularly acute. Since the time of Otto the Great, Germany had been a battlefield of petty princes and ambitious grandees. By the early sixteenth century a conglomeration of over 300 states of assorted sizes from large landed principalities to tiny imperial towns, vied with each other and with the emperor for political and economic supremacy or independence. Sometimes the rivalries between regions and dynasties was particularly intense. The Burgundian succession dispute following the death of Duke Charles the Bold (1477) stirred great upheavals, as did the attempts of the dukes of Bavaria to extend their power at the expense of the house of Hapsburg. And the Bavarian-Palatine War of 1504, over the succession in Landshut, illustrates the fact that not even foreign threats could stop the seeming necessity of internal war. Vertical rivalries were equally disruptive.

The princes were suspicious of the lesser nobles, who in turn resented the opulence and power of the magnates. Each distrusted the emperor and coveted the growing wealth of the imperial cities. Peasants hated both their aristocratic overlords and the miserly merchants who were interested only in riches. The imperial knights were no less restless than the peasants and were on the verge of war with the princes on many occasions.

• Rich and Poor in Germany

The widening economic gap in Germany was becoming dangerous by the early sixteenth century. The progressive expansion of European commerce since the dark decades of the Black Death had produced an extremely uneven distribution of wealth. While peasants and workers slid further into the mire of poverty, worsened by the break-up of feudal protectionism, ambitious merchant oligarchies were able to become wealthy in the cloth, salt, grain, and wine trades. They were favorably situated also to reap the greatest advantage from the new overseas expansion with its booming commerce in sugar, spices, silks and silver. The Hansa towns of the north, like Hamburg, Lübeck, and Bremen, profited from this trade, as did the merchant princes of the Rhineland and the Netherlands. But the most spectacular growth in corporate wealth in the empire took place in the south German towns, especially Nüremberg and Augsburg, where the Welser, Hochstetter, and Fugger families amassed vast fortunes from trade and financial activities. The opulence displayed by these successful businessmen, and the pageantry of the well-to-do nobles, was in stark contrast to the peasants whose very survival frequently depended on what they could steal from the manorial lords. The exploitation of these human resources was great in the early sixteenth century. In spite of their poverty and the oppressive rigidity of the class structure, the peasants bore the heaviest financial burden of any class, since all of the nobles, most of the clergy, and a large percentage of the imperial cities were exempt in full or in part from the payment of the direct taxes.

• German Hatred of the Papacy

The common element in this picture of political discontinuity and social unrest was the almost universal hatred of Italian, especially papal, interference in German affairs. The chronic rivalry between emperors and popes which had punctuated European relations for several centuries was hardly less violent now than it had been in Hildebrand's time. Pope Julius

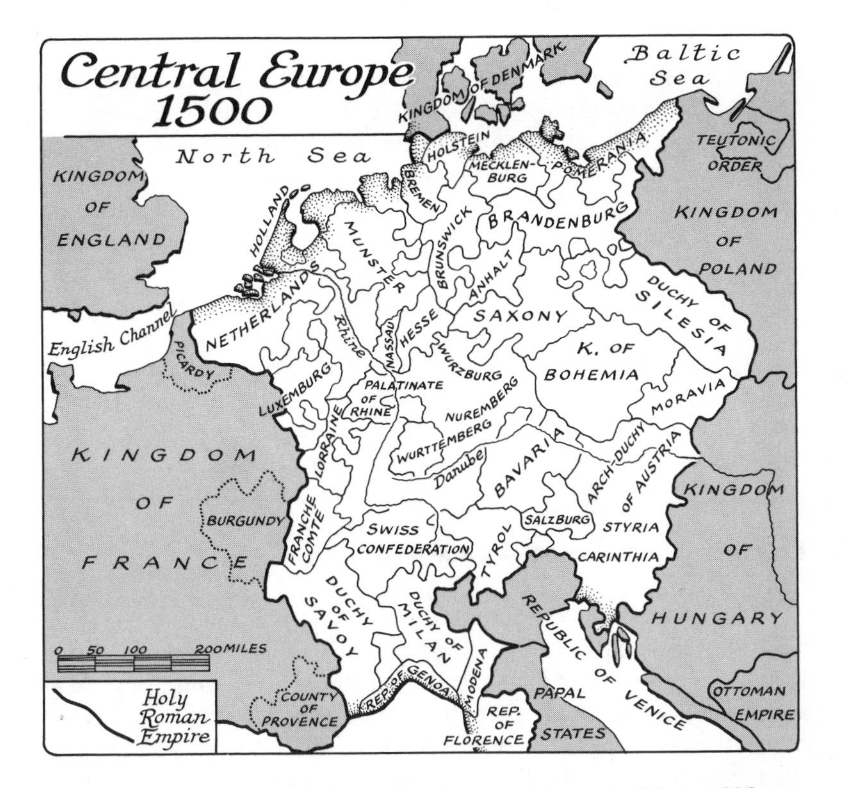

II, who succeeded the scandalous Borgia pope, Alexander VI, in 1503, was a cantankerous and belligerent militarist who, with remarkable energy and political intelligence, locked horns with several princes of Europe, including the chivalric German emperor, Maximilian I. The Medici pope, Leo X, who presided over the papal empire from 1513 to 1521, was even more contemptuous of "the barbarian Germans," considering them little improved since the days of their tribal wanderings. But the causes of German-papal dislike were grounded in more immediate and practical matters. Many kinds of papal dues flowed from Germany to Rome: services, annates, tithes and subsidies, procuration fees, visitations, and indulgences of various types. Thus, every level of German society, from emperor to peasant, had some reason for resenting the papacy.

Nor were the problems confined to political, social, and economic affairs. Religious unrest was rampant by the 1500's. Conflicts of ecclesiastical jurisdiction were frequent, caused both by territorial disputes between empire and papacy and by recurring contention over the rights of ecclesiastical appointment within the empire. Further antagonism arose over the extent of political authority exercised by ecclesiastical princes, and the religious jurisdiction of secular rulers. Finally, the serious clash of secular and ecclesiastical adjudication caused by the overlapping jurisdiction of civil and cannon law caused additional resentment and discord.

On the level of religious observance, the dissension was equally rampant. Nowhere in Christendom were religious ceremonies and practice more flagrantly abused. Priests were frequently ignorant and untrained; bishops prostituted their powers of priesthood and commercialized their ecclesiastical jurisdictions. Absenteeism, simony, and pluralism were common. Of course, not every bishop was a whoremonger, nor every priest an ignoramus. Yet there were enough of these to make a scandal of the church in many parts of the empire. The awareness of religious abuse was further exaggerated by the eager criticism of every clerical error. Humanists, orators, poets, pamphleteers, politicians, and gossipy stable boys were equally anxious to call attention to these malpractices.

• Erasmus and the Christian Humanists

The most alert and penetrating critics of clerical and monastic abuse were the Christian humanists, products of Italian humanism and of the New Learning of the northern schools, who based their reform ideas on an analysis of Christian sources as well as the Greek and Roman classics. They believed that reasoned learning, from original sources and correct translations, was an asset to the church and to Christian living. These dedicated scholars were deeply interested in applying their humanistic learning and style to the problems of Christian practice and understanding. In doing so they sharply criticized the hypocrisy of the monks, the lechery of the priests, and the ambitiousness of the princes. Appealing to reason and justice, they advocated greater emphasis upon Christian morality as taught in the Sermon on the Mount than on the outward ceremonies and rituals of the established church.

To Desiderius Erasmus, the leading humanist of Europe, it seemed that the popes and priests had turned religion into an empty ceremonialism devoid of true worship and without moral direction. Erasmus was a classical scholar, interested in the literature and wisdom of the Greek and Roman writers. But he was also a devoted Christian, hoping to influence other Christians to study the scriptures, lead moral lives, and promote peace and brotherhood. Born at Rotterdam in 1465 or 1466, and orphaned at age thirteen, Erasmus travelled widely and studied incessantly. Directed toward a religious life by the Brethren of the Common Life at their Deventer school, he was convinced by brief experience as a monk that he was not suited to the monastic life. Finally, he was stimulated

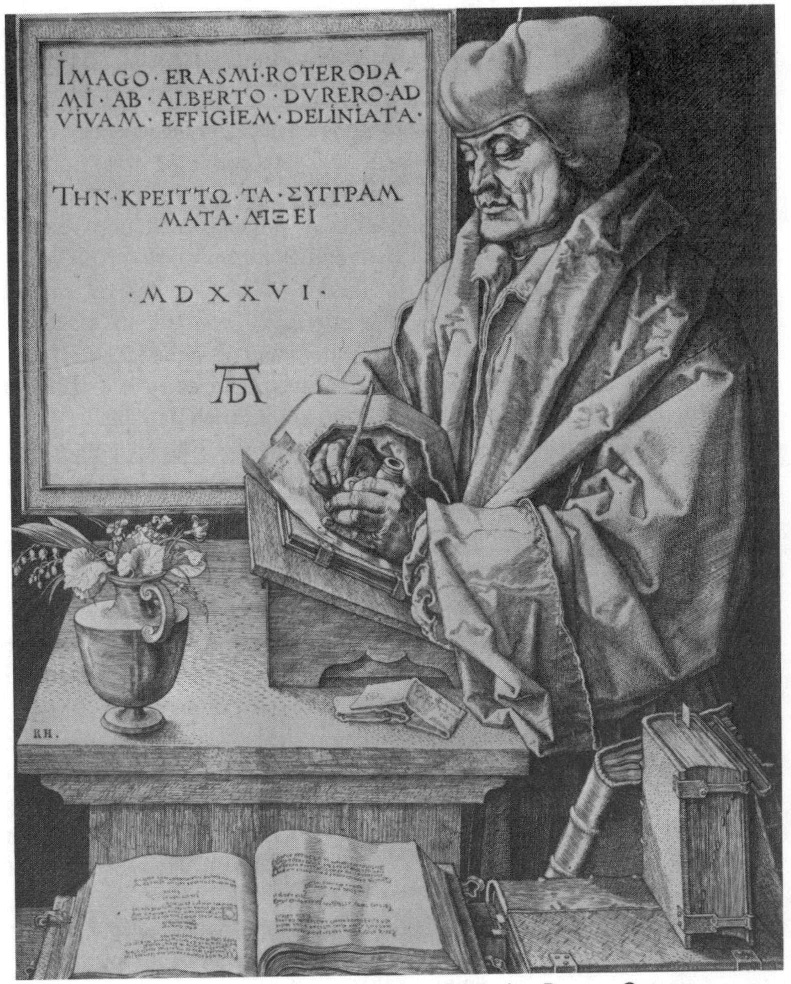

Erasmus, from an engraving by Albrecht Durer. Courtesy, Museum of Fine Arts, Boston.

toward scholarship and humanism by his studies in Paris and Italy. His close acquaintance with John Colet and Thomas More in England further strengthened his resolve to devote himself to a reconciliation of faith and reason, devotion and scholarship, scripture and literature. He thus became the great synthesizer of the northern Renaissance.

Eramus's writings, as well as his life, reflect this harmony of religious and secular thought. One of his earliest books, which he continued to expand and republish, was the *Adagia,* a collection of adages from classical sources with interpretative commentaries for the purpose of teaching moral and ethical values. More satirical in style are his *Colloques* and the still popular *Praise of Folly,* in which he effectively drew attention to the ignorance, folly, and corruption of men, particularly the churchmen. In the *Enchiridian* Erasmus pleaded with people to be concerned with the meaning of religious devotion, and to practice their beliefs instead of merely professing them. "What point in being sprinkled with holy oil unless you were to wage unremitting war upon your vices?" he reasoned, and added, "What point is there in your being showered with holy water if you do not wipe away the inward pollution from your heart? You venerate the saints and delight in touching their relics, but you despise the best one they left behind, the example of a holy life." Erasmus advocated the reading of scripture and promoted scriptural scholarship by his own translation and critical edition of the New Testament (published in 1516). He also edited and made available many of the early Church Fathers.

The religious concerns of Erasmus and the other Christian humanists were reflected in many ways in early sixteenth century Europe. They published widely, promoted and influenced elementary school education, and occasionally occupied chairs of literature, language, and classical studies in the universities (although the theological faculties generally remained conservatively scholastic). Johann Reuchlin, for example, taught Greek at Tübingen University. Mutianus Rufus was leader of the humanist circle at Erfurt. Juan Luis Vives was for a time professor of belles-lettres at the University of Louvain and subsequently fellow of Corpus Christi College, Oxford. Several Spanish humanists taught at the new University of Alcalá, established in 1509 by Cardinal Ximénez de Cisneros. Similarly, John Colet founded St. Paul's School in Westminster and directed its course toward the New Learning. Others could be mentioned: Lefèvre d'Etaples at Paris, Martin Cordier at Nevers and Bordeaux, and Hernán Núñez at Salamanca.

Parallel to this spreading humanism among the upper and middle classes was a growing devotionalism and desire for genuine spiritual expression among the masses. This yearning for devotional piety may have been caused in part by the aloofness and neglect of the clergy, but it was certainly intensified by the prevailing eschatology of the time. Belief in the imminent second coming of the Savior, in power and glory to annihilate the wicked and establish his kingdom, drove many believing souls to frenzied searching for spiritual expression through religious exercises and devotional rituals. Thus, the tensions of religious uncertainty were mounting at the same time that political disorders, economic and social strains, and ecclesiastical contradictions and abuses were reaching a peak. Germany in the early sixteenth century was a sprawling tinderbox waiting for someone to drop a match.

• Martin Luther and the Upheaval in Germany

In 1483 Martin Luther was born at Eisleben in Upper Thuringia, son of sturdy peasant stock. His father had become a fairly successful miner during the years just prior to Luther's birth and was therefore able to provide his son with some of the educational advantages he himself had not acquired. Luther's first fourteen years were spent in nearby Mansfeld, and his education was continued at Magdeburg and Eisenach. At seventeen, young Luther entered the nearby University of Erfurt where he moved quickly through the bachelor's and master's degrees in liberal arts. He had no sooner begun his subsequent study of law, when he abruptly abandoned the university and entered the Black Cloister of the Augustinian Eremites.

Luther's sudden decision to become a monk puzzled his companions, enraged his father, and has confused historians ever since. Luther was a very devout boy and tried hard to please God as best he could. But to no avail. The older he became the more he feared for his salvation as he became convinced that in the world he was unable to satisfy the demands of a just and all-knowing God. He experienced in extreme the fear of Christ's coming and the quick judgment that provoked his contemporaries to frenzied devotions and worship. He entered the monastery for safety's sake, but even within the quiet serenity of the cloister walls Luther could not find peace. He was tormented by the image of almighty God judging his sins and punishing him for them. Eventually he returned to the university, this time to become a doctor of theology, but still the agony persisted. He even reached the point of confessing his hatred of God before he finally discovered an answer to his dilemma which satisfied him and convinced him ultimately that the church, misled by false doctrines and evil men, had abandoned the word of God.

Luther's solution was a simple reinterpretation of the meaning of "justice of God," which he now came to view in an Augustinian manner not as punitive or retributive justice, in which sin and righteousness are weighed in a balance, but in a philanthropic sense in which God bestows faith on weak and fallen man through the divine grace of Jesus Christ. Thus, salvation is not something merited or even earned by man through good works, but rather a free gift from God, bestowed upon whom he will for his own purposes. This "discovery" of divine grace was the turning point in Luther's life and the nucleus of the Protestantism to which it gave birth. Because, if this interpretation of scripture is true, there is no need for treasuries of merit, indulgences, sacraments, priests, nor popes.

The next four or five years of Luther's life was the time of developing, testing, defending, and proclaiming his doctrines. In so doing he clashed head-on with the clergy (especially the Dominicans), the scholars of the universities, the pope, and finally the emperor. This conflict was punctuated by several landmarks and would-be turning points: indulgence sales and the *Ninety-Five Theses,* violently worded exchanges, disputations and interviews culminating in the Leipzig Debate (1519), and the burning of books by both sides. All of these led irrevocably to a final confrontation at the Diet of Worms between Luther and the Holy Roman Emperor. The result of that face-to-face confrontation was the dissolusion of Catholic Christendom.

At Worms Luther held stubbornly to his written words, refusing to retract or retreat in the least, unless he were convinced by scripture, reason, and conscience that he was in error. Upon these three principles he was prepared to defy anyone. For it was plain to him now that the word of God was explicit, authoritative, and unmistakable. On the other hand, the young emperor, Charles V, king of Castile and Aragon, archduke of Austria, duke of Burgundy as well as monarch of the New World and the "Islands of the Ocean Seas," although he had no great regard for the Roman pontiff, had no intention of resigning his position as secular guardian of the faith. He answered Luther's stand with an equally dogmatic declaration against all writings of the heretic professor. This Edict of Worms was published in several countries of Europe, but to little avail. The condemnation was too sweeping and extreme to be enforceable even if the emperor had not been sucked into a protracted war with France, a chronic rivaly with the pope, and a dangerous and immediate threat from the Ottoman Turks. After 1521 the cleft in Christendom soon widened into a permanent chasm.

• The Protestant Revolt Deepens

In the meantime, while the emperor's forces were diverted and divided into sundry campaigns to protect Christendom from the Turks and the dynasty from the French, Lutheranism itself entered a period of crisis and trial. Christian humanists had already pointed the way to the Protestant revolt, or as contemporaries put it, "Erasmus laid the egg that Luther hatched." Luther's reformation, however, was quite a different reformation than the one the humanists had in mind. They had hoped to bring reason, justice, unity, and peace into the existing church. It was the abuses and malpractices that they opposed not the theology nor organization of the church. But Luther had gone much further in his criticism of doctrines, organization, and authority. To him peace was not the paramount consideration, but rather truth – God's word. The parting of the ways

Portrait of Martin Luther, from a woodcut by Lucas Cranach, Sr. Courtesy, Museum of Fine Arts, Boston.

between humanists and Lutherans is vividly illustrated in the mounting disagreement between Luther and Erasmus, culminating in their sharp exchanges on the issue of human will.

But what appears radical from one point of view may be moderate or even conservative when viewed from another. As Luther returned to Wittenburg after a year's exile at Wartburg Castle in Thuringia (during which he completed his popular German translation of the New Testament), he found that many of his followers and associates had gone far beyond his own intentions in "reforming" the church. Andreas Karlstadt, who with Philipp Melanchthon had long been Luther's closest Wittenberg associate, and was his aide at the Leipzig Debate, was already caught up in a more radical revolt. Like the so-called Zwickau prophets, and others with whom he was associated, Karlstadt believed in the supremacy of the spirit over the letter, and determined to follow it "wherever it leadeth." He was likewise prepared to pursue Luther's criterion of reason further than Luther himself was. The resulting disorders and destruction of images and property in Wittenberg forced Luther to part company with these evangelical puritans and take up a middle ground somewhere between the cautious humanists and the spiritual and social activists.

• The Peasants' Revolt

The revolution that followed soon became the most serious threat to the integrity of Luther's revolt and precipitated a new crisis in the empire. The German peasants had much cause for despair in the conditions and hardships of their life. Some of their problems grew worse with the decline of feudal protectionism and the rise of commerce and money economy. The peasants were hard-pressed to survive without the use of the common lands and woods, and some of them struck out in sporadic uprisings against the landowners and princes. In some parts of Germany they banded together into revolutionary organizations using the emblem of the peasant boot, the *Bundschuh,* as their symbol.

Increasingly these peasants came to associate Luther's message of salvation by faith and the priesthood of all believers with their own social cause. They took his defiance of the pope and emperor as a call to resist authority, assuming (incorrectly) that they were acting according to Luther's gospel and that he would be their spiritual leader. In 1524, beginning in the Black Forest region of southwestern Germany, peasant uprisings spread rapidly into Swabia, Württemberg and Baden. Their demands were moderate enough at first, but as the movement spread northward it became more radical and more violent. This metamorphosis was accelerated in Saxony and Thuringia with the arousing of religious fanaticism by zealot reformers like Thomas Müntzer. At Alstedt and Mülhausen, Müntzer had already stirred the peasants to acts of violence and revolution with his inflamed oratory. Preaching the apocalyptic destruction of the wicked and the establishment of the Kingdom of God on earth, he now led them in a holy crusade against the ungodly.

The Peasants' War of 1524-25 brought terror and destruction to much of the empire; it also wrought a profound change in the direction and affiliation of Lutheranism. Deeply disturbed by the disorder of the peasant upheaval, Luther lashed out against those who had thus prostituted the gospel in the name of divine justice. In an unnecessarily violent tract, *Against the Murderous and Thieving Hordes of Peasants,* Luther called upon the princes to strike down the rebellious insurgents before it was too late. "Let everyone who can, smite, slay, and stab, secretly or openly, remembering that nothing can be more poisonous, hurtful, or devilish than a rebel." But the princes needed no such encouragement. The war was brought to its inevitable conclusion in a veritable blood-bath. Over five thousand peasants were butchered at Frankenhausen, including Müntzer himself, and in all some 100,000 are estimated to have been killed in the first violent months of 1525.

• Lutheranism as a State Religion

Luther was never again as popular as he had been between 1517 and 1525. Many people interpreted his role in the peasants' revolt as a betrayal of the people, when in fact they had misinterpreted his message. His revolt was a theological issue, not a social, political, or economic revolution. He believed in the same socio-political order that had prevailed for centuries, and his economic views were as conservative as were those of the majority of his contemporaries.

During the later 1520's, Luther was drawn ever closer to the German princes as his theological break with Rome required more and more administrative direction. Luther was not an "organization man," nor was he interested in politics or in political power. He was a scriptorian, a theological scholar, and a teacher. As Lutheranism spread through the northern German states it came to be organized and administered as a state church by the various princes and magistrates who ruled in their territories "as instruments of God." The invisible church, the Kingdom of Christ, the ultimate brotherhood of the elect, requires no institutionalization, Luther maintained, but he also conceded that the visible church, the Kingdom of the World, the temporal congregation of believers and worshipers, does require organization, laws, and government. It is this area of ecclesiastical and civil jurisdiction that Luther was willing to have handled by the magistrates and princes. It was their calling to rule. Thus, the spread of Lutheran ideas and attitudes through Germany, Scandinavia, and even into eastern Europe was closely allied with the interests of the ruling classes, whether noble or burgher, and wherever Lutheranism succeeded it was as a state religion, protected and promoted by the magistracy.

Lutheran propaganda, in tracts, pamphlets and vivid cartoons, poured through northern Germany in the 1520's, attracting thousands of adherents and, most importantly, converting many of the territorial rulers. Soon evangelical congregations were organized throughout the realms of converted princes and unified into territorial churches under the patronage of these rulers. Saxony was the first large state to be thus evangelized, but Lutheranism quickly spread to neighboring Hesse, Mansfeld, Brandenburg, Brunswick, Württenberg, Lüneburg, Anhalt, and eventually into all of northern Germany and Scandinavia. The Reformation also caught on rapidly in the Imperial Cities of Nüremberg, Augsburg, Ulm, Nördlingen, Heilbronn and Strassburg, and from these into many of the other towns and cities of Germany.

• The Augsburg Confession and the Schmalkaldic League

At the second Diet of Speyer, in 1529, the emperor attempted to enforce the Edict of Worms and extirpate heresy in the empire. A new imperial edict granting religious liberty to Catholics in Lutheran lands but denying it to Lutherans in Catholic territories was met with an immediate written protest by five of the Lutheran princes and some fourteen cities. This "protest" eventually gave the common name of Protestants to the scores of divergent Reformation movements of the sixteenth century. A year later another attempt to stem the tide of Reformation brought in response the Augsburg Confession, the first of several official statements of evangelical belief and practice. The Augsburg Confession was a moderate and conciliatory document, written by Philipp Melanchthon in the hope of placating the emperor and reducing the threat of religious war. But still it was a declaration of Protestant beliefs and as such it aroused as much Catholic opposition as it did Lutheran agreement. With their confession in hand, the Lutheran princes next formed a military alliance, called the Schmalkaldic League, for the purpose of defending their cause against the inevitable imperial attack.

But the emperor was in no position to attack. Amidst the endemic problems with France, the Turks, and the troublesome papacy, no sooner was one fire put out than another burst into flames. Peace was settled with France in 1526 only to have the Turks crash through the outer perimeter of Christian defense in the east and defeat the emperor's brother-in-law, Louis II of Hungary, at the Battle of Mohács, thus opening the empire to massive Turkish invasion from the southeast. At the time of the Diet of Speyer the Turks were already laying siege to Vienna itself. Meantime, imperial troops, campaigning in central Italy against Franco-papal armies, got out of control and put Rome to its most devastating sack since Visigoth and Vandal days. Thereupon, Henry VIII, frustrated by the failure of his initial attempt to obtain a papal divorce from Charles's aunt, Catherine of Aragon, joined with Francis I in a new war against the emperor. And thus Charles V was forced to turn his attention and resources from one troubled spot to another as the weeks turned to months and the months into years.

Persistently, the emperor also pressured the pope to summon a general council for the purpose of eradicating the still flagrant abuses of the Church – especially in Germany – as well as solving the problem of the Lutheran heresy. Charles and his humanist advisors believed that a willing and conciliatory attitude on both sides could result in a healing of the religious schism. Pope Paul procrastinated, for he feared the jurisdictional threat of a general council. Yet he also knew the church needed reform and hoped the schism might be healed through arbitration rather than war.

By the autumn of 1544 the fourth of the Hapsburg-Valois wars between Francis I and Charles V was drawing to a close. Suleiman and his Turkish hoards were still a threat in Hungary and Austria but Francis was brought to heel in the Treaty of Crespy. Things now seemed to be turning in Charles's favor. Pope Paul agreed to aid the emperor in a crusade against the Protestants; Maurice of Saxony agreed to join in an attack on his cousin, the elector and leader of the Schmalkaldic League; Martin Luther died, followed soon by Henry VIII and Francis I. Late in 1546, more than fifteen years after the formation of the Schmalkaldic League, the emperor finally struck in force against the now almost solidly Protestant north. He reached the peak of his success in April 1547 at the Battle of Mühlberg, where the army of the Schmalkaldic League was put to flight and the Saxon elector captured. Shortly thereafter Philipp of Hesse also surrendered, and the emperor issued a conciliatory edict, known as the Interim of Augsburg (1548) which he hoped would heal the doctrinal disputes until the Council of Trent reconvened and completed its work.

But the wheel of fortune turned fast in Reformation Europe. Four years later the whole situation was reversed. Maurice of Saxony betrayed the emperor and switched sides, signing an alliance with the French king and leading an attack on Charles's northern flank. In 1555 peace was finally restored in the empire with a compromise settlement. By this Religious Peace of Augsburg, each prince of the empire was free to chose his own religious preference, Catholic or Lutheran, and dictate its observance in his territories. Ecclesiastical property acquired by Protestant princes before 1552 was to remain Protestant. Lutheran subjects of Catholic ecclesiastical states would not be required to renounce their faith, but by an "ecclesiastical reservation" any Catholic prince becoming a Protestant was required to give up his ecclesiastical see, which would then be awarded to a new Catholic beneficiary. The settlement was imperfect, but it did bring relative tranquility to a land torn by dispute and war. Until the early seventeenth century it continued as the legal basis of religious politics in Germany.

Within four months after the peace of Augsburg, Charles V had abdicated all of his crowns, and the center of religious dissent shifted westward to Switzerland, France, and England.

• Zwingli and the Reformation in Switzerland

Luther was not a lone voice crying in the wilderness. Even before his indulgence hassel with Tetzel, other humanists and reformers were challenging Catholic doctrines as well as calling attention to clerical abuses. Thomas Wyttenback, in Basel, for example, was denouncing "the fraud of indulgences" as early as 1507, and a few years later Ulrich Zwingli, priest of Glarus in northeastern Switzerland, vehemently rebuked the indulgence hawker, Bernardino Samson, urging the people to put their trust in Christ rather than in papal certificates. Zwingli later maintained that in 1516 he had already begun preaching the gospel before Luther was even heard of.

Zwingli, who was born in 1484 just seven weeks after Luther's birth, was attracted by the writings of Erasmus, and became a member of the circle of humanists associated with the Froben printing house in Basel. Educated in Basel, Bern, and Vienna, Zwingli became priest of Glarus in 1503 and of Einsiedeln ten years later. As he became increasingly concerned with the spiritual welfare of his parishioners he moved gradually from Erasmus's aristocratic humanism to a more direct criticism of the doctrines of the church. He never entirely abandoned his humanistic orientation, however, and carried out a reformation in Zurich and surrounding regions that in its rational and systematic approach combined the practical piety of Erasmus with the Biblical fundamentalism of Luther. But Zwingli also went beyond the Wittenberg reformer in his rejection of ecclesiastical authority and in his willingness to act politically (even militarily) in defense of Christian truth. In this sense Zwingli was an interesting combination of the humanist, the theologian, and the radical.

In December, 1518 he became priest of the Grossmünster in Zurich, and from this post he expounded the principles and carried out the reforms that gradually drew the western Swiss cantons out of the Roman orbit. Within a year after the Diet of Worms, Zwingli was strongly criticizing many ecclesiastical observances. He also condemned the system of Swiss mercenaries, especially when they served the papacy. Through the use of public disputations, and with the support of the Zurich Council, Zwingli carried out an extensive reform of the church during the next few years, culminating in the abolition of the mass in 1525.

Pope Adrian VI (1521-23), the Dutch mentor of Charles V and friend of Erasmus, tried to persuade Zwingli to remain obedient to Rome and faithful to the Catholic Church. But the Zurich reformer paid no attention to the papal pleas of either Adrian or his successor, Clement VII (1523-34). The papal dependence upon Swiss mercenaries was too great for the pope to risk upsetting the system by a rash reaction against Zurich. However, some of the neighboring Swiss were greatly disturbed by the rebellious actions of the canton. The diet of the Swiss confederation, meeting in Luzern, reprimanded Zurich for its religious innovations and warned it against further reforms. At the same time, the cantons proposed, since the pope is "silent and asleep," to legislate for themselves in many matters of religious practice. Several of the northern, so-called forest cantons (Luzern, Uri, Schwyz, Unterwalden, and Zug) thereupon formed a separate alliance of their own to combat heresy and reformation, thereby driving Zurich to find allies among the more sympathetic cantons of Bern, Basel, Solothurn, and Schaffhausen, and among the Lutheran cities of southwestern Germany.

In spite of their apparent common cause, the Swiss and German reformations remained remarkably separate. For Zwingli as for Luther, the Bible was the divine word of God, presenting a unified and comprehensible body of teaching and law. Furthermore, both denied the salvational merit of good works, or of the saints, relying solely upon faith and divine grace to justify and redeem. But beyond that their doctrines began to diverge. Zwingli's underlying humanism persuaded him to believe there was some human predisposition to do good and led him to recognize the existence of will. He dissented sharply from Luther's view of the Lord's Supper, particularly in the meaning of the words "This is my body," which he interpreted as a symbolic presence of Christ in the sacrament, not a "real presence" as Luther insisted upon. At the Marburg Colloquy (1529) an attempt was made to reach a general agreement on doctrinal matters, but the effort foundered on this issue of the Eucharist. "You have a different spirit from us," Luther charged, "One side in this controversy is of the Devil and is God's enemy."

While Zwingli lived, the civil authority in Zurich worked hand in hand with him in organizing and supervising the church. After his death in the second Kappel War of 1531 (fought between Zurich and the army of the Catholic cantons), the Reformed congregations of western Switzerland and Alsace each found their own working relationship under the guidance of capable and dedicated men who had been motivated and trained by

Zwingli. Heinrich Bullinger ably carried on at Zurich for the next forty-four years; Johannes Oecolampadius and Wolfgang Capito led the Reformation in Basel; Berthold Haller carried it to Bern, Vadianus to St. Gall, and Sebastian Hofmeister to Schaffhausen. Mattew Zell first brought the reformed gospel to Strasbourg, and was soon joined there by Capito and later by Martin Bucer, whose leadership at Strasbourg made it the most tolerant Protestant city in Europe and the haven for religious exiles of every kind.

• Anabaptism

Switzerland also spawned another form of religious and social revolt, Anabaptism. Mavericks as far as the mainstream of the Reformation went, these unorthodox reformers and rebels were outcasts among Protestants as well as among Catholics. Furthermore, they differed a great deal with one another both in doctrines and practice, making them difficult to identify and describe. Their most distinguishing characteristic was their conception of the church as a brotherhood, a body of believers, disciples of Christ, separate and distinct from the secular state and autonomous in its organization and government. Membership in such communities was symbolized by baptism, and since baptism resulted from hearing the word and believing, it followed that infant baptism was vigorously rejected by the Anabaptists. Their name derives from their insistence upon adult baptism, following conversion, which in practice meant re-baptism since all Christians of the time had been baptised as infants.

Collateral with their belief in the autonomous community of believers was their rejection of the authority of the state. They declined to take oaths to civil authorities, refused to recognize many laws, and resisted paying taxes. It is not surprising that they seemed to everyone else as dangerous, radical, conspiratorial rebels. Their predominantly lower class composition, their frequently communal life, and their occasional rabid eschatology further combined to make them feared and persecuted.

Anabaptism arose first in Zurich, where Conrad Grebel, and others, crossed swords with Zwingli in their public disputations. In spite of strong opposition (even attempts at extermination), the Swiss Anabaptists quickly organized themselves into congregations, practicing believers' baptism and teaching the gospel of discipleship based on the Sermon on the Mount.

Persistent persecution forced many of the Brethren to flee to other parts of the empire where the movement grew like scattered seeds. Michael Sattler moved into the Schwartzwald and valley of the Neckar, where his followers gathered and proclaimed, in 1527, the Schleitheim Confession, consisting of seven articles of faith outlining their beliefs and objectives. Balthasar Hubmaier, another Zurich convert, became leader of a similar movement in Moravia after a long trek eastward. He was soon joined by Hans Hut, who, imbibed with Thomas Müntzer's zeal, radicalized the movement there and contributed to its negative image. George Blaurock went south from Zurich into the high Tyrol where the movement grew rapidly among the discontented peasants and found its greatest early leader in Jacob Hutter. When persecution by Austrian authorities intensified, Hutter led his followers eastward into Moravia where they combined with the remnant of Hubmaier's congregations to form the large Hutterite communities recognized by their passive, pastural lives and by their close communal society.

The spread of Anabaptism northward down the Rhine and into the Lowlands was accompanied by several new and less attractive adaptations, including an intense millenarianism. The initiator of this phase of the movement was Melchior Hofmann, a wandering furrier from Swabia. In 1529 he associated himself with the Anabaptist community in Strasbourg, but was expelled from that relatively tolerant city for his rabble-rousing oratory. Drifting through the Netherlands and East Friesland, he began prophesying the approaching Last Judgment, which he set for 1533, and designated Strasbourg as the New Jerusalem. He was arrested when he returned there, but the flame of eschatological enthusiasm that he had lighted was not easily extinguished. It flared up next in the Netherlands. As persecution mounted, two new and fanatical leaders, converts during Hofmann's Dutch sojourn, came to the front. Jan Matthys, a Haarlem baker claiming to be the reincarnated Enoch, and his companion Jan van Leyden, a tailor, led the Dutch Anabaptist communities to the Westphalian city of Münster, where they announced the foundations of yet another New Jerusalem. The bizarre episode of Münster from February 1534 until June 1535, as it fell under the hypnotic spell of Matthys and then of Leyden, who had himself proclaimed prophet-king, is a classic example of fanaticism feeding on fanaticism until reality is abandoned and either self-annihilation or destruction from outside become inevitable. Besieged for more than a year by armies of Philipp of Hesse and the bishop of Münster, the city finally collapsed and its inhabitants were put to the sword.

Those who managed to escape from the Münster holocaust, along with many persecuted congregations from other parts of the Lowlands, eventually found a new and inspiring leader in Menno Simons, a former parish priest of West Friesland. Under the sensitive and dedicated Menno Simons these Mennonites, as they came to be called, revived the earlier principles of sobriety, meekness, pacifism, and long-suffering, as being the attributes of Christ's disciples, and dedicated themselves to a simple life detached from the world. Their peregrinations across three continents and four centuries is a modern odyssey worthy of a new Homer.

• John Calvin

In the meantime, in March 1536, a Basel publisher issued a small octavo book, entitled *Institutes of the Christian Religion.* Its author, a twenty-six-year-old French exile by the name of John Calvin, was destined to infuse a dynamic new dimension into the Reformation, giving it a vitality that would carry it into all parts of Europe and beyond the seas. The *Institutes* was a forthright book written in clear, descriptive Latin as a catechism of Christian doctrine and a manual for church organization. It contained a dedicatory introduction to the king of France, then proceeded systematically and succinctly to outline the principal points of the law and the gospel. The impact of the *Institutes* was both immediate and lasting because it summarized the whole of Protestant theology in a logical and manageable way.

Calvin reached Switzerland for the first time in 1535 after fleeing France, where he had become too closely associated with the reform party at the University of Paris. Calvin was born in Picardy and had gone to school in Paris, Orléans, and Bourges, studying law under some of the most renowned teachers of the age. His conversion to Protestantism is shrouded in mystery, but by the time he published the *Institutes* he seems to have freed himself totally from Catholic thinking. Later in 1536 he found himself in the city of Geneva where, through the entreaties of Guillaume Farel, a fiery minister sent by Bern to convert the semi-imperial city to Protestantism, he began his ministry.

The first phase of that ministry lasted less than two years as Calvin and Farel clashed head-on with the Genevan Council over jurisdiction and ecclesiastical discipline. At Easter 1538 they were both expelled from the city. Thereupon, Calvin accepted Bucer's invitation to join him in Strasbourg and a new phase of the Reformation began. At Strasbourg Calvin further expanded and clarified his theology while developing a sharper notion of religious politics and ecclesiastical organization. When he returned to Geneva three-and-one-half years later it was with a clear conception of the gospel and of his role as an organizational as well as a theological reformer.

• Church and State in Geneva

Through his "Ecclesiastical Ordonnances" Calvin established a theocratic regime in Geneva that was unequalled in its effective jurisdiction.

The Ministry, staffed with carefully chosen pastors and teachers, was the pastoral and educational arm of the visible church, guarding its doctrinal purity and giving instruction in faith. The Consistory was its disciplinary arm, overseeing and correcting the lives of the people. Composed of both ministers and lay elders, the Consistory kept a close eye on every facet of Genevan life and brought quick and severe punishment to violators of its strict code of conduct. Heresy was looked upon without the least degree of tolerance, being punished in extreme cases by death. Even minor infractions of the ecclesiastical law were treated as serious offenses. The most famous heresy case occurring in Calvin's Geneva was that of the Spanish physician-theologian, Michael Servetus, who was burned to death in 1553 for his writings against the doctrine of the Trinity. One of the few contemporaries who raised their voices against this action was Sebastian Castellio, a Savoyard humanist who taught that the burning of heretics was contrary to the teachings of Christ. Castellio's advocacy of religious toleration was strongly opposed in Geneva and did not receive much better reception elsewhere.

In Calvin's mind the relationship between church and state was close, but it was not identical. He distinguished between spiritual and temporal jurisdictions and considered their respective callings distinct and complementary. "As soul and body constitute one man," he said, "so church and state constitute one society, distinct in function but inseparable in being." Furthermore, since the authority for both jurisdictions comes from God, and since the Bible is the word of God to magistrates and laymen as well as to the church and its clergymen, it was evident to Calvin that the church, as custodian of God's word, held a clear preeminence over the civil magistry in all matters of faith and morals – and even of law. Thus, if the civil authority should violate the laws of God or abuse its divinely ordained function, it is the responsibility of the church, or its representative, to override that civil power, the Bible being the final authority in all matters.

This doctrine marks a clear distinction from Luther's submission of the church to the jurisdiction of the state. It also accounts in part for the potentially revolutionary spirit of Calvinism as it spread across Europe. But Calvin was no more a political revolutionary than Luther was. The Genevan reformer made it clear that God did not condone civil disorder. Simple people are never justified in disobeying their rulers or in initiating action against them. Only clearly constituted and divinely sanctioned authority have the right to resist or oppose a government, even if that government is tyrannical. In such a case the people's duty is then to the resisting authority, since God must be obeyed above all. Even then Calvin was cautious in applying even this conservative resistance theory to particular political situations. Many of his followers were not so circumspect.

• The Spread of Calvinism

As Calvinism rapidly made its way from Geneva into the neighboring cantons, and from Switzerland into France, the Netherlands, Scotland, England and eastward into Germany and beyond, it was obvious that the Calvinist congregations possessed a dynamic motivation that gave them a greater impact than their numbers would indicate. This success may be due in part to the tight organization and rigid discipline of the Calvinist forces, but it was surely furthered through their active social ethic stemming from Calvin's theology. The crux of that theology was the belief in an omnipotent and omniscient sovereign God who "in His own wisdom, has from the remotest eternity, decreed what He would do, and now by His own power, executed what He has decreed." Furthermore, being a God of justice as well as majesty, he has of necessity condemned all mankind, because man is "impure, profane, and abominable to God," meriting nothing but eternal damnation. Man's spirit is so alien to God, according to Calvin, "that he conceives, covets, and undertakes nothing that is not evil, perverse, iniquitous, and soiled." His will is so obstinate "that it cannot excite itself . . . to anything but what is evil." Thus, mankind's condemnation is a tribute to God's justice.

Nevertheless, God also ordains some men to eternal salvation, not through their merit but through his mercy. For those whom he elected to salvation God provides a means of rescue through the redemption of Jesus Christ. By this vicarious transfusion of grace the elect are reborn and are made "partakers of the divine nature." This divine election, or predestination, was fundamental to Calvinist dynamics. It meant that those who were thus regenerated and justified constituted a chosen people of God, totally indebted to him, dedicated to his service and directing their energies to the single purpose of carrying out his will. The social effects of this belief were profound. It produced a movement that could not be halted nor deterred.

France was the first target of Calvinist proselyting efforts outside of Switzerland. In 1541 the first French edition of the *Institutes* (enlarged now to several times its original size) was published and distributed widely. The next decade was the germination period of Calvinism in France. By 1555 there were Calvinist congregations all over the country. In that year a national synod met in Paris, where a Calvinist confession of faith was drawn up. Between 1555 and 1562 a great number of French nobles joined these Huguenot congregations, giving an aristocratic and volatile flavor to French Protestantism, and ensuring the outbreak of civil war.

Calvinism grew rapidly in the Netherlands also, due to Protestant emigration from France and to the dispatch of ministers from Geneva itself. Protestant literature had been circulating in the Low Countries for many years in spite of Charles V's repressive measures to curtail it. After the emperor's abdication in 1556 and the accession of his son Philip II, Calvinism seemed to spread even more rapidly as the homeland of Erasmus reacted favorably to Calvinist logic and organization. A Belgic Confession was written in 1561 and adopted five years later in the Synod of Antwerp.

Across the Channel, Calvinist literature infiltrated into England during Edward VI's reign (1547-53) and following Mary Tudor's death in 1558 returning English divines who had spent their exile in Geneva added a new vitality to English Protestantism. Elizabeth I (1558-1603) was able successfully to contain Calvinist Puritans during the first half of her reign, even though her northern neighbor succumbed to Calvinism, but in the later years she was hard-pressed to keep them in check. The "Thundering Scot," John Knox, was largely responsible for the success of Calvinism in Scotland. Trained in Geneva at the feet of Calvin himself, Knox led a relentless and ultimately successful crusade against the Catholic nobles of the north country and against the ill-starred regime of Mary Queen of Scots, achieving in the 1561 Kirk of Scotland the first fully successful Calvinization of a whole kingdom.

In Germany Calvinism penetrated into the Rhineland Palatinate first under the protective cover of Elector Frederick III, count Palatine of the Rhine. Even though there was no accommodation for Calvinism in the Peace of Augsburg, it spread rapidly from the Palatinate into neighboring Nassau, Hesse, Anhalt, and Cleves. In 1563 the Heidelberg Catechism was adopted by the Rhenish reformers giving a valuable doctrinal guide for all the Reformed churches of the empire and aiding its continued spread eastward into Brandenberg and even into Poland, Bohemia, and Hungary.

• Ecclesiastical Rebellion in England

The church in England was also rife with corruption and abuse. Although seldom as powerful and independent as their German counterparts, the English bishops had nevertheless succeeded in amassing great wealth and prestige. Church courts were notoriously corrupt in Renaissance England, and the administration of ecclesiastical finances was subject to scandalous abuse, as was the operation of the monasteries. These and many other infractions were seen and criticized by concerned observers. English humanists were aware of the abuses and vigorously denounced them. As early as 1511 John Colet challenged the prelates to make amends and reform the church by reforming their own lives.

The consequence of an avaricious clergy was to drive an ever widening wedge between the institutional church and the people, causing them to lose faith in religious rituals and to turn elsewhere for guidance and solace. Many English worshippers found devotional satisfaction with the Lollards, whose underground cells continued to harbor religious dissidents since Wyclif's time. Others turned to less organized forms of individual spiritual devotions. When Lutheran literature began circulating in the 1520's some of it was smuggled into England where it was avidly read by reform-minded dons at the University of Cambridge. Among these early proto-Protestants were Hugh Latimer, Thomas Cranmer, Robert Barnes, Thomas Bilney, and William Tyndale. The latter became a very important figure in the English Reformation because of his prolific pamphleteering and his stirring English translation of the New Testament. More than anyone else, Tyndale was the intellectual bridge between England and the German Lutherans.

• Henry VIII and the Break with Rome

But it was neither Luther, Tyndale, nor Colet who caused the English Reformation. They and many others had a part in its shaping, but it was the king, Henry VIII, who was most responsible for the ecclesiastical break with Rome. In sixteenth-century England the king had great authority. The crown commanded in all things and demanded both respect and obedience from its clergy. But the churchmen owed allegiance to the pope as well as loyalty to the king. Nothing illustrates this dichotomy more vividly than the rise and fall of Henry's lord chancellor, Cardinal Thomas Wolsey. Not only was Wolsey the most honored and powerful of the king's servants, he was also archbishop of York, cardinal, and permanent papal legate in England, making him the supreme ecclesiastical authority in England next to the pope. But in his attempt to dominate both church and state he failed effectively to control either one. His fall in 1530 carried the English clergy with him, for they were both associated in everyone's mind with the hated Roman pope.

The cause of Wolsey's demise was his failure to obtain from Pope Clement VII a divorce, or annulment, of the king's twenty-one year marriage to Catherine of Aragon. Henry needed a male heir; his wife had produced only a daughter and four still-born sons. Now she was beyond childbearing age – and Henry's emotions were caught by the vivacious eyes of Anne Boleyn. The king tried to free himself from his wife by legal means. But Catherine's resistance and the pressures of her nephew, Emperor Charles V, on the pope were too much for Henry to overcome. So he resorted to counter pressure and then to force.

• Thomas Cromwell and the Reformation Parliament

When the venerable archbishop of Canterbury died in 1532 Henry appointed to succeed him a malleable and soft-spoken scholar who had no love for the pope and who could be counted on to obey the king's wishes. Thomas Cranmer was the choice. To assist him Henry brought forward Wolsey's former secretary, Thomas Cromwell, who had gradually risen in the king's estimation to become principal secretary and Lord Privy Seal. Cromwell was a capable administrator and a clever politician. He had the intellectual capacity to plan whatever objectives the king required and the cold determination to carry them out. Above all, he was industrious and completely loyal to the king.

Parliament was convened and became the instrument through which Cromwell executed the king's will. First the papacy was declared guilty of violating the English Statute of Praemunire, which prohibited appeals to Rome without royal consent; then Henry was declared "Protector and Only Supreme Head of the Church and Clergy in England"; the payment of annates to Rome was curtailed; and an act in restraint of appeals to Rome crowned the work of this Reformation Parliament. As far as England was concerned the Roman pontiff had been removed, and his place taken by the king. Now Henry married Anne Boleyn and had his archbishop pronounce the marriage to Catherine "null and absolutely void," and the one to Anne "good and lawful."

The enactments of the Reformation Parliament were significant constitutionally as well as religiously. For in effect the king and parliament had not only legalized the king's moral actions and completely repudiated the authority of Rome, they also declared the autonomous sovereignty of the English state. To make its enactment secure Parliament passed a final Act of Supremacy, declaring the king "Supreme head in earth of the Church of England," a Succession Act, and a Treason Act defining the bounds of loyalty.

• Thomas More and Opposition to Henry VIII

A few people – very few – would not submit to the king's will. Most prominent of these were John Fisher, bishop of Rochester, and Henry's former lord chancellor, the renowned and beloved humanist, Sir Thomas More. Years before, in his remarkable little book, *Utopia,* More had debated the issue of whether or not a good man should serve a bad master. "Don't give up the ship in a storm because you cannot control the winds," he concluded, "For what you cannot turn to good, you can at least make less bad." But as moderately and gently as More tried to influence the king toward less bad government he was still caught in the undertow of the Henrician Revolution. He refrained from opposing the king, but he likewise refused to take the oath condoning Henry's actions. Henry wanted and needed More's support; he demanded total allegiance or death. On July 6, 1535 Thomas More was beheaded.

The financing of the English Reformation was achieved by the cool logic of Thomas Cromwell. Between 1536 and 1539 the monasteries – first the smaller then the larger ones – were systematically suppressed and became the property of the crown. Now, for the first time, the king's high handed measures were met with something approaching popular opposition. Already in bad humor over newly imposed taxes and rents, a motley array of people in Lincolnshire took up arms in protest. The revolt, known as the Pilgrimage of Grace, gained momentum as it spread into Yorkshire, Lancashire, and East Riding. But, poorly directed and uncertain about its aims and objectives, the revolt disbanded in December 1536. Its leaders were sacrificed to Henry's revenge.

Others in turn fell victim to the king's capricious will. Anne Boleyn was beheaded only three years after her spectacular triumph; in 1541 Henry's fifth wife, Catherine Howard, followed her cousin to the block; Robert Barnes lost royal favor and his life in 1540; and in the same year Cromwell himself, the mastermind of the Henrician Reformation fell to the ax. Just as wives and ministers rose and fell, so did Henry's policies fluctuate with his changing whims and the shifting balance of powers. He tried alternately to side with the Schmalkaldic League, support the emperor, fight for France, and stalk the pope. Whatever he did he hoped to win glory and fame for himself. In January 1547, Henry VIII died, leaving the country weak from financial mismanagement and reckless foreign encounters, and at the mercy of court factions eager to gain the upper hand in a government that now passed to Henry's haughty nine-year-old son, Edward VI.

• The Edwardian Reformation

A council of regency, headed by Edward Seymour, duke of Somerset (the young king's uncle, and brother to Jane Seymour, Henry's third wife) directed the government and presided over the second phase of the English Reformation. Under Henry VIII almost no doctrinal changes had taken place. His was an ecclesiastical not a theological revolution. Henry had harshly prosecuted those who expressed Protestant views. Now the pent-up feelings of Protestant-prone clerics and laymen, and returning exiles from Germany and Switzerland, carried the English church toward continental Protestantism. The Edwardian Reformation was also carried out by acts of Parliament. Under Archbishop Cranmer's supervision the dissolution of the monasteries was completed; the Lord's Supper was administered in both kinds and celebrated in English; a Book of Common Prayer, drawn largely from Lutheran and Zwinglian sources, was published in 1549; clerical celebacy was ended; and images were removed from the churches.

In 1551 the winds of power shifted again and Somerset was swept from office. The new man at the helm was John Dudley, earl of Warwick and duke of Northumberland. Ruthless and ambitious, Northumberland was nevertheless a strong administrator who was able to make some headway against the continuing chaos of English finances. Under Northumberland the Reformation continued. A new, even more Protestant oriented Prayer Book was compiled by Cranmer in 1552; another Act of Uniformity made the English liturgy compulsory; and a new confession, known as the Forty-two Articles, was published. But neither Edward nor Northumberland lived to bask in their creations. Sickly throughout his short life, the king succumbed in July 1553. Caught in a plot to advance his son to the throne through marriage to sixteen-year-old Lady Jane Grey (who had a claim to the throne if the direct line succession to Henry's daughter, Mary, were by-passed), Northumberland's career suddenly ended. The succession was not by-passed. Mary expected and wanted the throne, and the people of England wanted her more than they wanted the scheming duke, even though she was openly Catholic. The failure of Northumberland's plot cost him his life and that of his unfortunate son and daughter-in-law.

• Bloody Mary

Securely on the throne, Mary tried to halt the movement of Reformation and initiate a return to Rome. It was expected that she would restore Catholic worship to the realm, but it was hoped she would do it smoothly and without undue subservience to Rome. Many features of the Reformation would have to be retained; everyone knew that, and they hoped the queen knew it too. Mary was sincere and devout, but she was also overly zealous in religious matters and lacked the flexibility and political judgment necessary to pursue a safe course through such dangerous times. She was not cruel or vindictive as she is popularly portrayed, but her ardent dedication to an unpopular cause led her to extreme actions that should never have been taken. Both bloody and tragic, Mary's reign solved few of the problems inherited from her brother and father, and added more for her sister to resolve.

Again the religious realignment was carried out by Parliament, and with less travail than might be expected. The supremacy acts of Henry's reign were removed, and the Edwardian doctrinal reforms were repealed. Picking up momentum, Parliament authorized the reconciliation with Rome and the restoration of the rights and authority of the Holy See. Pope Julius III, a gentle and conciliatory pontiff, reciprocated by confirming the secular possession of previous church properties, thus avoiding the upheaval that certainly would have followed Mary's attempt to restore monastic lands to the church. Cardinal Pole, the highest ranking English Catholic, was brought back from exile to direct the intricacies of doctrinal recovery. But Mary became impatient with the pace of restoration and began to push faster than the religious community was willing to move. Reluctance was interpreted by her as refusal, and disagreement taken for opposition. Soon the ax began to fall again, and many capable clerics who might have contributed to the restoration lost their lives. Others escaped into Swiss exile.

Mary's greatest blunder was her marriage to the emperor's son, Philip of Spain. From Charles's point of view the alliance made good sense. It insured English allegiance to imperial-Spanish policy and it guaranteed her cooperation in the impending war with France. But the English resented it vehemently. To them it meant the vassalage of England to Spain. Civil uprisings in the Midlands and in Kent had to be put down by force. Violence spawned more violence. Stronger opposition by the Protestant bishops caused the queen to turn her wrath against them. The bishop of London was put to death, as was Hugh Latimer, the bishop of Worcester, and finally even archbishop Cranmer. Mary was determined to follow the course she had marked out regardless of the cost. When the final phase of the Hapsburg-Valois Wars began in 1557 she complied with her husband's wish and brought England into the conflict on the side of Hapsburg Spain. But she did not live to see the conclusion of the war in 1559 with its spectacular Spanish victories in Italy and in France. She did survive long enough, however, to learn of the humiliation of English arms and the loss of Calais to the French. She died on November 17, 1558, mourned by a few, hated by many, pitied by all.

• The Catholic Reformation

The response of the Catholic Church to the spread of Protestantism was both negative and positive. Clerics, theologians, and friars from every country joined in writing against the reformers. Laymen, too, rose to defend the faith. Even Henry VIII answered Luther's *Babylonian Captivity of the Church* with a vituperate *Defense of the Seven Sacraments against Martin Luther,* for which he was awarded the title "Defender of the Faith" by Pope Leo X. As the Reformation spread so did reactions to it.

Notwithstanding these negative responses to the Reformation, there were at the same time many moves from within the church toward reform and reconciliation. The Christian humanists had exerted pressure in that direction for decades before Luther's time. Their writings were not all criticisms of the faults of the church; they frequently made concrete proposals for its improvement. Positive steps toward reformation were being taken on other levels too. The moving examples of saintly persons, such as Saint Teresa of Avila and San Juan de la Cruz, led many people closer to God. But canonization came to only a few; there were others who contributed in more immediate ways to the betterment of life and worship. Bishop Giberti of Verona, for example, demonstrated what could be done to improve and strengthen the church. Setting a standard of enlightened reform, he founded orphanages and schools, relief for the poor, better education for the clergy, and put an end to many of the clerical abuses that had existed. And in doing this he infused a more spiritual atmosphere into the entire diocese. The Venetian, Gasparo Contarini, was another who aspired to improve the church, not just criticize it. Through a long career as a distinguished diplomat and man of letters he influenced many people for good. When he became a cardinal he applied his energy and talents to reforming the church at the highest levels.

Reformation of the monastic and mendicant orders also took on vitality in the early sixteenth century, but even more significant was the founding of new orders dedicated to promoting internal reform and increasing spirituality. The simplest of these new orders, in terms of its goal, was the Capuchins, a reform offshoot from the Franciscans. It was devoted to serving the downtrodden and poor through acts of charity, piety, and compassion. Several new brotherhoods, designed to regulate and spiritualize the lives of the laity and secular clergy, were also founded. The Oratory of Divine Love was one of the earliest and most effective of these. It aspired to harmonize the faith and culture of the time and promote reform in the church through devotions, prayers, and exemplary lives. It numbered among its adherents some of the highest officials of the church. Closely related to it were the Barnabites, Somaschi, and the Theatines. The latter was founded by Gaetano Thiene, a mild and gentle layman from Vicenza, and Gian Pietro Caraffa, the tempestuous and brilliant Neopolitan bishop who, when he became a cardinal, was one of the most dedicated reformers in the curia, and subsequently as pope the most vehement champion of Catholicism.

The Jesuits

A new direction to the reforming movement in the church was taken in 1540 by the establishment of the Society of Jesus, or Jesuits. Its founder was Ignatius Loyola, a Basque soldier from the northern Spanish province of Guipuzcoa. Seriously injured in the battle of Pamplona (1521), Loyola turned his thoughts, and his life, toward religion. Resolving to devote himself to the church, he began preparing for whatever call he might receive. In addition to devotions, prayers, and pilgrimages, he trained his mind and spirit by systematic and arduous education – ten years of study at Barcelona, Salamanca, Alcalá, and the University of Paris – and by the application of spiritual exercises designed to discipline and direct the will toward God. Published as a handbook for spiritual training, Loyola's *Spiritual Exercises* became one of the most effective instruments of the Catholic Reformation. The purpose of the *Spiritual Exercises,* unlike Thomas à Kempis's *Imitation of Christ,* and other devotional books, was not just the salvation of men's souls but to prepare them for more effective service to God and the church.

Likewise, the Jesuit Order, which developed out of Loyola's association with a handful of followers at Paris, was dedicated to service and to actively promoting and defending the teachings of the church. The Jesuits soon became the most zealous and effective instrument of reform, a company of religious soldiers sworn by vows of obedience to defend the church. They thought of themselves as teachers, and established grammar schools and seminaries throughout Europe. As defenders of the faith they were effective and dedicated missionaries, both among faltering Christians in Europe and the heathen nations as far away as China, Japan, and South America. Some Jesuits became priests and expounded the gospel from the pulpit, some were confessors to princes and rulers, others became inquisitors in the Holy Office, and still others occupied chairs of theology at the great universities. In all of their activities they maintained the rule that results counted more than methods. They combined high ideals with practicality. Efficiency, dedication, flexibility, and utility were their guidelines. And their results were impressive. The work of two Jesuits alone, Francis Xavier and Peter Canisius, accounted for the winning of a million new souls to the church and the gaining of thousands who had fallen away.

Pope Paul III and the Council of Trent

To be correctly understood, the Catholic Reformation must be viewed at another level as well. The Renaissance popes from Martin V to

Leo X were notoriously unspiritual and neglectful of the religious needs of the people. The first reforming pope to mount the throne was Adrian VI, in 1521. He was an austere and pedantic Dutch prelate who taught humanism to his prize pupil, Charles V, and served the emperor as both statesman and priest. Had he lived to carry out his plans the story of the Reformation might have read differently. He was succeeded by Leo X's Medici cousin, Clement VII (1523-34), whose weak character and irresolute mind brought nothing but embarrassment to the church and humiliation to the papacy. The first reforming pope, in any meaningful sense, was Alessandro Farnese, Pope Paul III (1534-49). He enlarged the curia with reformers of the calibre of Contarini, Caraffa, Jacopo Sadoleto, and Reginald Pole, and appointed a reform commission to study the causes of corruption in the church. The commission's report laid the primary blame right at the pope's door. The root of all errors, it said, was the papacy itself, ambitious, proud, and blind to its faults. A major step had been taken toward church-wide reformation, but it was not followed up.

Finally, in 1545, Pope Paul convened a general council at Trent. The first assembly lasted until 1547, and, in spite of the efforts of a strong reform faction, directed its deliberations more to confirming dogma than to correcting abuses. In 1551-52 a second assembly of the Council resumed its work at Trent. Protestant delegates were invited to attend, but there was no common ground nor enthusiasm for understanding the chasm that now divided Christendom. After a long interlude the council met in its third and last assembly in 1562-63. Catholic doctrines were dogmatically defined and Protestantism condemned; the authority and responsibilities of the clergy were circumscribed; and the practices of the church clarified. The pope was firmly sustained at the head of the universal body. And thus renovated, with a new spirit of dogmatic certainty, the Catholic Church was prepared to carry the religious fight to the enemy. Now the real Counter-Reformation began.

• The Roman Inquisition

The main weapons of the religious war against Protestantism – and against anyone now who deviated in the least from approved Catholic dogma – were, in addition to the Jesuits and the decrees of the Council of Trent, the Roman Inquisition and the Index of Prohibited Books. Courts of inquisition had been established many times during the Middle Ages to ferret out heretics and religious conspirators, but these were not permanent, continuing institutions. Not until the establishment of the Spanish Inquisition in 1478 did any country have a permanent bureaucratic structure for that purpose. In 1542, Cardinal Caraffa proposed a comparable organ for the Roman papacy, and it was established as the Holy Office of the Universal Church. Through this instrument Caraffa hoped to centralize and modernize the heresy hunting machinery and make it more effective throughout the church. Caraffa himself became the first inquisitor-general.

In 1555, the trenchant Caraffa became Pope Paul IV. He was seventy-nine years old then, but he still grasped the reigns with energy and enthusiasm. He had been a reformer all his life, and since his elevation to the cardinalate he had been one of the moving spirits of the Catholic Reformation. But as pope his cantankerous personality and self-righteous zeal did as much as anything to pervert that reformation into a bigoted Counter-Reformation against Protestantism. In 1559 he compiled and published a list of "dangerous and unholy" books that he had issued while he was inquisitor-general. This *Index Librorum Prohibitorum* became the first church-wide *Index* published by the papacy. It was continued as a permanent fixture with frequently updated editions to counteract the latest errors.

Paul IV's pontificate marked the transition in papal policy from reform to Counter-Reformation, from an emphasis on humanism and unity to dogmatism and conformity. Thenceforth the attitude of the popes was aggressively militant. Additional reforms improving the effectiveness of papal government were instituted by Pius IV (1559-65) and Pius V (1566-72), who used the Inquisition and any other means at his disposal to root out heresy in Italy while cracking down on church corruption and abuse with equal fervor. The papal diplomatic service was modernized and the calendar reformed by Pope Gregory XIII (1572-85), and Sixtus V (1585-90) further tightened control of financial and administrative affairs. The Counter-Reformation papacy energized the church with new vitality and dedication preparing it to resume (for a short time, at least) an active role in European affairs and in the grandiose artistic and architectural expressions of the Age of Baroque. Nevertheless, in spite of renewed papal vigor and aggressiveness, the Protestant Reformation and its accompanying fragmentation spelled the end of Catholic dominance in Europe. This led in turn not only to further religious diversity but eventually to the secularization of thought and life.

• The Culture of Reformation and Counter-Reformation Europe

The Reformation did not suddenly put an end to Renaissance culture, but it did contribute heavily to changing that culture in some very definite ways. Humanism, for instance, was diverted from a classics centered intellectual-literary movement to an active religious partisanship. As the Reformation spread and intensified, few humanist writers could remain aloof from its influence. They frequently took sides (usually the Catholic) and soon many of them were as deeply entangled in religious tirades as anyone else. Some humanist converts to Lutheranism, like Ulrich von Hutten, turned almost entirely to sectarian writing, although the greatest of them, Philipp Melanchthon, not only retained his fine Latin style, he maintained a moderate and conciliatory attitude through most of the turmoil. Sebastian Castellio, a humanist convert to Calvinism, displayed eloquence as well as feeling in his defense of religious toleration against Calvin's dogmatism. Humanists were prominent in the high echelons of the Catholic church, for a time. The emperor Charles V always relied on humanist trained secretaries and advisors. But the fervor of the Counter-Reformation all but extinguished humanism as a movement in the Catholic church by the close of the Council of Trent.

In the second half of the century the mounting violence of religious confrontation produced a predictable backlash in the form of secularism and scepticism. Michel de Montaigne is an example of the humanist turned sceptic. The cancerous conflict in France had all but destroyed the vital organs of government when Montaigne wrote in 1588: "The sanest party is still made up of members of a decrepit and worm-eaten body. In such a body the least infected member is called healthy." (*Essays,* III, 9). Yet in spite of growing rationalism and secularism toward the end of the sixteenth century, this was also the flourishing period of European demonology and witchcraft mania, a blight in Western history that was not overcome until late in the next century.

The influence of the religious upheaval on the literature of the sixteenth century was profound. It took many forms and directions in producing some of the greatest literature of all time. As the literary vehicle of the church, Latin played a unique role in this outpouring. It was also the language of the humanists and was avidly cultivated by them. Yet in spite of the distinquished Latin writings of Erasmus, More, Vives, and Lefèvre d'Etaples, and the profound theological works of Luther, Melanchthon, Zwingli, and Calvin, Latin had passed its literary peak. Its greatest impact in the sixteenth century was its influence on the rapidly developing vernacular languages. The sixteenth century was the first great age of vernacular literature.

In France that literary flowering came earliest in poetry. Out of a long tradition of medieval lyrical and court poetry, sprinkled with the poignant raw-life ballads of Francois Villon (1431-c. 63), French poetry came of age under the patronage of Francis I. Clear yet subtle, tender and witty, French poetry acquired its first master in Clément Maro

(1496-1544). He was not the last. Saint-Gelais and the king's own sister, Marguerite of Navarre, added much depth and pathos. A broader and more exalted conception of French poetry was introduced after mid-century by the *Pléiade,* a school of poets, led by Joachim du Bellay (1522-60) and Pierre de Ronsard (c. 1524-85), dedicated to making French the supreme vehicle of poetic literature. Ronsard was particularly successful in describing beauty and in depicting the most personal yet universal emotions.

Vernacular poetry flourished outside of France also, but not with the same balance of beauty, content, and form. The great period of Italian poetry ended with Lodovico Ariosto (1474-1533), whose masterpiece, the romantic epic *Orlando Furioso,* was the culmination of the medieval chivalric romances and the epitome of Italian Renaissance manners, morals, and splendor – a literary mirror of the age. Another peak was reached later in the century with Torquato Tasso's heroic epic, *Jerusalem Delivered,* depicting the story of the reconquest of Jerusalem in the first Crusade. The best Spanish poet of the Reformation age was Garcilaso de la Vega (1501-36), an erudite young Latin and Italian scholar, orator, musician, diplomat, and soldier, whose poetry was a model of tranquility set with deep feeling. Late in the century, lyric poetry found its chief Castilian exponent in Luis de Góngora (1561-1627), who, in his attempt to lift Castilian verse to new heights, succeeded by his verbal extravagances in drawing a curtain of obscurity between poetry and all but a narrow clientele of readers.

In the north, vernacular languages were less fully developed by the early sixteenth century and consequently produced less significant poetry and almost no top-ranked poets. Important because of its contemporary polemical impact, however, is Sebastian Brant's (1457-1521) *The Ship of Fools.* Doggerel poetry, *The Ship of Fools,* nevertheless, was effective social satire, and went through many editions. More lyrical were the German *Meistersingers,* popular composers and singers of light verse, who produced their most famous member in the shoemaker-poet, Hans Sachs (1494-1576), remembered still as the sympathetic protagonist of Wagner's *Die Meistersinger von Nürnberg.* Latin retained its primacy as the literary language of England far into the sixteenth century, but by the 1540's at least two writers had acquired some renown as English poets. These were Sir Thomas Wyatt (1503-42), a courtier of Henry VIII and admirer of his second wife, Anne Boleyn; and Henry Howard, earl of Surrey (1517-47), son of the powerful duke of Norfolk and cousin to the king's fifth wife, Catherine Howard. When the Howard star fell with the execution of the queen, Surrey lost favor and he too was beheaded, at the age of twenty-nine. Versatile and precocious, he introduced blank verse into English and composed graceful and polished sonnets. With Philip Sidney (1554-86) and

Edmund Spencer (1552-99) English poetry reached its Renaissance peak. Spencer was undoubtedly the finest of the Elizabethan poets, and his *Faerie Queen* ranks high among the literary creations of that day.

The crowning glory of the Elizabethan age, however, was secular drama, expressing to the fullest the emotional energy and intellectual versatility of the time. A galaxy of dramatic writers, culminating in Christopher Marlowe (1564-93) and William Shakespeare (1564-1616) set the tone and gave momentum to this popular medium. In Spain, too, drama reached its golden age in the last half of the sixteenth century and the beginning of the seventeenth with the compositions of Lope de Rueda (1510-65), Lope de Vega (1562-1635), Tirso de Molina (1571-1658), and Juan Ruiz de Alarcón (1581-1639).

Even more than in drama, Spain was preeminent in the development of the novel. From Fernando de Rojas' *La Celestina* (1493) to Michel de Cervantes' masterpiece, *Don Quixote de la Mancha* (1605-15) the Spanish novel set the pace for others to follow. Spain also pioneered in the creation of the "picaresque novel," exploring the adventurous lives of lowborn rogues and social outcasts to uncover the sham and pretense in society. The first of these entertaining and insightful novels was *Lazarillo de Tormes,* and the best is perhaps Mateo Alemán's *Guzmán de Alfarache.*

French prose was more influenced by the Reformation than was Spanish, and it often reflected the clash of religious ideologies. The most delightful and robust novelist of the period was Francois Rabelais (1494-1553). Enthusiasm, satirical humor, and rebellious freedom characterize Rabelais and his lusty giants *Gargantua* and *Pantagruel.* Condemned by the Sorbonne and added to the papal *Index,* Rabelais' books became "best-sellers" in their time. A unique genre of French literature reaching its zenith in the second half of the century was the essay. Its creator and most gifted exponent was Montaigne (1533-92), whose vivid and pithy insights into human nature have seldom been equalled and never surpassed.

Finally, the theological works of Luther and Calvin, and the vernacular translations of the Bible by Lefèvre, Luther, Tyndale, and Coverdale helped establish the literary preeminence of modern French, German, and English. Style, orthography, syntax, spelling, and vocabulary continued to change, as they should in living languages, but the direction and pattern of those changes owe much to the literary craftsmanship of the great sixteenth century writers.

• Mannerism

In the expressions of art, Italy set the style and tone just as she had for over 150 years. The splendor and glory of the High Renaissance would never again be attained, but new moods and motivations prompted new and interesting artistic responses. One of these is called mannerism, a term derived from the Italian *maniera,* or style. In the sixteenth century this was an artistic movement growing out of the High Renaissance, with certain characteristics in common with it (grace, refinement, attraction to the human figure, etc.), yet also an exaggeration and repudiation of it. The virtuosity of Michelangelo's later paintings, for example, helped make virtuosity a conscious objective. This in turn led to capriciousness, distortion, and eccentricity. In the early sixteenth century the artists were gradually liberated from total dependence upon the patron's commission and they emerged as creative masters in their own right, free to chose their own medium, subject matter, and theme. Mannerist painting of the period 1530-1570 reflected this freedom. It also revealed very pronounced emotional stresses and unresolved tensions, expressed in visual distortion, the elongation of graceful but sensuous human figures, and the idealization of forms beyond the natural.

The leading mannerist painters of Florence and Rome in the generation after Andrea del Sarto and Raphael were Jacopo Pontormo (1494-1556) and Rosso Fiorentino (1494-1540), who tried to create emotional experiences rather than to depict events or scenes. Similarly, Giulio Romano (1495-1546), Francesco Parmigianino (1503-40), and Agnolo Bronzino (1503-72) elaborated the style in their exaggerated elegance and idealized portraits. Mannerism was carried to France by Rosso and by Francesco Primaticcio (1504-70) who served Francis I for many years. The best example of the spread of mannerism into other parts of Europe may be seen in the paintings of El Greco (1541-1614), a Cretean artist trained in Italy and living most of his life in Spain. El Greco's technique was predominantly mannerist, and shows a strong religious emotion springing from the tensions of the Reformation and Counter-Reformation. The strain of his elongated and tortuous figures reveals not only mannerist stylism but suggests a deep religious imagery and a close identification with mystical experiences.

It should not be thought that all artists of the sixteenth century were mannerists. The Venetian tradition was largely unaffected by it (except for Tintoretto) and continued to flourish alongside mannerist art for most of the century. Venetian art, as exemplified in Titian (1477-1576), the most versatile and powerful painter of the century, Lorenzo Lotto (1480-1556), and especially Paolo Veronese (1528-88), emphasized vivid color and grandiose composition in perpetuating the High Renaissance through the stresses of the sixteenth century. For Venetian artists, as well as for others like Francois Clouet (1505-72) in France, Antonio Moro (1519-75) in Flanders and Spain, and Sanchez Coello (1531-88) in Spain, this was also the first great age of European portraiture.

"Knight, Death and the Devil," from an engraving by Albrecht Durer. Courtesy, Museum of Fine Arts, Boston.

• The Arts in Northern Europe

Further north a different spirit pervaded the world of art. In Germany, Switzerland, and the Netherlands art was not just influenced by the Reformation, it was overwhelmed by it. Few, if any, of the leading German artists, from Altdorfer and Grünewald to Holbein and Dürer, were unaffected by the religious upheaval. Albrecht Dürer (1471-1528), the greatest of the Renaissance German artists, was one of the first northerners to catch the spirit and vitality of Italian creativity, and the first to grasp the possibilities of printing and engraving as artistic media. But the Reformation overtook Dürer, forcing him to compromise his Renaissance confidence in man's will and power of achievement. His growing preoccupation with themes such as his *Melancholia,* the memorable *Knight, Death and the Devil,* and the *Four Horsemen of the Apocalypse* reveal his deep concern for the spiritual dilemma of man. Lucas Cranach (1472-1553), and many others like him, gave themselves entirely to the Reformation, using their artistic talents almost exclusively for pictorial polemics. Cranach provided the visual accompaniment to Luther's robust tracts. The Reformation likewise influenced the work of the greatest Dutch painter of the century, Pieter Bruegel the Elder (1528-69). But Bruegel remained the master painter of sixteenth century life, especially the personal lives of the simple Dutch country folk as he depicted them in his *Country Wedding* and *The Peasants' Dance.*

It is unnecessary to elaborate further the impact of the Reformation on sixteenth century painting. All of the arts were influenced and altered by the religious upheaval, and all forms of art responded in their own ways. Northern building and design underwent gradual change as Protestant services required a new form of emphasis and decor. In Catholic lands the effect was less pronounced until the second half of the century when the Counter-Reformation sparked a renewed enthusiasm for building and launched a dynamic new architectural style that would dominate southern Europe for almost a century. This was the beginning of the Baroque. It was first seen in Giacomo della Porta's façade of the Gesù in Rome (built by the Jesuits in 1568-73), in the rhythmic unity of Vignola's interior of the same church, and in Carlo Maderno's pulsating façade of Santa Susanna a few years later.

Of all the arts, music was the best suited to become an integral part of the religious experiences of the century. Luther took a great interest in church music and, although the musical role in the liturgy was altered in the Lutheran worship, it remained an important part of the religious service. Luther was the leading spirit in this musical renovation, from polyphonic chorals and liturgical chants to the hundreds of congregational hymns that became a hallmark of Protestant worship. Catholic music was associated closely with the mass and with the singing of large, trained choirs. The greatest of the Catholic composers was Palestrina (1524-94), organist and choir-master of the papal choir. His music expressed the vitality and grandeur associated with the Catholic Reformation and with the ensuing age of European Baroque.

11

National Monarchy and Religious Wars

AT THE CLOSE of the fifteenth century the territorial states of France, Spain, and England developed rapidly toward centralized, bureaucratic monarchies. Not yet "absolute," as they came to be called in the seventeenth century, they were gaining strength by consolidating national territory, controlling more effectively the centrifugal forces trying to pull them apart, and developing the institutional bureaucracy necessary to rule a modern state.

Monarchs in the Middle Ages were handicapped by the independent power of the nobles and by the unreliability of feudal military contracts. They did have a number of long-range advantages, however. The law of *escheat,* for example, allowed a fief to revert to the crown if the fiefholder died without heirs. Favorable financial arrangements between the king and the towns also worked to monarchical advantage when the merchants were willing to extend credit and loans to the king, or when the towns rallied to his support. The monarchs also profited from the rise of representative institutions, such as the Parliament in England, the Estates General in France, and the Cortes of Aragon and Castile, because through these bodies came the authorization for valuable taxes. Therefore, the keys to increasing monarchical power in the fifteenth and sixteenth centuries were the ability to raise royal revenues and the skill to limit or control the nobility. In most cases the two went hand-in-hand. One other asset, which some rulers took greater advantage of than others, was the increasing popularity of monarchy. For the ordinary man of the sixteenth century a strong crown usually meant more just laws, more equitable treatment, and no heavier taxes (if he lived in one of the remote provinces far from the capital they could even be lighter) than if he were under the jurisdiction of a feudal lord.

• The Development of Monarchy

Success in capitalizing on these advantages, and making others, depended largely upon the skill and ingenuity of the monarchs themselves – and upon their success in maintaining and prospering their dynasty through advantageous marriages. Among the most successful at all of these were the Spanish monarchs, Ferdinand of Aragon (1479-1516) and Isabel of Castile (1474-1504), King Louis XI of France (1461-83), and the founder of the Tudor dynasty in England, Henry VII (1485-1509).

Headway in limiting the power of the nobles came slowly in some cases, and was achieved only at great cost in others. Louis XI pressed too hard in 1465 and found he had a rebellion on his hands. The nobles in England were in continuous civil war between 1455 and 1485 (the Wars of the Roses), and weakened themselves accordingly. Henry VII was able to limit the nobles' right to maintain private armies in defiance of the crown, while Louis XI's son, Charles VIII (1483-98), diverted the energy of the French nobility into foreign war in Italy. Queen Isabel placed her husband, Ferdinand, at the head of all three orders of knighthood in Castile, thus assuring their loyalty in times of stress. The Spanish rulers still had many problems to overcome, however, because of the many institutional and traditional differences between the two kingdoms of Castile and Aragon. Gradually, they shifted much of the political jurisdiction of their realms from the nobles to royal councils, like the Council of Castile, the Council of Aragon, and the Council of the Inquisition. The latter was the first institution with jurisdiction in both kingdoms. Louis XI met the challenge of his most powerful vassal, the duke of Burgundy, by surrounding him with a cordon of diplomatic alliances and entangling him in a web of political intrigue. In 1477 the colorful Burgundian duke, Charles the Bold, was defeated and killed in battle and the duchy reverted to the French crown. Other Burgundian territories, however (Franche-Comté, Luxemburg, and the Netherlands), passed from Charles's daughter, through her marriage to Maximilian of Austria, into Habsburg hands. Nothing could prevent the duchies of Anjou, Maine, and Provence from becoming French by *escheat,* and no one did forestall the incorporation of Brittany by marriage.

• The Royal Revenue

Increasing the royal revenue was no easy matter for any of the monarchs. Henry VII was able, both by tight-fisted management and clever maneuver, to build up a tidy reserve, only to have his prodigal son squander it all on his first continental campaign. The French crown was financially more fortunate in that it had acquired the right to exact a direct general tax, called the *taille,* without recourse to the Estates General. With this additional income Louis XI and his successors were able to create the nucleus of a standing royal army and free themselves from total dependence upon the feudal levy. Money was, as a contemporary remarked, the sinews of war. The Spanish kings were hard pressed for cash – since neither they nor their French and English counterparts were strong enough yet to force the nobles to pay their share of the taxes – but received sizeable sums from the church (the *cruzada,* a "crusade" tax for war against the infidel, for example) and after the discovery of the New World began to supplement their income with American silver.

There remained, of course, many limitations upon the power of the crown, both theoretical and real. In all countries the nobility remained strong and relatively independent, although in the sixteenth century they identified more and more with the crown. Successful monarchs were those who could find ways of winning their allegiance and making them king's men. A more serious practical handicap for the rulers was the inadequacy of royal officials and the absence of an institutional bureaucracy for administering the laws. Finally, poor transportation and communication facilities further hampered the effective operation of government as national territories increased in size and widened further the separation between the king's theoretical and actual power.

With the French invasion of Italy in 1494 a new era opened in the political evolution of Europe. During the first half of the sixteenth century the war in Italy drew almost all of the European powers into its mire. International diplomacy, developed to a fine point of performance on a smaller scale in Renaissance Italy, expanded now to accommodate the practical needs of the ambitious and growing monarchies.

• France

At the center of this states system, both geographically and politically, was France. With fifteen to sixteen million people, it was the largest of the territorial states. It was also the wealthiest. To further increase its wealth and to occupy the restless nobility, Charles VIII had marched all the way to Naples in 1494. For the next half-century the two pivot-points of French policy were the attempt to dominate Italy and to prevent the Hapsburg encirclement of France. In 1515 the young and dashing count of Angoulême became King Francis I. His first gesture as king was a glorious new campaign into Italy, establishing his renown as a warrior and projecting France into another costly and eventually disastrous military involvement in the peninsula. The cultural consequences were more encouraging, for with renewed contact with Renaissance Italy came an artistic and architectural flowering in France, supported and encouraged by the king. Francis I was charismatic enough to enable him to retain the loyalty of the nobles even under adverse conditions, but he was also wise enough to maintain and develop strong organs of government, such as the *Conseil des Affaires.*

• Spain

His life-long rival, Charles V, was not so favorably endowed, yet the emperor made more of his gifts than did Francis. Through the complicated entanglements of marriage diplomacy, Charles of Ghent (born in 1500) gradually came into possession of more territory and potential power than any European ruler since Charlemagne. But Charles was not gifted with more than ordinary wisdom and ability. Slow at speech and thought, he succeeded by the strength of his character rather than by the sagacity of his mind. The chart below shows the steps by which Charles became, in turn, duke of Burgundy upon the death of his father, Philip of Habsburg-Burgundy (ruled by a regent during Charles's minority), king of Castile after the passing of his grandmother, Isabel, and the mental collapse of his mother, Juana (with his grandfather as regent until 1516), of Aragon with the death of Ferdinand, and archduke of Austria upon the death of Emperor Maximilian.

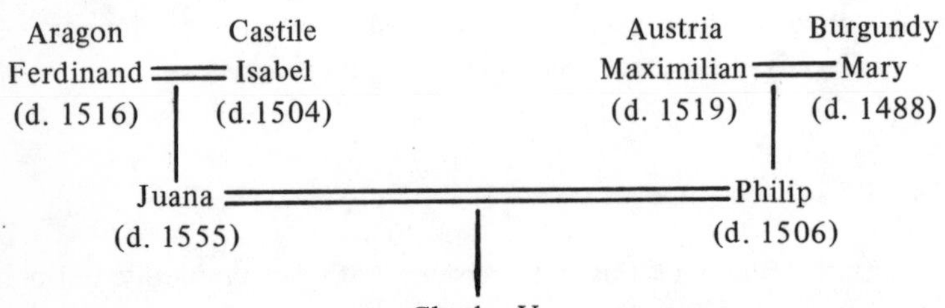

Maximilian's demise also vacated the imperial throne, and Charles was elected to succeed him (over rival candidates Francis I and Henry VIII) in July 1519. In addition, Charles V inherited all of the Aragonese claims to the Balearic Islands, Sardinia, Sicily and Naples, and the New World conquests of Castile.

But Charles's power was more theoretical than real. Each territory was held by separate right, and there were no unifying institutions of any kind for collecting taxes, enforcing laws, or fighting wars. He had to be a dozen different rulers, speaking a score of languages, in order to rule successfully. In Spain his reign began in civil war as the Castilian *comuneros* rose against his rule, and were joined by an equally serious Valencian uprising. Only gradually did it become apparent, both to the Spanish and to the emperor, that Spain was the most important part of his empire. He came to rely more heavily upon Spanish manpower and moneypower to maintain his position. Through the governing structure and economic machinery developed under Ferdinand and Isabel, Charles was able to rule effectively in spite of his long periods of absence from Spain. He was wise enough not to try to draw Castile and Aragon too close together, letting them retain their separate institutions, laws, and customs. The rapidly growing overseas empire was ruled primarily through Castilian institutions and by Castilian personnel. The system had many flaws but it was superior to most others of the time. Under Charles's hand Spain advanced to the rank of a major power.

• England

Of the other national monarchies only England aspired to the first rank during the early sixteenth century, although Scotland, Denmark, and Portugal also attained considerable importance. Henry VIII was responsible for giving England weight in international affairs, but he was likewise the cause of its greatest humiliation. England was small (some three million people at a time when there were six million in Spain, fifteen million in France, thirteen to fifteen million in Germany, and even four million in the Netherlands), but she played an important part in the diplomatic, religious, and governmental development of sixteenth-century Europe. English parliamentary rule, although not unique, was becoming more active and deeply established at a time when representative government seemed to be losing ground on the continent. Although Henry ruled despotically and capriciously, he received remarkable support and strength from Parliament and, consequently, continued to involve it in all of his affairs. By the time his daughter, Elizabeth, came to the throne, Parliament was more firmly a part of English government than it had ever been.

• Economic Growth and Social Unrest

To account for the rise of monarchy in the sixteenth century it is necessary to examine the changes taking place in economic and social affairs. Most of the 62,000,000 people of Europe were still engaged in agriculture, just as they were in the Middle Ages, producing wheat, rye, barley, beans, and peas for food, and flax, hemp, and other fiber crops for clothing, rope, and building materials. But in the sixteenth century some agricultural lands were being converted into more profitable use. One of these was the production of wool. Many landowners in England were enclosing the common lands to provide more grazing area for sheep. This enclosure of farm land brought huge profits to some but it had harmful effects on agriculture and even destroyed some of the small tenant farmers who depended on the soil for their survival.

In Spain the results of wool growing were even more detrimental because of the power of the sheep-raisers guild, the *Mesta,* which grew with the monarchy and soon dominated land policy in Castile. The unique migratory pattern of Castilian sheep-raising destroyed thousands of acres of farmland as the herds moved south in the autumn from their Leon and Soria grazing areas to sunny Andalucia, then north again in the spring.

Even without the encroachments of sheep and the devastations of war, European agriculture in the sixteenth century was seriously underproductive and unable to supply the demands of an expanding population. Industry, too, was unable to provide the basic essentials to achieve a well-fed and clothed society. Some ate and dressed sumptuously, but the majority of the population survived at a subsistence level. In the second half of the century important improvements in mining and metallurgy accompanied technological progress in the cloth industry, but they did not greatly alter the methods of production nor the patterns of consumption.

• Trade and Commerce

What did change dramatically in the sixteenth century was trade and commerce. Beginning with the discovery of America and the opening of an all-water route around Africa to India and southeast Asia, Europe experienced a veritable commercial revolution. This revolution took many forms and stimulated accompanying transformations in financial exchange, banking, and the distribution of wealth. The first impact of the European expansion was limited in scope but vast in its ultimate economic and political implications. Portuguese spice from the Malibar Coast of India, and later from the far off Moluccas, began the shift of trade from the

Mediterranean to the Atlantic (via Cape Horn and the Indian Ocean). This change was intensified by the discovery of America and the beginning of its trans-Atlantic commerce.

With the exploitation of New World silver, a boom in trade relationships and techniques followed. An international financial network developed, with trading houses from Cadiz to Amsterdam trading not only in commodities and wares but also in bills of exchange, loans, discounts, notes, and insurance. Lisbon flourished, Seville boomed like San Francisco in the gold rush, and Genoa got its share of the action via loans to Castilian entrepreneurs. But the greatest financial beneficiary of the Atlantic trade was Antwerp, where Charles V's favor, the Portuguese spice staple, Spanish and English wool, and the international monetary exchange all crossed. The "spin-off" from the Antwerp bourse was enough to make many cities in the Netherlands wealthy. Lyons, too, and the cities of south Germany profited from the financial activity. The Fuggers of Augsburg, who helped Charles V win the imperial crown became the chief bankers of the empire.

• The Price Revolution

Among the many related consequences of the commercial expansion was the rapid increase in prices throughout Europe, and especially in the south. This movement of prices began early in the century, reaching inflationary proportions after 1560, and was most extreme in foodstuffs, especially grain. This so-called price revolution fluctuated greatly in different regions and times, but it amounted to an overall increase of approximately 400 percent in the price index for the century. Wages did not keep pace with these prices and as a result most wage-earners were caught in a serious wage-price squeeze that diminished the real value of their money and lowered their already precarious standard of living. Also, those landowners who could not raise rents were caught in the same squeeze and frequently forced into bankruptcy or poverty. On the other hand, many of the well-to-do gentry, some nobles, and most of the merchant adventurers profited from the financial situation as they were able to use the inflation to their advantage. Governments, too, were affected by inflation, causing taxes to be raised and creating even greater difficulties in the payment of debts. By the end of the century Spain had gone bankrupt four times.

The causes of the sixteenth-century price revolution were multiple. The rapid influx of bullion from the New World had traditionally been identified as the principal culprit. It is now believed that other factors such as the shortage of land, the competition for jobs, and increasing population may have had more causal effects than the import of precious metals.

It is certain however, that the flood of silver into the European economy after mid-century helped to maintain and probably increase the inflation that had already begun.

• The Growth of Population

The economy is always closely linked with the density and movement of population. Evidence is abundant that the population of sixteenth-century Europe increased by eighteen or twenty million souls (or about 30 to 40 percent). A comparable increase in our time would be considered stagnation, but in the 1500's, after a century or more of declining population, this growth represented a veritable population "explosion." The increase was not uniform nor steady. It seems to have been the greatest in France during the first part of the century, and in Germany, Italy, and England in the latter half.

The demographic movement also seems to have been toward the cities, making some, like Seville and Madrid, that were little more than rural towns when the century began, large and thriving centers at its end. The great cities of Italy – Naples, Venice, Milan, Genoa, and Florence – continued to grow during the period, as did Palermo, Messina, and, spectacularly, Rome. Many northern cities now became economic and political crossroads, and some of them cultural centers as well. Paris, which had long been the largest city north of the Alps, nearing half a million inhabitants by 1600, was a teeming metropolis with every virtue and vice known at the time. Antwerp thrived on finance and trade, as did Amsterdam a generation or two later. London quadrupled its population in little over a century.

The surge to the cities was part of the broader economic and social unrest of the time. It came partly from the population pressure on the land and on the food supply and from the widespread desire of men to seek their fortunes in the cities. The Reformation also contributed to the growth of cities as converts to new faiths sought strength and solace in numbers. With the decline of feudalism, most peasants in western Europe were now free to move about, to compete with others for employment, and to choose their professions. But without money, in a money economy, these "freemen" were no freer than their ancestor serfs had been. Many of them became rural workers, struggling to make enough pennies a day to keep themselves and their families alive. Those who went to the cities without money and without a trade soon became lost in the jungle of nondescript buildings and inhospitable people.

Both town and country provided raw material for civil unrest and disorder, and, when a cause was provided, open revolution. It is small wonder, then, that most sixteenth-century governments interpreted their primary functions to be maintaining order at home and preventing attack from abroad. But disorder came, nevertheless. Hardly a year passed without insurrection or revolt in some part of the land. No country was exempt. Causes were never the same, but among those most frequently expressed were excessive taxation, political or social oppression, religious restraints, or the violations of some medieval rights. The *comunero* revolt and *Germanía* shook Spain in 1520, five years later the Peasants' War afflicted Germany, and recurring upheavals in the empire, in Italy, and in England reveal the social unrest of the times. Up until 1562, France had been relatively free from major disturbances. But its time of sorrows was about to begin.

• France and the Wars of Religion

During the second half of the sixteenth century, the French monarchy experienced its most serious crisis. Well-established and generally popular by 1559, it was subjected to extreme challenges thereafter when King Henry II (Francis I's son) was accidently killed in a tournament celebrating the end of the Hapsburg-Valois Wars (Treaty of Cateau-Cambrésis, 1559). He left the throne to a succession of immature and weak-charactered sons and a Florentine wife whose maternal concern for her children caused irreparable damage to them and to France.

Henry's and Catherine de Medici's oldest son was fifteen-year-old Francis II. Sickly and dominated by his wife's uncles (of the house of Guise), Francis lived less than two years. The throne then passed to nine-year-old Charles IX, who was only slightly more healthy than his brother and possessed no attributes of kingship. Catherine de Medici ruled as regent until Charles came of age, and after that as queen mother, telling her son what to do. When Charles IX died in 1574 he was succeeded by yet another son, Henry III, who was strong-willed, robust, and intelligent. But, being completely untrustworthy, dissolute, and psychotic, he proceeded to dissipate his reign until he was assassinated in 1589. Only the strong will of the queen mother and the institutional strength of the monarchy as established in earlier reigns carried it through these disastrous decades.

In 1562, Calvinist Huguenots in France accepted the challenge hurled by the extreme Catholic faction in France, led by the duke of Guise, and civil war broke out. It was a bloody orgy for France, self-inflicted and seemingly interminable. In additon to being a religious war fought between militant Calvinists and rabid Catholics, it was a factional struggle between rival nobles. The house of Guise represented one extreme, with the Bourbons of Navarre and Bearn (particularly Henry of Navarre and his cousin the Prince of Condé) on the other. The Montmorency, Chastillon, and the Valois were arrayed on one side or the other.

Economic distress and social dislocation added further causes for rivalry and war. Recurring financial crisis contributed to fear and distrust, and the heavy imposition of taxes added resentment and defiance. The spiralling inflation, which was reaching serious proportions, further diminished wages and profits, causing widespread despair. Some of these factors led many French nobles, who were caught by inflation and had lost their land to the speculators, to join the Huguenot ranks following the peace of Cateau-Cambrésis.

Catherine de Medici tried hard to prevent civil war. She negotiated incessantly with all parties in an effort to reduce tensions. But when she gave concessions to the Protestants the Catholics became aroused, and when she leaned toward the latter the opposite occurred. By 1572 peace finally seemed within grasp. A treaty was signed and, as was the custom, it was sealed in a marriage alliance between the former foes. Henry of Navarre, leader (with Gaspard de Coligny) of the Huguenots, was wedded to Marguerite of Valois, daughter of the queen mother. To celebrate the occasion thousands of Huguenots were in Paris on St. Bartholomew's Day (August 24). Jealous of the influence Coligny exercised over her son, the king, and fear that Charles might succumb to Coligny's pressure for war on Spain, Catherine abandoned her usual level-headedness and convinced herself that the safety and security of France depended on the assassination of Coligny. Henry of Guise willingly accepted the assignment, which he then botched. Coligny was only wounded. The Huguenot nobles reacted spontaneously with demands of punishment and threats of retaliation. Catherine panicked, issuing, instead, an order for the extermination of all Huguenots in Paris. From the capital the carnage spread into the provinces. The Massacre of St. Bartholomew's did not end the civil wars, it rather guaranteed that they would continue on for many years to come.

So successful was the Huguenot resurgence after St. Bartholomew's that in the next peace settlement in 1576 they were granted broad freedoms and guarantees. In reaction, Catholics formed a league to resist Protestant advances and assure the succession of a Catholic king. Henry III being without children, the heir to the throne became Henry of Navarre, leader of the Huguenots. The Catholic leaguers were alarmed. With the duke of Guise at their head they negotiated a treaty with Spain to come to their aid. Philip II sent diplomatic advice and occasional money, but when the crisis occurred in 1588 he was too involved launching his own Armada

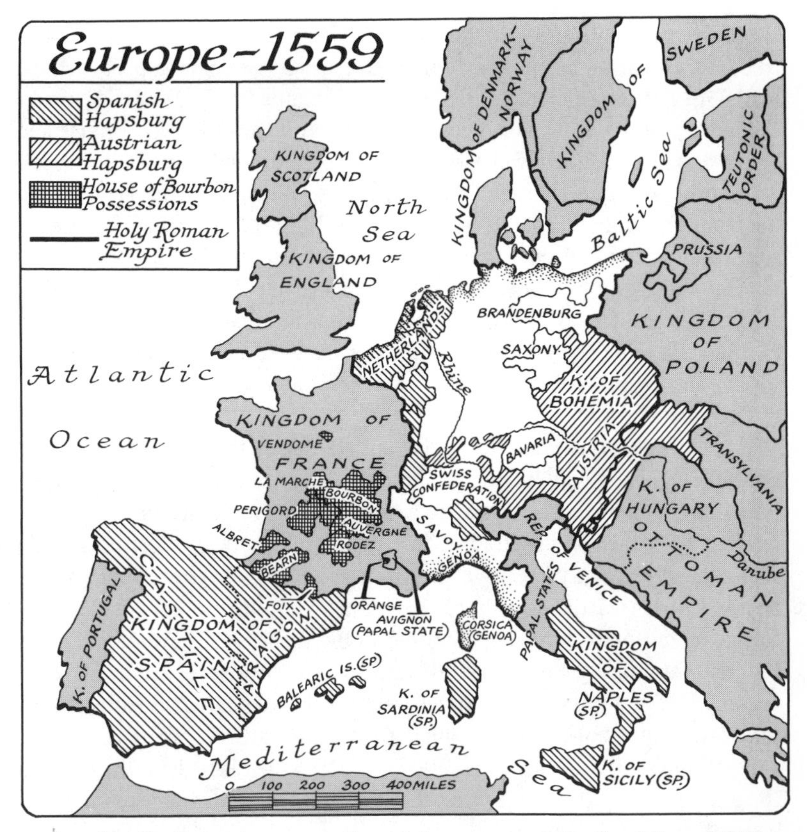

against England to give more than token support to the duke of Guise. Paris responded on the "Day of the Barricades" by supporting Guise; King Henry fled for his life, and the Catholic League became the ruler of northern France. Nine months later (December 1588), Guise was assassinated by order of the king and the wars suddenly took a new turn. Henry fled to the camp of his former foe (and brother-in-law), Henry of Navarre, and together they began the siege of Paris. When the last Valois was in turn assassinated in August, 1589, Navarre declared his accession as Henry IV. But it still required six years of struggle, and his own submission to the Catholic Church (recognizing that "Paris was worth a mass") before Henry IV was finally accepted and crowned king.

• Henry IV and the Edict of Nantes

The recovery of France under the first Bourbon monarch was spectacular, but not totally sound. It was achieved largely through Henry's administrative skill and his charismatic ability to unite the dissident factions into a nation again. Energetic and magnanimous, he approached his task with enthusiasm and confidence. He concluded the war with Spain by the Treaty of Vervins, which restored the status quo between France and Spain as it was following the wars in 1559. Safe now from foreign intervention he was free to attack the domestic problems at hand. He placated his former Huguenot friends by issuing the Edict of Nantes, giving a measure of religious and civil freedom to the Protestants. Nantes was important in the history of religious toleration because it allowed a minority religious group to exist and practice a faith other than the official religion of the state. The Huguenots were further declared eligible to hold public offices and guaranteed the right to use schools and other facilities the same as Catholics.

Henry demonstrated his willingness to uphold the edict by raising his trusted Huguenot lieutenant, the duke of Sully, to the high post of superintendent of finances (he was already director of communications, superintendent of fortifications and buildings, and grand master of artillery). The role played by Sully in the centralization of French government under Henry IV was particularly large. He immediately instigated monetary reforms, established a bureaucratic order in the financial structure, and made the tax farming system more efficient than it had ever been. He even accumulated a surplus in the royal treasury. By removing previous restrictions on grain exports, reintroducing silkworm cultivation in the south, and reclaiming thousands of acres of wasteland, he made agriculture flourish once more – thus prompting the king's promise of a chicken in every peasant's pot every Sunday.

Sully's promotion of the famous "Paulette" may not have been so wise. By this system of sanctioned venality, purchased offices became hereditary and their tenure secure upon the payment of an annual fee to the government. This practice added money to the royal coffers, thus assisting the Bourbon rulers to their claim to absolute power, but it also curtailed that power by depriving the king of complete authority over administrative offices.

By 1610 French recovery had been successful enough for Henry to resume an aggressive role in foreign affairs. In his memoirs, Sully attributes to Henry a "Grand Design" to neutralize Hapsburg power through a system of protective alliances and European-wide councils. It is doubtful that Henry's grand design was so comprehensive, although he did fear Habsburg power and aimed his diplomacy to counter it. But at that moment his life was cut short by an assassin's knife. His brief, turbulent reign ended in turbulence. When the aggrandizement of France and the French crown was resumed by Richelieu fourteen years later, it was along the lines already begun by the illustrious Henry, whom Frenchmen still lovingly refer to as "Henri le Grand."

• The Influence of Spain and Philip II

The rise of Spain in the sixteenth century, from a conjunction of poor and sparsely populated kingdoms inhabiting the Iberian highlands to become the leading power in Europe, is certainly spectacular. When Charles V abdicated his thrones in 1555-56, his Austrian territories went to his brother, Ferdinand, who was also elected Holy Roman Emperor. The Burgundian (Netherlands and Franche Comté) and Spanish realms, with their empires, went to Charles's son, Philip II.

Philip was a reserved, solitary, intensely serious man, slightly built and distinctively Hapsburg appearing, with his light hair, protruding jaw, and thick lower lip. Outwardly cold and impassive, Philip was sensitive to the world of literature and art, and he was an avid patron of letters and science. His personality pervaded much of Spanish society during the forty-two years of his reign; it was particularly felt in government, where austerity, formality, and frugality were the marks of the regime. Philip took his duties as king seriously, working long hours himself and expecting his subordinates to do likewise. He was so meticulous about every detail of government that at times the wheels of administration almost ground to a stop while he read memoranda, dictated replies, and penned scrawling annotation in the margins of diplomatic correspondence.

Philip ruled through the system of councils established by Ferdinand and Isabel and expanded by his father. Chief among these were the Council of State, composed largely of Castilian nobles, and smaller administrative councils responsible for the affairs of Castile, Aragon, Italy, and the Indies. These were made up primarily of trained legal personnel (*letrados*). Liaison between councils and crown was provided by secretaries of state, who also served in a broad field of responsibilities from simple private clerks to advisors on royal policy. For the first half of his reign Philip was served in this capacity by Gonzalo Pérez and his capable but overly ambitious son, Antonio Pérez. After the latter's fall in 1578, several men of varying abilities shared the secretarial office. Philip's closest personal advisor on high policy matters was Antoine Perrenot, cardinal of Granvelle, until he died in 1586.

• The Spanish Empire

In Philip's reign the overseas empire became increasingly important. It represented not only Spanish dominion and power, it furnished increasing amounts of valuable silver to replenish Spain's over-committed coffers. Wool had been, along with wine and olives, the principal source of export income. With the developing of the Guanajuato and Potosí mines, silver now began to flow in. From something like nine million ducats value in the first five years of Philip's reign, it rose to twenty million during 1575-80, and surged to forty-two million in 1590-95. This represented no more than 11 or 12 percent of the annual crown income, but it was an important 11 percent. With it the king was able to borrow on the expected return and finance projects that he should have left alone. Inflation ate up a large share of the increase, and the rest went to Genoese and German bankers to pay previous debts. Thus, neglect of agriculture, as population shifted to the cities, the displacement of the Moriscos, and the costly military escalation in the Netherlands, Portugal, England, and France all had disastrous effects on the Spanish economy, forcing Philip to resort to higher taxes and seek help from the church to finance his government.

• Spain and the Catholic Church

The working relationship between Spain and the Catholic Church was close. Their cultural affinities were deep and their political ties necessary. The Spanish people were devoutly Catholic and their rulers had always been defenders of the faith. Philip was no less dedicated than his ancestors had been in fighting heresy and rooting out corruption. Religion was an integral part of everything done in Spain, by monarch and people. It was natural, therefore, that Spain should become the backbone of the Counter-Reformation and Philip the champion of Catholicism throughout Europe. To say Philip was devoted to the church, however, does not mean he was subservient to the will of the papacy. Frequently their policies clashed and on occasion (during the pontificates of Paul IV and Sixtus V) Spanish-papal relations were openly hostile. Philip was always ready to submit to God's will, but he was not always convinced the pope knew that will any better than he did.

A chronic religious and social problem of Philip's reign was the presence of hundreds of thousands of Moriscos (Moors converted to Christianity) who continued to revert to Islamic practices and worship while outwardly observing Christian rituals. Government pressure to bring them into line resulted in open rebellion in 1569. The revolt was serious and widespread, requiring almost two years of military campaigning to suppress. The Morisco revolt was doubly dangerous because it coincided with the new Turkish offensive in the Mediterranean, which overran Cyprus and threatened to cut off Christian trade to the Levant. In 1570 Spain joined with Venice and the papacy in a new Holy League against the Turk. In early autumn 1571 the combined armada, commanded by Philip's twenty-four year old half-brother, Don Juan of Austria, met and defeated the Turkish fleet of over 300 galleys in the Bay of Lepanto. The victory at Lepanto secured Philip's Mediterranean flank and allowed him to turn his attention again to his serious problems in the north.

• Spain's Relations with England and the Netherlands

The Treaty of Cateau-Cambrésis had brought peace with France in 1559. But it was a precarious peace, one that required constant vigilence during the French civil wars. Closely related to the situation in France was Philip's relations with Scotland and England. Civil war and religious upheaval in Scotland drove Mary from the throne and presented Spain with a major dilemma. Not to help Mary meant victory for the Calvinists, but to assist her would give support to France and to her ambitious Guise relatives. Similarly, Philip had to pursue a cautious policy with Elizabeth of England. He hoped to keep England as an ally, as she had been during his father's reign, but Elizabeth was clever enough to keep him guessing about her intentions and thereby neutralize his strength. The most vital area of Philip's affairs was the Netherlands. As the richest part of his empire, and the most difficult to rule, it presented to the Catholic King a problem of growing concern.

The revolt of the Netherlands against Philip's rule began gradually and picked up momentum as the king tried awkwardly to counter Dutch demands and tighten royal control. In 1566 he sent the stern duke of Alba to establish law and order there. Alba succeeded only in pouring fuel on the fire by his ruthless regime, and soon half of the provinces were in arms against the king. William of Orange (William the Silent) became the hero of the Dutch as he took up their cause with vehemence and skill, riding the crest of the revolt to become stadholder and commander of the armies of Holland, Zeeland, Friesland, and Utrecht. Alba was recalled in 1573, but his more conciliatory successor died of typhus three years later. Don Juan of Austria was then assigned the onerous task, and he died two years later, after having accomplished little. Finally the duke of Parma, Philip's young nephew, Alexander Farnese, was sent to try his luck. Parma was a statesman and diplomat as well as a military man, and came as close as anyone could to ending the struggle. But he arrived too late. No one in the Lowlands was willing to compromise any more. Parma did draw together most of the southern states in the Union of Arras (1579), which was quickly countered by William of Orange with a rival league of the north, known as the Union of Utrecht, dedicated to opposing and overthrowing the Spanish rule. In 1581 the States General of the northern league formally deposed Philip II and began looking around for someone else to reign. Although it was not apparent yet, this Act of Abjuration marked the beginning of Dutch independence. From this point on the United Provinces, as they were called, grew and flourished in a remarkable way.

• The Spanish Armada

Spain was not able to prevent the loss of the Netherlands because she could not control the Channel and prevent the almost constant reinforcement of materials and men from Elizabeth's England. Eventually Philip became convinced that the key to the Netherlands was England. To crush the Dutch rebels by putting a stop to Elizabeth's aid, and at the same time topple her heretical reign and restore Catholicism to England, Philip ordered the preparation of the Spanish Armada. Its aim was to sail up the English Channel, rendezvous with Parma and escort his army across the Channel for an invasion of England. English Catholics were expected to rise to their support and the whole affair would be over in a few weeks. It turned out to be the most costly blunder of Philip's reign.

Building a fleet of the size required was impossible. Compromises had to be made. In 1580 the crown of Portugal passed to Philip, giving him a second nucleus around which to construct the fleet. When it finally sailed in July 1588, under the command of the duke of Medina Sidonia, the Armada was composed of some 130 vessels, but only twenty or so were front line war galleons. The rest were large cargo hulks, galleys, and small flyboats. The English fleet, commanded by Lord Howard of Effingham, was equally as large, and much closer to replenishing supplies. But the failure of the Armada was not due to the English fleet, although on the last day of the encounter it did inflict heavy damage on the Armada, nor to the "winds of God," although the northern gales did nearly destroy all that was left of it as it limped around Scotland and Ireland on its long voyage home. The cause of defeat was Philip's failure to secure a suitable Channel port for the rendezvous with Parma's army. Without it Parma could not move, and without Parma, Medina Sidonia had no choice than to return to Spain – by the only route left. The war with England, thus foolishly begun, dragged on for the last ten years of Philip's life.

Queen Elizabeth, from an engraving by Crispin van de Passe, Sr. Courtesy, Museum of Fine Arts, Boston.

• The England of Elizabeth I

Elizabeth dominated the English scene in the second half of the sixteenth century just as Philip did in Spain. She was a strong-willed, mercurial monarch, yet capricious and often irresolute. She was intelligent, witty, and charming when charm was required. She was also thrifty, even parsimonious, with the finances of state, but when it came to the royal wardrobe the queen was prodigal in the extreme. Believing that the people vicariously identified with their monarch, and that even her lavish dress and display became personalized in each of her subjects as they beheld her, she accomplished many extravagant processions and progresses through the cities and provinces in order to see and be seen.

The society ruled by Elizabeth was in chronic ferment, yet remarkably stable. The top ranks of the structure – peers and titled nobility – were compact and influential. They possessed privilege and power as well as extravagant wealth. Yet, in some ways their position was precarious. Depending upon royal preferrment and patronage, as did all office holders in the realm, they had to watch their step carefully to keep their place. Below them in rank was the amorphous body of landed gentry, knights, squires, and gentlemen, who possessed heraldic arms but not aristocratic titles. Their ranks were in constant agitation as money, preferrment, and differences in skill caused fluctuations in the fortunes of many. The Elizabethan yeomen were also more flexible than their ancestors had been, but the unpredictable nature of the times made their life critical too.

The city merchants formed an aristocracy of their own, based on money and credit. During Elizabeth's reign they made solid gains – which they usually converted into land and became "respectable" gentry. Artisans and urban wage earners could not so easily control their lot. With their country cousins, the propertyless peasants, they made up the bulk of Elizabethan society – poor, wretched, and hopelessly confined to their miserable condition. Indigence and vagrancy were common, even though they were cruelly punished. Not until the Elizabethan Poor Law of 1598 was legitimate unemployment acknowledged and a small step taken to ameliorate it.

The structure of Elizabeth's government was essentially the same as that of her predecessors, except that she reduced the size of the Privy Council and used it more effectively. Her chief minister and confident was Sir William Cecil, principal secretary and lord treasurer, who in 1572 she made Lord Burghley. Other key figures in her personal rule were her long-time favorite, Robert Dudley, earl of Leicester, and the inexorable Sir Francis Walsingham, principal secretary after 1572. Parliament was summoned thirteen times in Elizabeth's forty-four year reign, but for a total of only three years in session. It played an important role in providing money for the queen, although it was not allowed to discuss many matters of state which Elizabeth considered to be her prerogative alone. By the end of the reign the House of Commons, especially, was becoming increasingly stubborn about granting the queen's wishes. Her successor reaped the results of her tight rein.

• Elizabeth's Religious Policy

Elizabeth's settlement of the religious dilemma when she became queen in 1558 was wisely conceived and skillfully engineered, steering a careful middle course between Catholic and Protestant extremes. Moderation and expedience were the principles of the queen's reign in religious matters as well as in politics and diplomacy. The legislating of the religious settlement was provided by two acts of Parliament: the Act of Supremacy, which repealed Mary's religious legislation and designated Elizabeth "Supreme Governor of the Realm," and the Act of Uniformity, which restored the general liturgy and doctrines of Edward VI's reign. In 1562 a new Anglican confession of faith, known as the Thirty-Nine Articles, was adopted. This confession was a revised edition of Cranmer's Forty-Two Articles, with three of the more anti-Catholic sections removed in order to make it more palatable to them. Elizabeth chose the moderate Protestant divine, Matthew Parker, as archbishop of Canterbury to help implement her policy of compromise. Still, the settlement was a precarious balance at best, aided in some measure by the unpreparedness of either extreme to capitalize on Queen Mary's sudden death.

During the next few years religious tensions increased again. Factional disagreements arose over such matters as the form of the communion service and the use of clerical vestments and the chalice. Furthermore, Catholics became increasingly disillusioned as the English church took an unmistakable Protestant direction. At the same time, radical Protestants and Puritan reformers, including Marian exiles now flocking back from Geneva and other Calvinist refuges, advocated a more thorough-going reformation. After 1570 both Papists and Puritans became threateningly vociferous in their demands.

As English Catholics became more disruptive, with the infiltration of Jesuit trained missionaries, and as Puritan influences in the government increased, the severity of anti-Catholic laws grew correspondingly. The crisis came in the 1580's in conjunction with the rising international tensions involving Spain, France, and the Netherlands. Many heads rolled, most of them Catholic priests', as the threat of foreign invasion became imminent. Still, the fact that both Papists and Puritans continued to subsist in England, and that many shades of theological divergence were still tolerated within the Anglican Church, makes the Elizabethan religious settlement remarkably successful.

• Elizabeth's Foreign Policy

Elizabeth's foreign policy, like her religious management, was predicated on political expediency and characterized by caution, ambiguity, and even dissimulation. She was faced with the traditional enmity of France and Scotland, hostility from Rome, and at best the uncertain friendship of Spain. Elizabeth met these challenges with forthright indecision. As with her dilatory marriage policy, which she used to great advantage in foreign affairs, the queen retreated from any situation that would commit her to an inflexible course or that would force the hand of her enemies. Her policy was preventative: to impede a possible alliance between Spain and France; weaken the Spanish position in the Netherlands without strengthening that of France; glean as much economic and strategic advantage as possible from limited assistance to the Dutch rebels, without provoking Spain to attack; and to play off the Scottish nobles against one another, thus safeguarding her vulnerable northern flank.

Until the mid-1580's Elizabeth was successful. But eventually she was drawn into the European ideological conflict on the side of the Protestants by the combination of Spanish truculence, Anglo-Spanish maritime rivalry, Puritan pressures, Catholic plots, French impotence, and Dutch persistence. In 1585 the queen reluctantly committed her resources to a formal alliance with the Dutch. The following year an expeditionary force under the earl of Leicester landed in the Netherlands to assist in driving out the Spanish. Peace did not return during the remaining eighteen years of Elizabeth's reign.

• Hawkins and Drake

In the meantime, "beyond the line" (on the open sea) there was never peace. To augment the nation's meager economic income from relatively stagnant agricultural production and a narrowly-based wool and cloth trade, Elizabethan merchants gradually began to diversify and expand their commercial operations. Interest in the newly discovered Russian trade led to the founding of the Muscovy Company. Sir Humphrey Gilbert and The Merchant Adventurers sent expeditions to discover a northwest passage to India. Martin Frobisher and other English seamen sailed to the New World. Economically, the most successful of the English ventures was John Hawkins's thriving slave trade with Spanish America. The enterprise was illegal but it brought handsome profits to Hawkins, and to the queen. In 1568, one of Hawkins's expeditions was surprised by a Spanish flotilla in the harbor of San Juan de Uloa. Only two of his ships managed to escape and return to England; one of those was commanded by Sir Francis Drake.

For the next twenty-eight years Drake carried on a relentless personal feud against the king of Spain. In 1571-73 the Devonshire seaman was again in the West Indies, this time looking for plunder not trade. From 1577 to 1580 he pillaged the Spanish ports of Peru, captured a silver galleon off Panama, and then sailed for the Moluccas. When he returned to England after circumnavigating the globe he became the greatest English hero alive. His feats stimulated the English imagination and spirit as nothing else had done. He excited Elizabethan England in the manner Columbus and his immediate successors had awakened Spain. Soon other English seamen were venturing into the unknown seas and taking part in the free-lance war against Spanish shipping and trade. When war came, the English fleet was reaching its pinnacle.

The Armada encounter of 1588 was not decisive, even though the English fleet did inflict heavy damage to the Spanish. The ensuing naval war was even less conclusive. The following year, Drake led the "English Armada" in a counter-attack on Spain. His mission was to destroy the remnants of the Spanish Armada and land an invasion army in Portugal. It was as unsuccessful as the Spanish had been. Nearly half of its 25,000 men and 120 ships were lost. In 1595 Drake and Hawkins led a new expedition to the West Indies intending to capture the Spanish treasure fleet and devastate its American bases. This venture was not only a failure, it was an English tragedy, since both Hawkins and Drake died before the fleet returned. A year later another English fleet, under Lord Howard, the "Armada victor," sailed into Cadiz harbor. The town was sacked, but the victory was hollow for the fifty or more loaded merchantmen Howard had intended to capture were burned by the commander of the Cadiz garrison – who was none other than the duke of Medina Sidonia. Philip II retaliated with two more armadas in 1595 and 1597, but violent storms drove them both from the English Channel. The naval war was still a stand-off – profitless and disappointing for both England and Spain – when the two monarchs passed from the scene at the turn of the century.

• Sixteenth-Century Science and Thought

The sixteenth century was preeminently the century of religious thought and controversy. The Reformation and Counter-Reformation pervaded all aspects of life during that age. Religion was a motivating factor in politics and in war. Nevertheless, it was also an age of diversity and expansion. The discovery and conquest of new worlds across the seas opened new vistas and suggested new possibilities for human endeavor. Growing awareness of the complexity and diversity of nature and the aspiration not just to imitate nature but to transcend it, led to challenging new ideas and novel approaches to long-held notions. This was the age of Renaissance as well as Reformation. And the Reformation, too, represented the courageous questioning and challenging of traditional ideas.

The sixteenth century was not an age of great scientific discovery and thought, but it was a time of innovative suggestion and of intellectual preparation. The marvelous strides in scientific method and achievement taken in the seventeenth century did not come about in a vacuum. They developed out of the thinking and questioning of previous ages. The Renaissance humanists contributed to the inquisitive spirit of the time by making available to study for the first time the entire canon of Greek scientific writings, from Archimedes and Appolonius to Eratosthenes. By their enthusiasm for Plato, the humanists also revealed Plato's fascination with numbers, forms, and mathematics, which in turn affected all phases of scientific thought in the following centuries.

The desire to know and understand stimulated many men of the sixteenth century to investigate phenomena written of by the Greeks and the Arabs, and to push on into new territory themselves. Such a man was Nicholas Tartaglia (1500-57), who demonstrated the solution of cubic equations, and Girolamo Cardano (1501-76), his brilliant but erratic pupil. Pioneering work in chemistry and medicine was done by the bombastic and controversial Paracelsus (1493-1541) while he pursued his mystical formulations as an alchemist. More substantial was the anatomical study and teaching of Andreas Vesalius (1514-64) as he meticulously dissected cadavers and described the details of their structure to his students. His *Fabrica* (1543) carefully describing in words and pictures the parts and functions of the body, is a noteworthy achievement of Renaissance science.

• Copernicus

A very different kind of achievement was the *De Revolutionibus* (*On the Revolutions of Heavenly Bodies*) of Nicolaus Copernicus (1473-1543), also published in 1543, at the time of his death, but written in 1530. Copernicus was an Italian educated Polish mathematician, lawyer, physician, and priest, who spent the last thirty years of his life making such stellar observations as his poor eyesight would permit, and compiling his computations and thoughts into his magnum opus. He put forth the view that the sun was motionless at the center of the universe, that the earth revolved in a circle around it (while rotating on its own axis every twenty-four hours), and that the stars were motionless at the circumference of the universe.

There was something "revolutionary" in Copernucus's suggestions, but he did not intend it to be too radical. He was essentially conservative, hoping to rectify and fulfill the Aristotelian-Ptolemeic system rather than replacing it with another. The elements and conditions remained the same, the circular and uniform motion of the planets was retained, and the teleological assumptions of the system were unchanged. The only real difference between Copernicus's universe and Ptolemy's was his interchange of the sun and earth, with its accompanying simplification. However, in his having the earth move instead of the sun there were some religious implications. This prompted Copernicus to postpone publication of his work (when it was published it was put forth simply as a mathematical proposition rather than as a fact), and helped keep it from general acceptance thereafter. But the main reason for its unpopularity was that it raised insoluable new problems and failed to explain many of the old observable phenomena. In the second half of the century the Danish astronomer Tycho Brahe (1546-1601) provided careful observations and detailed stellar tabulations that made possible the revolutionary contributions of Galileo and Kepler.

In the meantime, the role of Copernicus, like that of Tartaglia, Paracelsas, Vesalius, and other sixteenth-century scientists was important, although for different reasons than are commonly given. In each case these men brought the scientific work of the Greeks and Arabs to its logical culmination and perfection. In so doing they also raised issues and problems that helped stimulate renewed activity during the following century.

• Sixteenth Century Philosophy

The most ambitious attempt to reconcile the dichotomies of science and religion in the sixteenth century was launched by the restless Italian philosopher Giordano Bruno (1548-1600). Bruno liked the heliocentric system of Copernicus but carried it much further by claiming it as fact, and by asserting the infinity of the universe, unlimited by crystaline spheres, and containing innumerable planetary systems like our own. Bruno anticipated many notions that were later established by observation. His conception of infinity and the imperishability of matter infused his philosophy of God with a new "scientific" speculation, and led him to conceive of God as the infinite cause that permeates and energizes the universe. But Bruno's attempt to articulate his religious ideas in terms of the Copernican universe eventually got him into serious trouble with the Inquisition. He was arrested in Venice, spent eight years in Venetian and Roman prisons, and finally burned at the stake.

Two other philosophers helped bridge the gap in scientific thought from Copernicus to Bacon and Descartes. The first of these was Bernardino Telesio (1508-80), who insisted that nature must be understood in her own terms according to experience and observation. Telesio attacked Aristotle's conceptions of matter and form, and his denial of a Creator. He substituted a conception of the universe composed of divinely created matter acted upon by the force of heat and cold to produce, through expansion and contraction, all motion and objects in the universe. His very independent disciple, Tommaso Campanella (1568-1639) held that all knowledge was founded on experience and conscious reasoning, and that knowledge, along with power and will, were the principles of being. For Campanella, nature was as direct a revelation of God as was the church, and should be read and obeyed with equal devotion. Although he was a devout Catholic, this conviction did not endear him to the Roman authorities and he spent much of his life in prison. Campanella extended his speculations into the realm of politics, his *City of the Sun* being the most serious attempt since More's *Utopia* to describe the ideal society.

• Sixteenth Century Political Thought

Political thought followed many avenues in the later sixteenth century due to the multiplication of loyalties created by the Reformation, but they led to some original and significant contributions. The cockpit of political controversy was France, where the wars of Religion gave theoretical disagreements a knife-like edge. Huguenot pamphleteers were among the first to stress the limited nature of monarchical government and even brought the idea of kingship itself into question. Francois Hotman (1524-90) argued in his *Francogallia* (1573) that the monarch was historically limited by law and by custom, and advocated the election of kings in France and their supervision by the Estates General. Theodore Beza (1519-1605) maintained that the authority of the king was granted by contract and if he fails to observe his political and religious duties he could be removed, through the proper divine authority. By similar arguments, the pseudonymous author of the *Vindiciae contra Tyrannos* (1579) limited the power of the monarch through a double contract, one between God, the king, and the people, and the other between the king and the people (as a community not as individuals).

Surprisingly similar to these revolutionary views of the French Protestant *monarchomachs* (monarch haters) were the anti-royalist writings of the Spanish Jesuits, Juan de Marina and Francisco Suárez, and the Italian Roberto Bellarmino. Like Hotman, Mariana (1536-1624) advanced the thesis that the king derived his authority from the people through a contract, and could be deposed by them. He even justified tyrannicide under certain circumstances (see *On the Authority of the King,* published in 1595). Suárez (1548-1617) advocated the limitation of monarchy in a more traditional way, arguing that the pope possessed the right to regulate the authority of the secular rulers, since he was the universal head of Christendom. Cardinal Bellarmino (1542-1621) also espoused the universal authority of the pope, in spiritual matters at least, but affirmed that the secular rulers derived their civil power from the community by contract.

Yet, in spite of these and other arguments for the limited and contractual nature of monarchy, the trend by the end of the century was unmistakably in the other direction, toward strong, centralizing governments and monarchical absolutism. Both in practice and in theory this was an age of enlarging authority rather than extending liberty. The most systematic and influential elaboration of a theory of strong central government came from the French jurist Jean Bodin (1530-96). The key to Bodin's justification was his definition of sovereignty as the power of a monarch to make laws binding upon everyone but himself. This sovereignty, Bodin explained in his *Six Books of the Commonwealth* (1576), comes to the king by natural law, not by contract or agreement. It is perpetual and inalienable, and the ruler is accountable only to God for its use. For that reason, no individuals or corporate groups have the right to oppose or resist the king. This right of sovereignty, which Johannes Althusius (1557-1638) defined as the "preeminent, supreme and universal power which governs all that concerns the spiritual and temporal welfare of the subjects," points directly to the seventeenth-century elaboration of Divine Right and other justifications of absolute monarchy.

Suggestions for Further Reading

Grimm, Harold J., *The Reformation Era, 1500-1650* (1965)

Elton, G. R., *Reformation Europe, 1517-1559* (1964)

Koenigsberger, H.G., and G. L. Mosse, *Europe in the Sixteenth Century* (1968)

Holborn, Hajo, *History of Modern Germany: The Reformation* (1959)

Spitz, Lewis W., *The Religious Renaissance of the German Humanists* (1963)

Bainton, Roland H., *Erasmus of Christendom* (1969)
Schweibert, Ernest G., *Luther and His Times* (1950)
Brandi, Karl, *The Emperor Charles V* (1954)
Rupp, Gordon, *Patterns of Reformation* (1969)
Rilliet, Jean, *Zwingli, Third Man of the Reformation* (1964)
Clasen, Claus-Peter, *Anabaptism: A Social History* (1972)
Dickens, A. G., *The English Reformation* (1964)
Scarisbrick, J. J., *Henry VIII* (1968)
Mattingly, Garrett, *Catherine of Aragon* (1963)
Pollard, Albert F., *Wolsey* (1966)
Chambers, R. W., *Thomas More* (1958)
Ridley, Jasper, *Thomas Cranmer* (1962)
McNeill, John T., *The History and Character of Calvinism* (1967)
Walzer, Michael, *The Revolution of the Saints* (1969)
Daniel-Rops, Henry, *The Catholic Reformation* (1962)
Dickens, A. G., *The Counter Reformation* (1969)
Brodrick, James, *The Origin of the Jesuits* (1960)
Shearman, John, *Mannerism* (1967)
Elliott, J. H., *Europe Divided, 1559-1598* (1968)
Heritier, Jean, *Catherine de Medici* (1963)
Mahoney, Irene, *Royal Cousin: The Life of Henri IV of France* (1970)
Elliott, J. H., *Imperial Spain, 1469-1716* (1966)
Lynch, John, *Spain under the Habsburgs,* vol. 1 (1964)
Kamen, Henry, *The Spanish Inquisition* (1965)
Ortiz, Antonio Dominguez, *The Golden Age of Spain, 1516-1659* (1971)
Geyl, Pieter, *The Revolt of the Netherlands* (1966)
Mattingly, Garrett, *The Armada* (1965)
Neale, Sir John, *Queen Elizabeth I* (1957)
MacCaffrey, Wallace K., *The Shaping of the Elizabethan Regime* (1968)
McGrath, Patrick, *Papists and Puritans under Elizabeth I* (1967)
Wernham, R. B., *Before the Armada* (1966)
Fraser, Antonia, *Mary Queen of Scots* (1969)
Williamson, James A., *The Age of Drake* (1965)
Allen, John W., *A History of Political Thought in the 16th Century* (1960)
Boas, Marie, *The Scientific Renaissance, 1450-1630* (1962)
Bonansea, Bernardino, *Tommaso Campanella: Renaissance Pioneer of Modern Thought* (1969)

THE SEVENTEENTH CENTURY

12

Absolute Monarchy at Its Height

AFTER THE TURBULENCE of the sixteenth-century's religious wars, the period from 1600 to 1715 looks like an age of retrenchment, with a consolidation of power so great that we call its products "absolute monarchies." Defined briefly, absolute monarchy was the old royal form of government, but with its ruler claiming full sovereignty over his territory and subjects. This meant that no subject or internal group such as a church could have a loyalty outside the state greater than to the ruler. It meant also that the ruler was freed or absolved (hence the term absolute) of all theoretical controls by his subjects or their assemblies, though in fact the royal will was sometimes bent by powerful pressure groups. Finally, it intensified international conflicts, as princes tested their growing power in clashes between their states.

As we shall see, the most effective of these absolute monarchies was France, which fought off internal rebellion and external threats from Spain and Austria during the Thirty Years' War of 1618-48, and then, under Louis XIV, became the model of that type of government. That monarch also took on most of Europe's other states in a series of wars, although this unwittingly helped the emergence of England and Austria, major opponents, as great military powers. To the east, Russia at long last began to realize its potential as a great, European power.

In order to understand these developments, it is necessary first to examine the background of the seventeenth-century economy, society, and political ideas. Economically the century was a period of prolonged depression reaching its low point around the 1640's and 1650's. This was in sharp contrast to the sixteenth century's economic boom of rising population, agricultural expansion, and the influx of New World silver and gold. Seventeenth-century society was, of course, substantially the hierarchical one of clergy, nobles, townsmen, and peasants that had existed during the immediately preceding centuries. Yet the way in which the various social groups clashed with each other and with the state was very distinctive of the hard times of the 1600's. Political ideas were framed as a response to social clashes, economic stagnation, and the religiously motivated foreign wars and internal revolts that swept across western and central Europe.

• The Economic Situation

By 1600 Europe had gone about as far as it could with medieval banking, industrial, and commercial techniques. The New World's silver mines that had primed the economic pump during the sixteenth century began to run dry, leaving the continent without the coinage that had helped inflate prices and the economy. Prices slumped, and there were few private banks and fewer state ones that could pick up the slack by providing alternatives to cash, such as loans and bills of exchange. The one hopeful sign in banking circles was the emergence of the semi-state Dutch Bank of Amsterdam. It served as the normal exchanger of Europe's many state monies. This enormously boosted international commerce. Merchants could trade easily across borders, and seller and buyer alike figured profits and costs with precision since all foreign coins exchanged through the Amsterdam bank were listed in terms of its own bank money. Toward the end of the seventeenth century, the Bank of England, established in 1694, showed that semi-state banks could serve another purpose. For it was the intermediary between merchants eager to have a sure investment and a state that badly needed to borrow regularly at a low interest rate.

• Industry, Agriculture, Trade

Industrial and agricultural production did not, in general, advance during the seventeenth century. Indeed, there was a striking setback in southern Europe, especially the Italian peninsula, whose woolen, silk, and metallurgical industries produced as little as a tenth of what they had a

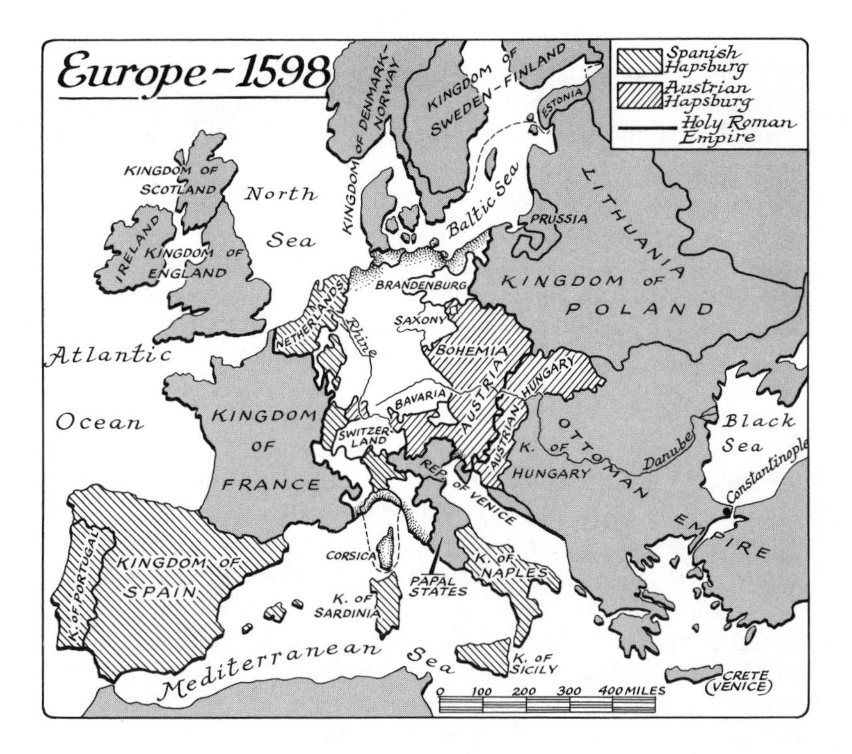

century before. In eastern Europe, where the raw products of the field, stream, and mines were crucial to the economy, the "solution" to a slackening of prices and demands in western Europe was a dismal one: rather than improve agricultural methods noble owners of estates tried to get the most of the soil by turning their working peasants into unfree serfs. Western European agriculture was slightly better off. The centuries-old trend from serfdom to free peasant status continued, and in the Netherlands some initiative was taken in improving crops. Northwestern Europe was the main bright spot in industry also. Ironically, this may have been partly due to almost continuous warfare. Soldiers needed guns, uniforms, and other equipment, and as the century wore on and states increased the size, discipline, and equipment of their armies, the cloth, mining, and metallurgical industries benefited. Another factor in the industrial development of northern Europe was the influx of skilled workers and wealthy entrepreneurs from the south. These people were eager to flee to places with a greater interest in investing in commerce, industry, and mining (rather than country estates, purchasable government office, and church buildings), and greater religious and intellectual tolerance. England, Holland, northern German port towns, and Sweden reaped the greatest economic windfalls from this population shift. Amsterdam alone grew from a quiet town of three thousand households to some hundred thousand persons, many of them refugees from the southern, Spanish Netherlands.

We quite rightly think of the seventeenth century as part of the golden age of European expansion, citing the foundation of East India Companies by England, France, and Holland, as well as the colonization of the northern, central, and southern American coastlines. However progress was often superficial. The French traced the course of the Mississippi river but established only two thousand settlers in Canada by 1660. In Spanish-dominated central Mexico, sixteenth-century colonization was followed by a fivefold drop in the European and native population to 2.5 million, disease and economic collapse providing the new world with its first local "depression" in modern times. European penetration of Africa was limited to parts of the west coast, while in the far east Dutch, English, and Portuguese traders fought among themselves for the "prize" of paying out badly needed silver and gold for Asian products. In truth, trade between western and northeastern Europe was more significant economically for Europeans than the scramble for furs, silks, tobaccos, and spices of the nonEuropean world. Even that European trade went into the doldrums during much of the seventeenth century, with the notable exception of the Dutch (who managed to become important middlemen in the exchange of goods as well as of monies) and, at the century's end, of the English.

• Human Misery

It is difficult for us to sort out the causes from the symptoms of the economically depressed conditions of the 1600's. But some things are clear. There simply were not the manpower, money, and food to keep Europe even on the moderately prosperous level it had reached by the 1500's. In particular, the population levelled off, and then fluctuated wildly between lows caused by terrifying plagues and crop failures brought on by a century of cold, damp weather, and highs produced by good crops and the natural tendency of the population to double itself in a generation unless checked by natural disasters. In human terms, the misery was greater than in economic statistics, but we can grasp the picture if we realize that a person was considered old at forty, and that babies surviving their first year were only one-third of those born. Medical practices did little to help. Louis XIII of France ruefully noted on his deathbed that he would have lived much longer if it had not been for his physicians! War was a grim reaper, of course, even if we can doubt the figure of a 40 percent loss of the German population during the Thirty Years' War. Plague was another grim reaper, reportedly carrying off 130 thousand souls in Naples in the single year of 1656. The population of many areas was decimated by such general crop failure periods as 1648-52, 1660-63, 1675-79, 1693-94, and 1709-10.

The poor were struck more savagely than others by the vagaries of fate, a staggering generalization when one notes that even in economically advanced England, those on relief amounted to one-sixth of the population at the century's end, while fully one-half of the people were too poor to pay for the "poor" through alms and other donations. As we move up the social scale, we find better diets, sanitation, and access to food in times of scarcity; hence one French town could save 60 percent of its bourgeois children before age fifteen, as opposed to only 40 percent of workers' offspring. Probably the aristocracy were the most fortunate. In England, at least, the aristocracy seem to have shown their optimism by having larger families than their social inferiors. And princely and noble families could somehow escape the summertime stinking, smog- and disease-infested air of Paris, London, Florence, and a dozen other major cities by retreating to the clear air of their country estates and palaces. Even so, Louis XIV saw death carry away all his legitimate children, and all but two of his grandchildren and greatgrandchildren, as well as his first wife. Little wonder that nobles, office holders and merchants frequently established family memorials in the form of chapels in the corners of great churches, or that educated and unlettered alike could make witchcraft a popular belief, and desperately looked to palmistry, astrology, and even the elixir of life as ways of either explaining cruel fate or trying to outwit it. The terrible economic and social conditions make it perfectly intelligible why there were more witches in the seventeenth than any other century – they were a convenient scapegoat.

• Popular Rebellion

Another "escape" was rebellion, for it was easy to give vent to one's angry frustrations by killing tax collectors, and turning harvest festivals into a bloodbath against one's landowner and master. "Popular rebellion," that is uprisings by the towns' wageearners and the rural peasants or serfs, were almost constantly on the minds of rulers, nobles, and merchants. The Anglican church service tried to instill the "people" with the idea that they must obey their social and political authorities, while in France Richelieu viewed the poor as mad dogs who needed to be chained, or at least kept working and uneducated. We can list a few of the popular revolts: the tax revolt of the "Barefooted Ones" in Normandy in 1639; uprisings in Sicily and Naples against foreign Spanish tax collectors and hated local nobles a decade later; mob uprisings that tore apart the already assassinated body of a French royal favorite, Concini, in 1617, and killed two Dutch political leaders, the de Witt brothers, then removed their fingers as souvenirs in 1672; the widespread south Russian revolt of Cossack nomad-warriors and their peasant followers against the Polish state in the 1650's; and the massive uprising of down-and-outs under Stenka Razin against the Russian state and higher society in the 1670's.

• Rebellion and Stability among the Middle and Upper Classes

Some of these revolts involved a few of the middle and upper classes as well, especially when the target of revolt was the state. However, rebellion led and composed of the wealthy and titled was usually a different kind of phenomenon, even when it occurred at the same time and place as lower-class uprisings. It was not as terrifying or bloody as a rule, since its armed rebellion was often by relatively organized armies (sometimes whole companies of the state's army seduced into rebellion by loyalty to the noblemen-captains), and the opposition often worked peacefully through regular channels, such as assemblies of the well-to-do (England's Parliament) or law courts (the Parlement of Paris). The major revolts can be listed here, and will be noted again when we deal with individual states: the "Time of Troubles" in Russia, 1605-13, concerning a dispute amongst nobles and others over succession to the throne; the war of independence by Portugal against Spanish rule, 1640-52; the abortive constitutional revolt of the Parlement of Paris and succeeding military rising of the French nobility, together called the Fronde (1648-53); the Puritan Revolution that temporarily abolished the English monarchy, 1640-60; the brief but fierce war by Bohemian nobles for automony from Austria, 1618-23; and a similar Hungarian uprising against the Austrians in the 1670's and again in the 1680's.

For the most part, however, bourgeois and noble subjects did not take out their frustrations in rebellion like the artisans and peasants. Middle-class people, whether merchants, government officials, or members of medical or other professions, were more interested in improving themselves socially by the peaceful means of buying patents of nobility from their king, purchasing noble estates and dressing like noblemen, or buying the highest governmental posts that included the right to call their holders noblemen. As for the nobilities, they had already arrived at the top socially, to be envied by every ambitious social-climbing peasant, merchant, or craftsman. Unless they were stripped of their political and social roles at royal courts, or deprived of their time-honored right to duel among themselves, turn their castles into impregnable fortresses, or tyrannize over their peasants, they remained relatively peaceful.

The main incitement to middle- or upper-class revolt was still the religious hatred that continued from the Reformation well into the seventeenth century. Here was a real "cause" to be fought over, a motive that could make persons of every walk of life forget the age's ingrained belief that everyone should remain submissively in his social class and respectful of his political superiors whether these were parish priest, lord of the village, town mayor, provincial governor, or king. Religious passion led to the following bloody deeds, listed chronologically: the assassination of Henry IV of France in 1610, the revolt of Protestant Bohemians against Catholic Austrians in 1618, the resumption of the Calvinist Dutch war of independence against Catholic Spain in 1621, and the Puritan Revolution against the Anglican state culminating in the execution of Charles I in 1649.

• The "Divine Right of Kings" Theory

The main political idea that arose to meet this social unrest and economic depression was the famous divine right of kings. In order to fend off the assassin's dagger, and make subjects contented with their lot, royal propagandists simply extended the medieval belief that God favored the royal form of government, thereby making the king's person as well as his office look divinely inspired. Thus in the words of the French prime minister and cardinal, Richelieu, "the king is the likeness of God, God's regent on earth and the one who works out His providence." How then could seventeenth-century persons question divine-right absolutism, let alone begin to think of any viable alternative?

The deep religious roots of absolute monarchy, and especially the notion of destructive human will going back to Adam's Fall, made it natural to think of the state's purpose as restraining the beast in men and women. The old medieval principle of "natural law" was also brought up to date as further support for absolutism. Originally natural law had meant those principles of morality and justice that human beings could come to know through their God-given rational faculty. In its secular seventeenth-century version, "natural law" became transformed into the set of principles that the observation of human nature deemed necessary for human survival. For example, the great English absolutist Thomas Hobbes, in his

Leviathan (1651), observed that man's selfish tendencies made for a "war of all against all" in the "state of nature." Hobbes concluded that this human instinctive right to do anything had to give way to a more practical set of natural laws. Basically these called for persons to give up their rights to an all-powerful state in return for protection of life.

• Locke's Theory of Individual Rights

As the seventeenth century progressed, however, both divine-right and natural-law defenses of absolutism began to lose their appeal, partly because they had done their work in calming down subjects, and partly because they became less meaningful in a changing intellectual climate. There was a gradual secularization of European society, illustrated by the fact that Louis XIV referred to "God" far less frequently in his letters than Louis XIII had. Hence to speak of one's divine right made less sense. Then, too, Hobbes' version of natural law dissatisfied persons who were beginning to realize that the growth of the centralized state made it possible to hope for more than merely law and order. In short they suggested that if subjects were to give up some old-fashioned freedoms, they should expect to receive back more than just the guarantee of life.

These developments set the stage for the most famous book on political thought in the century, and probably the most influential of all time, John Locke's *Two Treatises of Government* (1689). Locke boldly stated that humans are born with "natural rights" to life, liberty, and property. He was also firmly convinced that most human beings would respect these rights, that is, that the "state of nature" was not a state of constant fighting as Hobbes thought, but one of basic trust. This made it possible for Locke to establish his famous social contract. That agreement let the people keep their natural rights while giving up to a government the power and right to protect and enforce those rights. The implications of Locke's natural rights' philosophy were startling. First, he made government the servant of the people, rather than assuming that persons were born into and automatically beholden to governments. Secondly, he paved the way for an increasingly optimistic view of what governments could do, anticipating the notion that government can help humans in the right to "life, liberty, and the pursuit of happiness." Third, in the short run he strengthened the position of the well-to-do in society and politics. His idea of natural rights really meant that those who had property (a distinct minority in his day even in England) had it purely of their own doing, and owed nothing to government or society for it. This "self-made" man ethic

The Gold Weigher, from an etching by Rembrandt. Courtesy, Museum of Fine Arts, Boston.

made him also assume that property owners alone should partake in government by electing representatives from among themselves to legislate, and watch the royal executive branch of government. But, fourthly and finally, Locke's stress on human dignity and respect for others made it possible for the individual liberties of the few to be broadened eventually into the human rights of the many in a democratic society. It should be heavily underscored however, that Locke's main influence was on eighteenth-century thought, while most seventeenth-century thought centered on divine-right absolutism. Hence we should think of divine right, the Fall of Adam, and political turmoil in trying to make sense of the activities of rulers in the 1600's.

• Mercantilist Doctrines of the State

Just as rulers thought of their divine right to impose order on their rebellious subjects, so too, they considered it their prerogative to control all economic activities within their states. The basic assumption behind this principle of "mercantilism," or state-controlled economy, was that there was a fixed amount of wealth in the world. It naturally followed that if rulers were to have a strong army and peaceful, if not happy, subjects, they should try to secure as much as they could of this total. The crudest version of mercantilism was called bullionism, which tried to stockpile bullion or the raw metal for gold and silver coins by preventing the import of goods from other states if paid for in coin, and seeking to sell as much as possible outside the realm for cash.

Bullionism was associated most closely with Spain's rise to power through New World bullion during the late sixteenth century. Hence the collapse of Spanish might in the seventeenth century as bullion supplies dwindled necessitated a more sophisticated version of mercantilism. States fought to achieve a favorable balance of trade, and therefore an increase of bullion, by making certain that imports be somehow offset by exports. In France native luxury items, such as silks, were developed by state aid and protected by tariffs against Italian silk goods. Everywhere native shipping was developed to seek out markets, and England insisted on regulating shipping interests even after it dropped some other economic controls in the late seventeenth century. Water ways were dredged in France, and a canal dug to link Prussia's main rivers, the Elbe and Oder, thus facilitating trade within states. And, as every American student knows, Spanish, French, and English colonies were meant to supply raw materials and purchase the home country's manufactures, in both cases keeping wealth within the confines of the state.

Only the Dutch managed to escape the rigors of mercantilism, and that was because they knew that as the world's greatest coinage broker, trading middleman, and possessor of the largest merchant marine, they could afford to let trade flow freely: after all much of it passed through their hands, and they profitted handsomely. At the other extreme were eastern European states, notably Prussia, Sweden, and Russia, which went beyond western European regulation of the economy by having the state run its own industries and mines, largely because they lacked the bourgeois wealth and skill to let private entrepreneurs do the job.

The significance of mercantilism should be kept in perspective. It was designed to serve the state, not its subjects. Hence it was not a cure-all for the century's social and economic ills, though it did help to damp down the flames of unrest by protecting the economy and even distributing some of the wealth among subjects. In the words of the English statesman and philosopher, Francis Bacon, money was "like muck; good to be spread around." Just how far was this money spread? Poor and rich commoners alike knew that the nobility still counted most with rulers, economically as well as socially and politically. The poor might, if lucky, receive help from state and private charity, especially in Holland, England, and France. The rich commoner might, if lucky in his contacts at a royal court, receive a monopoly on making soap or mining copper, while other merchants had to fend for themselves. Meanwhile the nobility, from Spain to Sweden, and from Russia to Naples, received court pensions, government sinecures, and tax exemptions, all of which were paid for ultimately by the rest of society.

• The Thirty Years' War

Economic, social, and political problems came to a head most spectacularly in the Thirty Years' War of 1618-48, especially in the confederation of states called the Holy Roman Empire. These lands were constantly crisscrossed by rival Protestant and Catholic armies made up of fellow Germans, only to suffer the further injury of invasion by foreign armies on behalf of the Catholic and Protestant German sides. Before the fighting was over the Holy Roman Empire had been the victim of no less than four phases of the war: an abortive Protestant revolt in the kingdom of Bohemia against the Catholic Holy Roman Emperor; the ill-fated intervention by the Danish king against the Emperor's side in support of the survivors of the Bohemian cause; the more successful intervention by Sweden's king on behalf of German Protestants against the Emperor and other Catholic German princes; and, finally, the involvement of Lutheran Sweden and Catholic France for their own interests and the rights of individual German princes against the absolutist drive of the Holy Roman Emperor.

• The Holy Roman Empire

The Holy Roman Empire was tailor-made for this conflict which we call the last of the religious wars and the first modern, secular conflict. It was a loose confederation of states or principalities whose princes were virtually autonomous of the power of their titular ruler, the Holy Roman Emperor. This made for tension between the "German liberties" or right of self government by these various dukes, electors, archbishops, and bishops, on the one hand, and the desire of the Emperor Ferdinand (1619-37) to impose his will on them, in other words to turn the Empire into an absolute monarchy. The tension was all the greater, since many of the princes were Protestant while Ferdinand was a dedicated Catholic who was every bit as interested in saving the souls of his Protestant princes and their subjects as he was in being politically absolute.

Most of the trouble arose from the patchwork settlement of 1555 that had ended the earlier religious war of the German Reformation with the general provision that each prince could impose either Catholicism or Lutheranism on his subjects. Lutheran princes, notably the Electors of Brandenburg and Saxony, constantly broke one of the subordinate clauses by taking charge of church lands, that is, lands ruled secularly as well as religiously by Catholic bishops or archbishops. Naturally Catholics wanted to uphold the 1555 principle that church lands were very different from secular ones, and hence should remain Catholic. Calvinists led by the Elector of the Palatinate were even more resentful of the 1555 arrangements, since these made it technically illegal for Calvinism to exist in the Empire, or for a prince to be Calvinist. And if those political and religious sparks were not enough to explode the German powder keg, the Holy Roman Empire's lack of strong central government and state army like those in France, Spain, and Sweden, was enough to invite trouble.

Those three states and others were eager to send their troops into the German lands in the name of religion and for the sake of territorial conquest, if the settlement of 1555 should ever break down completely and bring civil-religious war to Germany.

• The Bohemian Revolt, 1618-23

The war began with a revolt by the Bohemian subjects of Ferdinand. In 1618 that Austrian Hapsburg prince was not only about to be elected as Holy Roman Emperor, but was in the process of bringing together under his personal rule some key family territories previously divided among his relatives. The most important were Austria, Hungary, and Bohemia. The trouble was that Ferdinand's Catholicism and absolutism ran headlong into the privileges of his Protestant noble subjects in Bohemia. Their revolt started spectacularly with the famous "defenestration of Prague" in 1618: representatives of the Austrian Hapsburgs were tossed out of a window of the Prague palace, escaping with their lives, but sustaining a loss of dignity and an insult to princely authority.

The rebellion was ill-fated however, since it never managed to get enough outside support to match the power of Ferdinand. He was able to enlist the support of major Catholic princes of the Empire constituting a Catholic League, complete with army and the leadership of the Duke of Bavaria. This was enough to win the battle of White Mountain late in 1620 against the Bohemian nobles and outside Protestant forces led by the Calvinist Elector Frederick of the Palatinate, who had made the mistake of accepting the Bohemians' offer to be their king in place of the deposed Ferdinand. By 1623, the Bohemian revolt was over, and the Calvinist Palatinate was turned over to Maximilian of Bavaria and the Spanish branch of the Hapsburg family that had also helped Ferdinand as relatives and territorial opportunists.

• The Rise of Austria

The Bohemian revolt really began the rise of Austria to major-power status, as the Austrian Hapsburg, Ferdinand, imposed absolutism on his Bohemian subjects during the rest of the 1620's. Noble lands were turned over to Catholic carpetbaggers who swarmed in from all across Europe and Protestant worship was all but obliterated. The Bohemian assembly or diet was stripped of essential powers. And Ferdinand made certain that there would be no further revolts or depositions of rulers in Bohemia by changing its constitution so that the Bohemian crown would henceforth pass down through the male Austrian Hapsburg line in hereditary succession.

• The Danish Phase, 1625-29

Ferdinand may have started the rise of Austria, but his success against his Bohemian subjects and the Elector of the Palatinate caused a backlash in the northern states of the Holy Roman Empire and beyond. Terrified by the northward march of the Catholic League's armies and fearful lest their religious and political liberties be also crushed, the north German princes fought back. The war entered its Danish phase as king Christian of Denmark placed himself at the head of these German Protestants. His position resembled somewhat that of the hapless Elector of the Palatinate. As a Lutheran and a prince of the Holy Roman Empire (he was duke of Holstein) he had two good reasons to support German Protestant princes. And he also wanted to take over some Catholic church states to round out his kingdom. Unfortunately for Christian, the Catholic League's army and a second force under the Emperor's personal commander, Wallenstein, were able to overwhelm the Protestant coalition within four years.

In 1629 Ferdinand was at the height of his power. Denmark was forced out of the war. German Protestant seizures of Catholic church lands since 1555 were declared illegal by the Emperor, and repossession proceedings began. Nearby, the Spanish branch of the Hapsburgs, fresh from their takeover of the Rhineland holdings of the Palatinate were sending troops from Spain's Italian possessions along the Rhine to the Netherlands in an attempt to reconquer the Dutch provinces that had broken from Spain in the sixteenth century.

The Swedish Phase, 1630-35

Ferdinand's successes brought another Lutheran ruler, king Gustavus Adolphus of Sweden, into the war. This "Lion of the North" who already had conquered most of the Baltic shores from his neighbors and turned Sweden into a great military and economic power took over key German ports on the Baltic, and then swept southward. Until his mysterious death in battle in 1632, Gustavus Adolphus was well on his way to dominating the Empire, so much so that he frightened his German Protestant allies almost as much as his Austrian and other Catholic foes. His death shifted back the balance to the imperial Catholic side. By 1635 Emperor Ferdinand was in the enviable position of being able to expect concessions from German Protestantism, while his Spanish cousins were still hopeful of subduing the Dutch rebels.

The Franco-Swedish Phase, 1635-48

Abruptly, the Swedish phase became the Franco-Swedish phase. Though a Catholic state, France felt that it had to intervene against Catho-

The Siege of La Rochelle, from an etching by Jacques Callot. Courtesy, Museum of Fine Arts, Boston.

lic Austria and Catholic Spain. Otherwise those two Hapsburg states would become so successful against the Swedes and the Dutch that they would, together, encircle France and threaten it with annihilation. That fear had already prompted France's chief minister, Cardinal Richelieu, to give financial support to both the Dutch and the Swedes. He had also attempted (unsuccessfully) to wrest from Spain some key Swiss and Italian posts on the Spanish supply line from Italy to the Netherlands. Now in 1635, Richelieu had to intervene openly and more directly against the Hapsburgs. French forces teamed up with the Swedes and some German states against the Emperor, while French and Dutch forces held off the Spaniards. In 1648 the German side of the war came to an end by the treaties of Westphalia. The same year Spain recognized definitively the independence of the Dutch republic. France continued to fight with Spain until the Peace of the Pyrenees in 1659.

The Peace of Westphalia in Germany

What had been accomplished by the Thirty Years' War and the accompanying Dutch-Spanish and Franco-Spanish conflicts? In the first place, the Holy Roman Empire had escaped Austrian imperial absolutism, and the famous "German liberties" of the princes were strengthened, announcing the emergence of absolutist princes within the formal structure of the Empire. German princes henceforth could virtually dictate their own foreign policy as well as control their own taxing, judicial, and military affairs. Moreover, their religious rights were broadened in the sense that now a prince could impose Catholicism, Lutheranism, *or* previously outlawed Calvinism on his subjects. Catholic church lands were parcelled out to the state, Catholic, Lutheran, or Calvinist, that had actually held them in 1624, a compromise that satisfied the princes in general, regardless of their faith.

Religious rights of subjects were another matter. These went against the grain of the emergence of princely absolutism at Westphalia, and specifically against the principle that the ruler would determine (impose) the religion of his subjects. All that princes would concede were the right of subjects to move to a more religiously congenial state, and the right of practitioners of the prince's faith to toleration if he adopted another faith. In practice, many princes did decide that war had proved the futility of forcing conformity to one church. The Elector of Brandenburg in particular became famous for tolerating all faiths, and of inviting religious refugees to his realm. The Holy Roman Emperor in his capacity as prince of Austria, Hungary, and Bohemia, was more typical however. He insisted on ramming his religion (Catholicism) down the throats of his subjects, especially the Bohemians.

Miseries of the War – The Hanging, from an etching by Jacques Callot. Courtesy, Museum of Fine Arts, Boston.

• The International Settlement of Westphalia and the Pyrenees

Internationally, the settlements demonstrated the emergence of absolutism on an even grander scale than within each principality of the Holy Roman Empire. Several of the European states that had intervened in the war became much stronger as a direct result of the wartime disciplining of economic resources and strengthening of border defenses. Sweden reached the height of its power, establishing bridgeheads at the mouths of key north German rivers, and at home utilizing its copper and other mines for war industries and trade with other states. France pushed its frontiers into the Rhineland, the Spanish Netherlands, the Savoyard Alps, and the Spanish Pyrenees mountains. Other states held their own. The Dutch republic (though not absolutist) showed that a country with the economic know-how we have already seen could survive the fury of the Spaniards even with a weak federal constitution. And Spain, though shorn of its Dutch provinces, battered by French forces, and in severe economic decline, at least managed to maintain the political absolutism that king Philip II had achieved by 1598. Europe was on its way to becoming a continent of sovereign military states driven by secular motives and their internal power to fight among themselves. The stage was set for the secular wars of Louis XIV's time and the emergence of a balance-of-power principle as a way of regulating relations among predatory powers.

• The Decline of Religious War

Clearly, too, in this process of the rise of secular absolutist states religious motives were on the wane. Within the Holy Roman Empire itself, religious issues had, to all intents and purposes, been settled. Internationally, the initial fighting for God and absolutism (or God and "liberties") had given way to straight absolutist conflicts. The war between the Dutch and the Spaniards had some religious content, Calvinism rallying against Catholicism, but the conflict between Catholic France and Catholic Spain was a secular struggle for external security on the part of France. And as the Swedish involvement against Austria became deeper and deeper, the cause of Lutheranism became secondary to the Swedish drive for strategically and commercially important ports.

• Economic and Social Impact of War

The economic and social ramifications of the Thirty Years' War are more difficult to assess. However, an entire generation of Germans was scarred by the military and psychological ravages of the conflict. Poorly disciplined armies numbering into the tens of thousands, with their youthful and female campfollowers, and under the banner of adventurer-generals like Wallenstein simply could not be contained by moral precepts or orders from princes. They looted, burned, raped whenever they took over a hitherto untouched city; they forced countryside inhabitants to feed, quarter, and even pay the infamous "contributions" of the war, and thought nothing of burying alive peasants who were so discourteous as to kill, maim, or torture foraging soldiers. Can one fail to understand the exaggerated stories of destruction that have come from this German war, which in some accounts killed off one-fourth of the population and left more wolves than people in some towns?

Outside Germany, the scars were less deep and easier to heal. But the Spanish and Dutch Netherlands suffered from the siege warfare that wore down the populations of beleaguered towns; and eastern France suffered the incursions of marching armies on more than one occasion, as Spanish forces came within a few miles of Paris itself.

Probably, the indirect effects of war on economy and society were greater than its direct impact. War forced rulers to increase taxes at precisely the time when the European economy was becoming depressed. This intensified the social unrest and political revolts of the age. But conversely, the social and political discontent throughout early seventeenth-century Europe actually strengthed the absolutist forces in the long run. Rulers discovered how to tax, how to use armies against subjects, how to play nobles against peasants. Subjects began to feel that princely order was preferable to the ravages of rebellion. In Sweden, Denmark, Prussia, Austria, the prince emerged stronger than ever from the political and social tensions. And as we shall see, the absolutist forces came out on top in France. The absolutist results of social unrest also were reinforced by the demise of religious passions. The last of the religious wars bred almost the last of religious revolts. The Bohemian rebels had waved the flag of religion, and had seen it trampled upon. In the last half of the seventeenth century, there was no ideological motive like religion to capture the imagination and inflame the passions of would-be rebels. Rebellions were fewer and less serious as a result.

• France: the Model Absolute Monarchy

At the very beginning of the seventeenth century, France had a strong, centralized monarchy and a powerful, charismatic king, Henry IV (1589-1610). He brought an end to the French religious wars a generation before they stopped in the Holy Roman Empire, and with a far more satisfactory religious settlement. This Edict of Nantes (1598) gave the French Protestant minority of Huguenots military power to defend themselves, the privilege of worshipping in select places, and the right to be considered for government offices. Not surprisingly, this settlement lasted, with some modification in 1629, until 1685. For the Huguenots now had as much as they could expect in a state whose population was 90 percent Catholic. Catholics were placated by the edict's retention of Catholicism as the official state religion and the awarding to Catholics of the lion's share of state offices. The edict also placed the monarchy in control of the religious situation, for a Catholic king had imposed his political solution to religious differences, instead of being controlled by one or the other religious group. So powerful was Henry IV that he could show his independence of the international head of the Catholic church, the Pope, by imposing a national solution to the French religious problem regardless of the Pope's feelings. This was in the tradition of French royal and priestly semi-independence of the Papacy, the so-called Gallican tradition.

Henry IV had limited success in tackling other deepseated French problems. One was the issue of the power and lawlessness of the nobility. His princely relatives and great nobles retained the memories of being independent warlords during the Middle Ages and rebel chieftains during the more recent religious wars. They also held important posts as military governors of French provinces, commanders of the king's armies, and holders of seats on the royal council. The king's own civil government also proved troublesome to the crown at the local level. Officials in regional law courts or Parlements, and in taxing bureaus were virtually irremovable, having bought their offices and the privilege of bequeathing them at death to a son or close relation. Moreover, local tax bureaus were inefficient and corrupt, while the law courts headed by the famous Parlement of Paris clung to the tradition of judicial review, that is, they decided whether any new royal law or tax deserved to be registered with the courts, a procedure which most subjects considered necessary before they would obey these laws.

• The Reign of Louis XIII (1610-43)

Louis XIII added "law and order" policies to Henry IV's legacy of religious peace. However these came mainly after the first part of Louis' reign, when he was growing up under the influence of his rather weak mother, Marie de Medici, and then some unimaginative chief ministers. Together, these people barely held on to Henry IV's achievements against rebellious nobles, Huguenots, and Parlements.

• Richelieu versus Rebellion

Royal fortunes brightened considerably when the mature Louis XIII chose Cardinal Richelieu as his chief minister in 1624. Until his death in 1642 a few months before the king's own demise, Richelieu bent every nerve in his physically frail body to make his royal master obeyed by subjects and respected by fellow rulers. The key Huguenot town of La Rochelle was captured in 1628, allowing Richelieu to strengthen the Henrician settlement at Nantes. By the Peace of Alais, 1629, Richelieu let the Huguenots retain their right to worship, while taking away their military power. The results were to be dramatically shown after the deaths of Louis XIII and Richelieu: the Huguenots were the only major group within France that did not rebel. Louis and Richelieu handled Catholic noblemen more ruthlessly. For example, the death penalty for the nobles' favorite pastime of dueling was strictly enforced: to the shock of one "veteran" dueler, who tried to test the minister's and king's will by dueling in front of Richelieu's residence, that bold soul was quickly condemned and dispatched from this life. The executioner's axe swung down also on a number of noble hotheads who dared to plot against Richelieu's life or rebel against Louis' authority. Only members of the royal family (who also hated Richelieu and plotted against him) were spared that fate, and even the king's brother and mother had to leave the realm, the one temporarily in disgrace, the other permanently in exile.

Louis and Richelieu also took some measures to enhance the central organs of government, notably by turning the temporary agents of the crown, called intendants, into quasi-permanent local officials. These intendants now saw that the regional courts and tax bureaus did their work, and, if not, they assumed the tasks of judging and taxing themselves. Further centralizing steps on behalf of royal absolutism were prevented by France's war against Spain and Austria, which we have already noted. Both Louis and Richelieu knew that the military drive to prevent Hapsburg encirclement of France took financial and other resources which otherwise could have gone into the task of revamping the financial and judicial apparatus. However the wars, increased taxes, and intendants fanned the flames of rebellion amongst tax-weary peasants in many areas, and embittered the Parlements which were forced to register taxes and accept supervision by intendants. The king and his famous minister barely kept matters under control by exiling the most obstinate judges and hanging batches of peasants as "examples" for the rest of the population.

• Mazarin and the Fronde 1648-53

A reaction against Louis XIII's "law and order" policies was almost inevitable. It came against the king's widow, Anne of Austria, and her chief minister, Mazarin, who ruled for the now child-king, Louis XIV, between 1643 and 1661. This revolt was called the Fronde, after a game in which Parisian boys threw stones at passersby from their slings (Frondes), only to scamper away when the police arrived. In a way, this name was an appropriate one, since the Fronde of 1648-53 was a futile uprising that petered out when Mazarin finally brought military force to bear on the opposition. However, before this happened France experienced two phases of the Fronde that made a lasting impact on the kingdom.

First came the Parlementary Fronde of 1648-49, which imposed on the monarchy a set of reforms drawn up by the Parlement of Paris and other law courts. Arbitrary imprisonment or exiling was severely restricted. All but six of the realm's intendancies were abolished. And taxes were subject to judicial review. One can easily see how the parlementarians were striking back at the absolutist policies of Louis XIII. These reforms continued to be enforced to a large degree during the second phase of the revolt, called the noble Fronde (1650-53). Mazarin had his hands full, trying to play off one noble faction against another, while fighting against Spain as well (the war with Austria had ended in 1648).

• The Legacy of the Fronde

Eventually the coalitions fell apart, as parlementary judges hated noble "lawlessness" (that is, fighting the crown), and the nobles became contemptuous of judges who rebelled with the pen but not the sword. The mass of the French population was thoroughly alienated by the purely destructive actions of the nobles. Parisians were particularly horrified to

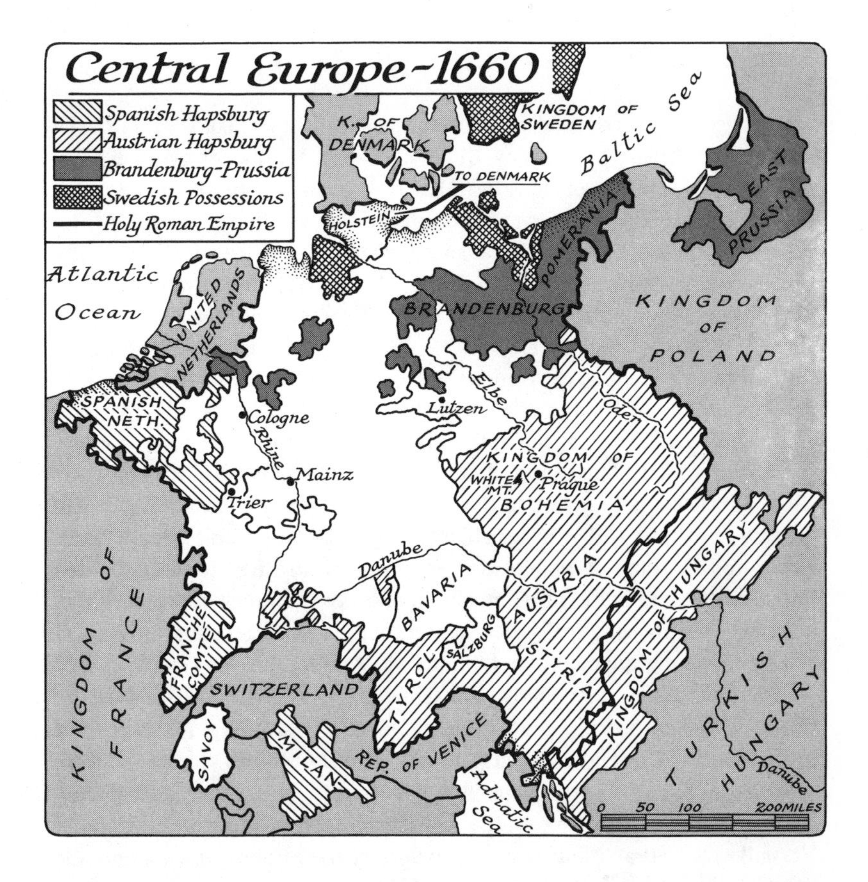

see the nobles' followers set fire to the city hall while the elite of the capital were inside debating how to end the Fronde. And the parlementarians came in for their share of criticism; every time they talked reform, it seemed that the result was more civil war. So when Mazarin put down the noble forces with royal armies, and forced the Parlement of Paris to capitulate, French subjects of every walk of life were prepared to have royal absolutism rather than suffer destruction and anarchy. Never again would the French nobility dare take up the standard of armed revolt. Never again would the parlementarians entertain such sweeping reform proposals. Rebellion was "out of season," as one of Louis XIV's ministers later declared. Mazarin could also boast of having put the finishing touches to Richelieu's foreign designs. Following his peace with Austria in 1648, he imposed a treaty on Spain in 1659, pushing back the French borders on all sides just as he had pushed back the forces of internal opposition.

• The Personal Rule of Louis XIV (1661-1715)

The work of Richelieu and Mazarin made the task of Louis XIV much easier than that of any other late-seventeenth-century ruler. The man who reigned personally after Mazarin's death for the incredibly long period from 1661 to 1715 was quite appropriately called the Sun King. He radiated self-confidence, fully believing that God had called him to a lifetime of work that was "grand, noble, and delightful." For the first part of his personal reign, up to about 1685, it really seemed all that.

The power and majesty of the absolute monarchy was above all symbolized by the palace, gardens, and courtly life at Versailles, a grandiose expansion of his father's small hunting lodge. It was said that you could tell what was happening at Versailles merely by consulting a calendar and a watch! This referred to the fact that Louis had an elaborate ritual which included rising in the morning and going to bed at night – in the presence and with the assistance of the greatest nobles of the land. These nobles, some of whom had been rebels during the Fronde, delighted in handing the king his shirt, in gambling away the hours of boredom, in hunting with the physically near-perfect king, and in dressing up like ancient gods at masquerades where Louis was Apollo, the Sun God. Did they realize that while they enjoyed the highest social place yet devised by Europeans, they were cut off from the business of ruling, reserved for a professional class of bureaucrats? In any case, Louis was able to domesticate the nobility, to put them in a gilded cage as it were, so that they could not think of repeating the Fronde. The other great significance of Versailles was that its dazzling splendor, centered as it was around the king, elevated him above all subjects. This was the ceremonial counterpart of the theory of divine right: both aimed at awing subjects into submission and obedience.

• Louis XIV's Government and Colbert

Louis XIV's government was admired by fellow monarchs almost as much as his courtly life at Versailles. Perhaps his greatest achievement was in being his own prime minister, no mean feat in view of the fact that it broke with the tradition of the rule of prime ministers Richelieu and Mazarin. Louis really wanted to rule personally, and during his first decades all but achieved that by carefully selecting three or four ministers to work closely with him, but always with the king having the final say, as well as the option of dismissing a minister at any time.

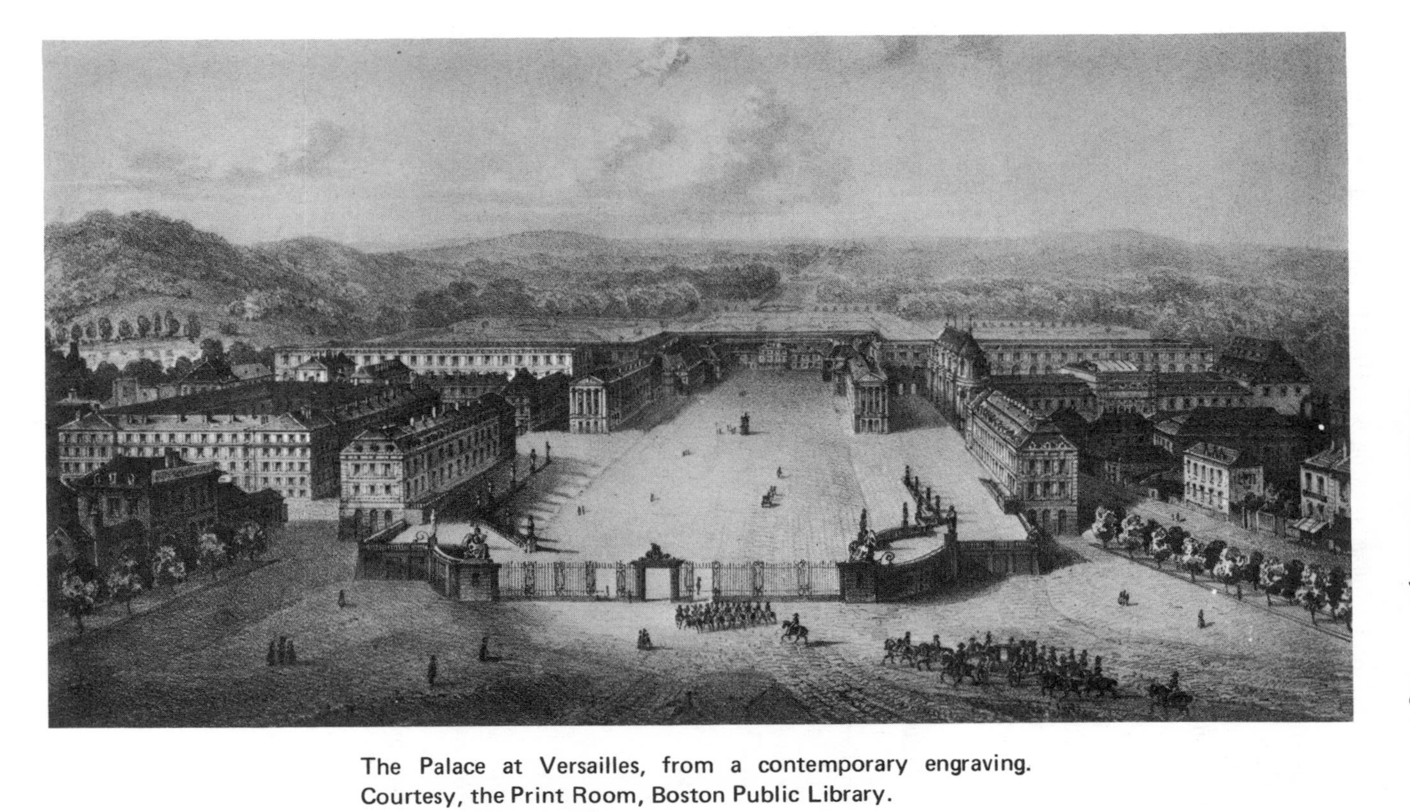

The Palace at Versailles, from a contemporary engraving.
Courtesy, the Print Room, Boston Public Library.

His most famous minister was Jean-Baptiste Colbert, a brilliant mind, but a cold, self-effacing, almost machine-like workhorse. Colbert was the brains behind two reforming, unifying schemes of the personal reign. Through him, the civil and legal procedures were codified throughout the realm, though the actual laws continued to differ from region to region. Through him also, mercantilist measures appropriately called Colbertism, were undertaken. Treasure was amassed (later to be used for Louis' wars), the navy rejuvenated, a tapestry works established, and the tariff structure streamlined. Colbert also had much to do with the reestablishment of the intendants after their removal by the Fronde: these eager state servants poked their noses into the financial and other records of supposedly independent town government, supervised the building of roads, interfered with the work of law courts and assumed control of most tax machinery, as well as being census takers. They were the eyes and ears of the royal government. In a sense, Colbert had another task, that of cultural coordinator. Louis XIV could claim credit for discovering the brilliant playwright Molière, whom many of the religious and courtly establishment found overly critical. However, Colbert was closely associated with the host of academies that sprang up during the reign. France could now boast of having academies for painting and sculpture, science, literature, an observatory built beyond the Paris smog, and a special school for French artists in Rome.

• Louvois' Brutal Policies

Colbert died in 1683, and even before then another of Louis' ministers was beginning to loom as the most important man in the king's team of advisors. This was the minister of war, Louvois, a hard-driving, ruthless person who completed the work of his father, Le Tellier, in organizing, disciplining, and placing under civilian control the military machine of 400,000 effectives that Louis assembled. Louvois and Louis were closely associated with the brutal tactics of destroying German towns that, as we shall see, brought upon France two gigantic wars which turned the Colbertian promise of economic prosperity into a nightmare of death and destruction. Louvois was equally brutal in pushing the king's policy of restoring religious unity to France. While Louis seemed contented to bribe and cajole Huguenots into turning Catholic like the rest of the French population, Louvois and some of the intendants were busy billeting the dreaded dragoons in Huguenot households. After harassment by those soldiers, or other forms of persecution, many a Huguenot family fled to the local Catholic priest for absolution of their sins and baptism into the Catholic faith. Finally, Louis, thinking that there were few Huguenots left, revoked the edict of Nantes in 1685. No longer could a subject worship except as a Catholic.

• The Achievements of Absolutism

The 1680's, marked as they were by the Revocation of the Edict of Nantes, the onslaught of major wars, and the death of Colbert, are normally viewed as the turning point in the Sun King's reign. This meant that the older Louis presided over a decline of the very absolute monarchy which he had taken to the height of its potential. The decline was not only economic and military; it also involved the ossification of personal monarchy conscious of the needs of state and subjects into a monarchy that appeared autocratic, capricious, and even tyrannical.

We should also note the positive aspects of the record. The monarchy had streamlined economics, law, and – distasteful as this seems to twentieth-century readers who fail to appreciate the seventeenth-century quest for religious unity – religion as well. The ossification of personal monarchy itself was both inevitable, and, in part, a good thing. Government became too complex for Louis and a few men to handle. Hence the army of bureaucrats who served the ministers when the government and court moved into Versailles. Hence, too, the bureaus established locally by the intendants to assist them. Bureaucracy changed the whole tone of government; for not only did it rigidify, and in a sense chain the ruler since he had to act through slowmoving, literal-minded, petty officials; it also imposed the will of the monarch on his subjects far more effectively than a single king could by running around his realm as earlier monarchs had tried to do. It was entirely appropriate for Louis to say that he was to die but the state would go on.

• Absolutism's Limits

Louis showed the limitations as well as the strengths of absolutism. He failed to overhaul the tax structure, largely because this would have required taxing the nobility and turning the clergy's meager donations into major financial obligations. To the Sun King who believed with his age in an hierarchical society, such an attack on upper-class privilege was almost inconceivable.

Louis also failed to control troublesome elements within the Catholic church. The Jansenist movement which stressed original sin and deemphasized the role of the church in the individual's quest for salvation could not be eradicated, even after the king destroyed Jansenism's buildings at Port Royal and scattered the bones of its departed saints. The Pope, too, proved impossible to manipulate. Louis did have his French clergy proclaim the so-called Gallican articles of church and state autonomy from Papal dominance in 1682; but by the end of the reign the king had backed down from enforcing the articles, and actually begged the Pope to help him suppress Jansenism.

Nor could he regiment public opinion, which during his last decade spoke out in popular songs, in doggerel verse, and in books smuggled into the kingdom, all directed against his relations with the opposite sex, with the persecuted Huguenots, and with surrounding states victimized by his aggression. Louis simply lacked the techniques to control thought that are placed at the disposal of both democratic and totalitarian modern states.

• Louis XIV and the European Balance of Power

Louis XIV is almost as well known for his wars as for his court and government. Little wonder, since he managed to take on most of Europe in a series of conflicts that looked as if they would give France domination over the continent. As we shall see, the War of Devolution (1667-68), the Dutch War (1672-79), the War of the League of Augsburg (1688-1697) and the War of Spanish Succession (1701-1714) created an entirely different situation from what was feared. Europe rallied against France, working out a principle or rule of thumb for international relations: whenever a state threatened to become overly powerful internationally, the other states would ally diplomatically and militarily to create a balance of power. If necessary they would redraw boundaries to give some states enough land and resources to counter the power of the aggressor-state. Later on we will trace the internal developments connected with the rise to great-power status of such states as England, Austria, and Russia. Here it is more important to see their role in the international conflicts centered on Louis XIV's France.

• Louis' Military Ambitions

In the 1660's, Louis XIV was young, ambitious, and eager to test his state's power in Europe. He was especially anxious to uphold his "gloire," a seventeenth-century word which did not mean personal glory or egocentrism but rather the full potential of one's office, in this case that of a warrior-king. He had the greatest army assembled since the days of the Roman Empire, the best generals that had been schooled in the mid-century civil and international wars, the best siege expert, Vauban – of whom it was said that if he fortified a place it was impregnable, and if he stormed one, it was doomed.

To be sure, his military machine could not sweep across a continent the way twentieth-century armies could, since it was composed of lumbering cannon, slowmoving infantry, and not always reliable horses of the cavalry. Nor could it undertake the annihilation of an enemy: armies were better disciplined than during the Thirty Years' War, but except for noble officers, soldiers were picked from the bottom of society by force and bribery, and even then it was difficult to find replacements when soldiers fell in battle. Lacking the unlimited "pool" of modern military drafts, Louis XIV tended to settle for limited maneuvers, concentrating on hopping from one captured fort to another. He was especially interested in strengthening France's border defenses to the east against the Spanish Netherlands, the German Rhineland, and Spanish Franche Comté. He was ambitious and naive enough to think that he might even become Holy Roman Emperor since it was an elective office, and at one point he had several of the electors bribed. (They took his money and voted for the Austrian Hapsburg line to continue.) He looked even more confidently to the day when the sickly, childless Charles II of Spain (reigned 1665-1700) would die; for Louis had so much Spanish blood in his veins through generations of Franco-Spanish royal marriages that he assumed the dynastic right of a Bourbon offspring to occupy the Spanish throne when the latter's Hapsburg line died out.

• War of Devolution (1667-68)

Louis could not wait for Charles II of Spain to die. Instead he launched his War of Devolution to take over parts of the Spanish Netherlands. He contended that by local Netherlands law some lands "devolved" on the female offspring of a first marriage (on Louis' Spanish wife) rather than on the male offspring of the second marriage (on Charles II of Spain). Fresh from imposing this legal sophistry on Spain, the Sun King sought revenge against the Dutch republic, which had organized a coalition to keep Louis from claiming any more devolution territory.

• The Dutch War (1672-79)

To his surprise, this Dutch War had a very uneven outcome. The Dutch stopped Louis' armies in their tracks by letting water from the sea through the famous Dutch dykes into the flat countryside. They also replaced their peace-and-commerce minded leaders with the great military figure, William III of Orange, a true descendant of the William of Orange who had led the Dutch revolt of the sixteenth century against Spain. France had to settle at the war's conclusion for non-Dutch territory: it rounded out its borders with the Spanish Netherlands, and took over Franche Comté.

Then, in the 1680's Louis XIV blundered badly by virtually tearing up the treaty of Westphalia that had rearranged the Franco-German borders in 1648. Special French tribunals declared that certain Rhineland territories were French "dependencies," or had been in the medieval past. As soon as the French judges declared for annexation, French troops took over the disputed lands to the astonishment of the German states in the Holy Roman Empire. Further "peacetime" acquisitions took place: in 1681 Strasbourg on the Rhine and Casale in the Savoyard Alps became French. Next came most of Spanish Luxembourg. The aggrieved states did temporarily acquiesce through the Truce of Ratisbon in 1684, but European events and human hatred of Louis quickly worked against peace and France.

• The Emergence of Austria and England

One "event" was the Turkish siege of Vienna in 1683. Louis had hoped that the Ottoman Empire of the Turks would keep the Austrian Hapsburgs under Emperor Leopold too busy to worry about the Rhineland. Instead, a European crusade of great powers threw back the besiegers in what became a rout. Austria expanded its Austrian, Bohemian, and Hungarian possessions to include former Turkish Hungary and Transylvania. On the Danube emerged the great power of Austria, appropriately called by some historians the Danubian monarchy. And throughout Europe, Catholic Louis was taunted for his secret support of the Moslem Turkish cause with the nickname, "the Most Christian Turk" (his official European title was the Most Christian King).

The other "event" was the Glorious Revolution of 1688 in England. On the invitation of dissatisfied subjects of the English king James II, the Dutch leader and son-in-law of James, William III, invaded England. James fled, William and his wife Mary were declared joint rulers of England, and in the ensuing settlement between the leaders of the English Parliament and William, the state was vastly strengthened. Poor Louis XIV might have aided James, but he mistrusted that ally, and banked on a long civil war between James and William. Instead William III, the military figure of the hour, and enemy of Louis XIV, was now at the head of the two greatest commercial states of the age, England and the Dutch Republic.

• War of the League of Augsburg (1688-97)

These events, plus Louis' attempt to overawe his enemies by devastating German Rhineland towns, brought about the long War of the League of Augsburg. Austria, England, the Dutch republic, Spain, and even the Holy Roman Empire as a unit became the major ingredients of a grand coalition to push France back to its former boundaries. By the treaty of Ryswick in 1697, France was able to salvage Strasbourg, but lost other Rhineland and Savoyard acquisitions. And Austria and England were well prepared for the next battle over the balance of power.

• The Spanish Succession Problem

This was the Spanish Succession question, which came to a climax in 1700 with the long expected death of Spain's Charles II. The French, English, and Dutch politicians had tried to head off a succession war by agreeing to partition the Spanish Empire between the Austrian Hapsburg and French Bourbon dynasties. But Charles upset their plans by bequeathing his entire possessions to Louis XIV's grandson. After a week of agonizing deliberation, Louis XIV threw open the doors of his palace chamber and announced to the assembled diplomats, "Behold the king of Spain" (his grandson now Philip V of Spain).

Louis hoped that this decision would be accepted by Europe, since it had the backing of both Spain and France, would probably be accepted by England and the Dutch republic so long as the French and Spanish crowns and states remained separate, and was totally unacceptable to only one man, Emperor Leopold I who felt his second son was robbed of the Spanish inheritance. Louis' thinking was sound, but his subsequent actions defied all logic. He sent advisors to dominate the Spanish government, secured special trading privileges with the Spanish empire for French merchants, and arrogantly took over Spanish Netherlands' fortresses that had been manned by Dutch forces.

• The War of Spanish Succession (1701-14)

Hence the War of Spanish Succession erupted, pitting England, the Dutch republic, the Holy Roman Empire, its Austrian Hapsburg emperor, and most individual German states against France and Spain. The military and economic destruction on both sides was enormous. Warfare was finally reduced to head-on battles, like Malplaquet in 1709, which claimed almost 40,000 casualties on both sides. Obviously this type of fighting could solve nothing, even if the brilliant English general, Marlborough, claimed victory in bloodbaths like this. Somehow the allied forces could bring neither France nor Spain to its knees. The Spanish succession question had to be solved by diplomacy, though this was trickier now than in 1700, most of the claimants and their close relatives having died.

• The Utrecht Settlement

Peace treaties in 1713 and 1714, commonly called the Treaty of Utrecht, resolved the succession problem in such a way that Europe now had a balance of power. Spain and her overseas possessions were retained by Louis' grandson, Philip V. However, there was a provision that the French and Spanish crowns and states would remain distinct. To further balance the power of these Bourbon states, the already large Danubian monarchy of Austria was awarded Spain's holdings in the Spanish Netherlands and Italy, while the emerging commercial empire of England was enhanced by the award of the Asiento (slave and other trading within the Spanish empire), Mediterranean posts of Gibraltar and Minorca, and New World territories of Newfoundland, Nova Scotia, and Hudson's Bay. In a separate Great Northern War of 1700-1721, to be discussed later, a final great power, Russia, was added to France, England, and Austria, to round out the balance of power. Spain and the Dutch republics still remained as important powers, but the wars of Louis XIV, the lack of natural resources, and commercial competition, especially from England, reduced them to mere shadows of their former selves. The same happened to Sweden, replaced by Russia as the great power in the north.

• English Absolutism, 1603-1640

England stands out as the most turbulent, and at the same time, the most successful seventeenth-century state in terms of grappling with internal problems. It began the century with a growing crisis of authority between kings James I (1603-25) and Charles I (1625-49) and their wealthy subjects in Parliament. The overly clever and irritating Scotsman, James, quarreled with Parliament constantly over his desire to increase taxes, his weak stand against Catholic Spain, and his hostility toward the Puritans who wanted to simplify the services and organization of the state Anglican Church.

Charles was even more disliked, for he continued the same stands, and tried between 1629 and 1640 to enforce them through royal appointed judges and special state and church courts, without even calling Parliament. Subjects called this the "eleven years' tyranny," retaining vivid memories of the forced collection of "Ship Money," that is contributions for a navy against an unnamed danger. They also recalled that Puritans were whipped, branded with red hot irons, even mutilated by the loss of their ears for writing pamphlets against Archbishop Laud's "High Church" policy of making the Anglican church more ritualistic and administratively authoritarian, that is, closer to Catholicism, than ever. And they worried when another Caroline administrator, Strafford, imposed an authoritarian regime on Anglican and Catholic Irish subjects, fearing that this abuse of military-judicial power might one day be turned against Puritan English subjects.

In short, many English subjects feared that Charles was turning their government into an absolute monarchy like those emerging on the continent. They did not of course advertise the fact that they had far greater political power than any subject body of the day: the important merchant and landed families controlled the unpaid local offices like Justice of the Peace, and Lord Lieutenant; they had a powerful national assembly, Parliament, to represent their interests, and sooner or later Charles would have to call it; and they were the most undertaxed elite in Europe.

• The Puritan Revolution, 1640-1660

Charles was forced to call Parliament in 1640 when a disastrous war with Scotland and rebelliousness in Ireland necessitated military and financial assistance on a massive scale. The Long Parliament, which lasted on and off from 1640 to 1660, was in no mood to give him the aid that might really make him absolute. Instead they abolished the most hated, arbitrary elements of his government in 1640-41. The special courts were destroyed, arbitrary detention halted, and taxation without parliamentary approval declared illegal. Strafford was executed, and Laud placed in jail.

These reforms were followed by civil war between Charles' supporters, called "Cavaliers," and parliamentarians with their own army of "Roundheads," so named because of the way they shaved their hair. The parliamentarians won, and in 1649 beheaded Charles.

The republic of 1649-60 established a degree of religious toleration after destroying the Anglican Church, and worked out a practice of taxing the well-to-do as well as the poor, a remarkable feat for the age. Externally, the regime emerged victorious in conflicts with the Dutch commercial rivals and the old English foe, Catholic Spain. But somehow the regime never outlived its first leader, Lord Protector (former civil war commander) Oliver Cromwell. His regime became too dictatorial even for his supporters, the well-to-do landed and merchant interests. Cromwell died in 1658 and in 1660 Charles I's son was placed on the restored throne as Charles II.

• The Restoration Monarchy, 1660-88

The Restoration settlement retained the moderate revolutionary gains of 1640-41, that is, they placed monarchy under the restraint of ruling with the assistance of Parliament and through the regular law courts. The Anglican church was restored, but with somewhat less power than before.

During his relatively peaceful reign from 1660 to 1685 Charles II learned how to work within this system, even though he was a secret Catholic and really wanted to make the monarchy absolute. Perhaps it was typical of him that he balanced Catholic mistresses with Protestant ones, just as he drew back from tolerating Catholicism and appointing Catholics to office whenever the Protestant Parliament threatened to attack his remaining powers.

His brother James II (1685-88) was not so diplomatic. Within three years this avowed Catholic had antagonized both emerging political parties in Parliament, the anti-absolutist Whigs as well as the divine-rightist, Anglican Tories. They did not want another revolution, but had to oppose James in 1688 when a male, Catholic heir was born, taking the imminently expected succession (James was not expected to live much longer) from the king's oldest daughter, the Protestant Mary.

• Glorious Revolution of 1688

As we have seen, Mary's husband, William III of the Dutch republic, helped out the Whigs and Tories by engineering the Glorious Revolution, a military take-over with continental troops unopposed by the English people. The subsequent Bill of Rights in 1689 strengthened the moderate revolutionary gains of 1640-41 and the Restoration settlement of 1660. England became a limited monarchy with three technically independent branches of government, the executive crown, the parliamentary legislature, and the judiciary balancing each other.

In practice, Parliament and Crown cooperated closely, thereby making the parliamentary monarchy far more cohesive than continental absolute monarchies. The well-to-do controlled tax legislation in Parliament, and influenced the way the king used tax money. Hence they were willing to tax themselves, and even support a semi-state Bank of England which loaned money at low rates of interest to the crown, an enormous help during the costly wars against Louis XIV. England also became a model of liberty, boasting the existence of widespread religious toleration, freedom of the press, and trial by peers. Finally, by crushing an Irish rebellion in 1689 and by uniting the English and Scottish crowns in 1707, the English state became the much larger, internally secure kingdom of Great Britain.

• Early Seventeenth-Century Russia

The other surprising political phenomenon of the seventeenth century was the Europeanization of Russia. That culturally backward, economically underdeveloped, crudely governed state was scarcely part of Europe in 1600. It had escaped the Renaissance and the Reformation, and was now escaping the revolution in science which was sweeping through western and central Europe.

However, a new dynasty, the Romanovs, ended the succession dispute called the Time of Troubles (1605-13) that almost tore the country apart at the beginning of the century. Then, at mid-century there was a modest reformation of the Russian Orthodox church. By changing the ritual somewhat to conform to the parent Greek Orthodox church, this reform broke down Russian resistance to change and innovation. Finally, near the end of the century Russia experienced the dynamic reign of Tsar Peter the Great.

• Peter the Great (1682-1725)

Peter was no Sun King, no lover of courtly ways, but in his own, pragmatic way he uplifted his society. He was especially interested in naval and military matters, a love which came to him as a youth when he wandered through the foreigners' suburb outside Moscow. Peter learned how to march his playmates like western soldiers, took apart and put together again a sailing boat, and boasted of knowing over twenty trades. (His courtiers naturally scattered when he produced a pair of pincers to demonstrate his "skill" as a dentist.)

• The Great Northern War (1700-21)

In 1695-96 Peter tested his army and navy, now much expanded, against the Ottoman Empire to the south. He was disappointed that all he could seize was the port of Azov leading to the Black Sea, but became more optimistic when he found that a coalition of northern European states could be formed against another enemy, Sweden. Peter's entry into this Great Northern War was initially a disaster. He lost the battle of Narva in a blinding snowstorm to an army only one-eighth the size of his forces. Undaunted he brought in European military advisors to revamp his army, and eventually emerged at the Treaty of Nystad with sizable gains. He acquired territory on the Baltic Sea, a warm water port providing commercial and cultural contact with the west, and a brand new capital, St. Petersburg, which he had built without waiting for the peace.

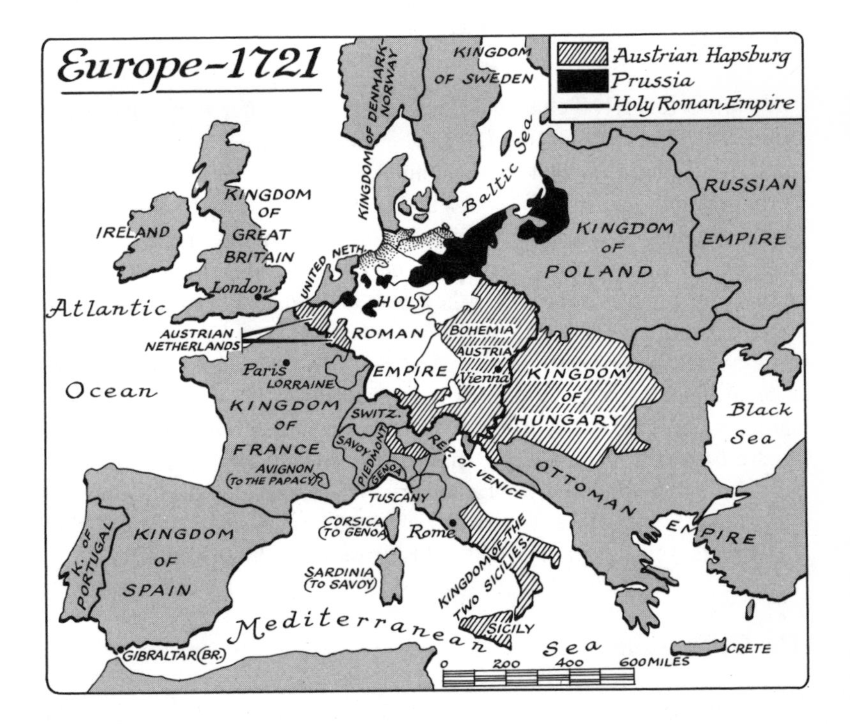

• Europeanization of Russia

This new territory signalled Russia's emergence as a great European power, and its ruler's determination to turn it toward European culture. Peter had also visited Europe to recruit western technicians and learned at first hand how Dutch shipyards and European mining and manufacturing worked. When he returned to Russia, just before the northern war, he established a series of technical plants and schools for the furthering of war industries like textiles and cannon-making as well as war techniques of the artillery, navigation, engineering, and so forth. He also tried to make his courtiers look like westerners, cutting off their beards, placing them in western dress, and putting pipes in their mouths. Little did he know that he was beginning to make them think like westerners as well. His emphasis, pragmatic and unintellectual as it was, set the stage for the entry of European literature in the decades after his death.

• Petrine Government and Society

Unfortunately Peter could not substantially alter the social or governmental structures of his state. The trend of the peasants from free status to being serfs tied to their noble master's lands was accelerated. Peter probably had no choice, for it was the sure way to be able to know peasants could not escape the tax collector or the military recruiter. But it had the effect of placing the nobles between the state and the peasant mass of the population, whereas they were being tamed in western Europe. Peter did make his nobles a service nobility, that is, their social rank was determined by their state service. And he turned the church into virtually a department of state by placing a civil servant at the Russian Orthodox church's head. However, the governmental apparatus itself remained haphazard by western standards. Officials were corrupt, and had to be supervised by native spies and foreign experts. There was no systematic bureaucracy, like Louis XIV's, and in the place of French intendants and their staffs there were governors who tried to govern over huge territories.

• The Other States

The pattern of absolutism, as shown in France and Russia, can be illustrated also by tracing the emergence of Austria and Prussia. As we have seen, the Austrian Hapsburgs not only held on to their rather formal role as head of the Holy Roman Empire, but crushed a Bohemian rebellion, threw back the Turkish siege of Vienna, and incorporated Turkish Hungary and Transylvania in their multinational Danubian monarchy. Prussia's real emergence was to come in the eighteenth century, but already in the seventeenth, the Hohenzollern dynasty brought together by marriage the scattered north German lands of Cleves and Mark in the west, Brandenburg in the center, and Prussia, in the east. Princely leadership, an aggressive foreign policy, and an ability to impose military rule on the restive nobles and townspeople made Prussia an important power by 1715. In 1701, the prince acquired a crown, becoming "King in Prussia." If space permitted, we could also discuss the fascinating constitution of the Dutch republic, which appeared very decentralized but allowed political shifts from peace-minded merchant leadership to military domination under the House of Orange, depending on whether peace or war was "the order of the day." Until overtaken by the English at the century's end, the Dutch also utilized the connection between politics and commerce to maintain a leading role in the economic and fiscal affairs of Europe. Spain's "decline" is another interesting subject. Suffice it to say here that it survived the successful revolt of Portugal (1640-68), the abortive revolt of the province of Catalonia (1640-52), and the dreary reign of Charles II (1665-1700). Under the Bourbon Philip V (1700-46), what remained of the empire after the Spanish succession revived economically and even achieved a degree of centralization modelled after Louis XIV's France. It is with good reason that we call the period when absolutism reached its height the "Age of Louis XIV."

13

The Age of Scientific Revolution

So SPECTACULAR were the achievements of the thinkers and artists of the seventeenth century that we often refer to it as the "century of genius." But even more appropriate is the term "age of the scientific revolution," since this genius was most clearly demonstrated by the scientists, who vastly increased our knowledge of astronomy, physics, and mathematics. At the other side of the intellectual spectrum, painters, sculptors, and architects developed the striking new artistic style of the baroque. In both science and art there was a trend away from religion, even though scientists and artists did not always realize this, and despite the fact that often they worked with problems which were, in their origins, distinctly religious. In the course of this chapter we will see the underlying struggle between the traditional religious idea that God controlled the ultimate destiny of man and the emerging secular notion, expressed best in the philosophy of the time, that the physical world was governed by fixed laws, which human beings could use to improve their lot on earth.

• The Scientific Revolution

When historians speak of the "scientific revolution" of the seventeenth century, they mean that science destroyed basic theories about the heavens and the earth, going back to Ptolemy's astronomy and Aristotle's physics during ancient history. They also mean that the new theories replacing ancient-medieval science made up not just "new" ideas but constituted a fundamentally different way of looking at science and physical phenomena. In other words, a critical and quantitative approach, called the "scientific method" was developed. Of course scientists had always sought to be methodical but the changes in assumptions about the way in which the universe operated made it possible to have a much more accurate and useful methodology by the 1600's.

In a sense, the scientific revolution began with the so-called Copernican revolution of 1543. Copernicus had placed the sun at the center of the universe, no mean feat in view of the fact that most scientists going back to antiquity had assumed that the sun, planets, and fixed stars went around the earth. In so doing that sixteenth-century astronomer had defied not only ancient authority but the human senses, which perceived the sun rising and setting, while the earth appeared to be motionless at the universe's center.

What Copernicus could not do, however, was break with still more fundamental tenets of Ptolemaic astronomy or Aristotelian physics. Specifically, the Copernican revolution retained Ptolemy's notion of the perfect heavenly bodies going around their center in circular motion. (Circular motion was assumed to be perfect, fit for the heavens.) He also retained Aristotle's idea that motion on the imperfect earth was different. In the Aristotelian scheme the earth was composed of four elements, the heaviest being earth proper, surrounded by the next heaviest, water, and with two outer layers, lighter air, and, lightest of all, fire. Of course, these elements had become confused a bit, some earth in particular (the continents and islands) being above water. However, the natural tendency of all substances of these qualities was to go down, if earthy or watery, or upward, if airy or fiery.

Unfortunately it was hard to see just why the earth's four elements should move rectilinearly while according to Copernicus the earth itself moved circularly around the sun. This central problem of reconciling the types of motion on earth and in the heavens could not be resolved until scientists understood that the entire universe was one, regulated by the same laws of motion, and that these laws explained not only circular and rectilinear motion, but the many other types of motion, including elliptical ones, which in the Aristotelian and Ptolemaic schemes, were "unnatural." (That is they required some special explanation, divine intervention causing fire, in the form of lightning, to fall, and human action, the tossing of a ball in the air, causing upward earthy motion).

• Kepler and Galileo

Within a span of ten years early in the seventeenth century, the sun-worshipping Johannes Kepler laid down three laws that brushed aside the remaining debris from Ptolemy's scheme. In their stead he had the planets moving about the sun in elliptical orbits, whose speed and dimensions could be determined with mathematical precision. His contemporary, Galileo, added more tangible support to the heliocentric or sun-centered theory. Training his self-made telescope on the heavens, he saw a miniature planetary system in Jupiter and its moons that demolished the old notion that the earth could be the only center of heavenly motion. And his discovery of sunspots and the moon's imperfect surface added credence to those who were beginning to doubt that the supposedly "perfect" heavens were all that different from this corrupt, earthy globe of sinful creatures.

Galileo was equally famous for his work in physics, which came close to the modern view of motion. In contrast to the ancient Aristotelian idea that assumes most motion to be unnatural, the modern inertial theory assumes motion to be natural. More precisely, it contends that a body which is not influenced by other bodies will be in a state of rest or moving at a constant speed and in a straight line. While Galileo did not make the test attributed to him of dropping weights from the leaning tower of Pisa, he did work out mathematically various terrestial motions: of projectiles, balls rolling down inclined planes, bodies dropped from heights in free fall, and the swing of the pendulum of a clock.

• Newton's Law of Gravitation

The synthesis of Keplerian astronomy and Galilean physics was made by perhaps the most brilliant, and clearly one of the most eccentric of seventeenth-century scientists. Sir Isaac Newton grasped the essentials of the principle of gravitation as a young man, yet had to be goaded by paranoic reaction against a rival scientist before he worked out the details, some twenty years later. There is probably no truth to the idea that his inspiration came from a falling apple. But his famous *Mathematical Principles of Natural Philosophy* (1687) showed that the same gravitational principles governed the motion of the apple, moon, planets, and the infinite universe. It was now possible to conceive of the universe as a single system, with one set of laws, a mathematical language to describe them, and an unerring predictability of all physical objects.

• Other Sciences

Much of the revolutionary work in physics and astronomy was aided by breakthroughs in mathematics. The calculus, coordinate geometry, slide rules, and the decimal system permitted scientists to make complicated calculations without agonizing expenditures of time as previously was the case, and also to work out mathematically, on paper, various types of curved movements, which had defied analysis in early ages. Human biology also made the breakthrough of William Harvey's theory that the heart acted like a pump, circulating blood through the body. Meanwhile botanists and zoologists were still working at the elementary level of classifying plants and animals and setting up zoos. Chemistry was beginning to deal with gases, but had not yet arrived at a sophisticated conception of elements capable of replacing Aristotle's earth, water, air, fire. And geologists had yet to puzzle out the existence of fossils on mountain tops, and the fact that the earth's history was much longer than the usually accepted birthdate of 4004 B.C. In most of these sciences, existing assumptions (like the sudden Creation and short history of the earth) blocked basic revolutionary changes comparable to the theory of inertia's overthrow of the old idea that most motion was unnatural.

• The Scientific Method

One of the reasons science became all the rage when the scientific revolution broke on Europe was its method of arriving at truth. Europeans felt that science could actually tell truth, a sharp contrast to the impossible squabbles among theologians of varying churches, the habit of university professors answering questions by falling back on an ancient or medieval authority and statesmen's habit of engaging in wars. Confidence in scientific method arose also because scientists concentrated on answering the question "how" something works and how its movement is related to other objects' motions. This could be answered by observation, experiment, and mathematical description. In the process, scientists discarded as irrelevant (or unanswerable by human beings) the old scientific question of "why" something happens, that is, what are the purpose and meaning behind the phenomena of nature.

Two philosophers are most closely associated with this scientific method, Francis Bacon and René Descartes. Bacon was no scientist, reputedly dying from the effects of his one experiment, going out into the snow to preserve a chicken. Yet his *New Organon* of 1620 put the right stress on science's need to build up generalizations gradually from a factual base. His model scientist was like the bee, which took an ingredient from one object (nectar from the flower) and produced something entirely new, the honey. And he ranted against two false models: (1) the spider, which like the ancient Aristotelian scientists, kept spinning old material from inside himself, instead of looking outside his own thoughts for the facts, (2) the ant, which simply piled fact on fact like some contemporary observation-crazed astronomers.

The more theoretical, mathematical aspects of the scientific method, which Bacon slighted, were stressed by Descartes, a brilliant mathematician. His *Discourse on Method* of 1637 was a model of how one should logically proceed to scientific generalization. Descartes' only methodological weakness was that he virtually ignored the facts which Bacon stressed as the primary stage of scientific knowledge. Descartes thought that one could start with a self-evident truth, comparable to a mathematical axiom, and deduce complicated conclusions, like theorems, and only then glance back at the phenomena to see whether theory squared with the facts.

Luckily for both Bacon and Descartes, Sir Isaac Newton pulled together their two approaches. In Newton's words, "the whole burden of [science] seems to consist in this – from the phenomena of motions to investigate the forces of nature, and from these forces to demonstrate other phenomena." This approach gave ample room for formulating theories and working them out mathematically, once the facts were established.

• Popularization of Science

The eighteenth-century writer Voltaire said that no one understands Newton, but everyone talks about him. It was almost literally true, at least among the literate minority of the European population. By the eighteenth century even those French and German intellectuals whose national pride or other reasons had made them prefer Descartes or some other continental to the English scientist, came around to accepting his clock-like universe which was kept going by mysterious, invisible gravity. An Italian book was entitled *Newtonism for Ladies.*

The craze involved not just an acceptance of a watered-down Newton, but the entire gamut of new scientific laws and inventions. Academies for experimenting and disseminating information sprang up, first in Italy, then in France and England, and finally ranging from eastern Europe all the way to the New World. Their functions are told by the very title of the

English academy, the Royal Society for Improving Natural Knowledge, and by the mandate of the French Academy of Sciences to "work for the perfection of the sciences and arts and to seek generally for all that can be of use or convenience to the human race, and particularly to France." These were very broad instructions, typical of the period's enthusiasm for science even if unrealistic about what could actually be accomplished in the immediate future.

• Practical Scientific Benefits

Still, there were practical as well as theoretical advances in the realm of the sciences. Barometers and thermometers improved human knowledge about the weather, astronomy explained seasonal changes, and the study of atmospheric pressure resulted in the first steam engine, announcing that human beings were on the threshold of emancipating themselves from less reliable water, wind, animal, and human power. Equally profound in its implications was the development of accurate timepieces, for they would one day give modern, urban society the means to organize a daily schedule with greater efficiency. The seventeenth century saw the development and widespread use of pocket watches that kept fairly good time. The still more famous pendulum clocks of the period are interesting simply because they were the first important industrial invention fashioned by theoretical science rather than by practical-minded craftsmen. And even one of the most primitive of all the sciences, medicine, which was associated as much with causing death as preserving life, was on the verge of using innoculation to prevent smallpox. (Unfortunately, when innoculations began in the early eighteenth century, the habit of treating an individual with a mild dose of another's disease sometimes innoculated the person a little too well!)

• The Scientific Spirit

The influence of the "scientific spirit" was broader than the application of pure, theoretical science to practical matters. Precision and accuracy which were the hall marks of science crept into the vocabulary and work of geographers, economists, and military writers. Improved surveying and mapmaking helped property owners, tax assessors, and international treaty makers, who finally discovered the convenience of appending maps to treaties. "Political arithmetic," or the application of statistics to the economic, social, and political spheres, was another important development, even though the politicians did not alter their states' policies in line with the information garnered about death-rates, the actual wealth of subjects, and commercial trade. By contrast, Dutch businessmen did put vital statistics to use in developing life-insurance schemes, some city blocks were using numbers instead of signs to distinguish houses, and gunners replaced quaint names like "cannons petro" and "bastard cannons" with more precise terms like "twenty-four pounders" and "forty-two pounders."

The scientific emphasis on rationality and uniform laws can also be credited in large part for the demise of witchcraft by the eighteenth century after it had reached its very peak in the previous decades. Sorcerers and other agents of evil supernatural forces or beings like the Devil could not coexist in a universe ruled by Newtonian natural laws. And an English judge peremptorily threw out of court one of the last witch trials with the caustic comment that there was no law against a woman travelling between London and Oxford on a broomstick. There were limits to such a rational approach however. While some advances were made in helping deaf mutes, society retained its fears and prejudices about mentally handicapped individuals.

The scientific spirit spread very broadly among the literate, educated minority of Europeans. Even kings became involved. While Charles II of England went around laughing at the thought that his scientists were weighing air, Louis XIV was visiting his new observatory. There is a story about a lady who kept a cadaver in her carriage for experimental work in anatomy. Perhaps the most charming story was a fictitious one, Fontenelle's *Conversations on the Plurality of Worlds* (1686). During a series of nightly dialogues, the author removed the fears of a fashionable lady that she was in danger, now that the world was not at the center of the universe, but whirling around the sun. Gradually she gave up her need for the Indian theory that the world was held up by elephants, and at last she triumphantly proclaimed about the universe: "I value it the more since I know it resembles a Watch, and the whole order of nature the more plain and easy it is, to me it appears the more admirable."

• Religion and Science

The path to acceptance of the new science was not entirely smooth, however. Many tradition-minded university professors continued to teach their Aristotle into the eighteenth century. And religious critics were many, especially during the early stages of the scientific revolution when it was hard to sort out the good things in science from the apparent threat it posed to religion. Galileo's quarrel with the Catholic church over his *Dialogue on the two chief cosmic systems, the Ptolemaic and the Copernican* (1632) was the most spectacular example of the confrontation. While Protestants had been the original leaders of religious reaction against Copernican ideas, Galileo clashed with Catholic authorities. He suggested that the Bible should not be taken literally when it alluded to the physical universe. (It suggested that the earth was the center, and that the sun moved.) This was galling enough to those close to the Pope who feared that criticism of Biblical "science" might undermine the average Christian's belief in the religious and moral aspects of God's Word. Even more irritating was Galileo's suggestion that his sources, human mathematical reasoning and sensory knowledge, could not err (he did err, frequently) while the Bible could, even though it was divinely inspired.

It took little to stir up the Pope, an erstwhile benefactor of Galileo, to turn against him when it was suggested that the buffoon of the *Dialogue,* "Simplicio," was meant to be none other than the Pope. (It actually was an hypothetical simple-minded defender of the Ptolemaic system.) The Catholic authorities had previously declared that the heliocentric theory could not be taught as "truth," just as an hypothesis; now Galileo, supporting heliocentrism and ridiculing Ptolemaic geocentrism in his clever dialogue, was muzzled, placed under house arrest, and ordered to say the Penitential Psalms.

The irony of this destructive, polarizing controversy was that it need not have taken place, or could have been worked out to save the authority of the churches and the *religious* message about human destiny (the question of "why") in the Bible and yet keep the validity of the scientific quest for truth about *how* the universe functions. Somehow both areas of knowledge had become more obstinate and sweeping in their claims than was healthy or correct. As time went on religion did retreat to a more reasonable posture, Sir Isaac Newton actually being buried in Westminster Abbey, usually reserved for royalty and clergy. Science on the other hand became more pervasive, having an impact on all other intellectual realms, including philosophy, political thought, and religion itself.

The clock-like universe of the scientific revolution led many literate Europeans to believe in a "natural religion," that is the idea that God simply created the world with its fixed laws, and gave humans the ability to understand how they worked and the reason to figure out natural, moral ways of living together. There was no room in such a natural religion (called Deism in the eighteenth century) for a God who intervened to defy his own scientific laws through miracles. And, by implication, there was not even room for belief that the Bible was divinely inspired, by God for man's use; or for accepting the central Christian idea that God sent His own son to teach, die for men's sins and return to his Father. In short, religion was reduced to morality – a matter of individual reason and conscience rather than a relationship between omnipresent deity and frail humans needing faith and outside help to get through life.

• The Impact of Critical Religious Scholarship

In addition to science, other sources of knowledge worked to undermine traditional religion. One was the growth in critical analysis of the past, which had become popular during the Renaissance. By the seventeenth century, university scholars were exposing myths about Greek and Roman history (including the story of Romulus and Remus and the birth of Rome). Father Jean Bolland delved into medieval saints' lives and banished spurious saints from the list with the hope that the true saints who remained would be an inspiration rather than a scandal. However, many Christians thought the Bollandists were simply undermining belief in sainthood.

Then along came the supreme skeptic of the seventeenth century, Pierre Bayle. His *Critical and Historical Dictionary* (1697) examined microscopically and with acid wit the morals of thousands of figures from the Christian past, pagan antiquity, and the Old Testament. Though Bayle was a Christian, and probably meant to show that there were high ideals set by God even if men did not meet them, his criticism of specific Biblical humans tended to undermine religious belief. His favorite Old Testament figure was David, who was castigated for "his adultery with Bathsheba, the murder of Uriah, and the proscription of the people" along with his general interest in war. In another way Bayle edged toward natural religion by suggesting (to the scandal of his age) that a society of atheists could be just as moral (maybe more, he added) as a Christian society. Few caught Bayle's inference that Christians ought to be more moral than others, and could if they actually practiced their beliefs. Equally misunderstood was the brilliant Biblical analyst, Richard Simon. His several critical histories of the various parts of the Bible tried to buttress Christianity by purging it of literal belief in those contradictory passages and other inconsistencies which had always been embarrassing. All he accomplished was the undermining of confidence in the Bible.

• Knowledge of Non-Christian Cultures

As Europeans delved into the non-Christian past and the non-European present they added doubts to old Christian belief. How could one believe in Adam and Eve if Egyptian accounts went so far back that those "first" humans were later comers? How could one square wars of religion between professed Christians with the supposed "inferiority" of contemporary peoples in other continents who were now known to live more moral, peaceful lives – without any knowledge of the Christian God or His son, Jesus. This was the time when the North American Indian was emerging in European literature as the Noble Savage, and when the Confucian was being dubbed the Sage Chinese.

In an unconscious move towards the eighteenth-century idea that all religions are essentially the same, if stripped of everything beyond their "natural" elements, the Jesuit missionaries in China tried to write the Chinese population into the Catholic church. The Jesuits failed to convince the Pope that the Chinese secular customs were harmless, their morality essentially Christian, and only a few pagan (religious, but non-Christian) rites deserved to be purged. But this "Chinese rites" controversy poured forth hundreds of books from the European presses, most of them turning people toward fascination in Chinese culture and belief that the Chinese Confucians were every bit as good, if not better than European Christians.

• Formal Philosophy

The seventeenth century was one of the great periods of philosophy, the last age when philosophers attempted to bring together all past knowledge and present ideas in grand philosophical syntheses. Their task was a staggering one because of the weight of past knowledge, including ancient moral philosophies revived during the fifteenth and sixteenth centuries to look just as convincing as Christian ideas. They had to contend with Stoicism's belief in human struggle with a hostile universe, Epicureanism's interest in moderate enjoyment of life, and Pyrrhonism's suggestion that morality is relative since neither the senses nor reason can arrive at any absolute truth. Furthermore, these philosophers had to accommodate the philosophical implications of the scientific revolution, which banished man from the center of a world created by an aloof deity.

• Descartes

Where did human beings fit into the cold, mechanistic scheme of a clock-like universe? The most influential philosopher of the century, Descartes, placed *homo sapiens* in a far more glorious role than either the ancient pagan philosophies or medieval Christianity's view of man as a combined beast and angel.

Descartes started by questioning everything he could: the knowledge accumulated from the past (professors constantly quarrelled); the physical world (since the human senses were imperfect and might be seeing something that did not exist); and his own physical body (perhaps he was in a dream, and his body was not really there). Then he arrived at one absolute truth, something that was so self-evident, like a mathematical axiom, that it could not be doubted. He had to accept the fact that he was thinking as he questioned all these things. His famous aphorism was: "I think; therefore I exist." What Descartes was really saying was that human beings were thinking, even rational beings, something that the ancient pagans and Christians had shied away from asserting.

Now all Descartes needed to build up an optimistic view of human potentiality was to fit God and the physical world into his man-centered philosophy. His God was really an abstraction of pure wisdom, a being who simply set up the universe, and – more crucially in view of Descartes' initial skepticism about what his senses told him about the physical world – one who could not deceive human beings about that world. In other words, scientists could now rest assured that when they observed, experimented, and deduced principles or laws about matter in motion, these really conformed to reality. Far from being the frail, fallen creatures of Christian thought, or beings battling against a hostile world as some pagans had suggested, people could become the "masters and possessors of nature."

• Leibniz and Spinoza

Descartes' "Cartesian" philosophy had one flaw that perplexed European philosophers until John Locke came along a generation later to straighten it out. The Cartesian dilemma was how to fit together the essential part of the human being that was pure mind or soul, and the body that was somehow attached to the human mind. One answer was given by Leibniz, a brilliant thinker about virtually all intellectual issues and inventor of the calculus (Newton discovered it independently). The Leibnizian universe was composed of "monads," centers of energy rather than separate minds and bodies. Though each monad goes its own way, they all interract harmoniously through God who has preprogrammed their coordination through a "pre-established harmony." Unfortunately, this theory tended to make humans subject to God, something Descartes had implicitly rejected.

Spinoza's pantheism fell into an opposite trap; his God was in Nature, seemingly swallowed up by or identical with the world, rather than independent of it. This theory did solve the relationship of mind and body, since in Spinoza's world, the physical and psychical or mental phenomena are really only two different views of the same deity, rather than two distinct, Cartesian substances. But Europeans were horrified that God could be reduced to substances in this world, and called Spinoza an atheist.

• Locke's Common Sense

John Locke's *Essay Concerning Human Understanding* (1690) was just the right book at the right time to put European philosophy back on a common-sense course. Brushing aside the impossible question of how mind and body could interact, Locke asked pragmatically what can we imperfect human beings know? In answering, he rejected the notion that some ideas could be innate, that is here from birth (a pet notion of Descartes). He sidestepped the question of whether "revelation," which is knowledge from God, mainly through the Bible, can add to human knowledge or merely fortify what we already know ourselves. Boldly, he proclaimed that knowledge is composed of "ideas" which come from "experience." This means that the outside world provides the human senses with the data which the mind sorts out into working knowledge.

Locke's common-sense philosophy took Europe by storm in the eighteenth century, and with good reason. By evading the age-old stress on revelation, he allowed humans to believe that they, and not God, were responsible for pushing back the frontiers of knowledge. By burying Descartes' belief in innate ideas, he made people think that they did not have to settle for the knowledge of the past; ideas could change simply by changing the experiences of society. In other words, human beings' education and hence their very actions could be altered. It was an exhilarating thought that Locke expressed when he said that the difference between a

Hottentot and an Englishman was education. This made it possible for Europeans to believe in material, intellectual, and moral progress. In short, the old search for the magical elixir of life would be largely replaced by a confidence in human perfectibility.

• Ancients versus Moderns

Locke's philosophy fitted nicely with the "Moderns" in the famous late seventeenth-century literary Battle of the Ancients versus the Moderns. Those scholars who claimed that the ancient Greeks and Romans had asked and answered all the great questions and reached perfection in literature were answered by the moderns' modest but devastating answer: We are greater, for we stand atop (ancient) giants; we not only know what they knew, but have learned by their errors, and added our own knowledge to theirs. As the author of Mother Goose stories, Charles Perrault, said in a popular poem, "And one can compare, without fear of injustice; the Age of Louis XIV, to the fair Age of Augustus."

• Traditional Religion

Formal religion was not entirely divorced from the intellectual vitality of the age of the scientific revolution. Indeed, the seventeenth century was a time of intensely heated religious controversy, a carryover from the Reformation of the sixteenth century. The main difference was that while in the 1500's the major arguments had been between churches, for example between Catholicism and Lutheranism, now they were often between factions within a given church. One key issue arose over salvation. In France and the Spanish Netherlands, Catholic Jansenists stressed the Fall of Adam and played down the hope of salvation, except for the few lucky enough to receive God's grace, while Catholic Jesuits emphasized God's mercy and the joy of life in this world. In the Dutch Netherlands, the officials in control of the Calvinist (Reformed) church took a stand close to Jansenism by stressing predestination, while their rivals within the church, the Arminians, emphasized man's free will, much like the Jesuits.

In England, the quarrel within the Anglican church between the semi-Catholic High Church supporters and their Puritan opponents involved both theology and ritual. The Puritans wished to purify the church, that is strip it of all its High Church emphasis on what they considered idolatrous, Catholic externals: the clergy's beautiful vestments, the use of the ring in marriage, the stress on organ music, and the inference that salvation was an easy thing to obtain by merely going through religious ceremonies. These Puritans were close to the Jansenists and Dutch Reformed leaders in their emphasis on predestination and the will of God.

The Russian Orthodox church had its own quarrels, but these were mainly over the wording and forms of the church service. The reforming Patriarch Nikon turned many tradition-minded Russians into hostile Old Believers by making the Russian church conform to practices in the Greek Orthodox church. He altered the number of Hallelujas and genuflections, the spelling of Jesus' name, and other externals, all of which were deeply symbolical to the Old Believers.

Much of this intensified religious interest was constructive in its effects, making Christians more aware of their beliefs. Many people tried to act out their beliefs by more regular churchgoing, increasing their gifts to the poor, visiting hospitals or caring for the sick. English, Dutch, and French charity of the period was especially striking, though some middle- and upper-class do-gooders were a bit sanctimonious and even condescending toward those less fortunate than themselves.

There was a divisive effect of this religious turmoil. Many were turned away from the formal churches and Christian theology, some toward the emerging "natural religion" of simple morality, others toward highly emotional and personal religious experiences, still others toward a desperate effort on behalf of religious toleration.

• Religious "Enthusiasm" and Toleration

The emotional "wing" of seventeenth-century Christianity is a fascinating phenomenon. Its devotees were often called "enthusiasts" because they were en-thused, that is, literally filled with God. American students may recall reading of religious fanatics running naked through the streets of Salem, Massachusetts, when "drunk with God." Their brand of enthusiasm, which freed them from polite Christian society's scruples was at the opposite extreme of Quaker enthusiasts, the followers of George Fox's Society of Friends, whose emotional communion with God made them far more moral than the society about them. Different again were the Pietists, German Lutherans who stressed mysticism, piety, and humanitarianism. There were many other sects, including Quietists, Molinosists, Lapadists, Ranters, and some Baptist groups. All found the rigid, intellectual, and ritualistic approach of the main churches irrelevant to their own emotional needs.

Much more subdued were the scholarly persons who sought with pen and voice to bring the churches together. Locke wrote a famous *Letter on Toleration,* which argued for toleration of all but Catholics and Atheists. He thought both were potential enemies of the state. Pierre Bayle went much further, contending that since God alone knows absolute truth, every one's belief should be tolerated; it was enough that one sincerely believed what he or she professed. Unfortunately for the basic beliefs which were the driving force and grandeur of Christianity, the move to tolerate and to accept differences had the effect of watering down religion to the common elements, which meant stripping it of everything except the morality of "natural religion."

Unfortunately, also, most rulers did not believe toleration to be practical. They remembered too well the religious wars of the sixteenth and early seventeenth centuries and the rebellions that stemmed from religious differences! Instead of seeing toleration as a way to internal and international peace, they clung to the seventeenth-century motto of "One King, One Faith, One Law." Louis XIV banned Huguenot worship, Leopold I tried to uproot Protestantism in Hungary, and William III persecuted Irish Catholics. The Dutch republic, Prussia, and at the end of the century the English state, were exceptions, largely due to the economic motive of tolerating talented persons and to the strong will of political leaders.

• The Baroque Style of Art

The artistic style of the seventeenth century, the baroque, takes its name from a Portuguese word for deformed pearls. Somehow the term was applied, rather nastily, to the art: critics assumed that baroque painting, sculpture, and architecture, were a rejection, or at least a debasement of the Renaissance style of classical naturalism, harmony, and proportion. There is some truth to this charge. Instead of stressing these orderly traits, baroque painters and sculptors seemed bent on distorting human figures to accentuate their emotions. Its architects stressed movement rather than repose, by using light and shade to play on facades, and by stringing out an entire wing of uniform windows. Its planners of urban squares or palace grounds refused to settle for working with a single building, insisting on integrating it on a grandiose scale with courtyards or gardens through paths, canals, or balustrades. Often, this integration, at least on canvas and in the interiors of churches, was achieved by dramatically emphasizing some focal point of the scene, or the high altar, in contrast to a Renaissance painting which can often be cut up into parts, or a Renaissance church, which is centered on the plan of an even-armed cross.

We will have a more rounded, fairer assessment of baroque if we realize that these traits of emotionalism, movement, exaggeration, and unity on a grand scale were not "bad" or "inferior" but simply attempts to express the artistic feeling of a new age. Some of the baroque's technical origins lay in the Renaissance style, but naturally these were expanded, modified, altered, distorted, at times rejected as baroque artists worked within the intellectual, social, and political context of their own age.

• Religious Baroque

The most spectacular influence was religious. It derived from the sixteenth-century Reformation's focus on salvation, the interplay of God and humans, and the sheer unleashing of emotional conflict between Protestants and Catholics. The Catholic church was most adept at capturing this spirit of intense feeling and drama. The Jesuit order became famous for its baroque churches, especially the parent church of the Gesu in Rome. Its interior captured the imagination and won over the hearts of the curious visitor and devout worshipper alike. There was a soaring dome and barrel vault to awe the viewer, and the human eye could trace its way along columns at the side of the curving front wall which nestled the high altar. The facade combined different styles in its two stories to achieve both movement and unity. Despite the clustering of columns and pilasters in a way that defies the Renaissance's classical canons, the observer's attention is somehow drawn upward from columns to pilasters, and from the straight sides through second-story ends to the triangular top.

Perhaps an even better example of religious baroque is the sculpted altarpiece, the Vision of St. Teresa, by Lorenzo Bernini. Set in a chapel of the Roman church, Santa Maria della Vittoria, the ecstatic saint is inextricably connected with the angel aiming his arrow at her heart. This dramatic story is connected with the background architecture by billowing clouds beneath the figures and shafts of gold light above them. Bernini's overly elaborate setting for St. Peter's chair, in St. Peter's cathedral, shows that baroque religious feeling could be combined with Renaissance harmony. The chair is suspended above temporal church figures mounted on the altar and below a heavenly scene, while clouds unite the entire piece.

The Church of St. Peter's, Rome. Courtesy, Italian Government Travel Office.

• Baroque and the State

Second only to religion as a molder of baroque was politics. The emerging absolute monarchy's wealth and power allowed rulers to patronize painters and erect new palaces, as well as to infuse art with a little of the sense of their own grandeur and power. The best examples come from Louis XIV's France, notably the classical columned facade of the Louvre done by Perrault, and the equally classical wings of Versailles. It is often said that France rejected the baroque and voted for a refined classical style stemming from the Renaissance. The Louvre facade and Versailles do reflect classicism's sense of symmetry and balance, but both architectural masterpieces also convey a sense of power and movement that is more baroque than Renaissance, and above all reflects absolutism. And anyone who has glanced at the colorful, richly ornate ceilings of the Hall of Mirrors at Versailles or Apollo's Gallery at the Louvre, knows that palace interiors could be flamboyantly baroque, even if their exteriors were restrained.

It is more difficult to fit baroque into the intellectual context of the age. However, one senses in the painting, especially Rembrandt's penetrating portraits and dramatic scenes such as the "Night Watch," a fathoming of human actions beyond Renaissance naturalism. It could well be that all the political, social, economic, and religious unrest noted in this and the previous chapter forced painters and sculptors of the 1600's to show inner turmoil in the people of the day. Certainly the scientific revolution had an impact. It was shown dramatically in the late seventeenth century's emphasis on motion, on controlling and organizing earthly space (including the geometrical clipping of hedges in palace gardens), and the infinite universe (by the use of domes, billowing clouds, and sweeping curves).

• Literature

So far we have limited this analysis of baroque to painting, sculpture, and architecture. Literature and music also displayed baroque traits, though one should not try to force too rigidly either field into that style. Words which describe baroque writing in the early decades of the seventeenth century are elaborate, emotional, complicated, even bombastic. The Italian poet Marino thought the very purpose of poetry was to astonish the reader, while the Spaniard Gongora used metaphors and allusions in such a way that the reader was almost lost. Perhaps the greatest baroque vehicle of literature was the stage. England's Shakespeare, France's Corneille, Spain's Lope de Vega all concentrated their plays on a single emotion of the hero, whether this was passionate love, noble honor, or a death-defying quest for fame. As the century wore on, the literature did become more subdued, more polished, and less vulgar. This was also the century when the French Academy disciplined the French language so that it was clear, precise, and, eventually relatively unemotional. This was in keeping with the change in tone of royal courts from the barnyard manners and conversation of 1600 to the elegant, refined talk of 1700.

• Music

Music contributed the baroque's most typical creation, opera. It combined an enormous number of arts: elaborate stage scenery, instruments, the human voice, acting, costumes, and some semblance of a story. Like its religious version (the oratorio), the secular opera played on the audience's emotions by effective use of the human voice, going so far as to "produce" male adult sopranos whose unnaturally high but rich and powerful voices had a devastating effect on many operagoers. Musicians also began to work out the implications of the current transition from polyphonic to monodic music, and the technique of combining strong melodies with some dissonance. The development of instruments, especially strings (including some of the best violins made, highly prized today, like the Amati and Stradivari) complemented the human voice better than ever. At Louis XIV's court, as many as one hundred violins were combined with twenty piano-like clavecins, giving the effect of a thunderstorm. The orchestra was also emerging, though the notion of a conductor to discipline a performance was rather difficult for many musicians of the age to take.

• Baroque, Society, and Time

Essentially, all forms of the baroque were for the elite, just as government and society were dominated by the wealthy and the titled. Yet it should be remembered that church interiors were meant for the worship of both the prince and the pauper, and the goal of dazzling the eyes and evoking the deepest feelings was certainly set with all walks of life in mind. Moreover, this still largely preliterate age directed its church music at the average churchgoer who had to rely on nonliterary vehicles for his religious education. Even in painting, which so often depicted the high and mighty of the current and previous times, mythology as well as religion, there were glimpses of the suffering poor, ranging from Caravaggio's pilgrims to Le Nain's peasants. In short, the baroque reflects all aspects of the seventeenth century.

It also changed with the times. At the beginning of the century it was difficult to tell whether the art was "baroque" or what is called "mannerism" – a transitional stage between Renaissance and baroque that stressed extremes of emotion, distortion of figures, revolt against artistic rules. That was natural, fitting in with the turmoil of the late religious wars and political upheaval. As the seventeenth century came to a close all the arts underwent another shift. We have noted how courtly language became refined. Turbulence and warfare on canvas gave way to subdued portraits. Mathematics and rationality became keys for understanding music and for writing prose. In a broad sense these developments reflected the order that secular states had imposed on their subjects, an order which forced many artists and the public from an obsession with violence and emotion. Concurrently, the scientific revolution's suggestion that the world was regular and its human inhabitants capable of understanding and even controlling it gave Europeans freedom to engage in a less frantic, perhaps more superficial, and probably more enjoyable analysis of the human race on canvas, in music and on paper. This was fully in keeping with the age that read its Locke and believed in a rational, natural man who could create political society in an orderly fashion and learn to tolerate other peoples and other beliefs.

Suggestions for Further Reading

Clark, G.N., *The Seventeenth Century* (1947)

Aston, T., ed., *Crisis in Europe, 1560-1660* (1965)

Trevor-Roper, H., ed., *The Age of Expansion: Europe and the World, 1559-1660* (1968). Essays on individual countries.

Moote, A.L., *The Seventeenth Century: Europe in Ferment* (1970)

Sabine, G.H. *A History of Political Theory* (1955)

Wedgwood, C.V., *The Thirty Years' War* (1938)

Wedgwood, C.V., *Richelieu and the French Monarchy* (1949)

Moote, A.L., *The Revolt of the Judges* (1971)

Wolf, J.B., *Louis XIV* (1968) France and European states-system.

Hill, C., *The Century of Revolution, 1603-1714* (1963). England.

Wilson, C.H., *England's Apprenticeship (1603-1763)* (1965). Economic and social.

Sumner, B.H., *Peter the Great and the Emergence of Russia* (1950)

Butterfield, H., *The Origins of Modern Science* (1965)

Koestler, A., *The Sleepwalkers* (1959). Astronomers.

Tillyard, E.M., *The Elizabethan World Picture* (1961)

Grimmelshausen, *The Adventurous Sumplicissimus.* Novel of the period.

Hazard, P., *The European Mind, 1680-1715* (1953)

Gay, P., *The Enlightenment: An Interpretation,* vol. I (1967)

Bronowski, J., and Mazlish, B., *The Western Intellectual Tradition: From Leonardo to Hegel* (1960)

Tapié, V.L., *The Age of Grandeur: Baroque Art and Architecture* (1960)

THE EIGHTEENTH CENTURY

14

The Eighteenth Century

In 1715 when the aging but still vigorous symbol of royal absolutism, Louis XIV, finally breathed his last at Versailles, Europe was enjoying one of its rare intervals of peace. King Louis is reported to have confessed at the end that he had loved war too much, but the peace that prevailed in 1715 was probably more the result of the monarch's financial extremities than any genuine repentance. Even though the concept of total war or even the nation-in-arms was still far in the future, by 1715 armies had increased in size to the point where the financial burden of continuous large scale warfare was so great that occasional respites were essential for all participants. The peace treaties of 1713 and 1714 which ended Louis' last war were to usher in the longest period of real peace that the eighteenth century was to experience. It is hard for us to imagine a world in which war was looked upon as a normal state of affairs and periods of peace as exceptional. Yet this was generally the situation at the beginning of the eighteenth century in Europe. The large and increasingly powerful dynastic states which emerged in the sixteenth century looked upon military competition between rulers as a sort of royal prerogative – the true sport of kings – to be enjoyed whenever royal resources permitted. To fight was necessary to survive, and if rulers sometimes made treaties or alliances it was usually not with the intention of securing permanent peace and friendship, but was generally a matter of tactical or strategic necessity.

But if war was the normal state and peace the exception, what were the factors which produced the relatively peaceful interlude between 1715 and 1740? In order to answer this question we must turn to the internal situation of the major powers and try to see why at this point in history they chose to follow the paths of peace rather than war.

• Louis XV and Cardinal Fleury

At Louis XIV's death his legal successor was his five-year-old, great-grandson, Louis XV. This meant that there would have to be a regency until the young lad attained legal age to rule (thirteen for kings of France). Because of his dislike for his dissolute nephew, the Duke of Orleans, Louis had tried to exclude him from his rightful position as head of the council of regency (as nearest male relative), and to put his own illegitimate sons in control. But when the Duke agreed to restore to the Parlement of Paris their right to review royal laws which Louis XIV had suppressed, the court declared Louis' will invalid and confirmed Orleans as chief regent. But he could never feel as secure as a regular monarch and was not inclined to take any bold initiative in foreign affairs. In spite of the Duke's unsavory reputation, his relations with the young king seem to have been cordial and proper. Although the Regent's scheme to increase the participation and influence of the old nobility in royal administration proved to be a failure because of the noblemen's quickly demonstrated lack of ability and application, he demonstrated his own perceptiveness by moving at once to end the experiment and restore control to experienced ministers. And in spite of the ultimate collapse of the radical financial schemes of his protégé, the Scotsman, John Law, the economy of the country made a good recovery from the financial chaos brought on by the preceding half century of war.

In 1723 the Regent died and Louis XV assumed his full powers. After a brief interlude he appointed his former tutor, Bishop Fleury, to act as his chief minister, though in the tradition of his predecessor he always refused to have a chief minister in name. Bishop Fleury who was soon made a cardinal proved to be a most worthy successor to Colbert and Richelieu. In a quiet but effective way he gradually took control of more and more aspects of policy as it became clear that the young king had inherited none of his great-grandfather's zest for the dreary details of government. From the beginning Louis XV much preferred the pursuit of game and women to the exercise of power and accordingly he came to depend more and more on Fleury and his ministers to carry on the business of government. Fleury, by temperament a moderate and conservative man (he was 73 when he took office), had seen enough of the vicissitudes of life to learn that in most instances the best policy was to avoid rocking the boat. In diplomacy this meant that France should strive to maintain her position but do everything to avoid open warfare.

But in 1733 he was unable to resist the pressure of a pro-war faction at court which took advantage of the death of the king of Poland to urge that France support the candidacy of the queen's father, Stanislas Lezcnski, who had held the elective throne briefly once before. Although legally elected by a portion of the Polish nobility, he was forcibly deposed by the combined military efforts of the Austrians and the Russians who had their own candidate. The cautious Cardinal authorized only token military support but utilized it so effectively that France emerged from the conflict with the prospect of the ultimate acquisition of the valuable Duchy of Lorraine (the deposed king was to have the Duchy as consolation for the loss of his throne and on his death it would go to his daughter, the queen of France).

In 1740 the Cardinal was again drawn into war. Before the Hapsburg emperor, Charles VI, died, he had made agreements with all the major powers to accept his daughter, Maria Theresa, as the legitimate and rightful successor to his title and his lands. But when he died the temptation to take advantage of a traditional enemy at a moment of weakness was too strong for the young and ambitious king of Prussia and the war hawks of the court of France to resist. Fortunately for the Cardinal he did not live to see the ultimate failure of France's effort in the war which he tried as long as he could to avoid.

Internally what France needed after the severe drain of Louis XIV's wars and the disruptions caused by speculation during the Regency was a period of financial order and stability. Although Fleury made no dramatic innovations, he did succeed in stabilizing the value of French currency (devaluations had been a favorite device for meeting the unusual expenses of war) at the level it was to hold until the French Revolution. By carefully cutting expenses and improving the collection and utilization of existing revenues Fleury was able to balance the French budget for the only time (1738) during the eighteenth century.

By the time of his death Cardinal Fleury's conscientious attention to the details of government and his cautious but effective foreign policy had brought the monarchy to a new peak of prosperity and popularity. When Louis XV became seriously ill in 1745, the apparently spontaneous outburst of sympathy and concern indicated by the number of prayers and masses said for his recovery seems to suggest that Fleury had done his work well. But unfortunately no successor combining all his favorable talents appeared. For a time the monarchy could live on the store of good will accumulated by the Cardinal, but the supply was quite quickly exhausted.

• England and the Hanoverian Succession

By the Act of Settlement of 1701 the English throne on the death of Queen Anne was to go to the Protestant Electress of Hanover or her heirs (descendants of James I's daughter, Elizabeth). When Queen Anne died in 1714, the transition to the Hanoverian line went more easily and smoothly than most expected. George, the Elector of Hanover, was accepted as the only viable alternative to civil war (an abortive attempt of the old pretender, James Edward Stuart, to launch an invasion from Scotland in 1715 failed miserably), but as a middle-aged foreigner (he spoke no English) he was never able to exercise really effective control of the government. This left a vacuum of power that was finally filled by Sir Robert Walpole who was called to the chancellorship of the Exchequer in 1721 to clean up the mess left by the collapse of the wave of speculation in stocks known as the "South Sea Bubble." Certain members of both Parliament and the royal council had been involved in the affair and it was felt to be necessary to bring in new men, including a new Chancellor, who were not tainted with involvement in the disaster. Sir Robert was not only not involved but had even given public warnings of the potential dangers in the situation. Within a few years he was assuming such a predominant role in the royal council that he seemed to be acting very much like a prime minister – although at that time the title did not exist officially.

• Ministry of Walpole, 1721-42

From 1721 to 1742, Sir Robert Walpole in his position of leadership established both internal and external policies remarkably similar to those of his contemporary in France, Cardinal Fleury. Walpole had even more compelling reasons for caution, however. He had to try to conciliate the numerous "interests" or power groups which could exert influence through either the House of Lords or the House of Commons, as well as satisfy the king (he was still a minister only at the king's pleasure), and allow nothing to be done that might arouse the people (popular outcry forced him to abandon his proposal for an excise tax in 1734). Sir Robert accomplished these tasks with consummate skill. He was even more successful than Fleury in avoiding armed conflicts, but like the latter found his hand forced by powerful pro-war forces in 1739-40. English merchants who found their illicit but formerly condoned trade with the Spanish colonies suddenly drastically curtailed by a new and rigorous enforcement policy on the part of the Spanish government, demanded that England undertake armed retaliation against what were described as Spanish atrocities. These traders were able to stir up enough support in Parliament to force a declaration of war in 1739. When England's traditional ally, Austria, was attacked by France and Prussia in 1740, the war against Spain was expanded to include both those countries. Like Fleury, Walpole retired before the end of the conflict which, as he predicted, brought little gain or glory to his fellow countrymen.

His skill at using every resource of patronage and influence to keep the government running smoothly under his control made his system a model for all political and factional leaders in the eighteenth century. Fortunately for Walpole both the first two Georges (1714-27, 1727-60) were satisfied with simply having things go smoothly and during his regime made little attempt to initiate policy. When George III later attempted to take a more independent line it produced the tensions and crises which troubled British political life in the second half of the eighteenth century.

• The Holy Roman Empire and the Hapsburg Succession, 1715-50

The Archduke Charles, the younger brother of Emperor Joseph I (1705-11) had been the Hapsburg candidate for the Spanish throne and had seemed to find some support, especially in Aragon, during the War of the Spanish Succession. He therefore found it distasteful to have to abandon his hopes at the peace table in 1714, even though in the meantime he had unexpectedly become Emperor on the death of his older brother in 1711. While Charles was not as eager for peace as his two contemporaries, Fleury and Walpole, he had an Achilles heel which forced him to moderate any aggressive designs. Charles' problem was that for the first time the ruler of the Hapsburg lands in Europe had no male heir to succeed him. Since the law of succession in several key areas of the realm specifically forbade inheritance by a female, something had to be done if the fragmentation of the Hapsburg inheritance was to be avoided.

Charles' legal advisors came up with a device which would solve the problem, if he could get accepted. This was a document called a "Pragmatic Sanction" which provided that those signing would agree to recognize the right of his daughter, Maria Theresa, to inherit all the Hapsburg lands without regard to any contrary legal custom or tradition. Charles, in his anxiety to get the document approved, on several occasions bargained away military and territorial advantages. It was this situation which tended to make Hapsburg policies more moderate up until his death in 1740. At that point Maria Theresa found how little to be trusted was the word of kings and diplomats, when the temptation to share in the spoils of the Hapsburg territory brought a quick end to almost three decades of relative peace. Europe was not to know such a luxury again until the end of the Napoleonic Wars in 1815.

• Prussia and Frederick II, 1740-86

The most immediate threat came from the young Frederick II of Prussia (1740-86) who had inherited the superb military machine developed by his father, Frederick William I (1713-40) who had built it but never could bring himself to the point of risking it in battle. Frederick William I, a subject perhaps more suited to study by a psychiatrist than a historian, had all the attributes usually associated with the word "Prussian." He was fanatical in his devotion to the interests of his kingdom and ruthless in his methods of organizing it for war. His army was far larger in proportion to population than any other in Europe, and it was raised and supported by the most rigorous utilization of both material and human resources. But even if one concedes that such Spartan policies were essential to the survival of Prussia, one can hardly excuse the physical abuse which he often meted out to those who displeased him, or his cruel treatment of his own children. The young Prince Frederick often suffered under the blows of his father's cane and when he failed in an attempt to flee the country, he feared for his life. His father spared Frederick's life but forced him to witness the execution of the friend who had accompanied him. After this traumatic episode the young man bowed to his father's will and began to devote the conscientious attention to military and civil affairs which was to characterize the rest of his long life. And when an opportunity came in 1740 to sieze the neighboring Austrian province of Silesia from the young and seemingly defenseless Hapsburg empress, Maria Theresa, Frederick was quite prepared to place what he considered to be the future security and well-being of his kingdom above any moral considerations. He moved with a ruthlessness which his father would have applauded, but which sent a thrill of horror through all Europe.

• Silesia and the War of the Austrian Succession

When Frederick was quickly joined by France, Maria Theresa and the Habsburg inheritance seemed to be doomed. England's honoring of her long-standing Austrian alliance seemed to offer little prospect of help. England's land forces were pitiably small, and the Hanoverian rulers were generally more anxious to guard Hanover than to launch any offensive that might really help the hard-pressed Empress. The most immediate threat came from the Elector Maximilian of Bavaria who with French support invaded Habsburg territories and succeeded in getting himself elected Holy Roman Emperor. At this critical moment the future Empress managed to rally the traditionally hostile and rebellious Hungarians to her support and by a combination of military and diplomatic moves successfully turned the tide – at a price, however. Peace with Frederick was gained by accepting his occupation of Silesia. When the new Bavarian Emperor died suddenly in 1742, Maria was able to get her husband, the Duke of Tuscany, elected as Emperor and her position thus made more secure. The French were driven out of Habsburg lands by 1744 and thereafter the fighting between England, France, and her ally Spain was primarily concerned with overseas or colonial conflicts and had little effect on the ultimate terms. The final treaty of Aix La Chapelle in 1748 did confirm Frederick's successful siezure of Silesia – a crucial factor in the rise of Prussia and so of all European history.

• The Extension of European Conflicts

It was not until the wars associated with Louis XIV that European conflicts, as a matter of course, tended to have worldwide reverberations but by 1715 this had become a permanent fact of international relations even though the consequences of this development were not generally understood by European statesmen and diplomats until the emergence of William Pitt the Elder as the war leader in Great Britain in 1757. Generally, until the second half of the seventeenth century none of the powers had settlers enough in the territories they claimed nor, with the exception of Spain and the Dutch, did their territories produce enough wealth to make them worthy of serious consideration. But by 1700 the products of the French and English plantations, especially in the West Indies, had become so valuable that these two countries became increasingly aware of their economic importance. While their possessions in North America were less immediately valuable, the steady growth of population in the English colonies was to make it increasingly difficult for the mother country to ignore their interest and concerns in future conflicts. The increasing importance of commerce and of colonies, in the eyes of English political leaders, was shown by the emphasis upon securing commercial concessions and strategic maritime posts in the treaty of Utrecht. The most significant of these was the *asiento,* the privilege of supplying slaves to the Spanish colonies on the New World.

• Overseas Strategies

Although the War of the Austrian Succession was primarily concerned with continental issues, it actually merged with the commercial and colonial war between England and Spain. England's alliance with Austria involved her on the continent as did Spain's anti-Austrian objectives in Italy. France and England only began hostilities in 1744, and although they fought some important land battles, their overseas interests in both North America and India involved major commitments of manpower and material. However, as usual, the peace settlement of 1748 was determined by the military situation in Europe without regard to the actual success or failure of operations overseas. The British colonists were infuriated to find that the key French fortress at Louisburg at the mouth of the Saint Lawrence River which they had taken with great effort was to be returned to the enemy – seemingly without consideration for their investment of time, blood, and money or their interests. But their indignation could not be entirely ignored at home and it probably contributed to the change in attitude manifested when hostilities were resumed in the Seven Years War (called the French and Indian War in America) in 1756.

• The Philosophes and the New World-View

In the sixteenth and seventeenth centuries the traditional Christian-Aristotelian-Ptolemaic world-view had received a series of shattering blows. The full effects of these were not felt until the eighteenth century when intellectuals (both amateur and professional) began to explore, discover, and then explain to the literate public the truly vast implications of this new scientific view of the world. The leaders of the movement have generally been referred to by the French term "*philosophes,*" although many to whom it has been applied were not philosophers in the formal or professional sense. Their most important role was as popularizers of the radical new-world view and its implications through both the written and spoken word. In doing this virtually all literary forms were utilized and one reason the *philosophes* were so successful was that with a few exceptions, they all wrote with such style and grace that they managed to make even the most dry and abstruse subjects relatively lively and interesting.

The most famous of the *philosophes* was Francois Marie Arouet, better known as Voltaire (1694-1778). Of bourgeois origin and moderate wealth, as a young man he offended a nobleman in some of his writings and was forced to take refuge in England. He there became acquainted not only with the intoxicating air of free expression, but also first came to be aware of the new theories of Newton and Locke. Convinced of the absolute validity of the idea of the world as a great machine run by natural laws, he devoted the rest of his life after his return from England to defending this view against all attackers and preaching it to all who would listen. A master literary artist, he used all the forms – essay, drama, poetry, and novel – for the spread of these new ideas. Because they seemed to threaten traditional religion he found it safer to live most of the later years of his life just across the border in Switzerland. Friend of kings, princes, and aristocrats as well as the literary elite, he was the acknowledged leader of all those trying to move people toward a happier existence by making known to them the laws of nature and nature's God.

But Voltaire was not alone. His contemporary, Diderot (1713-84), who really was a philosopher, devoted his life to disseminating the new world-view of the enlightenment through the publication over almost twenty years of a multi-volumed encyclopedia which contained in its many articles written by experts such as the famous mathematician, D'Alembert (1717-83) the sum total of knowledge available to the enlightened man. As each volume appeared, Frenchmen would line up at the public reading rooms to await their turn to read the new volume like a novel. Two other *philosophes* more famous for their political and social views, the Baron de Montesquieu (1689-1755) and Jean Jacques Rousseau will be discussed in detail later on.

The establishment of Newton's theory of universal gravitation seemed to place the cap-stone on the view that the universe was a marvelous machine operating according to regularly established laws which could be expressed mathematically and were completely intelligible to human reason. As a contemporary poet ecstatically expressed it, "God said, 'Let Newton be' and there was light." No longer was the universe dark and mysterious and knowable only to God. With the scientific method developed by Newton and his predecessors, there was no limit to what man might be able to discover about the universe in which he lived. The formerly unfathomable abyss between lowly man and the omnipotent creator seemed to be closing – or at least it appeared that it might be as man continued to extend the limits of his knowledge. Intoxicated with this idea and its tremendous boost to man's self-esteem, the philosophers began to dream of a perfect world here and now – rather than as something only obtainable in the heavenly realm of future existence. There were two critical assumptions which most seemed to accept with a remarkably unscientific lack of rigor. The first one was that the creator God who made this marvelous machine for man must be beneficent. That is, he intended the well-being and happiness of man. What malevolent God could ever have produced such a marvel for man's enjoyment? The second assumption was this wonderful universe designed for man's happiness and well-being operated in the area of human relations according to the same regular natural laws as in its physical aspects. Or at least it could if man by study and proper education would only learn what these "natural" laws of the universe in the area of human (including political, social, and economic) relations were, and put themselves in harmony with them. For most of the *philosophes* it was the disharmony between the human laws and institutions which was the source of all man's ills and the solution was to bring these laws and institutions into accord with those prescribed by nature.

• Religion: Deism

The first problem of those who adopted these new views was to establish some relationship to the traditional Christianity which they all had been brought up in. For most it was a question of modifying traditional Christianity to the degree necessary to make a comfortable accommodation. This meant maintaining a belief in a beneficent Creator God who might continue to be identified with the God of the Bible so long as the miracles could be dismissed as the fantasies of people who were carried away by religious enthusiasm. This belief was known as Deism and it was undoubtedly a position knowingly or unknowingly held by millions who still considered themselves good Christians. Many like George Washington continued to be churchgoers, but like him discreetly separated themselves from the supernatural elements of the faith (he withdrew during the administration of Holy Communion). Some Deists like Voltaire rejected institutional Christianity vehemently and completely, and a very small number of the *philosophes* even professed atheism.

• Freedom of Belief, Speech, and Press

Since the differences between the traditional churches and sects revolved around issues which were ultimately theological and therefore supernatural, to the *philosophes* there seemed to be no basis for establishing the absolute validity of any one set of beliefs as opposed to another. Therefore it clearly was totally irrational and unjustified to persecute anyone for his religious beliefs or to attempt to control them. The only natural and accordingly proper attitude was complete toleration of all views. Similarly there could be no justification for censoring the writing or speech of anyone on religious grounds. Since the church had been responsible for most restrictions on speech and press, the *philosophes,* most of whom at various times suffered from the effects of this censorship, were enthusiastic supporters of these two civil liberties.

• Faith in Progress

It was assumed that like the physical laws of the universe the laws governing human relations and activities would apply universally. From this it followed that man and societies when organized "naturally" would basically be all alike, since men from the Eskimos to the South Sea Islanders were intrinsically similar in their human condition and the fundamental rules of human conduct would be the same wherever the enlightened congregated. The result (along with the acceptance of French as the language of culture) gave the eighteenth century a cosmopolitan aspect that has never existed since. Intellectuals moved freely from one country to another and even between continents, as shown by the experiences of Franklin and Jefferson in Europe.

Because of the belief that men had discovered the key to the unlocking of the secrets of the universe with the scientific method, and through education could hope to make the conditions essential to human happiness known and actively sought, it was a century of optimism. Achievement of the golden age was just a matter of time and progress toward it was inevitable. A few, of course, were more impressed by the obstacles than the prospects, but generally complacency or acceptance of the *status quo* was apparently very rarely felt and even less seldom expressed. Even Voltaire who in his fable *Candide* seemed to end up by saying that with all the evil in the world one should limit oneself to cultivating one's garden, obviously never took the advice seriously himself. He never stopped fighting for causes that seemed to him to be just.

• Enlighted Despotism

All the *philosophes* agreed that given the new world-view's stress on individual rights, the aim of the political order was to allow the greatest possible freedom to individuals with only the very minimum of restrictions absolutely essential to the protection of society's interests. Since this was the most desirable situation, it was assumed that this was the one which would be attained if the laws of a country were brought into harmony with the natural laws of the political order, as far as they could be discerned by a truly enlightened sovereign. Because there would always be some groups and individuals with a vested interest in preserving the old order, the ruler would have to be strong enough to overcome this opposition – even absolute power might be necessary. But since the properly enlightened ruler could always be expected to know and follow the interests of his people (with whom obviously his own interests as an enlightened ruler were identical), there was no danger of an enlightened despot abusing his power.

This classical theory of enlightened despotism, as just described, has been applied to certain monarchs of the eighteenth century who seemed to make an effort to apply the political principles of the enlightenment to their countries.

The three foremost examples of enlightened despots are Frederick II (The Great) of Prussia, Joseph II of Austria (co-ruler with his mother 1765-80, ruler 1780-90) and Catherine II (The Great) of Russia (1762-1795). If one were to judge by her policies and accomplishments, the Empress of Austria, Maria Theresa (1740-80) might well be included in this list, but her strongly traditional Catholic religious beliefs led her to reject the ideology of the Enlightenment.

• Frederick the Great of Prussia

Thanks in large measure to the work of his father, Frederick inherited a kingdom which although made up of disparate territories, nevertheless had received a relatively high degree of administrative centralization. The Prussian bureaucracy was already becoming a model for all Europe, and as long as an active energetic ruler coordinated the administration of the kingdom, it was successful in getting more out of its limited resources than any other country in Europe. The cost was great but at least it was fairly evenly distributed between the towns and the countryside. Even though the Prussian nobility were exempt from regular taxes, they were all required to serve the state in either a civil or military capacity. While it was true that they held extensive powers over the serfs on their estates, they were also held responsible for furnishing police, justice, and administrative services at the local level as well as for collecting the taxes from their own serfs. Because of the effectiveness with which this obligation of service was enforced it could perhaps be described as the least unjust social system in eighteenth century Europe.

Frederick II consciously embraced the principle of enlightened despotism that the first obligation of the ruler is to live and rule only for the well being of his people. This principle Frederick expressed most aptly when he described himself as the first servant of the state. For rulers who repudiated traditional Christianity and its doctrine of obligatory obedience to sovereigns, some logical justification for the obligation of obedience to their rule had to be found. Mere hereditary right was not sufficient since in the bright lexicon of the Enlightenment no legal claim was valid unless it could be supported by some principle of justice or utility. Frederick in a sense had to prove his right to the throne by what he did rather than what he was – a most revolutionary idea if one considers its possible implications. Although it has always been said that the *philosophes,* with the exception of Rousseau, were not revolutionaries, their doctrine of enlightened despotism, although conservative as long as hereditary and traditional rulers were willing to become enlightened, was bound to be subversive of rulers who refused to accept its demands.

Since natural laws were expected to be applied universally, it is obvious that throughout the lands of a single ruler all laws should not only be just but uniform. In a state like Prussia made up of a conglomeration of territories extending over 500 miles with quite different historical backgrounds and traditions, the tremendous disparity in laws could only be an offense to the enlightened. Unfortunately for Frederick he could not claim the initiative in starting the vast codification of Prussian law. It had been begun by his singularly unenlightened father, but Frederick gave the project his blessing and as much material support as he could spare. The task was not finally completed until after his death, but he clearly deserved the credit for seeing it through. The fact that this enlightened step also greatly improved Prussian civil administration and made the task of government easier was perhaps just a happy by-product.

• Religious Toleration and Education

Frederick II also received high marks as an enlightened ruler for his policy of religious toleration. In a Europe where religious prosecution was still very much alive, Frederick welcomed the exiled Jesuits and offered to build a mosque in Prussia if any Moslems would be willing to come settle there. His record in this area is slightly tarnished by his strong prejudice against Jews, however. The indifference to the tenets of traditional religion which underlay his policy, also led him to virtually suspend censorship of all religious books and to this degree support freedom of speech and thought. Whether this would have been so freely granted had the speech been critical of him or the Prussian state is an open question, but one could say as nasty things as one wished about revealed religion.

Since education was to provide the means for producing the perfect society, according to the tenets of the Enlightenment, it was also to Frederick's credit that he attempted to extend the opportunity for education in his state and to recognize an obligation of the state to support it. Although here again his father had anticipated him by initiating an elementary school provision, Frederick greatly extended state responsibility for education in 1763 – at least in theory. With his limited resources, support was always meager and practical results below aspirations. Furthermore, Frederick's statements made it clear that he supported education because of the greater practical utility of educated citizens rather than as an instrument of social improvement.

• Joseph II of Austria

Although Frederick's adherence to enlightened ideals was impressive, in no case did this require any notable sacrifice of either his own or his kingdom's interest – quite the contrary. This was not the case with Joseph II, however, and accordingly he is usually recognized as a much more sincere advocate of enlightenment than his Prussian counterpart. It is also true that his innovations were both more numerous and more radical. His mother, Maria Theresa had made numerous innovations in the Hapsburg state which were perfectly in harmony with the political objectives of the enlightened despots. The bitter experience of the threat to her realm in 1740-48 had made the necessity of radical revision of the fiscal, administrative and military structure only too evident. What Maria found was that, except for her Bohemian lands which had lost most of their traditional self-governing privileges in the Thirty Years War, ruling Austria was like having to negotiate with separate independent states so strong and extensive were the powers of local representative estates. The recently acquired territories in the Netherlands and Lombardy, the traditionally separate kingdom of Hungary, the nuclear lands of Upper and Lower Austria, the

Tyrol, Styria and Carinola, as well as Bohemia, Moravia and Silesia, were all virtually autonomous units controlling their own fiscal, judicial, and military affairs. The still existing representative assemblies in these areas were completely dominated by the local nobility who generally had no aim other than to safeguard their own local rights and privileges.

As soon as the war was over in 1748, with all except Silesia still intact, Maria ordered the trusted advisers to whom she felt she owed her survival to proceed with the process of modernizing the Hapsburg state. Since this meant removing power from the privileged at the local level and transferring it to Vienna, it required a high order of political skill to accomplish it without throwing the state into turmoil. But Maria Theresa, in spite of her impatience to settle with her arch enemy, Frederick II, carried out the process of centralizing power with consummate skill. While the administrative reforms did not attempt to establish anything approaching complete equality of taxation, they did assess the burden more equitably than in most other countries. Hungary required special treatment as its special claims to autonomy had been recognized as recently as 1723. But what the Empress could not do directly she accomplished indirectly. Like Louis XIV she began a policy of buying the support of the Hungarian nobility by attracting them to Vienna with promises of favors both of money and power. More and more Hungarians appeared in positions of authority in both the civil and the military administrations.

As a result of his mother's efforts and with his own active participation as co-ruler after 1765, Joseph in 1780 found himself at the head of a state which had accomplished in twenty years what had taken almost a century in France and Prussia. While this undoubtedly helped to make Joseph's program all the more difficult to achieve but it did not cause him to slacken his determination to go ahead. Joseph II's experience furnishes a striking example of the dangers and difficulties of attempting to realize good intentions in an imperfect world. Impatient with his mother who tended to delay the introduction of reforms because she feared the consequences of too rapid change, Joseph attempted to introduce social and economic changes that were not being finally achieved in eastern Europe for another half century. These included the abolition of the degrading conditions of serfdom which existed throughout the Hapsburg Empire, and the establishment of equal liability to taxation of all land holders, regardless of social rank. A secondary and permanent reform was to remove justice at the local level from the hands of the nobility and give it to a government appointed and supported judge. The emperor also pushed for new law codes, some of which were established during his reign and others after his death. In economics Joseph tried to move his realm from the traditional government controls of cameralism to the more liberal policies advocated by the Physiocrats.

In his religious policy he moved with as much daring as seemed feasible in a dynastic state where the Catholic religion provided the single bond of unity besides common allegiance to the ruler. Although he made repeated protestations of his loyalty to the Roman Church, he did not hesitate to regulate church affairs in ways that were highly distasteful to church authorities, and even to treat the pope with studied insolence when he came to Vienna to see if he could persuade Joseph to modify some of his policies. In 1781 he issued an edict which not only sanctioned private religious observances, but opened both the universities and the ranks of the civil service to non-Catholics. He also closed down those still existing cloistered religious orders which had been declining drastically in numbers and religious zeal since the sixteenth century. He applied their wealth to the improvement of social welfare programs. He also restricted the number of religious holidays and attempted to regulate religious ceremonies and processions. Unfortunately these last steps provided a means for his opponents to stir up peasant resentment against the Emperor in spite of his other attempts to improve their conditions. As one would expect of an enlightened ruler, he increased government support of education and particularly of the University of Vienna.

Joseph's attempts at reform in the social, economic and religious structure of the Hapsburg realm aroused intense and widespread opposition – unfortunately from all ranks. The nobility understandably objected to their losses resulting from the abolition of serfdom and the establishment of equal liability to taxation. The serfs found that the new situation did not automatically bring an end to their problems and blamed the government for lack of sincerity as well as effectiveness. They also resented government regulation of religious observances which had resulted in the abolition of many longstanding and cherished local traditions. Although the bourgeoise might have been expected to support Joseph, its numbers were relatively small except in Bohemia and the Netherlands, and its economic position was often not strong enough to benefit very much by the introduction of his limited laissez-faire policies. As opposition mounted Joseph became more determined to use his power to see that his will was carried out. Police power became more oppressive, and this in turn provoked more opposition, even from those who otherwise were sympathetic with the aims of the reforms. Outlying portions of the empire such as the Netherlands, Lombardy, and Hungary where ties to the crown were weaker or less well defined, were in open revolt at the time of Joseph's death in 1790. No wonder he died feeling that he had failed in everything he attempted. His younger brother succeeded him, and although an equally strong partisan of enlightened policy (his Duchy of Tuscany was considered by many to be a model) was forced to rescind major portions of Joseph's program in order to re-establish internal peace and order. But those portions which were retained, such as the judicial reforms, did represent a permanent contribution to the continuing viability of the Hapsburg state.

• Catherine the Great of Russia

The Tsarina, Catherine II, is traditionally included among the enlightened despots, although all authorities agree that she is least deserving in every respect except her willingness to subsidize the *philosophe* writers who established her reputation. Even so she is usually excused for her shortcomings on the grounds that conditions in Russia and her somewhat shaky claim to the throne made it difficult if not impossible for her to attempt any truly radical enlightened reforms. Because she had occupied the throne only with the acquiescence of the Russian nobility when her husband died under mysterious circumstances (she had a living son who might have been considered to have a better claim to the throne with his mother relegated to the position of regent) it was reasonable that she would be extremely cautious about doing anything that would arouse opposition. Besides relieving the nobility of any obligation to service in the army or the government – obligations which Peter the Great had rigorously enforced when he had formalized their ranks and privileges – she also confirmed the extended rights over their serfs which they had gradually usurped since Peter's death. Even the confirmation of the rights of the towns which the Tsarina issued in 1775 made no change in the basic character of an administrative system which gave preponderance to the nobility at the local level.

The chief reasons for including Catherine among the enlightened despots were her well-publicized but ultimately abortive attempt to codify Russian law, and her policies toward the church. Although she seems to have read many of the works of the *philosophes* and invited them to visit her so they could instruct her, she seemed to have been most influenced by Montesquieu whose ideas that governments must be suited to the physical and social environment of the people they ruled, seemed to offer a convenient justification of autocracy in Russia. The size of the country and the variety of its people seemed to indicate that only autocratic rule could be effective. With the church she continued Peter's policies of secularization by taking over the lands of the church and making all clergy simply civil servants of the state. The confiscated property was used for the most part for beneficial social welfare projects. Although Catherine II seems to have been aware of the importance of education and the desirability of its support, it remained understandably low on her list of priorities and little progress was made in this field.

• Development of Laissez-Faire

By the mid-eighteenth century it was being urged that the economic interests of governments and people were identical. It was presumably impossible to have a rich state in a poor country and, the argument went, the state should therefore pursue those economic policies which would bring maximum prosperity to its citizens. This could be best achieved by allowing them to pursue their natural instincts for profit since these would automatically guide them toward the best investment of their money and their labor, provided they were not hindered in their efforts by government regulations. One group of economists in France called the Physiocrats developed the theory that if all would follow their instincts and enlightened self-interest, the economy would function like a great machine which would in the end bring the greatest prosperity to all. A Scotsman, Adam Smith (1723-90), developed the notion of this wonderful machine a step further by arguing that the pursuit of enlightened economic self-interest, far from being harmful to the interest of society as traditional Christian economic ethics had held, would be reconciled with the interest of society by the operation of a wonderful and even sort of magical "invisible hand" which could effectively reconcile the most flagrant pursuit of self-interest with the maximum economic advantage of society as a whole. Adam Smith's theory that the wealth of nations (the title of the book he published in 1776) could best be obtained by allowing economic freedom to their citizens, became the basis for the dominant stream of economic thought throughout the nineteenth century and much of the twentieth. The similarity between Adam Smith's ideas and those of the Physiocrats is shown by the fact that we use the latter's term "laissez-faire" (allow one to act freely) as a convenient description of Smith's theory.

• Social Structure of Eighteenth Century Europe

The social structure of most countries in Europe was extremely complex by the eighteenth century but there was a kind of general pattern. At the top was the relatively small aristocratic or noble class which for the most part derived its wealth from land and in most cases possessed certain formally recognized or even legalized rights or privileges denied to other classes. One of the most common of these was exemption from taxation. This privilege was based originally on the idea that this class by fighting for the crown (its primary function in the Middle Ages) made its contribution in blood rather than money. Over the years other forms of service besides military had likewise been recognized as deserving of the rank and privileges of nobility, and in some cases money alone became sufficient to gain admission to its ranks. Originally this noble class had actively shared powers of government with the crown, but in western Europe they had generally lost this position by the eighteenth century. In the eastern part of the continent (east of a line running roughly from the Elbe River to the Adriatic) however, where for local reasons the system of serfdom had been reimposed in the seventeenth and eighteenth centuries, they still played a key role as administrators and judges for their rulers. Originally in the Middle Ages the only other class (excepting the clergy who were a corporate group into which one entered by choice rather than birth) were the serfs who by virtue of their status were required to perform certain services (later transformed to money payments as serfdom disappeared in western Europe) for the lords who protected them and provided rudimentary government services. Most oppressive servile aspects (such as uncompensated labor) had disappeared by the eighteenth century in western Europe, but this seemed to make the few remaining obligations, such as payments when land was inherited, all the more objectionable.

Between lords and serfs there had come to intrude a new class, the class in the middle, the new townsmen – the bourgeoisie. Over the centuries this class had grown markedly in size and importance because of its increasing wealth, but by the eighteenth century it probably still constituted less than 15 percent of the population. As members of the class achieved wealth through their handicrafts or in commerce or banking or governmental finance, the upper ranks found it not too difficult to move into the ranks of the nobility. While it is clear that as a group this class was generally cut off from the privileges and honors of the nobility, many members, by virtue of membership in guilds or professions or other corporate groups, shared in the special rights or distinctions of these groups – and these were not inconsiderable. The largest, most significant, and most highly privileged of all these corporate groups was the clergy, although their privileges were not shared equally between noble and non-noble members. The status and privileges of the clergy varied greatly from country to country, but in all they constituted a separate and distinct order.

• The Implications of Enlightenment: Social Theory

Although the *philosophes* generally were not equalizers or social radicals – quite the opposite in most cases – their doctrine was bound to be revolutionary in its implications when applied to a traditional society. Since their doctrine affirmed that all men are created free and equal in rights, special rights or privileges could be only rationally justified as a reward for special talents or contributions to the state – in which case they should be only personal and not transmissible – or when such privileges could be justified on the basis of social utility – perhaps as a means of getting some distasteful or socially necessary task accomplished. The implications of this doctrine therefore were to place in jeopardy all special rights or privileges that were held solely on the basis of hereditary or prescriptive right, or any other such irrational justification. While the *philosophes* did not push the implications of this doctrine very hard, since most of them lived happily on intimate terms with persons of noble status, they always remained in the background as the ultimate justification for proposals for social reform such as the abolition of serfdom and equality of taxation. The degree to which the doctrine of social equality had pervaded not only intellectual circles but French society as a whole became quickly evident during the Revolution when all former social distinctions were abolished in June of 1790 and equality became one of its watchwords.

• Critics of the Enlightenment World-View

Although the great majority of those whom we would call intellectuals enthusiastically embraced the new world-view in the eighteenth century and worked valiantly to spread its message through all available channels of propaganda (Diderot's *Encyclopedia* was only the most famous), there were some, however, who rejected it completely as well as some who refused to accept certain particulars, or interpreted its implications differently. Probably the largest group of dissenters was made up of those who remained strictly loyal to some form of traditional Christianity. There were significant numbers of Catholics in France who remained staunchly loyal to the faith. Although they never attained the intellectual preeminence or reputation of the *philosophes,* they did try to continue to keep a pro-church viewpoint alive and before the public. In addition, in both England and Germany movements developed in the eighteenth century which placed emphasis on the importance of emotion rather than reason as the key element in religious commitment.

Besides the supporters of religious orthodoxy, even adherents of the basic tenets of the Enlightenment differed in their positions on particular topics. Although both Voltaire and Montesquieu were admirers of the English government in the form it assumed after the Revolution of 1688, Voltaire recognized that it was unrealistic to propose it as a model for the traditional monarchies on the continent. The lawyer and judge, the Baron Montesquieu, on the other hand, perhaps because he recognized that the natural laws of politics were not nearly so easily determinable as his other *philosophe* friends thought, judged that it might be well to maintain some kind of check on the absolute power of government, no matter how enlightened it might be. He advocated a constitution providing for a separation of powers and a system of checks and balances such as he thought he saw operating in England after 1688. Or as an alternative a system providing for a powerful, privileged aristocracy which could provide a necessary and salutary check on absolute monarchy.

Another dissenter from the political orthodoxy of the *philosophes* was Jean Jacques Rousseau (1712-78). He did not dissent from the idea of the existence of a universal, natural law, he merely disputed whether this was identifiable with human reason. For him the emotions were much more important in determining what was natural than reason. Rousseau also rejected the rules and regulations of eighteenth-century society as artificial and corrupting and urged that men seek a new basis for morality. Contrary to popular view he did not find it in the example of the "noble savage," since he was well aware that laws and conventions had contributed to man's moral improvement. But Rousseau's chief distinction was his insistence, in his since famous but then relatively little known book, *The Social Contract,* that no government was legitimate unless all men living under its jurisdiction had a direct voice in the making of its laws. His insistence on the right of every individual (male) to such participation, and his insistence on the immorality of any other system, made him the first modern advocate of the one man-one vote principle. His advocacy of radical democracy put him completely outside the mainstream of eighteenth-century political thought. Generally, even the most liberal political writers took it for granted that the right to vote would be limited to the educated and/or well-to-do.

• Diplomatic Revolution, 1756

The brief interval of peace during the first half of the century was interrupted in 1740 when old rivals went to war again. France, allying with

Frederick II, resumed her long standing conflict with the Habsburgs, and England renewed her old rivalry with Spain. In the end the Empress Maria Theresa was the only loser at the peace table, and understandably she thought of the peace as only a truce to be maintained until she was ready to make Frederick II pay for his evil deeds. Her chief adviser, Prince Kaunitz (1711-94), recognized that it would be very difficult to accomplish this aim if opposed by the two best land armies in Europe, France and Prussia. Accordingly, the Empress was persuaded to end the long-time feud with France and seek her as an ally. Frederick played into their hands by initiating a shift from a French to an English alliance in 1756, and a complete reversal of alliances was quickly accomplished with an abandoned France now joining with Austria. When the Tsarina Elizabeth of Russia also joined the attack on Prussia, it seemed as though Frederick's situation was hopeless. But during the next seven years he showed his true military genius by marching his army from one border of Prussia to the other and always managing somehow to hold off the attacks of his three opponents.

• Seven Years War, 1756-63

The opening phases of this war were disastrous for England overseas with Braddock's defeat in America only one of several setbacks. Public opinion soon demanded the inclusion of William Pitt, the Elder (1708-78), into the cabinet, and he quickly assumed control of both diplomatic and military operations. For the first time the colonial aspects of a war were given higher priority than the European on the grounds that these colonial areas were of greater importance to Great Britain and that any conquests overseas could, if necessary, be used as bargaining points in any settlement of affairs in Europe. In the meantime France, as usual, continued to divide its support between large-scale land operations on the continent and naval and land operations overseas. In the end the result completely vindicated Pitt's judgment. Spain's entry into the conflict on France's side in 1761 was too late to have any effect on the outcome and served only to provide more spoils for England. By 1763 the French had been defeated both at home and abroad, and with Russia pulling out of the war in 1762, Maria Theresa had to admit that once again she failed in her effort to force Frederick II to return Silesia. The success of Frederick II and Pitt had almost been too great, however. A frustrated and humiliated Austria and France were sure to want to fight again as soon as they had recovered, but the wily Frederick II for the remainder of his reign was able to forestall Austrian efforts to find some compensations for their loss. On the other hand in 1777 the success of the American colonists in their war for independence convinced the French that this offered an opportunity to humiliate their old rival, England. Their intervention on behalf of the colonists was effective for them, but gained nothing for France but some dearly bought solace for past defeats.

• French Military Reorganization

One positive benefit for France did emerge, however. As a result of her defeat in the Seven Years War, France undertook a drastic reorganization of her military machine. Its chief aims were to make forces more mobile and battle more decisive. Eighteenth-century armies tended to be very unwieldy and immobile, as commanders were reluctant to move far from their supply bases, and it was difficult to force the enemy to join battle if he wished to avoid it. If battles were fought, they frequently brought no decisive result. In order to facilitate greater mobility a new command structure was evolved using the division as the basic unit. Each division was given all the necessary supporting units (artillery, cavalry, quartermaster, medical, etc.) to enable it to operate as a self-sufficient unit which could be relatively easily maneuvered by commanders. Some new weaponry, such as lighter and more mobile artillery, was also developed. These innovations, along with experience gained in the American War and some additional innovations by the revolutionary government, were what provided the basis for French military domination of Europe down to the end of the Napoleonic wars.

• Partition of Poland, 1772

In the late 1760's it appeared that Poland under an enlightened king was making an effort to repair some of the most critical weaknesses of its government which had made it the prey of its stronger neighbors throughout its history. An elective kingship and a representative assembly which gave each of its members a personal veto had made any really effective government impossible. But none of the great powers wished to see real reform unless they could continue to dominate the stronger state. And unfortunately rival reform elements within Poland were also unable to unite behind their ruler. In order to avoid anyone's taking advantage as Frederick had done with Silesia in 1740, Poland's three neighbors, Russia, Prussia, and Austria, agreed in 1772 that each should take an agreed upon portion of Polish territory and thereby avoid the dangers of a quarrel over the spoils. Since Poland's forces were inadequate to resist even one of these powers, there was no alternative but to submit. This so-called "partition of Poland" stands as the eighteenth century's classic example of the continuing and constant predatory instincts of all great powers in this century. The means of satisfying them changed from time to time – becoming more effective – but the instincts didn't.

• England and the Agricultural Revolution

As a result of its victories in the Seven Years War, Great Britain and Prussia dominated the period between 1763 and 1789. Frederick the Great continued his buildup of Prussian power, and skillfully used it to defend the territory which he had acquired at such great cost to his obedient subjects. Great Britain also continued to grow in wealth and power, even though her progress at times seemed to be threatened by internal political tensions. Her trade continued to grow spectacularly – in part as a result of her victories in the competition for colonial areas – but in large measure because of the remarkable economic development of the whole European complex.

England was in a particularly favorable position because since the beginning of the century she had been going through an agricultural revolution which not only provided the food base for the remarkable increase in population which becomes evident in the second half of the eighteenth century, but also had the effect of making agriculture increasingly profitable. This helped to provide additional capital for the support of commercial ventures, or after 1780 for the new machines which were just beginning to revolutionize the production of textiles. The agricultural innovations such as the use of lime, marl, or other chemical fertilizers, the use of root crops to restore fertility, the use of horse-drawn implements such as harrows, rakes and seed-drills, seem hardly extraordinary to us. But these steps, when applied to the larger and larger farms which could be developed by combining holdings and enclosing former communal lands, along with the scientific breeding which became possible with enclosed lands, all resulted in a truly revolutionary increase in agricultural production. Other effects were perhaps not so beneficial. The small independent farmer usually found it almost impossible to compete since he lacked the capital to enclose and fence his land. He either had to become a renter, a day-laborer, or go to the city and provide the labor supply for the newly developing industry. Fortunately the peak of the enclosure movement did

"Gin Lane" in London, from an engraving by Hogarth. Courtesy, Museum of Fine Arts, Boston.

not come until the very end of the century when the demand for factory labor was beginning to be quite strong.

• Colonies and the Constitutional Crisis

The only dark spot in this bright picture was the problem of England's relations with her North American colonies. During the first half of the century, although the colonies were theoretically restricted by mercantilist colonial trading policies, the government generally was tolerant of violations so long as they did not adversely affect English interests. The fact that the colonists used money gained by illicit trade with the French and Spanish colonists in the West Indies to pay for products bought in England helped to make a policy of "salutary neglect" beneficial to both. The situation changed after the Seven Years War, however, when Britain felt it only reasonable that the colonists should bear part of the burden of paying for the war which had so successfully defended them. This, however, raised the question of just what were the exact powers of the mother country over her colonies, and it turned out in the end that this issue could not be resolved peaceably.

Part of the difficulty was that Great Britain herself was going through a kind of constitutional crisis and this tended to complicate markedly the problem with the colonies. During the reigns of the first two Georges the broad lines of cabinet government and ministerial responsibility had developed under Walpole's skillful handling. Unfortunately, on his death there was no single politician able to carry on as effectively, with the result that control was generally exercised by combinations of interests or factions which tried to establish policies favorable to their groups. Although this worked well enough in times of peace, it failed when war came in 1756 and the leaders of the various factions were forced to turn to William Pitt, an individualist whom none of them trusted, but whose ability to arouse the people they all feared. His brilliant management of the war effort made him popular with the masses but not with the young George III who succeeded to the throne in 1760. The new king had visions of ruling England as a kind of "patriot king" who, by holding himself above all factional interests and party strife, would appoint only ministers with similar ideals and would use his extensive powers of patronage to insure that only men with the proper view of the national interest were elected. If only George III had possessed the capacity (or perhaps charisma) to induce people to trust him and accept his views, he might have succeeded. But to a large number of Englishmen, and especially the Whigs whose forebears had revolted in 1688, the question of who had the right to define the national interest had been settled then in favor of Parliament. It seemed to many that if George III's views prevailed, English political liberties were once again in danger. Even though most of George III's opponents supported him on the issue of coercing the American rebels, if there had been a better political climate in England, the issue might either have been settled or avoided altogether. It was failure in the war that finally brought down the king's man, Lord North (Prime Minister, 1770-82), and when George III turned to the young William Pitt

(1759-1806), whom both sides felt they could trust, the crisis was over. Although Pitt and some of the older opponents of the king made gestures toward introducing reforms that would have made a revival of the king's attempt at "enlightened despotism" impossible, these were quickly forgotten when it became evident that all concerned felt safer living with the known short-comings of the old system rather than risking the unknown dangers of trying to bring into being a more truly representative government. The riots in support of John Wilkes, the member of Parliament who defied George III, had perhaps been useful in the struggle against the king, but there was some fear that they had also perhaps afforded an accurate foretaste of what it might mean to give power to the people. Because the turmoil in France after 1789 only tended to confirm that view, England had to wait until 1832 for her first real Parliamentary reform.

• The Decline of France

It was hard for contemporaries to understand what had happened to France between 1748 and 1763. At the former date she was still living on the capital of prosperity and stable government provided by Cardinal Fleury and his wise administration, and although she did not gain anything in the war of the Austrian Succession, she had not lost anything either. But gradually the ineptitude and shortsightedness of the rival court factions that contended for control of the key ministries after Fleury's death began to have its effect. Louis XV persisted in his decision to appoint no chief minister, and when Cardinal Fleury died no one appeared to take over the authority which he had exercised *de facto.* There were able individual ministers at various times, but none of these were successful in organizing a team that could coordinate effectively all phases of the government behind a single policy. Absolutism without a single initiating and coordinating force at the top turned out to be perhaps the worst kind of government. Louis XV understood his role and at times bestirred himself to play it, but for the most part he refused to do the hard kind of royal homework that was required if France was to maintain its pre-eminence.

The difficulties of Louis' government were legion, but most of them could be traced back to one cause – lack of money. The irony was that France was unquestionably the richest country in Europe in terms of wealth and resources. So obviously the problem was caused by the royal government's inability to tap this wealth. In spite of the efforts of Colbert and others, the collection of taxes remained very costly and inefficient. One of the expedients which the monarchy had resorted to in its desperation for money was to sell offices, including that of tax collector. This meant that the government had little or no control over these agents or their performance. Although the exemption of noblemen from the single most important tax, the *taille,* was the most important factor in reducing revenues, the tremendous variation in the amounts imposed on those who paid the *taille* was equally disadvantageous. The amounts, levied by the government on the various provinces were not for the most part based on wealth or population or other reasonable indices, but simply on what had been paid by that province over the preceding years. Certain areas of the country retained the privilege of negotiating with the government over the amount of the tax they were to be required to pay, and understandably these areas usually paid only one-half to one-third of the amount paid by those not enjoying this privilege. Although Louis XIV had attempted toward the end of his reign to introduce new taxes which would have to be paid by all individuals and classes (except churchmen of course) the one that was most effective was abandoned as soon as the war which it was supposed to pay for was over in 1714. There had been an attempt to reimpose it at a reduced level in 1725, but it aroused too much opposition. In 1748 the matter came up again, this time sponsored by the royal comptroller. The levy was supposed to amount to one-twentieth of income, but the Parlement of Paris, the highest court in the land which, after the death of Louis XIV had recovered its right to "remonstrate" against royal acts, refused to register the new tax. The clergy also refused to pay it. The king, who tried to coerce Parlement by ordering it to register and then exiling its members from Paris when it didn't, was finally forced to accept a compromise. The tax would be paid thereafter, but always in the same amount as in 1748. The attempt to force the clergy to accept it also failed. Later on during the century in times of special need (usually war) a second levy of one-twentieth was added on top of the first – but always only with the Parlement's approval.

The failure to find new sources of revenue meant that every year the deficit grew larger as each year's deficit had to be covered by borrowing which in turn added the additional interest cost to current expenses. Wars only intensified the problem as they always required additional loans and so ultimately higher interest expense. It was this vicious cycle of deficit borrowing – higher interest payments – larger deficits, that plagued the monarchy throughout the century. Fortunately the state of the French economy was such that French and foreign financiers were willing and able to provide the loans that were annually required.

• The French Parlements

The principal obstacle to change in France was the Parlements, with the Parlement of Paris having the largest jurisdiction and the greatest influence and prestige. During the reign of Louis XIV these courts had timidly registered all laws without "remonstrance" after Louis early in his reign had lectured them on their duty to their sovereign. But France was only too well aware that under Louis XV royal authority was flaunted in ways that Louis XIV would never have tolerated. Even Louis XV finally lost patience as resistance grew even stronger in the provincial parlements as well as Paris, and in 1771 he dissolved all the old Parlements and established a new system of law courts without the power of remonstrance. His death in 1774, however, put an end to this attempt to restore the absolute power of the monarchy. When the young Louis XVI ascended the throne, he was assured by counselors sympathetic to the former Parlements, that if he wished to get his reign off on the right foot, he should restore the Parlements to their former position and powers. Louis XVI was sadly deceived if he believed that by doing this he had earned the court's gratitude and support. Within a year the Parlement of Paris was attacking the reform proposals of his comptroller, Turgot, and it continued to harass his government until it provoked the final crisis of 1787-89.

• Louis XVI

All France had breathed a sigh of relief on the death of Louis XV in 1774. Like his great-grandfather he had lived far too long. The young Louis XVI was welcomed with enthusiasm and with great hopes for the restoration of France's power and prestige. The victory of the American colonists with France's backing restored some of the lustre to the French image, but it was a very costly venture with no solid or strategic gains to show for it. When the young king appointed first the experienced administrator Turgot, and then the Swiss banker, Necker, who were both known as advocates of enlightened reform, it seemed as though enlightened despotism had perhaps at last reached France. But when vested interests at court and the Parlements were able to bring about the dismissal of both (Turgot's proposal to extend the annual road tax to the formerly exempt nobility was denounced as in effect "taxation with representation") hopes for a new day for France plummeted once again. With the long cycle of prosperity coming to an end in the seventies and with continuing recession in the eighties it was a decade of uncertainty and watchful waiting.

Although neither Louis XV nor XVI could perhaps qualify as "enlightened despots," it should not be assumed that France was badly governed when one got below the top echelon. Recent studies have shown that the intendants in charge of local administration were generally conscientious and able. Even those holding purchased offices at the municipal level seemed to have functioned reasonably well. The chief problem was that the tax structure was incapable of producing the sums of money needed to maintain the kingdom even in times of peace. But understandably all those who possessed any kind of privilege or exemption were reluctant to accept change and they found in the Parlements powerful supporters of their traditional rights and privileges. But they also had no conception of the seriousness of the crisis which was soon to break upon France and Europe.

15

The Era of the French Revolution and Napoleon

THE CONVOCATION of the Estates General for the first time in almost two centuries has traditionally been thought of as marking the beginning of the French Revolution. In fact, however, it actually began in 1787 when the near bankrupt monarchy found itself compelled to find some means to deal with its financial crisis. With hindsight we can see that the conditions which led to the crisis of 1787 had existed for a century or more, but few people had any comprehension of the possible effects of their cumulative impact with the result the revolution of 1789 came as a complete surprise to contemporaries.

On the surface France's social, political, and economic institutions seemed to be functioning reasonably well. Although some people had complaints, has there ever been a period of history when they haven't? And while it was true that the government had been forced to seek loans more and more frequently at rising interest rates, there was little or no reason for the general public to suspect that a crisis was imminent. Just before his dismissal in 1781, the comptroller-general, Necker, had issued the first public statement on the state of royal finances which indicated that the king's treasury could expect a surplus of income in a normal year. Calonne, the comptroller since 1783, was supporting an extensive program of public works which seemed to suggest no need for economizing on the part of the royal government.

• The First Assembly of Notables

There was therefore little reason to anticipate the dramatic announcement on the last day of 1786 that the king planned to convene an Assembly of Notables (all but four of the one hundred and fifty members were nobles) to advise the king on fiscal and administrative changes. Since an Assembly of Notables had not met for more than a century and a half, it was a highly unusual step to take, even if not revolutionary. What had happened was that Calonne had exhausted the traditional expedients used by the treasury to meet the continuing and mounting deficits, and the monarchy faced the threat of immediate bankruptcy unless some way could be found to increase revenues.

When this situation was revealed to the Notables by Calonne at their first session in February, 1787, the shock effect on both the members of the Assembly, and very soon on France itself, was unprecedented – especially in view of the recent optimism of both Calonne and Necker. The first reaction of the Notables was to disbelieve the report, but when the existence of a substantial deficit was verified, they next blamed Calonne. As a result, when the comptroller introduced his reform proposals, they examined them with prejudiced eyes. These reform proposals were extensive and detailed, but the most crucial one was a proposed new land tax which would be paid by *all* landholders regardless of status (including the church). Most members of the Assembly were willing to go along with the new tax provided the king was willing to establish a kind of "watch-dog committee" to keep an eye on the treasury. When the king refused to agree (at that point he was unwilling to consider allowing any group to have permanent surveillance over the crown's expenditures) the Assembly refused to endorse the new taxes and was dissolved (May, 1787). But the crisis remained unresolved.

• The Failure of the Techniques of Absolutism

At this point, the only course open seemed to be for Louis XVI to force the acceptance of the necessary reforms using the traditional techniques of royal absolutism. This meant issuing new laws and decrees that would have to be registered by the Parlement of Paris if they were to have legal validity. The Parlement, made up of judges who had bought their office and who had noble status, had been trying throughout the eighteenth century to affirm its right to the power of judicial review of all laws proposed by the crown. Ever since its success in opposing the reforms of

Turgot at the beginning of Louis XVI's reign, the Parlement had shown itself more and more inclined to challenge royal financial decrees. Now it not only refused to register the new taxes but called for the convocation of the Estates General as the only body legally authorized to sanction new taxes. This was a truly revolutionary stand since both Louis XIV and XV had introduced new taxes at will without convening that body. Louis XVI went through the traditional forms of directly ordering the Parlement to register the decrees. When it then declared this forced registration to be null and void, Louis ordered the members of the court to leave Paris and to cease their functions – the usual means used to force the Parlement to do the king's bidding. Although a compromise was patched up and the court returned to Paris in September 1787, the fundamental issue was not resolved. Could the crown levy new taxes without the approval of an Estates General?

Over the next six months the king made several unsuccessful attempts to reach an agreement with the Parlement on this issue, but when these failed he once again was forced to resort to absolutist techniques. On May 8, 1788 he ordered the establishment of a new system of law courts which would deprive the Parlements of most of their business and also established a new supreme court to take over the Parlement's old power of registration. Probably because of the popularity of the Parlement's stand against new taxes these decrees provoked immediate widespread and vocal opposition all across the country. Most of the provincial Parlements protested vigorously, and in some instances were supported by popular demonstrations. Many lower courts also joined the protest. Many of the Parlements published their official protests in pamphlet form. In some instances they were joined by the lower courts and other official bodies such as town councils, as well as many individuals. There was an unprecedented flurry of protests in the form of pamphlets during June, July, and August. Since the Parlements were the traditional agents of censorship there was nothing to stop anyone from publishing his views – and hundreds did – especially in Paris and the provincial cities where the Parlements were located.

Although the royal government hired writers to publish pamphlets in support of its action, the vast majority of the pamphlets were so hostile to the government's action – even the clergy who happened to be meeting in a special assembly joined the protest – that clearly something had to be done to try to win public support. Accordingly the king on July 5, 1788 issued a decree calling for officials having access to records concerning prodecures to be followed in convening an Estates General to forward them to Versailles. When this hint that a convocation of the Estates General was contemplated failed to have any appreciable calming effect, a second decree was issued on August 8, 1788 formally proclaiming the convocation of an Estates General for May of 1789. When the king followed this up quickly with the reappointment of Necker as comptroller, the public's attitude toward the government quickly changed from hostility to extravagant praise.

• The Revolution of 1788

And well it might since a revolutionary victory had just been achieved as bloodlessly as the English one a century before. The foremost absolute monarch in Europe had just proclaimed his willingness to consult with representatives of the people in an Estates General! What could have been more revolutionary? But whereas England in 1688 had a representative government whose powers and role in government had been clearly defined over a period of four hundred years, the Estates General had not met in 175 years. And since the Estates General had never succeeded in becoming anything more than an ineffective and little used adjunct of the French monarchy, no one could say with certainty how it should be convoked, how it should proceed, or just exactly what should be its powers and its relationship to the monarch. But the evidence is overwhelming that the vast majority of Frenchmen in 1788 jumped to the conclusion that the Estates General when it met would have legislative powers comparable to the English Parliament, and that its meeting would be merely the first step toward the development of a constitution providing for limited constitutional monarchy. But how was this transition to be achieved? How was this body to be organized and how elected? Suddenly for the first time in their lives Frenchmen were faced with practical political questions and very few had any real political experience except in those few provinces which still had their local representative Estates. Even there virtually their only function had been to negotiate the annual tax levy with royal officials.

Now the French were confronted with the most crucial and difficult of political questions – how was the power which everyone assumed the monarchy was relinquishing to be divided between the various classes and interests? The problem had to be at least partially settled before the Estates were either elected or organized, since the mode of election and initial organization would well be decisive in determining the future structure of the government. As in England the initiative in convocation and electoral procedure had to come from the crown, and therefore the problem was how to influence the royal government. At first some of the most influential element, the "patriots" or the "*faction americaine*," in the Parlement of Paris, who had taken the lead in calling for the Estates General, feared that the king would try to organize the coming assembly in such a way as to favor royal interests. Accordingly when the king revoked the decrees of May 8 and the Parlements were restored to their former position, this faction probably was responsible for the demand by the Parlement of Paris that in organizing the convocation the king adhere strictly to the procedures used in the last Estates General of 1614. But no sooner had this demand been publicised than it became the subject of a violent wave of protests in the pamphlets which now began to pour from the presses in even greater volume. Since traditionally the three orders of clergy, nobility, and Third Estate had an equal number of representatives, some of the pamphleteers quickly pointed out that the procedure followed in 1614 had been grossly unfair to the Third Estate which represented 98 percent of the people but had only one-third of the deputies. These partisans of the Third Estate immediately accused the Parlement of attempting to organize the coming assembly in such a way as to assure the preponderant influence of the nobility and clergy. This accusation whether justified or not quickly ended the popularity of the Parlement.

• Vote by Order or by Head?

In some assemblies of the old regime it had been the practice to have twice as many representatives of the Third Estate as either the clergy or the nobility, and a surge of popular feeling now developed in support of this ratio between the number of deputies of each order. Coupled with this, however, was the more radical demand that voting be by head rather than by order. The popular view was that under the old system of voting in the Estates General any action required the approval of each order voting separately – which of course had the effect of giving each order veto power. If, however, the voting was done with deputies of the three orders sitting together as one body, the Third Estate, if it had double the number of deputies, could with the support of known sympathizers in the other orders always expect to have a majority. This then became the key issue around which all others revolved.

The king, now uncertain about the procedures to be followed in the convocation, decided to reconvene the Assembly of Notables and ask their help. They worked assiduously all through the month of November and finally decided that organization and voting should be by order. By this time a flood of petitions had poured into Versailles from all over the country urging the doubling and the vote by head, so there was little doubt but that this was the popular view. But the leading and most influential noblemen had just recommended the opposite. What was to be done? With a rising tide of pamphlets demanding doubling and the vote by head, the king at the end of December on Necker's advice ordered the doubling of the Third, but prescribed no change in the manner of voting. This turned out to be the worst course. The Third Estate was angry because he didn't go the whole way, and the nobility was angry because they thought that he intended at some point to go the whole way (otherwise what was the point of doubling). Because of the ambiguity of this decision, leadership, instead of being firmly in the hands of the king tended to fall into the hands of local leaders. These often were men of high ideals and great intellect but as yet without the experience or the breadth of vision to assume the position of national leadership that was slipping from Necker and the crown.

• The Meeting of the Estates General

Beginning in February 1789 the nation began the long and complex process of electing deputies. Only the nobility elected representatives directly to Versailles. Both the other orders went through a process of indirect election in which individuals at the local level chose electors who in turn joined with other electors to choose the deputies. At every level in each order *cahiers,* or lists of grievances and recommendations, were drawn up and these were finally combined into a summary statement which the deputy was to carry with him to Versailles. What the *cahiers* make absolutely clear is that all France, including the nobility and the clergy, wanted to see the establishment of some form of limited, responsible government which could maintain the monarchy, but associate the people with it in some constitutional manner. Although there were, of course, wide variations in details, the degree of unanimity even between the orders on major points is what is most striking. Although some of the recommendations might seem to threaten long standing rights and privileges such as the traditional noble exemption from some taxes, one is impressed by the moderation of both the demands themselves and the tone in which they were made.

What happened then to the nation that was seemingly ready to make peaceful but revolutionary change by common consent in May of 1789? Unfortunately below this general level of agreement there was the problem of implementation. How were these general principles and aims to be

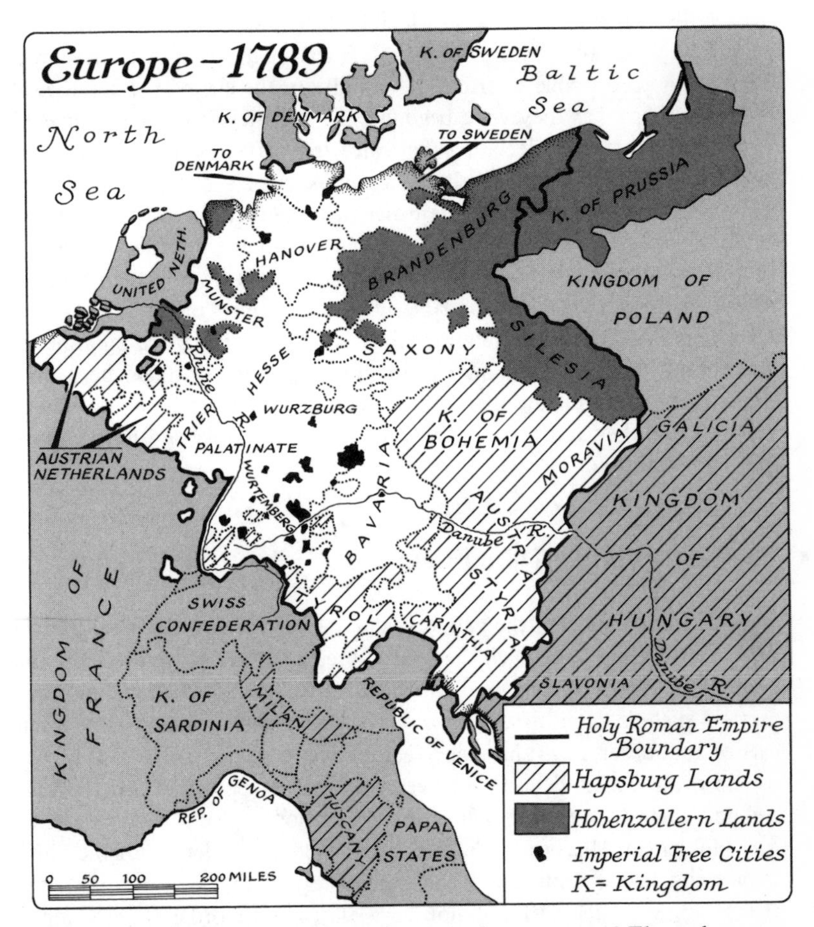

realized in an effective working structure of government? The only means possible in this instance was the Estates General which in the eyes of the majority of Frenchmen was itself not organized in such a way as to give just and proper weight to the wishes of all citizens. Since the Third Estate had neither organization nor arms, nor even the will for violence at this point, the only possible technique was passive resistance – the deputies could abstain from doing anything after the opening ceremony on May 5, 1789, and thus force the king to change the rules. This was the course they followed and for six weeks there was a stalemate. Nothing could be done because the deputies of the Third Estate refused to organize unless it was agreed that credentials would be verified by a committee of the whole body rather than just by each order verifying its own. This action was revolutionary in the sense that it was a defiance of royal orders, but it was passive disobedience of the kind which Parlements had used effectively for centuries. When the royal government failed in its attempt to develop a compromise acceptable to either the nobility or the clergy, the deputies of the commons – as they were beginning to call themselves – on June 17 took the bold step of declaring that since they effectively represented 98 percent of the people, they should be considered a National Assembly. They also invited deputies of the other two orders to sit with them. Some of the most enthusiastic sympathizers from the other two orders (members of the lower clergy particularly) did begin to drift in, and their number increased daily. It is understandable why the members of the Third Estate were apprehensive when they arrived at their meeting place on June 20 and found it closed and under guard. Fearing that this might be merely preliminary to dismissing them, they adjourned to a nearby indoor tennis court where they joined in a solemn oath to never disband until France had a constitution.

• The Victory of the Third Estate

It turned out that the hall was merely closed to prepare it for a royal session on June 23 at which the king offered a further compromise on the issue of the vote. His proposal which called for the vote by head on some matters such as taxation and by order on matters involving only the interests of that order, might have been acceptable in the first days of May, but by now the Third Estate had begun to feel its power. When the king ordered them to leave the hall at the conclusion of the session, the renegade nobleman, Mirabeau, who had been elected as a deputy of the Third Estate and had quickly established leadership of that body refused, and the faltering Louis XVI did not have the will to order them forcibly expelled. They felt confident of the support of the Parisians and strong in their own solidarity. The following weekend there was rioting in Paris when a rumor of Necker's dismissal circulated, and for the first time members of the Parisian guard openly fraternized with the rioters. A frightened royal government finally capitulated to the pressure of the Third Estate and on June 27, 1789 ordered the nobility and clergy to join with the Third Estate in a single assembly which now became truly national.

Because no legitimate means seemed to be available, the Third Estate had resorted to the extra-legal means of passive disobedience and had succeeded in forcing the royal government to accept its demands. To many in the privileged orders this seemed to confirm their fears that the Third would have little respect for tradition or precedent. The nobility in the Estates from provincial areas were generally far more conservative than the liberal, more broad-minded nobility of Paris, and the tactics of the Third convinced many both within the Assembly and outside that further deviation from old customs and traditions was too threatening to be risked. There was a resultant solidifying of resistance to change among those who held favored status under the old regime which was ultimately to make nobility synonomous with counter-revolution and to make it, along with the clergy, the objects of a social revolution carried out by act of the Assembly which stripped them of their privileged status.

Another effect of the royal order of June 27th was to change the nobility from the foremost opponents of royal absolutism – a role they had played ever since the feudal era – to the most ardent and persistent defenders of the king and his royal authority. Since they both based their position and power on inheritance and tradition they obviously had a common enemy in any class or a group that wished to establish other criteria such as ability or talent as a basis for political power or social prestige. Unfortunately, Louis XVI did not see the danger of this embrace by the nobility, and ultimately it cost him his life.

Despite the king's concessions a majority in the royal council believed that the Third Estate could be controlled with a threat of force. Regular troops were moved into the vicinity of Versailles and Paris and no one was really convinced when the king declared that they were there to protect the Assembly. Finally on July 12 some members of the royal council who were alarmed at the direction events seemed to be moving persuaded the king to dismiss Necker and replace him with someone who would stand firm. When this news reached Paris, the citizens, seeking means to defend themselves against an anticipated attack by royal troops, sought arms in the various royal buildings in the city – among them the Bastille. When the governor of that formidable fortress refused admittance, the mob proceeded to storm it. During the bloody events of that day (some of the defenders of the Bastille and some public officials were lynched) cooler heads used the occasion to seize control of the city from its royal officials and establish a new popularly elected governing body with its own citizen militia – soon to be called the National Guard. Louis refused to send troops to the city against "his people," and the next day went to the city hall in Paris to help them celebrate their victory. When he was persuaded to pin on the new red, white and blue cockade (the white of the Bourbons combined with the red and blue of Paris) it was only the first of many efforts by leaders of the Third Estate to identify Louis with the new forces now at work in France, but it was a role he never could bring himself to play convincingly.

• The Spread of Revolutionary Action

After the capture of the Bastille and the establishment of the new municipal government in Paris, the tempo of revolutionary action greatly accelerated. Hearing of events in Paris, eager supporters of the Third Estate in provincial towns and cities proceeded to democratize their own municipal governments. The occasional violence which resulted undoubtedly contributed to the phenomenon which swept the countryside during the last weeks of July now generally known as the "Great Fear." The fall of 1788 had been marked by an unprecedented failure of crops coming on top of a general economic recession which hit when the nation was only beginning to recover from the depression of the 1770's. By the following summer there were serious shortages of grain and prices had skyrocketed. As a result there seems to have been an unusually large sort of floating population of migrant or displaced persons who were mixed with the usual rural underworld of beggars, smugglers, and petty thieves. Given the state of tension which had existed in France for more than a year – and the process of electing deputies and drawing up *cahiers* made even the remote rural inhabitants aware that momentous events were underway – it is understandable that rumors that neighboring villages had been attacked by "brigands" could easily sweep across the countryside in a wave of fear and panic. It is also understandable that the villagers could reasonably believe that the nobility who seemed most threatened by the events of the preceding months were responsible for the instigation of these attacks. When the villagers picked up staves and pitchforks, or whatever was at hand, and banded together to defend themselves they quickly saw an opportunity to free themselves from the bitterly resented monetary obligations which they still had to pay to the local holder of seigneurial rights. In many instances they marched to the seigneur's residence, demanded the legal documents upon which their obligations were recorded and proceeded to burn them. Except in a very few instances where the seigneur resisted, there was no bloodshed and very little actual violence. But the number and extent of these illegal acts of defiance led to the impression that the whole countryside was in arms and was in the process of attacking the unpopular vestiges of the old feudal seigneurial system.

To all responsible officials and to all citizens who believed that respect for the rights of property was a fundamental prerequisite for any

Storming the Bastille. Courtesy, the Print Room, Boston Public Library.

society, it was obvious that something had to be done to restore order. On the night of August 4 in accord with well laid plans a number of noble deputies arose in the National Assembly in turn and voluntarily renounced the seigneurial obligations which they held personally. Others quickly followed the example and someone then proposed that such obligations be legally abolished. By the early morning it was said that the vestiges of the feudal regime had been destroyed in France. Actually the detailed laws took several days to work out and in the end it was found that the members of the Assembly had not been so radical or so generous as first appeared. The rights which infringed on personal freedom such as the prohibitions against having arms or hunting, or requiring the performance of any demeaning personal services were abolished outright. But those obligations which arose from property such as the *cens* or quit-rent, or the payments due when lands changed hands, all of these were to be redeemed – meaning that the peasant landholder had to buy them off over a specified period. Furthermore in the case of dispute about obligations, the burden of proof was to be on the peasant. Even though the results were obviously far short of what the peasants would have liked – and what they eventually got in 1793 – they were too radical for the king. For the whole month of September the Assembly waited in vain for his approval.

• Declaration of the Rights of Man and the Citizen

Meanwhile for the rest of August the National Assembly worked on a declaration of the principles which they would follow in drawing up their constitution for France. Collectively these principles were based on the fundamental beliefs of the Enlightenment respecting man's rights as a human being and as a citizen. Starting with the inherent freedom and equality of man, the declaration went on to spell out what the majority of the Assembly felt were the necessary conditions to secure these rights. Men need to be secure in their persons and property, but able to enjoy the right to do anything which is not expressly forbidden by law. Law is the expression of the general will. All citizens have a right to take part in the making of this law either directly or through their representatives. Citizens are entitled to freedom from arbitrary arrest or the presumption of guilt until proved. They are also guaranteed freedom of speech, press and religious opinion. Taxes must be approved by all citizens and must be apportioned equally according to capacity to pay. No one can be deprived of his property without due process of law. All citizens are eligible for any public office for which qualified, but are accountable to the people for their actions. As might be expected the main points of the Declaration were directed chiefly toward specific grievances against the old regime, but it was broad enough to provide a general basis for liberal movements throughout the next century.

As hunger got worse during September and the king delayed his approval of the August 4 decrees, popular tension once again erupted and the women of Paris staged a march to Versailles. With a minimum of violence they succeeded in getting both the Assembly and the royal family moved to Paris where the sovereign people would presumably be better able to keep an eye on them. This was to be the last serious instance of violence for the next two years while the Assembly completed its work.

• The Work of the Constituent Assembly

The National (also called Constituent) Assembly then set about the difficult task of not only drawing up a constitution but also trying to deal legislatively with the most pressing problems of the moment. The first serious rifts in the ranks of the supporters of the Revolution began to appear in September when the question of the position of the king with respect to the Assembly was being debated, as well as the question of whether legislative power should be in the hands of one or two houses. These were, of course, fundamental constitutional issues and when the body had decided on a unicameral system and only a suspensive veto, some deputies who believed in the necessity of strong monarchy for stability felt that the decision would so fatally flaw the new constitution that they turned against the Revolution. This pattern was to be repeated again and again as legislative decisions were made. The result was a continuing draining away of revolutionary support not only in the Assembly but in the country as a whole. The narrowing base of popular support for the Revolution was to make the problem of governing France increasingly difficult and the trend was not to be successfully reversed until the Terror – and then only temporarily.

The Declaration of the Rights of Man and the Citizens had stated the principles on which the new structure of society and government were to be based and it was the task of the Assembly to establish the laws necessary to put them into effect. This meant uprooting the many aspects of the old regime which violated the principles of freedom and equality and introducing the new elements necessary to secure them.

In government and administration the general pattern followed was to try to reverse the long-term pattern of centralization which had been characteristic of the monarchy. Eighty-three departments with uniform structure were established in place of the old provinces with their wide variations in traditions, rights, and privileges. The departments were to be governed by elective assemblies as were towns and cities. All local officials including mayors, judges, tax collectors and ultimately even priests were to be locally elected.

In one critical respect the Assembly seemed to depart from its stated principles. Rather than universal male sufferage and eligibility for office, qualifications for voting were set up which divided France into "active" (those with the right to vote) and "passive" citizens. Although the property qualification was set relatively low (payment of taxes equal to wages for three days labor) it was still true that about one-third of the male electorate was effectively disenfranchised. The qualifications for eligibility to hold office were much higher and limited the number eligible to about 50,000 (out of a potential electorate of about six million).

The major economic problem was the deficit. What had been the king's problem now became the Assembly's problem. It is usually the policy of revolutionary governments to repudiate the debt of the government they overturn, but in this case the revolutionaries were not really overturning the king. Besides a large proportion of the money he owed was owed to them or members of their class. The only solution to the immediate problem seemed to be to borrow more money to tide the Assembly over until the new government could restore fiscal health. Unfortunately those with money were not impressed with the new government's prospects and initial attempts to float loans were only partially successful. Then in November the Assembly, with the financial crisis in mind, passed an act placing the vast property of the church at the disposal of the nation. Within a few months they were using this property as security, first for government bonds and then for actual negotiable paper money called *assignats.* The extensive lands of the church were to be sold off and paid for with *assignats* which would then be destroyed. In this way the amount of *assignats* in circulation would gradually be reduced. At first the system worked well with *assignats* circulating at nearly face value, but as opposition to the revolution mounted confidence in the *assignats* fell to such a degree that by 1792-93 they were circulating at about one-third of their face value. But in the meantime they had enabled the Assembly to survive the financial crisis.

• The Civil Constitution of the Clergy

But only at inestimable cost, however, for the appropriation of church lands immediately involved the Assembly in religious affairs. Because it took over the source of much of its income, the government felt obliged to provide financial support for the church and as long as it was paying the bill it seemed only reasonable to reorganize the church along lines more in accord with the principles of the revolution. All priests and other officials were to be elected like other civil servants and their salaries fixed by the state. The Assembly was surprised to find that many churchmen conscientiously refused to accept the new arrangement called the Civil Constitution of the Clergy and began to agitate against the Revolution. The government responded by requiring all priests to take an oath affirming their support of the Civil Constitution. When some of the clergy refused, conscientious Catholics sought them out rather than receive the sacraments from priests that had capitulated to the state. The climax came when the papacy formally condemned the Civil Constitution and other acts of the National Assembly directed against the church such as the abolition of monasteries. This made it impossible for a conscientious Catholic to support the Revolution any longer. The cause of counter-revolution thus received its greatest assist and French society was cleft by a rift that still has not healed.

• Opposition of the King

The most important conscientious Catholic was the king himself. The decision of the pope plus the other actions of the Assembly which had restricted his traditional powers made him easy prey for those members of the court and the nobility who wanted to use him in the cause of counter-revolution. By June, 1791 he had decided to try to escape from the control of the Revolution in Paris and seek refuge across the border where all who deplored the course of events in France could rally around him. When this well planned and very nearly successful escape effort failed France was in trouble. The Constituent Assembly had just about completed its work on a constitution in which the monarch had to play a key role. Yet the monarch had not only attempted to abandon his post, but in a statement left behind him strongly criticized many of the actions of the Assembly and the provisions of the proposed constitution. It may seem surprising in view of this that the Assembly did not just let him go and wish him Godspeed. But for over eight centuries France had followed the principle of hereditary monarchy, and many otherwise very radical revolutionaries were as yet unwilling to deviate from the monarchical principle. Therefore when Louis XVI showed himself willing to reconsider, the Assembly was willing to go along with the patently false explanation that the king had never intended to leave France. For both the king and the National Assembly there seemed to be no alternative but to appear satisfied with each other. The Revolutionaries, however, obviously could never completely trust Louis XVI again in spite of his outward acceptance of the new constitution.

• The Counter-Revolutionary Movement

The new constitution went into effect in September of 1791 and the newly elected body called the Legislative Assembly began to try to deal with the legacy of problems left to it by its predecessor. The most pressing of these was the growing disillusionment with the Revolution and the growing strength of an active counter-revolutionary movement. The first counter-revolutionaries were noblemen who found themselves unable to accept the events of Bastille day. The foremost examples were the king's brothers, the Count of Artois and the Count of Provence and as the revolutionary program unfolded other noblemen and their families followed their example and went into exile. Even after the decrees abolishing nobility were passed in June, 1790 the numbers leaving were not large, but these were not ordinary people. Many were among the oldest and most illustrious members of the European aristocracy. These *emigrés* gathered around the Count of Artois in Coblenz not far from the French frontier and began organizing a military force. The king's escape attempt involved the help of French troops whose noble officers considered their foremost loyalty to be to the king and not to the Assembly.

A steady barrage of counter-revolutionary propaganda was kept up from just across the border of the Empire. So long as Louis XVI had maintained an outward appearance of accepting the changes being made in France, the other rulers remained officially perfectly correct in their attitude toward developments in France and generally rebuffed the attempts of *emigrés* nobles to get support for a counter-revolutionary offensive against France. But once Louis' escape attempt seemed to show that he was an unwilling participant in events in France, the other crowned heads in Europe began to show more concern. Louis' acceptance of the constitution made it difficult for them to be too openly hostile, and there is reason to believe that the declaration drawn up at a meeting of the Emperor Leopold II, the queen's brother, with King Frederick William II of Prussia, in the summer of 1791 was intended as a sop to the *emigrés* rather than a genuine threat to France. What the joint declaration that emerged from the meeting said, however, was that the two rulers deplored what was happening in France and urged that action be taken jointly by all powers to try to restore the king to his former position. Since it was known to the makers that several powers, including Great Britain, had no intention of taking action and that accordingly joint action was impossible, it was clearly intended to give the *emigrés* the illusion of support without the substance. But when the document was published and circulated in France by counter-revolutionary agents, it must have sounded like a very real and dangerous threat to the average Frenchman.

• Revolutionary Reaction Toward Other Powers

Up until this time the Revolutionaries had matched their revolutionary fervor for internal change with an equally revolutionary pacifistic policy in foreign affairs. In the spring of 1790 in reply to an inquiry from Spain whether France would honor the long-standing alliance with Spain and join the latter in a war on England, the National Assembly replied with a ringing declaration renouncing the use of force except in self-defense. But with the seemingly mounting hostility of Austria and its ally Prussia, the new Legislative Assembly began to experience a change of attitude.

Although it is now recognized that the declaration made by the rulers of Austria and Prussia at Pillnitz in August, 1791 was only meant to sound threatening, the Legislative Assembly and most Frenchmen were not aware of this. But whether intended as a real threat or not, it provided a basis for supporting a war initiative by a faction of the Assembly which wanted to take aggressive action against the growing threat of counter-revolution. It was too tempting not to use the patriotic appeal of the "country in danger" in order to get the popular support needed to force their more radical views on the more conservative members of the Assembly. When they were joined in turn by some of the conservatives who hoped to use the war as an excuse for a conservative military takeover, as well as by supporters of the king who thought that a war would provide the best means to reverse the course of the revolution, war became almost inevitable. On April 20, 1792 a declaration of war against Austria was passed with only a handful of members dissenting. Prussia in accordance with its alliance with Austria in turn declared war on France.

At first the strategy of the radical faction known as the Girondists, seemed to have backfired when the initial military operations ended disastrously. But they were able to attribute the blame to the alleged treason of the king who was suspected by many to be conveying military information to the enemy. When a large Austro-Prussian force crossed the eastern border on the road to Paris at the end of July, tension mounted. Petitions demanding the removal of the king and the establishment of a new constitution were presented to the Assembly and these began to get vocal support from the populace of Paris. When the commander of the invading army, the Duke of Brunswick, issued a proclamation at the end of July threatening the citizens of Paris with dire punishment if they harmed the royal family, the complicity of the king seemed to be confirmed. Preparations for an insurrection were started by the radical group known as the Jacobins which at this time included most of the Girondists.

On the night of August 9 well organized forces attacked the royal residence, the Tuileries, and the royal family was forced to take refuge with the Legislative Assembly. Unfortunately the order to cease fighting never reached the king's Swiss Guard and casualties were heavy on both sides. The following day the Assembly declared the king removed and called for the election of representatives to a new constitutional convention which would be charged with establishing the government of the first French Republic. In effect a second French Revolution had been accomplished by the Parisian populace along with the detachments of army volunteers from the provinces which were passing through Paris on their way to the endangered frontier. The most famous of these was the detachment from Marseilles which brought its stirring new revolutionary song with it.

• The First Republic

Although the principal reason for the second revolution was the impossibility of maintaining a constitutional monarchy without the willing cooperation of the monarch, it is also true that its fall was initiated and supported by many whose main objective was to obtain a much more radically liberal regime – one more democratic, more egalitarian, and more anti-religious than the one that had just fallen. But when the National Convention met for the first time on September 20, 1792 and was given a chance for survival by a victory at Valmy over the Austro-Prussian invaders on the same day, it became evident that even a body which had been elected for the most part by what was probably the radical minority of the French electorate, could not agree on policy. The Girondists who had been the radicals in the Legislative Assembly quickly became the right wing in the Convention. The new radical wing was called the Mountain because its adherents sat in elevated seats to the left of the speaker's rostrum. As the Convention had to deal with different issues such as the fate of the king (he was executed in January, 1793 for treason against the people of

France), the prosecution of the war, control of the economy, and control of counter-revolutionary activities, the divisions within it became ever sharper. Generally the Mountain pressed for tighter control by the Convention over the departments, especially where fighting or counter-revolutionary activity was going on, and more rigorous economic controls to assure supplies for the military and cheap food for the masses. Increasingly frustrated during the spring of 1793 in its efforts to get its policies adopted, the Mountain appealed to the radical revolutionaries of the city for support. They responded by surrounding the Convention building and demanding the exclusion of those Girondist deputies opposed to the Mountain's program. The Convention made a feeble show of resistance but soon gave in to the pressure. As a result from the beginning of June 1793 the Mountain was in control.

• The Reign of Terror

Outside of Paris there was considerable opposition even from loyal supporters of the Revolution to a government in Paris controlled by the radicals of the Mountain with the support of the Parisian mob, and at one time as many as half the departments were refusing to obey the Convention's orders. This situation in combination with the threat of invasion from without led the Convention to adopt the policy of terror. Beginning in July, 1793 actual control of the country was put in the hands of a committee made up of twelve members of the Convention called the Committee of Public Safety. It had full control over both military and civil affairs. Following a policy of conciliation on the one hand by offering amnesty to those who were willing to cease their opposition to the rule of the Convention and terror on the other in dealing with those who refused to lay down their arms, the Committee managed to keep France from collapsing internally while at the same time seeing that the army's ranks were filled (general conscription of manpower was introduced) and its soldiers supplied with food, clothing, and weapons (the government had the power to requisition any needed items).

Altogether about 17,000 persons were executed during the Terror and although Revolutionary justice was inevitably crude and guilt by association was an accepted principle, probably most of these were guilty of overt acts against the government. Many like the former queen, Marie Antoinette, were not guilty of any overt acts but certainly guilty of hostile feelings toward the Revolution. With the help of deputies sent out directly from the Committee and the ranks of the Convention the crisis appeared to be under control by the spring of 1794. There was mounting criticism from some members of the Convention who believed that the Terror and other controls over individuals (both economic and personal) should be relaxed. On the other hand there were some groups both inside and outside the Convention calling for even more radical measures. Maximilien Robespierre, prominent member of the Jacobins since the early days of the Revolution and a leader of the Mountain who had great influence both in the Convention and in the Committee of Public Safety persuaded his colleagues on the Committee to send to the guillotine those who opposed the policies of the Committee from either the right or the left. Thus in the spring of 1794 the Terror was turned into a political weapon. Up until this time it had been directed primarily against those who either had or threatened to take up arms against the Revolution, and most of the executions had taken place in the rebellious departments. In the spring most of the executions took place in Paris and more often these were the result of a threat or supposed threat to the authority of the Convention. Since this posed a potential threat to all members of the Convention, some began to think about ways to rid themselves of the Committee. By July, with French troops everywhere on the offensive outside France, a successful plot was developed within the Convention by members who as representatives of the Convention in rebellious areas had incurred the wrath of Robespierre because of cruelty or corruption. Although it was not the intention of these conspirators to end the Terror, but only Robespierre's control of it, the Convention seized the opportunity to re-assert itself and proceeded to dismantle the machinery of control. Reaction against not only the Committee of Public Safety but also against the Mountain and its policies soon followed. Those ousted Girondists who had managed to escape execution were allowed to return to take their seats.

• The Directory

Thus when the Convention finally completed its task of making a new constitution in the spring of 1795, the result was a document far less radical than the one drawn up while under the domination of the Mountain in 1793 and never put into effect. It called for a bicameral legislature, and executive authority was to be wielded by a council of five men called the Directory. This title was given to the whole government which took power in September of 1795 – but not under the most auspicious circumstances. The members of the Convention wished to forestall the possibility that free elections under the new constitution might lead to the election of a royalist majority. For this reason they proposed that two-thirds of their number should be guaranteed seats in the new legislative bodies. Although this proposal won a slight majority in the nationally held referendum on the question of accepting the new constitution, it lost heavily in Paris and especially in the conservative, well-to-do districts. When the results of the vote were announced, the conservative sections of Paris attempted to organize a popular movement against the still sitting Convention, but they were thwarted by the effective defense of its building by a young general of artillery named Buonaparte. As a result a month later the Directory was able to formally assume power with two-thirds of the members of the Convention in seats in one or the other of its two legislative bodies, the Council of Ancients (limited to married men over forty) or the Council of 500.

What was desperately needed in France was a government of reconciliation, a government that could re-unite the country and restore a sense of national community. Unfortunately the circumstances of its inception made it virtually impossible for the Directory to accomplish that task. Unsure of itself from the beginning, the government struck out violently, using extra-legal procedures to void elections and thereby making itself vulnerable to those who in turn believed themselves thereby justified in using violence against it. In 1797 the Directors even had to go so far as to call on the army to support them in a coup directed against a resurgence of the Right in the elections of that year – certainly a dangerous procedure for a government which supposedly based its power on the will of the people.

Historically the Directory has had a bad name. No great leaders emerged from its ranks, and generally its members have been accused of venality and corruption. They were mostly middle-class men of property with little inclination to try to win over or even to understand the mass of the people. They placed stability before democracy when they found they couldn't have both, but in the end they had to give way to one who seemed to offer even more stability than they – Napoleon Bonaparte.

• The Rise of General Bonaparte

General Bonaparte had deserved a reward for saving the Convention in 1795, and finally accepted the offer of the command of the Army of Italy in the dual attack on Austria planned for the summer of 1796. One army was to drive due east across Germany, and the other was to advance north from Italy. At that point the Republic had been at war for almost four years and had achieved spectacular success. French armies occupied both the Austrian Netherlands and virtually the whole left bank of the

Rhine. Prussia, along with Spain and Sardinia which had entered the war at the same time as England in February, 1793, had dropped out of the war during 1795, but Austria and the British refused to accept any peace which left France holding the Austrian Netherlands. France, proud of the success of her citizen armies, felt that there had to be some compensation for the blood and money she had expended since 1792. To suggest the relinquishing of any gains simply to achieve peace was looked upon as unpatriotic. Accordingly the only alternative was for the war to continue.

General Bonaparte in his first field command showed himself a master at using the new army, fashioned by combining the new tactics, organization, and weapons developed after the disastrous defeats of 1756-63, with the masses of skilled, well-disciplined, and highly motivated soldiers provided by the Revolution. It was a combination unmatched by any other power in Europe and was to provide the basis for French domination for the next twenty years. In a series of lightning-like attacks which saw troops moved with unprecedented speed to decisive strategic points, Napoleon in the summer and fall of 1796 quickly defeated the forces of the Austrians and their Italian allies.

As General Bonaparte gained control of northern Italy he proceeded to reorganize the former hereditary principalities into republics with new names and new governments. Although the Directory had little interest in the future of Italy, it had no alternative but to accept Napoleon's actions. Could the Revolutionary Republic of France deny the benefits of liberty to other people? More importantly satellite governments could be more easily exploited as they were forced to supply both money and ultimately troops to their French liberators. By his victories and his levies on the new republics, as well as by unofficial looting of works of art, Boneparte made war pay – a factor of crucial importance to the financially hard-pressed Directory. When the General made peace with Austria in 1797 the terms gave France more than she wanted in Italy and less than she wanted on the west bank of the Rhine, but the Directory was again forced to go along. Later after he supplied military support to the Directors in the crisis of September, 1797 Napoleon became even more difficult to control. By this time he was a national hero in France, but the defeat of Austria had left only Great Britain in the war. Bonaparte's strategy of attacking her through the Suez life-line to India led to the disastrous Egyptian expedition of 1798. Cut off by Admiral Nelson's destruction of the French fleet, Napoleon was lucky to get safely back to France after having abandoned his army in the summer of 1799. He attempted the risky journey because Austria had renewed the war with France and had been joined this time by Russia which resented the French foray into the eastern Mediterranean.

"The Skirmish of the Pont d'Arcole" during Napoleon's Italian campaign, from a sketch by Raffet. Courtesy, the Fogg Art Museum, Harvard University.

• Napoleon Takes Power

When Napoleon landed in France, he found the Directory shaken though still in power. Some of its members who had lost faith in it approached Bonaparte to see if he would be willing to provide the military force needed to overturn the Directory and replace it with a new and stronger government which could provide greater stability to the country. The General agreed to go along but showed himself to be much less adept at planning a political coup than a military campaign. Although no one had any real enthusiasm for the Directory, it was still the legal government and some of its members simply refused to bow to Bonaparte's demands for special powers to save the government from an alleged conspiracy of leftists. Even though Napoleon himself fainted away at a crucial moment during the attempted *coup d'etat,* his brother who was chairman of the Council of 500 kept his head and saved the day. On his order last ditch resisters were chased out of the assembly hall at bayonet point by Bonaparte's men and the General's supporters who remained proceeded to vote him the power to draw up yet another new constitution for France. This one, with modifications, provided the basis for Napoleon's rule until 1814.

• Napoleon Reorganizes France

The new government was known as the Consulate, after the title of the holders of executive power. Although there were three Consuls only the First Consul had any real power, and it represented very little change for Napoleon to simply change his title to Emperor in 1804. The constitution that Napoleon constructed returned to the tradition of absolutism and centralization that had been pursued by French kings since the Renaissance. But Napoleon's regime (his first name became his official designation after he became Emperor) had more of the characteristics of the enlightened despotism which France had missed out on in the eighteenth century. His government was a regime of intelligent and conscientious administrators who approached problems with the rationality expected of men who had been educated in the era of Enlightenment. There was just enough popular participation to give the illusion of responsibility, but not enough to impede the rational treatment of problems. The public was allowed to approve by plebiscite important constitutional matters, such as the establishment of the position of emperor, and also to elect a permanent body of electors which provided members for various legislative and executive bodies. The legislative bodies were supposed to rubber-stamp the acts of the elite Council of State, but when they showed slight signs of independence in 1808, Napoleon abolished them. In order to insure the execution of policy down to the lowest level, department and district heads as well as mayors were all appointed by the government in Paris. It seemed as though the old intendant had merely been given a new title, the prefect. But Napoleon read the temper of the French people unerringly. What they really wanted was stability – the kind of stability that would result not only from a firm hand restoring order in areas still in armed revolt, but also from the capacity to effect a reconciliation between the various factions of a highly fragmented French society. This service Napoleon was in a unique position to supply. He owed his elevation to no particular class or group and therefore could act completely independently using men of talent of any background. On several occasions he took pains to dissociate his regime from either republican or royalist factions.

Napoleon's reorganization of the government, his legislation, and his policies soon established his popularity. It was evident that he meant to preserve the major changes of the Revolution while rejecting its extremes. By a concordat with the papacy which accepted the Revolution's disposition of church lands, he healed the long standing schism with the church. Catholics could now support a French government with enthusiasm for the

Spanish Guerillas Fight the French, in "Disasters of War," from an etching by Francisco Goya. Courtesy, Museum of Fine Arts, Boston.

first time since 1790. At the same time owners of former church lands were confirmed in their possession. The abolition of the vestiges of the seigneurial regime also remained in force, thus insuring the support of the peasantry. Honors and titles were revived, but only as rewards for merit. The equality of all citizens before the law was confirmed by the series of law codes drawn up at the instigation of the Emperor who personally participated in the discussion of several of their provisions. The famous Napoleonic code constituted the Emperor's most enduring monument.

On the other hand, some elements of the new regime were not so favorable. The liberty of speech, press, and assembly which had been enjoyed during most of the Revolution were increasingly restricted. Also as the wars went on the levies of men and money which the Emperor required became more and more burdensome. But to most Frenchmen these disadvantages were a small price to pay for the stability and glory which the great Emperor brought to France, and there was almost no evidence of serious discontent until the very end of his regime.

• Napoleon and Europe

As a result of his victories Napoleon seemed to have many opportunities to make peace if he had been willing to put a halt to the arbitrary changes he kept making in the map of Europe. These seemed to be without any clear purpose, unless it was – as many feared outside France – to establish France's domination of the continent.

Immediately after he assumed power he made another quick campaign in Italy and once again forced Austria to accept peace. England too at this time seemed receptive to peace terms, and in 1802 at Amiens she signed perhaps the most unfavorable treaty Great Britain has ever knowingly accepted. But Napoleon, seemingly could not quietly accept the *status quo,* and almost immediately he began to make unilateral changes in the boundaries of his various satellite republics in Italy and central Europe. The English could only conclude that peace with Napoleon on any terms except complete surrender was impossible. Consequently in 1803 they resumed their long struggle to free the continent of his domination – as the principle of the balance of power required. But Napoleon's subsequent victories over combined Austro-Russian forces at Austerlitz in 1805, over Prussia in 1806, and Russia in 1807, made him master of Europe. At a meeting with Tsar Alexander I of Russia after that defeat they rearranged boundaries and rulers to satisfy their mutual interests. Napoleon who was already dreaming of establishing a dynasty placed his brothers on the thrones of Holland, Spain, and Westphalia. Meanwhile he consolidated dozens of the smaller states in the Holy Roman Empire into a number of larger principalities which were then arbitrarily reassigned to rulers who would agree to support him. These were then joined together in what was called the Confederation of the Rhine – thus, ironically, probably speeding up the process of German unification by at least a half century.

• The Continental System

After 1806 Napoleon's policies were more and more governed by his new strategy for the defeat of England. Although French ships were superior in design (the best English fighting ships were those captured from the French) the English remained masters of the sea – as was proved conclusively at Trafalgar in 1805. Even if Napoleon had used his far larger land base to build a huge fleet, he would still have needed the trained men to man it, which might take longer than building the ships. A quicker and less risky course seemed to be to use the weapon of economic warfare. Trade

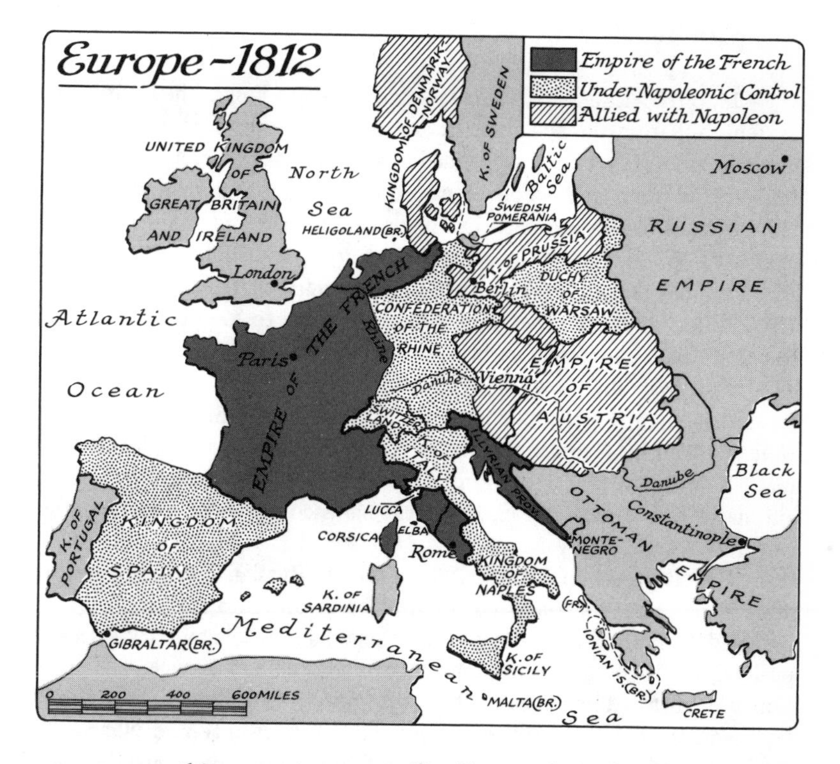

wars were nothing new to mercantilist Europe, but what Napoleon proposed was on a larger scale than ever before. The aim of what became known as the Continental System was to close the continent of Europe to English trade completely, since her economic viability depended on her commerce with the continent. While the project seemed theoretically sound, its success depended on whether he could really shut off English trade significantly. For the next six years implementation of this policy by any and all means was his primary objective. When Portugal refused to close her ports to British ships, they could be forced to do so only by forces moved through France's old ally Spain. But even after Napoleon placed his brother on the Spanish throne, French troops were unable to move safely through Spain because of underground resistance supported by regular English forces operating out of Portugal. The attack on Portugal was a complete failure, and the guerilla war in Spain was to be a continuing drain on his resources until his downfall. As part of his effort to shut off the ports of the west coast of Italy, as well as those of Holland and northern Germany, he incorporated these territories into France proper – seemingly confirming France's imperialist intentions in Europe.

• War With Russia

In 1807 Alexander I of Russia had agreed to join in the Continental System, but from the beginning he encountered protests from the Russian nobility whose livelihood depended upon the export of Russian grain, timber, and furs, and whose comfort depended on the import of the luxury goods usually supplied by English ships. Alexander had reasons to mistrust Napoleon's intentions in eastern Europe as well, and this provided an additional reason for announcing his withdrawal from the system in 1811. Since other countries were equally anxious to escape if they could, Napoleon had no alternative but to try to force Alexander's compliance. The result was the invasion of Russia in the summer of 1812 by the greatest land army assembled up until that time (more than half the troops were supplied by Napoleon's satellite states or allies). Although this army reached Moscow, the Tsar refused to surrender and the troops had no alternative but a long and bitter retreat harassed by both an early winter and the Russian cavalry.

Napoleon was in critical straits after the Russian fiasco, but it took more than a year for a new coalition to be organized (for the first time it included all four of the great powers at once) and for its military forces to push him from eastern Europe back to the borders of France. The coalition was always threatened with disruption until Castlereagh of England finally persuaded the members to join in a firm twenty-year alliance directed against any renewed threat from France – the traditional disrupter of Europe.

The members of the alliance completed their mission with the capture of Napoleon and his exile to the small Italian island of Elba in May, 1814. The peace terms imposed were remarkably mild considering the grief and suffering which an aggressive France had caused during the preceding twenty-five years, but the Austrian foreign minister, Metternich, and Castlereagh saw no point in making a treaty that was so vindictive that Frenchmen could never accept it with honor. It was only after Napoleon's escape from Elba in March of 1815, his resumption of power in France and his ill-fated attempt to reopen hostilities against the coalition with its disastrous ending at Waterloo in June that stiffer penalties were imposed on France – minor loss of territory and an indemnity with occupation by coalition troops until paid.

• Spread of Liberalism and Nationalism

With Napoleon deposed and Louis XVI's brother re-established on the throne of France as Louis XVIII (Louis XVI's son, Louis XVII, had died in prison in 1795), the next step was to revise the boundaries of the map of Europe in accordance with the interests of the members of the victorious coalition. It is clear that Europe could never really go back to the way of life it knew in 1789 much as some (and perhaps a majority) of those living in 1815 would have liked. The French Revolution had brought fundamental changes to France which even the reactionary Louis XVIII had been forced to accept in an official document known as the Charter, before he could be restored to the throne of France. The Charter reconfirmed those aspects of the Revolution established by Napoleon and in addition guaranteed responsible government with appropriate constitutional provisions for civil liberties and elected assemblies. There was to be no turning back in France. And even though it was possible to dismantle the satellite governments established by Napoleon, it was not possible to so easily erase the memory of the benefits of the application of Revolutionary principles in these countries. Policies such as the abolition of the vestiges of feudal land tenure, the secularization of church property, the establishment of equality before the law and the opening of careers to talent rather than birth continued to have wide appeal. These principles would provide a basis for future liberal efforts to change the old governments and social structures that were now being restored.

One of the most powerful forces unleashed by the Revolution was the patriotic fervor generated as a result of the establishment of a democratic state toward which all Frenchmen for the first time felt a total commitment. The new spirit of brotherhood and community may have been nurtured by the breakdown of the old corporate social structure of the old regime, but whatever its source, the intense feeling of loyalty and devotion which Frenchmen developed toward their nation and its interests was unquestionably a major factor in enabling it to establish its dominance over Europe for almost two decades. But more importantly the intensity of this feeling provoked a corresponding counter-reaction in many of the areas occupied by French forces, but most notably in Spain, Italy, and Germany. Since at this time Italy and Germany were only geographical terms, the appearance of this feeling constituted the first step in a long and difficult struggle to achieve nationhood.

Some historians have argued that, seen in its proper perspective, the French Revolution was only part of a broader revolutionary movement which affected not only France but many other countries both in Europe and America, in the second half of the eighteenth century. While it can be helpful to our understanding of this period to see the movement in its broadest perspective, it was events in France which dominated the history of both Europe and the world from 1789 to 1815. The most significant developments in other countries generally came in reaction to events in France. At first this took the form of an instinctive but sterile defense of old institutions against the dangers of any French innovations, but as time went on and France again and again demonstrated her military superiority, her opponents were forced into the painful process of self-examination which in numerous instances resulted in the adoption of "revolutionary" principles. To cope with the mass armies of the French, military conscription was adopted in several countries and became a permanent aspect of European life. The support of mass armies also required the mobilization of material resources on an unprecedented scale. In Prussia an attempt was made to broaden the base of popular support for the government by alleviating conditions of serfdom and restricting some privileges of the aristocracy.

Resistance to change generally, except where demonstrably essential to survival, remained strong, however, outside France. The experience of France seemed to furnish compelling evidence of the potential dangers of drastic changes in a country's government and society. As early as 1790, Edmund Burke, the famous member of the English Parliament, had pointed out the mistakes of the French Revolutionaries and in so doing provided a sound intellectual basis for a policy of conservatism. It is, therefore, easy to understand why the era that followed the final defeat of Napoleon and France, the symbols of revolution, is often designated as the Age of Conservatism.

Suggestions for Further Reading

Rude, G., *Revolutionary Europe, 1783-1815* (1964)

Gershoy, L., *The French Revolution and Napoleon* (1964)

Thompson, J. M., *The French Revolution* (1966)

Palmer, R. R., *The Age of the Democratic Revolution,* 2 vols. (1959-64)

Higgins, E. L., *The French Revolution as Told by Contemporaries* (1938)

McManners, J., *The French Revolution and the Church* (1969)

Palmer, R. R., *Twelve Who Ruled* (1968)

Thompson, J. M., *Robespierre and the French Revolution* (1964)

Markham, F., *Napoleon and the Awakening of Europe* (1964)

Oman, C., *Studies on the Napoleonic Wars* (1930)

Connelly, O., *Napoleon's Satellite Kingdoms* (1966)

Bryant, A., *The Years of Endurance* (1942)

Bryant, A., *The Years of Victory* (1945)

The Horizon Book of the Age of Napoleon (1963)

Anderson, M. S., *Eighteenth Century Europe* (1966)

Behrens, C. B. A., *The Ancien Regime* (1967)

Becker, C. L., *The Heavenly City of the Eighteenth Century Philosophers* (1932)

Roberts, Penfield, *The Quest for Security, 1715-40* (1947)

Dorn, W. L., *Competition for Empire, 1740-63* (1940)

Gershoy, Leo, *From Despotism to Revolution, 1763-89* (1944)

Cobban, Alfred, *The Eighteenth Century: Europe in the Age of the Enlightenment* (1969)

Williams, E. N., *The Ancien Regime in Europe: Government and Society in the Major States, 1614-1789* (1970)

Plumb, J. A., *England in the Eighteenth Century* (1950)

Cobban, Alfred, *A History of Modern France, 1715-99*, Vol. I (1965)

Holborn, Hajo, *A History of Modern Germany: 1648-1840* (1964)

THE NINETEENTH CENTURY 1815-1914

16

The Aftermath of Upheaval

THE CENTURY after 1815 saw the widespread acceptance of many of the forces and values released in Europe since 1789. An era of such political, social, and economic change occurred that we may well understand why the nineteenth century has been hailed by many as an Age of Progress. Living conditions during earlier generations had changed at a snail's pace compared with what happened between 1789 and 1914. European cultural achievements were unparalleled and an age of progress appeared to have dawned. A substantial intellectual effort was even dedicated to trying to understand the well-springs of this change. The spectacular nature of Europe's obvious progress, however, obscured much of the variety of nineteenth-century experience and especially blurred the real extent to which the new values were only partially applied. While the gospel of machine production became well-ensconced in much of western Europe by 1914, there remained large areas still virtually untouched by new outlooks and new technologies. Such contrasts underline the caution which must be kept in mind when generalizing about the nineteenth century and yet, the identification of these very contrasts allows us to examine the spread of new ideas, to explore the literal unfolding of Progress in all its variety.

• Social and Economic Conditions

The nineteenth century was characterized by an almost explosive population growth. Thanks to agricultural, hygienic, and scientific advances, Europe's 188 million souls doubled to over 400 million, besides sending another 18 million overseas. At a time when an industrial revolution multiplied the effectiveness of labor, more workers were available and productivity spiralled upward. The population boom occurred first in western Europe, then spread eastward. Substantial growth of cities and commerce developed in the West while in the East a vast migratory work force sprang up as more peasants began to acquire freedom. The Napoleonic Wars had stimulated English manufacturing and commerce; with peace in 1815, industrial development in western and central Europe followed the English model. Capital to fund industrialization came from western Europe and by the 1880's most major governments had to be concerned with such by-products of industry as urban crime, overcrowding, rioting, and general social unrest.

The expansion of industry led to a series of evolving trade patterns. England maintained a strong position in South and Central American trade and the opening of the Suez Canal in 1869 further stimulated English overseas economic activity. Russia became an important exporter of wheat and the tottering Ottoman Empire appeared to be a potentially lucrative market, especially for England and Russia. In this case an economic competition had been added to international rivalries already centuries old. French businessmen found many opportunities in central Europe which influenced her diplomacy in the Germanies and northern Italy. Perhaps the most dramatic result of economic growth was the formation of the Zollverein, a customs union supported by Prussia. It eventually embraced most of non-Austrian Germany and is often regarded as a prelude to German unification. Only one of several attempts at a German customs union, it became dominant and securely established by 1844. Austrian economic policy was to remain aloof during these developments as though her rulers were unaware of the great political potential involved. Through trade Prussia had received a striking advantage over Austria in their long-standing competition for control of Germany.

• The Liberal and the Socialist

Along with industrialization came two quite different spokesmen for change, the liberal and the socialist. The liberal saw himself as a defender of property and property rights. With roots in the thinking of John Locke, he found his economics in Adam Smith. Laissez-faire was his watchword as the businessman was to be free to do all he could in a marketplace where economic laws were unhampered by government controls. The political liberal thus was the spokesman for the newly emerging business elite which sought an identity in the new political order. Often liberals were able to find allies among the older commercial aristocracies. In crucial situations their opposition to arbitrary authority, such as divine-right monarchy, brought them support from Jacobin-type radicals. Hardly a democrat, the liberal usually couched his opposition to traditional aristocracies in language stressing human equality and natural rights. Despite the limited liberal objectives, these ideas were easily taken over by lower-class spokesmen and proved effective in broadening political equality and opportunity.

Unlike the liberal with his emphasis on the businessman's essential freedom, the socialist was concerned mainly with justice for all, especially those who labored without being adequately rewarded. The socialist regarded the liberal emphasis on property as responsible for the most callous disregard for human life and dignity. Laissez-faire was merely a device to assure economic slavery as thousands of workers could be controlled by a handful of factory owners. The socialist answer was to emphasize the distribution of profit. Early socialists ("utopian") believed that an altruistic appeal to the conscience of society's leaders would be sufficient – if not, then government, rather than being laissez-faire, should actually regulate business. A number of early socialists were concerned with devising ideal communities where the emphasis was on planning to achieve social and economic justice. As industry expanded, socialist theory became more refined, and, with Karl Marx, took on a highly sophisticated character. Similarly liberal theory was made more precise by the so-called "classical economists" and the Manchester School. The science of economics lent itself to many ramifications and both the liberals and socialists diligently pored over the implications of new data and techniques which were appearing in rapid profusion. In the nineteenth century both liberals and socialists multiplied as industrialization spelled the decline of agrarian society and its institutions.

• The Vienna Settlement and the Metternich System

The fall of Napoleon was correctly regarded as a crucial event in European history, spelling the end of a quarter century of nearly continuous warfare. It was appropriate that an international congress be called to review thoroughly the state of Europe and its problems. Accordingly, statesmen gathered in Vienna between September, 1814 and June, 1815 to arrange a basic peace settlement. Imperfect in many ways, the agreements defined power relationships clearly enough so that Europe was spared another continent-wide power struggle for a century. Diplomacy for a hundred years was to deal with issues as devised – or omitted – at Vienna.

Punctuated by sumptuous balls and banquets, the work of the congress was carried on largely by the spokesmen for the major powers. Most prominent was Austria's foreign minister, Prince Clemens von Metternich, who hosted the affair for his virtually bankrupt government which could ill-afford such extravagance. Contributing to the proceedings were Russia's Tsar Alexander I, Prussia's King Frederick William III, and England's foreign secretary and leader of the House of Commons, Viscount Castlereigh. These and their aides were members of a charmed inner circle which, with some consultation with spokesmen of secondary states, made most of the basic decisions. An initial outsider who became an insider was the French delegate, the intrepid Prince Talleyrand, who managed to parlay his nation's position of weakness into one of strength. It was an impressive gathering of statesmen. Many had been erstwhile allies of Napoleon and the assemblage even included Napoleon's step-son, the former viceroy of Italy, Eugene Beauharnais.

The peacemakers approached their task with a common antipathy to Bonaparte and also the legacy of several wartime agreements. They sought, above all, to secure themselves against future French or Bonapartist aggression. Vacant thrones or those with rival claimants were to be filled, as much as possible, by consideration of the principle of legitimacy, a handy concept which Talleyrand promoted mainly to assure the restoration of the Bourbons. In addition, several powers expected explicit compensation for their sacrifices against the French. From these multiple and often conflicting demands a series of agreements were arranged in 1815 at Vienna and signed either then or shortly thereafter.

France escaped with little punishment. In an indemnity she paid only for the cost to the allies of the Hundred Days, that brief period after Napoleon's escape from Elba which had culminated in the battle of Waterloo. Her boundaries were set as they existed in 1791. The brunt of anti-French feeling proved to be mostly against Napoleon and consequently the Bonapartes were banned from the thrones of Europe. As a barrier to any future French expansion, Sardinia was enlarged to the status of a second-rank power and the Netherlands were strengthened through the

addition of the Belgian provinces, the former Austrian Netherlands. Thus two important buffer states would receive the first shock of any French move either to the mouth of the Rhine or toward northern Italy. Further securing central Europe from France, Switzerland was slightly enlarged and given guarantees while Prussia shared an important boundary with France. The principle of legitimacy was most evident in the restoration of Bourbons in France, Spain, and Naples. The concept was only partially applied as Metternich himself doubted the wisdom of blindly restoring dynasties. The congress ended up accepting most of the amalgamations of small German states instituted by Napoleon and in Sweden, Bernadotte, the marshal raised to royalty thanks to Napoleon, retained his crown. In territorial realignments Sweden lost Finland to Russia but emerged with Norway; Austria gave up her claim to the Belgian provinces and received Lombardy-Venetia, basic footholds in Italy. Britain received assurances of security for the ancestral home of her dynasty, Hanover, and made scattered overseas gains, Malta and the Cape Colony being the most important. Dutch overseas losses were supposed to be balanced by the gain of the Belgian provinces. In central Europe the Germanic Confederation was established with Austria in a dominant position.

The most serious problem concerned Russian demands for control of Poland. Prussia had acquired large areas of Poland in the late eighteenth century partitions, territories she had then lost during the Napoleonic Wars. Now the principle of compensation required that Prussia either receive her Polish territories back or else be given other territory for her losses, but dispute arose over exactly what lands would be adequate. Prussia argued that Saxony would be a fair equivalent but Austria was apprehensive of this accretion to Prussian strength in Germany. Russia wanted control of Poland and proposed that Prussia seek her compensation to the west where England became worried over the safety of Hanover. For a time the dispute threatened to destroy the constructive work of the congress and at one point the allies were so split on the issue that a secret treaty was negotiated between France, England, and Austria against the pretensions of Prussia and Russia. It was the Polish question which encouraged the victorious powers to allow France to participate in policy discussions and Talleyrand made the most of his opportunity. Napoleon's reappearance from exile on Elba served to make all parties to the dispute more amenable to compromise and a modified "Congress Poland" controlled by Russia emerged, Prussia being compensated by portions of Saxony and lands along the Rhine.

To provide teeth to the overall settlement a Quadruple Alliance pledged the powers of England, Austria, Prussia, and Russia to police the several agreements for twenty years and to consult regularly on European problems. A moralistic and impractical Holy Alliance promoted by the Russian tsar further pledged the monarchs (England declining) to support Christian love and brotherhood by helping each other. The over-all settlement paid scant attention to the seeds of nationalism planted by the French in much of Europe, especially in Italy, Germany, and Spain. Economic progress was not discussed, nor was the Ottoman Empire in Europe an important consideration as the main intent was to restore as much as possible the map of 1789.

The immediate consequence of the peace settlement was that the unenlightened social values of Austria came to dominate much of Germany. Reforms stemming from the French Revolution were stopped short and even reversed in some areas. A system of spies and forcible control of ideas attempted to stamp out liberal doctrines while Metternich was at the height of his power. Within the Germanic Confederation the Carlsbad Decrees (1819) constituted specific legislation authorizing repression and through the Holy Alliance the Austrian statesman managed to arrange a broader international sanction, the Troppau Protocol (1820), a document which explicitly bound the various German princes to help him in repressive policies within their own lands. He had claimed to be the spokesman of small states' rights when arguing against Prussia on the Polish compensation issue but now he acquired the power to intervene arbitrarily in those same states on a systematic basis. In the new order Metternich had so manipulated things that two of Austria's most obvious rivals, Prussia and Russia, were the most steadfast supporters of his system.

The working of the so-called "Congress System," especially the meetings shortly after Vienna – Aix-la-Chapelle in 1818, Troppau in 1820, Laibach in 1821, and Verona in 1822 – spelled the gradual disenchantment of England and the loss of her cooperation as a Quadruple Alliance power. This encouraged a concomitant coalescing of policy among Russia, Prussia and Austria, the Holy Alliance powers. At Aix-la-Chapelle the congress system functioned well as France officially joined the other powers in a Quintuple Alliance and a number of minor problems were settled. In later congresses England and even Bourbon France withheld support for Metternich's reactionary policies. The Austrian's consummate skill as a diplomat came out in 1822 when he gained Russian agreement that he should send Austrian arms alone to put down uprisings in Italy while at the same time he persuaded Tsar Alexander I to refrain from using force in the Danubian provinces of the Ottoman Empire. The Tsar's forces could have been embarrassing for Metternich in either Italy or the Balkans but Metternich talked him into inaction in both areas. Against such effective reactionary leadership, liberal opinion made painfully slow progress in the decade following 1815.

• Russia

After 1815 most of Europe's domestic regimes mirrored the conservative values Metternich was promoting internationally. Alexander's Russia was a bastion of rigid authoritarian rule. His main advisor, Count Arakcheiev, was a brutal reactionary who easily countered the Tsar's occasional liberal instincts. Earlier hints of practical serf reforms (an 1803 law freed 37,000 in the course of 20 years) were largely fruitless as the society remained rigidly hierarchical. A massive system of peasant military conscription cut into the agrarian labor force and the expense of maintaining troops quartered on the population fixed the grip of the autocracy ever more solidly on society. Meanwhile bribery and corruption honeycombed the whole bureaucratic establishment. After 1816 a handful among the educated nobility formed secret organizations to plot schemes for change but they were divided in their prescriptions for a better society. In three border areas, however, Alexander's rule was more enlightened. Finland, which had only recently been acquired by Russia, was allowed a considerable amount of autonomy. In Estonia, Kurland, and Livonia the Tsar even carried through a program of serf emancipation. The Poles were granted a great deal of autonomy although the uglier features of an authoritarian regime became progressively apparent. Overall, Alexander's record is one of rigid autocracy, punctuated here and there by occasional indications of a sentimental interest in something more humane.

• Austria

In the enlarged, post-Vienna Austria there was no ambiguity regarding domestic policy. Under Francis I the entire bureaucracy stood resolutely against any change whatever. When Count Sedlnitzky became minister of policy in 1817 he brought refinements and efficiency to a system of censorship, police spies, and surveillance. Within the government Metternich had a competitor after 1826 in Count Kolowrat; both saw a need for some reform but neither was able to counter the ultraconservative attitudes of their Emperor Francis. The growth of trade and industry was handicapped by a system of high tariffs which prevented the middle class from becoming either numerous or powerful. The Germanic nobility administered and controlled a polyglot empire where the overwhelming danger was diagnosed as nationalism. This was indeed the problem as Poles, Bohemians, Hungarians, and Italians were only the more prominent of the various peoples chafing under Viennese control. The Emperor's unenlightened social attitudes were supported in other German states through Austria's diplomacy and influence in the Confederation. The same values were also promoted in Italy, not only in Lombardy-Venetia under direct Austrian control, but in the Papal States and Naples. Austrian spies seemed to be everywhere in Italy, indirectly instilling an anti-Austrian sentiment over the length of the peninsula.

• Prussia

In Prussia the French occupation had resulted in many reforms. Large areas of north Germany looked on Prussia as a liberating power, and there were widespread expectations of Prussian initiative in the formation of national, liberal political institutions. To these hopes for further reform Frederick William III turned a deaf ear once Napoleon was defeated. University students took up the liberal cause, forming clubs (Burschenschaften) and sponsoring rallies to protest the reactionary policies of Metternich. This threatening unrest led explicitly to the previously mentioned Carlsbad Decrees which were aimed mainly at the universities. Liberal hopes for a Prussian national representative body made up of delegates from provincial assemblies were dashed as the King allowed Metternich to convince him of the danger of ideas which had come to central Europe from France. Thus an interminable speculation about how the ancient medieval estates would fit into a new system or whether peasants ought to be represented at all became beside the point. Prussia had been much enlarged by the Vienna Congress with substantial gains in Saxony and along the Rhine. The new lands to the west brought into the kingdom a substantial liberal middle class as well as a large number of Catholics. As Prussian administrators married local girls, a religious problem developed over control of the education of the children, with Catholic bishops regularly clashing headlong with the government. The new territory was welcome but brought special problems so far as Berlin was concerned. After 1815 Prussia's only major policy initiative was limited to the Zollverein, a bold and successful foray in economic policy which was totally out of character with the lethargy and general mood of reaction otherwise present in government policy-making.

• Spain

Repression in its most vitriolic form occurred in Spain during the restored regime of Ferdinand VII. With Napoleonic blessings the Cortes had formulated the promising Constitution of 1812. Borrowed from French, English, and American experience, it was a reasonable document which provided for a hereditary but limited monarchy and a legislative body. Feudalism and the Inquisition were both abolished and the Rights of Man proclaimed. This Constitution along with the French Charter of 1814 were to stand as liberal rallying cries. Ferdinand canceled the Constitution, disbanded the Cortes, and instituted a reactionary, repressive program of harassment directed against all moderate and liberal influences. After four unsuccessful revolts led by army officers, Colonel del Riego managed to restore the Constitution and the Cortes in 1820. Ferdinand bowed to the necessities of the moment but asked the major powers for help, and in 1822 the Congress of Verona sanctioned French aid. The

French army easily defeated the insurgent forces at the battle of Trocadero (August 31, 1823) and Riego's regime ended. Ferdinand's revenge included the hanging and dismemberment of Riego which started five years of terrorism, dwarfing in brutality the atrocities reported from Russia and Naples. Every effort was made to root out all vestiges of constitutional government, and torture, exile, and imprisonment became the lot of thousands of liberals.

• France

In France after Waterloo the forces of reaction and revenge were kept under reasonable control by Louis XVIII who was satisfied to sit on the throne and accept in good faith the more pronounced changes wrought by the Revolution and Napoleon. He "granted" the Charter of 1814, a reasonable document which established a constitutional monarchy and incorporated many revolutionary ideals. His main problem was in restraining ultraroyalist emigré agitators who had a forceful leader in the figure of the King's brother, the Count of Artois and future Charles X. These proclerical and almost medieval advocates of divine-right monarchy demanded vengeance and a White Terror began in 1816. Before the movement could be blunted by the crown, Marshal Ney had fallen as one of its republican and Napoleonic victims. The nation then enjoyed four years of moderate and responsible government by so-called "Constitutionals," a regime of upper-middle-class moderates. The Ultras continued to plot against Louis' moderation and in 1820 their efforts, combined with two scandals (the assassination of the Duke de Berri and the election to the Chamber of the Abbé de Grégoire, a prominent regicide), succeeded in swinging opinion to support a more reactionary policy. Thus, until 1824 when Louis XVIII died and on until 1830 under Charles X, France was guided for ten years by a proclerical, reactionary, and revenge-oriented leadership. Characteristically, this was the France which sent an army to Spain to restore Ferdinand to absolute power in 1823. On the surface France seemed to be moving in the same direction as other reactionary regimes to the south and east but there was a major difference. France had a substantial middle class and the revolutionary principles in the Charter were by now entrenched. Disregard of this point was to lead to revolution in 1830 as Charles X seemed to have learned little from the decades after 1780.

• The Netherlands

The seeds of revolution were also being cultivated in the Belgian provinces of the newly enlarged Netherlands. Historically the Belgians had been fairly compliant subjects under many regimes, but King William I managed after 1815 to follow a course which infuriated them on a number of accounts. They complained of unfair taxation and inadequate representation. His decrees on equality of creeds were particularly offensive and his educational policies appeared to be a deliberate attempt to turn Belgians into Dutchmen. William promoted extensive programs of public works and saw himself as a benevolent enlightened monarch but unfortunately he offended the sense of pride and self-assurance of a population which was able and resourceful. All through the 1820's there were a succession of provocative incidents which alienated all classes of Belgians. By 1830 William had unwittingly created a complex revolutionary situation.

• England

Even in England there was a similar conservative orientation in government circles. The Tories had won the struggle against Napoleon and although political reform was long overdue, there was little inclination for them to move in this direction. An 1815 Corn Law kept grain imports low, bread prices high, and agricultural landlords financially secure. Poor harvests added to the discontent and rioting became more common. At the Peterloo Massacre (August 16, 1819) cavalry was used against a mass protest meeting, spurring a formal government response which was frankly authoritarian. Coercive legislation (the Six Acts) limited freedom and produced martyrs. The repression was much milder than that on the Continent but for England it was severe. Still reasonably secure in power in the early 1820's the Tories gingerly embarked on a series of reforms. The criminal code was updated to remove death as the penalty for over 200 crimes and the mercantile system was modified as many import duties were reduced, a first step on what proved to be a policy of free trade by mid-century. The hour, however, was late and conditions cried out for far more constructive change.

• The Romantic Movement

Both the particular features of the diplomatic settlement and the domestic regimes in most of Europe after 1815 were either conservative or outright reactionary. Meanwhile the liberal revolutionary impulses of 1789-1815 had not ceased to exist and were to burst forth in 1830 and 1848. Thus the general aura of conservatism present in most of Europe's ruling circles after 1815 was only partially an adequate indication of Europe's values. The dominant intellectual mood was Romanticism and in it a variety of opinion can be clearly seen. Romanticism knew no national boundaries and could be politically both conservative and liberal. It placed a strong emphasis on one's feelings, one's sense of identity with one's fellows and with nature. The earlier Enlightenment reliance on data as a source of knowledge was now challenged as many intellectuals saw life as much broader and richer. Stemming largely from the ideas of Jean Jacques Rousseau, Romanticism was steeped in history and purportedly found great moral purpose in cases where some solitary individual struggled valiantly against nature. One could find a sense of life's purpose in a large group or collective; or, just as consistently, with some solitary genius who struggled alone against vast numbers. Romanticism bolstered both the one and the many, as well as both right and left.

In politics and diplomacy worthy models abounded. Napoleon seemed the very essence of a modern hero. The "people" and the "nation" were sources of identity for many while others found a smaller group (such as a club like the Jacobins) more congenial. Some found the spread and planting of French Revolutionary values during the wars of Napoleon as noble and a service for previously shackled humanity, while similar romantic values were clearly present in the national struggles of the Russian and Spanish peoples against these self-same principles and procedures. Those opposing the French conquests found solace in such historic institutions as the monarchy and the Church. The Holy Alliance was an international conspiracy of thrones against peoples and the Napoleonic Legend helped keep alive the sense that one man alone might change things for everyone. Various political restorations were characterized by close cooperation between throne and altar. Many people found comfort in a religion which was fundamentalist and historically medieval while others found true religion practiced close to nature in outdoor services. Revivalism and piety flourished.

The basic romantic themes were apparent in much of nineteenth-century literature. Man in nature, his past, his present, and his sense of identity found eloquent expression in writers as diverse as the aristocratic defender of divine-right monarchy, Joseph de Maistre, and Jules Michelet, who passionately portrayed the heroic and suffering "people" of the French Revolution. Both Félicité de Lamennais and René de Chateaubriand were devout Catholics who absorbed much of the liberal ideas around them and tried to incorporate them into their distinctive religious orientation. Writers like Samuel Coleridge, Lord Byron, and William Wordsworth used imaginative and intricately descriptive prose to present and explore the awesome beauty found in nature. Stendhal (Marie Henri Beyle) wrote novels indicting the regimes following Napoleon by showing how sadly they were in need of the values the Emperor had promoted. All facets of life and nature were rigorously explored in a profuse torrent of writing which continued unabated through the entire century.

Romanticism was especially pronounced in music. Coming from the carefully structured order of the Enlightenment highlighted by Johann Sebastian Bach, Wolfgang Amadeus Mozart, and Franz Joseph Haydn, the romantic era put great emphasis on originality and feeling. Ludwig van Beethoven's prolific career presented a dramatic transition from the order, balance, and clarity of eighteenth century musical expression to the romantic soul-searching values of the nineteenth century. His early work was strongly influenced by the formal grace and order of Haydn and Mozart while in his later compositions he was pioneering in the depths of human emotion capable of being tapped by music. The development of the piano gave greater potential to composers and there was a flowering of emotional compositions. Italy and Germany dominated the musical scene and Gioacchino Rossini, Giuseppe Verdi, Richard Wagner, Franz Schubert, and Felix Mendelssohn were only a few among a large number of composers. Frederick Chopin was a Pole whose music was vigorously and intensely patriotic. Countering the great imaginative flourishes of many of his contemporaries Hector Berlioz tempered his romanticism with a concern for realism. He also explored the potential impact on the listener of massive and grandiose orchestrations. Out of this abundance of talent and productivity came a host of nationalistic schools of composition as patriotism was an obvious source of both individual and collective feeling. In music a new dimension of man could be explored and secular music now overshadowed the church choir or the madrigal.

Romanticism made a serious impact on religion. Friedrich Schleiermacher, a philosopher-theologian at the University of Berlin, concluded that the best religion was that which nurtured one's sense of piety and dependence on an absolute being. This perspective was part of a resurgence of pietism sweeping through central Europe and Schleiermacher's ideas permeated many theological training programs in Germany. This pulled religion still further from deism and from aged proofs of God's existence and also helped make religion more impervious to new facts being discovered by an expanding science. This primary emphasis on feeling rather than knowing gave formal religion a new source of strength.

Romanticism in philosophy may be seen in the resurgence of idealism, an idea-oriented view of the world as distinguished from the empiricism of the Enlightenment. In the eighteenth century David Hume had criticized data as a source of knowledge and Immanuel Kant observed that while data was important, abstract ideas and concepts were equally so. Thus time, space, duty, and justice were as fundamental and real as the factual details of the world as commonly observed. In a bold formulation Kant opened the door to a flowering of idealist thought. G.J. Fichte and Friedrich W.J. von Schelling added seminal insights to Kant's position but idealism's most distinguished proponent was Georg Wilhelm Friedrich Hegel whose imaginative writing both astounded and attracted the finest minds of several generations. Among the practical consequences of his work was a defense and encouragement of Prussian nationalism and a number of the basic ideas in the thinking of Karl Marx. Arthur Schopenhauer also articulated a major idealist position.

The Romantic movement extended through the entire century, coloring and conditioning a broad range of activity. Favoring neither right nor left, it gave encouragement to those both in and out of power and in fact provided an overall setting in which varieties of change could take place.

• Independence in Spanish America and Greece

Between 1820 and 1832 Europe's conservatively oriented structure was broadly challenged. Internationally the system of cooperation through great power decisions arrived at through congresses foundered on the independence movements in Spanish America and in Greece. After 1808 much of South and Central America experienced revolt under the leadership of Simon Bolivar, Francisco de Miranda, José de San Martin and others. England and the United States encouraged the insurgents as both nations aspired to replace Spain in doing business in South America. According to Quadruple and Holy Alliance principles, the powers should aid in helping Spain to resume control of her former colonies. However, in a complex diplomatic sequence England's refusal to support the congress decisions was clear. Further, she appeared ready to oppose such efforts by force. In the Monroe Doctrine of 1823 the United States warned all European powers against further colonial aspirations in North or South America and England's George Canning, Castlereagh's successor, tried to take credit for this defiance by the New World of the Old, even though the Doctrine was aimed also at England. By 1829 all of Spain's New World holdings, save Cuba and Puerto Rico, were independent as the government in Madrid lost all control.

The Greek struggle for independence from their Ottoman overlords was equally destructive of the system devised at Vienna. In open revolt after 1821, the Greeks enjoyed considerable public sympathy in western Europe where they were seen as descendants of those ancient peoples who so greatly contributed to western civilization. The Russian Tsar was less romantic but he aspired to aid fellow Orthodox Christians in order to weaken a historic enemy, the Turk. By the standards of the Congress of Vienna, the Sultan was a legitimate monarch but when Greek Christians were trying to be free from the yoke of non-Christians, legitimacy was a hollow concept that even Metternich was unable to view with enthusiasm. He knew that success for the Greek insurgents meant an increase in Russian influence in the Balkans, and yet he could not in good conscience support the Sultan who was regarded as essentially non-European as well as non-Christian. Nationalism triumphed as direct aid from England, France, and Russia helped assure the founding of modern Greece, a kingdom with the Bavarian prince Otto as its first king. Independence for the new state was achieved by 1830 and validated by separate treaties with England, France, and Russia. The congress system of Metternich had given way to overlapping bilateral agreements.

• The Decembrist Revolt

Defiance of the established order was widespread. In Russia after 1816 secret societies were promoting ideas of liberal reform and even, in the Southern Society led by Paul Pestel, republicanism. Members of these societies were largely young noble officers with an intellectual bent. They were inexperienced in the devious ways of plotting a revolution and they had little contact with the peasantry, urban dwellers, or even the common soldiers they commanded. It is no wonder that they failed when on December 26, 1825 they challenged the accession of Nicholas I. Alexander had unexpectedly died on December 1 but there was a hiatus until December 24 before doubt was dispelled that Nicholas was the successor. His older brother, Constantine, the viceroy of Poland, had privately renounced his claim to the succession but few knew this. The officers decided to challenge the succession so they arranged for the palace troops to refuse allegiance to Nicholas, thereby hoping to create a constitutional impasse. Nicholas brought in other troops and crushed this "Decembrist" revolt. The leaders were swiftly tried, some were executed including Pestel, and others were sent off to Siberia. It was a pathetic and naive episode. Nicholas thereafter suspected his officers and turned to Germans for administrators. The revolt was the first attempt in Russia to use palace troops to support an ideological revolt.

• French Revolution of 1830

In France after 1824 Charles X ruled as though the world had changed little since 1789. Closely cooperating with the clergy, he ignored and irritated a new elite in Parisian society, the prosperous businessman. When the King attempted to restore pre-Revolutionary inheritance laws which favored the eldest son, he defied the nation's egalitarian instincts. He manipulated bond rates to indemnify émigré families at the expense of bond holders and bankers. He never really accepted the basic principles of the Charter and acted like a divine-right monarch, appointing ever more reactionary officials, a process which culminated in August, 1829 with the selection of a ministry under the Prince de Polignac, an arch reactionary. There was an immediate storm of liberal protest.

Widespread unemployment and hunger followed the cold winter of 1829-30 and a season of poor crops. When the Chamber of Deputies convened on March 2, 1830, both Peers and Deputies criticized the ideas in Charles' traditional address from the throne. On this occasion the King presented his legislative program and 221 members of the Chamber openly reproved him. In response he called for new elections, hoping for a more compliant body; instead, the new chamber included 270 opponents to royal policy. Charles then issued a series of ordinances (July 25) restricting the press, changing electoral laws, and canceling the scheduled meeting of the newly elected chamber. These ordinances triggered insurrection as laborers, especially unemployed printers, went into the streets while liberal journalists published in defiance of the King. After four days of insurrection which royal troops could not control, Charles abdicated. In a French version of the English revolution of 1688, the throne was offered to the Duke of Orleans, Louis Philippe, who accepted it on August 9, 1830. Thus mob rule, aided and abetted by a liberal commercial aristocracy, drove a legitimate monarch from power. His successor was chosen by the business elite rather than the workers and there was a lingering resentment among worker spokesmen that their hopes for a republic had been sabotaged – their revolution had been taken over by their employers. As the price of his accession Louis Philippe acknowledged the Charter in revised form whereby there was firmer press freedom and a guarantee that there would be no return to divine-right monarchy. Despite the 1815 Vienna agreements, France had changed her ruler by force but the revolution in Paris was over so quickly, from Metternich's view, that it was easier to ignore than to coerce; after all, Louis Philippe was royalty and the nation was still a monarchy. Besides, Metternich's main concern was Italy.

• Belgian Independence

More serious for the international order was the Belgian Revolution which broke out in Brussels on August 25, 1830, in the wake of the revolution in Paris. Insurrection in Brussels triggered revolts in most of the major Belgian cities as pent-up frustrations came out into the open. King William's attitude was to attempt to suppress the revolt by force, but to the amazement of most, including many insurgents, Dutch troops were beaten in a series of skirmishes in Brussels and forced to withdraw, whereupon civic leaders organized a provisional government. A national congress was elected and between November 10, 1830, and July 21, 1831, it prepared Europe's most liberal constitution and selected a monarch (Leopold of Saxe-Coburg) to rule as the first King of the Belgians. Not to be so readily brushed aside, William appealed to the great powers for help but England and France refused aid. Louis Philippe twice sent the French army into Belgium to oppose Dutch efforts to crush the revolution and England cooperated with the French in sending naval units to hamper the Dutch. Thus the liberal powers aided an insurrection against a legitimate monarch and contemporaneous insurrection in Poland and Italy made it nearly impossible for the conservative powers to agree on putting down the Belgians. Meanwhile in London conferences, the diplomats of the major powers debated the question of Belgian independence until 1839, finally agreeing that Belgium should be independent and forever neutral. Freedom had come through force and a new dynasty established – another challenge to the order of 1815 had taken place.

• The Polish Revolt

While the Belgian revolution was posing problems for Metternich in the West, the Poles rose in revolt. Led by students, army officers, and most of the aristocracy, the upheaval was supported by urban workers but lacked peasant support. The Polish Diet formally declared Nicholas deposed on January 25, 1831, and a provisional government headed by Prince Czartoryski and General Chlopicki vainly sought help from abroad. Apprehensive of the lower classes, the aristocratic leadership offered to negotiate grievances but the Russian Tsar refused to deal with revolutionaries. Though winning a few minor engagements, the Polish army was an easy prey when its leaders divided over the matter of whether to make further approaches to Nicholas. The dreaded disease, cholera, killed many on both sides, but the issue was decided once substantial Russian forces arrived. Some Polish zealots hoped for help from France but Louis Philippe refused to become involved. In the fall of 1831, the Tsar vigorously restored Russian control, clamped down martial law, and executed many insurgent leaders. Poland lost the special status which Vienna had conferred on it and became a harshly ruled part of Russia. Nicholas stood revealed as a despot and militarist.

• Revolt in Italy

Metternich's main problem proved to be Italy where there had been sporadic unrest through the 1820's. Among other liberal secret societies, the Carbonari were plotting a major upheaval and a coordinated revolt over the whole peninsula. The leading figure was Guiseppe Mazzini, an idealist and humanitarian, who founded the Young Italy movement. Other insurgent leaders cautiously accepted the idea of help from Duke Francis IV of Modena since he could bring to the cause the resources of an established government, an asset lacking in earlier unsuccessful revolts. When the French were followed in revolution by the Belgians and the Poles, the moment for Italy seemed at hand. In February, 1831 the Italians rose in revolt but were handily put down by the Austrians. Duke Francis turned against the conspiracy when, at the last moment, aid which had been expected from the French was withheld by Louis Philippe. The Carbonari failure raised questions about whether such secret societies could really accomplish a major task such as expelling the Austrians. Metternich saw the situation simply as a matter of applying the earlier international agreements such as the Troppau Protocol which allowed outside powers to intervene in a state to counter liberal ideas. From his view the conservative principles of Vienna had been shaken by the events of 1830-31 but essentially non-liberal regimes still governed central and eastern Europe. Revolution was a widespread danger which had been controlled everywhere but in France and Belgium. Much remained of the old order.

17

The Problems of Progress

IN THE SECOND third of the nineteenth century enormous strides were made in industrial progress. The earlier industrial revolution in England, northern France and Belgium was dwarfed by the enormous growth of business in most of Europe. Heavy industry began to emerge in the Ruhr area and in northern Italy, a vast and progressively better-off middle class grew rapidly, and the grimy factory town with its slums became a regular feature of much of the European landscape. The construction of rail networks was significant; now products and produce could be moved more quickly. Consumers had a wide range of goods to purchase and with mass marketing came department stores. At the same time, the railroad brought these goods and various opportunities to many a stagnating community. There was relatively little interest in colonialism in this period as Europe tended to be absorbed in dealing with the various domestic problems of an evolving and growing economy. Free trade came to be gospel in England while on the Continent socialist theory was feverishly developed by many zealots. Nationalism triumphed, most notably in Germany and Italy, in this era of ferment and vitality.

• Tory Reform

Much of the Continent sought reform through violence and revolution in the 1820's and 1830's, and many of the same stimuli for change were present in England. Here an established parliamentary system was similarly pressured to liberalize. George Canning, the foreign secretary and prime minister briefly in 1827, supported his fellow ministers, Sir Robert Peel and William Huskisson, in launching England on an era of reform. The Tories recognized the new importance of manufacturing and that agriculture now provided a direct livelihood for only a third of the population. Beginning with their moderation of tariff and navigation regulations and enlightened adjustments of the criminal code, they started a wave of legislative change which extended into the 1840's. The Tories went so far as to respond to a poor harvest in 1826 by modifying the force of the restrictive Corn Law. When this helped to bring quick relief in the form of lower bread prices, the continuance of the Corn Law in any form seemed immoral. Every subsequent major electoral campaign until 1846 was to have Corn Law repeal as an issue and in 1839, the Anti-Corn Law League was formed, a powerful and united source of propaganda against the Corn Law.

Shortly after the death of Canning in 1827, the Duke of Wellington became the Tory leader. Far more conservative than his predecessor, Wellington found himself caught up in circumstances which led him to endorse Catholic Emancipation, an issue alienating many Tories. The Test Act of 1673 had insisted that all officeholders be receivers of communion as sanctioned by the Church of England. This statute had been effectively used to keep Catholics from office but otherwise had long been ignored – many non-Anglican protestants had held various posts. In 1828 the law was revised so that non-Anglican protestants were formally granted equal political privileges. Naturally Catholics felt that they too should enjoy full political rights, but Catholic rights were embroiled in the whole complex issue of Ireland. Bringing the situation to a head, an Irish leader, Daniel O'Connell, ran for a seat in Parliament in full knowledge that, because of his religion and his consequent inability to take the required oaths of allegiance and Anglican Church supremacy, he could not be seated if he won. His success in County Clare forced Wellington to face the problem directly. The prime minister decided that concessions had to be made if civil war were to be avoided in Ireland and, to the consternation of the most conservative elements among his Tory colleagues, he pushed through a Catholic Emancipation Bill (1829). The Irish believed their defiance had paid off. Instead of the Irish people being virtually unrepresented, now there would be Catholics in Parliament who could be expected to air Ireland's other grievances – and Tories faced this prospect with their ranks split.

An Engine House in England in the mid-nineteenth century. Courtesy, the Print Room, Boston Public Library.

• The Reform Bill

By their enlightened legislation during the 1820's the Tories had encouraged a reform spirit which by 1830 burgeoned into broad demands for the liberalizing of Parliament itself. Under criticism was the "pocket" and "rotten" borough system where privilege and corruption made a mockery of the idea of representation. There had been no modernizing of the formulas for representation in Parliament and former towns almost completely depopulated had spokesmen in Parliament while newer manufacturing cities, such as Leeds and Manchester, had virtually no voice. The call for parliamentary reform was taken up by the Whigs who saw it as an opportunity to grasp power. Between 1829 and 1832, while revolution and revolt plagued much of Europe, electoral campaigns in England were waged to the accompaniment of widescale rioting and many feared that England might go the path of her neighbors. The Whigs won and Earl Grey, who became prime minister in 1830, introduced a Reform Bill. Stubbornly fought by Tories, especially in the House of Lords, it took special pressure from the crown, including the threat of creation of new titles if need be, to get the bill in a third version passed through Parliament in 1832. The electorate was nearly doubled (to 814,000) and the way opened for further reform. A more democratic Commons assumed a legislative ascendancy over the Lords as England's landed aristocracy found its power significantly curtailed.

• Additional Reform

The Whigs, now calling themselves Liberals, were firmly in power and embarked on further reform which they directed until 1841. A series of half measures dealt with religious grievances in Ireland where the established church served less than 12 percent of the population. Adding to other festering grievances, in a Tithe War in 1831 the government assigned troops to aid in the forced collections to support the hated church. The Liberals eased the burden somewhat by reducing the number of bishoprics and archbishoprics to be supported but such a half-measure merely engendered further ill-will among the Irish, inviting additional unrest. More successful was the 1838 abolition of slavery in all lands under the British flag. An indemnity was provided for plantation owners who had lost "property" and slaves became wage laborers. (In many cases their lives changed little.) Humanitarianism also found its way into other reform legislation, particularly the Factory Act (1844), aimed mainly at the textile industry. Providing for inquiries into child labor practices with inspectors and thorough reports, it was a blow to the unrestrained freedom of employers. Extended to other industries (such as in the Mining Act of 1835) such legislation provided voluminous reports to Parliament. (These reports have allowed historians to present a detailed picture of modern capitalism in an early stage. Karl Marx also used them to pinpoint his savage indictment of capitalism.) To cope with the growing slums which clustered about the new factories, a Poor Law Admendment Act in 1834 was passed. Like much humanitarian legislation, some intellectuals opposed it on the grounds that as the population grew it was natural that the number of poor would increase. It was thus unnatural to help them and a flouting of natural law. A Municipal Corporations Act (1835) corrected many abuses in city government and made possible rule by the rising middle class. England thus proved flexible enough to accomplish basic reform without revolution.

• The Liberal Regime of Louis Philippe

Across the Channel in France, Louis Philippe reigned as a "liberal" to please the business interests. Under the Charter as modified in 1830 hardly 3 percent of the adult males could vote so that real democratic control was not the issue. Elections were usually corrupt with the votes of the tiny electorate being bought or otherwise solicited in an open and shameless competition between the upper middle class and the middle and lower middle class. The main spokesman for the former was Francois Guizot while Adolphe Thiers represented the interests of the latter. These two vied for control of the cabinet with Guizot dominating policy most of the time.

Domestic violence was common. In an 1832 counter revolutionary attempt in the Vendée, the Duchess de Berri tried unsuccessfully to restore the Bourbons. Bloody uprisings occurred in Lyon in 1831 and 1834 and in Paris in 1831, 1832, and 1834; there were also numerous attempts to assassinate the King. During his reign workers became more articulate and politically conscious, many going over to socialism and republicanism. Liberal reform in France meant a substantial broadening of public education and government modification of laissez faire through protection of many business interests. A major railway network, sponsored by the government, was begun in 1842, and French industry grew rapidly, though at a substantially slower rate than in England and Belgium.

Along with industrial growth came a new concern for the worker. The Catholic Church worried over a growing secularism and many young priests dedicated themselves to service among the workers. Foremost among these was Félicité Robert de Lamennais, the outspoken priest, who advocated in the columns of his paper, "L'Avenir," that the papacy endorse both political and social democracy, which alienated the hierarchy in France as well as Rome. The pope, Gregory XVI, responded by excommunicating Lamennais and reasserted a rigidly conservative position. Lamennais failed in his immediate effort but the lower priesthood and the working population looked on him as a martyr in their cause.

Also aimed at correcting the ills of a manufacturing society was the "utopian" socialism of Henri de Saint-Simon and Charles Fourier who thought that if society were responsibly governed the workers would live in an environment of social justice, happiness, and progress. Saint-Simon sponsored a kind of new feudalism, where business leaders were at the apex of society protecting and taking care of the workers, a mild and elitist form of socialism. He believed in unleashing the constructive talents of the entrepreneurs and many industrial projects of the nineteenth century – railway and canal construction, including the Suez Canal – were carried through by Saint-Simonian believers. Fourier's planned communities (phalanstres), of about 1600 people each, promoted the virtue of work and fair distribution. He wanted all to work and to like their work, with dirty jobs either carrying greater rewards or being done by children who traditionally seem to love filth. Another early socialist theorizer was Louis Blanc who promoted plans for producer cooperatives supported initially by government funds. These socialist writers won many converts in their indictments of the uncontrolled growth of industry.

There were other critics of the system. Pierre Joseph Proudhon condemned injustice, associating much of it with the abuse of property. When he saw property being used to enslave men, he bluntly branded it as theft, which disturbed many property owners. Criticism also came from Louis Napoleon, a nephew of Bonaparte, who wrote that by applying "Napoleonic Ideas" would occur "The Extinction of Pauperism" as well as a restoration of the national honor. His appeals were to right-wingers generally, to nationalists, but also to the business community at large; for this Napoleonic pretender was in truth a Saint-Simonian by instinct. After two abortive coups, he was imprisoned between 1840 and 1846 at the fortress at Ham where he wrote extensively, his social ideas attracting many prominent people, including Louis Blanc.

While promoting business, Louis Philippe carried on a lackluster and contradictory foreign policy. He had supported the Belgians in their

The French Legislature in the 1840's as portrayed by Honoré Daumier. Courtesy, Museum of Fine Arts, Boston.

revolution and he also pushed forward the Algerian conquest which Charles X had initiated in 1829. These initiatives were balanced by his retreat in 1840 before threats of a general war with Russia, England, and Turkey in another perennial crisis over the Ottoman Empire. He joined England in supporting the liberal side in Spain's dynastic struggle, the Carlist War, in the mid-1830's but managed to alienate the English in the frustrating episode known as the Spanish Marriages. Betraying earlier agreements, one of Louis Philippe's sons, the Duke de Montpensier, married the Queen's younger sister, putting him in a position of undue influence, from an English point of view. Thiers and the Bonapartists attacked the colorless monarch for emphasizing peace (cowardice) rather than honor while perhaps the most telling observation was to come from the republican poet Alphonse de Lamartine who declared, "France is bored." During the 1840's there were appalling crop failures (especially the potato) which settled on northern France, the mid and lower Rhine, Low Countries, England, and Ireland. These touched off a widespread depression and nature itself seemed to have turned against Louis Philippe.

• Conservative Reaction to New Forces

While liberal policies held sway in France and England, to the east ultra-conservative attitudes were dominant. In Austria the bureaucracy kept the population largely cut off and immune from outside ideas. In Prussia, aside from the Zollverein, liberal progress was slow, more because of lethargic leadership than the systematic repression of ideas, as in Austria. Russia was openly hostile to new forces, with Nicholas I insisting on a rigid autocracy. Against any concessions to principles of the French Revolution, his regime was based on the concepts of orthodoxy, autocracy, and nationality. The Russian emperor believed in divine-right monarchy and added a political police, the "Third Section," to augment his repressive bureaucracy. Secret agents and spies permeated Russian society. His deeply religious faith was simple and he was unquestioningly absorbed by ritual. Nicholas was interested in military affairs but concerned himself mostly with petty details while gross inefficiency went uncorrected.

During Nicholas' reign two literary groups sprang up which probed the Russian character. The "westerners" found Russia lagging behind western Europe which they wanted to imitate while the "slavophiles" nationalistically emphasized Russia's uniqueness. Serfdom was the compelling social problem and Nicholas himself appointed some ten special committees to examine peasant emancipation, but the nobility frustrated his tentative reform efforts. After 1848 he became more rigidly conservative and his reign was characterized by cruel and inhumane punishments. Abroad he was a consistent spokesman against revolution yet because of religion as well as Russia's anti-Turkish policies, he supported the Greeks in their struggle against the Turk. Foursquare against liberalism, he managed to blunt its progress in eastern Europe for decades.

• Revolution of 1848 in France

Despite appearances of stability, in 1847 the monarchy of Louis Philippe was very insecure. The nation's economic ills were publicized widely in a series of protest banquets where republican orators criticized the failure of Guizot's government to deal with flagrant electoral corruption, the limited franchise, and personal scandal. In February, 1848, when a banquet was scheduled in Paris, the government would not permit it, whereupon its sponsors urged workers to riot. When members of the National Guard came out against Guizot, Louis Philippe sensed that his cause was lost and fled to England. A provisional republican government was established, made up of both republican and socialist leaders, the most prominent of whom were Alphonse de Lamartine and Louis Blanc. As in 1830, rioting workers helped topple the government but this time they were represented in the new regime. This coalition of republicans and socialists was uneasy and soon became a struggle between the republican defenders of property and the socialist critics of property. An early decree guaranteed work for all with socialist inspired "workshops" to provide labor where needed. These workshops soon attracted thousands of vagabonds and when there were not enough jobs to go around, partial payments were made. The system took on the appearance of a modified dole and in the plotting between republicans and socialists the republicans publicized the workshops as examples of the failure of socialism. In elections for a constituent assembly (April 23) the republicans were successful and the socialists felt that now their only recourse was to take to the streets. They had demonstrated earlier on March 17 and April 16 and now again on May 15 but were dispersed in each instance. The republican dominated Assembly decided to close down the workshops completely, leading to a massive and savage uprising in Paris (June 23-26) which was vigorously crushed by the army commanded by General Cavaignac. The republican leaders were appalled by the extent of the bloodshed (1500 dead) and now turned the government over to Cavaignac, giving him complete executive powers until a new constitution could be framed and implemented. The slaughter of the workers was seen by socialists as an example of the republican propertied classes using the army in an open struggle against the propertyless masses. (The events of 1848 in France lend themselves to an analysis based on class warfare – the most expressive version of this viewpoint was to be written by Karl Marx.)

While the republicans and socialists were competing for power, the Bonapartists were also active and several Bonapartes managed to win seats in the Assembly. Prince Louis Napoleon, son of Napoleon Bonaparte's brother Louis, took his place in the Assembly in September and began to campaign for the presidency. Since his escape from Ham he had been living in London, but his supporters had been publishing newspapers and otherwise propagandizing on his behalf. His main opponent was Cavaignac who was thought to be an easy winner because of his June services in defense of public order, but to everyone's amazement Louis attracted about 5.5 million votes while Cavaignac only received 1.5 million. It was a tribute to the name of Napoleon since Louis had been out of prison only two years and, except for his name, was unknown in France. On December 20, 1848, he formally became President of the Second French Republic.

It had been a tumultuous year for France. It was no less so for central Europe as well. After Louis Napoleon's victory, many feared the new republican France would once again assume an aggressive posture. The new foreign minister, Lamartine, effectively calmed these apprehensions but the changes in France helped to bring out lingering discontents in much of Europe. There were local economic problems in Belgium and in the Rhine and Moselle valleys, and despite Lamartine's reassurances to the contrary, the French government sent agitators into these border areas to promote revolution and republicanism. Local regimes were generally maintained but there were many reforms in a number of small German states whose rulers were fearful of the spread of revolutionary contagion from France.

• The Frankfurt Assembly

In Frankfurt, a liberal parliament – the so-called Frankfurt Assembly – convened on May 18, 1848, to debate the constitution for a new "Germany." Its leaders were intellectuals – some like Heinrich von Gagern were veterans of the earlier Burschenshaft movement – and lacked practical political experience. After extensive debate (May-December) they drafted a Declaration of Fundamental Rights which asserted middle-class values. However, they disagreed on the composition of the new Germany as well as on the role Austria should play. They ended by offering the crown of "Germany" to Prussia's Frederick William IV but since the tide of revolutionary fervor was on the ebb the king brusquely refused this offer "from the gutter." Chances for a liberal Germany had passed and the movement collapsed; the liberals at Frankfurt had no army, could not tax, and controlled no bureaucracy. They could not survive without help from either Prussia or Austria – and such help was denied them.

• Revolt in Prussia

With insurrections spreading in Europe, on March 13, 1848, the venerable Metternich resigned after thirty-nine years in the Austrian foreign ministry, and like Charles X and Louis Philippe before him, fled to London. On the heels of Louis Philippe's fall, news of this unexpected surrender triggered more unrest. In Berlin long-frustrated liberals went into the streets to call for a national legislature and a constitution. Their actions cowed the king, the uninspiring Frederick William IV, and after some initial bloodshed when his troops fired into the crowd, he shrank from using his army and granted the demands. In the course of the upheaval the liberals were joined by a horde of workers who threw up barricades. Their passionate intensity worried upper-class, educated agitators who now softened their position. Thus Prussia managed to escape without massive bloodshed and without extensive restructuring of her basic government. A constitution had been assured and the monarchy had betrayed a posture of weakness in crisis.

• Revolt in Austria

In France, the year 1848 had seen liberals (republicans) and socialists in competition. In Prussia those calling for change had been emphatically liberal. In Austria there were no socialists and few liberals, but many nationalists. Austria's polyglot empire of different cultures and peoples seemed about to disintegrate as Hungarians, Czechs, Italians, and others mirrored the Viennese in challenging the imperial government. Complicating Austria's problem was widespread agrarian unrest. The insurrection in Vienna was an open student revolt which the government handled timidly, further emboldening the dissidents, while Metternich's flight left the Emperor exposed and on the defensive. Under Louis Kossuth's leadership the Hungarians were demanding almost complete autonomy for themselves and other areas of the empire. The voices for independence were raised in Bohemia and in Italy, and there were Serb and Croat demands for freedom from Magyar control. The barricades were up around the empire with the nerve center of the system, Vienna, in confusion. At this critical juncture appeared four able leaders who were to restore Vienna's power. Prince Felix von Schwarzenberg managed to blunt demands for sweeping reforms. An assembly to draw up a constitution took so long that its product, the so-called "Kremsier Constitution" was out of date on March 1, 1849, when it appeared and Schwarzenberg simply issued his own authoritarian document. He also replaced the weak emperor Ferdinand I with a younger nephew, Francis Joseph, who seemed more alert. The Bohemian revolt was crushed by Prince Alfred Windischgrätz on June 17, 1848. He then joined the Croatian governor, Joseph Jellachich in attacking the Hungarians and also moving against the insurrection in Vienna. South of the Alps Marshall Joseph Radetzky struggled against local insurrections while also being attacked by Sardinia's King Charles Albert. By heroic exertions he managed to crush Charles Albert at the battle of Novara on March 23, 1849, restoring order in Italy.

In 1849 it looked as though the conservative forces were returning to power everywhere in Austria except Hungary. Russia's Tsar Nicholas now came to Austria's aid, sending an army to Budapest and restoring Vienna's control. Thus autocracy was restored in central Europe; there had been few changes, the most important the end of serfdom in the Austrian empire. In France, too, liberalism appeared blunted as Louis Napoleon quickly converted the Second Republic into a Napoleonic empire. In 1848 liberals had felt their hour was at hand but by 1851 it seemed that at one of history's great turning points, history forgot to turn.

• Midcentury Progress in England

Despite the widespread violent upheavals of 1848, in England, France, and Russia the second third of the century saw a considerable amount of social and economic progress. In 1837, Victoria, the eighteen-year-old niece of William IV, became Queen. During much of her reign she tried to protect royal prerogatives. Her early years saw the rise of the Liberal and Conservative parties, formerly the Whigs and Tories. The reforming zeal of the early 1830's continued, highlighted by the Factory Act of 1844 which regulated child labor in industry and established inspection procedures to guarantee safety standards. The epochal repeal of the Corn Law occurred in 1846, a major triumph for Sir Robert Peel. As in the earlier case of Catholic Emancipation, the most conservative and reactionary wing of his party viewed repeal of the Corn Law as unacceptable, and internal dissension weakened the party to the point where Peel fell from power. He had had an extraordinary career of public service – under the Conservative banner in the 1820's he had ushered through Parliament the first of Tory reforms and helped to launch England on an economic policy of free trade.

The 1840's were difficult for many workers as poor crops contributed to economic hardship. Yet enormous industrial progress was taking place. Between 1830 and 1850 production in many industries doubled and some, like pig iron tonnage, tripled. A sense of worker solidarity was developing; the Chartist movement for parliamentary reform consisted of a massive petition sent in to Parliament. Despite the fear of violence, especially in 1848, Parliament failed to act on each occasion (1838, 1842, 1848) a petition was presented. Free trade's success was almost instantaneous; as in the case of the Zollverein, the reduction of trade barriers markedly increased the flow of goods which resulted in a substantial rise in profits. The same result followed the enlightened

Cobden-Chevalier treaty negotiated with France in 1860. The generation of those admitted to the vote in 1832, the liberal manufacturing elite, was now dominant in the House of Commons and riding high on a wave of prosperity.

After Peel the next major political leader was the Liberal Lord Palmerston. As foreign secretary he had frequently alienated Queen Victoria by not clearing ambassadorial instructions with the palace. She stubbornly refused to name him as prime minister until forced to by scandals in the midst of the Crimean War. After Palmerston's death in 1865 parliamentary reform again surfaced and another Reform Bill doubling the electorate was passed in 1867. This was the setting for a classic rivalry between Benjamin Disraeli and William Gladstone as English politics entered a new era.

• Domestic Progress in France

Louis Napoleon had hardly taken the oath of office as President of the Second Republic when he moved to place Bonapartist sympathizers into positions of power. Shortly he was on a collision course with the Assembly which ended when he staged a coup d'etat on December 2, 1851. The republic was phased out a year later as he declared the founding of the Second Empire and took the title of Napoleon III. After the turmoil of 1848 a Bonaparte seemed at least to be a guarantee of social order and many of Europe's aristocracies breathed easier.

The Second Empire of Napoleon III was a period of substantial industrial and economic growth. The government was authoritarian through 1860 when systematic political liberalization began. In both the authoritarian and the liberal phases of the empire the government was used in Saint-Simonian fashion to promote and finance widescale economic and social projects. A great many construction programs were conceived, largely funded through joint stock companies such as the Credit Mobilier and the Credit Foncier, new and daring innovations in credit banking. The system of rail construction started under Louis Philippe was dramatically extended, with the 1900 kilometers completed by 1848 increased to almost 16,000 by 1870. Extensive canal construction coupled with highway improvements also tended to bind the nation closer together. The business elite found a plethora of worthy projects for investment, including the rebuilding of Paris. A maze of dank and winding alleyways, replete with all sorts of stenches, was replaced by open squares and majestic boulevards which literally let light into the heart of the city. Material progress was evident on every hand. New department stores exhibited a large array of goods for the middle-class consumer and international exhibitions in Paris (1855,1867) publicized advances from an expansive technology. The Empire was an entrepreneurial paradise as the Saint-Simonian Emperor gave his blessings to all sorts of business enterprise, including construction of the Suez Canal.

Politically the Emperor faced growing opposition as the years went by and various foreign adventures disappointed one group after another. In an attempt to maintain popularity, he slowly liberalized the apparatus of government in the 1860's. Subject to declining health, criticized as a shabby roué, badgered by self-seeking relatives and hangers-on, and attacked by a slowly growing number of republicans, he even lost clerical support, formerly one of the mainstays of his power. Thus while the regime was losing its political control, the nation was undergoing a striking economic transformation, much of which must be credited to Napoleon III. He believed in free trade, in free nationalities, and in international congresses. In these respects he was as much a forerunner of the future as he was a child of that Napoleonic political past he so assiduously publicized.

• Reform by Decree in Russia

Nineteenth-century reform in Russia is associated with the twenty-six-year reign of Alexander II who came to power in the midst of the frustrations of the Crimean War. A number of factors impelled him to face up to the problem of serfdom. The war had discredited both the military and the bureaucracy and sentiment for emancipation and modernization was widespread. In addition, Alexander's mother and sister were both German and regarded serfdom as uncivilized. As was to be expected, the nobility proved unwilling to free their serfs voluntarily and a host of study committees urged reform that stopped short of freeing the serfs. The Tsar had to intervene with decrees freeing crown serfs. Eventually (1861) all peasants, some forty million, were freed but in such a way as to create more problems. The nobles were to be compensated for the lost services through bonds, paid off over forty-nine years by local communities, the *mirs,* which were to pay for the bonds through peasant labor. Thus the peasant was free, but now economically tied to the *mir* – the *mir* had replaced the noble in control of the peasant.

While the country was adjusting to the problems of serf emancipation, judicial reform was carried out. Courts were made independent and trials public, with judges secure in office. The legal code was westernized, jurisdiction in minor crimes was taken away from the landlords, and jury

A demonstration of the new electric lights at a nighttime balloon ascension. From *Illustrated London News,* August 25, 1849.

trials with formal defense procedures were instituted, securing for the average citizen a considerable increase in protection. In 1874 military reform attempted to make military service more efficient and less onerous. The formal length of full-time service was set at six years instead of twenty-five. The more barbarous aspects of punishment were eliminated and more care was given to officer training. The army also instituted a formal program of education. Many peasants now became literate and even began to imbibe liberal and revolutionary ideas.

Alexander instituted regional assemblies (*zemstvos*) to consider local problems such as road building, education, and health regulations. These were composed of representatives from the *mirs* and functioned well, with both nobles and peasants acquiring some political experience. Meanwhile newspapers sprang up under a relaxed censorship and Russians began to be exposed to new ideas from western Europe, such as socialism. The Tsar's reforms failed to include a national *zemstvo* and accordingly were not liberal enough for many intellectuals who began to protest. An anarchistic movement, nihilism, turned its back on all organized government and called for the forceful destruction of existing institutions, while social critics like Michael Bakunin, Nicholas Chernyshevsky, and Peter

Lavrov could not agree on how to attack the regime. In a naive episode between 1872-1875, two to three thousand student intellectuals appeared in the villages in peasant dress and tried to get the peasants to revolt. This Narodnik (to the people) movement failed dismally when the apprehensive peasants turned the students in to the tsarist police. When such good intentions failed so badly, the radicals turned to terrorism, and murdered a number of prominent officials. Meanwhile the Tsar had received a formal report from General Loris Melikov, a responsible and far-sighted official, which recommended a modified version of a national *zemstvo.* Alexander approved of the proposal on March 13, 1881, but on the same day he was murdered by terrorist bombs. While his reforms had not come fast enough for the radicals, his death put an immediate stop to further liberalization.

• The Crimean War

The confusion and disorder in the wake of the revolutions of 1848 had hardly settled when another crisis appeared, this time rooted in the so-called Eastern Question. For centuries the French and Russians had intermittently served as spokesmen and protectors for Catholic and Orthodox Christians respectively, in their relations with the Turk, mostly regarding worship privileges of pilgrims visiting various Holy Places in the Ottoman Empire. As head of the French state, Louis Napoleon promoted a vigorous restatement of French rights, triggering a similar Russian response. Thus, contradictory demands were made on the Sultan who really cared little about who worshipped in Christian shrines. England's economic interests and concern for power arrangements in the eastern Mediterranean brought her into the dispute on the side of France, and both sides made a show of force, an Anglo-French fleet passing through the Dardanelles violating the Straits Convention of 1841 and the Russians occupying Moldavia and Wallachia. In October, 1853 Turkey declared war on Russia. In April, 1854 the English and French formally declared war on Russia, claiming to be protecting the sovereignty of the Ottoman Empire.

The war which followed, the Crimean War, was characterized by general inefficiency and incompetence. The "Charge of the Light Brigade" reflected great heroism but abysmal leadership and Florence Nightingale's nursing served to point up the amateur hospital facilities in England's army. The war settled into an eleven-month seige of Sebastopol which finally fell on September 8, 1855. The French provided much of the manpower and their army proved to be up-to-date in terms of logistics and ability to live in the field. The English mainly provided naval transport.

The Russians had so grimly hung on that even when they gave up Sebastopol they could claim a moral victory. Nicholas had died in March, 1855 and all were ready for peace at the Congress of Paris (1856), which among other stipulations, neutralized the Black Sea.

During the struggle Austria had remained neutral, antagonizing Russia's leaders who expected aid from the state they had recently saved from disintegration by crushing the Hungarians. Austria's reward for her neutrality was to be cast adrift, free of alliances and an easy prey for future nationalistic attacks. Sardinia had joined the war against Russia and lobbied members of the Congress to end Austrian aggression in Italy. The big winner seemed to be Napoleon III whose army had been equal to the task. He had humbled Russia and could claim to have broken the system of Vienna.

• The War for Italian Independence

The war was hardly over when Napoleon III found himself drawn to the cause of Italian freedom from the Austrians. He had vaguely promised "to do something for Italy." In January, 1858 an Italian nationalist, Orsini, attempted to assassinate Napoleon and almost succeeded. This was a rude reminder of his own personal stake in Italy. In 1830-31 as a member of the secret society of Carbonari, he had fought the Austrians in Italy and of course his family's roots were firmly Italian. He felt that he could no longer refuse to help and so he began negotiations with Camillo Cavour, Sardinia's premier, and at Plombieres on July 20, 1858, he and Cavour secretly plotted war against Austria. Often seen as a highpoint in a whole series of machinations on Cavour's part, Napoleon was every bit as shrewd. Cavour goaded the Austrians to war in late April, 1859 and Napoleon then came to the aid of the Sardinians who appeared to many of Europe's statesmen as innocent victims of Austrian arrogance.

During the Crimean War Napoleon III had wanted to join the army at the front but had been dissuaded. In Italy, Napoleon insisted on leading the army. There were two bloody victories (Magenta on June 4, Solferino on June 24) and he played a major role at Solferino. After these engagements the French and Austrian emperors met and arranged an armistice at Villafranca on July 12 which Cavour condemned as betrayal – the French had negotiated peace before the whole of Italy was free of the Austrians. At the time a wave of revolutionary outbreaks occurred in the rest of the peninsula and Napoleon suspected that Cavour had a hand in these. The colorful Garibaldi was conquering Sicily and most of southern and central Italy which he gave to Sardinia. The new Italy was thus born on March 17, 1861. It was really a greater Sardinia which, thanks to French help, embraced all but Rome and Venetia; these would join the new kingdom in 1870. For his efforts in Italy, Napoleon acquired Nice and Savoy for France.

• The Mexican Expedition

The Italian war had unfortunate consequences for Napoleon III. The papacy saw the new Italian kingdom as a threat and the elevation of Sardinia from fourth to second rank status rankled ardent nationalists in France. Napoleon thus appeared somewhat suspect as a steward of the national honor and as a friend of the Church. As the 1860's wore on, he liberalized his regime at home while in one diplomatic crisis after another, he kept losing public support. Between 1861 and 1867 his prestige suffered from an involvement in Mexico where, to satisfy the Church and some business interests, he sponsored Maximilian, an Austrian archduke and brother of Francis Joseph, as emperor. After the end of the American Civil War, Maximilian's position in Mexico became tenuous and Napoleon decided to end the adventure and recalled his troops. When Maximilian refused to abdicate, Mexican republican forces led by Benito Juarez easily overthrew his regime and shot him on July 15, 1867. To the embarrassment of Napoleon the news of the execution arrived in Paris while the Exposition of 1867 was in progress, a time when much of Europe's royalty was gathered together. The cost and futility of the Mexican venture became a telling point of Napoleon's political critics who were on the increase during the 1860's.

• Bismarck and German Unification

While Napoleon was trying to regain domestic support, Prussia was on the move. In 1862, Otto von Bismarck became the minister president of Prussia and at once set the nation on an aggressive path. Despite being a former delegate to the Frankfurt Assembly, he was a thoroughly Junker aristocrat and had little respect for the liberal objectives and gains of 1848. During Austria's struggle in Italy in 1859, Prussia had mobilized. While this succeeded in worrying the French, the Prussian military staff had noted serious deficiencies in the army. When the Prussian ministry asked for funds to carry through military reforms urged by the generals, liberals in the lower house balked. At this point the vacillating King William I had called Bismarck to office. In a characteristic act Bismarck simply ordered collection of the needed tax money, in defiance of the liberals, and instituted the military reforms. As the army was being modernized, Bismarck's diplomacy followed an opportunistic path, his goal being an enlarged Prussia. In finally creating a new German Empire, he was successful far beyond his hopes or expectations.

In 1863 when the Poles rose in a bloody revolt against Russian domination, the Prussian statesman passed word to Tsar Alexander that any Poles trying to escape into Prussia would be turned over to Russian forces. By this act Bismarck claimed to be purchasing Russian friendship but this irritated the French who, along with the Russians, were his natural allies against Austria, the major foe of Prussia in any struggle for control of central Europe. It was a vain gesture in reality for Alexander needed no help and even resented Bismarck's offer.

By 1864 Prussian army reforms were well-along and the new army was ready to be tested. Toward the end of 1863, a dynastic and constitutional dispute arose over whether both of the provinces of Schleswig and Holstein should be incorporated into the Danish monarchy. The German population of the provinces was enflamed and Bismarck intervened in this most recent episode of one of Europe's most aged and complex disputes. Despite a Confederation policy which dispatched Hanoverian and Saxon troops into the disputed territory, Bismarck set Prussia on an independent course in the crisis and managed to drag Austria with him. In a brief struggle, where Austrian troops played a negligible part, the Prussian army moved into the disputed area and crushed the Danes, taking their stronghold of Düppel on April 18, 1864. A feverish diplomacy followed, calculated mainly to isolate Austria. By acting bilaterally both Prussia and Austria had weakened the German Confederation and it was clear that a showdown for control of central Europe was at hand.

Bismarck now sought out Napoleon III at Biarritz in southwestern France and came away with the feeling that France would not oppose Prussia in a struggle with Austria. Napoleon had long seen Prussia as the state capable of building a united Germany. The French emperor now managed to get agreements from both Prussia and Austria that in any struggle between them, Italy would get Venetia, thus virtually completing Italian unification (an act which would make up for his earlier desertion of Cavour). Italy was pledged to enter the coming war against Austria. Napoleon III stood to gain no matter who won and expected to play a substantial part in the peace, possibly acquiring lands for France along the Rhine. This was a major miscalculation on Napoleon's part for Prussia soundly defeated Austria in the so-called Seven Weeks War, essentially settled July 3, 1866, at the battle of Königgrätz (Sadowa). Prussia had become the dominant German power and Austria was forced out of German affairs just as she had been earlier driven from a dominant position in Italy. Most European statesmen were as surprised as Napoleon at the swiftness of the Austrian demise. French nationalists criticized the Emperor for not gaining something for France out of such a profound change across the Rhine. Napoleon had not mobilized and when he made belated inquiries to Bismarck regarding compensations (such as Luxembourg) Bismarck turned him down, making the French emperor look like a scheming and shabby beggar.

Bismarck now established the North German Confederation, embracing most German lands north of the Main River, and began plotting a showdown with France, a war he seems to have regarded as inevitable and necessary to bring him control of the South German states. Austria meanwhile came to terms with the Hungarians granting them a large degree of autonomy and, being forced out of major German affairs, began, with Bismarck's blessing, to build a new structure of power oriented toward the Balkans. At home a successful Bismarck finally won approval for the funds he had been illegally collecting since 1862.

In 1868 the vacated throne in Spain occasioned the final chapter in German unification. A revolution had forced out Queen Isabella and the question of who was to rule in Madrid plagued the chancellories of Europe. French ineptitude played into Bismarck's hands. The leading candidate was Prince Leopold of Hohenzollern-Sigmaringen, a relative of William of Prussia and a brother of Charles whom Napoleon had aided in becoming king of Rumania. The Hohenzollern candidate was the center of controversy for the French saw the possibility of being nearly surrounded by the Prussian dynasty. By editing a telegram from King William in Ems, Bismarck implied the French had delivered an unreasonable ultimatum against the Hohenzollern candidate. By mid-July, 1870, a mood of jingoistic defiance prevailed and France and Prussia went to war.

With the declaration of war Prussian troops moved at once toward France, triggering a decision by the South German states to join Prussia in the struggle. In a series of victories the Prussian army outclassed the French. Their movements showed logistical skill in use of the railroad and their staff planning showed the fruit of their reforms and experience against Denmark and Austria. In the Crimean War there had been some attempt to bring industrial and scientific advances to the waging of war, but the Franco-Prussian War is most commonly regarded as the one where

A sardonic commentary on the reign of Napoleon III by Honoré Daumier. Courtesy, Museum of Fine Arts, Boston.

such applications were first made on a large scale. This is especially seen in troop movements, communications, and in weaponry.

The French troops fought well but were indifferently led and very poorly supplied. The aging and sick Emperor left Paris by train with his son, the Prince Imperial, to join his army at the front. Nearly all the fighting was on French soil and the French suffered a series of defeats. Napoleon had for some time been calling for military reforms but the appropriate funds were not voted by his liberalized legislative body; his republican opponents in recent elections had even argued for doing away altogether with a standing army. They were soon to raise their voices condemning Napoleon for the fall of France which symbolically was linked with the Emperor's personal surrender of himself and an army at Sedan on September 2, 1870, and with Marshal Bazaine's capitulation of Metz in October. The Second French Empire was ended and a new German Empire was born, being formally proclaimed at the palace of Versailles on January 18, 1871.

• Intellectual Vitality: Charles Darwin

In spite of the stability provided by the settlement of Vienna, there had been domestic revolts, revolutions, and open limited wars of aggression. Appropriate to such an age were two intellectuals who recognized in competitive struggle a basic key to survival and progress, Charles Darwin and Karl Marx.

Darwin's genius was to reformulate ideas on biological evolution in a way which could also explain human and social progress. A meticulous collector and naturalist, Darwin was convinced that species, rather than being fixed as earlier presumed, actually were undergoing change and he concluded that the explanation lay in a struggle for survival. Influenced by Thomas Malthus' much earlier studies which foresaw an inadequate food supply for humans as populations increased, it seemed to Darwin that in a grimly competitive world, only the fittest survived. The unfit and marginally competitive tended to disappear, accounting for changes in life forms over the centuries. Taken up by social scientists this sort of thinking could be used to explain and justify ruthless capitalistic competition, imperialism, and even neglect of the poor and weak. The enormous span of time needed for some of the change of species studied by Darwin prompted more sophisticated study of earth formations. Pioneering work by Charles Lyell had established geology as a scientific field. Before Lyell changes in the physical structure of the earth were often explained as occurring swiftly through some violent catastrophe. Lyell's work, along with Darwin's, tipped the scales in favor of the theory that uniform forces were going on the same everywhere with change coming slowly. Life of all sorts, including man, seemed to have been proven to advance slowly – thus by inference any rapid change in man's institutions, whether social, economic, or political, was explained as often emerging from violence.

• Karl Marx

Karl Marx also recognized the role of competitive struggle as an essential ingredient to social progress. Marx believed that economics was the mainspring of human activity (economic determinism). He built on many earlier ideas and added an extensive array of data which suggested a scientific validity to his "scientific socialism." Marx wrote that insufficient wages (robbery) at the hands of the capitalists tended to grind down workers in a vicious though natural exploitation. Since greed drove factory owners, inevitably the sheer need for survival dictated that the workers would organize and rise in bloody revolution, led by the socialist party. Looking at history he saw wars as having clear economic motivations. The French Revolution and other recent upheavals seemed to make more sense when viewed as the middle class protesting artificial restrictions and privilege. Together with Friedrich Engels, he managed to change the whole character of the socialist movement. The workers must control the means of production as well as profit distribution. Utopian socialism was branded as impractical and class warfare was widely presumed to be natural and extending across national lines. Wars were international conspiracies of the middle and upper classes and the victims were usually the workers or peasants. Religion, laws, government, and traditional standards of morality were all bourgeois creations intended to deceive and subjugate the masses. Questions at once came up on whether Marx was to be taken absolutely literally. For example, was a bloody revolution truly inevitable? Were there no possibilities for compromise? As industrialization spread, socialist parties became stronger with Marx being the seminal father-figure whose ideas were religiously quoted and debated.

• Advances in Science

The sheer accumulation of new information in the nineteenth century led to the organization of knowledge into the more clearly defined fields we are now familiar with. While Lyell was studying the earth's structure, many of its surface features were being detailed by the geographer Alexander von Humbolt, an indefatigable traveler who meticulously recorded all he observed of flora, fauna, and natural conditions. His work helped to awaken Europe to a renewed romantic interest in the broader world. In physics and chemistry problems associated with heat, energy, and movement prompted many studies; of incalculable importance were the first and second laws of thermodynamics. The first, enunciated by Herman von Helmholtz in 1847, said that the amount of existing energy remained constant. The second law, formulated by Lord Kelvin in 1852, noted that practical loss of energy does occur, prompting a vision of the earth gradually cooling off to become eventually lifeless and frigid. Atomic and molecular theory, electricity, and magnetism were all explored. Lord Kelvin remained a forerunner in scientific research, in 1881 concluding that an atom's diameter was less than a hundred-millionth of a centimeter. Louis Pasteur contributed enormously to bacteriology, especially in his development of a vaccine for rabies which led to other vaccines and a systematic attack on many diseases. Darwin's contemporaries in biology worked with plant and animal cells; in the atom and the cell the chemists and the biologists believed that they had discovered two of nature's fundamental building blocks.

• Philosophy and Literature

European intellectual life in the second third of the century was vigorous. In philosophy Hegel's shadow was imposing but Sören Kierkegaard, Auguste Comte, and Friedrich Nietzsche all formulated perspectives on life with far-reaching impact. Kierkegaard emphasized the painful reality of decision-making and his ideas were the seminal statement for twentieth century existentialism. Comte was an optimistic believer that scientific knowledge could be used for man's good. He argued for a highly structured world where intellectual elites (scientists, engineers, educators, sociologists) organized and ran society – all for the greater good of all. His writings constituted the definition of positivism as well as leading to the foundation of sociology. In Nietzsche evolution was worked into philosophy. He glorified the use of force, what he called the will to power, and developed an ideology for a sort of fascist autocracy. While Nietzsche was praising power and Bismarck was using it, in music Richard Wagner was evolving powerfully romantic expressions of German nationalism. A talented operatic producer, he absorbed much from other composers (especially Hector Berlioz and Giacomo Meyerbeer), coming out with a new intellectual product which blended music, literature, and the theater in striking fashion. A Wagner cult was testimony to the growing vitality of nationalism as a force; fifty years later the Nazis used his compositions in their propaganda films.

In literature, romantic themes continued but there also appeared an interest in depicting life as it really was. Among the greatest of the nineteenth-century writers were Victor Hugo, Charles Dickens, Gustave

Flaubert, Feodor Dostoyevsky, and Henrik Ibsen. Such names make clear the impossibility of an adequate brief analysis of literary developments while underlining the point that it was a golden age for literature. More comprehensive educational systems were preparing Europe's people for this literature and a rapidly growing public press was making them more conscious of problems and perspectives in their daily lives. Meanwhile Europe's cultural norms were being spread overseas by a massive stream of emigrants, while a vibrant technology was changing many of the contours of life.

18

Toward a New Upheaval

IN THE FORTY YEARS after 1870 European society was heading inexorably toward war, a holocaust unlike any preceding struggle, largely because the capabilities for destruction had become so awesome. The nineteenth century had witnessed the spread of the industrial revolution and by 1914 the strongest contending powers were fully industrialized. Their mass armies possessed fire power unthinkable only a half century before. An apt illustration of the changed conditions is the contrast between Lord Nelson's cumbersome sailing fleet in the Napoleonic Wars and the battlefleets of World War I with their steel-plated dreadnoughts. Napoleon had been closer to the technology and the problems of command of the Renaissance than he was to 1914. Technologically, the bulk of this change had occurred after 1870.

• Economic and Social Conditions

After 1870 the progress of industrialization dwarfed what had gone before. Technological and scientific advances enabled Europe's entrepreneurs to create a massive outpouring of goods. The highly sophisticated electrical and chemical industries rivaled in importance steel-producing complexes such as the Ruhr. The steel industry profited from a series of new techniques, mainly the Bessemer and the Siemens-Martin processes which yielded higher grade steel. The result was an enormous increase in production, a doubling between 1860 and 1880, but over a thirty-five-fold increase between 1870 and 1913. This meant cheaper and safer rails for railroads, larger more powerful warships, and stronger building materials. The steam engine also became more efficient thanks largely to Charles Parsons who in 1884 devised a steam turbine. By 1910 steam turbines could generate over 100,000 horsepower compared with 1,000 forty years earlier. In the chemical industry, research in dyes resulted in many new products, as well as improvements in explosives and pharmaceuticals. The chemists discovered a number of important new metals, such as aluminium, chromium, and magnesium. Refrigeration was a boon since many foods could now be shipped long distances.

These industrial developments had a major impact on the European landscape. Factories sprang up everywhere and even backward Russia developed a significant industrial plant. The demand for skilled workers skyrocketed and there was a comparable rise in literacy rates and public education. Germany led the way in establishing a comprehensive network of technical schools to organize and disseminate the flood of new information. Labor unions had had a spasmodic existence, but by the eve of World War I they were a major element in European society and rapidly becoming stronger – England's union membership doubled from 2 million to 4 million between 1900 and 1914. Both French and German unions had political ties and were wracked with debates over socialism. The French, however, were more divided, making a national stand by labor difficult. In Germany there was more sense of worker solidarity and the socialists were stronger, with union membership numbering three million by 1914. Most of these workers lived in dirty squalid slums which clustered about the factory sites. In Paris the rebuilding of the city had placed factories and working quarters on the fringes, keeping the center for tourism, entertainment, and the governmental bureaucracy. All these working districts came to be sources of left-wing socialist strength.

With a literacy rate as high as 90 percent in many areas, ideas could be spread by paper and a massive popular press flourished. There were 12,000 newspapers in Europe in 1900 compared with 6000 only twenty years before. Journalism was often a recitation of lurid scandals as the main object, of course, was for the papers to make money. Europe's economies were expanding (French investment doubled between 1900-1914 and world trade also doubled in the same period), and the lower classes were becoming more literate, politically more important, more secular, and capable of being moved by slogans relating to worker's rights, national goals, or imperial ventures. It was a society unlike any before. Yet on the surface, a cultivated aristocracy exercised a leadership which only partially understood the social frustrations and explosive qualities in the ranks below. This world was to end between 1914 and 1918.

• Christianity's Problems

Among the by-products of French national failure in 1870 was an isolated papacy. French troops which had long been protecting Rome were recalled, leaving Pope Pius IX alone and at the mercy of the new Italian state. Pius had waged a losing struggle against secular forces for many years. Regarded as a liberal at his elevation in 1846, the insubordination, rioting, and bloodshed of 1848 made him a determined conservative who regularly pronounced against liberal influences. In 1864 his criticisms appeared in comprehensive form entitled the *Syllabus of Errors.* Here he placed the Church squarely against rationalism in religion, free choice in one's selection of a religion, government control of either the clergy or clerical education, the right of rebellion, democratic procedures, divorce, and marriage as a civil contract. He even declared it to be an error to believe that the papacy should come to terms with progress and with liberalism. Pope Pius reasserted papal authority, struggling against the powerful secular tide which was fostering a decline in the unquestioning authority of established religions.

Both Protestants and Catholics faced criticism on several fronts. Darwin's theory of evolution produced much soul-searching regarding many details of established belief. The world clearly seemed older than previously thought and quite possibly man was a mere animal reacting to natural laws. He appeared no different than other animals and hardly divine. Too often the pulpit's response was shallow and emotional, disregarding the findings of modern science.

Christianity was also attacked on the accuracy and authorship of the Bible. German scholars, including Julius Wellhausen, F.C. Bauer, and D.F. Strauss, showed the Bible to be an amalgam of songs, myths, and literature, containing contradictory accounts by many authors. The Old Testament was especially suspect as a document to be taken literally. A movement developed championing the Bible as primarily a moral, inspirational work, to be appreciated as myth and perhaps symbol. To some Jesus became a human, understandable prophet, but hardly divine. Such textual and interpretive challenges were especially trying for Protestants who at the time of the Reformation had insisted on the literal truth of the Bible ("This *is* my body, this *is* my blood"). The Catholics were more fortunate since they had always adopted a broader view, seeing the Bible as a source of God's word accompanying the writings of the Church Fathers and the history of the Church.

Meanwhile anthropological insights were implying a relative view of ethical standards. Correct action in one society was often reprehensible in another; so, clearly, a religious fiat defining correct moral action was hardly acceptable. At the same time a dechristianization or paganization process was rapidly growing in the developing industrial slums. Construction of new urban churches failed to stem the growing human brutalization encouraged by the factory system and Christian values suffered substantial setbacks among the laboring population. Religious responses to the problem, such as the Salvation Army, were often only marginally effective.

To all these difficulties the Catholic Church had the additional problem that it was under attack by secular states, hence the vigor of Pius IX's defiance. In Italy, except for the Vatican itself, all the Papal States, lands controlled by the Church for centuries, had been lost and in Germany, Bismarck directly attacked Catholic interests in the May Laws (1873, 1874, 1875) designed to hamper their political activities. To his *Syllabus of Errors* Pius had added (1869) the doctrine of Papal Infallibility when speaking *ex cathedra* on faith and morals. He doggedly refused to grant any concessions to the newly unified states. At his death in 1878, he was succeeded by Leo XIII who moved quickly to restore normal relations with Germany. In France the Church had supported the cause of monarchism even while the Third Republic was becoming more firmly established. Leo counseled the French clergy to accept the republic but he continued Pius' refusal to acknowledge the new Italian state. In 1891 he issued an encyclical, *Rerum Novarum,* formally committing Catholicism to do all it could for the industrial worker, who was seen as a transplanted peasant. A number of Catholic labor unions appeared and several versions of Catholic socialism helped to build a broader base for the Church. Leo also promoted modernism, a belief that both humanistic and scientific study should be encouraged since both sought truth. Both Catholics and Protestants became involved with problems of social welfare. Here they met the socialist on his home ground. Neither Christians nor socialists were adequately supported by the politicians or capitalists; they were lonely competitors in efforts to bring relief to the urban poor.

• Italy After Unification

The completion of Italian and German unification was the fulfillment of decades of national and liberal ambitions; it was assumed that unity would bring both areas internal stability and prosperity. Ever since Charlemagne's empire had been split up, struggles had occurred for portions of it, usually involving strife over control of much of Germany or Italy. Now, since these areas were united and would be able to protect themselves, a major cause of war in Europe had vanished. Unfortunately, the unifications created new difficulties. Pope Pius IX's refusal to deal with the new secular state denied the government the talents of many able men. Further, unification had joined an economically backward south to an industrial north which now had to pay for the problems of literacy and corruption in the whole peninsula. Seeing modern Italy as a major state, the politicans' sense of pride led them to authorize a considerably oversized army, creating more of an economic burden and forcing high taxes on the peasantry. The salaries in the new bureauracy especially attracted southerners into the civil service. Bringing their special codes of family loyalty, they soon changed the system of government employment into a sort of corrupt relief system. Parliamentary life was characterized by obstructionism, bribery, and the alignments and realignments of cliques and personal power blocs. Politicians angled to obtain and manipulate power and there was little concern for the general welfare. As the north continued to industrialize, improved living conditions gradually spread into the south but unification in Italy in the decades after 1870 failed to live up to liberal expectations.

• Germany After Unification

In Germany the Prussian state had absorbed its former partners in the Zollverein and consequently the new federated empire came into being as a powerful and unified economic unit. Regional free trade had been dramatically successful and now industry surged forward on a scale to amaze the most optimistic observers. The middle class enormously increased along with a corresponding rise in socialist strength. Unification brought Bismarck, now the Imperial Chancellor, a more complex political environment with the appearance of two new parties, the Center or Catholic party with special strength in Bavaria and along the Rhine, and the Social Democrats with a growing influence in the industrial areas. The days of unchallenged control by Prussia's landed Junker aristocracy were passing but, nonetheless, Bismarck lashed out against both new forces. Regarding both Catholics and socialists as non-nationals and hence citizens of questionable loyalty, he moved against both through the enactment of restrictive and coercive legislation, first (1873-75) the Catholics (the

Kulturkampf) and after 1878, the Socialists (the Exceptional Laws). However, both parties grew as voters returned more of their deputies to the Reichstag. When the Chancellor had clearly failed in his attack on the Catholics (the Black International), he covered his failure by lashing out against the socialists (the Red International) where he also failed.

Out of Bismarck's struggle with the socialists came a body of enlightened social legislation (1881, 1883, 1889). Designed to improve the lot of workers (and to make them less susceptible to socialism) they constituted, in effect, the core of what came to be called state socialism, providing for insurance to cover old age, accidents, and illness. Despite its narrow objectives it was one of the most enlightened moves by an industrial state in the century. The workers, however, continued to support socialism and by 1912 the Social Democrats attracted four and a half million votes. The socialists everywhere debated whether or not to revise Marxian tactics; a revision of Marxian thought would allow socialism to be evolutionary, growing peacefully and operating within the law by participating in elections and trying for more influence in the avowedly bourgeois instruments of government. Marx, however, had insisted that socialism should be revolutionary, refusing to cooperate in elections and with elected chambers of government. In Germany, as in most areas outside Russia, the so-called revisionists were successful.

In German industry the large corporation evolved rapidly. There was little emphasis on laissez-faire and natural competition – the growth of monopolies seemed both natural and efficient. Large vertical and horizontal cartels were encouraged, with government support, to control whole industries, particularly the chemical and electrical industries, as well as steel and mining. Companies made agreements on prices and systematically divided the market, further putting a damper on competition and assuring a large measure of corporate control of the nation's economic life. Sensing the possibilities for far more profits in world markets, business leaders supported a more aggressive German effort to acquire overseas colonies with an adequate navy to assure access to raw materials. Bismarck had always thought in terms of power in central Europe and he tried to reduce or ignore such ambitious pressures from the business community. The new Kaiser, William II, however, was of the new generation and sympathetic to the vision of Germany as a *world* power and dismissed Bismarck in 1890 as being out-of-step with the times. As Bismarck had predicted, the colonies that Germany acquired put her in competition with England, and the building of a naval fleet was to contribute to the tensions leading to World War I. German industry successfully competed in world markets, even winning a substantial share of the English home market.

The Avenue de l'Opéra in Paris lit up by electricity in 1878. From *La Lumière Electrique*, 1881.

German economic vitality, coupled with her colonial program and the new world orientation of her monarch called for a tactful foreign policy which unfortunately was lacking.

• France After 1870

After the fall of the Second Empire a new assembly was elected on February 8, 1871. It proved to be dominated by monarchists who had campaigned on platforms promising peace rather than continuance of war. By early March the assembly accepted the vindictive terms of peace offered by Bismarck, but the terms (loss of Alsace and some of Lorraine, an indemnity of 5 billion francs and an occupation until it was paid) offended the sense of national pride of the Parisian workers. Adolphe Thiers was made chief executive provisionally by the assembly and cancelled a moratorium on rents and debts, cut off dole payments to the National Guard and ordered its arms taken. The result was an urban revolt; the working class of Paris rose against the assembly and proclaimed themselves a self-governing commune, and Thiers was forced to use the army to restore order. The Commune of Paris lasted from March 26, 1871, until the city fell to Thiers on May 28, 1871. A bloody clash with overtones of class warfare, it was also a cause committed to municipal liberties. Minor uprisings in a number of other French cities were even less successful.

After crushing the Commune, Thiers completed the peace treaty with Germany and the state began a soul-searching effort to establish a permanent form of government. Monarchists could not cooperate in backing a single pretender and each election showed increasing republican strength. Accordingly France literally drifted into the foundation of the Third Republic, a middle-class regime characterized by lack-luster, revolving-door ministries. Thanks to an efficient bureaucracy, the government managed to stagger through various crises and scandals. In 1887 the president's son-in-law, Daniel Wilson, was exposed selling his influence in elections to the Legion of Honor, and 1892 was highlighted by revelations that entrepreneurs promoting Panama Canal construction were deceiving the public and investors. Between 1886 and 1889 General Georges Boulanger, a popular minister of war, maneuvered to take power to restore national honor, but fled the country when challenged by the senate. His strident nationalism and calls for revenge against Germany attracted the support of many right-wing opponents of the republic. His flight left them disillusioned but still convinced of the weakness of the government.

The celebrated Dreyfus Case, which dragged on from 1894 to 1906, was by far the most excruciating crisis for the republic and for French society in general. Discredit fell alike on the clergy, monarchists, nationalists, royalists, and the military. Captain Alfred Dreyfus, a patriotic Jewish officer serving on the General Staff, was charged with transmitting military information to the Germans. He was convicted but further probing showed him to be the victim of forged documents. In the ferreting out of the guilty party and the exoneration of Dreyfus, all Frenchmen took sides – the republicans supported Dreyfus while most right-wingers were against him, with anti-Semitism an ugly factor. Dreyfus was finally vindicated but France had been through a soul-wrenching experience. A similar crisis would have toppled earlier regimes but the republic emerged strengthened, though divided.

A thirst for revenge for the defeat in 1870 added an abrasive element to the nation's political and social life. Anticlerical legislation culminated in the separation of church and state in 1905. A bitter revolutionary sentiment permeated the labor movement as the June Days of 1848 and the Commune of 1871 were continuously recalled as instances when those in charge of the government, the property classes (managers), had used the army against those lacking property. French unions had evolved from a tradition of syndicalism which emphasized direct action as the most effective bargaining tool, specifically, sabotage and the strike. Nearly all workers were included in the massive General Confederation of Labor which was dedicated to direct action. When a general strike occurred on May Day of 1906, French labor had clearly acquired vast new potential.

• Britain After 1865

After Palmerston's death the witty, urbane, conservative Benjamin Disraeli fought for power with the dour, moralistic liberal, William Gladstone. Their competition brought both to the high office of prime minister while the nation profited from a wave of reform legislation. There was spreading prosperity, a rapidly expanding middle class, and an extended overseas empire with Irish problems providing a somber backdrop. Disraeli had brought conservative support for the Second Reform Bill but the new electors voted for the Liberals. In Gladstone's first ministry (1868-1874) Parliament enacted a monumental number of reform measures dealing with domestic problems. Public education was broadly extended, the secret ballot adopted in local elections, and major military reforms enacted. All these measures were under continuous and scathing attacks by Disreali who ridiculed such prosaic and undramatic concerns, making fun of debates which concentrated on the width of desks in schools while a new Germany had upset Europe's power structure. When he became prime minister, he launched England on a series of brilliant diplomatic coups. He gained control of the Suez Canal for Britain, acquired the title of Empress of India for Victoria and managed, despite Bismarck, to be the key figure at the Congress of Berlin in 1878. All the while Ireland remained an issue and finally home rule seemed a reluctant road which had to be followed. In 1890 Gladstone at last faced the issue and following his death home rule won steady support until in 1914 its success was nearly assured.

By 1910 the era of enormous profits flowing from free-trade policies appeared at an end. Both the United States and Germany loomed as competitors in the world's major markets and all of England's earlier commercial advantages disappeared. Her products were no longer the best and the Americans and Germans showed more consideration for customers, both in designing goods for particular needs and in finding flexible methods of payment. They were also more dynamic salesmen. England needed to update her productive plant, found technical schools, and adopt more imaginative sales techniques. England's decline in trade came at a time when she was forced to give up her long standing policy of no entangling foreign alliances. In the Boer War, England's showing had been embarrassing, but more important, her leaders realized that in a dangerous world she had no friends. Both apprehensive and cautious, they began to seek firm commitments and by 1914 England was a major partner in the Triple Entente.

• Russia After 1881

Alexander III was embittered by his father's murder and convinced that liberalism was a mistake. His autocracy and police oppression were grimly efficient and for years effectively eliminated the free expression of ideas. Minorities were savagely treated, especially the Jews. Russification meant orthodoxy in religion and the outlawing of various languages, such as Polish in Poland. An arch reactionary, Constantine Pobodonostsev, helped direct the persecution of all suspected of harboring liberal or western sentiments, and he was against western influences such as jury trials, freedom of the press, and elections. There was strict censorship in the universities, and many offenders were shipped off to Siberia.

Capital began to flow into Russia from western Europe, powering industrial development. Under economic policies promoted by Sergius Witte, the finance minister, this growth was nurtured as part of an attempt to promote the iron and steel industries and railroad building, and in the 1890's some 1500 miles of railways were built. Peasants moved in large numbers to the cities, becoming part of the new proletariat, while those remaining in the countryside were victims of rising population pressures and lived a precarious and marginal existence.

Nicholas II, who came to the throne in 1894, was less set against liberal ideas but was largely ineffectual. Completion of the Trans-Siberian railway in 1903 helped attract Russian imperial ambitions toward Korea where a Chinese power vacuum had also attracted Japan. Russia and Japan went to war in 1904 and to the amazement of the Russians and many other westerners, the Japanese were successful in encounter after encounter on both land and sea. Russia was embarrassed by being the first major European state to be defeated in war by an oriental power and at home criticism became open and intense. Strikes and riots led Nicholas to agree to freedom of speech, assembly, and the press and to call a national representative body, the Duma. Liberals were satisfied but not the radicals. Marxism in Russia took the form of the Social Democratic Workers Party which split into two groups, dividing over the question of violent revolution with Nicolai Lenin, the major leader of the more radical Bolshevik group. Looking ahead, it was ironic that a militant Marxism was to succeed most dramatically in a nation far less industrially advanced than England, France, or Germany. Accordingly, it was perhaps natural that Russian Marxism was to be far more concerned for the peasant than other Marxist parties which were urban-worker oriented.

• The New Imperialism

The industrial progress which powered the growth of Europe's cities and middle classes also prompted a new wave of imperialism. The Suez Canal had spurred new interest in Asia as the shortened voyage opened up more of Asia to European entrepreneurs. At the same time, explorers like David Livingston who travelled for twenty-two years in Africa (1849-1871) were writing hundreds of books and articles. A new awareness of China and Japan, coupled with a fresh knowledge of different cultures in Africa, led European merchants to see opportunities for capital investment – and economic exploitation went comfortably with a vigorous nationalism. Trunk railways and steam transportation expedited the acquisition of raw materials while European technological superiority in weaponry made quick work of subduing many of the world's native peoples. Gunboats often sailed up rivers and shelled villages along the shore with no danger of any return fire – in 1880 a French force of 800 dispersed 40,000 Chinese cavalry. The temptations for plunder were enormous and governments rapidly becoming more democratic at home established and promoted harshly exploitive and autocratic colonial regimes abroad. Native handicraft economies were destroyed in the face of European machine-made goods, and the native systems were integrated into the economy of the Europeans. The result was often complete economic servitude. At times the Europeans achieved their will by working through native elites but often they implanted their own official bureaucracy. The army was a standard feature of the European presence as well as the Christian missionary who gave the movement the suggestion of a moral dimension usually lacking in fact. Back in Europe many people truly believed in colonization as a civilizing mission. Bringing enlightenment to savages was thought of as "the white man's burden" which happily coincided with enormous fortunes acquired from products such as ivory, rubber, gold, and diamonds.

Among the most vicious examples of rapacious exploitation was the Belgian experience in the Congo. Leopold II personally directed the venture. Under the guise of humanitarianism – to end the slave trade and to bring Christianity to the natives – Leopold's International Association of the Congo negotiated treaties with chieftains and set up trading posts. In 1885 the Association was recognized as the Congo Free State, a personal holding of King Leopold. The natives were forced to collect and deliver rubber and ivory and when quotas were not met, their women were often taken as hostages. Sometimes cannibal tribes were turned against the offending natives and grisly orgies resulted. It was a ghastly regime, which went unchecked for years with no formal courts where victims could complain. Enormous personal profits were made, though the Belgian government lost substantially through having to bear military costs.

Between November 16, 1884, and February 28, 1885, at Berlin, Europe's leading statesmen met and agreed on basic ground rules regarding what constituted proper claims to land in the ensuing "scramble for Africa." The French and the British were equally aggressive colonizers, creating vast African empires, while the Germans, Portugese, and the Italians were lesser partners in the feverish European rush for profits. A surge of romantic excitement accompanied these new colonial gains, and until the Germans moved into Tanganyika in 1890, the British dreamed of a Cape-to-Cairo railroad. In Asia trade concessions and spheres of influence were usually sought rather than vast amounts of territory. The French extension of their Southeast Asian holdings was an exception and followed the general imperial pattern common in Africa.

By 1890 European leaders were beginning to be apprehensive lest, despite the ground rules, an incident between European forces on some remote colonial frontier (as indeed occurred between French and British units at Fashoda in 1898) might lead to a military confrontation in Europe itself. Diplomacy resulting from colonial competition served to sharpen and refine Europe's evolving treaty structure. War was to come, however, from an incident in Europe.

• The Background of the First World War

For two decades after the Franco Prussian War in 1870 Bismarck dominated European diplomacy. Because of French hostility he tried to come to terms with powers the French might seek as allies. Since Britain was pursuing a policy of splendid isolation, he arranged a loose Three Emperor's League (Dreikaiserbund) between Germany, Austria-Hungary, and Russia. This left only the possibility of Italy as a French ally but Bismarck believed that Italy was too weak to be of much help to France in a war of revenge against Germany. Bismarck's system was in danger in the Balkans where Austrian and Russian ambitions collided. In 1877 Russia went to war with Turkey. After taking Plevna, following a five-month siege, Russia negotiated the treaty of San Stefano which called for a much enlarged Bulgaria bordering on the Aegean. Presumably Bulgaria would be a satellite state of Russia's which alarmed Europe's statesmen. Accordingly, in 1878 a congress met at Berlin to consider the whole problem. Not only was Austria disturbed by this extension of Russian power in the Balkans, but Britain also was concerned over the implications of the Ottoman defeat. Disraeli emphatically wanted no increase in Russian strength in the eastern Mediterranean. Russia came to the conference having only one chance of maintaining what she had won in battle; Germany had to support her. Bismarck, to his chagrin, was forced to choose between his two allies. Claiming to be the "honest broker" with no stake in the Ottoman issue, he insisted that he was neutral. In the circumstances, however, this amounted to a pro-Austrian stance. He later claimed that he chose Austria-Hungary because in any alliance she could be dominated by Germany and crucial policy decisions would be made in Berlin. Russia, on the other hand, could not be dominated and would insist on an equal voice in any partnership.

After the Congress of Berlin, Bismarck negotiated an Austro-German Dual Alliance in 1879. Italy made it a Triple Alliance in 1882 and Rumania joined in 1883. The Three Emperors League was resurrected in 1884 but by 1887 it had disintegrated over mutual Russian and Austrian suspicions. Bismarck saw all these treaties as aimed at French isolation and he became alarmed at the idea of Russia's being formally uncommitted. Further, French capital was finding its way into Russia and in feverish anxiety he negotiated a German-Russian pact, the Reinsurance Treaty. This secret agreement of 1887 was fraught with risks if Austria and Russia actually came to blows over the Balkans. When Bismarck was dismissed in 1890, his successors allowed the Reinsurance Treaty to lapse, a particularly short-sighted decision in Bismarck's opinion. By 1890, then, the Central Powers had come together, the core of their relationship being the Dual Alliance of 1879.

Bismarck was hardly out of office when what he had feared for twenty years took place, France found an ally, Russia. In 1894 Russia and France signed a military agreement aimed at the Triple Alliance powers. Meanwhile British statesmen had decided that splendid isolation was no longer a viable policy. An approach to Germany was rebuffed so they turned to France. In Africa at Fashoda (September, 1898) both French and British forces met face to face, each claiming the area, creating a colonial crisis which served to make both countries reconsider the entire range of their basic interests. Egypt and Morocco were particular problems involving economic penetration but eventually these were compromised and an Entente Cordiale was negotiated in 1904. From this agreement until the supreme crisis of 1914 the French and English diplomats worked closely together, a circumstance unlikely in Bismarck's day. The British and Russians then compromised several "sphere of influence" issues (Tibet, Persia, Afghanistan) between them and in 1907 comprehensive agreements were signed. Thus two massive alliance structures had evolved and a "Triple Entente" faced a "Triple Alliance." A major continental war could now result from some relatively small incident.

By some miracle a general war was avoided for seven years, but several crises occurred, testing and straining the wisdom of Europe's statesmen. A complex diplomacy centered on the Balkans where Austria-Hungary absorbed Bosnia-Herzegovina, in 1908 and two Balkan wars were fought in 1912-1913. Over the years, territories slipping from the grasp of the Turk were infected with nationalism; the Greeks, Serbs and Bulgars all coveted more land. The Serbs, especially, wanted to create a greater Serbia, including Serb-inhabited lands controlled by Austria-Hungary, such as Bosnia-Herzegovina. Serbian nationalists explicitly wanted a seaport, but although they had been on the winning side in both Balkan Wars, their objectives were unfulfilled. Blocked to the south, Austria-Hungary stood in their way to the west and was now their obvious enemy. They hoped for aid from their Russian ally should a real showdown occur. A second Moroccan crisis (1911) resulted in moving France and Britain closer together. All the time economic competition was further separating Britain and Germany, and under the abrasive William II a new and ambitious program of naval construction added a pronounced truculence to German policy.

The final crisis came in July of 1914. At Sarajevo in Bosnia on June 28, the next in line to the Hapsburg crown, Archduke Francis Ferdinand, was assassinated. The archduke was on record as favoring an answer to the Serb problem which would make the sort of concessions which had earlier been made with the Hungarians; that is, a triple monarchy. Since this would have effectively blunted the national ambitions of Serbia, the Serb extremists collaborated in the plot to kill Ferdinand. In the crisis which followed. Austria-Hungary issued an unacceptable ultimatum to Serbia, who asked for help from Russia, and all the powers looked to their alliances. Ironically, Germany told Vienna she would stand behind her in whatever she felt she must do, thus granting her a "blank check." The decision of what to do was therefore made in Vienna and not in Berlin, an absolute reversal of Bismarck's policies. In 1908 Russia had let the Serbs down by not preventing the Dual Monarchy's absorption of Bosnia-Herzegovina. Russia now felt she could not again be wanting and still pretend to be a protector of the Slavs. Accordingly, after agonizing about whether to mobilize or not, on July 29 Russia began partial mobilization against Austria-Hungary. August 1 saw Germany declare war against Russia and two days later against France. Great Britain entered the war on August 5 and the continent-wide struggle statesmen had dreaded for decades began.

• The End of an Era

The war of 1914 ended a long era of optimism about future progress. Even before the struggle, thoughtful observers had become despondent about the viability of Europe's social structures. The gap between upper and lower classes seemed to be entirely too great considering the productive potential of the economic system. Not only was there an acute awareness of the depravity in the industrial slums but publicity about brutality overseas also gnawed at the conscience of many Europeans. Leo Tolstoy and Peter Kropotkin found new virtues in anarchism. Meanwhile, industry continued to grow at an amazing rate, producing all sorts of goods, and many in the upper classes viewed life from a stance of lighthearted and irresponsible gaiety, symbolized perhaps by England's Edward VII. The war was to put an end to this superficial society. There had seemed some hope in a revised form of socialism that even elites could live with and yet, of all things, it was a socialist dominated Reichstag that voted for war.

Nationalism was the dominant force. The Kaiser could look out over the Reichstag and see neither right or left but "only Germans." This overpowering nationalism now led Europe's peoples at each other's throats with deadly new weapons, such as the submarine and chemical warfare. Millions were to be killed in a nightmarish, suicidal orgy of destruction on a scale completely unheard of and unforeseen.

Was this what western civilization had been aiming for? Was this the fruit of progress? Was this what the bitter struggles for constitutional liberties added up to? In many ways much of Europe had entered a new era between 1890 and 1914. Conservatism in politics was in massive retreat and old Metternich-type formulas for peace and control belonged to another world. Even the Eastern Question was in its last throes. City-life and city values were dominant, and with widespread literacy a public press was far more critical of society. The world of the nineteenth century can be said to have ended symbolically with the discharge of Bismarck in 1890. William II typified a newer and broader world-view, but also one of gnawing uncertainties, where the price of failure was to be catastrophic, on a scale undreamt of before 1890. It was a bigger world in which Europe played a correspondingly bigger part. The situation called for extraordinary leadership which was unfortunately in small supply.

Suggestions for Further Reading

Altholz, J. L., *The Churches in the Nineteenth Century* (1966)

Artz, F. B., *France under the Bourbon Restoration 1814-1838* (1931)

Aydelotte, W. O., *Bismarck and British Colonial Policy* (1937)

Barzun, J., *Darwin, Marx, Wagner* (1941)

Bell, H. C. F., *Lord Palmerston* (2 vols., 1936)

Briggs, A., *Victorian People: A Reassessment of Persons and Themes 1851-1867* (1954)

Cameron, R. E., *France and the Economic Development of Europe, 1800-1914* (1961)

Chapman, G., *The Dreyfus Case* (1955)

Eyck, E., *Bismarck and the German Empire* (1950)

Fay, S. B., *The Origins of the World War* (2 vols., 1930)

Gooch, G. P., *History and Historians in the Nineteenth Century* (1949)

Hearder, H., *Europe in the Nineteenth Century* (1966)

Howard, M., *The Franco-Prussian War* (1961)

Hughes, H. S., *Consciousness and Society* (1958)

Kissinger, H. A., *A World Restored* (1957)

Langer, W. A., *European Alliances and Alignments, 1871-1890* (1951)

May, A. J., *The Habsburg Monarchy, 1867-1914* (1951)

Medlicott, W. N., *The Congress of Berlin and After* (1938)

Mosely, P., *Russian Diplomacy and the Opening of the Eastern Question in 1838 and 1839* (1934)

Mosse, W. E., *Alexander II and the Modernization of Russia* (1959)

Nichols, J. A., *Germany after Bismarck* (1958)

Petrovich, M. B., *The Emergence of Russian Pan-Slavism, 1856-1870* (1956)

Plamenetz, J., *The Revolutionary Movement in France 1815-1871* (1952)

Power, T. F., *Jules Ferry and the Renaissance of French Imperialism* (1944)

Puryear, V. J., *International Economics and Diplomacy in the Near East 1834-53* (1935)

Rath, R. J., *The Viennese Revolution of 1848* (1957)

Riasanovsky, N. V., *Nicholas I and Official Nationality in Russia, 1825-1855* (1959)

Robertson, P., *The Revolutions of 1848: A Social History* (1952)

Schmitt, B., *Triple Alliance and Triple Entente* (1934)

Schorske, C. W., *German Social Democracy 1905-1917* (1955)

Seaman, L. C. B., *From Vienna to Versailles* (1955)

Setson-Watson, R. W., *Britain in Europe 1789-1914* (1937)

Simon, W. M., *European Positivism in the Nineteenth Century* (1963)

Slade, R., *King Leopold's Congo* (1962)

Smith, D. M., *Cavour and Garibaldi in 1860* (1954)

Sontag, R. J., *Germany and England: The Background of Conflict 1848-1894* (1938)

Stearns, P. N., *European Society in Upheaval: Social History Since 1800* (1967)

Steefel, L., *The Schleswig-Holstein Question* (1932)

Taylor, A. J. P., *The Struggle for Mastery in Europe 1848-1918* (1954)

Temperley, H. W. V., *England and the Near East: The Crimea* (1936)

Thompson, J. M., *Louis Napoleon and the Second Empire* (1955)

Webster, C. K., *The European Alliance 1815-1825* (1929)

Williams, R. L., *The French Revolution of 1870-1871* (1969)

Woodward, E. L., *The Age of Reform, 1815-1870* (1941)

Zetlin, M., *The Decembrists* (1958)

DEATH OF AN OLD WORLD
1914-1945

19

The Beginning of the End: World War I and an Unsuccessful Peace Settlement

SCARCELY ANYONE foresaw the holocaust of the First World War. Before it ended, the incredibly destructive war which lasted from 1914 to 1918 had devastated all of the belligerent nations and caused such ruin that European civilization never totally recovered. This war was a new phenomenon – a mass, industrial war draining all the energies of a nation and involving total populations, civilian and military alike. Ultimately it engaged most of the independent states of the world. Europe was no longer insular – the imperialistic ventures of the nineteenth century had drawn the entire globe into the European orbit.

• The Belligerents

At the outset the opposing camps – the Allied and the Central Powers – possessed reasonably equal military advantages. The Central Powers – Germany, Austria-Hungary, Bulgaria and Turkey – had a combined population of 150,000,000; the Allied and Associated Powers had 300,000,000. From first to last, the Central Powers mustered 21,000,000 soldiers, the Allied Powers 40,000,000. The Allied superiority in manpower, however, was offset by the weakness of Russia's industry – most of the Russian soldiers were poorly armed and easily mowed down by German machine guns. Nevertheless, the Allies had other advantages. Their ability to draw on their colonial possessions vastly increased their potential for a sustained war. England's control of the shipping lanes greatly facilitated Allied endeavors to draw men, food, and war material directly into the conflict. The Central Powers, on the other hand, suffered from shortages in all natural resources except coal and iron.

The Central Powers gained a significant advantage from their location at the center of Europe. They had considerably less difficulty with communication, not only because of interior lines but also because of the linguistic and cultural affinities between Germany and Austria-Hungary. The efficiency of the German military machine and coordination of the war effort strengthened their fighting potential. Throughout the first years of the war, England, France, and Russia cooperated with difficulty, which seriously hampered their military effectiveness. The problem of collaboration among the Allies was not satisfactorily resolved until 1918. By that time Russia had been removed from the coalition by revolution at home and the United States had taken her place, a decisive turning point in the war.

• The Failure of the Schlieffen Plan and the Stalemated War

The German government had recognized and feared for decades the possibility of a two-front war against France and England in the West and Russia in the East. To cope with this contingency a German Chief of Staff, General Alfred von Schlieffen, had drawn up a plan for a short war, based on a quick victory over France before England could come to her assistance and then, keeping only a small German force in the West, a concentrated attack and quick defeat of Russia. The Schlieffen Plan called for the main German striking force to hit France through Belgium and then to drive straight to the channel coast to prevent British forces from landing. The German army would then swing around Paris, separate the capital and the government from the rest of the country and catch the French army in a pincer grip. The plan nearly succeeded. England did not declare war until August 4 when German forces were already in Belgium, but the Belgian fortresses held out longer than the Germans expected. The Schlieffen Plan failed primarily because the Belgian's delaying tactics allowed the British to rush troops quickly to France's aid and because, at a crucial moment, a Russian invasion in the East caused the Germans to withdraw several divisions from the western front. The Russians as well as the British had mobilized their armies far more rapidly than the German strategists had believed possible.

The failure of the initial German offensive was the first indication that victory would not be easy for either side. The British and the French maintained a stubborn resistance to repeated German onslaughts. Neither side won a clear-cut victory at the First Battle of the Marne in September, 1914. The opposing armies held their positions, dug into long ditches protected by barbed wire and a stretch of continually-shelled territory called "no-man's land." Germany had failed to prevent the two-front war and settled down to trench warfare on both her eastern and western fronts.

Throughout 1915 and 1916 the war remained a stalemate while the trenches were extended from the channel coast to the Swiss border – 500 miles of ditches where men lived like animals. In the East the lines extended fully 1200 miles. More and more troops were hurled into futile assaults and the trenches became more elaborate as armies, kitchens, hospitals, and command areas moved underground. Men learned to exist with mud, human waste, ice, and the putrid smell of bloated, unburied bodies of the dead. Artillery fire constantly threatened – on a twenty-mile section of the front an army might fire 6,000,000 artillery shells in one month (in some places there was one gun for every nine years of front) Life expectancy in the trenches dropped to less than six months for privates and to about two months for lieutenants as millions of soldiers died on the western front without succeeding in moving the lines more than seven miles in either direction. The populations of Europe decimated their youth, destroyed their leadership, and drained their economies in a war which neither side could win. At the Battle of Verdun in 1916, 700,000 men were killed or wounded and the Battle of the Somme caused one million casualties. On the eastern front, in one single offensive in Galicia, the Russians lost two million men. Where the fighting was heaviest in France, the topsoil was simply blown away – the land became a desert. Lice, flies, and rats spread disease in both armies, killing nearly as many soldiers as the bullets.

• The British Blockade

Although there was only one major naval battle, the war at sea proved to be decisive to the final outcome. The Battle of Jutland, the only serious engagement, was a tactical victory for the Germans but a strategic victory for the British; the German navy extensively damaged the British naval forces, but after the battle the German fleet never again left its home ports and the British continued to control the oceans of the world. British ships imposed a tight naval blockade around Germany, limiting the ability of the Central Powers to import war materials and food. So effectively did the British succeed in cutting off Germany's food supplies that malnutrition reached epic proportions – the German people were to remember for years the "Turnip Winter" of 1916.

In order to break the British blockade, the German navy developed a new weapon, the submarine, which seriously challenged British naval superiority. The Germans never had more than sixty submarines operating at any one time, however, and the Allies were able to develop anti-submarine defenses which diminished their effectiveness. German foolhardiness in employing without restraint a weapon which antagonzied not only the belligerent but also the neutral nations was a major factor causing the final defeat of the Central Powers. As early as 1915 the Germans began unrestricted submarine warfare, attacking not only British ships, but those of neutral nations. In May, 1915 the English passenger ship *Lusitania* was torpedoed and sunk, killing more than a thousand civilians, including

A Germany Company at Rest, from an etching by Otto Dix.
Courtesy, Museum of Fine Arts, Boston.

many women and children (more than a hundred were Americans). President Woodrow Wilson made it clear to Germany that such acts would force the United States into the war, and for nearly two years the Germans discontinued their attacks against noncombatant shipping. However, in January, 1917 Germany's military situation forced her to resume attacks against all shipping, and during that year German submarines sank nearly 3,000 ships, including American and other neutral vessels. Unrestricted

German submarine warfare brought the United States into the war on April 6, 1917. By that time Allied sub-chasers, depth charges, and the convoy system allowed American ships to carry two million American soldiers successfully into the European war.

The Russians, struggling with revolution at home, had removed themselves from the war in March, 1918 when the Bolsheviks signed the Treaty of Brest-Litovsk, ceding vast Russian territories to the Germans. The two-front war was over, and Germany was able to concentrate her full military attention on the western front. The Americans arrived barely in time to meet the all-out German offensive in 1918.

• America Enters the War

During the years of the stalemate which had destroyed the economic resources of both the Allied and Central Powers, the United States had experienced a period of unprecedented economic growth and expansion. America brought all her wealth and power to the war effort and brought as well American soldiers fired with a new zeal, a determination to defeat the German Kaiser and "make the world safe for democracy." Their enthusiasm injected fresh energy into the war-weary British and French fighting men. The Americans, too, contributed a powerful new weapon, President Woodrow Wilson's Fourteen Point Plan for peace, which in the Spring of 1918 demanded a "peace without victory" and had a powerful appeal to the war-weary in Germany. The Fourteen Points called for an end to secret diplomacy and secret treaties, for freedom of the seas, the development of free trade, armaments reduction, national self-determination, and creation of a League of Nations to keep the peace. With her allies rapidly capitulating in the East and internal revolution brewing at home, the German High Command urged the government to sue for peace on the basis of the Fourteen Points. In November, unable to continue the struggle, the Germans signed an armistice which actually amounted to unconditional surrender. The long war had ended, and a sombre, shattered world turned to the problems of peace.

• The Peace: Optimism and Disillusion

More than ten million men were killed in battle during the four years of World War I and some thirty million more were wounded, many maimed for life. Countless others died of causes indirectly related to the war. The war had not only ravaged the populations of Europe – devoured its youth and consumed its future statesmen – it had caused enormous financial and economic damage. In France alone more than seven million acres of farmland were so devastated that for years they were lost to agriculture. Thousands of factories and mines were completely destroyed all over Europe, and with them raw materials, consumer goods and potential jobs. The psychic damage suffered by populations which had endured starvation and dietary deficiency diseases cannot be measured.

The intensity and destructiveness of the war had inflamed the passions not only of the leaders of the belligerent nations, but of all members of their populations, and when the guns stopped, such passions did not abate. The desire to punish the defeated powers made peacemaking difficult and the German assumption that Wilson's idealistic Fourteen Points would be the basis of the peace compounded the difficulties of creating a settlement which would satisfy anyone.

Negotiations for the treaties which ended World War I were conducted in Paris in 1919 (the victorious Allies refused to permit representatives of the defeated powers to attend). The English and French delegations, headed by Prime Minister David Lloyd George and Premier Georges Clemenceau, were determined to command harsher peace terms than Woodrow Wilson had outlined. Wilson, who wanted above all to establish a League of Nations that would arbitrate international disputes and prevent future wars, was forced to compromise most of his principles to the ambitions of the European powers and to France's demands for security against another German invasion. The resulting settlement did establish a League of Nations, an international body with little real authority and further weakened by the fact that the United States refused to join. The settlement also promulgated a series of treaties which tried to provide self-determination for Europeans, with the glaring exception of Germans.

The Treaty of Versailles, forced on the defeated Germans, created deep and lasting bitterness in Germany because it refused self-determination to 60,000,000 Germans. The majority wished to be joined in a single unified German state, but were kept divided in Germany and Austria, with large minorities in Czechoslovakia and the free city of Danzig. Germany was compelled to return Alsace-Lorraine to France, to cede to Poland territories taken from her in the eighteenth century and, in order to give Poland access to the sea, to relinquish the area of the Polish corridor, which meant dividing Germany into two parts. The Treaty took all of Germany's colonies from her. It curtailed Germany's armed power – severely restricted the size of her army, disbanded the navy, and forbade rearmament. But the most severe blow to German national pride was

Article 231, which forced Germany to accept full responsibility for the war. The "War Guilt Clause" also meant that Germany had to agree to repay the full cost of the war – an economic penalty that Germany, weakened by the war and by her territorial and industrial losses, would find impossible to bear. Moreover, the total amount of the reparations was left unspecified. The German government recognized the injustice of the assertion that Germany alone was responsible for the outbreak of war in 1914, but her representatives accepted the terms of the Treaty of Versailles because they had no choice. The German people never accepted it – they sustained a deep and lasting resentment of its terms.

With the exception of the German provisions, the Versailles Peace Treaty, although not the settlement Wilson had envisioned, reflected reasonably accurately his ideals, as did the treaties with the other defeated states – the Treaty of Saint Germain with Austria, the Treaty of Neuilly with Bulgaria, and the Treaty of Trianon with Hungary. The Austro-Hungarian Empire was shattered into a number of new sovereign nations – Czechoslovakia, Hungary, and Yugoslavia, with Poland, Estonia, Latvia, and Lithuania carved out of former Russian territory (most of these new states were to survive autonomously for less than a generation). The Paris peace settlement, conceived in idealism but born in compromise, did not provide stability in Europe. Instead, it contributed to the chaos which not only prevented security, but prepared the breeding ground for new and not too distant conflicts.

• Revolution in Russia

Of all the European powers embroiled in World War I, the most backward – politically, socially, and economically – was Russia. All authority rested in the hands of the Tsar, Nicholas II, a weak and vacillating individual who could not wield power effectively. Russia had a parliamentary body, the Duma, created in 1906, but such an infant legislature had neither the experience nor the authority to force Nicholas II to make needed social and economic reforms. Russia needed munitions plants, railroads, a modern system of food supply and distribution, an improvement in working conditions, education, and justice, but her government blindly ignored the need for change.

Despite increasing dissatisfaction, however, the Russian people had responded to the war. Some 15,000,000 men were called to the colors and when the first year was over, some 4,000,000 were casualties. During the early months the Russian army fired more shells every day than Russian

munitions factories could produce in three months. The army was so poorly equipped that at times the soldiers in the trenches faced the Germans with only one man in three holding a rifle. As the shortages of munitions and food, gross disorganization and lack of leadership became clearer to the soldiers and to the public, the demand for reform increased.

In March, 1917 workers struck a factory in the capital city, Petrograd, and the hungry and angry workers of most of the other factories in the city joined them in bread riots and violence. Troops sent to shoot down the rioters chose instead to join them, and within a few days the city was paralyzed. The movement spread to other parts of Russia, and still the Tsar's government proved ineffective. Before the month was out the Duma appointed a Provisional Government to function as Russia's executive power, and the Tsar abdicated. The Provisional Government and the Duma represented the moderate middle classes, and it appeared for the moment that they could achieve a political revolution which would place them in power without any danger of a really violent social revolution. They intended to carry on the war, write a liberal constitution, and even to provide for a major land reform, but the revolutionary Social Democrats (Marxists) were determined to create a complete social and economic revolution. They organized soviets (committees) all over the country to provide a broad base among the people and prepared to force radical change.

The problems besetting the Provisional Government multiplied in April when Vladimir Ilyich Ulianov (Lenin) returned to Russia from exile in Switzerland. Lenin, a professional revolutionary since the 1880's, had recognized at once the possibility of turning the situation to the advantage of his party, the Social Democrats, and immediately upon his arrival in Russia he attracted a large following. His inflammatory speeches and his slogans, "Land, peace, bread" promised the people exactly what they craved and had a wide appeal to the masses who were desperate for a resolution of the crisis.

During the summer of 1917 while the Germans marched into Russia, starvation and hunger increased, and the revolutionaries demanded that all power be handed over to the soviets. The Provisional Government proved unable to provide adequate leadership, and by November Lenin and his colleagues felt that they had gained enough support to challenge the Provisional Government. In a few hours the Bolsheviks, with army support, successfully accomplished a take-over which placed Lenin and the Bolsheviks in control of all key positions in the government.

• War Communism

Lenin immediately tried to put the ideas of Karl Marx into effect throughout Russia. He nationalized (seized into government ownership) almost all private property, completely abolishing private ownership of land, and expropriated all wealth. "War Communism," this attempt to transform without delay the national economy, caused widespread poverty and hunger, maddened the peasants, who resented having to turn their crops over to the government without getting money in return, and nearly destroyed the Russian people. At the same time Lenin concluded a humiliating peace with Germany. The Treaty of Brest-Litovsk, signed in March, 1918, ceded to the Germans nearly one-third of Russia's population, 1,300,000 square miles of territory, 80 percent of her iron and 90 percent of her coal – vital resources for industrialization. The treaty fanned hatred of Lenin's regime to violence.

Opponents of the new regime, calling themselves "White Russians," as opposed to the "Red Bolsheviks," used the bitterness generated by War Communism to organize a counter-revolutionary movement, and civil war broke out between the "Whites" and the "Reds," which lasted until 1920 – the bloodiest phase of the revolution. Millions, including the Tsar and all his family, died in the conflict – victims of terror perpetrated by both sides.

During the same period Russia faced the shock of foreign invasion. Troops from the United States, England, France, and Japan entered various areas of Russia in support of the anti-Bolshevik forces. The foreign invaders and the Whites never developed a cohesive alliance, however, and the foreign intervention aroused Russian nationalism. Many Russians who would not otherwise have supported the Bolsheviks fled into their ranks to fight the foreigners. Using thousands of former Tsarist Army officers, Leon Trotsky, as Minister of War, organized and trained a 3,000,000 man army and defeated both the Whites and the occupying forces.

• The New Economic Policy

World war, revolution, civil war, and invasion – all these between 1914 and 1921 – proved terribly destructive to the Russian people and their economy. When Lenin imposed War Communism, the system broke down – the peasants refused to turn their produce over to the state without payment, workers resented their conscript status, the new managers proved incompetent. Famine resulted and incalculable suffering turned the people away from the new experiment – between 1914 and 1921 some 28,000,000 Russians died. In order to regain the support of peasants and workers and to get the economy moving, the Bolsheviks retreated toward capitalism. In 1921 Lenin introduced the New Economic Policy (NEP) which lasted until 1928. Under the NEP the peasants paid a fixed tax, then were free to sell any surplus produce on the open market. Private property was re-instituted, small factories and businesses were returned to private management, while the government kept control of heavy industry, banking, transportation, and foreign trade. The NEP proved effective and by 1927 Russia had again reached pre-war levels in industrial production, although agricultural production remained about one-fourth lower than it had been in 1913.

In 1922 Lenin suffered the first of a series of crippling strokes which caused his death in 1924. His illness set off a gigantic power struggle for his position between Leon Trotsky and Joseph Stalin. Trotsky had strong support because he had organized the Red Army and achieved the victory over the Whites and the invading foreigners. He agreed with Marx and Lenin that socialism could not survive in Russia unless the socialist revolution occurred elsewhere. Stalin's power rested on his position as Secretary of the Party, which permitted him to put his own followers into key positions throughout the country. He had rejected hope of immediate world revolution, and believed that Russia must concentrate on establishing "socialism in one country." When Russia had achieved that, she would be in a position to lead and direct the world revolution as the proletariat of other countries proved ready to revolt. Gradually Stalin's control over the Party apparatus (he became Chairman of the Politburo) gave him the victory in the power struggle, and Trotsky was expelled from Russia. He was assassinated in Mexico in 1940.

After defeating Trotsky, Stalin consolidated his iron grip on the Communist Party machinery; only members of the Communist Party could hold any position of leadership or authority. The Party represented only a small percentage of the Russian population (about one percent), but its pyramidal structure penetrated down to the village level, controlling all institutions and dictating all policy. Whoever controlled the Party controlled Russia. Stalin gained total control and by 1930 forced out all opposition and filled the Party with his followers. Once he had assured his personal rule, Stalin was able to turn his attention to creating the socialist state. His ruthless pursuit of the total destruction of all vestiges of capitalism and simultaneous rapid industrialization in Russia meant further misery for the Russian people, and even greater loss of any liberties they had once dreamed of attaining.

• Fascism in Italy

Russia's feeble attempt at democracy had ended in failure. Italy was the next nation to choose totalitarianism. Economically and politically far less advanced than the other western nations, Italy could not overcome the chaos and confusion of the post-war world. Within four years after the cessation of hostilities, Italy, like Russia, had moved to a dictatorship. But Italy chose another type of totalitarian state – a dictatorship of the right. Whereas the Bolsheviks had attempted to establish a socialist utopia patterned on Marxist ideas, the Italians clung fiercely to capitalist ideology, carrying nineteenth-century, middle-class goals to a warped and politically unrecognizable extreme.

Although Italy had fought on the side of the victorious Allies, her gains were small, and many people believed that the western powers had betrayed her. The Italian government had made no real effort to pay for the war – Italy's economy was far too poor, and the Allies had loaned her vast sums. With peace, the government faced an enormous debt and a serious inflation. These economic ills weighed most heavily on those segments of the population who could least afford it – the middle and lower classes. With industry reconverting from wartime to peacetime manufacture, and agriculture retarded by an archaic and inequitable land distribution, jobs were scarce. Soldiers returning home discovered that society could not honor them – it could not even provide them with a living. Unemployment reached staggering proportions.

Those who had jobs were little more satisfied with conditions than those who had none. The failure of the government to fulfill wartime promises of land redistribution and industrial reform created intense frustration in both the rural and urban working classes. Many of the peasants, in bloody rural rebellions, simply seized the land they had expected to acquire. At the same time city workers began a series of violent strikes to stress their loss of faith in the government and to insist on immediate redress of grievances. Lawlessness, aggravated by brigandage, already an Italian tradition, became a vicious counterpart to government in many areas – sometimes whole towns defied the forces of law and order. The success of the Bolsheviks in Russia, the loud-mouthed rhetoric of the small number of communists in Italy, and the chaotic government combined to convince the aristocratic and upper-middle classes that their entire way of life faced extinction. The threat was more imagined than real, but the established classes sought to protect their privileged position and bring order to the nation.

None of these conditions need have been fatal, but the government failed. The political parties fought each other rather than cooperate to solve problems. The Christian Democrats opposed the Socialists, who hated the Liberals' resistance to any government interference in the economy. The entire political system simply incapacitated itself while events moved beyond its control. When unemployment rose, the government did nothing; when gangs of thugs, cut-throats, and brigands terrorized towns and country-side until no one was safe, the government followed a policy of strict non-intervention; when the Treaty of Versailles failed to provide vast additions to Italy's territory, the government sulked. Alienation grew in every class of society. The upper middle classes, wealthy landowners, and industrialists began seeking a strong man to protect their property. The frustrated nationalists, who had pushed Italy into the war, sought a leader who would act to redeem the national honor. Returned veterans looked for one of their own to provide them jobs. The peasants and the workers clamored for peace, security, and economic stability. All of these dissident factions found the leadership they sought in a new faction, the Fascists, whose violence masqueraded as strength. Their founder and creator would, by 1928, became the undisputed leader of Italy – the strong man everyone wanted. His name was Benito Mussolini.

• The Rise of the Fascist Party

In 1919 Mussolini organized the first *fasci di combattimento* – combat groups – of unhappy and discontented citizens. The Fascists, as they became known, capitalized on the dissatisfactions of all the various segments of the Italian population. A small faction in 1919, by 1920 they numbered 30,000; by 1921, nearly 300,000. They began to attract to their ranks representatives of the upper classes and even had adherents in the Italian aristocracy. Government and propertied classes turned to Mussolini, this man of action, who claimed he could protect them from the danger of Bolshevism, and the other classes approved of action rather than the "do-nothing" policies of the existing government. With the consent of the army, the police, and the law courts, Mussolini and his "Black Shirts" – Fascist troops – began a genuine reign of terror against the only groups which showed any inclination to oppose him, the Socialists and Christian Democrats. Labor union offices were burned, newspaper presses destroyed, socialist party headquarters demolished. Anti-Fascists were beaten, had castor oil poured down their throats, their teeth pulled with pliers – many were openly murdered. During 1921 and 1922 the Fascists killed hundreds of people with the active and passive support of those who were supposed to preserve law and order.

Mussolini was elected to Parliament in 1921, along with many of his followers, and by 1922 had enlisted the tacit sympathy of the monarchy and the church. In October, therefore, when the Trade Unions called a General Strike, Mussolini and his Black Shirts swarmed into Rome – the riot later became famous as the "March on Rome" – and the King invited Mussolini to form a cabinet. As Prime Minister, Mussolini formed a coalition government (the Fascists still did not command a majority in the legislature) and then, cloaking his tactics in legality, used his position to gain control of the entire governmental structure. By changing the electoral laws and continuing the terror, the Fascists gained a clear majority in both houses of the legislature. Mussolini demanded and received dictatorial powers, imposed a rigid censorship, and abolished all opposition parties, making the Fascists the only "legal" political party in Italy. Proclaiming himself the *Duce* (Leader), Mussolini rapidly tightened his control of the Italian state until, by 1928, he had completely reorganized the Italian political system.

• The Fascist State

Fascism had no well-thought-out doctrines, no clear ideology. It developed according to the needs of the moment, distinguished, in the beginning, only by its reactionary policies and its determination to achieve power. As it developed, though, patterns began to emerge. It glorified the state above all else – the individual had no significance and no rights except to advance the glory of the state. Fascism therefore denied completely the western concepts of individual freedom and dignity, subordinating the individual to the needs of the state. Along with liberalism and democracy, it vehemently rejected socialism and the economic doctrines of communism. Although Mussolini subjected every aspect of society – politics, economics and cultural life – to a strict authoritarian control, allowing no opposition of any sort, he maintained a state-dominated capitalism. Fascism, then, as developed by Mussolini, became a totalitarian state system which ruthlessly suppressed dissent, glorified nationalism and the nation-state, and adhered rigidly to private (but not free) enterprise and profit. The leadership principle became an essential element of Fascism. Mussolini – the *Duce* – assumed almost mystical leadership over the nation, possessing an emotional and irrational grip over the people. He required total and unquestioning obedience from everyone in Italy – "You must obey because you must."

At first Mussolini retained the appearances of the established Italian political system. Instead of immediately destroying parliamentary institutions, he allowed them to remain in existence but, by filling the cabinet and the legislature with party affiliates, transformed them into sycophantic organizations whose only function was to applaud Mussolini and his policies. Even the King and the Church condoned his usurpation of power. The King remained Monarch, but retained no power or authority – he did whatever Mussolini told him to do. In 1929 Mussolini signed the Lateran Treaty with the Pope, in which Church and State formally recognized each other. Mussolini granted the Church concessions regarding education and marriage law, and the Pope declared that Catholics could in good conscience support Mussolini.

After Mussolini had subjugated the Monarchy, the Church, the Legislature, the Courts and the law enforcement agencies, he began a reorganization of the economy. The Corporate State, the complex economic and political system Mussolini created, was primarily an elaborate justification for economic dominance by the large landowners and wealthy industrialists. In 1925 Mussolini and the Italian industrialists sealed a mutually advantageous pact, the Palazzo Vidoni Agreement, which provided for a highly privileged position for organized industry in return for industry's full support of Mussolini. Mussolini subjugated labor by replacing the old labor unions with Fascist Labor Unions, the only organizations with the right to establish wages, working conditions, and contracts.

Economic and political regimentation, despite the brutality with which it was imposed, did bring order to the former turmoil in Italy and enlisted support for the regime from the lower and middle classes. Moreover, Mussolini silenced any protests which might have arisen by launching an ostentatious program of public works intended to display Italy's prosperity. He built roads, grand new public buildings, improved transportation facilities, and brought water and electricity to rural villages which had never had them before. He encouraged trade, drained marshes and swamps, reclaimed formerly useless land, and subsidized public health programs. At the same time, he staged impressive public spectacles, parades, and party rallies to stir the emotions and the enthusiasm of the population. His propaganda agencies and his censorship program controlled every possible vehicle of influence, and publicized Mussolini and the Fascists. Textbooks, literature, the stage, movies, radio – all proclaimed the glories of Fascism. All the while, the Secret Police assured that no one voiced dissent or even questioned national policy. By 1938 Fascism seemed to have not just the support but the acclaim of every segment of the Italian population. Many thought that Italy had never been as well-run or as prosperous as under Mussolini. Liberty was forgotten – and Fascist propaganda succeeded in convincing the majority of Italians that liberty was not only unimportant, but really undesirable.

Mussolini's glorification of nationalism and his exaltation of the state meant a new surge of imperialism and militarism – expansion by military might of the Italian state. Spurred on by those dissatisfied nationalists hungry for territorial acquisition, Mussolini undertook a policy of military aggression aimed at making Italy the dominant nation in the Mediterranean. Although he did not openly break with the League of Nations, he despised it, and ignored the League's condemnation of his actions when he brazenly and without justification attempted to seize Ethiopia in 1935. In 1936 he violated League neutrality by openly aiding the Franco faction in the Spanish Civil War. After the Nazis attained power in Germany, Mussolini's aggressive foreign policy, which had alienated him from the western European nations, led him into an alliance with Hitler, his Fascist neighbor. Although Mussolini never quite trusted Hitler, both the imperialistic foreign policy and the domestic policies he had launched forced him into tighter and tighter friendship with Germany. The liaison was an extremely dangerous one for Mussolini – ultimately it would prove fatal both to the *Duce* and to the Fascist regime he had constructed.

• The Weimar Republic

The First World War had brought not only defeat but internal chaos to Germany. The long-suffering German people had never been informed of the impending disaster – they were led to believe, until the very end, that Germany was conquering the Allies. At the end of September, 1918, the German Army High Command suddenly and without prior warning informed the Kaiser that an armistice must be arranged without delay, and that the authoritarian government should be changed into a more constitutional and liberal structure to broaden popular support for the Emperor's regime. Prince Max of Baden, a member of the royal family and a liberal statesman, therefore formed a coalition government which had the support of the Social Democratic Party, the largest political party in Germany. As the negotiations for an armistice continued, President Woodrow Wilson made it quite clear that the war would continue until the Kaiser abdicated. The German people, stunned at the sudden reversal of everything they had been told, wanted peace more than anything and believed that only the Kaiser's refusal to abdicate prevented peace. Public discontent intensified and quickly reached a revolutionary stage. When the Naval officers ordered the German fleet to put to sea, the sailors mutinied. At the same time rebellion flared in other portions of Germany. Popular dissatisfaction forced even the Social Democrats, although members of the coalition government, to support the plans for a general strike in favor of abdication. As the rebellion spread, the Kaiser abdicated. Prince Max then handed the reins of government over to Friedrich Ebert, the leader of the Social Democratic Party. Ebert accepted power on the firm promise that he would support the existing constitution.

Conditions throughout Germany, and particularly in Berlin, however, forced the Social Democrats to move toward a democratic republic in order to maintain popular support. Ebert therefore ordered the election of a constituent assembly to draw up a constitution, with all Germans over twenty years of age eligible to vote. Before the election, however, a group of revolutionaries called Spartacists tried to establish by violence a communist government which would have changed the entire social structure of Germany and given power to the working classes. In order to prevent such radical change, the Social Democratic government turned to the old Army under Gustav Noske, self-styled "Bloodhound of the Revolution," who brutally wiped out the uprising.

In southern Germany, Bavaria experienced a particularly brutal civil war during the Spring of 1919 and hundreds of people died in Munich. The defeat of the communists, however, contributed to the development of powerful right-wing organizations which claimed that the Jews were responsible for the attempt to establish a communist government in Munich and in Bavaria. The Social Democratic government was finally victorious over the rebels all over Germany, but only after more than 1,000 people had been killed.

These events of 1918 and 1919 have been called "the German Revolution." The "revolution" was, rather, an attempt to preserve exactly those institutions -- the Monarchy, the Army, and the social structure -- which a genuine revolution would have destroyed. The changes which had occurred in Germany had not basically altered German society. After 1919 Germany had a new and more democratic government in place of the old authoritatian empire. But democracy in Germany was only superficial. It was tolerated by the ruling classes only to defeat the clamor for more extreme change and in the hope of achieving more lenient treatment from the Allies.

On January 19, 1919, elections were held for a National Assembly which met at Weimar on February 6, a coalition of the major political parties in Germany. By the middle of the year the Assembly had provided the legal establishment of the Weimar Republic resting on the people, and operating under the democratic Weimar Constitution. The new Constitution provided for a president to be elected by the people for a seven-year term. Article 48 granted the president the power to govern by decree in the event of a sudden crisis which threatened the republic. Legislative power was vested in a Reichstag, to be elected by universal suffrage, and a Reichsrat, representing the states. A cabinet, headed by a chancellor, was responsible only to the Reichstag.

• Problems Facing the New Republic

From its inception the Weimar Republic faced nearly insurmountable problems. The Allied Powers forced the new government to sign the dictated Treaty of Versailles with its historically false and psychologically unsound clause (Article 231) concerning Germany's sole guilt in causing the war. Resting on that article were the reparations clauses, which stated that Germany must pay the total costs of the war to the victors. All Germans, from extreme left to extreme right, united in bitter opposition to the terms of the treaty. The Chancellor, Philip Scheidemann, and his cabinet resigned rather than sign it. But it had to be signed; the only alternative was military occupation by the victorious troops of the Allied Powers. Nevertheless, the German people refused to accept that reality – they felt that in accepting the treaty the new Government had betrayed the German nation, that Germany had been "stabbed in the back," a constantly repeated phrase. From this time forward far too many Germans accepted the myths constantly dinned into all German ears, that the "November Criminals," the Weimar Constitution, the democrats, and the Jews were responsible for the hated treaty.

The Republic was blamed, too, for the failure to annex German Austria. As the old Habsburg Empire broke into its component national entities, the German portion declared itself part of Greater Germany and requested that the new Weimar government accept it. But the Allies refused to agree to the union of Germany and Austria on the ground that it would be a violation of the Treaty of Versailles. The Allies, and France in particular, feared a large, economically strong German state.

Economic problems of vast proportions plagued the Weimar government. The Reparations Commission immediately took all of Germany's gold reserves and then began to confiscate her capital goods, that is, those items which produce wealth. Specifically, it seized the merchant marine, the fishing fleet, entire machine shops, locomotives, railroad cars, trucks, and any other facilities which could be used to produce goods. Germany thus had to pay an enormous debt, without any of the means necessary to acquire the capital to pay it.

At the beginning of the war the value of the German mark was approximately 25 cents in American currency – four to the dollar. Naturally there had been inflation during the war – there has never been a war without inflation. But the loss of the war and the removal of the gold backing of paper currency inflated the mark to sixty-two to the dollar by May, 1921. At that time the Reparations Commission ordered immediate payment of one billion gold marks and two million per year thereafter, under threat of invasion of the Ruhr Valley, the most highly industrialized area left to Germany. The mark began an immediate slide in value. By June, 1922, scarcely a year later, the situation had deteriorated to such an extent that Germany asked for a moratorium, suggesting that the Allies were killing the goose which laid the golden egg. While England showed signs of agreement, France flatly refused, arguing that Germany really could pay the full amount, that she simply was not trying. Unless Germany paid in full and on time, France insisted that she would occupy the Ruhr and force payment. When this threat failed to produce the desired results, the French moved into the Ruhr area in January, 1923. This step caused more bitterness and hatred in Germany than the entire four years of actual warfare and completed the destruction of the currency. By November 15, 1923, $1.00 would buy 4,200,000,000,000 marks. Some 2,000 printing presses worked twenty-four hours a day stamping paper money – a streetcar ticket cost 16,000,000,000 marks and trade was reduced to barter. The inflation shook Germany to her very roots. The lower middle classes were destroyed – their invested savings wiped out, their pensions and government bonds worthless. Unemployment skyrocketed and soon, in many areas of Germany, three-fourths of the children were suffering from malnutritional diseases and tuberculosis.

Such economic difficulties contributed to the political problems facing the Weimar Republic and many doubted whether the democratic system could survive. As the inflation approached its peak in November, 1923, a right-wing effort was made to overthrow the Republic. A tiny dissident group had formed in Munich immediately after the war, one of many which developed overnight out of the dislocations and distress of the time. Like the others it lacked leadership, followers, or money. But unlike the others, this one came under the leadership of Adolf Hitler, an Austrian German who had moved to Germany shortly before the outbreak of the war, who had served in the German army, and who had elected to remain in Munich after the war. Hitler proved to have a special and hypnotic effect upon those who heard him speak, and by 1923 he had gained almost complete control over the party, which he renamed the National Socialist German Workers Party (Nazi Party). Hitler firmly established the leadership principle – everyone in the party was totally subservient to "Der Führer," the leader of the party. The authoritarian rule which Germans had accepted under the Kaiser was thus reinstituted, but in a harsher and far more dictatorial manner. Neither Hitler nor the Nazi Party had any coherent political philosophy. They were primitive, ardently nationalistic, and passionately anti-semitic. Above all else, they were men of violence and force. The Nazis organized a private army, called the Brown Shirts, which used violence to intimidate not only the Communists and the Jews, the scapegoats of the German populace, but the government officials themselves.

Bread! Depression in Germany in 1924, from a lithograph by Kathe Kollwitz. Courtesy, Museum of Fine Arts, Boston.

With the support of one of Germany's World War heroes, General Erich von Ludendorff, Hitler and the Nazis attempted to overthrow the government in the famous beer-hall *putsch* in November, 1923. The effort failed, primarily because of lack of preparation, and Hitler was convicted of treason and imprisoned in Landsberg Castle, where he dictated *Mein Kampf* (My Struggle). In this work the Nazi leader outlined the propaganda techniques which would play a powerful role in bringing him to power in 1933, and laid down the outlines of his future aggression and his justification for it. At the same time he made his decision to come to power by legal means, operating at least theoretically within the framework of the Weimar Constitution. This would require careful organization. Hitler had learned from the failure of the Munich *putsch* – he would not make the same mistakes again.

By firm discipline and the introduction of a new currency called the *Rentenmark,* the Weimar Republic pulled out of the inflation and put an end to the internal rebellion. The Allies cooperated, with the Dawes Plan of 1924, which provided for loans from Allied governments to help reestablish German industry and trade. Private capital began to flow into Germany and Germany regained her economic balance – by 1929 her industrial production exceeded that of 1914.

Just when the German people were beginning to feel safe again, the Wall Street Crash in October, 1929 in the United States began the Great Depression which quickly spread to Europe, affecting all the industrialized nations. The short-term credits which had been the foundation of German economic recovery were recalled and within six months the German banks began to fail. By 1931, 17,000 companies had gone bankrupt; during the following year bankruptcies reached the rate of 3,000 per month. Unemployment reached 6,000,000 and many of those who had jobs worked only part-time. At one time, late in 1932, 96 percent of all people who had been employed in the building trades were out of work. The German people once again faced economic collapse. Those classes hardest hit in the inflation of 1923 were now wiped out by the depression. Politics polarized – the moderate political parties lost their support to the extreme parties of both the right and the left. In the September, 1930 election the Communists picked up 77 seats in the Reichstag while the most extreme right-wing party, the Nazis, increased from 12 Reichstag seats to 107 and became the second strongest party in the Reichstag. The parties refused to form an effective coalition which could gain a majority in the legislature, creating extreme political instability. Article 48 – the emergency decree clause – now came into regular use, not for the purpose intended in the constitution, but because of the failure of a majority. In 1932 the Reichstag passed only five laws during the entire year, but the President issued 59 decrees under Article 48. The legislature had ceased to function, and German democracy, ill and weak from birth, died.

• The Western Democracies in the Post-War World

England and France had plunged into the First World War without clearly formulated goals or aims. But, before the end, the war became, in the minds of the populations of the western democracies, a fight for democracy against German autocracy. As the devastations of industrial warfare were slowly realized, it became something else as well – a war to end all war. But the savage recriminations between nations continued after the war, resulting in an unjust and vindictive peace settlement. The realization that the war had not created a better world, indeed, had left a heritage of economic and political turmoil affecting all of Europe, created intense disappointment in the West. The European nations which had entered the twentieth century with unbounded optimism, faced the 1920's in a mood of disillusion and despair. Politically and economically they clung to patterns which were time-tried and tested, fearful that experimentation would open the doors to anarchy and revolutions of the kind wracking Eastern Europe. Socially and culturally they abandoned tradition with an almost frenzied fervor.

The 1920's in America and western Europe have been variously described as "the Jazz Age," "the Long Week-end," or "the Lost Generation." Certainly they were years of rapid bewildering social change. Revolutions in transportation, social customs, dress and entertainment transformed the outward pattern of life. Four years of living face-to-face with imminent death were followed by the threat of death from peace-time disease (the flu epidemic of 1918-1919 killed twenty-seven million people in the world – in England alone 200,000 died). The people of the western democracies sought escape from misery by plunging into materialistic indulgence.

War had reinforced strains of doubt beginning to surface in the pre-war decade. Sigmund Freud's theories of the subconscious, known only to the intellectual elite before 1914, now filtered down to the general public and became a popular topic of conversation. Freud's ideas challenged accepted modes of sexual behavior and contributed to a more relaxed moral code, as well as striking a severe blow against the concept that man is a rational being.

Art, music, poetry, and literature mirrored the confusions of the post-war world. Traditional representative art, which depicted a stable, orderly world, was engulfed by the new abstract schools of Cubism, Surrealism, and Expressionism which shattered space and portrayed a fragmented, chaotic universe. Picasso, the foremost painter of the age, led the way in the artistic exploration of modern culture. The Surrealists, like

Salvador Dali and Jean Cocteau, exhibited nightmarish canvasses proclaiming the irrationality of modern man.

Poets articulated the moral despair of the time – T. S. Eliot's *The Waste Land* and *The Hollow Men* described a defeated world peopled with paralyzed, defeated men. Free experimentation with new techniques characterized music and the theatre as well. "Modern" music, to many ears, sounded like the modern world – all dissonance and discord. All the arts reflected the complexities and the bewilderment, the lack of guidelines and the fragmentation of life in the twentieth century.

Yet, along with the rejection of the older moral and social values, there was a simultaneous reassertion of political and economic values. The victory of the Bolshevik regime in Russia powerfully strengthened the conviction, in England, France and the United States, that institutions should not be changed. The western Establishments became quickly convinced that the greatest danger of all was social revolution – that social change would ultimately bring communist revolution.

But the lower classes had discovered their potential during the war, when, through the attrition of upper-class leadership by mass slaughter, officers and government officials had to be drawn from the lower classes. Death had its own equalizing effects. When the soldiers returned home after four years of dreaming of a better life (and propaganda had encouraged those dreams), they did not return easily and quietly to their previous subservience. Demobilization created enormous social tensions, as men returned home to discover that the old class structures still prevailed, and, frequently, that jobs were not available. The result was seething restlessness in the lower classes. During the war women had been employed in all the western democracies in jobs which had formerly been reserved for men. When the men returned to the work force, women were thrown back into their traditional roles. They did not take lightly to the idea of returning to the fireside. In the years following the war women contributed to the social unrest that threatened security by their continuing refusal to be put "back in their place."

In England, in France, and in the United States the social repercussions of the war lasted long into the peace. As the democracies entered the new decade each was faced with social tumult that produced fear and insecurity, and an accompanying nostalgia for the past. Every new demand from any segment of the population, whether it was the right to vote by women, better pay for work, improved working or housing conditions, appeared to the upper class establishments as a dire attack on everything of value in the culture of the "golden years" before the war.

All of the democracies experienced serious economic problems after the war. Each faced rising prices, reconversion of industry to peacetime production, rising unemployment, large public debts and shrinking international trade. During the war, England, France, and the United States had resorted to governmental regulation of the economy and central planning to boost the war effort. Instead of retaining planning to solve the economic dislocations of the peace, each nation rapidly rejected war-time controls. Their adherence to limited government intervention failed to resolve the problems of peace. As economic structures broke down, unrest in the populations increased, along with more and more strident demands for change.

• England

Over two million British citizens were killed or wounded on the battlefields of World War I. Moreover, England had invested forty-four billion dollars in the war effort – increasing her national debt ten times over pre-war levels. Although her property damage was not nearly as great as that of Germany and France, her economic difficulties were severe. In the years immediately following the war the Labour Party, born in 1906, attracted enough electoral support to become the largest opposition party in the House of Commons. The Labour Party, after 1918 a self-proclaimed socialist party, demanded radical methods of attacking economic troubles, such as nationalization of industry. Conservatives and the old Liberal Party viewed such drastic measures with great antipathy, but were unable to combat Labour's growing attraction to workers, farmers, trade-unionists, and those of the middle and upper classes who were insistent on economic reform.

Immediately after the war a Liberal-Conservative Coalition government, under the leadership of David Lloyd-George, tackled the initial problems of the peace. By 1921, however, its efforts had proved so disappointing that the coalition collapsed. In the 1922 election Liberals and Conservatives both campaigned on fears of the new Labour Party and the dangers of Bolshevism. So real was the fear, although of course not the reality, that even Labour moderated its economic proposals and vehemently denied any ties to communism. The emotional issue, however, catapulted the Conservatives into power under Bonar Law. Law was already seriously ill with the cancer which would kill him in 1923 and proved an ineffectual leader in a time of mounting discontent. When his illness forced his resignation in 1923, the King called on Stanley Baldwin to form a government. Baldwin, who would be a dominant British political figure during the crucial decades between the wars, was an old-line Conservative who viewed the rise of Labour as an unmitigated disaster for England. A rather apathetic individual whose most distinguishing trait was mediocrity, he marshalled the Conservative troops in the fight against change. He offered the electorate empty slogans – "Faith, Hope, Love, and Work" – instead of vigorous solutions. His failure to solve the deep-seated problems facing Great Britain turned voters increasingly in the direction he most feared – to Labour. In 1924 Liberals and Labour aligned against his government and brought it down. For the first time, the King called on the leader of the Labour Party, Ramsey MacDonald, to form a government.

Although conservative Englishmen deplored the move, fearing "the horrors of socialism and confiscation," there was no real danger. Labour's rhetoric was more radical than its sentiments – it was firmly rooted in democracy and enormously susceptible to the blandishments of the middle class. Moreover, since the Party had no clear majority, it had to rely on Liberal support. There were, however, some domestic reforms. Some of the wartime tariffs were abolished. The government provided extended educational opportunities for laboring class children, built new housing at controlled rents for workers, and increased payments for unemployment. But attention rested primarily on foreign, not domestic, policy. Britain, convinced that German economic reconstruction was essential to her own recovery, played a significant role in drafting and supporting the Dawes Plan, which eased the German reparations payments somewhat. At the same time England encouraged France to remove her troops from the Ruhr Valley. MacDonald's determination to settle the international tensions left by the war in order to improve the economic situation at home led him to grant full recognition to Soviet Russia. He also signed treaties providing large loans to Russia because he believed that the Russians would then be enabled to purchase British goods and improve England's lagging export trade. But both Liberals and Conservatives vehemently opposed such close relations with the outlaw communist nation. Fearing Labour's seeming alignment with Bolshevism, they brought down the Labour government with a vote of no confidence. In the resulting election, again under Stanley Baldwin's leadership, the Conservatives campaigned on a program of saving England from Bolshevism and won a clear majority. Thereafter, for several years, the Conservatives maintained almost complete control of the government.

British industry continued to fail miserably to move with the times. Equipment, machinery, and methods, all lagged behind other countries. The dole, unemployment, falling exports – in short, economic ill-health –

endured. Politically, as well, England could not pull out of the doldrums. A weary electorate returned Labour to power in 1929, again with Liberal support. In 1931, however, England was engulfed in the Great Depression and a genuine crisis forced MacDonald's resignation. A "National Government," a coalition of all three major parties, was formed to deal with the situation, and made token efforts to cure England's economic diseases. But British statesmen, no matter what the party stamp, paralyzed by their fear of radical change, could not alter their basic economic assumptions sufficiently to get England back on her feet. Gradually, Conservative domination of the coalition gave way to Conservative control of the political system which endured through the 1930's. England in the 1920's had hesitantly and reluctantly experimented with minor innovation by twice voting Labour into office, but had finally rejected even the desire to try new approaches. Tired and apathetic, England moved into the 1930's with little vigor to fight the challenge of Fascist aggression.

• France

France suffered severe physical and psychic damages during World War I. She put eight million men into uniform and five million were casualties – in a country which already had a low birthrate and in which women outnumbered men by about 2 percent. During the war the population declined by four million; in the civilian population there were one and a half million more deaths than births, and by 1921 France had a female population which exceeded males by 15 percent. More than three quarters of a million buildings had been destroyed, along with roads, bridges, railroads, and mines. The animal population had also sharply declined. Industrial and agricultural production suffered irreparable damage. Almost immediately after the war vast numbers of peasants flocked to the cities and towns and since most had no marketable skills, they joined radical unions which became communist strongholds. The polarization of politics into a loudly protesting left and a sometimes violently defensive right occurred more drastically in France than it did in England.

The government of the Third Republic contained fatal weaknesses. The executive, directly responsible to the legislature, could be turned out of office immediately, as in England, but the legislature was elected for fixed four-year terms. Unlike England, the cabinet could not call a new election to determine the wishes of the population. The existence of over two dozen political parties, no one of which could ever claim a clear majority, worsened the situation. Every cabinet had to be a coalition cabinet, and most did not last long enough to do anything constructive. The governments of France in the years after the war demonstrated extreme instability of leadership, of policy, and vast inefficiency. Between 1919 and 1933 France had twenty-seven different cabinets. The real conduct of affairs was left to civil service officials, who provided the only degree of continuity and stability the system possessed, but who opposed any changes in policy.

The government seemed utterly incapable of solving the problems that rocked France after the war. Almost everyone was imbued with a sick fear of Germany and a determination to insure that Germany would never again invade France as she had in 1870 and 1914. A passion for security gripped Frenchmen and blinded them to the need for reform. This became clear even at the peace conference when it appeared to England and the United States that France wanted to ruin Germany. France wanted reparations, she wanted buffer states, she wanted a strong Poland, and she wanted the colonial empires of Germany and Turkey. But at the same time, Frenchmen needed to relax after the years of terrifying destruction of World War I. Soldiers impatiently awaited demobilization, businessmen wanted relief from taxes, and workingmen wanted to improve their standard of living. France had problems of such enormity even a young, dynamic leadership would have found them overwhelming. Instead, they had to be solved by old men, who faced the twentieth century with fear and trepidation, and with outdated answers.

Rigid enforcement of the Treaty of Versailles took precedence over all else in the immediate post-war years. France's vehement policy of kicking the dead German horse came into direct conflict with England's policy of restoring Germany in order to rebuild the world economy and caused mistrust between the two European nations. The climax of dissension occurred in 1923 when France, under the leadership of the arch-conservative Raymond Poincaré, an aged man with residual hostilities toward Germany from the pre-war period, invaded the Ruhr in an attempt to force full German payment of reparations. The United States and England opposed France, and the French people, bitterly resenting further military expenditures, became increasingly dissatisfied with the government and its policies.

In 1924 Aristide Briand became Premier and for a time succeeded in establishing a more rational foreign policy. Briand believed strongly in reconciliation. Cooperating with Gustav Stresemann, then German Foreign Minister, he ended the French occupation of the Ruhr and concluded the Treaty of Locarno, which initiated a period of reduced international tensions and surface harmony. Briand also recognized the

Soviet government in Russia and regularized French relations with that country.

Briand's domestic policies met with considerably less success, however. The inflationary spiral affecting all of Europe hit France with extraordinary severity. The franc, worth twenty cents before the war, devalued to a low of two cents in 1926. The crisis brought down Briand's government and returned Poincaré to office. Through a new tax program and vigorous economic measures Poincaré managed to stabilize the French currency and prevent disaster. By 1928 the new currency rate was established at just under four cents, or 20 percent of its pre-war value. But the inflation caused wide suffering. Small investors and many moderately prosperous members of the middle-class were wiped out and lost their remaining faith in the government. The very class which had most vigorously supported republican principles and ideals, in their fear of being pushed down into the lower classes, moved sharply to the conservative right and became almost fanatical opponents of any change which seemed to issue from the left.

As the decade of the 1920's neared a close, France faced economic and political tensions of even greater severity than those debilitating England. When depression struck France in 1932, she was already largely immobilized by political and economic dislocation. She would not be able to pull out of the decline, and the international crises of the 1930's would ultimately sound the death knell of the Third Republic.

• The United States

Unlike her European allies or the defeated Central Powers, the United States did not suffer greatly from World War I. She emerged from the war victorious and unhurt, with enormously increased international prestige, undisputed economic leader of the world. After a brief depression in 1921 as war-time economic controls were abandoned and demobilization caused some unemployment and labor unrest, America entered into a period of unrivalled economic growth and expansion. Yet Americans shared the disillusionment that gripped the western world after the war. She had escaped most of the horrors of war and did not want to take on the responsibilities of peace.

Determined not to get involved in any further European conflicts, Americans refused to ratify the Versailles Treaty or to join the League of Nations. In 1920 voters turned Woodrow Wilson and the Democrats out of office, handing the reins of government over to the Republicans, who would keep them for nearly twenty years. The Republican candidate, Warren G. Harding, a political unknown with the ability to say absolutely nothing while sounding profound, won a resounding victory in a campaign which pleaded a return to pre-war security. "America's present need," he said, "is not heroics but healing; not nostrums but normalcy; not revolution but restoration; . . . not surgery but serenity."

Normalcy meant complacency. It meant a return to a government policy of allying with big business to remove controls. Corruption, bribery, and attacks on personal liberties marked the Harding administration. Calvin Coolidge's administration which followed continued the patterns established under Harding without the corruption. Coolidge supported business totally, and efforts on the part of labor to improve its position found no sympathy either in the government or the population.

Normalcy also meant intolerance. Fear of change plus social and economic unrest caused a desperate effort to force adherence to traditional values. Hundreds of innocent aliens were deported; the National Origins Act prevented immigration of any but White Anglo-Saxon Protestants (WASPS); and the Ku Klux Klan boasted a membership approaching 5,000,000 across the country. The Eighteenth Amendment made alcohol unconstitutional. New York State's Assembly expelled five properly elected representatives simply because they were socialists, and a Tennessee court convicted a high school teacher for teaching Darwin's theory of evolution.

The United States withdrew from the position of leadership in world affairs which her successful intervention in the war had won. She continued to participate in the attempt to stabilize international relations, however, by encouraging disarmament and combatting militarism. In 1922 at the Washington Conference the United States, China, Japan, and six European nations met to consider naval armaments and the settlement of problems in the Far East. The Conference resulted in an agreement to respect the integrity and territorial independence of China, and it established naval ratios among the world powers intended to prevent any naval armaments race. Significantly, Russia was not invited. In 1926 the American Secretary of State, Frank B. Kellogg, together with Aristide Briand of France submitted to the nations of the world a naive proposal outlawing war as a means of settling international disputes. Twenty-three nations signed the Kellogg-Briand Pact. Throughout the decade the United States worked with England and France to solve the problem of German reparations.

Yet Americans, despite these efforts to encourage world-wide cooperation between nations, shared a growing conviction that the United

States must remain uncontaminated from the virulent diseases striking Europe. Reluctant to face the fact that in the twentieth-century world no nation can remain truly independent, she continued to pursue policies aimed at keeping uninvolved. The immigration restrictions of the 1920's were an expression of defensive American nationalism and growing isolationist sentiment – so were the high protective tariffs enacted at a time most damaging to world trade. Isolationism in the 1920's was not so extreme as it became in the 1930's, but the seeds of America's abdication of responsible leadership were sowed in the post-war decade. And America's failure during those same years to solve her own economic ills, eating away beneath the surface at the foundations of her booming prosperity, was a primary cause of Europe's final collapse.

20

The Lights Finally Go Out: International Anarchy, 1930-1945

IN OCTOBER, 1929 the New York Stock Exchange collapsed. America had experienced stock market declines before, along with economic depressions, but never one of this magnitude. A decade of over-extended credit and complacent confidence that American prosperity was boundless had resulted in an economy that was entirely out of balance. The Stock Market Crash set off the worst depression in United States history. In the twentieth century, with its interdependent industrial economies, the American economic disaster soon affected most of the industrial nations of the world.

By 1931, as Americans withdrew the capital they had invested in Europe and recalled loans at a rapid rate, major European banks began to fail. Because of the crisis the United States agreed to a one-year moratorium on war debts, since the European nations, without the help of American capital, clearly could not pay. But it was too late; the depression had already struck.

• The Great Depression and World Repercussions

As the depression spread throughout the world, the major governments took measures which made the situation worse. At a time when an increase in world trade was most needed, governments raised tariffs, introduced quotas, and insisted on economic self-sufficiency. Almost every country instituted "buy-at-home" programs. But the economic crisis was too severe to be easily overcome. And it brought in its wake a wave of radicalism in the lower classes which awakened a fierce reaction to the right, and a renewed faith in authoritarian concepts. The political tensions which had simmered below the surface in the 1920's erupted into full boil in the 1930's – a direct response to the economic collapse.

• The New Deal

In the United States the depression deepened between 1929 and 1932 and the government, handicapped by its conviction that government should not play too direct a role in the economy, seemed incapable of finding a solution. President Herbert Hoover refused to allow direct government relief for the unemployed and insisted that the federal budget must remain balanced. As his correctives proved increasingly ineffectual, Americans began to examine more carefully the concept of government economic controls. The crisis made the public aware that the new industrial society had invalidated the old policies of laissez-faire.

In 1932 Americans voted the Democrats back into office. President Franklin Delano Roosevelt emerged as a dynamic leader who initiated a program of vigorous action which gave the public new hope. His New Deal program aimed at modifying the capitalist system in order to save it. Although they did not immediately conquer all the problems of the depression, within a short time Roosevelt's policies began to rejuvenate the American economy. The success of his program undermined extremism in American politics, and the United States survived the 1930's without the political upheavals the European nations were to experience. The economic crisis had caused Americans to shift slightly to the left – in the direction of greater government control of the economy. Americans did not entirely reject economic liberalism, but realistically accepted the fact that modern economies must be organized.

• England's National Government

In England the Labour Party had come to power just a few months before the Wall Street crash. Despite the radical economic program proposed after 1918, Labour, again led by Ramsay MacDonald, proved to be as reluctant as Herbert Hoover to take vigorous action. MacDonald pursued a policy of retrenchment and, when he refused to increase government aid to the unemployed, his cabinet fell. A National Government, theoretically a coalition of Conservatives, Liberals, and Labour, took its place. By 1932 England had abandoned her long-standing, free trade position, enacted protective tariffs, and joined the other European nations and the United States in an excess of economic nationalism.

By a desperately needed housing program which helped reduce unemployment and by keeping interest rates low so that purchasing power was extended, the National Government created a slight recovery by 1936, but unemployment still remained discouragingly high, and production low. England, typically, managed to muddle through without political crisis. By 1937, as a measure of prosperity returned, it was evident that striking changes in attitude had occurred and the government had entered more strongly into economic regulation. But recovery was slow, and Englishmen, as they increasingly accepted the necessity of centralized economic planning, demanded further extensions of government responsibility. The attitudes which would ultimately initiate the welfare state in England took shape during the depression decade.

• Popular Front in France

The depression hit France somewhat more slowly than the other European states. By 1932, however, the collapse of world markets, falling exports, and the declining tourist trade had pulled France into the economic slump. The conservative orientation of French politicians and the instability of French politics made it exceedingly difficult to cope with the depression. A small, wealthy clique of 200 families controlled most of France's capital, and vehemently resisted rigid governmental controls. The rest of the population feared further devaluation of the franc, and the government resisted deficit spending. Consequently, nothing effective was done to curb the deepening economic decline in a nation which had scarcely recovered from the war.

At the same time France watched with fear and apprehension the rise of the Nazis in Germany. Caught in the conflict between the communist system in Russia and the threatening Fascist systems in Germany and Italy, French policy vacillated, hesitated, and floundered. The economic collapse created a more extreme polarization of political opinion in France than it had in England and the United States, and France struggled through the thirties, rocked from left and right. As the depression dragged on, Frenchmen increasingly sought drastic solutions. Active organizations of the right, such as the reactionary *Action Francaise,* an extremely nationalistic, royalist group, clashed disturbingly with a rapidly solidifying left.

In 1934 a scandal in high government circles demonstrated clearly the malaise affecting French politics. The government was implicated in the murder of Serge Alexandre Stavisky, a financial swindler with numerous connections in government. The government, dominated by the middle-class Radicals, seemed riddled with corruption. Public indignation reached fever pitch and riots broke out nightly.

The cabinet resigned, and was succeeded by a series of weak governments which were utterly incapable of remedying the political or economic situation. The left insisted that France was being run by Fascists; the right declared that the Socialists and Communists were menacing the state. Hitler's successful remilitarization of the Rhineland in 1936 intensified the struggle.

The government's continuing failure to bring stability to France had caused the parties of the left to solidify into a weak union called the Popular Front. Although Socialists and Communists remained bitter enemies, and the moderate-center Radical Party supported the union indecisively, the Popular Front won a clear-cut electoral victory in 1936. For the first time, France had a socialist Premier. Leon Blum was by no means a representative of the radical left, however. He was neither a Marxist nor a revolutionary, but had joined the Socialists out of his conviction that France desperately needed reform.

Under Blum's leadership the government undertook a program of social reform. He ordered the leaders of capital and labor to sit down with him to work out compromises which would modernize France's economic system. The resulting Matignon Agreements laid the foundations for the future welfare state in France. Representatives of the managerial class agreed to the eight-hour day, forty-hour week, minimum wage scale, paid vacations, and the right to collective bargaining. But many employers used every possible method to evade the new regulations.

The Conservatives reacted furiously and "Better Hitler than Blum" became a prominent slogan. The Radical Party, hesitant from the beginning and committed to principles of laissez-faire, pulled out of the coalition, bringing the cabinet down. The Blum government, the only French cabinet in the inter-war period to attempt to come to terms with the modern world, had lasted just over a year. After its fall in 1937 the French people drifted more and more to the right, without vitality or strength, which resulted in their rapid capitulation to Hitler in 1940. Faced with economic crisis, France proved incapable of even the compromises England and the United States had reluctantly accepted. The failure of the French system to adapt to changing times marked the final disintegration of the Third Republic.

• Responses Around the World

All over Europe democracy was in crisis. The depression gave impetus to extremism and violence against which the frail democratic systems established after World War I could not prevail. Socialist parties grew rapidly in response to the obvious failure of the older economic policies to restore prosperity. The left, ordinarily splintered into rival factions, consolidated in an attempt to gain strength through unity. These coalitions of the left – Popular Fronts – gained power only briefly, however. A Popular Front emerged in Spain in 1934 and managed to initiate some reform in that extraordinarily backward state, but the opposition to reform policies was so strong that Spain became embroiled in civil war.

In other areas of Europe the depression undermined confidence in political institutions, causing varying degrees of change. The smaller western nations, Belgium, Switzerland, and the Scandinavian countries, managed to cling to their long-established democratic institutions by accepting the idea of government intervention in the economy and state regulation of business. The newer democracies of eastern Europe, however, moved rapidly toward authoritarianism and dictatorship. In the 1930's dictatorships arose in Yugoslavia, Rumania, Bulgaria, and Albania. Austria attempted to retain a modicum of democracy, but it was shaky at best. Only Czechoslovakia succeeded in preserving a democratic state, but it was constantly threatened by factionalism.

The impact of the depression was not limited to Europe and the United States – the economic collapse sent shock waves around the world. The industrial nations were most directly affected. Between 1918 and 1930 Japan seemed to be moving in the direction of liberalism and parliamentarianism. But the government faced enormous difficulties. Wealth and power were concentrated in the hands of a few individuals reluctant to share it, and western traditions were alien to Japanese culture. In 1931, when Japanese export trade had so sharply declined that the entire economy suffered, extremist elements fatally attacked Japanese democracy. The Prime Minister, Hamaguchi, who had pursued liberal, pacifist policies, was assassinated and in the ensuing crisis the reactionary elements in Japan gained control. The new government was an ultranationalistic, military dictatorship, intent on spreading the "New Order" to all of Asia. That meant expansion of the Japanese state and Japanese domination of the Far East.

• Solutions in Germany

In 1930, as banks and businesses failed, and unemployment climbed above 3,000,000, the German people elected 77 Communists and 107 Nazis to the Reichstag. Since no coalition of parties could be formed to provide majority support for a cabinet, the people accepted a presidential cabinet which ruled by decrees issued under Article 48 of the constitution. The moderate parties permitted the failure of the democratic process because they feared that another election would establish a dictatorship of either the Communists or the Nazis.

The presidential cabinet, however, could not solve the economic and social problems; unemployment continued to rise, going above 6,000,000 in 1932, while the private armies of the Nazi and Communist Parties carried on pitched battles in the streets, and murdered their opponents. Hitler's propaganda machine worked overtime to convince the people of all classes that the Nazis could and would solve all problems and that order and security depended on a Nazi government. In July, 1932 the Nazis elected 230 members to the Reichstag, thus becoming the largest party in Germany.

A small group of men, representing the Army, the aristocracy, big business and the bureaucracy convinced President Hindenburg that Germany faced civil war and Bolshevization unless the Nazis were brought into the government. They believed that they could control Hitler and the Nazis in the cabinet. On January 30, 1933 President Hindenburg appointed Hitler Chancellor, heading a cabinet of Nazis and Nationalists, and within little more than a year Hitler had established a totalitarian dictatorship.

The reasons for the failure of the Weimar Republic are numerous and complex. But the central fact is simply that the democratic process failed in Germany. The events surrounding Hitler's appointment as Chancellor have far less significance than the failure of the democratic leadership throughout the fourteen years of the Republic. Too many Germans opposed the Weimar Republic for too many reasons. The Social Democrats lacked the courage and vision to introduce socialism, and many workers who wanted socialism believed Hitler would establish it. Many leading Nazis before 1933 were genuine socialists, disenchanted with the Social Democrats' failure to live up to their rhetoric. Monarchists opposed the republic without the courage to restore monarchy. Big businessmen opposed the idea of a republic, or the democratic process, and especially of giving any role to the labor unions, but they lacked the ability to suggest any positive alternatives. So with the army, which supported Adolf Hitler, the one man who guaranteed action. Ultimately the Weimar Republic failed because its leaders could not solve the problems which plagued the German people, and thus permitted a drift into demagogic rule.

• Totalitarian Germany

From the moment of his appointment as Chancellor, Hitler showed himself to be intensely activist. His was to be a "do-something" regime. In Prussia every office was filled with Nazis and Nazi supporters, and the Brownshirts (the Nazi private army) were deliberately loosed upon any opposition with instructions to shoot left-wing opponents. A reign of terror developed throughout Prussia, and spread into the other German states. In the midst of the disorder Hitler called for another election to the Reichstag, to be held in March, 1933. When, shortly before election day, the Reichstag building burned, the entire Communist Party received the blame, and was outlawed; thousands of Communist and Socialist leaders were arrested, and all left-wing newspapers were banned. On the pretext that the Communists and Socialists had jointly planned a civil war, the government suspended the constitutional guarantees of basic human rights. The Nazis gained several million more votes in this election than they had previously garnered and Hitler now demanded that the Reichstag pass the Enabling Act of March, 1933, to give him dictatorial powers for four years. With the Communist Party outlawed, and with many Social Democrats under arrest, the Reichstag overwhelmingly passed the Enabling Act.

Hitler used his new powers to abolish all political parties except his own, to destroy the separate existence of the individual German states, to wipe out all labor unions, and to bring every single facet of German life under totalitarian Nazi control. In the place of the traditional labor unions the Nazis established the German Labor Front, which incorporated both labor and management in a single organization completely controlled by the party. Thus strikes and lockouts were outlawed. A special law was promulgated which unified party and state and, after President Hindenburg's death in 1934, even the offices of President and Chancellor were merged in the person of Hitler. Schools, newspapers, radio, drama, cinema, every means of communication, came under the control of the Ministry of Propaganda, and many Germans joined in burning outlawed books. All children from the age of ten years were forced into the Hitler Youth to be molded into Nazis.

By June, 1934 Hitler faced the inevitable development in any revolutionary situation – some wanted the revolution to go further, while conservative elements wanted to pause. Hitler moved swiftly. On the Night of the Long Knives, June 30, 1934, his personal henchmen killed off the leadership of the radical wing, and included a number of conservatives to indicate that he would not tolerate opposition from any direction. Hitler announced to the German people that the hundreds who had been slaughtered were killed on his orders, and that he was entitled to administer justice on his own authority. The German state and the German people had been mastered.

• Economic Solutions

Probably none of Hitler's actions would have been sufficient to maintain his control had he not solved many of Germany's more serious problems. When he came to power, almost 4,000,000 Germans were out of work. Hitler set out to bring Germany to full employment, and in this he was largely successful. Vast public works projects employed many men, who then became consumers, priming the economic pump. A highway system, the best in the world at that time, used huge numbers of laborers, as did reforestation projects and the draining of swamps. A housing program reached its peak in 1937 with the construction of more than 300,000 houses, mostly one and two family units, complete with gardens. At the same time organizations such as "Strength Through Joy" provided paid vacations for workers which they could never have dreamed of under earlier regimes. Such tactics helped Germans forget that they were being taxed excessively and that much of the money used for their vacations came from confiscated property of other Germans who languished in concentration camps or who had been killed. By 1936 there was a labor shortage, especially in skilled occupations, and the depression had been solved.

Millions of Germans from every economic and social class in the state actively supported Hitler and the Nazis. Hitler fully understood how to use propaganda to convince the masses that he knew exactly what their needs were and that he was fulfilling them. Those who opposed the new regime ended up in concentration camps or were shot by the Gestapo, the secret police. People were arrested, tortured, and thrown into concentration camps without trials or any semblance of legality. Thus even those who did not actively support Hitler quickly found it expedient to go quietly about their business.

Propaganda hid the fact that the Nazi movement lacked any ideological base. The Nazis were essentially activists, using whatever came to hand in lieu of ideology. After January, 1933 anti-Semitism was consciously developed as part of the Nazi program. By 1935 the Nuremberg Laws proscribed marriages between Jews and Aryans and placed numerous restrictions on their lives. Soon no Jew could be employed in Germany and Jewish children could not attend school with Aryans. But they could not leave Germany without leaving all their property and often had no place to go anyway. By 1938 officially sanctioned pogroms against the Jews were commonplace, and the Nazi government placed a billion-mark fine on the whole Jewish community on the pretext that a Polish Jew had killed a German diplomat in Paris.

After World War II began, it was decided to exterminate all the Jews in Europe. At first the Jews were marched into ditches and shot. Gradually the Germans refined their techniques until they developed gas chambers and crematoria such as those at Auschwitz, where at least 3,000,000 people were slaughtered, all but some 20,000 of them Jews.

• Hitler's Foreign Policy

Part of Hitler's appeal to the German people rested on his foreign ambitions. All Germans could applaud the idea of breaking the chains of the hated Treaty of Versailles. Germany must be rearmed, German territory must be reclaimed, and German people brought back under the protective mantle of the Fatherland. As early as October, 1933 Hitler flamboyantly withdrew Germany from the League of Nations, and pulled out of the Disarmament Conference then going on, on the popular grounds that both these bodies intended to keep Germany disarmed, while other nations rearmed. German industry was given huge government orders for armaments, a road system was designed for military purposes, and in 1935 Hitler announced to the world that he was building an air force and a navy. To provide manpower for them, he reintroduced universal military training and conscription. Conservative economists objected that the armaments projects disrupted the reviving economy, and the generals objected on the grounds that Germany might have to fight a two-front war which she would lose. Hitler responded by establishing a Second Four-Year Plan, designed to place Germany in readiness for war within four years. This move placed effective control over the economy in the hands of the Nazi Party, masterminded by the brilliant Dr. Hjalmar Schacht. Hitler himself directed that Germany was to be completely independent of all foreign powers as soon as possible in all the materials which might be needed for war. The scientific community bent every effort to creating substitutes for those raw materials which Germany lacked. Artificial rubber, synthetic fabrics, plastics, and numerous other developments cut down Germany's need for imports. Having firmly established totalitarian control over Germany, Hitler now prepared for mastery of Europe.

• The Soviet Industrial Revolution

During the 1930's the western nations moved at varying rates of speed toward state controlled economies. The example of the soviet system which had emerged in Russia between 1917 and 1923 served a paradoxical function: ultra-right-wing groups in Germany and Italy had utilized fear of Bolshevism to precipitate the establishment of totalitarian, statist regimes, but the western democracies, equally fearful of Russian Communism, had shied away from further centralization of state power and from much-needed government economic planning. At the same time, all of the European nations isolated Russia from international affairs, and softened their resistance to Fascist aggression. Developments in Russia between 1928 and 1939 gave impetus to each of these reactions.

While Russia had moved to political dictatorship after the Bolshevik revolution, between 1923 and 1928 the Soviet Union had not established a socialist state, although few in the West recognized that fact. The New Economic Policy, instituted after the failure of War Communism, had preserved many elements of capitalism, and retarded progress toward the socialist goal. Under the NEP industrialization had progressed only slowly, and the policy had permitted the growth of the Kulak class – peasants who owned their own land and sold their products on the market, and who vehemently opposed further socialization. The economic agencies of the state did not in reality control the Russian economy.

In 1927 Stalin determined to forcefully establish a pure socialist economy in Russia. His goal was to turn Russia from a backward, rural, agricultural economy with little industry into a highly industrialized state with centralized economic organization and planning, and to wipe out the remains of capitalism, private ownership, and profit. To effect such a transformation, Stalin had to accomplish two formidable tasks: agriculture had to be collectivized – that is, brought under state ownership and control – and industrial facilities had to be built. An economic revolution of such magnitude creates extreme difficulties for a population. But Stalin was not the man to allow humanitarian concerns to deter him. In a period of just ten years, he achieved his economic goals, but at an enormous cost in human misery and suffering.

• Collectivization of Agriculture

The collectivization of agriculture and an increase in agricultural production were necessary first steps toward creating the socialist state. Agriculture remained fantastically primitive, with even the best Russian farmers producing only about 15 percent as much as their American counterparts. Earlier efforts to gain the support of the peasants had actually decreased the size of farms, which were far too small to make efficient use of machinery. Russian farmers marketed less than half as much grain in 1928 as they had in 1913. Kulaks often refused to sell their grain at government pegged prices and strenuously resisted attempts to merge their property into large, state-run farms.

The effort to collectivize Russian agriculture turned into a veritable civil war between the middle and upper level of peasants on the one hand and the poorer peasants and the government on the other. Entire Kulak villages were destroyed and the Kulak class was entirely wiped out. In the conflict crops and livestock perished, causing famine and starvation. During the period of enforced collectivization five million Russians died, along with half of all the livestock in the country. Many other peasants were sent to forced labor camps in Siberia, where they were forced to open up new lands to agriculture.

Between 1933 and 1935 a new Russian agricultural system emerged. The collective farms were large estates, averaging well over one thousand acres each, farmed by several families according to central planning. Tractor stations issued heavy equipment to all farms and insured control by refusing it if a farm did not conform to government policies. Individual families were permitted to own only small plots of land for home gardens and livestock for family use. By 1933 more than 50 percent of Russia's agricultural families lived on collective farms, and by 1939, when war interfered with further extension of the program, 95 percent of all Russian agriculture had been collectivized.

• The Five Year Plans

The creation of a new industrial society caused as much hardship as had the agricultural revolution. Russia had few skilled laborers and technicians, and had to hire them from the more industrially advanced nations. Furthermore, enormous capital was required to create the bases of an industrialized economy – machines, tools, electrical generating plants, oil refineries and steel mills. Stalin decided to sacrifice housing and consumer goods to the production of the necessary basic elements of the new economy.

In 1928 Russia launched the first of the Five Year Plans, the most massive program of economic restructuring ever undertaken. Under the direction of the *Gosplan,* the state planning agency, the First Five Year Plan, which ran from 1928 to 1933, was succeeded by the Second (1933-1937). World War II prevented completion of the Third.

The Soviet State engaged all of its energies in realizing Stalin's economic goals. Soviet propaganda ceaselessly proclaimed the worthiness of the Five Year Plans. Absenteeism, slow-downs, incompetence – all suddenly became crimes against the state and drew heavy penalties, frequently up to twenty years at hard labor in Siberia. A person convicted of stealing state-owned property could expect the death penalty, no matter how small the value of the stolen object. At the same time, those whose production exceeded the average or who contributed to increasing efficiency received special rewards. Pay was made proportionate to production, and highly efficient teams of workers received the glory and publicity accorded military heroes in war-time.

Measured by industrial achievement, the Five Year Plans were an overwhelming success. Thousands of new factories were built, new agricultural areas opened, new industrial complexes created. In ten years Russia became one of the front-ranking industrial powers in the world. In 1939 only two countries reported greater industrial production than the Soviet Union – the United States and Germany. The cost to the individual had been great, but the response of the Russian people had been surprisingly cooperative; the effectiveness of the propaganda program and the obvious industrial achievements had generated an excitement for the projects and the long-range goals. Simply to be part of such an endeavor attracted many to its support.

• "Socialism in One State"

The consolidation of the Soviet police state ensured cooperation where it did not develop voluntarily. Stalin's war on capitalism meant the extermination of the "bourgeois mentality" and the creation of an entirely new society. All the social institutions of the past came under attack, and centralized control of every aspect of soviet life accompanied centralization of the economy. Family life weakened as the soviet agencies actively worked to undermine parental and traditional authority. Strict censorship insured that the newspapers, literature, movies, the theatre, art and music applauded and proclaimed the Soviet ideology. In the schools teachers were closely supervised and textbooks were written to indoctrinate young Communist minds.

Since religion was considered a stronghold of traditional thought, the Soviet leadership sharply curtailed religious activity. Church property was confiscated and churches converted into museums or other types of secular buildings. Religious publications were forbidden, civil marriages encouraged, and religious instruction outlawed.

After Hitler's advent to power in 1933, however, and the increase of Japanese aggression in the Far East, the Soviet leadership realized that it needed widespread support for the regime in case of war. The announced success of the First Five Year Plan permitted a slight relaxation of the ruthless drive toward industrialization. Government social policies eased, and propaganda began to insist on the importance of healthy family discipline and the recognition of parental authority. Even the attack on religion was reversed to the extent that at one time the Party-sponsored Atheist Society was ordered to rehabilitate the church. Perhaps most significantly, emphasis changed from the international revolutionary nature of the Communist movement to old-fashioned Russian nationalism. Old heroes, even those from Tsarist times, were dusted off and refurbished, and used as examples of good communists. All this meant that Russia was moving farther and farther away from the kind of international proletarian society Karl Marx had envisioned and was developing a new system marked more by Russia's national heritage than by socialist philosophy. The Russian Soviet State, as it emerged, blended a harsh political dictatorship with a socialist economy, but the chances that the state would ever "wither away" as Marx had predicted diminished yearly.

• The Constitution of 1936 and Stalin's Totalitarianism

The Constitution of 1936 contributed to building support for the Soviet regime. It served well the propaganda interests of the communists abroad, as well, for it seemed remarkably democratic to outsiders, and it seemed to signify the end of the harsh struggle to establish the society. Although guarantees of the basic freedoms considered essential in the West were absent, fewer Russians than we might imagine were distressed by the omission. The Constitution appeared to provide for the participation of the individual citizen in the political system. It did guarantee "universal, direct and equal suffrage by secret ballot" and decreed that all citizens of eighteen years or older, "irrespective of race, nationality, religion, educational and residential qualifications, social origin, property status or past activities, have the right to vote . . . and to be elected. . . ." In practice, during the first elections, each electoral district presented several candidates. The Party selected one for each position, the ballot showed only one name, and the voter could vote yes or no. Ninety-six percent of the eligible voters cast ballots; of those, 98 percent voted yes. The existence of only one party obviously precluded the possibility of the democratic process, but to the vast majority of Russians the system was infinitely superior to anything else they had known.

In reality the new Constitution marked very little change in the rule of force which characterized Stalin's regime. At the very time that the document was being praised by westerners, Stalin set out to eliminate the Old Bolsheviks, who retained ideas antithetic to Stalinist communism. In a series of purges which lasted from 1934 to 1938, Stalin reached into every segment of the governmental structure to eradicate deviation and brought even high officials to trial. Western observers were astonished at the eagerness with which most of the accused pleaded guilty to the charges, and with the rapidity with which they were convicted and sentenced. Nearly all were executed. Through the purges Stalin destroyed all opposition to his personal rule, and removed all the old idealists who had dreamed of establishing a truly democratic system of socialism, with the state withering away, and with even high government officials receiving no more privileges than laborers. Perhaps Stalin genuinely feared conspiracies from both right and left opposition forces to his dictatorship – and certainly he later developed a distrust of everyone which bordered on madness. Before the purges ended, Stalin bore the responsibility for the deaths of three-quarters of a million party members.

After the purges new young men trained and brainwashed in the Stalinist era refilled the ranks of the party. By 1939 Stalin's totalitarian control was unchallenged, with the dictator revered almost as a god. Any new opposition would have to be secret and desperate, and would risk torture and death. The purges ended finally and completely any possibility of change by discussion, compromise, or yielding on the part of government. Henceforth Stalinist totalitarianism became increasingly rigid and inflexible, and Russia a closed society. Each new step in the direction of Stalinist communism further alienated the West – and added fuel to the fires the Fascists built to weaken opposition to their expansionist exploits.

• Clash of Ideologies: Aggression and Appeasement

The "Era of Locarno," that period of apparent peace and reconciliation between the European powers in the years after 1925, did not last long. It was, in reality, a period of false security – the calm before the storm. England and France, undisputed leaders in the diplomatic maneuverings of the European nations after 1919, could not develop a cooperative policy. Because their underlying convictions about Germany were fundamentally irreconcilable, they frequently pulled in opposing directions rather than exerting firm leadership together. They did, however, agree completely about one thing – the necessity of isolating Russia from European affairs. At the same time the United States withdrew deeper and deeper into isolationism and abdicated responsibility in European concerns. The failure of these four powers to consolidate their combined strength and forcefully oppose violations of the peace made World War II a certainty from the time of the first Fascist challenges of the peace.

The weakness of British and French foreign policy was not immediately obvious. The League of Nations had been created to provide collective security against aggression. The smaller nations in particular had high hopes that it would do so. But the League got little support from the Great Powers. Neither the United States nor Russia was a member, and England supported it only when it suited her to do so. By the early 1930's France's domestic problems had so absorbed the attention and energies of her statesmen that she felt incapable of strong action without British support, and Britain refused to take a strong stand against Fascist expansion.

During the years after World War I the western democracies, struggling with internal economic and political dislocations, developed a policy of conciliation in the face of aggression which the Fascist dictators understood only as weakness. The policy of granting concessions to a dictator's demands when threatened with force became known as the appeasement policy. Appeasing the dictators generated from a genuine fear of another war, a fear complicated by the conviction, in the leadership of both England and France, that a new war would open the floodgates to Bolshevik revolution all over Europe. In England, the unquestionable leader in the genesis and evolution of the appeasement policy, a sincere conviction that Germany had been badly treated by the Versailles peace settlement contributed to the belief that a restitution of Germany's honorable position would satisfy her ambitions and eventually result in stability in Central Europe. The English belief that Hitler represented "the last bulwark against Communism" further reinforced the policy. All of these factors combined to paralyze British diplomacy, and the British refusal to act paralyzed the French. In short, American and Russian isolation, the weakness of the League and the British and French abdication of strong leadership convinced the Fascist aggressors that no real opposition to their ambitions existed. They gradually moved more and more openly down a path of aggression that finally led to war.

• Early Aggression

The inability of the League of Nations to deal effectively with outright aggression was clearly demonstrated in 1931 when the Japanese seized Manchuria. China appealed to the League for help. The League took months to adopt a report which mildly criticized the Japanese for their tactics but suggested that the Chinese concede to Japanese demands. Individual states such as England chose to refuse to sell arms to either side, a policy which assisted the industrialized Japanese whose resources required no outside assistance against economically backward China. The League's failure to resist the Japanese military threat caused a general loss of respect for the organization, as both great and small powers recognized its ineffectual nature.

After the Nazis attained power in Germany, aggression accelerated. In 1935 Adolf Hitler announced to the world that Germany would reintroduce conscription and universal military training. Such a direct violation of the Versailles Treaty would have merited instant reprisal from England and France had it been announced by the Weimar government, but the German democrats no longer represented Germany. An expansive, militant leadership, ruthless and totalitarian, now spoke for Germany to a world wracked by the Great Depression, serious domestic problems, and often a number of Fascist sympathizers. France wished to oppose the German decree but feared to take action alone. England responded by signing a treaty with Germany which allowed Germany to begin rebuilding her navy.

Hitler's next step was an even more serious violation of the Treaty of Versailles. Perhaps more significantly, it violated the Treaty of Locarno, which by no stretch of the imagination had been forced on the Germans. In March, 1936 German troops reoccupied the Rhineland, the area bordering France which had been demilitarized after World War I. Hitler could have been easily stopped at that time with any, even the slightest, show of force. His personal orders to his generals instructed them to retreat if they met any resistance at all. But, again, France found no support either in England or the United States, and she had no heart to move alone. Soon hundreds of thousands of German workers began fortifying the area which would protect Germany from possible attack while she pursued her adventures in the East and South.

• Italy's Ethiopian Venture

Germany was not the only country in Europe practicing aggression. Italy, like Germany a latecomer to the community of nations, felt that she, too, should have colonies. Particularly she believed that Ethiopia should belong to Italy, and had attempted in the late nineteenth century to conquer it. The Ethiopians at that time had proved too much for the Italian military, however, and the defeat had increased the frustration of those Italian nationalists who clamored for Italian territorial additions. Now Benito Mussolini made the decision to incorporate the Ethiopians into the Italian empire. In 1935 the Italians organized border incidents to provide an excuse for an invasion. The Ethiopian government, a member of the League of Nations since 1923, naturally appealed to the League; the League received the appeal but failed to act. In March, 1935 Ethiopia again appealed to the League with evidence that Italy planned immediate invasion. This time the League was busy with the fears which Germany's announced military draft had generated and again chose not to act. Only after the Italians had launched a full-scale invasion into Ethiopia did the League do anything at all and then its action approached the farcical. Economic sanctions were applied against Italy – that is, member nations of the League agreed not to sell the Italians munitions or materials which would aid their military efforts. The sanctions, however, carefully excluded oil, the one commodity most needed by the Italian war machine. Italy could also have been stopped cold simply by closing the Suez Canal to her military use, but that was not done. The Ethiopian capital fell in May, 1935 – shortly thereafter the entire country was incorporated into Italy's empire. Once again the aggressive power had achieved its goal while the democratic powers practiced appeasement, hoping that the dictators' desires would be satiated before they attacked the larger states.

• The Spanish Civil War

The year 1936 dealt another body blow to the League of Nations and to the hopes for peace and reasonable solutions to world problems. During that year the aggressor states formed an alliance which stretched across the world from Germany to Japan. In October, Hitler and Mussolini signed a formal agreement known as the Rome-Berlin Axis, which they intended to be the basis for determining European diplomacy. In the following month Germany and Japan signed a pact which had as its public clauses opposition to the world-wide communist movement, but which included secret clauses providing for military cooperation against Russia as a state. The imperialistic powers had joined together in the Rome-Berlin-Tokyo Axis – the nucleus for World War II.

Almost immediately, the new Fascist bonds were strengthened by joint participation in the Spanish Civil War. Spain had made little progress toward modernization until 1931. Most of her population were poor, illiterate peasants, miserably exploited by an arrogant nobility, a few wealthy capitalists, the remarkably corrupt officers of the army, and the determinedly medieval Roman Catholic Church. In 1931 a bloodless revolution established a new Republic, with a liberal democratic constitution. The new government immediately launched an effort to modernize Spain. Church and State were separated, the Jesuit order dissolved, and civil marriage permitted in an effort to break the Church's strangle-hold on the population.

Every new piece of social legislation and reform, however, angered the former ruling classes and made them more intransigent. The Land Reform Bill of 1932, an effort to redistribute the land, caused the entire right wing to coalesce into opposition to the government. Monarchists, landlords, and army officers joined with the most determined opponents of all, the Catholic Church, in opposition to the Republic. Bishops forbade Spanish children to attend the state schools, and Pope Pius XI issued an encyclical condemning the Republic and all its acts. The result was that in the general election of 1933, with the Pope actively participating in the electioneering, the right wing elements gained a majority in the government and promptly set about to turn the clock back. As they hastily undid everything the republican government had accomplished, the left wing opposition began to solidify. In 1936 the left formed a Popular Front and won a clear majority in the 1936 elections.

Rather than lose their positions of power and wealth, the Conservatives chose to overthrow the republic and restore the old regime by force. Under the leadership of General Francisco Franco, and with the active participation of the Spanish Fascist Party (the Falange), the right wing opened armed rebellion against the constitutional government, beginning the Spanish Civil War.

Hitler and Mussolini quickly recognized the opportunity to gain prestige for Fascism by adding another Fascist dictatorship to the growing

120,000 Nazi Storm Troopers under Review by Hitler at Nuremberg in 1938. World Wide Photos.

list. General Franco appealed for and at once received military support from both Germany and Italy. Germany sent the cream of her military to prepare them to serve later as training cadres for her own armies, rotating them, experimenting with new equipment, using Spain as a testing ground for her future military endeavors. Italy ultimately sent six army corps, fully equipped with planes, tanks, and artillery. In the decisive battles of the Spanish Civil War more Germans and Italians fought in Franco's army than did Spaniards.

The Loyalists appealed to the democracies for help, but they once more chose appeasement. England, France, and the United States insisted on strict neutrality, a hands-off policy which prevented any but a few Russian troops and scattered volunteer units from helping the Loyalists. By 1939, after incredible slaughter and vicious brutality, the Loyalists were destroyed and Franco established a dictatorship which has survived until today. Fascism benefitted enormously from the episode, but the morale and influence of the democratic countries suffered. The Spanish Civil War marks a turning point in the road to World War II.

• Germany Annexes Austria

Each successive step in the aggression-appeasement pattern strengthened the dictators and encouraged further challenges to the peace while at the same time weakening and making the appeasers more timorous. By 1937 Hitler was convinced that he could annex Austria and Czechoslovakia without provoking a general war. He saw England as the crucial opponent, and England had convinced him that she would not take action so long as Hitler's objectives lay in the center and eastern portions of Europe. Actually, England's leaders hoped that Germany and Russia, declared enemies, would go to war against each other. The Austrian Nazis belligerently insisted that all Austrians wanted to be joined to the Third Reich. Hitler provided them with moral support by making public speeches in which he proclaimed himself the protector of the millions of Germans living outside the Fatherland. In 1938 he demanded that the Austrian Chancellor, Kurt von Schuschnigg, appoint one of his henchmen to the cabinet. Schuschnigg feared to refuse, but feared also the consequences of giving in. As the Austrian Nazis went on a rampage, Schuschnigg in desperation decided on a plebiscite to determine whether the majority of Austrians really wanted to join the Third Reich and called an election on March 9. Afraid he would lose the vote, Hitler moved troops into invasion position on the Austrian border and announced that unless Schuschnigg called off the plebiscite, he would order invasion. Schuschnigg resigned and a Nazi became Chancellor and immediately invited the German army into Austria. France and England once again acquiesced rather than fight. Before the month was out, Hitler had ordered his military advisers to prepare the invasion plans for Czechoslovakia.

• Annexation of Czechoslovakia

Czechoslovakia, carved out of the old Hapsburg Empire after 1918, was made up of a number of drastically different peoples and economies. The highly industrialized Czechs tended to dominate the other nationalities and to insist on a highly centralized state with a large degree of socialism in the economy. The Slovaks, heavily rural and Catholic, wanted states' rights within the system. Even more serious were the differences between the Czechs and the Sudeten Germans. Some three and a half million Germans, occupying the Sudetenland, an area bordering Germany, had lost their special position in the Austrian Empire with its dissolution. Using the argument of self-determination, they demanded special privileges

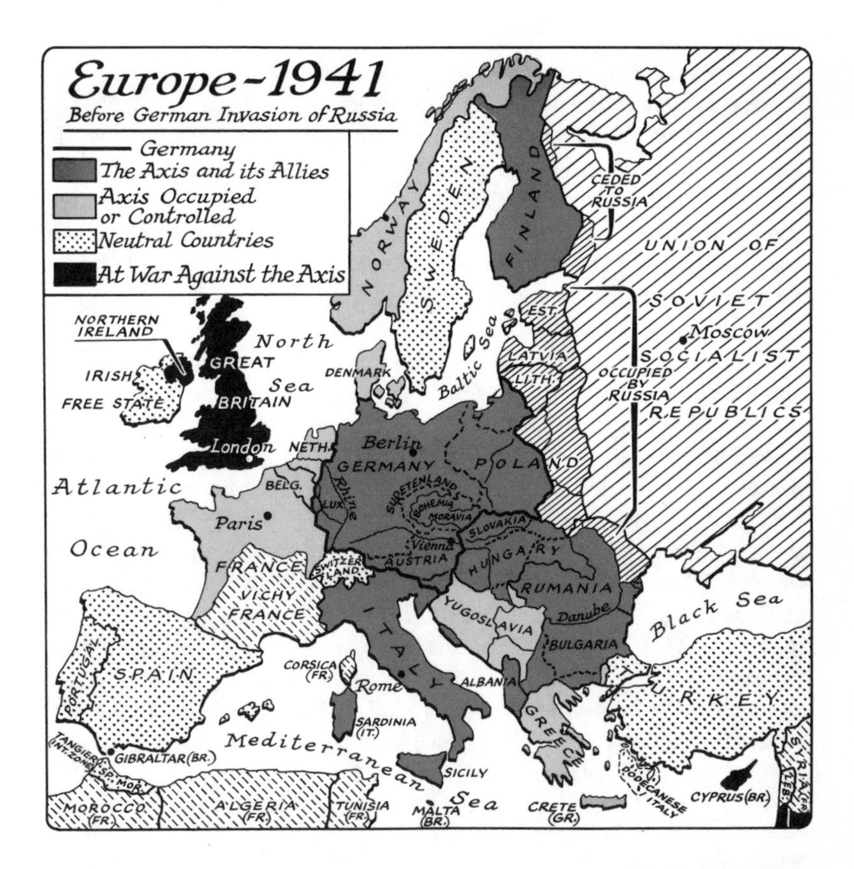

of the Czech government. By 1935, under the leadership of Konrad Henlein, the Sudeten Germans had formed a Nazi Party which looked to Hitler as its real leader, and which became the largest political party in the area.

Hitler's propaganda machine kept up a barrage of lies about terrible Czech mistreatment of the Sudeten Germans, insisting that the Czech government was a tool of Russia. Under such pressure, the government granted concessions to the Sudetens, but by 1938 Henlein refused to accept anything less than unification of the Sudeten area with Germany. After the Austrian *Anschluss* Hitler publicly stated that he would use force if necessary to bring about annexation of the Sudetenland.

Czechoslovakia prepared for war, and called on her allies, France, Russia, Rumania, and Yugoslavia, to fulfill their agreements to support her should Germany attack. But appeasement decreed otherwise. France delayed, looking to England for support, and England refused to fight to preserve the independence and integrity of Czechoslovakia. Instead of pledging resistance to the German demands, Neville Chamberlain, the British Prime Minister, sent a representative to Czechoslovakia to urge the Czechs to permit the country's dismemberment. Russia's firm offer of support caused the Czechs and the western nations more distress than did the possibility of another German victory. A frantic series of meetings resulted in a final conference at Munich in late September, 1938. Neither the Russians nor the Czechs were invited to attend the Munich Conference, the meeting at which the Germans were given one fourth of Czechoslovakia's land area, one third of her population, including many non-Germans, and all of her defenses.

Neville Chamberlain has received most of the opprobrium for this best-known example of appeasement and certainly he deserves some. But the Munich Cession was hailed at the time all over Europe and in the United States as the most suitable solution to a dangerous threat to world peace. Few could see that a peace bought with such dishonor would be shortlived, and that even the time bought worked in Germany's favor, as she was arming at a faster rate than the western democracies. Furthermore, Czechoslovakia had been a democratic stronghold, with a powerful, well-equipped army and rich industrial resources. Now that army, and the resources, went to the side of the Fascists. At the same time Russia, deliberately excluded from European decisions, properly decided that she would have to look after herself. A straight line runs from Russia's exclusion from the Munich Conference to the Nazi-Soviet Non-Aggression Pact of August 23, 1939.

• The Last Step

Although the western powers did nothing to oppose Hitler's annexation of the rest of Czechoslovakia in the spring of 1939, it was nevertheless now clear, even to Chamberlain, that Hitler must be stopped. Everyone knew that Poland was Hitler's next target. Awkward as it might seem at this late date, England, France, and Poland now signed a pact in which all agreed that an attack on one would be looked upon as an attack on all, and all would fight to prevent further aggression. England and France thereby guaranteed the independence of Poland. The British and French even attempted to negotiate with Russia, but the courtship was half-hearted and Russia's price had gone up after Munich – she demanded annexations to which England and France could not agree. Germany offered Russia the territory she demanded, and the two nations, once bitter enemies, quickly came to agreement. The Nazi-Soviet Pact of August,

1939, concluded in a matter of weeks, agreed that Russia could annex part of Poland and all of the Baltic states, Latvia, Estonia, and Lithuania.

Once Hitler was assured of Russian acquiescence to his further expansion, he no longer feared the opposition of France and England. Convinced, despite their guarantee to the contrary, that the western nations were effete and would not actually fight, he openly prepared for an invasion of Poland. One week after the Nazi-Soviet Pact was announced to a surprised world, the Germans advanced. On September 1, 1939, after twenty years of an unstable and constantly threatened peace, World War II began.

• World War II: The Old World Dies

German military leaders had learned well the lessons of World War I. Then, because the war had turned into a war of attrition and had lasted far beyond their short-range preparation, they had been beaten by superior economic and manpower resources. Now the Germans concentrated on developing a military machine which was specifically designed to prevent stalemate and trench warfare. World War I had been almost wholly defensive in its strategy. The Germans planned World War II as pure offense. Instead of using tanks merely as a protective wall (a mobile trench), the generals organized entire divisions of tanks designed to break directly through the defense of the enemy and to operate without immediate reference to infantry at all. The air force, limited in World War I to spotting for artillery, romantic dog-fighting, and tossing bombs out by hand, now was prepared to wreak major destruction by mass bombing and to support the infantry by strafing and bombing immediately ahead of its advance. The totality of offense came to be known as Blitzkrieg (Lightning War).

• Blitzkrieg and Sitzkrieg

A few individuals in the West had the same ideas, and the French built some excellent tanks, the British fine planes. But the mentality remained the mentality of World War I. The French, obsessed with defensive strategy, built the Maginot Line, massive fortifications from Switzerland to Belgium, and planned to wait for the Germans to wear themselves out against this impregnable fortress.

The Germans did not oblige. Leaving only token forces in the West, they struck Poland with almost the entire German army. Poland's air force never got off the ground and was wiped out on September 1, 1939. The tank divisions ripped through the Polish defenses with ease. By mid-September only Warsaw, completely surrounded, held out. Retreating Poles ran into the Russians, who had hastily advanced to be sure they got the territory they had been promised in the Nazi-Soviet Pact. Before the month was out Russia and Germany had divided Poland, wiping it off the map. Russia took a little more than half the territory and a little less than half the population. Germany got the rest.

Russia turned immediately to the establishment of military control over Latvia, Lithuania, and Estonia, with a series of treaties in September and October, 1939. Efforts to gain control over Finland and Turkey proved more troublesome. Turkey relied upon her alliances with the West and rejected the Russian demands, whereupon Russia let the matter ride. Finland chose war rather than to yield, and for a few months startled the world by her magnificent and futile efforts against Russia in the "Winter War." By March, 1940, however, the victorious Russians had forced even harsher terms than originally demanded from the Finns, and had left Finland largely defenseless.

During all this time the western states, theoretically in a state of war with Germany, had done nothing. Stunned by the awesome effects of the *Blitzkrieg* in Poland, western military leaders convinced themselves even more strongly that defense was the only possible weapon and so kept their increasingly unhappy soldiers hidden behind the Maginot Line. The winter of 1939-1940 came to be known as the *Sitzkrieg* – sitting war – or the Phony War.

• The Fall of France

The Germans were simply biding their time, however. The lightning struck again in April, 1940 – this time on Denmark and Norway. Denmark fell at once and although Norway resisted she could not last long under the new methods of warfare. Paratroops seized control of airfields which immediately received Nazi troops, transports, and equipment. The Germans were assisted by the treason of some Norwegians, most notably Vidkun Quisling, who were repaid by being permitted to establish a satellite regime after the conquest. After the attack on Norway, the word "quisling" entered the English language as a synonym for treason and fifth-column activity.

Having completely sealed his back doors, Hitler was ready to take on his major enemies and to invade the West. On May 10, 1940 he advanced into Belgium, Holland, and Luxemburg. Luxemburg chose not to fight, Holland lasted five days, and the Belgians surrendered on May 28. But the Germans had not waited for that event – they were sitting on the English Channel on May 20, already in French territory.

The speed of the German movement owed much to the rigid defense thinking of the Allies, particularly the French. The Maginot Line had magnificent defenses, but most Frenchmen had never bothered to worry that it extended only from Switzerland to the Belgian border. The Germans simply launched their attack around the end of the Maginot Line, where France, Germany, and Belgium met. The Belgian surrender, without prior warning to the Allies, left the British and French Expeditionary Forces exposed to a vastly superior German army, without support from the main French army. They were forced back to the Channel and stranded at Dunkirk. The English utilized every kind of floating vessel at their disposal and evacuated 230,000 British and French soldiers in a heroic rescue operation. But they left another half million behind, captured or killed. And all of their equipment, artillery, and supplies fell into German hands.

Meanwhile, ignoring the Maginot defenses, the Germans pushed rapidly on to Paris, occupying the city on June 13. The French, bewildered and demoralized by the failure of their defenses, hastened to make peace with Germany. A new government agreed to German occupation of more than half of France, including all her coasts, with the French people paying the occupation costs. The government of unoccupied France, established with the capital at Vichy, soon became nothing more than a dictatorial puppet of Adolf Hitler. A few French chose to fight on, and gradually grouped around an indomitable fighter, General Charles DeGaulle. Operating from London, DeGaulle's troops became the Free French forces who fought on with the English for the liberation of all France. Germany's rapid conquest of France, however, finally brought Hitler's ally, Mussolini, into the war.

After the fall of France England stood alone facing a Europe almost entirely occupied by Hitler's troops or his allies. Hitler's plans for the invasion of England depended on German control of the air and sea around the island. For months the German air force attempted to establish air superiority, bombing British industrial cities and towns daily and wreaking awesome damage. But the British, courageously rallying to defend their independence, shot down three German planes for every English plane lost. Hitler could never gain sufficient control to permit an invasion and lost the Battle of Britain. The Germans were running out of fuel, and abandoned the operations against England.

• The Russian Invasion

Hitler had never intended to abide permanently by his non-aggression pact with Russia – Communism had always been his most bitterly denounced foe. He had begun planning an invasion of the Soviet Union immediately after the conquest of France. In June, 1941 he put his plans into action, and turned to the invasion of Russia. In a very real sense, it marked a turning point in the war. As bitterly as Russia had been isolated and opposed by everyone in the western world in the years before the war, Hitler's attack enlisted the sympathy of the free world for Russia. In a surprising turn-about, the long antagonism between communism and democracy was forgotten, and Americans, British, and Free French began to hope that Russia would defeat Germany.

At first the *Blitzkrieg* appeared to have the same success in the Russian invasion that it had previously enjoyed in the West. By December, 1941 the Germans held an area of Russia equal to nearly 20 percent of the size of the entire United States. But the Russians had yielded ground without losing control; they had practiced a "scorched earth" policy, removing or destroying everything of use in the path of the Germans, and their armies remained intact. As winter weather slowed the German advance, the Russian defense tightened. In December the Russians launched a counter-attack all along a line from Leningrad to Moscow to the eastern tip of the Sea of Azov, forcing the Germans back until Hitler ordered his men not to retreat, even if it meant certain death. But the Germans were not prepared for a Russian winter, since Hitler had expected complete victory before the winter months, so they suffered heavily. After the spring thaw the Germans returned to the offensive and drove this time all the way to Stalingrad, where Stalin ordered the Russians to hold. Hold they did, in an awesome house-to-house battle which killed nearly 300,000 Axis soldiers and broke the German offensive. After the Battle of Stalingrad the Russians went on the offensive and did not stop until they were masters of Berlin.

• The United States Enters the War

In the United States, although the sympathies of the people clearly lay with England and France during the early phases of the war, isolationism had been responsible for legislation which forbade any action that might involve the United States in war. As the peace steadily deteriorated during the 1930's, Congress passed neutrality legislation aimed at keeping

America entirely out of the threatening European conflict. In 1935 a law prevented the sale of any goods to any country involved in war, and in 1937 further legislation made it clear that victims of aggression could expect no more help from the United States than could the aggressors. Exports could be made only on a cash-and-carry basis, and Americans, deluding themselves about Hitler's plans for world domination, believed that whatever happened in Europe was of no concern to them. American oil shipments gave tremendous support to Mussolini in his Ethiopian venture. During the Spanish Civil War American policy (specified by law in 1937) prevented the sale of arms even to the legal and constitutional government of Spain, although at the same time war materials were sold to Japan which aided in the conquests in China. Refugees with no place to go found no haven in the United States since the quota system limiting immigration permitted entry to very few Europeans.

After the fall of France, however, Americans recognized reluctantly that they could not remain totally uninvolved. As it became increasingly obvious that England could not indefinitely stand alone, Congress permitted the "destroyers-for-bases" deal, which traded half a hundred worn-out destroyers to England in return for U.S. control over English territory to be used for military bases. Finally, in March, 1941, in a sudden decision to make the United States "the arsenal of democracy," Congress authorized the President to lend or lease support to England, when it became evident that that country had food supplies for only a short time and would soon fall before the Nazi onslaught. After the invasion of Russia, Americans woke up to Hitler's goals of European domination. Congress repealed the neutrality laws, and the United States began a far more active participation in the effort to stop Hitler, sending money and supplies to both England and Russia.

Events in the Far East, however, finally brought America directly into the war. On December 7, 1941 the Japanese struck against the United States in the Pacific. Using aircraft carriers to bring their bombers and fighter planes to Pearl Harbor, they attacked and destroyed the better part of America's Pacific fleet and much of her air power. On the same day another attack did massive damage to American forces in the Philippines. The United States declared war on Japan the following day. Japan's allies, Germany and Italy, then declared war on the United States. Consequently, the Americans, drawn unwillingly into the European inferno, determined to cooperate with England and Russia in beating the Germans first, while operating a holding action against the other Axis powers.

American entry made a tremendous difference in the European theater of war. Turning her awesome industrial capacity into the war effort, she supplied her allies with vast quantities of armaments while she built her own army and navy into formidable forces. Before the war ended Americans built nearly 300,000 airplanes, some 3,000,000 machine guns, 85,000 tanks, 8,000,000 tons of ships for the Navy, and 55,000,000 tons of merchant ships.

In 1942 Americans joined the British in North Africa, until that time a dangerously weak area for the British army. With American support in new landings, the German and Italian forces in Africa were caught between American and British armies and forced to surrender. The Allies were still not ready, however, for a direct assault on the continent, and chose instead to move into Sicily. But that operation brought German troops far south into Italy, and an American force was landed on the peninsula below Naples. The British joined in the drive and gradually, at tremendous cost, the Allies pushed north. The Germans, however, were never cleared out of northern Italy until the end of the war.

In the meantime the great buildup for the direct invasion across the English Channel had been proceeding. On June 6, 1944, after heavy air and naval bombardment and simultaneous paratroop landings, the first wave of Allied soldiers hit the Normandy beaches, and soon secured a beach-head sufficiently strong to pack in the main invasion army and its equipment. A second landing took place from the Mediterranean, and soon more than two and a half million Allied soldiers were pushing the Germans out of France and looking toward an invasion of Germany itself. A desperate German counter-attack failed, and in the spring of 1945 the Russians and western Allies met in Germany. At about the same time Mussolini was captured and shot by Italian partisans. Hitler chose suicide rather than capture by the Russians as they destroyed Berlin. The Germans, without their demonic leader to push them to further destruction, surrendered on May 7, 1945.

• War in the Far East

In the Far East the United States remained on the defensive for the most part throughout 1942, although in two major sea-battles, Coral Sea and Midway, the American navy seriously damaged the Japanese navy. In 1943 the buildup was sufficient for American forces to take the offensive and recapture many of the islands which had fallen to the Japanese the previous year. The battles of the Philippine Sea and Leyte Gulf in June and October, 1944 broke the back of the Japanese navy and permitted American forces to retake the Philippines. By the spring of 1945 American planes were dropping bombs on Japanese cities, while plans were laid for the invasion of Japan. In the meantime, however, American scientists had perfected an awesome new weapon. In August, 1945 American planes dropped atomic bombs on Hiroshima and Nagasaki, literally destroying the cities and killing some 200,000 people. The Japanese surrendered on August 14, 1945, and the war was over.

• Assessment

But the full horrors of the war still had to be assimilated. The Second World War, more than the first, had indeed been global war, wreaking devastation, horror, and death that is difficult to comprehend even when the full evidence is presented. World War I challenged the Enlightenment beliefs in rationalism and progress which the nineteenth century had accepted with almost religious intensity, but did not destroy them. After World War II, the European world realized that the nineteenth-century certainties had been proven indisputably false. As the Allied armies advanced through German territory, the grisly obscenities of the Nazi regime were revealed to a world already stunned by the atrocities of war. The liberation of the concentration camps exposed in ghastly detail the extent of Fascist insanity. Some six million Jews from conquered German territories had been tortured and killed in Auschwitz, Bergen-Belsen, Buchenwald, Dachau, and similar camps. In Auschwitz alone in 1944 as many as 22,000 Jews were processed, gassed, and cremated every day. German industry and agriculture utilized slave labor, collected clothing and shoes of victims, used their bones for fertilizer. The bankers received gold fillings from the victims' teeth, while scientists practised gruesome experiments on their bodies. The barbaric cruelties in the camps provided horrifying evidence of the total breakdown of civilization in the twentieth century. World War II proved, even to those most reluctant to admit it, that twentieth-century man was not rational – that the forces of hatred, aggression, and cruelty had overwhelmed rationality and destroyed progress. No longer could man cling to the old solutions – the twentieth-century experiments had exposed the bankruptcy of most of the old verities. World War II left the world without illusions. In the post-war world, new hopes had somehow to be found.

Suggestions for Further Reading

Arendt, Hannah, *The Origins of Totalitarianism* (1968)

Fromm, Erich, *Escape from Freedom* (1941)

Sontag, Raymond, *A Broken World: 1919-1939* (1971)

Weber, Eugen, ed., *Varieties of Fascism: Doctrines of Revolution in the Twentieth Century* (1964)

Horne, Alistair, *The Price of Glory: Verdun, 1916* (1963)

Moorhead, Alan, *Gallipoli* (1956)

Roth, Jack, ed., *World War One: A Turning Point in Modern History* (1967)

Nettl, J. P., *The Soviet Achievement* (1968)

Rigby, Thomas, ed., *Stalin* (1966)

Von Laue, Theodore, *Why Stalin? Why Lenin?* (1964)

Wolfe, Bertram, *Three Who Made a Revolution: A Biographical History* (1966)

Kirkpatrick, Ivonne, *Mussolini: A Study in Power* (1964)

Macgregor-Hastie, R., *The Day of the Lion: The Life and Death of Fascist Italy, 1922-1945* (1963)

Bullock, Alan, *Hitler: A Study in Tyranny* (1964)

Halperin, S. William, *Germany Tried Democracy* (1965)

Simpson, Amos E., ed., *Why Hitler?* (1961)

Watt, Richard M., *The Kings Depart – The Tragedy of Germany: Versailles and the German Revolution* (1968)

Allen, Frederick Lewis, *Only Yesterday* (1931)

Allen, Frederick Lewis, *Since Yesterday* (1940)

Conkin, Paul K., *The New Deal* (1967)

Leuchtenburg, William E., *The Perils of Prosperity, 1914-1932* (1958)

Gilbert, M., and R. Gott, *The Appeasers* (1963)

Graves, R., and A. Hodge, *The Long Weekend: A Social History of Great Britain, 1918-1939* (1941)

Bloch, Marc, *Strange Defeat* (1945)

Greene, Nathanael, *From Versailles to Vichy: The Third French Republic, 1919-1940* (1970)

Thomas, Hugh, *The Spanish Civil War* (1961)

Benedict, Ruth, *The Chrysanthemum and the Sword* (1946)

Morris, Ivan, ed., *Japan, 1931-1945 – Militarism, Fascism, Japanism?* (1963)

Eubank, Keith, *The Origins of World War II* (1969)

Snell, John L., ed., *The Outbreak of the Second World War: Design or Blunder?* (1962)

Hersey, John, *Hiroshima* (1946)

Wright, Gordon, *The Ordeal of Total War* (1968)

GENESIS OF A NEW WORLD 1945 TO THE PRESENT

21

The Era of Cold War

WHEN THE GUNS stopped in 1945, the world rejoiced that the grueling years of the Second World War had ended. But the delirium was short-lived. The war left a legacy of almost total devastation in Europe and loosed a tidal wave of political and social unrest that swept every nation in the world. A new age began in 1945, although few realized it at the time.

The war's most obvious legacy was enormous material and social destruction. Reconstruction was the most pressing and most immediate task. Almost the entire European continent had to be rebuilt politically, agriculturally, and industrially. Many of Europe's major cities – Berlin, Warsaw, Dresden, Stalingrad – were in ashes; others, like London and Vienna, had suffered extensive and crippling damage. Many smaller cities in Germany, France, and Russia had been razed to the ground. In the battle zones little of anything remained – communication and transportation systems were ruined, industry destroyed. Restoration of agriculture presented staggering problems, as many areas were not in condition for cultivation, and livestock and machinery were unavailable.

• The Effects of War

The cost of the war had drained the monetary resources of the belligerent nations. Although estimates are not exact, war costs have been calculated at more than $1,000 billion. The United States and Germany contributed the greatest sums – Americans spent $317 billion, the Germans $273 billion – but every nation had squeezed its economy to the last penny to support the war effort. Damage to civilian property added several billion dollars to the total sums.

These figures indicate the economic exhaustion which the war caused in every nation in Europe. But human resources were as depleted by the war as were material resources; Europe's population declined by 30 million. Hitler's attempt to eliminate the entire Jewish race took six million lives. Admittedly uncertain statistics calculated military deaths at more than 15 million – Germany lost 3,500,000, while 7,500,000 Russians were killed. But concentration camp victims and military casualties only partially account for the victims of World War II. Civilian populations were more directly involved in this war than in any war in history, and it is impossible to calculate the lives lost in the air-raids and bombing of cities or through the starvation and disease which inevitably accompanied the war. The psychological effect of death in such staggering numbers is impossible to describe. Scarcely a single family in all of Europe emerged unscathed – in simple terms, this means that every individual member of the European population suffered the emotional after-effects of the war. The Nazi reign of terror left scars which many have not yet overcome.

Death accounted only partially for the decimation of European national populations – additional millions had been displaced from their homes. Prisoners, expatriated minorities, fugitives, refugees from every country crowded the roads of Europe. In the years immediately following the war, possibly 30 million people had to be relocated, or returned to their homes. The reintegration of these war victims posed formidable problems in housing, jobs, and social organization for governments already over-burdened with reconstruction problems.

And reconstruction included necessary political rebuilding. Many formerly strong nations – France, Italy, and Germany among others – were politically broken as well. The Fascist regimes and their puppet administrations had been destroyed and new governments had to be constructed to replace them. The border countries in East Europe struggled to reestablish political systems – most attempted for the second time since 1919 to broaden the base of political participation and to build democratic regimes. Even the British, so strongly united during the war, encountered forceful demands for change both at home and in the Empire. In the post-war decade economic reconstruction and political reorganization absorbed most of the energies of European statesmen.

• The Superpowers

Europe's exhaustion left a vacuum of power in world politics; the war destroyed the balance of power which formerly ruled international affairs. England, Russia, and the United States had controlled the Grand Coalition which dominated the war effort. But England's participation depleted her strength, and after the war her influence rapidly declined. In the two decades after the war the formerly great British Empire sank to the status of a minor world power along with the other European states. Only two nations sustained enough vitality to continue to exert leadership – Russia and the United States.

The United States was unquestionably the most fortunate of the belligerent nations to emerge from the war. Industrial production rose to new heights, and the demands of the American people for consumer goods curbed even the fear of post-war inflation. The war effort restored confidence in American institutions and produced a conviction that the country could and should play a large role in the post-war world. There were minor problems: demobilization had to be accomplished and the released veterans absorbed into the economy; inflation did exist; and a flurry of strikes indicated that the labor force intended to participate in the benefits of the new affluence. But on the whole Americans faced the peace confident, strong, and optimistic.

Russia, too, managed to avoid the psychologically defeated attitude which characterized the other European states. Although she suffered massive property damage in Western Russia and lost more dead than any country (15 to 21 million dead), her leaders and people convinced themselves that danger to her social experiment still existed, and she retained a strongly militant stand. She therefore continued to pursue an aggressive policy, determined to recover all the territorial losses she had suffered after World War I, and to establish a sphere of influence in Eastern Europe which would serve as an effective defensive perimeter between the Soviet Union and the West. Nor had Stalin completely abandoned the ultimate goal of world communist revolution. In pursuit of that aim he actively encouraged leftist revolts whenever the opportunity arose. Moreover, Russia's industrial machinery had been built only in the immediate pre-war decade. It was new, modern, and much of it had survived the war. Russia's productive capacity consequently remained strong at war's end, capable of supporting both Russian reconstruction and Russian imperialistic ambitions.

Japan's defeat in the Far East and China's continued weakness meant that Russian and American supremacy could not be challenged in the Pacific; Europe's exhaustion assured that no challenge would arise in the West. There arose, then, a new phenomenon – two superpowers, whose influence determined the course of world affairs. Bipolarity of power would be one of the distinguishing characteristics of the new era until cooperation between the smaller nations of the world began, in the 1960's, to indicate a new dissemination of power. When Russia acquired the atomic bomb in 1949, the Russian and American ascendancy was finalized – the two atomic powers indisputably held greater military strength than the rest of the world combined.

• The United Nations

Even before the final failure of the old international balance and the emergence of bipolarity the realization of the interdependence of twentieth-century nations, so clearly demonstrated by the Second World War, provoked a search for new forms of international organization. Although the League of Nations had singularly failed to preserve peace in the inter-war period, the concept of a multi-national arena in which sovereign states could work in harmony to promote the welfare of mankind survived, and created the United Nations.

In 1941 Roosevelt and Churchill issued the Atlantic Charter, an idealistic statement of war aims which recognized the importance of international cooperation in developing economic prosperity and preserving peace, and suggested "the establishment of a wider and permanent system of general security." The following year 26 states signed a "Declaration of United Nations," pledging united action against the Axis Powers. These states were to become the charter members of the formal body of the United Nations when it organized in 1945.

The formal proposal for "a general international organization" came from a Moscow conference of the United States, Russia, England, and China in 1943, and the following year the United States hosted a meeting to draft plans for the organization. When the leaders of the Allied Coalition – Roosevelt, Churchill, and Stalin – met to confer at Yalta in February, 1945, they acted on the proposals and scheduled an interna-

Prime Minister Winston Churchill. Wide World Photos.

tional conference to draft an official charter. In April half-a-hundred nations from Europe, Asia, Africa, and North and South America gathered in San Francisco to formally create the United Nations. The Charter was adopted on June 26, 1945.

The goals of the United Nations are the development of international cooperation in maintaining peace and security, in solving economic and social problems, and in promoting human dignity and freedom. Membership is open to all "peace-loving states" who abide by the obligations imposed by the Charter. The General Assembly, the representative body, meets annually in September at the U.N. Headquarters in New York, and special sessions may be called upon request of a majority of the members. Each state, regardless of size or power, has one vote. Action on major questions concerning international peace, or admitting new members, requires a two-thirds vote of the membership; a majority decides routine and minor questions. The General Assembly may discuss any matter which lies within the scope of the Charter, and make recommendations to member states and to the Security Council. As membership increased, these recommendations began to carry greater weight.

In the early days of the U.N. the Security Council dominated the organization. There the United States, Russia, England, France, and China, as permanent members, each had veto power on important issues, which tended to paralyze the Council's ability to act, and prevented significant action against any of the five. Therefore, although the Charter provided for six (later ten) members to be elected to the Council by the Assembly, the five permanent members effectively controlled the organization. More recently, however, the General Assembly has begun to act more forcefully, as new nations joined and began collaborating to offset the strength of the great powers. As the two superpowers courted them for support, their collective weight began to effect a significant change in the United Nations.

• The U.N.: Failures and Successes

The U.N. holds no authority over the sovereign rights of its members, and the Charter expressly forbids any intervention in a nation's internal affairs. These limitations severely restrict the U.N.'s jurisdiction, for, while the Charter obliges members to solve problems by peaceful means, it provides no method of forcing a state to abide by the obligation. Although members are required to furnish military assistance when necessity demands, the U.N. has no permanent military force under its own command. The absence of an international police force severely limits the ability of the U.N. to insure peaceful settlement of disputes quickly, but the Military Staff Committee has put together special forces for use in crises in Africa, Cyprus, and the Middle East. These precedents could ultimately evolve into the creation of an effective international security agency.

Joseph Stalin, with Nikita Krushchev in the background. Wide World Photos.

Although the U.N. has not been able to achieve its stated purpose of maintaining world peace and security, it has done outstanding work in other areas. The Economic and Social Council, working through a number of subsidiary agencies such as the United Nations Educational, Scientific, and Cultural Organization (UNESCO) and the World Health Organization (WHO), seek to produce economic and social progress in the underdeveloped nations. These agencies have scored noteworthy achievements in combatting illiteracy, controlling disease, improving communications and furthering economic development.

Despite its limitations, the United Nations represents a major step toward international cooperation. Unquestionably, both the advanced nations and the world's new states support it with enthusiasm as a forum in which world problems of every sort can be openly discussed. But, at the same time that the world searched for security through the creation and growth of the United Nations, the breakdown in relations between the superpowers made that hope more elusive than ever. Even before the Second World War ended, the alliance between Russia and the United States deteriorated and produced a new kind of conflict, a prolonged state of political and military tension and rivalry short of full-scale armed combat.

• From Coalition to Cold War

At the Yalta Conference in 1945 Stalin bluntly insisted on Russian domination of Eastern Europe. Since Russia had borne the brunt of the fighting against the Germans in that area, and since her continued assistance was essential to Germany's defeat, Roosevelt and Churchill suppressed their doubts regarding Russia's promises and tacitly acceded to most of her demands. The three leaders agreed to divide Germany into four zones, occupied by British, French, American, and Russian troops. Berlin was to be similarly divided, although it lay within the boundaries of the Russian occupation zone. Roosevelt and Churchill recognized the existing communist governments in eastern Europe, and did not examine too closely the terms "democratic" and "free elections" promised for other east European countries.

Later in 1945, after Roosevelt's death and Churchill's defeat as England's Prime Minister, another Big Three conference met at Potsdam. This time Harry Truman, the new President of the United States, and Clement Attlee, England's new Prime Minister, met with Stalin. By this time it was evident that the swords were drawn between Russia and the West. The difference in peace aims became so sharp that little agreement between the powers could be reached, except in regard to Germany. The three statesmen did agree that Germany should be demilitarized and deprived of any capacity to wage future wars, that she should pay reparations, that the Nazis should be removed from all positions of influence, and that German war criminals should be punished. During and after Potsdam the relations between East and West quickly deteriorated.

In 1946 the great war-time leader, Winston Churchill, speaking in Fulton, Missouri, said that "From Stettin in the Baltic to Trieste in the Adriatic an iron curtain has descended across the continent." Events proved him right, and the iron curtain marked the line between two drastically different ideologies which quickly became involved in the Cold War to determine which ideology would establish world hegemony. The struggle centered at first in Germany. Russia feared that Germany might again recover from military defeat, as she had after World War I, and again conquer Europe. From such a base she could once more attack Russia. Stalin, therefore, determined that Russia must retain absolute control over all of eastern Europe as a buffer zone, and if possible, gain control over Germany itself. Western European and American statesmen feared Russian control over Germany. From there she could easily dominate all of Europe, especially since France and Italy both already had communists in their governments.

• The Federal Republic of Germany

As recently as the Potsdam meeting the assumption had been that after a period of denazification, reparations payments, and firm evidence that she was no longer dangerous, Germany would be reunited into a single sovereign state. Such was not to be. From the beginning of four-power control Russian policy aimed at using her position to weaken Germany, and to establish a communist state. This policy reached its peak when, in 1948, the Russians closed all land approaches to Berlin. Instead of yielding to the Russian threat, the United States and Great Britain responded with the Berlin "airlift," supplying the needs of the western sector by air for nearly a full year. In fact, Russian intransigence and a continuing economic crisis convinced the western powers that they must unite their three zones in West Germany into a single economic and political unit, and in May, 1949, they handed over most of the responsibility of government to a newly created state, the Federal Republic of Germany, which comprised all of Germany except the Russian zone. The Basic Law (Constitution) provided for a two-house legislature, the Bundesrat (upper house, representing the German states), and the Bundestag (lower house, elected by universal suffrage at age 21, representing the people). Executive power rested in the Chancellor and Cabinet. They were made responsible to the Bundestag, but could not be overturned unless their successors could take over immediate responsibility.

The first elections established Konrad Adenauer as Chancellor, a position he held strongly until 1963. West Germany owes much of its fantastic rebuilding and its present economic success and political stability to Adenauer, who concentrated his efforts on establishing working relationships with other western governments, and especially that of France. He supported every effort to bring Europe closer to unity, and, since Germany was disarmed and had no military expenditures, she quickly rebuilt a strong economy, falling behind only the United States and Great Britain in volume of international trade.

• The German Democratic Republic

During the same year in which the Federal Republic was created by the western powers, Russia sponsored the formation of a satellite state in her zone of Germany. Called the German Democratic Republic, the new state was patterned on the Russian system, strongly centralized, and required to take orders from Russia, especially after an abortive revolt in 1953, which was harshly suppressed by the Russian army.

Such constant repression in the East, combined with a weak economy, caused many East Germans to leave the German Democratic Republic in the hope of finding a happier life in West Germany. This constant loss of manpower, and especially skilled labor and the educated classes, threatened the East German economy. In 1961, with Russian permission, East Germany built a wall across the entire city of Berlin and shot anyone who attempted to cross it. Gradually the East German economy improved, as the new state established trade relations with other states in eastern Europe and with Russia. In 1972 formal agreement was signed between East and West Germany which indicates that neither side is strongly interested in reuniting the two parts again.

• Soviet Eastern Europe

In the first three years after the war Russia, with the help of local communists, established "People's Republics" in eight countries in eastern Europe. Poland, Hungary, Czechoslovakia, East Germany, Bulgaria, Rumania, Albania, and Yugoslavia accepted dominance, although Yugoslavia later defected. In all of these states the Russian army had been recognized as the liberator from Nazi occupation and tyranny. Roosevelt and Churchill had officially recognized the area as Russia's sphere of influence, and merely satisfied themselves that Stalin would adhere to the democratic process in recreating the governments of these states. The belief was a delusion. Although the Russians allowed parliamentary processes to remain in existence for a few years, by the end of the decade the last vestiges of democracy had disappeared from eastern Europe.

Several factors contributed to Russia's victory over the eastern European nations: the economic and military weakness of small states devastated by war; the strength of local communist organizations which had gained support by leading the resistance against the Nazis; and the direct military and economic intervention of the Soviet Union. In most instances, communist leaders obtained key positions in the post-war governments. Once in positions of authority, the communists increased infiltration and directed policy until they were ready to assume domination. Only after they had forced the leading non-communists out of government and sufficiently usurped enough power to insure success did they openly assert control. The establishment of the Soviet sphere was thus by no means an unquestioned power-play of the Russian army. Instead, the foundations of freedom were crumbled from within, gradually enough to hold western intervention at bay.

• Poland, Hungary, Czechoslovakia

In 1945 communists in Poland announced the establishment of the Provisional National Government of the Polish Republic, which immediately received Russian recognition. The Polish government-in-exile, backed by Great Britain and the United States, refused to recognize the legality of the Polish communist government, and the issue came into discussion at the Yalta Conference. There it was decided that the two governments should coalesce, and hold new elections, with universal suffrage and protected voting privileges.

When the elections were finally held in 1947, terror, fraud, and violence insured the success of the communist forces. Purges ensued, in which non-communists and deviant party members fled or were killed or imprisoned, and Poland moved rapidly into totalitarian dictatorship, allowing no internal opposition at all. Following the Soviet model, the new government of the Polish People's Republic began the transformation of Poland from an agricultural to an industrial state.

In Hungary the government formed in 1944, called the Hungarian National Independence Front, was dominated by communists. The general elections in 1945, however, resulted in a coalition victory for the parties of the more moderate center. The monarchy was abolished, and a republic proclaimed. But anti-government elements fomented discord, until, in 1947, new elections which disfranchised some 6 percent of the electorate increased communist representation. Rapidly thereafter the non-communist parties were either disbanded or destroyed, until by 1949 the communists had obtained full control of the government and the country. In February, 1949, the People's Republic of Hungary was proclaimed. Vigorous efforts to collectivize agriculture and increase industry created discontent with the regime, but Russian support prevented serious revolt.

By 1948 Czechoslovakia had fallen to communist control. Factionalism within the state weakened the post-war National Front government, which struggled to reconstruct the economy along socialist lines but at the same time to maintain a compromise with western democratic principles. Cold War antagonisms, however, undermined Czechoslovakia's attempt to straddle the fence between East and West. Russia insisted that the Czechs refuse Marshall Plan aid, desperately needed to restore her economy, and, after 1947, launched a communist attempt to obtain governmental control of the state. Infiltrating the military, the police, and the communications media, the communists acquired a parliamentary majority and ultimately dominated the cabinet. Once in control, they quickly destroyed the political and intellectual freedoms protected by the post-war government. Jan Masaryk, the son of Czechoslovakia's first President and a leader of Czechoslovakian liberalism, committed suicide under extremely suspicious circumstances. In the ensuing years the government moved firmly into the Soviet orbit and increasingly tightened its grasp on Czechoslovakian society.

• Rumania, Bulgaria, and Albania

In Rumania a communist-dominated government, established in 1945, retained token participation from other parties until 1947. In that year, however, it moved openly to squash all opposition. In October, after the leaders of the Peasant and Liberal Parties were denounced and tried as traitors, the People's Republic of Rumania was proclaimed. In 1948 a new constitution established a severely repressive soviet-type governmental system, and another eastern state moved firmly into the Soviet bloc.

The Bulgarian People's Republic was established in 1946 and by 1948 the communist regime was firmly consolidated. As in the neighboring eastern states, rapid social and economic transformation followed. By 1956, 90 percent of all peasants had been forced into collective farms, and succeeding Five-Year Plans expedited industrialization.

Communist-controlled forces in Albania emerged victorious from a civil war in 1945 and in 1946 turned the country from a monarchy into an undisguised communist republic. Confiscation and redistribution of the land accompanied nationalization of industry. Ruthlessly pursuing socialization of the economy, the Albanian government demonstrated a brutality remarkable even in the Soviet camp. Economic difficulties with Russia caused friction between the two countries, however, and after 1960 dissension between them intensified into an open rift.

• The Soviet Bloc

As in the Soviet Union, real authority in the People's Republics of eastern Europe rested in the Communist Party. New constitutions provided for one-party control of all institutions and placed the economy under the direction of the state. Each of the new regimes launched industrialization programs aimed at transforming their previously agrarian societies into industrial states. A Soviet-controlled organization called Cominform (Communist Information Bureau) coordinated policy among the communist states and a military alliance under the Warsaw Pact provided a common defense system. The Soviet Union enjoyed economic as well as military advantages from her domination of Eastern Europe. The states of that area not only provided Russia with raw materials and markets on her own terms, but paid reparations to Russia at the same time. Moreover, the satellites of eastern Europe formed a ring of buffer states between Russia and the West – a strategic protection of immense significance to the Soviet Union.

But not everyone was happy with the new regimes. Opposition arose from independent peasant landowners who resisted nationalization of agriculture, and forced industrialization created strains as well, necessitating severe police methods to maintain order. The Churches resisted fiercely, causing the governments to repress religion and to persecute such high-ranking church leaders as Cardinal Mindszenty in Hungary and Cardinal Wyszynski in Poland. The imposition of Russian culture aroused local nationalism. A series of revolts culminated in 1956, when open revolt in Poland and Hungary required direct Soviet military intervention. The Russians, however, had the will to act quickly and with brutal thoroughness and brought the native populations to heel. Lenin's belief that imperialism was the last stage of decadent capitalism had been tossed aside. Russia introduced the world to a new and virulent variety of imperialism, and the horrors of earlier European colonialism were more than matched by the Russians as they exploited eastern Europeans, hammering down age-old cultures, traditions, and social arrangements. Totalitarian controls turned even Czechoslovakia, one of the most industrially advanced and democratic states in the world before the Nazi take-over, into a drab colony of Russia, where individual freedom and human dignity were impossible of achievement.

• Non-Soviet Eastern Europe

The Russian leadership expected to control all of eastern Europe after 1945, but they were foiled in Finland, Austria, and Greece, and Yugoslavia later withdrew its allegiance. Finland chose to resist being incorporated into the Soviet Bloc, and Russia did not make an issue of it because of the danger that if Russia attacked Finland, Sweden's fear would drive her into the western alliance. Besides, Russia had already gained most of what she wanted from Finland in a series of post-war treaties.

In Austria the two major political parties wisely chose to cooperate against Russian dominance instead of fighting each other. The Socialists and the People's Party formed a coalition which was so strong and so effective that it provided the country with its government and administration for an entire generation. Much of the economy was nationalized and even that which remained in private hands came under strong centralized control. By 1955 Austria regained full sovereignty by the Austrian State Treaty, which committed her to a neutral position in the Cold War and which clearly stated that Austria could never become a part of Germany. The Austrian economy quickly recovered. By trading with both East and West, the Austrians raised their standard of living to levels prevalent in the rest of free Europe.

Greece experienced a vicious civil war between communists and non-communists after the expulsion of the German invaders, despite the establishment of a democratically-elected government in 1946. England and the United States supported the government, while Russia's satellites in the area supplied and protected the communist insurgents, which had considerable success until American assistance became too great, and until Yugoslavia cut her ties with Moscow and ceased supporting the communists. Finally the non-communists won at least a temporary victory, but at the expense of any real chance for a decent government. The system which has evolved is strongly authoritarian, amounting to a military dictatorship which denies the most basic liberties to the people.

Yugoslavia's defection particularly surprised the Russians, and introduced the idea of "national communism," as opposed to "monolithic communism." When the Cominform attempted to enforce Russian policies and control over Yugoslavia, Marshal Tito, the beloved communist dictator and World War II hero of the resistance, balked. Stalin, failing to understand the strength of nationalism, tried coercion. But even strong non-communists supported Tito against all Russian efforts to subordinate Yugoslavia. Hoping to find an ally, and looking for propaganda advantages, the western states provided Tito with arms and money, and the Yugoslav state gradually established an independent existence. Tito remained firmly communist in his domestic policies and completely neutral in the Cold War diplomacy.

• The Truman Doctrine

Russia's imperialism and her refusal to permit the development of democratic institutions in the eastern European countries caused a strong reaction against her in England and the United States. The British, responsible for restoring Greek institutions after the Germans had been pushed out in 1944, found themselves involved in a civil war in which the guerillas were supplied by Russia's satellites, and by 1947 were too exhausted to handle the rapidly deteriorating situation. At the same time Russia, by demanding concessions from Turkey, indicated that she planned to take over that country. Here, too, England's support proved too much for her own economy. In 1947 the British government informed the United States that she could no longer carry the burden, and President Harry Truman responded to the situation by asking Congress for funds to permit the United States to intervene. In his speech he expressed the belief that ". . . it must be the policy of the United States to support free peoples who are resisting attempted subjugation by armed minorities or by outside pressures." Congress promptly gave the President the necessary legislation, and established what came to be known as the Truman Doctrine: that the United States would give military and economic support to defend non-communist countries against internal and external enemies.

• European Economic Integration

The Truman Doctrine was followed almost immediately by the Marshall Plan. Secretary of State George Marshall, arguing that "Our policy is directed not against any country or doctrine but against hunger, poverty, desperation and chaos," proposed to use American money to revitalize the economies of the European states. The Marshall Plan arose from the belief that communism spread quickly in areas of economic distress. In order to make efficient use of Marshall Plan aid, the interested governments created the Organization for European Economic Cooperation (OEEC), which directed the use of some $12,000,000,000 in U.S. funds in the next five years. This cooperation led naturally to Point 4 of President Truman's inaugural address in 1949, and to the Point 4 Program to provide economic assistance to the former colonial areas of the world.

The Marshall Plan had a profoundly beneficial effect on the European economies and governments. Recognizing that cooperation among themselves would facilitate restoration, the European governments, through OEEC, reduced tariff barriers and deliberately began a policy of integrating the economies of most of the western European states. The combination of American assistance and economic cooperation produced an amazing prosperity where there had been nothing but devastation, hopelessness, and economic chaos. Although the United States had not excluded eastern Europe from receiving Marshall Plan aid, Russia forbade her satellites to participate, thus increasing the gap between the forces on each side of the iron curtain.

The obvious successes of supra-national organization and planning, using Marshall Plan money, led European leadership gradually to transform OEEC into an organization for long-range European cooperation even without American assistance. By 1951 France, West Germany, and Italy joined the Benelux countries (*Be*lgium, *Ne*therlands, *Lux*emburg) in a new six-nation European Coal and Steel Community, which was designed to pool resources and markets in these two products. Again, success led to a broadening of cooperation. In 1955 the same six countries signed an agreement which established the European Economic Community (EEC), or Common Market. The purposes included the ultimate creation of a tariff-free area in western Europe, and while there were lots of problems to solve before that goal had been achieved, the European leaders genuinely recognized that such cooperation was essential.

Other European states soon felt the effects of the EEC on their economies, and, being excluded from membership, formed the European Free Trade Association (EFTA). The seven member states (Austria, Denmark, England, Norway, Portugal, Sweden, Switzerland) set about reducing tariffs, but did not attempt extensive economic integration, and the Outer Seven has been less successful than the Inner Six. In 1969 the EEC agreed to consider applications from several states for membership, and by 1972 England, Ireland, and Norway had been accepted. EEC and

EFTA now have mutual members, and others may join. Workers already can move easily throughout the Community and social security benefits can be transferred from any member state to a worker's home country. From such beginnings political unity may grow.

• NATO

Increasing prosperity alone could not dismiss the fear of Russia in the minds of Europeans. Military cooperation, as well as economic, was required. Some steps had been taken in this direction by 1948, but it was only with the American adoption of the containment policy that a significant structure was created. The containment policy proceeded from the assumption that Russia's imperialism could be stopped by "adroit and vigilant application of counter-force. . ." every time and every place Russia attempted to move out of the area she already controlled. With such a policy it was necessary to have highly mobile troops strategically located, and to have Russia fully aware of the capability of containment. In 1949, therefore, the United States and Canada joined most of the western European states in the North Atlantic Treaty Organization (NATO). NATO, like EEC, was based on close cooperation among the European states, and required all members to integrate their military planning for common defense. An attack on one member would be looked upon as an attack on all members, and NATO would respond accordingly. American support for NATO responsibilities added economic support to Marshall Plan aid, and the added security contributed to Europe's economic recovery.

• Japan's Recovery

While a resurgent western Europe moved toward economic integration and corporate security to curb the threat of the Soviet menace, the spread of revolutionary communism to the non-European world accelerated the buildup of Cold War tensions. As Europe's weakness became apparent immediately after the war, local communist forces grew strong in most of Asia. They argued for national self-determination, exclusion of foreign oppression, and major land reforms. Japan's wartime occupation of most of southeast Asia bred nationalism in those lands, and her early victories against the United States convinced many Asians that they, too, could end their old subservience to western dominance.

The association of communist nationalists with anti-colonialism frightened the American government and caused a drastic revision of original plans for the occupation of Japan. The occupying forces chose to rule through the established government, which it reformed along democratic lines, and this avoided much of the lasting bitterness usually associated with occupation of defeated countries. Vast American economic assistance (six billion dollars in a dozen years) enabled Japanese industry to develop widespread economic prosperity as it produced for the growing markets in the Far East.

While the United States and other industrial powers devoted ever-greater portions of their economies to the military in pursuit of Cold War aims, Japan, unhindered by any military expenditures, became a major industrial power and began to challenge even the home markets of its industrial competitors. In 1968 Japan by-passed West Germany to become the third-ranking industrial power in the world. Although her growing prosperity invalidated American fears that Japan would succumb to communism, in 1949 a revolution in China turned the largest nation in the Far East into the communist camp.

• The Communist Revolution in China

Chinese nationalism regenerated in the first decade of the century – in 1911 a republican revolution, led by Sun Yat-sen, brought the Kuomintang, or Chinese Nationalist Party, into power. But Sun's political successor, Chiang Kai-shek, failed to develop centralized authority sufficient to solve China's economic ills. An enduring feudal aristocracy resisted land reform and governmental corruption undermined support of the Kuomintang. Led by Mao Tse-tung, Chinese communists won the allegiance of the rural disinherited, disenchanted nationalists and humanitarian intellectuals. Having nothing to defend, the Chinese peasants did not oppose the communists, who promised to raise their standard of living. Of 450 million Chinese, only a handful actively participated in the Civil War, but as the communists took over a region the land-hungry peasants joined in revolt against the established authorities. In 1949 Chiang Kai-shek and a few devoted followers were driven to the island of Formosa (Taiwan) off the coast of China, where he established authoritarian control with the support of the United States. Despite the overwhelming evidence that he had no real chance of successfully returning to power in China, Chiang continued to claim legitimate authority over the mainland.

On October 1, 1949, the communists announced the establishment of the People's Republic of China. Sweeping land reform drew the support of the peasants and the government quickly established sufficient strength to launch a ruthless program of economic modernization without regard to cost in human life. Striking advances were made through five year plans which concentrated on agricultural collectivization and the development of basic industrial facilities. Before the end of the 1950's, Mao and his lieutenants had effected a radical transformation of Chinese society.

Russia immediately recognized the Chinese communist government and in 1950 signed a thirty-year treaty of friendship with the Red Chinese, but ideological differences soon caused a rift between the two. Communist China had no intention of becoming a satellite of the U.S.S.R. Adopting a fiercely militant revolutionary doctrine, the Chinese rejected the concept of peaceful co-existence and demonstrated a determination to control Asia which led to territorial clashes with the Soviet Union along their mutual borders. The Sino-Soviet split had wide-ranging repercussions as the east

European countries recognized a possible alternative to Russian dominance and a potential alternative leadership.

The United States refused to recognize the Chinese communist government, insisting that Chiang Kai-shek and the Nationalists were the rightful authority. Consequently, the U.S. signed a mutual defense treaty with the exiled government on Formosa and followed it with military and economic assistance. Defending Chiang's claim to legitimacy, the U.S. also took the lead in blocking Red China's admission to the United Nations. The Chinese revolution intensified American fears of communist expansion and caused an extension of the containment policy to include the Far East as well as Europe. When communist forces invaded South Korea in June, 1950, the United States resorted to direct military intervention to prevent a Communist take-over.

A former Japanese colony, Korea was divided along the 38th parallel at the Potsdam Conference, with the Soviets occupying the northern region and the Americans the southern. In 1948 the South Koreans established the Republic of Korea; North Korea responded by announcing the formation of the People's Democratic Republic of Korea. Both claimed sovereignty over the entire country. When the Soviet and American occupying forces withdrew in 1949, the crisis between the rival governments mounted. In June, 1950, a North Korean army suddenly crossed the 38th parallel and invaded South Korea. The United States immediately appealed to the United Nations, which called on U.N. members to aid in defending South Korea from communist aggression. Since the U.S.S.R. had temporarily withdrawn from the organization in protest against the refusal to admit Red China to membership, the Soviets could not block the action. Fifteen nations sent forces into Korea, but Americans provided the predominant military resistance. The war became chiefly an American struggle against the North Korean communists, supported by about 200,000 Chinese.

It ended in a stalemate. Frustrating negotiations dragged on for two years, and finally produced, in July, 1953, an armistice which retained the division of the country. The conflict, which ended with neither victors nor vanquished, resulted only in the devastation of Korean territory, the death of 3,000,000 Koreans and more than 100,000 Americans. It did, however, mark the United States as the world's police force against communism. Europe and the anti-communist factions throughout the world adopted a complacent assurance that Americans would and could contain communist aggression.

• The End of Bipolarity

Chinese aggrandizement provoked attempts to create regional security organizations in Asia patterned on the European NATO alliance. In September, 1954, the United States, England, France, Australia, New Zealand, Pakistan, the Philippines, and Thailand signed the Manila Pact, which provided for the formation of the Southeast Asia Treaty Organization. SEATO completed the division of the globe into rival blocs. Cold War competition had expanded to include the entire world.

But rapidly accelerating events were already undermining the foundations of bipolar domination. By 1954 both Russia and the United States had stockpiled sufficient nuclear weapons to destroy life on the globe. The military balance forced the conclusion that neither could emerge victorious from a nuclear confrontation – only annihilation would result. Recognition of the undeniable ecological devastation resulting from continued testing exerted further pressure to end the suicidal armaments race and produced negotiations which ultimately resulted in the nuclear test-ban treaty of 1963.

Simultaneously, nationalism operated to weaken the ties between the superpowers and their previously submissive allies and to create a new climate in international relations. The power of the United States and Russia began to decline relative to the growing strength and restiveness of the rest of the world and ushered in an era of global politics.

22

The Emerging Nations in the Contemporary Era

ONE OF THE MOST striking characteristics of the contemporary period is a shift in the focus of history from a European to a global perspective. For more than 400 years Europe dominated the historical stage. The last decades of the nineteenth century witnessed the rapid exportation of European authority to all corners of the globe. Europe's collapse in the twentieth century brought in its wake the disintegration of European world hegemony. Beginning after World War I and accelerating rapidly after World War II, a revolt against European domination and a strong assertion of national self-determination in the industrially under-developed nations swept the globe, crumbling the old colonial empires, and challenging the economic leadership of the industrially advanced nations.

Europe's loss of economic, political, and military power began a new era of world politics. Russia and the United States, the two superpowers, vied for supremacy, each pursuing the allegiance of the rest of the world. Bipolarity dominated world politics for over a decade, but by the 1960's a new power structure was clearly recognizable. It rested on a regenerated Europe and a new bloc of developing nations in Asia, Africa, and Latin America, called the "Third World." By 1970 this shifting coalition held the balance in the conflict between the Russian and American superpowers. The breakup of Europe's colonial empires generated the Third World bloc.

• The Twilight of Empire

Although economic necessities had undeniably encouraged the acquisition of empire, Europe's imperialistic motivations included a complex mixture of political and economic domination and paternalism. The "White Man's Burden" dictated an inculcation of western ideas and mores into native cultures and left a mixed heritage in the colonial areas. Lord Curzon, England's Viceroy in India (1899-1905), articulated the attitudes of the European masters when he described empire as the means of service to mankind as well as the key to glory and wealth. And imperialism did indeed spread Europe's advanced cultural concepts to the less highly developed areas of the globe. In most European colonies westernized elites, educated in European schools, absorbed the ideas of popular sovereignty, individualism, and self-determination asserted so vigorously by their imperial masters. Moreover, they determined to industrialize and modernize their homelands in order to share the material comforts of twentieth-century society. This urge quickened after Russia's rapid industrialization in the 1930's showed the way. Imperialism consequently sowed the seeds of its own destruction – it awakened slumbering societies to the benefits of modernization and at the same time, because of its frequently harsh economic demands, created a determination to throw off the yoke of foreign domination.

After 1945 the colonial empires disintegrated with a rapidity that astonished everyone. England led in relinquishing empire, as she had led in acquiring it – hers was the first of the imperial structures to crumble. Although a strong imperialistiic wing still existed in the British Conservative Party, Labour grasped control in the immediate post-war years and spurred imperial disintegration. Labour insisted that all people, of whatever race or color, had an equal right to freedom and national sovereignty. The British Commonwealth policy, instituted with the Statute of Westminister in 1931, facilitated England's withdrawal from empire. It declared that the dominions were autonomous states, equal in status with each other and with Great Britain, freely associated in common allegiance to the crown in the Commonwealth of Nations. Although the Commonwealth idea was adopted specifically in regard to Canada and Australia – western nations populated with whites – it established a precedent which later included non-western colonies as England considered them capable of self-rule.

France, more reluctant to give up her colonial possessions, pursued an ambivalent course. Although imperialism remained strong in conservative segments of the French population, the Second World War necessitated changes in France's colonial policies. A French Union preserved the French possessions and dominance from Paris, but allowed limited self-government and colonial representation in the French Parliament. Unlike the British Commonwealth, the French Union was a weak and unsatisfactory structure from the beginning and never attained viability. Belgium, the Netherlands, and Portugal, the remaining imperial powers, tried desperately to hold on to their colonies. Only Portugal succeeded.

• Southeast Asia

The challenge to European control began in Asia. China's nationalist revolution in the first decade of the twentieth century initiated a drive toward independence which gained impetus in southeast Asia in the inter-war period. India took the lead in discarding imperial rule.

Spurred by the leadership of Mohandas Gandhi, an ascetic, western-educated champion of Indian freedom, Indian demands for self-government began before World War I. Gandhi urged a policy of passive resistance, non-violence, and civil disobedience to British rule. Under pressure from Gandhi and his fellow nationalists, the British passed the Government of India Act in 1919, designed to train the Indian population toward independence. The Act established a parliament and elective provincial legislative councils. Limited self-rule did not satisfy the demands of the nationalists, however, and disorder increased. Religious and cultural differences between Hindus and Moslems complicated the situation and despite Gandhi's insistence on non-violence, terrorist acts frequently occurred. The Moslem League, a political party which opposed Gandhi's Hindu Congress Party, rejected co-existence with the Hindu majority and militantly insisted on partition of the territory and the creation of a separate Moslem state. Since complete division of the inextricably intermingled populations could not be realized, the British resisted the demands for partition.

In 1940 Indian nationalists, now led by Jawaharlal Nehru, an English-educated Indian aristocrat, rejected a British offer of semi-autonomy, belligerently insisting on full independence. As Hindu-Moslem differences continued to cause disturbances and riots the British reluctantly recognized that partition was inevitable. In 1947 England granted independent dominion status to India, the predominantly Hindu area, and to a new state, Pakistan, formed of the severed Moslem territories. Both republics became Commonwealth members.

• Independence and After

Independence and partition failed to resolve the religious and civil discord. Following England's withdrawal, violent civil wars broke out in India and Pakistan, as minorities clashed with ruling majorities. Territorial disputes further embittered relations between the two countries, as both claimed the province of Kashmir. Neither could quell the civil turmoil nor resolve the external conflict. At the same time, both nations struggled to solve monumental social and economic problems.

Modernization in India requires more than the development of industrial facilities and improved methods of agriculture. India has a population of more than 500 million, most of them underfed, illiterate, and with archaic religious and cultural traditions. In his attempt to advance the drive toward modernization, Nehru, India's Prime Minister from 1947 to 1964, utilized assistance in foreign aid from both the United States and Russia. Nehru's policy of non-alignment in the ideological struggle between the super-powers established a model emulated by most of the other Third World States.

Pakistan's division into two segments complicated her efforts to modernize. East and West Pakistan were separated by a thousand miles, united only by a common religion and rent with linguistic and cultural differences. Pakistani leadership could not cement the two. In 1971 dissension erupted into civil war and resulted in further fragmentation. East Pakistan announced its independence as a new state, and took the name of Bangladesh. Hindu minorities fled into India, creating a staggering refugee problem. Thousands starved to death, and the influx imposed a heavy burden on India's already over-taxed economy.

In other areas of south-east Asia new states arose in profusion. The British granted independence to Burma and Ceylon in 1948, and belatedly to Malaya in 1957 after a long war against communist guerilla forces. The United States, fulfilling a pre-war promise, granted independence to the Philippines in 1946. In 1949 after four years of bloody conflict, the Dutch finally retreated from Indonesia, and a federal republic was created.

In the years since independence each of these states has struggled to improve living conditions for populations which still live largely in a medieval world. Entrenched elites have resisted land redistribution and maintained a stranglehold on government machinery which has greatly hindered progress. The disinherited segments of these Asian populations have not acquiesced easily in socio-economic stagnation. Their demands for a share of the wealth have encouraged the development of Communist cadres which seek to undermine the established governments. Government corruption and refusal to reform have fed ever increasing numbers of normally quiescent peasants into the ranks of revolutionary movements seeking economic improvement. This characteristic pattern in the Asian world has been most insistently demonstrated in French Indo-China, now called Vietnam.

• Vietnam

During World War II the French possessions in Indo-China became the seat of a complicated power struggle between the French, the Japanese, and the natives, led by Ho Chi Minh, a Communist-trained nationalist who was determined to establish an independent native republic. When the French attempted to re-establish control over the area after the war, Ho and his insurgents, the Vietminh, resisted fiercely. In 1946 the French granted Vietnam semi-autonomy within the French Union, but the nationalist rebellion continued. Because of the Vietminh's communist orientation, the French refused to accede to the increasingly insistent Vietnamese demands for full independence. The struggle became full-scale war in 1946.

The war in Indo-China continued for eight years, becoming an interminable conflict which drained France's already depleted resources, and was enormously unpopular with the French people. In 1949 the Soviet Union and the new communist Chinese government recognized Ho's Vietminh regime as the legitimate government in Vietnam. The United States and England recognized Vietnam and the neighboring French Protectorates of Laos and Cambodia as member states of the French Union, and the United States poured vast economic aid into the French military effort. Nothing could stem the tide of Vietnamese nationalism.

From 1950 to 1954 Ho broadened his base of popular support and stepped up guerilla tactics. The absorption of French energies in the Vietnamese war allowed Laos and Cambodia to demand and receive greater sovereignty over their own affairs, thus preventing the outbreak of open conflict in those areas. In 1954, after a disastrous defeat at Dien Bien Phu, the French admitted their inability to continue the struggle and withdrew from Vietnam.

The fall of Dien Bien Phu marked the end of French imperialist control in southeast Asia. The Geneva Conference in 1954 partitioned Vietnam along the seventeenth parallel. The Communist Democratic Republic of Vietnam, led by Ho Chi Minh, was established in the North, and the Nationalist Republic of Vietnam in the South. Laos and Cambodia acquired full independence.

But the civil war in Vietnam continued after partition. Determined to unite the country under his leadership, Ho Chi Minh proclaimed a Fatherland Front and urged the South Vietnamese government to cooperate in unification, but the ruler of South Vietnam, Ngo Dinh Diem, refused to negotiate. Diem, a Catholic, issued a constitution and promised elections in South Vietnam, but assumed dictatorial powers. He received enormous aid from the United States because of his declared anti-communism, but was unable to win the support of his own people who charged him with religious persecution and vehemently protested his religious policies. Buddhist monks led the rebellion, sometimes resorting to such extreme protests as self-immolation. As Diem continued to resist demands for change, the civil war intensified, and the local communist forces, the National Liberation Front (NLF), gained more and more adherents.

• U.S. Intervention

The United States, having adopted the "Domino Theory" – a belief that the fall of one state to communism would inevitably result in the fall of all – chose to take France's place in South Vietnam. Gradually it became clear that Ngo Dinh Diem was insupportable and the United States participated in a coup which overthrew his government. Succeeding South Vietnamese governments accepted increasing American economic and military intervention until more than half-a-million American soldiers were fighting the Vietnamese insurgents. While the United States pretended that it was defending freedom and saving civilization from godless communism, the more experienced Europeans realized that much of Ho Chi Minh's support rested on a determined desire for Vietnamese independence from foreign domination. American involvement in Vietnam became the central international event of the decade between 1960 and 1970. Many Americans and most Europeans agonized over the United States' military policies, which resulted in defoliation of the Vietnamese forests, the use of napalm against villagers whose allegiance was uncertain, and the massacre of village populations, including women and small children, such as occurred at My Lai in 1968. As it became increasingly obvious that America's national and vital interests were not threatened by the civil war in Vietnam, increasing numbers of citizens questioned the justification of American involvement in a war which seemed not only imperialistic but interminable as well. As war costs mounted past $400,000,000,000 the

Terrified children fleeing after being burned by a misplaced American napalm bombing. Wide World Photos.

anti-war movement, dominated initially by the young, eventually enlisted the support of many influential leaders. In the presidential election of 1968 the war was a major campaign issue. Promising to withdraw American troops from Vietnam "with all reasonable speed," the Republican candidate, Richard Milhous Nixon, defeated the Democrats who bore the public responsibility for escalating the war.

Nixon's first administration proved as incapable of resolving the dilemma as had the preceding Democratic governments. His program, called Vietnamization, was a combination of reducing American troop levels, strengthening the Vietnamese Army, and negotiating for peace, all to be achieved at the same time. It met with little success. While ground troops were reduced, the American bombing of North Vietnam intensified. At Quang Tri in 1972 South Vietnamese soldiers threw down their weapons and ran from the communist forces. Despite recurrent promises that peace was imminent, negotations remained at an impasse until early in 1973, when the United States, North and South Vietnam signed an agreement ending direct American military involvement.

Europe shared America's perplexity concerning Vietnam. While most Europeans had vigorously condemned American involvement, many feared that U.S. withdrawal from the defense against communism in Southeast Asia would also mean withdrawal from Europe's defense. Europe feared that Vietnamization would be followed by Europeanization, and fears of Russian aggrandizement had not sufficiently abated to face such a prospect with equanimity. Increasing international tensions in the Middle East reinforced European fears for its security.

• The Middle East

The Ottoman Empire had extended over most of the Arab world, although England and France had established protectorates over portions of the Middle East. Turkish and European domination produced, even before the First World War, an Arab leadership determined to end foreign control and gain national independence. Allied with Germany in the First World War, the Turkish Empire disintegrated after the defeat of the Central Powers. Despite the efforts of Arab nationalists to unite the Arab lands of the Middle East into an independent state, the League of Nations extended European control, granting England and France mandates over Arab territories. Instead of unifying the Arab world, the League of Nations mandates divided it into a number of small, antagonistic states united only in their opposition to foreigners and in their determination to prevent the foundation of a Jewish nation in Palestine.

In 1917 the British government's Balfour Declaration announced that England favored the establishment in Palestine, the historic Jewish homeland now populated with Arabs, of a "national home for the Jewish people," and would support the creation of such a state. The Declaration promised, however, that all civil and religious rights of Arab residents would be protected. Encouraged by the Balfour Declaration, large numbers of Jews, especially from eastern Europe, migrated into Palestine between the wars. Many of the new settlers represented a literate, technically advanced class, imbued with the ideas of democratic socialism.

Tensions grew between the Jewish immigrants and the Palestinian Arabs as the culturally advanced Jews tried to turn economically backward Palestine into a modern nation. Between the wars Palestine developed more rapidly than other Arab regions, but inevitably the Arab people resisted Jewish dominance and the rapid change in their way of life. Clashes between the two groups occurred constantly.

After World War II vast numbers of Europe's surviving Jews poured into Palestine, fleeing the horrors they had endured under the Nazis, and seeking security and protection in a "national home." By 1947 tensions between Arab and Jew had reached such proportions that England decided to withdraw from the area, and asked the United Nations to resolve the problem. When England removed her troops in 1948, however, the U.N. had found no satisfactory solution, and the Jews unilaterally proclaimed the independence and autonomy of the state of Israel as a republic.

• Arab-Israeli Conflict

The immediate consequence was war between the Palestinian Arabs and the Israelis, quickly won by the latter because the Arabs were disunited and poorly equipped, and because Israel had the support of most of the western states. Nearly a million Palestinian Arabs fled Israel and established themselves in refugee camps in neighboring Arab states where they remain, living in misery and squalor, refusing assimilation, demanding to be restored to their lost home. The camps bred fanatical terrorist groups which intensified Israeli defensiveness. Arab terror tactics had world-wide repercussions as innocent non-Jew and non-Arab people were drawn into the conflict. Arab fanatics hijacked international airplanes and held the passengers as hostages to wring concessions from the Israelis. Bombings of planes and embassies aroused world-wide hostility. In 1972 Arab terrorists violated the traditional neutrality of the Olympic Games in Munich, Germany, and killed several members of the Israeli Olympic team. Such irrational activities have served to harden antagonism to the Arab cause, and to arouse sympathy for the Israelis. Europeans, genuinely distressed by German atrocities and pleased that the Jews had found a home in the Arab world rather than in Europe, tended to side with the Israelis against the Arabs. Arab terrorism strengthened European and American sympathies for the Jewish cause, but the Russian bloc supported the Arabs, supplying military equipment and moral support to the Arab League, a union of the major Arab states dominated by Egypt. The Arab-Israeli conflict thus became of major significance in international politics, and the tension aroused fears that the area would serve as the tinderbox for a new world war. These fears caused the United States, France, and England to agree in 1950 to limit their sales of military equipment to both sides, a decision which angered the nationalists and contributed to a dangerous situation in 1956.

• The Suez Canal Crisis

The Suez Canal Crisis greatly stimulated Arab nationalism, seriously damaged the western alliance, marked the decline of British power and influence in the Middle East, and fostered significant growth of presidential power in the United States at the expense of Congress. In 1954 an Anglo-Egyptian agreement provided for gradual withdrawal of British troops from the Suez Canal Zone, to be completed by 1956. Under the agreement the Suez Canal Company continued to operate the canal and both countries guaranteed freedom of its use to all countries. Egypt granted that in case of attack on any Arab country or Turkey, British troops might return to protect the canal.

The United States had helped in the negotiations, hoping to create a Middle Eastern Treaty Organization (METO) to fill the containment gap between NATO and SEATO. Iraq, Pakistan, Turkey, Iran, and Great Britain joined, but Egypt refused. She wanted weapons to use against Israel, not Russia, and she wanted the leadership of Arab nationalism. Russia saw the opportunity and agreed to swap Russian and Czechoslovakian weapons for Egyptian cotton. Egypt's flirtation with Russia caused the United States and England first to promise huge funding to build the High Aswan Dam in Egypt, then later, when the Egyptians failed to align with the West, to withdraw the funding. Bitterly seeking a way to retaliate, Egypt nationalized the Suez Canal Company in 1956, giving her control over shipping which passed through the canal. But about 60 percent of the oil used in France and England had to pass through the Suez.

Israel, too, worried about Russian arms in Egypt. After a series of conferences failed to impress the Egyptians, France, England, and Israel chose military force. The Israelis attacked Egypt across the Sinai Peninsula, and British and French troops, fully expecting American support, were sent to "protect the canal." But the United States joined Russia in a U.N. General Assembly order to cease fire, and the sending of a U.N. military force to the canal to replace Anglo-French troops in defending the canal. Under heavy world pressure the invaders returned home.

England's humiliation weakened the western alliance, METO lost much of its effectiveness, Egypt took the lead in Arab nationalism, and the U.S. government feared a Russian take-over of the entire area. President Eisenhower requested, and received from Congress in 1957, presidential authority to order U.S. military intervention to secure and protect the territorial integrity of any nation threatened with armed aggression by international communism. Former Secretary of State Dean Acheson suggested that this "Eisenhower Doctrine" amounted to a threat "to fight an enemy that is not going to attack with forces that do not exist to carry out a policy you have not yet decided upon." Egypt was not controlled by international communism. Her goals were the leadership of Arab nationalism and the destruction of Israel. Neither of Egypt's goals has been achieved, and the Eisenhower Doctrine later provided the foundation for the presidential escalation of the war in Vietnam.

Arab and Jewish animosity erupted into war again in 1967. Again Israel's disciplined, highly-trained, well-equipped forces defeated the Arabs and extended Israel's boundaries. In the "Six-Day War" the Israelis awed the world by their easy victory over an Arab army equipped with Russian tanks and airplanes. The Israeli triumph weakened Egyptian leadership, intensified Arab hostility, and exacerbated the crisis. Major foreign powers deplored Israel's action and the United Nations unsuccessfully demanded that she withdraw from the territory she had conquered.

• Underdevelopment in the Arab States

Israel's neighbors could not match her economic achievements. Despite vast mineral resources – the Middle East is one of the world's largest oil-producing areas, second only to North America – wealth has not extended to the masses of the populations. Economic progress in the oil-rich Arab states is seriously retarded by the opposition of dominating elites – tribal shieks, military oligarchies, and native aristocracies – who have subordinated their people's interests to their own in dealing with the oil-using western states. The need for oil and the area's strategic importance sustained vital interest in the area by the United States, Russia, and western Europe. Although the United States has done much to extend education and economic progress in the Arab nations, American support for Israel marks the United States as an enemy in the eyes of Arab statesmen, while Russia supports the Arab cause to provide a buffer zone between the West and Russia. Huge differences in levels of economic, cultural, and social development among the Arab states maintain division in the area and prevent common political action. The key to progress in the Middle East is unification of the Arab states to share technological knowledge, to expand markets, and to stimulate social reform. Egypt has tried to provide leadership for unity, but the Arab countries remain divided. The Arab League, established in 1945 with headquarters in Cairo, has not been able to overcome national self-interest in its member states. Formerly dominated by Egypt's dynamic Gamal Abdul Nasser, the League has effectively harassed Israel, but has not attracted the loyalty of all the Arab states. Nasser's dependence on Soviet technical and financial assistance alienated those nations determined to pursue a neutral policy in the Cold War conflict, and his undisguised desire to assume leadership of the Arab world offended other Mid-East statesmen. His prestige declined after the humiliating Arab defeat in 1967 and since his death in 1970 the Arabs have found no comparable leader.

Crisis has characterized the pattern of development in the Middle East since the turn of the century. In most of the Arab world pre-modern structures, illiterate populations, and inadequate distribution of enormous wealth predominate. The conflict with Israel has served paradoxical functions: it has, on the one hand, advanced consolidation in the Arab fight against a mutual enemy, and, on the other hand, absorbed energies and resources desperately needed elsewhere. The conflict itself has invited foreign intervention and keeps the danger of an international confrontation alive. Hope for peace in the Middle East remains a remote possibility as Arab nationalism and Israeli militarism intensify. Hope for international peace can only survive if the Soviet and American powers, together with the European and neighboring Third World states, exert strenuous efforts to restrain Arab-Israeli passions, and, in the process, change Cold War détente into cooperation.

• Africa

The determination to achieve modern economic comforts through independence and self-determination struck Africa with explosive force. Before the Second World War, four independent nations existed on the African continent; by 1960, 39 nations had emerged. The new African states passionately support the objectives of the Third World bloc: to pursue an independent course in evolving political systems which will serve their own unique needs, and to accelerate economic improvement for their impoverished populations. The nationalist revolution in Africa, however, faces severe internal challenges.

Immediately after the Second World War several African leaders began agitation for independence. Such men as Kwame Nkrumah of the Gold Coast and Jomo Kenyatta of Kenya not only provided leadership for their own people, but served as examples for other African leaders. In the 1950's and 1960's new states emerged from former colonial possessions with bewildering rapidity. Bloody tribal rebellion, violence of an extreme nature, brutal civil war, and territorial fragmentation accompanied

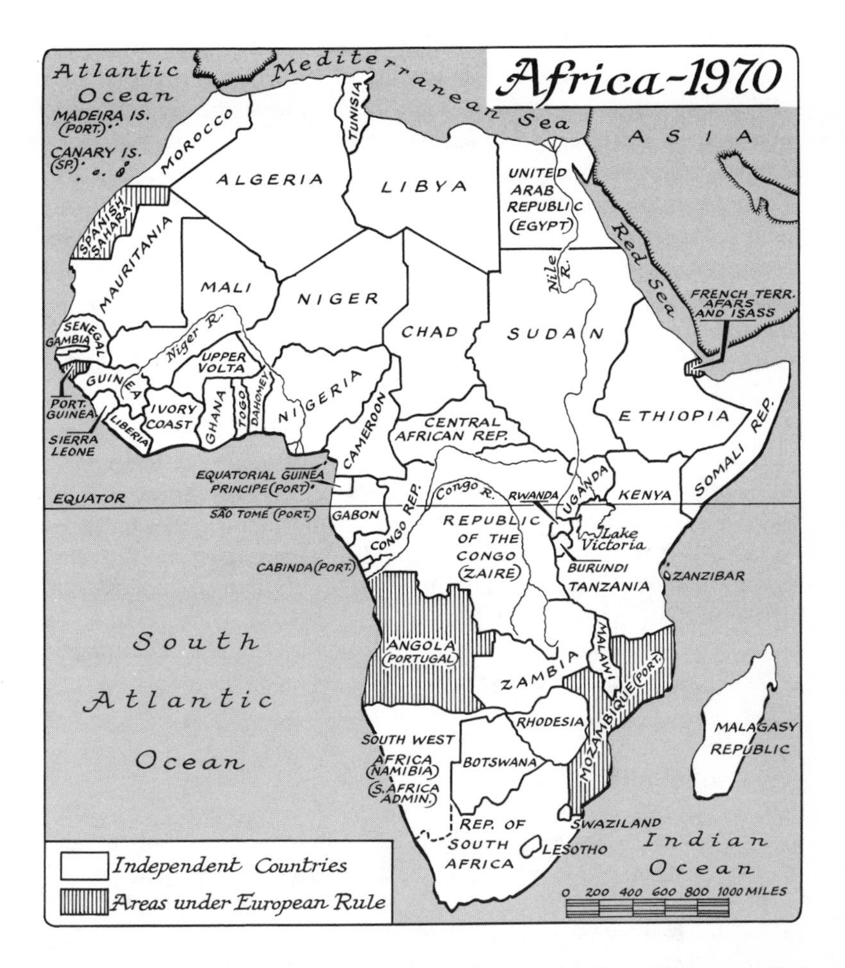

independence. In Nigeria in 1967 the Ibo, one of the three dominant tribal groupings, broke away from the state and formed the independent Republic of Biafra. The Nigerians coldheartedly and ruthlessly reunited the nation. A bloody tribal rebellion led by the Mau-Mau in Kenya lasted eight years. After Belgium abruptly broke her ties with the Congo, violence, horror and massacre required United Nations intervention. These events illustrated the enduring force of primitive traditions and patterns, and demonstrated clearly the weakness of African nationalism. Africans had to overcome not only their colonial experience, but perhaps more significantly, the handicaps of centuries of tribal allegiances which counter the movement toward modern nationalism.

In southern Africa white settlers refused to grant native demands for participation in government, and enforced a fierce and rigid policy of subjugation called *apartheid.* The British government demanded that the extreme racial segregation of *apartheid* be dropped, but in 1961 South Africa withdrew from the Commonwealth rather than yield. In 1965 Rhodesia unilaterally proclaimed her independence from British rule and joined South Africa in a fanatical determination to maintain *apartheid.* Despite censure by the United Nations and international economic sanctions, the two south African states defiantly persisted in their determination to keep the non-European population from political participation. The result is that both South Africa and Rhodesia have established vicious police state systems.

The French government faced special problems in her territories in northern Africa. Tunisia and Morocco, after years of internal discord and futile efforts by France to resist demands for self-rule, gained independence in 1956. But many French families in Algeria thought of themselves as French citizens and resisted demands for independence led particularly by the National Liberation Front (FLN), and a sanguinary civil war developed into terroristic tactics both in Algeria and in France. The terrorism and the government's brutal response led to chaos and ultimately toppled the Fourth French Republic.

• The Future in Africa

Most of the new African states attempted to pattern their governments on west European models, with all the institutions instantly created which had evolved in Europe over hundreds of years. They failed to realize that parliamentary democracy requires, for viability, a large degree of willingness to compromise, an educated citizenry, sufficient income to provide leisure time to devote to political and cultural pursuits. None of these requisites characterized the new African states. They have tended to develop into one-party systems, governed by charismatic leaders – native nationalists whose leadership frequently appears demagogic.

Democracy in the western European states and in America developed out of a long and gradual evolution toward popular sovereignty and did not reach full maturity even in the west until well into the twentieth century. But democracy as it evolved in the west is not presently a viable system for Africa's new nations. African statesmen face unique problems and monumental challenges in their drive to bring twentieth-century economic benefits to their people. These new states may evolve unique political solutions and patterns of self-determination out of their own cultural traditions as valid as the western variety. Popular sovereignty can assume different guises – and is attempting to do so in Africa whose experiments with social revolution have just begun. Unquestionably, self-determination in Africa will pursue a vastly different course than it did in the western tradition.

• Latin America

As in Africa, Latin American nationalism was first expressed by politically articulate elites in terms of territorial integrity. Despite overwhelming difficulties in overcoming particularism and internal division, many of the nations in Latin America have begun social revolutions and are engaged in widely divergent forms of political experimentation. As the most economically advanced of the Third World regions, its solutions will inevitably serve as models for the contemporary world's emerging states.

Like Russia and the United States, Latin America remained on the periphery of world affairs until the twentieth century. After the Second World War, however, developments there assumed a new significance. In 1942 a Pan-American Conference at Rio de Janeiro resulted in the closest ties among American states in their history. All except Argentina, which had a pro-fascist government, broke diplomatic relations with the Axis powers before the year ended and strong pressure brought even that country around early in 1945.

After the war the Latin American states faced many of the same political and economic difficulties found in other portions of the Third World. Their efforts to emulate European and American political movements had failed, primarily because of the weakness of their middle classes which tended to join authoritarian dictatorships rather than to lead genuine reform movements.

Grinding poverty, high illiteracy rates, and a medieval social structure contributed to the development of communist groups in the Latin American states. The 1956 Twentieth Party Congress in Moscow encouraged the idea of "national communism," appealing to hatred of foreign economic domination and the conspicuous wealth of the upper classes. The incredibly poor peasants and workers in Latin America turned to communism as a method of improving their miserable lot. Increasingly radical demands generated fears among the ruling elites, and in the United State, of a communist takeover.

Fear of communist advance in the western hemisphere produced the Inter-American Treaty of Reciprocal Assistance in 1947, which provided for collective defense of the American republics against internal as well as external communist threats. This was followed the next year by the Organization of American States which pledged consultation on matters of mutual interest and guaranteed that the United States would not interfere in the domestic or foreign policies of any Latin American state.

• The Cuban Revolution

U.S. policy-makers, however, paid little heed to their own promises, to the obvious distress of even the most anti-communist Latin American leaders. United States participation in the disastrous Bay of Pigs episode in 1961 caused grave damage to inter-American relations. Cuba's vicious right-wing dictator, Fulgencio Batista, was overthrown by Fidel Castro in 1959. Castro proclaimed himself a communist, expropriated the property of U.S. citizens, and killed or exiled thousands of his opponents. In April, 1961, Cuban refugees, with U.S. assistance, attempted an invasion to overthrow Castro. The ill-conceived landing, at the Bay of Pigs, miscarried miserably and the failure of the Cuban population to rise in support of the invading forces indicated that the people largely supported Castro's government.

A year later the Russians began establishing missile bases in Cuba. Success in such a venture would have given Russia a preponderance of power in the world, because from Cuba the missiles could threaten even the northeastern population centers of the United States, and because, too, Russia would have successfully interfered in the American sphere of influence. President John F. Kennedy threatened atomic war unless the Russian missiles were removed immediately, although he agreed at the same time that the United States would not invade Cuba. Russia complied with the demand and the diplomatic victory restored some of the previously lost prestige of the United States.

In an effort to prevent the spread of communism in the Latin American Republics, the United States initiated a series of programs of financial assistance. Congress largely funded the creation of the Inter-American Development Bank in 1959 and 1960, and in 1961 the Kennedy administration launched the ambitious Alliance for Progress, which has poured more than five billion dollars into all the Latin American countries except Cuba. But the economic factors retarding progress in Latin America have not been eradicated. Extractive economies dependent on limited markets, deficiencies in scientific and technological personnel, and lagging inter-regional cooperation maintain social conditions which form breeding grounds for revolutionary doctrines. After more than a century of independence, political maturity in Latin America still proves elusive.

• The Third World Presence in International Affairs

Unquestionably, the nations of the Third World bloc are politically and economically diverse – distinctions rather than similarities prevail. Solidarity is only a semblance. Their impact on international politics has nevertheless radically altered contemporary power alignments. In the United Nations small, poor countries account for 97 of the 132 votes in the General Assembly. Such states as Zambia and Burundi voted with the majority 92 percent of the time in 1972, while the United States increasingly opposed it. Thus far the majority has been unable to enforce its will, because the small states lack the clout to make the great powers respond. Brazil's Ambassador to the United States spoke for many Third World leaders when he warned that "the U.N. is becoming irrelevant on matters of peace and security, and runs the risk of being converted into a sort of international institute of technology or into an ineffective chapter of the International Red Cross." But he also warned that such a development might force the world "toward a concept of new centers of power upon which to build a new structure for peace."

The possibility is recognized even by some Americans. A former Ambassador to the U.N. pointed out that "When the Assembly of 132 states adopts a resolution, that action represents, as nearly as any action can in a world of separate sovereign states, the predominant public opinion of the world. It may not have the force of law, but it often has the force of prophecy." The danger exists, if such countries as the United States continue, under Nixon's strategy of benign neglect, to ignore these new forces, that the conflicts between rich and poor, strong and weak, might become more difficult of resolution through the U.N., and force the Third World into a belligerent and united stance against the great powers.

Despite their diversity, the under-developed nations share important objectives. A passionate determination to protect national identity underlies a diplomatic policy of non-alignment in the Russian-American ideological competition. In all the Third World states, economic development is the most urgent imperative. Confronted with the necessity of seeking outside aid, most have resisted subordination into neo-colonialism and have sought instead to cooperate with each other. The Latin American

Free Trade Association, the Organization of African Unity, the Arab League, and other regional associations – ranging from customs unions to common markets – have accelerated progress in many areas. Although torn with dissension and internal conflict, these associations provide a basis for a developing unity in the Third World – a contingency which offers hope that the destructive Cold War competition between the superpowers will give way to a more creative future.

23

The Industrially Advanced Nations in the Contemporary Era

THE SEARCH FOR new forms of social organization worked profound change within Europe as well as without. In the immediate post-war years each of the major nations of western Europe moved rapidly into consolidation of the welfare state. With the aid of the Marshall Plan and the security provided against further Soviet expansion by NATO, economic recovery occurred with an awesome rapidity – in West Germany it has been called a miracle. In less than a decade after the war Europe was back on her feet, although she had not regained her pre-war ascendancy in international affairs.

• England

England turned to reconstruction immediately following the defeat of Germany. In July, 1945, a national election turned the indomitable war leader, Winston Churchill, and his Conservative government out of office. Labour, led by Clement Attlee, won a mandate for sweeping internal change and advanced the British movement toward a centrally controlled economy, a direction begun but not completed before the war.

Compensating the private owners for their property, the Labour Government nationalized the coal industry and began nationalization of the steel industries, and established government control over the railroads and other segments of England's transportation facilities. But socialization of the economy stopped with nationalization of the essential primary industries – England retained a mixed economy, with ownership still largely in private hands. Government economic planning expanded England's already progressive system of social welfare – initiating a National Health Service in 1948 which provided free medical care, hospitalization, and drugs to all citizens. Educational reforms democratized public schooling and provided increased educational opportunities – the number of university students in England tripled in twenty years, creating an enormous demand for schools, teachers, and educational facilities. Government subsidies greatly increased the amount and quality of housing available to England's working classes, and social legislation provided benefits for unemployment, sickness, child care, and old-age pensions.

The expansion of government subsidized benefits meant sharply increased taxation for the British citizen. The cost of social services rose sharply, at the same time that England struggled to regain a favorable balance of trade in order to remedy the dislocations in the British economy. Yet, despite a few strident critics, the British people overwhelmingly supported England's transformation into a welfare state. Labour's reform program ended in 1951, when the Conservatives returned to power, but the Conservatives retained almost totally the changes Labour had initiated.

English democracy became stronger than ever in the post-war years. The old Liberal Party, already weak before the war, now practically disappeared, and the Labour and Conservative Parties dominated British politics. By 1951 Labour had achieved the goals it had demanded since its inception and evolved an increasingly moderate, middle-class orientation. At the same time, the Conservatives adopted much of Labour's earlier philosophy, accepting without further resistance the necessity of a government controlled economy. After the 1960's both parties operated in the moderate center of the political spectrum.

England's post-war economic revolution did not immediately solve all her economic ills, although it reduced the gap between rich and poor and advanced prosperity and security for the British people. In the 1960's England exhibited all the symptoms of economic old age. Her industrial facilities, the first to be built, required extensive modernization. The breakup of her colonial empire reduced both her access to raw materials and the availability of guaranteed markets. Her exclusion from the European Economic Community further handicapped economic growth, and her ties to the Commonwealth and to the Outer Seven (EFTA) proved less stimulating than she had hoped. In an effort to share the economic

President Charles de Gaulle. Wide World Photos.

progress which distinguished the EEC, England, after years of debate and the final consent of France, voted to become a Common Market member. Participation in the European economic union draws England inextricably into the European community and finally marks the end of her traditional reluctance to identify with Europe's destiny. Despite her economic decline after the war, England remained an industrial innovator, developing strength in such technological fields as computers, jet aircraft, and other advanced transportation facilities. England's admission opens the EEC members to the benefits of her continuing vitality; integration into European affairs places England with her natural partners.

• The Fourth French Republic

France's recovery from the devastation of the war was more difficult. For over a decade political stability proved as elusive as in the inter-war period. The end of the Vichy regime, the Nazi puppet government in France, meant that France's governmental system had to be organized anew; with overwhelming concensus, the French established the Fourth Republic. But the Fourth Republic, like the Third, retained a weak executive, with the seat of power still in the legislature. Charles de Gaulle, elected President in 1945, failed to convince French voters that constitutional revision was a necessary prerequisite to effective government and retired in frustration in 1946.

Wracked by both internal and imperial crises, the Fourth Republic proved incapable of bringing order to France. A growing Communist Party threatened revolutionary change, and the new imperial French Union was an unstable edifice from its inception. Although France made progress in economic reconstruction, nearly doubling her industrial production by 1951, the national budget remained unbalanced and the French population strenuously resisted increased taxation. Social legislation was nevertheless increased – social security, health insurance, unemployment benefits, government subsidized housing, and agricultural programs placed great strains on the economy. Between 1945 and 1958 succeeding administrations struggled to maintain stability, but cabinets fell on the average of two a year.

Imperial crises, however, finally caused the Fourth Republic's collapse. The Indo-Chinese War combined with rising inflation and continued economic instability to create grave tensions, but the colonial conflict in Algeria finally overwhelmed the government. A revolt of French Army officers in Algeria in 1958 created an extreme crisis and the French people turned once more to Charles de Gaulle for leadership. On June 1, 1958, the National Assembly voted de Gaulle dictatorial powers for six months. He immediately turned to restructuring the French political system. In September the French approved a new constitution, the basis of the Fifth French Republic. The Constitution greatly increased the power of the president, who was now elected by the people rather than by the legislature. The parliament, consisting of a National Assembly and a Senate, retained legislative control, but could be dissolved by the President and the Premier. Furthermore, in a crisis, the President could rule by executive decree upon approval of the French legislature.

• The Fifth Republic

De Gaulle, the first President of the Fifth Republic under the new Constitution, retained the executive office until 1969. He ruled with great authority, but France was still undeniably a democratic republic. Stubborn, nationalistic, often narrowminded, de Gaulle was nevertheless firmly committed to democracy and was determined to guide France toward democratic stability. Under his leadership France experienced political security and economic growth and expansion for the first time in nearly a century.

By 1962 de Gaulle had settled the Algerian crisis, although not, as many Frenchmen had assumed he would, by retaining colonial control. Instead, he granted Algeria independence and ended the drain on France's human and economic resources. In foreign relations with the western powers he pursued a firm and independent nationalistic course. His insistence on developing atomic power for France irritated the United States, already annoyed with his challenges to American predominance in Europe's defense policies. Moreover, although French statesmen had led the development of the European Economic Community, de Gaulle opposed its evolution into a politically United Europe, insisting instead upon a loose union of sovereign states – a "Europe of Fatherlands." His refusal to agree to British entry into the Common Market severely retarded progress toward supra-nationalism in Europe, an evolution necessary to the reconsolidation of power for the European continent.

In 1969, nearing 80 years of age, de Gaulle retired once again. Political observers, impressed with the stability and prosperity France had achieved under the Fifth Republic, wondered if it could be maintained without de Gaulle's firm control. Since 1969 France has moderated her recalcitrance concerning European integration, but she has continued her prosperity. Her future political course, however, remains to be proved.

• The Rebirth of German Democracy

West Germany experienced a remarkable economic resurgence after the war. The newly established Bonn Republic was headed by the

73-year-old Konrad Adenauer, who firmly guided Germany's young democratic regime through its difficult early years. In 1963 Ludwig Erhard replaced Adenauer as Chancellor. Under Adenauer and Erhard the German government expanded social services and struggled to deepen the roots of democracy in the previously authoritarian German population. Germany faced unique social problems in assimilating the refugees who swarmed into the western sectors from Eastern Europe, placing great strains on housing and employment. Furthermore, many Germany people remained bitter about the division of the country, and continued to insist that the parts be reunited. But the threat of Soviet domination counteracted the possibility of any revived excess of nationalism, and by 1970, when Chancellor Willy Brandt signed the Moscow Treaty with Russia, accepting existing boundaries of all European states (but without interfering with the four-power responsibilities toward Germany), the West Germans seemed reconciled to the partition of the German nation.

West Germany in the 1970's is a thriving, energetic state, with extensive social welfare services, and a healthy capitalistic economy. In 1945 the area was an economic vacuum. Within fifteen years West Germany had more gold per capita than did the United States; the Federal Republic ranked third in the world in industrial power, and second in trading power. During that period the German currency became the most stable in Europe, and the rate of growth of her gross national product was more than double that of the United States. German technology moved into the vanguard of industrial nations and drew Germany into a position of strength in Europe's evolving economic union, which caused even France, traditionally Germany's most bitter enemy, to recognize that no viable European Union can develop without the inclusion of West Germany. Brandt's signing a non-aggression treaty with Russia in 1970 indicates that West Germany can today largely ignore the lead of the United States. Two decades after the war the western portion of Germany had moved, politically and economically, firmly into the western bloc. The middle classes came to full power, without the authoritarian ruling class of the past – aristocracy, army, and civil service – to provide its value system. For the first time Germany could genuinely try to establish the democratic process. Individuals had become citizens rather than subjects.

• Italian Reconstruction

In Italy, after Mussolini was killed in 1945, King Victor Emmanuel III abdicated in favor of his son, Humbert II. But a plebiscite in 1946 turned Italy into a republic, and Humbert II moved to Portugal. The Constitution of the new Italian Republic vested legislative power in a bicameral assembly, composed of a Chamber of Deputies and a Senate. As in West Germany the President held largely ceremonial powers – executive authority was controlled by a cabinet and a prime minister. Numerous parties developed, from neo-fascist on the right to communist on the left, but the Church-supported, middle-of-the-road Christian Democratic Party drew more votes than any other. Italy's Communist Party, the strongest in free Europe, provided a strong challenge, because it proved to be remarkably un-revolutionary and firmly nationalistic. The socialists constantly weakened their potential by factional disputes and splits, but one or another socialist group often participated in coalitions. Although Italy has averaged more than one cabinet a year since World War II, the democratic process appears to rest on a more solid foundation than before the war. Much progress has been made in economic and social reform. The government participates in a mixed economy, a combination of government ownership, private ownership, and extensive government regulation and planning. In 1962 the entire electric power industry was nationalized. Housing projects have high priority, and many of the larger landholdings have gone into development projects, both public and private, to improve conditions in southern Italy, and the differences between northern and southern Italy gradually are disappearing.

• Europe: A New Vitality

The general standard of living rose throughout Europe in the 1950's and 1960's, including the formerly excluded social groups in the overall prosperity. Although class consciousness remains strong nearly everywhere in Europe, political and economic participation in the social system is shared by all members of the population in most countries. Western Europe, despite her terrible experiences of the early twentieth century, has shown astounding recuperative powers. The two most awesome wars in all of man's history did not destroy her intrinsic vitality. Europe has ceased to be subject to the whims of the two superpowers, and has helped to end bipolarity. As economic union strengthens, European policies should play a role in attempting to solve the world's basic problems – global pollution, racial conflicts, and the revolution of rising expectations. Europe may once again show the way, but without the imperialism of the previous era.

• The Soviet Bloc

Besides the millions of lives lost as a result of World War II, more than 20,000,000 Russians were without housing of any kind. Probably 25 percent of the pre-war wealth of the country had been destroyed and the industrial labor force declined by more than 10,000,000. Yet the Soviet Union recovered with amazing rapidity, and within little more than a decade the Russian people had more of the basic consumer goods available than at any time in their history. Agriculture remained the most serious problem. Despite continued efforts to increase the efficiency of the Kolkhozes, agricultural production did not meet the needs of the populations, and Russia depended on large imports of grain to satisfy food demands.

To achieve such recovery required harsh discipline and the conviction that Russia's war continued. The government convinced the people that the country was in constant danger from the capitalist and imperialist enemies surrounding her and appealed to Russian nationalism to inspire the people to greater efforts. A comprehensive anti-American propaganda campaign insisted that wartime conditions must prevail until Russia could defend herself against the imperialist threat. With such incentives the government not only maintained defense spending, but in the 1950's launched an expensive but spectacular space program. At the same time she rebuilt her entire economy. The drain on Soviet economic resources prevented the country from achieving the standard of living characteristic in western Europe. But by the end of the 1960's, the Russian people enjoyed many of the material benefits of "bourgeois" society, and the grim, cruel years of the transition to communism became one more period in Russia's unhappy past.

• De-Stalinization

Politically, as well, tensions in Soviet society gradually diminished after Stalin's death in 1953. In his last years Stalin's paranoia reached a pathologic level, culminating just before his death with the threat of another purge. When Stalin died, in March 1953, fear and apprehension relaxed, but were replaced by a struggle for the succession which was not resolved until Nikita Khrushchev emerged in 1955 as the acknowledged leader of the Soviet state. In 1956, in a speech at the Twentieth Party Congress, Khrushchev astonished the world by denouncing Stalin, his tyranny, and his "cult of personality." The speech marked the beginning of a program of de-Stalinization – a relaxation of controls in Russian society.

Although Khrushchev alleviated despotism in Russia, he nevertheless reigned as a dictator until 1964. He filled party ranks with his supporters and expelled opponents from positions of power. He did not, however, execute them as Stalin had. Krushchev relaxed censorship in art and literature, but serious dissent still would not be tolerated. In 1958 Boris Pasternak won the Nobel Prize for literature for his novel, *Dr. Zhivago,* which attacked the Russian revolutionary experience. Pasternak was not permitted to accept the award and the novel was not published in Russia. But courageous Soviet writers continued to smuggle manuscripts to the West, criticizing aspects of the Soviet regime. The novelist Alexander Solzhenitzen, in *One Day in the Life of Ivan Denisovitch* and *Cancer Ward,* exposed the fundamental oppression which characterized Soviet life. The poet Yevgeny Yevtushenko attacked Soviet policies which stifle freedom of expression. Although the right to dissent has by no means been established in the Soviet Union, the very existence of such voices indicates a moderation of political tyranny in Russia and offers hope that the future will witness a further evolution toward freedom.

Khrushchev embarked on a program of economic, administrative, and cultural reform within Russia. He attempted to solve Russia's agricultural difficulties by opening up new lands to cultivation, and he initiated a program of administrative decentralization, creating regional ministries to supervise economic concerns. Both programs proved unsuccessful, and their failure helped bring about his downfall in 1964.

• Satellite Rebellion

As a result of de-Stalinization and relaxation, revolts erupted in the satellite states of Poland and Hungary. The Soviet government reacted strongly. In Poland, Wladislaw Gomulka led a series of strikes and riots which exhibited a resurgence of Polish nationalism, and seized control of the Polish government. He remained, however, unquestionably dedicated to the communist ideology, and the Russians allowed him to remain in power. The Hungarian revolution of 1956 was put down with ruthless brutality. The Hungarian revolutionaries denounced Russian supremacy and moved toward a renunciation of communism and removal of the state from the Soviet bloc. The Russians responded with savagery. Soviet troops rolled into Hungary and the free world recoiled in shock at pictures of Russian tanks gunning down students and young children whose only weapons were rocks and home-made gasoline bombs.

Although cracks in the structure of monolithic communism did indeed appear, the Soviet government demonstrated clearly in 1968 that it would not tolerate serious deviation from the Communist ideology. In 1967 the Czechoslovakian people, under the leadership of Alexander Dubcek, began a program of political liberalization. Dubcek did not intend to revise radically the Czechoslovak socialist economic system. Nevertheless, his demands for greater political freedom within Czechoslovakia antagonized the Russian government. Czechoslovakia's strategic importance in the Russian defense system meant that Russian domination of the Czech state could not relax. In the spring of 1968 Russian tanks moved into Czechoslovakia and Soviet control was forcefully reconfirmed. Dubcek was removed from office and sent into retirement in the country and a tame government put into his place.

During the decade of the 1960's Rumania achieved at least a partial independence of Soviet control. She denounced the invasion of Czechoslovakia without being herself occupied. The Sino-Soviet split improved her bargaining position, and recently she has experienced a considerable relaxation of censorship and secret police activities. Her large oil fields serve as the basis for an extensive industrial development and a western-oriented, as well as eastern trade. In 1969 military clashes between Russians and Chinese along their common border blew long-developing ideological differences between the two countries into a serious split, and Russia has consequently found it advisable to moderate her militancy toward the West.

• Cracks in the Structure

The treaty between East and West Germany at the end of 1972 illustrated the increasing awareness among governments that détente was essential and possible. It opened the way for international acceptance of East Germany, which had been an outlaw state to the West, acknowledged only by the communist and Arab Blocs. The treaty made it possible for the western states to exchange ambassadors with East Germany before her entry into the United Nations in the Fall of 1973. Russia's acquiescence indicates a major change in attitude since the days of the Berlin Blockade.

Russia's continued strength depends in large measure, of course, on control of eastern Europe by communist parties at least friendly to, if not dominated by, Russia. Eastern Europe provides the strategic guarantee of security she deems essential for her protection. As early as 1947 the satellite countries bought one-half of Russia's total exports, and provided more than a third of her imports. When the Marshall Plan aid proved effective in the West, Russia countered in 1949 with the Council for Economic Mutual Assistance (COMECON), designed to tie the economies of the satellites to Russia. While there is no question but that the system operated to Russia's advantage, major economic growth characterized the satellites. They now produce several times their pre-war levels.

By 1956 a clearly evident movement toward local autonomy emerged and Russia chose to accept a large degree of independence among the eastern European states. Certainly the Russians must maintain some control over the area and its economies, but nationalism has proved an effective counter-force to total Russian subjugation. The communist nations of eastern Europe must be considered from now on as forces in their own right – not merely as colonial adjuncts of an all-powerful Russian state.

• The United States

Americans entered the post-war era in a mood of confidence and optimism which absorbed even the shocks of the Cold War. After Roosevelt's death in 1945, Harry Truman, a blunt, outspoken midwestern statesman, became President and steered the country through the years of adjustment following the war. In foreign affairs Truman demonstrated a strong resistance to communist expansion. In domestic affairs he attempted to extend New Deal policies and to provide more equitable justice. Americans, however, content with the changes of the Roosevelt administration, and comfortably certain that post-war prosperity would continue, defeated Truman's domestic proposals. In 1952 Americans rejected Adlai Stevenson and a Democratic social welfare platform, electing the Republican war-hero Dwight Eisenhower as President. Eisenhower retained the presidential office throughout the decade of the 1950's, a period marked by increasing affluence for the majority of Americans.

In direct opposition to the developing of central planning which even the United States insisted upon for European countries, the American government turned back toward cooperation between government and big business. The huge industrial plants which had been built by tax money during the war were now sold at a tiny fraction of cost to private interests and turned to domestic production. Middle-class complacency with accelerating economic growth bred the assumption that American prosperity would inevitably extend to every citizen, and contributed to indifference to reform. Fear of the communist ideology, now bolstered by Russia's expansive power, became pathological, and caused Americans to identify all reform with "creeping socialism."

Senator Joseph McCarthy of Wisconsin convinced the majority of Americans that the Democratic Party was engaged in a conspiracy to overthrow the American Way of Life. McCarthyism resulted in a witch hunt so extreme that by 1953 an inevitable reaction among enlightened leadership set in, which ultimately ended McCarthy's support, and permitted the country to turn again to an examination of surviving inequalities in American social and economic life.

The most obvious issue was the place of the nation's disinherited blacks. Although President Truman's civil rights program of 1948 found little support at that time, it did awaken some American leaders to the problem of Negro inequality. Congressional rejection left the matter to the courts, and in 1954 the Supreme Court ruled against continued segregation in southern schools. The Supreme Court decision marked the beginning of an awakening of black political, social, and economic consciousness. The failure of the administration to implement the decision led to the rise of effective individual black leaders, such as Martin Luther King, Jr., who adopted Mohandas Gandhi's tactics and preached non-violent resistance to prejudice. The success of economic boycotts, sit-ins and civil rights marches generated fear among the white, middle-class establishment and led to ugly, violent confrontation, riots, and murder.

• The 1960's: Polarization and Paranoia

The presidential election of 1960 revealed a sharp division in the American people. The Republican candidate, Richard Nixon, known primarily for his support of McCarthyism and his Eisenhower economics, was devoid of charisma. His opponent, John Kennedy, a dynamic young Senator from Massachusetts, led the Democrats to victory on a reform platform. For the moment it appeared that the reform ethos had once again emerged as a dominant strain in American political thought. But Kennedy's clarion call to Americans to put into practice the rhetoric of the American Constitution ushered in a period of social conflict and violence, culminating in a series of assassinations which profoundly shocked the population. Kennedy himself was assassinated in 1963; Martin Luther King, Jr., a leader of the black civil rights movement, in 1967; and Robert Kennedy, the former President's brother, and himself a presidential candidate, in 1968. The profound split in American opinion, centering on the participation of blacks in the benefits of the American system, became increasingly apparent.

Vice-President Lyndon Johnson quickly asserted himself as President upon Kennedy's death. He used all his power with Congress to reduce taxes on less affluent Americans, and to pass the Civil Rights Act of 1964. The Civil Rights Act provided the federal government power to guarantee voting rights, equal educational and job opportunities, and use of public facilities to all citizens. He proposed his own "War on Poverty" program and pressured Congress into establishing the machinery and appropriating money to implement it. The people responded by giving him the greatest landslide victory in American history in the 1964 election.

Johnson proposed in his State-of-the-Union Message that Americans build "the Great Society," and his first Congress passed a series of bills which laid the foundations: federal aid to education; medical assistance for over-65 year olds; abolition of poll tax, literacy tests, and other methods of preventing Negro voting; and cabinet level for Housing and Urban Affairs and for Transportation.

But the split in society became more evident during these years. A series of massive civil rights demonstrations and vicious riots spread across the nation. In Los Angeles, Cleveland, Chicago, and in New York, particularly violent confrontations occurred. Urban whites in the northern cities responded with bitter prejudice and hatred for the blacks who seemed to endanger their status. At the same time the Johnson administration increased the number of Americans in Vietnam by more than a quarter of a million in one year, and growing numbers of the voters turned away from both Johnson and his conception of the Great Society. Escalation of the war in Vietnam exacerbated the already obvious schism between the middle-class establishment and growing numbers of dissident minority groups.

• The Nixon Years

The Republican Party, led by Richard Nixon, won the Presidency in 1968 on a platform of getting the country out of Vietnam, and of providing law and order for a nation in crisis. But Nixon failed to do either in his first term in office and the continuing tension threatened to rip the entire fabric of American society. Black demands that privilege broaden its base awakened similar demands from other subjugated groups, and America faced a cultural revolution in which women, ethnic minorities, and youth factions stridently insisted upon profound social change. The

Women's Liberation Movement, like the earlier civil rights movement, challenged some of the most basic concepts of the social structure. The consequent confusion in American thought produced rapidly accelerating change, and at the same time, a hardened adherence to traditional patterns within the established classes.

The tensions and frustrations of bewildering change, increased by the violent rhetoric and actions of discontented groups, caused a marked shift to the conservative right in American political behavior. The presidential election of 1972 demonstrated the polarization of American thought. Supported largely by the dissident factions, women, blacks, and ethnic minorities, the Democrats nominated George McGovern on a platform which recognized the dislocations in American life. American voters overwhelmingly defeated McGovern and reelected Richard Nixon who remained antagonistic to the cries of the discontented.

In foreign policy Americans showed a greater willingness to abandon outdated concepts and to reassess their position. In the years following World War II, containment of communism was a valid policy, particularly for a world disillusioned by the failure of the West to restrain the forces of aggression through appeasement. The Vietnam War, however, invalidated the basic assumptions of the containment policy, forcing Americans to recognize that social revolution in the emerging nations cannot be equated with communist expansion. Moreover, it challenged America's belief that her resources were infinite and brought the recognition that the United States neither can, nor wants to be, the world's policeman.

• East-West Rapprochement

As the Cold War moderated into détente, American statesmen faced the necessity of a drastic revision of foreign policy. In 1971 Americans suffered the shock of international opposition to U.S. policy, when the United Nations voted to admit Red China to membership. Within a year President Nixon had faced the realities of changed world conditions, and opened relations with the Chinese Communist state. While Nixon's visit to China served primarily as a beginning of relations between the two countries, that in itself signified a vast change in American policy, a recognition that the United States deplored its increasing isolation. Nixon's trip to Russia later in 1972 resulted in more immediate and tangible agreements. The attitudes on both sides showed marked change from those of 1968 and demonstrated a drive toward mutual self-interest. The Russians wanted American trade and a generally closer relationship with the West, which would permit them to share in technological developments and ease Cold War tensions. Nixon wanted to gain support for his tough line in Vietnam, where he had recently mined Haiphong Harbor and increased the heavy bombing of North Vietnam. Perhaps both wished to convince the world that there were still only two superpowers and that they could arrange world affairs by themselves.

In a series of highly publicized agreements Russia and the United States agreed to limit strategic nuclear weapons and to continue the Strategic Arms Limitation Talks (SALT). Although the agreement left both countries with sufficient nuclear arms to destroy human life, it did mark a distinct improvement in relations. Other agreements provided for the two countries to pool their resources to improve health and to protect the environment, and to rendezvous Russian and American spaceships in orbit in 1975, using crews trained together in both countries, and ships rigged to mutual compatibility in all essentials, such as radio frequencies and docking systems.

Perhaps more significant than all of the signed agreements, however, was the simple fact that the heads of two heretofore incompatible social systems examined the wishes and needs of both, found that they could agree on mutually advantageous matters while peaceably disagreeing on others. Nixon's visits to Peking and then to Moscow marked the inauguration of a new course in American foreign policy, one moved by the spirit of cooperation rather than antagonism.

• Contemporary Perspectives: The Scientific Revolution

Perhaps the most striking of the distinguishing features of twentieth century civilization is the advance in science and technology. The rapid acceleration of technological change, stimulated by the extension of scientific knowledge, has provoked a sweeping social revolution and profoundly affected politics and economics. The crises of the twentieth century – war, revolution, depression – have all had roots in the technological revolution which began in the nineteenth century, but dynamically increased since the middle of the present century.

There is little doubt that technological developments have greatly benefited mankind. Man's ability to manipulate and control his environment is greater than ever before in history. Bacteriology, microbiology, pharmacology, virology, and awesome progress in surgical technique conquered many traditional killers, while increased knowledge in preventive medicine and nutrition now control formerly lethal diseases which were still prevalent at the beginning of the century.

Transportation and communication facilities, particularly since the Second World War, have produced instantaneous communication with even the most remote corners of the globe. Continental and intercontinental travel have become commonplace. Consequently, the world has, in effect, become smaller, and events occurring half-way around the globe send repercussions not only to neighboring nations, but to the farthest corners of the earth. In the contemporary era, the interdependence of nations cannot be evaded nor denied.

New modes of production and increases in agricultural efficiency have brought material comfort to the majority in all of the industrialized nations. The inescapable evidence of a marked increase in the standard of living has produced the desire, in the under-developed nations of the world, to acquire equal scientific and industrial strength and the resulting material benefits for their own populations, and has been a major stimulus in generating nationalism in the Third World.

Perhaps the most spectacular developments in science have occurred in the field of space exploration. Formerly a subject only for science fiction, manned flight in space has extended knowledge in numerous areas, particularly in discovering the origins of the universe. The Space Age began in 1957, when the Russians launched *Sputnik*, a capsule which became the earth's first man-made satellite. *Sputnik* touched off a space-race between the Soviet Union and the United States which dominated the decade of the 1960's, affecting education, defense, and every area of scientific endeavor. In December, 1968, the United States sent the first space-crew into orbit around the moon and the following year the whole world watched as Neil Armstrong stepped down onto moon territory. His comment, "That's one small step for a man, one giant leap for mankind," articulated clearly the implications of man's victory over space.

• The Problems of Scientific Advance

But scientific progress has not been an unmitigated blessing. New methods of military defense obviously threaten the survival of mankind. The world first witnessed an atomic mushroom cloud as it hung over Hiroshima and Nagasaki in 1945. The residual horrors of atomic warfare were only gradually discovered as the poisoning effects of radioactive fallout became known. In 1952 the United States announced a new and even more powerful hydrogen bomb, and both Russia and the United States experimented with chemical and bacterial warfare. As other nations built atomic arsenals, the likelihood increased that a nuclear war would

The earth as seen from the moon. Wide World Photos.

destroy all life on the planet. The fear of a nuclear holocaust has diminished somewhat with the realization of the possibility of human genocide, but until strict controls over nuclear buildup are implemented, the ominous threat remains.

Extended life expectancy and the control of disease has caused a staggering increase in the world's population. A United Nations Conference on World Population held in Rome in 1954 established that the world at that time held 2.5 billion people, and predicted that there would be 6 billion by the year 2000. The figure is probably conservative.

Statisticians today generally believe that by the turn of the century the world's population will begin to double every generation. Thus by 2025 there would be 12 billion people, or four times as many as presently exist, and 25 years later the figure would be 24 billion. These estimates are given credence by the fact that in many areas of the world (including Mexico) the population is already doubling every generation. Death rates decline while birth rates rise, despite deliberate governmental policies in some countries to control population growth – Japan's government shortly after World War II legalized and encouraged abortion.

The population explosion created overwhelming social and economic problems. Particularly in the underdeveloped areas of the world, food production has lagged behind population increase, and thousands suffer from starvation and disease. The poorer classes in India consume only about 25 percent as many calories as the wealthier classes in the United States. But figures concerning other consumption are even more startling. Per capita, Americans use 20 times more energy than Indians, 80 times as much iron, and two-thirds of the world's total oil production. While the increase in population is rapidly depleting the world's resources, associated problems absorb the attention of national authorities. Major crises in over-crowded cities and a sky-rocketing increase in the crime rate are directly related to the demographic rise. Population control is consequently one of the contemporary era's most insistent imperatives.

Excessive population growth is also a major factor in pollution of every kind – air, water, noise. Many of the world's lakes and rivers have already lost all plant and fish life through discharge of poisonous wastes into them from factories, industrial complexes, and sewage lines. Smog and air pollution have turned whole cities into hazardous living areas. Noise levels in the large cities, and increasingly where supersonic planes fly, have reached danger levels. The search for new sources of energy has endangered wide geographical areas, and entire species of wildlife are threatened with extinction as man, in attempting to control his environment, faces the very real danger of destroying it.

• The Intellectual Revolution

Rapidly accelerating social change has produced a growing tendency to challenge traditional concepts. Culturally and intellectually, the questioning of western values and priorities which had emerged in the 1920's and 1930's accelerated in the 1960's and 1970's. As material comfort reached the majority in the advanced nations, it became increasingly clear that affluence did not insure spiritual satisfaction. Throughout the western states a rejection of traditional patterns of thought, which equated progress with Gross National Product, gained momentum. Cultural critics condemn the environmental and spiritual spoliation caused by modern technology, and decry the materialism which pervades western society. They argue that fear of a nuclear holocaust is an ever-present reality, but that industrial potential threatens life and freedom in subtler and equally dangerous ways.

As in the seventeenth and eighteenth centuries, the scientific revolution has produced an intellectual revolution in which serious thinkers seek to find a coherent body of principles to replace the invalidated former guidelines. Organized religion, under the leadership of theologians such as Karl Barth, Paul Tillich, and Pope John XXIII, is in a period of flux as it attempts to combat secularism and reconstruct religious doctrines meaningful to modern man. In philosophy, Existentialism has attempted to respond to the absurdities of contemporary life and to re-emphasize, despite the anguish of twentieth-century life, human freedom and dignity.

But the most profound challenge to the fundamental precepts of western civilization emerged in the 1960's in the ranks of western youth. A dissident younger generation, influenced by the obvious contradictions between their parents' rhetoric and practice, burst into rebellion as they rejected established creeds and life-styles. Student riots and demonstrations in Paris, Tokyo, Berlin, and all over the United States manifested a violent rejection of the established order. The movement alienated many of the older generation, who felt that their efforts to preserve western civilization against the onslaughts of depression, communism, and fascism have not been appreciated by their children, raised in greater comfort than any generation in history. But the older generation as well is affected by the proven validity of the criticism.

• Confronting the Future

Until the present century Europe and the West stood in the vanguard of progress. The experiences of two world wars, the emergence of a third world bloc of young nations, and the perplexities of an advanced technological society have necessitated fundamental adjustments in western social organization, and in political and economic thought. Neither the more advanced western states nor the emerging nations will abandon the undeniable benefits or material comforts of industrialization, but the technology must be controlled if civilization is to survive. The western world, the source of the ideas and knowledge which created the technology, consequently bears an awesome responsibility. Leadership in solving the problems of industrial society must come from the nations which gave it birth. If scientific knowledge and industrialization are not to become Frankenstein monsters, destroying their creators, then the western nations must awaken to the exigencies of modern civilization. In the contemporary world Europe and her step-children, Russia and the United States, face a formidable task: assuring the survival of the human race.

Suggestions for Further Reading

Barraclough, Geoffrey, *An Introduction to Contemporary History* (1967)

Boulding, K. E., *The Meaning of the Twentieth Century: The Great Tradition* (1964)

Gatzke, Hans, *The Present in Perspective: A Look at the World Since 1945* (1961)

Harrington, Michael, *The Accidental Century* (1966)

Adamic, Louis, *The Eagle and the Roots* (1952)

Alexander, Edgar, *Adenauer and the New Germany* (1957)

Carr, E. H., *The Soviet Impact on the Western World* (1947)

Churchill, Winston, *Closing the Ring* (1951)

Haas, E. B., *The Uniting of Europe* (1958)

Henderson, Gregory, *Korea: The Politics of the Vortex* (1968)

LaFeber, W., *America, Russia and the Cold War* (1968)

Latourette, K. S., *China* (1964)

Mayne, Richard, *The Community of Europe* (1963)

Pethybridge, Roger, ed., *The Development of the Communist Bloc* (1965)

Portisch, Hugo, *Red China Today* (1965)

Rees, David, *The Age of Containment: The Cold War* (1967)

Schram, Stuart R., *Mao Tse-tung* (1968)

Snell, John, ed., *The Meaning of Yalta: Big Three Diplomacy and the New Balance of Power* (1956)

Tuchman, Barbara, *Stilwell and the American Experience in China* (1972)

Willis, F. Roy, *Europe in the Global Age* (1968)

Barker, A. J., *Suez: The Seven Day War* (1965)

Busia, K. A., *Africa in Search of Democracy* (1968)

Carter, Gwendolyn, *Independence for Africa* (1960)

Dean, Vera Micheles, *The Nature of the Non-Western World* (1964)

Emerson, R., *From Empire to Nation: The Rise to Self-Assertion of Asian and African Peoples* (1960)

Fall, Bernard B., *Hell in a Very Small Place: The Siege of Dien Bien Phu* (1967)

Khouri, F. J., *The Arab-Israeli Dilemma* (1968)

Lacouture, Jean, *Ho Chi Minh: A Political Biography* (1968)

Purcell,V., *The Revolution in Southeast Asia* (1962)

Schram, Stuart R., *Mao Tse-tung* (1968)

Szulc, T., *The Winds of Revolution: Latin America Today and Tomorrow* (1963)

Tannenbaum, F., *Ten Keys to Latin America* (1963)

Ward, Barbara, *The Rich Nations and the Poor Nations* (1962)

Barber, Bernard, *Science and the Social Order* (1962)

Brzezinski, Z. K., *The Soviet Bloc: Unity and Conflict* (1960)

Crouzet, Maurice, *The European Renaissance* (1970)

Degler, Carl, *Affluence and Anxiety: The United States Since 1945* (1968)

Fromm, Erich, *The Sane Society* (1955)

Grosser, Alfred, *Germany in Our Time: A Political History of the Postwar Years* (1971)

Lichtheim, George, *The New Europe Today – And Tomorrow* (1964)

Maier, Charles, and Dan White, *The Thirteenth of May: The Advent of de Gaulle's Republic* (1968)

Little, Malcolm, with Alex Haley, *The Autobiography of Malcolm X* (1965)

Marcuse, Herbert, *One Dimensional Man* (1964)

Mayne, Richard, *The Community of Europe* (1963)

Moorhouse, Geoffrey, *Britain in the Sixties: The Other England* (1964)

Northcott, Jim, *Why Labour?* (1964)

Roszak, Theodore, *The Making of a Counter Culture* (1969)

Smith, Jean E., *Germany Beyond the Wall: People, Politics . . . and Prosperity* (1969)

Toffler, Alvin, *Future Shock* (1971)

Werth, Alexander, *De Gaulle: A Political Biography* (1966)

Willis, F. Roy, *Italy Chooses Europe* (1971)

THE ANCIENT WORLD, TO 800

THE MEDIEVAL WORLD

THE RENAISSANCE WORLD

THE SIXTEENTH CENTURY

THE SEVENTEENTH CENTURY

THE EIGHTEENTH CENTURY

THE NINETEENTH CENTURY

DEATH OF AN OLD WORLD, 1914-1945

GENESIS OF A NEW WORLD, 1945 TO THE PRESENT